MW01170871

Twelve Centuries of Persian Poetry
Eighth to 20th century
By Parviz Nezami

Twelve Centuries of Persian Poetry
Classics to Modern (8th to 20th century)

BY: PARVIZ NEZAMI

FRONT MATERIAL

Persian literature series by the same author (in Farsi)

سیروسفری درگلستان ادب پارسی از رودکی تا فروغ

سیروسفری درگلستان ادب پارسی ازسنایی تا توللی

سیروسفری در گلستان ادب پارسی از انوری تا نیما

سیروسفری در گلستان ادب پارسی از فردوسی تا بهار

سیروسفری در گلستان ادب پارسی از مولوی تا مشیری

سیروسفری در گلستان ادب پارسی از سعدی تا سپهری

سیروسفری در گلستان ادب پارسی ار حافظ تا حمیدی

دوازده قرن تاریخ شعروادب در ایران (قرن دوم تا قرن ششم)

دوازده قرن تاریخ شعروادب در ایران (قرن ششم تا قرن دهم)

دوازده قرن تاریخ شعروادب در ایران (قرن دهم تا عصرحاضر)

To order the books please email
parviznezami@yahoo.com
or call Parviz Nezami 1516 208 7787

Dedication

I dedicate this book to the young Iranian men and women living in countries beyond the borders of Iran, who due to no choice of their own, were deprived of the opportunity to learn to read and write their mother language 'Farsi'

Acknowledgement

I am indebted to Richard A. Lockshin Ph.D., and his wonderful wife Zahra Zakeri-Lockshin Ph.D. for their vital assistance in editing this book, and Ali Haghighi for providing invaluable computer services and support.

I am especially grateful to Mansour Zandieh MD; for his continuous support of my cultural contributions, this book included, over the past 15 years, in the task of promoting the magnificent and one-of-a-kind Persian literary heritage. Last but not least I wish to thank my wife Effat Nezami, my son Razi Nezami MD; & my daughter Shabnam Nezami for their understanding and patience that made it possible for me to devote colossal amount of time, energy, and resource to my cultural endeavor over the past twenty-two years. With special thanks to my loving sister Maryam Nezami who, with her delightful, kind and positive attitude, that gave me the moral support I needed to complete this difficult work.

Letter from technical assistant

September 9, 2021

Dear Parviz,

It was a pleasure assisting you in assembling *Twelve Centuries of Persian Poetry*. It was fascinating to read the chapters, and I learned a great deal. I am sure that the new generation of Persian-Americans and beyond will equally find it valuable, and that, thanks to you, the culture will persist in America. It truly is a magnum opus.

Yours sincerely,

Richard A. Lockshin, Ph.D.

FOREWORD

Parviz Nezami
The Voice of Persian Culture, Poetry, History and Philosophy,
in and out of Iran.

By:Dr.Hormoz Mansouri

Seventy two years ago, my family relocated from Isfahan to Tehran, Iran, as my father, a young educator, was assigned to Ministry of Education in Tehran. I have never forgotten my nervousness and anxiety, as I entered my new fourth grade class at Targhib elementary school, facing my strange classmates, a whole bunch of kids with backgrounds, traditions, habits and accents quite different from mine. Somehow there was a sense of inferiority, as outsiders were regarded, against the inhabitants of capital city of Tehran, and most definitely my deep Isfahani accent was to be subjected to ridicule and satire.

And, I will never forget the sense of relief, comfort and happiness when, I spotted somewhere in the back of the class, my own childhood playmate, my dear friend, my buddy and, then my savior, Parviz Nezami. Our fathers had been extremely close friends, then living in Isfahan, and we shared such delightful memories of our childhood, joyfully detached from the real world.

We separated from each other again, when we attended separate high schools and pursued different higher education, and we both left Iran for different countries, however, the undeniable, strong bonds of friendship and brotherhood had already held us together firmly.
Parviz went to England and I came to United States, and we somehow had lost each other for years. I completed my education in medicine and surgery and stablished my surgical practice on Long Island, New York. Parviz became a civil engineer and then immigrated to United States.

Call it destiny or coincidence or whatever, unbeknownst to us, for few years we were living only blocks from each other on Long Island. Contacts were made and we found each other, interestingly at a time when our parents had also immigrated to United States. A most delightful family reunion. Our fathers shared the same emotions after years of separation.

During ensuing years, I began to know my friend, Parviz, now a respected professional, a lot better than before, and soon I realized that our bonds of friendship had further strengthened by our mutual love and attachment to our homeland cultural, literary and historical heritage of Iran. Clearly what we had inherited from our parents' dedication to education and culture.

Parviz Nezami's remarkable dedication to Persian literature and poetry, many years of self-education, hard work and steadfast belief in the need for conservation and safeguarding of Persian culture, literature and poetry abroad, specifically for second generation Iranians born or raised in the western world, came to fruition about thirty years ago, when he, singlehandedly, established gatherings of Iranians for poetry readings, on a regular monthly basis. One cannot underestimate the perseverance, hard work, energy, dedication and sacrifice such worthy and laudable endeavor would require.

What has made his poetry reading nights so popular and pleasant, is the unique accentuation he applies to each word and sentence, the rhythm and inflection that brings out the impact of the poem, in a very pleasant tone, so specific for poetry recital.

Approximately twenty years ago he published a seven-volume collection of Persian poetry titled "A journey through the landscape of Persian poetry" in Farsi. (سیر و سفری در گلستان ادب پارسی). Each volume contained selected works of renowned Persian poets and philosophers going back more than a thousand years along with a brief biography of their life story, birth places, and some description of their literary contributions.

For a variety of reasons, including periodic invasions of Persian empire by barbaric neighboring countries from north, east and west and often total destruction of centers of knowledge, burning of libraries and books, there is a paucity of recorded biographies and life stories of the well-known masters of Persian poetry and literary pioneers going back many centuries. Numerous volumes of poetry books of famous Persian poets contain only their art of poetry with no reference to who they were, how they lived and how they survived in often hostile environments of dictatorial kingdoms and religious suppression. Nezami's remarkable seven-volume work of Persian poets is just as unique and informative for the poets' biographies as is the masterful selection of their poems.

These seven-volume series were well received and applauded by our fellow countrymen, however, Parviz found it necessary to embark on an extensive revision and re-arrangements of the topics in a chronological order starting from twelve centuries ago and his remarkable efforts that never knew the boundaries of a single human being physical and mental ability, energy, dedication, and focus on detail, accuracy and excellence resulted in a three-volume collection of a masterfully written document about the life history and lifetime literary works of more than one hundred and fifty Persian poets and philosophers. Hence, "Twelve Centuries History of Persian Literature in Iran" was published in Farsi. (دوازده قرن تاریخ شعر و ادب در ایران).

For a man with a lifetime love of his ancestral homeland and deep interests in culture, literature, poetry, history and philosophy, there seemed to be no rest when it came to his lofty goal of the preservation and safeguarding of Persian literature and poetry in foreign lands where millions of Iranians have settled for many decades and, specifically, their second and third generations are now mostly alien to or insufficient in Persian language, Farsi, and the knowledge of their homeland history and culture. Therefore, he soon realized that his massive works of Persian poetry and culture, written in Farsi, had to be translated to English.

In addition to that, our younger generation who had no education in Iran, required a minimum introductory knowledge in Persian culture and philosophy, so deeply embedded and masterfully expressed in the language of poetry.

Welcome to Parviz Nezami's masterpiece, "Twelve Centuries of Persian Poetry (Introspection) Classics to Modern (8th to 20th Century)".

The book you are reading now is a unique collection of biography, history and cultural works of about hundred and fifty famous Persian poets.

You will also read a brief history of Iran, going back to five thousand years BC, and how original geographical and historical formation of Iran came to be.

As you read through the Introduction, Parviz Nezami guides you through a fascinating course of tumultuous Iranian cultural history starting with Arab invasion about 650 C.E; the event that changed the course of history for the ensuing 1500 years. For almost two hundred years of Arab domination, severe cultural restrictions were imposed aimed at annihilating Iranian ancient languages of Farsi Dari and Pahlavi. Use of these languages were punished by death.

further devastations were brought about by four major invasions of the country by her barbaric neighbors destroying libraries, burning books and mass murdering the villagers and wiping out major cities and communities, starting with the invasion of Mongols from the north east plains of Mongolia in early years of thirteenth century. Then came invasion of Timor Lame in late fourteenth century, and invasion of Afghan tribes in mid-seventeenth century. All of these are explained in detail in this book. It is amazing that despite all these periods of mayhem and devastation, slaughtering of innocent inhabitants, including tens of thousands of scholars, scientists, writers and poets there remains a reasonable account of the life histories of Persian scholars, scientists, writers, philosophers and poets that have survived, thanks to a limited number of biographers known as Tazkereh-writers.

It should be noted that the renowned Persian poets, whose name and fame and literary works have survived the social and geographical turmoil going back twelve centuries ago, were not just simple, superficial poetry writers. They were great thinkers, philosophers and scientists who resorted to the cryptic and ambiguous language of poetry to shield themselves against the despotic rulers and oppressive religious leaders of their times.

As you read the last few pages of Introduction, Parviz Nezami will educate you in what he believes readers could not comprehend the depth of the thoughts, opinions and ideologies of famous Persian poets without a basic knowledge of psychology, philosophy, introspection, and recognition of "self", and the role of mysticism practiced by mystics and what exactly is "Erfan" (عرفان).

Chapter 1 is titled "A Brief History of the Persian Empire, How It All Began". Frankly, I don't find anything "Brief" in this chapter. This is a masterfully structured account of historical and geographical development of Persia, starting with second millennium BC going through a description of a variety of empires, dynasties, their culture, language and religion.

Likewise, in ensuing chapters you will read about the Basics of Persia, language and literature and the influence of Arab invasion. A description of Persian literature of the medieval period up to the contemporary and modern

Persian literature and influence of Persian literature on world literature. You will learn about the early writers of Persian poetry and the rebirth of Persian culture after the Arab invasion, what Nezami has coined as "The Persian Renaissance", starting with the Father of Persian Poetry, Rudaki Samarghandi, the 9th century poet.

The bulk of the material in this book is devoted to about one hundred and fifty prominent Persian poets including what is known today of their life story and their remarkable literary work.
Selected pieces of their poetry are beautifully translated to English, so descriptive and narrative of the essence of the poet's ideology and philosophy.

Considering the range of topics discussed in this book, from historical accounts of our mother land Iran, to her culture, literature, art, geography, poetry and her great thinkers, philosophers and spiritual leaders, this book is truly an encyclopedia that belongs to every library, school and book shelves of Iranians dedicated to their ancestral heritage.

Seventy two years since the days of my elementary school, where I found my dear friend Parviz Nezami, I am again walking into a delightful class, not with anxiety and nervousness, rather with joy, pleasure and anticipation. This is an immensely educational forum, now established by none other than Parviz Nezami himself, in which I seek to quench my insatiable appetite for Persian culture, literature and poetry.
The book is a treasure I relish for my remaining days as I approach the sunset of my life.

Hormoz Mansouri. MD., F.A.C.S.
September 6, 2021

Dr.Hormoz Mansouri is a poet, writer, and scholar of Persian literature He has written and published a number of books in Farsi & English. He retired from practice of medicine few years ago. His most outstanding creation has been "Candle of Heart, Collection of Poetry" published in New York a few years ago. He is also a skillful musician who plays Persian musical instruments; Tar & Setar.

Preface

By Dr. Minoo Varzegar

The purpose of this book is to present our magnificent literature and vast culture not only to our generation 1.5 and 2 but also those who come from other cultures and literary traditions. Our broad and deep culture needs to be manifested and presented to the world to enable people from other cultures to broaden their vision and to enhance their appreciation of its beauty and depth.

Mr. Parviz Nezami has done a miracle in presenting <u>The Twelve Centuries of Persian Poetry from Classic to Modern (8th to 21stth Century)</u>. Not only has he written this book on literature but he also has produced a collection of seven volumes of Persian Poetry titled "A Journey through the Landscape of Persian Poetry" in Farsi to enlighten Iranians who are craving for more literary information. These literary works are quite daunting to those who seek more information about our poets and writers from the past and present. They give a broad vision in literature to the lovers of our culture and civilization. These books have been praised by many literature lovers and critiques in Iran. In addition to these literary attempts, he has also compiled and written the above-mentioned book, a more comprehensive volume of poetry, to enrich and widen the literary horizon of those who are passionate about literature and poetry. This book portrays the large- scale view of different areas of poetry to provide an exhaustive view of different poets and their poetry in addition to the language of Persian speaking countries, history, culture and civilization of Persia.

This collection is designed not only for those who are novice but also for those who are well-versed in literature. It also intends to be a recourse book for those who seek more information and knowledge in Persian poetry. Additionally, it discusses the poetry of many prominent poets in detail with many examples from their poems. The literary work is very comprehensive and intends to enhance the readers' horizon of poetry.

Mr. Parviz Nezami, who has been delving into the different genres of Persian literature and organizing poetry sessions for more than thirty years, has done an unimaginable work of art. His lifelong devotion, perseverance, perfection have been the sources of creativity and uniqueness of this masterpiece, which made his dream materialize. This collection of poetry needs praise and acknowledgment and must be read by all literature lovers in general and poetry lovers in particular. I salute him for his love of Persian literature to the point that he has devoted many years of life to produce these literary works. He should be acclaimed and applauded not only for his most recent collection but also for all his other endeavors for producing his scholarly works.

Minoo Varzegar, Ph.D

Dr. Minoo Varzegar is a former professor of Tehran University, Iran and Rutgers University, New Jersey, USA .

Contents

Contents

Contents

Contents

Contents

Contents

Contents

Contents

INTRODUCTION

Following the 1979 Islamic Revolution in Iran a large number of Iranians migrated from their native land and settled in other countries throughout the world. The immigrants brought out with themselves their children whose ages varied from infants upwards. These children who were later classified by sociologists as "2nd generation naturalized Iranians" had undergone mostly little or no schooling during the short years of their life in Iran and lacked ability to read and write Farsi (their mother language). Most of the immigrants were also in their early or mid-years of their lives and had more children in their newly settled homelands. The newborns got their entire schooling in the new countries where their parents had settled and, naturally, acquired no ability to read or write Farsi, notwithstanding the fact that all these children had come from a land that was rich with a great cultural heritage going back almost three thousand years.

One living example is my own family; At the time of our arrival in the United States our children were of the ages of two, five and seven and although presently they speak Farsi but, to my great sadness and disappointment, are not able to read and write Farsi. The number of such children scattered around the world, who never had the chance to learn to read and write Farsi, with the greatest majority in the United States and Europe, easily runs in to thousands.

Upon taking retirement from my engineering career, almost twenty years ago, I did some soul searching to find out what would be a suitable occupation to keep me busy during the remaining years of my life going forward. I soon realized that the best choice would be to go back to literary writing, poetry, history and translation which was something that I enjoyed greatly back in Iran, during the early years of my life. The realization was like a dream coming true. It completely changed my life for better and forever. It is said that "Once you have found it don't ever let it go"

During the long and beautiful years that followed, I succeeded to write and publish in Farsi, my first book in seven volumes titled "Seir.o.Safari dar Golestan adabe Parsi" (A journey through the landscape of Persian poetry) and the second one; "Twelve centuries history of Persian literature in Iran" in three volumes. Shortly after I embarked upon writing the present book, in English, on the same subject.

Introduction

This book, in fact, is a concise version of the other two series, but it covers a wider range of subjects. It is specifically designed to benefit the second and third generations of Iranian youth who, because of the interruption that occurred in their education in Iran during the years following the establishment of Islamic Revolution did not have the opportunity to learn the history of their homeland, and discover the magnificent and beautiful cultural treasures of Persia. This book can also be helpful to English speaking enthusiasts of other countries with an interest in Persian history and literature to provide them with an opportunity to read, learn and enjoy the great literary masterpieces created by the Persian masters going back to the ancient and Middle Ages all the way up to the present time.

The subject material in this book as well as the selected poems were basically gathered and compiled from the contents of my previous books. It is useful to know that, during the past twelve hundred years Iran went through some of the most devastating invasions of its entire history in the hands of its neighbors to the west, the north, and the east. Each and every of these four attacks coupled with centuries of foreign barbaric domination that followed each invasion resulted in the burning, pillage and the loss of our cultural treasures created during its preceding periods. The invaders had no understanding of the values and the importance of books and libraries and the great and beautiful knowledge that they stored. The barbarians, randomly and savagely, burnt down and killed the inhabitants of every home and building that they came across. Great centers of culture such as Jundi-Shahpour, Balkh, Merve, Neishabour, Rey, Isfahan, Shiraz, Tabriz, Hamadan and many more other centers were completely destroyed and burnt to the ground. Many of our scientists, scholars, writers, philosophers and poets were tortured and killed and some who had the chance to flee took residence elsewhere in far off lands such as India's subcontinent and Asia Minor. The end result is that a comprehensive account of the Persian cultural treasures in the form of an accurately written and methodically preserved literary history does not exist today.

During these horrific and devastating times, a limited number of Tazkereh-writers (biographers) whose number does not exceed about 50 or 60 (at least to my knowledge) sporadically were able to compile life stories, accounts and reports of the life and works of the Persian scholars, scientists, writers, philosophers and poets as well as selections of poems from their Diva'ns

Introduction

(collection of poems). The accuracy of the contents of these Tazkerehs cannot even be completely verified. Furthermore, these tazkerehs which were mostly hand written by the professional copiers and not by the authors themselves were discovered hundreds of years later by European researchers and orientalists who had travelled to Persia with the sole purpose of finding the old and one-of-a-kind precious manuscript for export and sale to the museums and libraries in Europe. Very few original copies of such Tazkerehs are even to be found in Iran today. The Tazkerehs were originally written mostly in Farsi and some in Arabic. They were in recent years translated, analyzed and corrected by the Iranian and some European scholars and literary critics. It is unfortunate that most of this limited amount of information is not even easily accessible by the public at large. The reason being that the Tazkerehs, except for a limited number, have not been translated in to other languages nor been published and therefore are not available for purchase. The copies can mainly be accessed in the public libraries in Iran or some western universities abroad. In the Bibliography attached to this book I have included the titles of these tazkeras and tazkereh-nevisan (Tazkeras and their authors).

This book has been designed for the purpose of presenting the reader with a panoramic bird's eye view of a selected number of the works from the magnificent and one of a kind literary treasures of Persia in the past twelve hundred years. The existing diva'ns and writings of our great literary men and women are much larger in number and a lot more extensive than what is included in this book which, as mentioned before, is only a very concise and limited selection compiled from that vast literary treasure. A brief background information has also been included covering the original geographical and historical formation of Iran going back to the migration of the Arian tribes from Asian north and northwest plains in the Urals west of Caspian Sea that gradually moved south and settled in the Iranian plateau starting about four to five thousand years B.C. Two main branches eventually established the Median dynasty in the north west bordering Assyrian Empire and Persian dynasty in the south and south west. The story continues to the coming of Cyrus the Great, in 550 B.C with the establishment of the Achaemenid dynasty and eventually in 330 B.C Alexander the Macedonian's invasion of Persia, followed by the Selocid's rule, Parthian Empire defeating the Selocid's in 230 B.C, the Sassanid Empire taking over in 220 C.E and finally the Arab's invasion of Iran in 650 C.E; the Event that changed the entire course of history for the next 1500 years. We have also included in this section a discussion of the ancient language, religion and literature of Iranian peoples starting around

Introduction

750 B.C with the rule of Medians through to the Arab's conquest of Iran. From this point on, we continue with the introduction of an extremely important Event in the cultural history of Iran that we have called: "Persian Cultural Renaissance" following the Arab's invasion.

The Movement started during the rule of Safaris ruler Jacob Layse Safari around the year 850 C.E. Iranians for the first time after almost 200 years of Arab domination managed to break away from the cultural restrictions that were imposed by the rulers on the use of Iranian's ancient languages "Farsi Dari" and "Pahlavi". Iranians now once again were able to use these languages to speak and write. Poets and writers were allowed to write their poems and books in Farsi. The Renaissance was the start of the evolution of the golden ages of Persian culture and literature marking the rise of some of the greatest poets, writers, philosophers, and scientists and mystics of all times: Bayazid Bastami Rudaki, Ferdowsi, Omar Khayam, Khaghani Shervani, Nezami of Ganja, Sa'di, Shirazi, Mowlavi, Eraghi, Obeyd Zakani, Ha'fez Shirazi, Abdolrahman, Ja'mi, Kalim Kashani, Sa'eb Tabrizi, Foroughi Basta'mi,Gha'a'ni Shirazi, Iraj Mirza, Malek ol Shoara Baha'r, Parvin Etesa'mi, Ali Akbar Dehkhoda, Shahryar, Rahi Moayeri, Sohrab Sepehri, Fereydoon Moshiri, Forough Farokhzad, Simin Behbahani, and hundreds more. In this book we have included a brief introduction to the life and works of about a hundred of those great literary men and women.

As mentioned above, The Persian Renaissance movement which started with the gradual appearance of Persian poets and writers in the nineth and tenth centuries C.E. and continued through the following centuries up to the present time, completely changed the cultural landscape of Persian civilization, putting Iran at the pinnacle of the world's literary history.

The golden years of Persian culture came to a sudden and horrific stop in the early years of thirteenth century with the invasion of Mongols from the north-east plains of Mongolia headed by Chingiz khan. The barbarian united together a number of Mongol tribes and attacked Iran, killing, destroying, pilfering almost every town and village throughout the vast Iranian territories as far east as India, and as far west as Anatolia and Asia Minor. Everywhere he went he made sure that not one person was left alive. It is reported that he would even have all animals; slaughtered, not even sparing the cats and dogs. He would destroy all over ground and underground water canals, aqueducts and wells in order to turn fertile lands into desert for years to come. Libraries,

Introduction

mosques, schools and colleges were burnt down and completely destroyed. After his death Iran came under the rule of his family members and various Mongolian tribe leaders as well as his commanders and their descendants. This catastrophe continued for a period of more than two hundred years.

A second invasion came headed by Timor Lane around the end of the fourteenth century, that resulted in almost equal destruction, slaughter of the innocent men, women and children, and pilferage of all the cities that had been rebuilt in the interval between the death of Chingiz and arrival of Timur Lane. A third mayhem of similar nature occurred when Iran was attacked by Afghan tribes, in the mid-seventeenth century. The Afghan invaders brought less destruction than the Arabs, the Chingiz, and Timur Lane, but were as murderous and bloodthirsty as the other three. In the third or fourth day of their arrival in Isfahan, the splendid capital city of the Safavid dynasty, during a banquet at the royal palace, they savagely murdered every member of the royal family including children of the last ruling monarch, Shah Sultan Hussein who was made to witness the killing of his own young children. This tragedy was followed by slaughtering thousands of innocent inhabitants of the city of Isfahan, and other cities as far as the city of Shiraz four hundred kilometers to the south.

It is to be noted that all these savage barbarians in the process of slaughtering innocent inhabitants or destroying and burning down the cities did not differentiate between the scholars and men of science or the ordinary population. They randomly murdered every man, woman and child they came across and destroyed and put fire to every building regardless of that being a home, a library, school or a mosque.

It is truly a miracle that despite all these devastating invasions resulting in the loss of tens and tens of scholars, scientists, writers, poets, and the destruction of libraries and homes where thousands of books were being stored over the years, we still have inherited a sizable treasure of knowledge that can demonstrate to the world the creativity and genius of the people of this land and the great role that they played in the development of human culture and civilization from the early times in history up to the present time. It is my sincere hope that this book shall provide the readers in particular the young second generation Iranian immigrants scattered all over the world an opportunity to learn of at least part of what is left from that magnificent

Introduction

treasure of human knowledge that was created over the past twelve hundred years.

Introspection is the examination of one's own conscious thoughts and feelings. In psychology, the process of introspection relies on the observation of one's own mental state, while in a spiritual context it may refer to the examination of one's soul. Introspection is closely related to human self-reflection and self-discovery and is contrasted with external observation.

Introspection generally provides a privileged access to owns mental states, not meditated by other sources of knowledge, so that individual experience of the mind is unique. Introspection has been a subject of philosophical, Gnostic and Mystic discussion for thousands of years. The philosopher Plato asked, "why should we not calmly and patiently review our own thoughts, and thoroughly examine and see what these appearances in us really are?

While introspection is applicable to many facets of philosophical and Gnostic thoughts it is perhaps best known for its role in epistemology (the branch of philosophy that investigates the nature, limits, criteria, or validity of human knowledge; also, a particular theory of cognition); in this context introspection is often compared with perception, reason, memory, and testimony as a source of knowledge.

It has often been claimed that Wilhelm Wundt, the father of experimental psychology was the first to adopt introspection to experimental psychology. Though the methodological idea had been presented long before, as by 18th century German philosopher–psychologists such as Alexander Gottlieb Baumgartner and Johan Nicolas Tetens. Also, Wundt's views on introspection must be approached with great care. Wundt was influenced by notable psychologists, such as Gustav Fechner, who used a kind of controlled introspection as a means to study human sensory organs.

Building upon the pre-existing use of introspection was the ability to observe an experience, not just the logical reflection or speculations which some others interpreted its meaning to be.

Introspection was practiced in a number of Eastern rooted religions such as Christianity, Jains pracrice pratikraman (Sanskrit "introspection"), a process of repentance of wrongdoings during their daily life, and remind themselves

Introduction

to refrain from doing so again. Introspection is encouraged in schools such as Advaita Veddanta; in order for one to know their own true nature, they need to reflect and introspect on their true nature—which is what meditation is. Especially, Swami Chinmayaanda emphasized the role of introspection in five stages, outlined in the book "Self-Unfoldment". Starting with the advent of Islam in the 7th and 8th centuries C.E, in Persia, philosophers, mystics, and Gnostics developed this basically ancient concept to the practice of Mysticism ; "Erfan"(عرفان) ; Some of the more famous of these Mystics were : Habib Adjami, Mansour Balkhi, Aya'z Khorasani, Firoozan Irani, Bayazid Bastami, Abolhassan Kharaghani, Yahya Sohrevardi, Abu Saiid Abolkheir, Mansour Hallaj, Einolghozat Hamadani, Attar Neishabouri, Ibn-al-Arabi, Rumi, Eraghi and a great number of others of whom we shall be talking in the coming chapters.

As it was indicated, the term used in the contemporary philosophy of mind is that of the means of learning about one's own currently ongoing, or perhaps in the recent past, mental states or processes. You can, of course, learn about your own mind in the same way you learn about others' minds.

For a process to qualify as "introspective" as the terms ordinarily used in contemporary philosophy of mind, it must minimally meet the following conditions:

1.The mentality condition: Introspection is a process that generates, or is aimed at generating, knowledge, judgments, or beliefs about mental events, states, or processes, and not about affairs outside one's mind, at least not directly. In this respect, it is different from sensory processes that normally deliver information about outward events or about the non-mental aspects of the individual's body. The border between introspective and non-introspective knowledge can begin to seem blurry with respect to bodily self-knowledge such as proprioceptive knowledge about the position of one's limbs or nociceptive knowledge about one's pains. But in principle the introspective part of such processes, pertaining to judgements about one's mind—e.g., that one as the feeling as though one's arms were crossed or of toe-located pain – can be distinguished from the non-introspective judgement that one's arms are in fact crossed or one's toe is being pinched.

Introduction

2.The first-person condition: Introspection is a process that generates, or is aimed at generating, knowledge, judgement, or beliefs about one's own mind only and no one else's, at least not directly. Any process that in a similar manner generates knowledge of one's own and other's minds is by that token not an introspective process. (Some philosophers have contemplated peculiar or science fiction cases in which we might introspect the contents of other's minds directly for example in telepathy or when two people's brains are directly wired together-but the proper interpretation of such cases is disputable.

Mysticism is one of the major pillars upon which Persian classical poetry largely stands. Persian greatest classical poets and literary writers have been deeply inspired by monistic ideas and doctrines. Amongst these we can point to great Gnostics such as Ba'yazid Basta'mi, Ra'biyeh Ghozdari, Sanaii Ghaznavi, Ba'ba'Ta'her, S'adi, Mowlana Jala'l-ed Din Balkhi, known as Rumi, Eraghi, Abu Said Abolkheir, Attar Neishabouri, just to name a few. Mysticism has transcended the time starting in the Orient in particular in India two to three thousand years ago continuing into the present time. It is still very much alive amongst large number of devotees in India, south east Asia, countries in the Middle-East; Iran, Turkey and other. A major number of poems that the readers will come across in this book are inspired by mystic beliefs, sentiments and doctrines. To be able to understand and appreciate the beauty of these poems some understanding of the basic concepts and underlying principles of mysticism as well as some vocabulary used by Sufis and Gnostics in their writings is not only desirable but most of the times necessary. Some of the more common ones will be indicated later. In general, mystic pantheism or monism involves the following propositions:

1-There is One Real Being, the Ultimate ground of all existence. This Realty may be viewed either as God (The Divine essence) or as the World (phenomena by which the hidden Essence is made manifest)

2-There is no creation in Time. Divine Self-manifestation is a perpetual process. While the forms of the universe change and pass and are simultaneously renewed without a moment's intermission, in its essence it is co-eternal with God. There never was a time when it did not exist as a whole in his Knowledge.

Introduction

3-God is both Immanent, in the sense that he appears under the aspect of creation in all phenomenal forms, and Transcendent, in the sense that he is the Absolute Realty above and beyond every appearance.

4-The divine Essence is unknowable. God makes His Nature known to us (mystics in particular) by names and Attributes which He has revealed in the Qur'an. Though essentially identical, from our point of view the Devine Attributes are diverse and opposed to each other, and this differentiation constitutes the phenomenal world, without which we could not distinguish good from evil and come to know the Absolute Good. In the sphere of Realty there is no such thing as evil.

5-According to the Holy tradition, "I created the creatures in order that I might be known," the entire content of God's Knowledge is objectified in the universe and pre-eminently in Man. The Divine Mind, which rules and animates the cosmos as an Indwelling Rational Principle (Logos), displays itself completely in the Perfect Man. The Supreme type of the Perfect Man is the pre-existent Reality of Spirit of Muhammad, whose "Light" irradiates the long series of prophets beginning with Adam and, after them, the hierarchy of Muslim saints, who are Muhammad's spiritual heirs. Whether prophet or saint, the Perfect Man has realized his oneness with God: he is the authentic image and manifestation of God and therefore the final cause of creation, since only through him does God become fully conscious of Himself.

These are some of the themes underlying all the mystic beliefs, mystic writings, doctrines and related poetries starting with Ba'yazid Bastami and other mystic thinkers and poets. They may be regarded as having been gradually evolved by the long succession of Sufi thinkers from the ninth century onwards, then gathered together and finally formulated by the famous Andalusian mystic, Ibn al-Arabi (1165-1240), Who has every right to be the father of Islamic pantheism. He devoted colossal powers of intellect and imagination to constructing a system which, though it lacks order and connection, covers the whole ground in detail and perhaps, all things considered, is the most imposing monument of mystical speculation the world has ever seen. His two books Fusus al-Hekam (Bezels of Wisdom and al-Futuha't al Makkiya (Meccan Revelations) are considered by a large number of Sufis as textbooks in this particular field. However, Mowlavi as one example of the Sufis that were inspired by Ibn- al-Arabi, differs from him in that his mysticism is not "doctoral" in the catholic sense but "experimental."

Introduction

And appeals to the heart more than to the head. He scorns the logic of the schools, and nowhere does he embody in philosophical language even the elements of a system. He is the perfect spiritual guide engaged in making others perfect and furnishing novice and adept alike with matter suitable to their needs. Assuming the general monistic theory to be well known to his readers, he gives them a panoramic view of the Sufi gnosis (direct intuition of God; kindles their enthusiasm by depicting the rapture of those who "break through to the Oneness)" and sees all mysteries revealed. In the coming chapters we shall discuss in greater details the mysticism of Mowlavi. However, stepping back from consideration of mysticism solely in the context of Islamic philosophy and taking a look at it more broadly and universally, philosophical interest in mysticism has been heavy in distinctive, allegedly knowledge-granting "mystical experiences." Philosophers have focused on such topics as the classification of mystical experiences, their nature in different religions and mystical traditions, to what extent mystical experiences are conditioned by a mystic's language and culture, and whether mystical experiences furnish evidence for the truth of their contents. Some philosophers have questioned the emphasis on experience in favor of examining the entire mystical complex. Typically, mystics, theistic or not, see their mystical experience as part of a larger undertaking aimed at human transformation and not as the terminus of their efforts.

Mysticism is best thought of as a constellation of distinctive practices, discourses, texts, institutions, traditions, and experiences aimed at human transformation, variously defined. Generally, philosophers have excluded purely para-sensual experiences such as religious visions and auditions from the mystical. The definition also excludes anomalous experiences such as out of body experiences, telepathy, precognition, and clairvoyance. All of these are acquaintance with objects or qualities of a kind accessible to the senses, to ordinary introspection, such as human thoughts and future events. (A degree of vagueness enters the definition of mystical experience here because of what is to count as a "kind" of thing accessible to non-mystical experience.)

In the wide sense, mystical experiences occur within the religious traditions of at least Judaism, Christianity, Islam, Indian religions, Buddhism, and primal religions. In some of these traditions the experiences are allegedly of a supersensory reality, such as God or Brahman (or, in a few Buddhist traditions, Nirvana, as a reality.) Many Buddhists traditions, however, make no claim for an experience of a supersensory reality. Some cultivate instead

Introduction

an experience of "unconstructed awareness," involving an awareness of the world on an absolutely or relatively non-conceptual level. The unconstructed experience is thought to grant insight, such as into the impermanent nature of all things. This is more common amongst Buddhists.

A unitive experience involves a phenomenological de-emphasis, blurring or eradication of multiplicity, where the cognitive significance of the experience is deemed to lie precisely in that phenomenological feature. Examples are experiences of the oneness of all nature, "Union" with God, as in Christian mysticism. This signifies a rich family of experiences rather than a single experience. Union involves a falling away of the separation between a person and God, short of identity. Christian mystics have variously described union with Devine. Generally, medieval Christian mysticism had at least three stages, variously described, in the union-consciousness: quiet, essentially a prelude to the union with God, full union, and a rapture, the latter involving a feeling of being "carried away" beyond oneself.

Theistic mystics sometimes speak as though they have a consciousness of being fully absorbed into or even identical with God. Examples are a few in the Islamic Mysticism ; Ba'yazid Basta'mi, Husayn Mansur Hallaj (858-922), Ein al-Ghozat Hamada'ni proclaiming, "I am God". This was taken literally by some, when in fact what those mystics, including Halla'j said was: I am the Truth "ana'l-hagh" (ان الحق) in "Islamic pantheism". The utterance:" I am God "was in fact proclaimed by Pharaohs' of Egypt. Mowlana Jala'l-al-Din Rumi includes many references to Halla'j in the Mathnavi including some specifically to the utterance "ana'l-hagh"; (bood ana'l-hagh dar lab-e Mansur nur / bood ana'lla'h dar labe-Fer 'un zur, ("Mansur's "I am the Truth" was purest light, But Pharoah's "I am God" claimed his own might"). The Jewish kabbalist, Isaac of Acre (born 1291), who wrote of the soul absorbed into God as a jug of water into a running well." Also, the Hasidic master, Shneur Zalman of Liady (1745 – 1812) wrote of a person as a drop of water in the ocean of the Infinite with an illusory sense of individual "dropness". It is still controversial, however, as to when such declarations are to be taken as identity assertions, with pantheistic or acosmic intentions, and when they are perhaps hyperbolic variations on descriptions of union-type experiences.

There are other types of mysticism scattered all over the world amongst various peoples, and tribes, however this brief history that was included here should hopefully shed some light upon and explain those types of mysticism

Introduction

that were predominant amongst the Persian mystics covering the range mainly in Iran and within the scope of Islamic population of the Middle Eastern nations. Historically this covers mystics, their beliefs and practice starting with Bayazid Bastami, continuing with Mowlavi, Attar Neisha'bouri, Eraghi, Abu Saiid Abol-khayr, Abolhassan Kharaghani, Abdol-Rahman Ja"mi, and many others in between and after.

In this regard it is important to know that mystics have had their own diction in expressing their beliefs, feelings, sentiments, and style of worship in general. Poets and hymn writers, in particular, have traditionally been using certain symbols in addressing "God" in their prayers. As an example, God has been most frequently addressed as "Beloved" as well as other symbols some of which we shall mention below.
Rumi in his poetry has most often used "Beloved" when speaking of God:

The Beloved is all and the lover (but) a veil;
The Beloved living and the lover a dead thing.

Ba'yazid Bastami employed the term "eshgh" for love of God and insisted that divine love precedes man's love of God. Ba'yazid says: "In the beginning I was in error about four things: I imagined that I recollected God, knew Him, loved Him, and searched for Him. At the end I realized, however, that His recollection preceded mine, His knowledge was prior to mine, His love came before my own, and His search was there before I sought him" (Sahlaki, page 96; Atta'r, I, page.170). Ba'yazid defended the mystic's love of God as mutual love between God and man and maintained that "love consists in regarding your own much as little and your Beloved's little as much. When Yahya' Ibn.Moa'd confessed that he had become intoxicated in drinking from the cup of love of God, Bayazid replied that he had drunk empty the oceans of the heavens and the earth and still his thirst was not quenched and his tongue was hanging out for more Sahlaki, p. 136; Attar, I, p. 143)

Another very common word is "Wine" symbolizing the Divine intoxicant that makes the lover intoxicated with "Divine love" relieving him or her from self and all worldly desires around him or her. Some other similar symbols are: cup, eye, lips, face, hair, witness, beautiful woman, handsome youth, drunk, intoxicated, rose bud, amorous glance, unconscious, kiss, lock of hair, cheek, mole, heart, candle, tavern, magi, cloak, pot-house, light, idol, girdle (Christian's), unity, union, Simorgh (legendry bird), Pir (magi; mystic or

Introduction

religious guide) and more. When reading classical mystic Persian poems in this book you will inevitably come across such symbols. The English translation of the poems, if taken in context, should be helpful to somehow clarify the mystic intent of the symbols and to some extent that of the poet himself. There is of course plenty reading material available in libraries on mysticism as well as clarifications and analysis to help with understanding the true essence and intent of mystic poetries. It should also be pointed out that poetical symbols have always been widely used by a great number of poets throughout the world during the classical periods as well as recent times.

Finally, it is important to note that Persian classical literature (poetry or prose) is fundamentally built by its writers upon moral and spiritual foundations to promote spiritual, ethical, and humanistic principles based on individual integrity, loyalty, social justice, morality, truth and fairness. Family, honor, personal responsibility, good manners and character, humanity, love and mutual respect to preserve the health and welfare of individuals and above all education and proper upbringing of children to maintain order and discipline in the society. The ancient Iranian religion introduced by Zoroaster about 1000 years B.C. was based upon these three principles: good thought, good act, good talk. It promoted honesty, and truth. It condemned lying to one another and declared it to be a Satanic act.

CHAPTER 1: A BRIEF HISTORY OF THE PERSIAN EMPIRE; "HOW IT ALL BEGAN".

At the end of the second millennium BC the Iranian tribes emerged in the region of northwest Iran. These tribes gradually expanded their control over larger areas. Subsequently, the boundaries of Media (which is no longer a country) changed over a period of several hundred years. Iranian tribes were present in western and northwestern Iran from at least the 12th or 11th centuries BC. But the significance of Iranian elements in these regions was established from the beginning of the second half of the 8th century BC. By this time the Iranian tribes were the majority in what later became the territory of the Median Kingdom and also the west of Media proper. A review of textual sources indicates that the northwest, had a population with Iranian speaking people as the majority extending to the regions of Media and further west during the Neo-Assyrian period.

This period of migration coincided with a power vacuum in the Near East with the Middle Assyrian Empire (1365-1020 BC), which had dominated northwestern Iran and eastern Anatolia and the Caucasus, going into a comparative decline. This allowed new peoples to pass through and settle. In addition Elam, the dominant power in Iran, was suffering a period of severe weakness, as was Babylonia to the west.

In western and northwestern Iran and in areas further west prior to Median rule, there is evidence of the earlier political activity of the powerful societies of Elam.Mannaea, Assyria and Urartu. There are various and updated opinions on the positions and activities of Iranian tribes in these societies and prior to the "major Iranian state formations" in the late 7th century BC. One opinion of Hertzfeld and others is that the ruling class were "Iranian migrants" but the society was 'Autonomous' while another opinion of Grantovsky holds that both the ruling class and basic elements of the population were Iranian.

From the 10th to the late seventh centuries BC, the western parts of Media fell under the domination of the vast Neo-Assyrian based in Mesopotamia, which stretched from Cypress in the west to parts of western Iran in the east, Egypt and the north of the Arabian Peninsula. Assyrian kings such as Tiglath-pileser

Brief History of Persian Empire

III, Sargon II, Sennacherib, and Ashurbanipal imposed Vassal Treaties upon the Median rulers and also protected them from predatory raids by marauding Scythians and Cimmerians. During the reign of Sinsharishkun (622-612 BC) the Assyrian Empire, which had been in a state of constant civil war since 626 BC, began to unravel. Subject peoples, such as Medes, Babylonians, Chaldeans, Egyptians, Scythians, Cimmerian, Lydians and Arameans quietly ceased to pay tribute to Assyria

Neo-Asyrians dominance over the Medians came to an end during the reign of Median King Cyaxares, who, in alliance with King Nabopolassar of the Neo-Babylonian Empire, attacked and destroyed the strife-ridden empire between 616 and 609 BC. The newfound alliance helped the Medes to capture Nineveh in 612 BC. The Medes were subsequently able to establish their Median Kingdom (with Ecbatana as their royal capital) beyond their original homeland and had eventually a territory stretching roughly from northeastern Iran to the Kizilirmak River in Anatolia. After the fall of Assyria between 616 BC and 609 BC, a unified Median state was formed which together with Babylonia, Lydia, and Egypt became one of the four major powers of the ancient Near East

Cyaxares was succeeded by his son King Astyages. In 553 BC, his maternal grandson Cyrus the Great, the King of Anshan/Persia, a Median vassal, revolted against Astyages. In 550 BC, Cyrus finally won a decisive victory resulting in Astyages' capture by his own dissatisfied nobles who promptly turned him over to the triumphant Cyrus. After Cyrus's victory against Astyiagus the Medes were subjected to their close kin, the Persians. In the new empire they retained a prominent position; in honor and war, they stood next to the Persians; their court ceremony was adopted by the new sovereigns, who in the summer months resided in Ecbatana; and many noble Medes were employed as official satraps and generals.

Median dynasty

The list of Median rulers and their period of reign is compiled according to two sources. Herodotus calls them "Kings" and associates them with the same family, and the Babylonian chronicles which in "Gad's Chronicle" on the fall of Nineveh gives its own list. A combined list stretching over 150 years is thus:

Chapter 1

Deioces (700-647) BC
Phraotes (647-625) BC
Scythian (624-597) BC
Cyaxares (624-585) BC
Astyages (585-549)

However, not all of these dates and personalities given by Herodotus match the other near eastern sources. In Herodotus (Book 1, chapters 95-130) Deioces is introduced as the founder of a centralized Median state. He had been known to the Median people as "a just and incorruptible man" and when asked by the Median people to solve their possible disputes he agreed and put forward. They made him "king" and built a great city at Ecbatana as the capital state. Judging from the contemporary sources of the region and disregarding the account of Herodotus puts the formation of a unified Median state during the reign of Cyazares or later.

Culture & Society

Greek reference to "Median people", make no clear distinction between the "Persians" and the "Medians"; in fact, for a Greek to become "too closely associated with Iranian culture" was to become medianized, not persianized. The Median Kingdom was a short-lived Iranian state and the textual and archeological sources of that period are rare and little could be known from the Median culture which nevertheless made a" profound, and lasting contribution to the greater world of Iranian culture

Language

Median people spoke the Median language, which was an Old Iranian language. Strabo's Geographical (finished in the early first century) mentions the affinity of Median with other Iranian languages: "The name of Aryan is further extended to a part of Persia and of Media, as also to the Bactrian and Sogdians on the north ; for these speak approximately the same language, but with slight variations.

No original deciphered text has been proven to have been written in the Median language. It is suggested that similar to the later Iranian practice of keeping archives of written documents in Achaemenid Iran, there was also maintenance of archives by the Median government in their capital Ecbatana. There are examples of "Median literature" found in later records. One is according to Herodotus that the Median King Dioces, appearing as a judge, made judgment on causes submitted in writing. There is also a report by Dinon on the existence of "Median court poets". Median literature is part of the" Old Iranian literature" (including also Sakas, Old Persian Avesta) as this Iranian affiliation of them is explicit also in ancient texts, such as Herodotus' account that many Peoples including Medes were "universally called Iranian".

Words of Median origin appear in various other Iranian dialects, including Old Persian. A feature of Old Persian inscriptions is the large number of words and names from other languages and the Median language takes in this regard a special place for historical reasons. The Median words in Old Persian texts, whose Median origin can be established by "phonetic criteria", appear "more frequently among royal titles and among terms of chancellery, military, and judicial affairs.

Religion

There are very limited sources concerning the religion of Median people. Primary sources pointing to the religious affiliations of Medes found so far include the archeological discoveries in Tepee Nish-e Jan, personal names of Median individuals, and the histories of Herodotus. The archeological source gives the earliest of the temple structures in Iran and the "stepped fire altar" discovered there is linked to the common Iranian legacy of the "cult of fire". Herodotus mentions Median Magi as priests as a Median tribe providing priests for both the Medes and the Persians. They had a "priestly caste" which passed their functions from father to son. They played a significant role in the court of the Median king Astyages who had in his court certain Medians as "advisers, dream interpreters, and soothsayers"

Classical historians "unanimously" regarded the Magi as priests of the Zoroastrian faith. From the personal names of Medes as recorded by Assyrians (in 8th and 9th centuries BC) there are examples of the use of the Indi-Iranian word arta- (lit. "Truth") which is familiar from both Avesta and Old Persian and also examples of euophoric names containing Mazdakku and also "Ahura Mazda'". Scholars disagree whether these are indications of Zoroastrian religion amongst the Medes. Diakonoff believes that "Astyages and perhaps even Cyaxares had already embraced a religion derived from the teachings of Zoroaster" and Mary Boyce believes that "the existence of the Magi in Media with their own traditions and forms of worship was an obstacle to Zoroastrian proselytizing there". Boyce wrote that Zoroastrian traditions in the Median city of Ray probably go back to the 8th century BC. It is suggested that from the 8th century BC, a form of "Mazdeism with common Iranian traditions" existed in Media and the strict reforms of Zoroastrian began to spread in western Iran during the reign of the Median kings in the sixth century BC. It has also been suggested by some that Mithras is a Median name and Medes may have practiced Mithraism and had Mithras as their supreme deity.

Kurds and Medes (Origin of Kurds)

Russian historian and linguist Vladimir Minorsky suggested that the Medes, who widely inhabited the land where currently the Kurds form a majority, might have been forefathers of the modern Kurds. He also states that the Medes, who invaded the region in the eight century BC, linguistically resembled the Kurds. This view was accepted by many Kurdish nationalists in the twentieth century. However, Martin van Bruiniessen, a Dutch scholar, argues against the attempt to take the Medes as ancestors of the Kurds.

"Though some Kurdish intellectuals claim that their people are descendants of the Medes", there is no evidence to permit such a connection across the considerable gap in time between the political dominance of the Medes and the first attestation of the Kurds"-van Bruinessen.

Contemporary linguistic evidence has challenged the previously suggested view that the Kurds are descendants of the Medes. Garnet Wind fur professor of Iranian studies identified the Kurdish language as Parthian, albeit with a Median substratum. David Neil Mackenzie, an authority on the Kurdish language, said Kurdish was closer to Persian and questioned the "traditional" view holding that Kurdish, because of its differences from Persian, should be regarded a Northwestern Iranian language. Garnet Assatarian stated that "That the Central Iranian dialects, and primarily those of the Kashan area in the first place, as well as Azeri dialects (otherwise called Southern Tata) are probably the only Iranian dialects, which can pretend to be the direct offshoots of Median. In general, the relationship between the Kurdish and Median is not closer than the affinities between the latter and other North Western dialects— Baluchi, Talishi, South Caspian, Zara, Gurgani, etc

Brief History of Persian Empire

The Achaemenid Empire

By the seventh century BC the Persians had settled in the south-western portion of the Iranian plateau in the region of Persia which came to be their heartland.

The Empire that was also called the first Persian Empire was an ancient Iranian empire based in Western Asia founded by Cyrus the Great (Cyrus II) around 550 BC. It was from this region that Cyrus advanced to defeat the Medes, the Lydia, the Neo-Babylonian, and establish the Acheamenid Empire. He was succeeded by his son Cambyses in 530 BC.

Cambyses conquered the last major power of the region, ancient Egypt, causing the collapse of the twenty- sixth Dynasty of Egypt. Since he became ill and died before, or while leaving Egypt, stories developed, as related by Herodotus, that he was struck down for impiety against the ancient Egyptian deities. He was followd by the usurper Guava tama, and finally by Darius the great in 522 BC. Darius based his claim on membership in a collateral line of the Achaemenid Empire. Darius's first capital was at Susa, and he started the building program of Persepolis. He rebuilt a canal between the Nile and the Red sea, a forerunner of the modern Suez Canal. He improved the extensive road system, and it is during his reign that mention is first made of the Royal road, a great highway stretching all the way from Susa to Sardis with posting stations at regular intervals. Major reforms took place under Darius. Coinage, in the form that was invented over a century before in Lydia in 660 BC, was standardized and its administrative efficiency increased. daric (gold coin) and the shekel (silver coin) were standardized. Coinage had already been in use more or less throughout the empire.

The Old Persian language appears in royal inscriptions, written in a specially adopted version of the cuneiform script. Under Cyrus the Great and Darius I, the Persian Empire eventually became the largest empire in human history up until that point, ruling and administrating over most of the then known world, as well as spanning the continents of Europe, Asia, and Africa. The greatest achievement was the empire itself. The Persian Empire represented the world's superpower that was based on a model of tolerance and respect for other cultures and religions.

In the late sixth century BC, Darius launched his European campaign, in which he defeated the Panonians, conquered Thrace, and subdued all coastal

Chapter 1

Greek cities as well as defeating the European Scythians around the Danube River. In 512/511, Macedon became a vassal kingdom of Persia.

In 499 BC, Athens lent support to a revolt in Miletus, which resulted in the sacking of Sardis. This led to an Acheamenid campaign against the mainland Greece known as the Greco-Persian Wars, which lasted the first half of the 5th century BC, and is known as one of the most important wars in European history. In the first Persian invasion of Greece, the Persian general Mardonius resubjugated Thrace and made Macedonia a full part of Persia. The war eventually turned out in defeat. However. Darius's successor Xerxes I launched the Second Persian invasion of Greece. At a crucial moment in the war, about half of mainland Greece was overrun by the Persians, including all territories on the north of the Isthmus of Corinth, however, this was also turned out in a Greek victory, following the battles of Plataea and Salamis, by which Persia lost its footholds in Europe, and eventually withdrew from it. During the Greco-Persian wars Persia gained major territorial advantages, captured and razed Athens in 480 BC, However, after a string of Greek victories the Persians were forced to withdraw thus losing control of Macedonia, Thrace and Ionia. Fighting continued for several decades after the successful Greek repelling of the Second Invasion with numerous Greek city states under the Athens's newly formed Dolan League, which eventually ended with the peace of Callias in 440 BC, ending the Greco-Persian Wars. In 404 BC, following the death of Darius II, Egypt rebelled under Amyrtaes. Later pharaohs successfully resisted Persian attempts to re conquer Egypt until 343BC, when Egypt was re conquered by Artaxerzas III.

Greek conquest and Seleucid Empire (312BC-248BC)

In 330 BC, Alexander the Macedonian, an avid admirer of Cyrus the Great, attacked the western borders and defeated Darius the third the last King to rule the Acheamenid Empire. It happened mainly because of disloyalty and act of treason committed by his commanders. Darius the third was later murdered by three of his own generals and the tragic and devastating news spread fear throughout the empire. The guards responsible for the protection of Persepolis surrendered the city to Alexander, who simply walked in to the capital encountering no resistance. Thus the Greatest Empire of the ancient world collapsed. The invaders attacked the defenseless city, killing, raping and plundering the the citie's inhabitants. Twelve royal Palaces were plundered by the soldiers. The vast treasures containing deposits of gold, silver and priceless jewels were looted , loaded on to hundreds of carriages and taken to

Brief History of Persian Empire

Athens and Macedonia. Finally on a night of drinking mayhem, Alexander grabbed a torch and set fire to the Palace of hundred columns (Sar-sotune Palace); the private residence of Darius the Great. In that horrible night that will live in memory for ever, Alexander started a devastating and horrifying fire that soon engulfed all of the royal Palaces and gardens; spreading to the entire city. The buildings all over the city burnt out of control for days. By the time that the flames subsided, nothing was left but ashes from a spectacular architectural marvel of the ancient world that had been called "The richest city under the sun"

The Greeks and Macedonians who reported some details of this carnage and act of barbarianism as committed by Alexander and his soldiers, then declared Alexander a" Greek Hero" and called his victorious attack on Persian Empire "A Great Conquest". It must of course be rememberd that, there were almost no other history writers at the time other than Greeks to give a thorough, and unbiased report of the incident. The Greeks so far as we know, had in fact been the world's exclusive historians for centuries and it was them who wrote the story and credited Alexander, with the so called "Great Conquest of the Vast and Powerful Persian Empire". However, because of the rivalry and animosity that was predominant at the time between the Persians and the Greeks in general, it appears that the true story may have never been told; the entire empire was not in fact won by Alexander the way that was reported by the Greek historians. The empire was handed over to him in a silver plate by the three or four traitors, i.e., Darius's generals who betrayed him and subsequently murdered him. As indicated the fear and terror that quickly spread all over the Empire particularly in the eastern territories and satrapies must have caused the defenders of the provinces to prepare and surrender to Alexander and his soldiers once he set off finally, after a few months rest in Persepolis, continuing his murderous expedition throughout the Eastern Asian sub-continent under the Persian rule. Alexander did not meet any challenge or resistance by the Persians from the time he left Persepolis until he reached the Indian sub-continent and crossed over River Indie inside the territories under the rule of local Indian Kings. The territories that were part of the dissolved Persian Empire and had fallen on to his lap without any fighting! However the Indian kings and chieftains gathered forces numbering in thousands and gave Alexander the fight of his life. We should therefore ask: "What is the claim to the title of "The Great Conqueror of the Persian Empire" all about?" Furthermore, what special act of heroism did he commit that should have earned him the title of "Great"? Alexander, as said before was only able to defeat Darius in three battles in Asia Minor at the outset of his invasion. Even those early defeats were the direct result of the betrayal of Darius's generals. In his younger days Alexander had admired the kings of Persia and had probably dreamed of catching a glimpse of the magnificent palaces, and cities of the greatest empire ever created in the history of the ancient world. Before leaving Greece for Persia, he had set his greedy eyes on the treasures of unbelievable wealth gathered in Persepolis and other four capital cities of the empire. Alexander did not appreciate how much work, ingenuity, devotion, sacrifice, and knowledge had gone into the task of building such a great and magnificent civilization. This could explain among other factors the reason why this man in one night decided to commit such a barbaric act of the sort that Gingize Khan repeated few hundred years later when he set fire to many beautiful cities of Iran in Khorassan. The civilized world will never forget nor forgive the barbaric acts of vandalism and murder committed by these invaders causing the destruction of what it had taken thousands of people to build over hundreds of years.

Upon Alexander's death, his Empire broke up shortly. Most of the empire's former territory fell under the rule of the Ptolemaic Kingdom and Seleucid Empire. Seleucid tried to take control of Iran, Mesopotamia and later Syria and Anatolia. His empire was named after him the Seleucid Empire. He was killed in 281 BC by Ptolemy Karamus. In addition to other minor territories which gained independence at that time, the Iranian elites of the central plateau reclaimed power by the second century BC under the Parthian Empire'.

The Achaemenid Empire is noted in Western history as the antagonist of the Greek city-states during the Greco-Persian Wars and for the emancipation of the Jewish exiles in Babylon. The historical mark of the empire went far beyond its territorial and military influences and included cultural, social, technological and religious influences as well. Greek language, philosophy and art came with the colonists. During the Seleucid era, Greek became the common language of diplomacy and literature throughout the empire.

Parthian Empire (248 BC-224 AD)

The Parthian Empire, ruled by the Parthians, a group of northwestern Iranian people, was of the Arsacid dynasty, that reunited and governed Iranian plateau after the Parma conquest of Parthia and defeating the Seleucid Empire in the later third century BC and intermittently controlled Mesopotamia between 150 BC and 224 AD. The Parthian Empire quickly included Eastern Arabia.

Parthia was the eastern arch-enemy of the Roman Empire and it limited Rome's expansion beyond Cappadocia (central Anatolia). The Parthian armies included two types of cavalry: the heavily armed and armored cataphracts and the lightly- armed but highly-mobile mounted archers.

For the Romans, who relied on heavy infantry, the Parthians were too hard to defeat, as both types of cavalry were much faster and more mobile than foot soldiers, which proved pivotal in the crushing Roman defeat at the battle of Carrhae. On the other hand, the Parthians found it difficult to occupy conquered areas as they were unskilled in siege warfare. Because of these weaknesses, neither the Romans nor the Parthians were able to completely annex each other's territory.

The Parthian empire subsisted for five centuries, longer than most Eastern Empires. The end of this empire came at last in 224 AD, when the empire's organization had loosened and the last king was defeated by one of the empire's vassal peoples, the Persians under the Sassanians. However, the Arascid dynasty continued to exist for centuries onwards in Armenia, the Iberia, and the Caucasian Albania, which were all eponymous branches of the dynasty.

Sassanian Empire (224 CE-651CE)

The first shah of the Sassanian Empire, Ardeshir 1, started reforming the country economically and militarily. For a period of more than 400 years Iran was once again one of the leading powers in the world, alongside its neighboring rival, the Roman and the Byzantine Empires. The entire's territory, at its height, encompassed all of today's Iran, Iraq, Azerbaijan, Armenia, Georgia, Abkhazia, Dagestan, Lebanon, Jordan, Palestine, Israel, parts of Pakistan, Central Asia, Eastern Arabia, and parts of Egypt.

Most of the Sassanian Empire's lifespan was overshadowed by the frequent Byzantine-Sassanian wars, a continuation of the Roman-Parthian Wars and the all-comprising Roman-Persian Wars; the last was the longest-lasting conflict in human history. Started in the first century BC by their predecessors, the Parthian and Romans, the last Roman-Persian War was fought in the

Chapter 1

seventh century. The Persians defeated the Romans at the Battle of Edessa in 260 CE and took Emperor Valerian prisoner for the remainder of his life.

Eastern Arabia was conquered early on. During KhosrowII's rule in 590-628, Egypt, Jordan, Palestine and Lebanon were also annexed to the Empire. The Sassanians called their empire Iranshahr ("Dominion of the Arians"), i.e., of Iranians.

A chapter of Iran's history followed after roughly six hundred years of conflict with the Roman Empire. During this time, the Sassanian and Roman-Byzantine armies clashed for influence in Anatolia, the western Caucasus (mainly Lexica and the kingdom of Iberia, modern-day Georgia and Abkhazia), Mesopotamia, Armenia and the Levant. Under Justinian I, the war came to an easy peace with payment of tribute to the Sassanians.

However, the Sassanians used the deposition of the Byzantine emperor Maurice as a casus belli to attack Asiatic medieval art.the Empire. After many gains, the Sassanians were defeated at Issus, Constantinople, and finally Nineveh, resulting in peace. With the conclusion of the over 700 years lasting Roman-Persian Wars through the climactic Byzantine-Sassanian War of 602-628 which included the very siege of the Byzantine capital of Constantinople, the war –exhausted Persians lost the Battle of Al-Qadisiyyah (632CE) in Hellas (present day Iraq) to the invading Muslim forces.

The Sassanian era, encompassing the length of Late Antiquity, is considered to be one of the most important and influential historical periods in Iran, and had a major impact on the world. In many ways the Sassanian period witnessed the highest achievement of Persian civilization, and constitutes the last great Iranian Empire before the adoption of Islam. Persia influenced Roman Civilization considerably during the Sassanian times, their cultural influence extending far beyond the empire's territorial borders, reaching as far as Western Europe, Africa, China and India and also playing a prominent role in the formation of Europe, and the influence was carried forward to the Muslim world. The dynasty's unique and aristocratic culture transformed the Islamic conquest and destruction of Iran into a Persian Renaissance. Much of what later became known as Islamic culture, architecture, writing, and other contributions to civilization, were taken from the Sassanian Persians into the broader Muslim world.

Islamic conquest of Persia

Brief History of Persian Empire

In 633, when the Sassanian king Yazdgerd III was ruling over Iran, The Muslims under Omar the caliph invaded the country right after it had been in a bloody civil war. Several Iranian nobles and families such as King Dinar of the House of Karen, and later Kanarangiyan of Khorasan, mutinied against their Sassanian overlords. Although the House of Mihran had claimed the Sassanian throne under the two prominent generals Bahram Chobin and Shahrbaraz, it remained loyal to the Sassanians during their struggle against the Arabs, but the Mihrans were eventually betrayed and defeated by their own kinsmen, the House of Ispahbudan, under their leader Farrukhzad, who had mutinied against Yazdgerd III.

Yazdgerd III, fled from one district to another until a miller killed him for his purse at Marv in 651CE. By 674, Muslims had conquered Greater Khorasan (which included modern Iranian Khorassan province and modern Afghanistan and parts of (Transoxiana).

The Muslim conquest of Persia ended the Sassanian Empire and led to the eventual decline of the Zoroastrian religion in Persia. Over time, the majority of Iranians converted to Islam. Most of the aspects of the previous Persian civilizations were not discarded, but were absorbed by the new Islamic polity.

Umayyad era and Muslim incursions into the Caspian coast

After the fall of the Sassanian Empire in 651CE, the Arabs of the Umayyad Caliphate adopted many Persian customs, especially the administrative and the court mannerisms. Arab provincial governors were undoubtedly either Persianized Arameans or ethnic Persians; certainly Persian remained the language began at the capital, Damascus. The new Islamic coins evolved from imitations of Sassanian coins (as well as Byzantine), and the Pahlavi script on the coinage was replaced with Arabic alphabet of official business of the caliphate until the adoption of Arabic toward the end of the seventh century.

During the Umayyad Caliphate, the Arab conquerors imposed Arabic as the primary language of the subject peoples throughout their empire. Al-Hajjaj-ibn Yusuf, who was not happy with the prevalence of the Persian language in the divan, (Administration), ordered the official language of the conquered land be replaced by Arabic, sometimes by force.(None Arabs were forced to even speak Arabic inside their homes, and those violating the order would be prosecuted and punished). In Al-Biruni's "From the Remaining Signs of Past Centuries" for example it is written:

"When Qutaibah bin Muslim under the command of Al-Hajjaj bin Yusuf was sent to Kharazm with a military expedition and conquered it for the second time, he swiftly killed whoever wrote Kharazmian native language that knew of the Kharazmian heritage, history, and culture. He then killed all their Zoroastrian priests and burned and wasted their books, until gradually the illiterate only remained, who knew nothing of writing, and hence their history was mostly forgotten.

In the 7th century C.E when many non-Arabs such as Persians entered Islam, they were recognized as mawali ("clients") and treated as second-class citizens by the ruling Arab elite until the end of the Umayyad Caliphate. During this era, Islam was initially associated with the ethnic identity of the Arab and required formal association with an Arab tribe and the adoption of the client status of mawali. The half-hearted policies of the late Umayyad to tolerate non-Arab Muslims and Shiites had failed to quell unrest among these minorities.

However, all of Iran was still not under Arab control, and the region of Daylam was under the control of the Daylamites, while Tabarestan was under Dabuyid and Paduspanid control, and the Mount Damavand region under Masmughans of Damavand. The Arabs had invaded these regions several times, but achieved no decisive result because of the inaccessible terrain of the regions. The most prominent ruler of the Dabuyid, known as Farrakhan the Great, reigned (712-728), managed to hold his domains during his long struggle against Arab general Yazid ibn al-Muhallab, who was defeated by a combined Dailamite-Dabuyid army, and was forced to retreat from Tabarestan.

With the death of the Umayyad Caliph Hisham ibn abdal-Malik in 743CE, the Islamic world was launched into civil war. Abu Muslim was sent to Khorasan by the Abbasid Caliphate initially as a propagandist and then to revolt on their behalf. He took Marv defeating the Umayyad governor there Nasr ibn Sayyar. He became the de facto Abbasid governor of Khorasan. During the same period, the Dabuyid ruler Khurshid declared independence from the Umayyad, but shortly forced to recognize Abbasid authority. In 750, Abu Muslim became leader of the Abbasid army and defeated the Umayyad at the Battle of the Zahab. Abu Muslim stormed Damascus, the capital of the Umayyad caliphate, later that year.

Brief History of Persian Empire

Abbasid period and autonomous Iranian dynasties

The Abbasid army consisted primarily of Khorasanians and was led by an Iranian general, Abu Muslim Khorasani. It contained both Iranian and Arab elements, and the Abbasids enjoyed both Iranian and Arab support. The Abbasids overthrew the Umayyad in 750. The Abbasid Revolution essentially marked the end of the Arab empire and the beginning of a more inclusive, multi-ethnic state in the Middle East.

One of the first changes the Abbasids made after taking power from the Umayyad was to move the capital from Damascus, in the Levant, to Iraq. The latter region was influenced by Persian history and culture, and moving the capital was part of the Persian mawali demand for Arab influence in the empire. The city of Baghdad was constructed on the Tigris River in 762, to serve as the new Abbasid capital. The Abbasids established the position of vizier like the Barmakis in their administration, which was the equivalent of a "vice-caliph", or second in command. Eventually, this change meant that many caliphs under the Abbasids ended up in a much more ceremonial role than ever before, with the vizier in real power. A new Persian bureaucracy began to replace the old Arab aristocracy, and the entire administration reflected these changes, demonstrating that the new dynasty was different in many ways to the Umayyad.

By the 9th century, Abbasid control began to wane as regional leaders sprang up in the far corners of the empire to challenge the central authority of the Abbassid Caliphate. The Abbasid caliphs began enlisting mamlukes, Turkic-speaking warriors, who had been moving out of central Asia into Transoxiana as slave warriors as early as the 9th century. Shortly thereafter the real power of the Abbasid caliphs began to wane; eventually, they became religious figureheads while the warrior slaves ruled.

The 9th century also saw the revolt by native Zoroastrians, known, as the Khoramdinan against oppressive Arab rule. The movement was led by Persian freedom fighter Baback Khoramdin. Babak's Iranianizing rebellion, from its base in Azerbaijan in northwestern Iran, called for a return of the political glories of the Iranian past. The Khoramdinan rebellion of Babak spread to the western and central parts of Iran and lasted more than twenty years before it was defeated when Babak was betrayed by Afshin, a senior general of the Abbasid Calliphate.

As the power of the Abbasid caliphs diminished, a series of dynasties rose in various parts of Iran, some with considerable influence and power. Among the most important of these overlapping dynasties were the Tahirids in Khorasan (821-873); the Safarids in Sistan (861-1003), their rule lasted as maleks of Sistan until 1537; and the Samanids (819-1005), originally at Bukhara. The Samanids eventually ruled an area from central Iran to Pakistan.

By the early 10th century, The Abbasids almost lost control to the growing faction known as the Buyid dynasty (934-1062). Since much of the Abbasid administration had been Persian anyway, the Buyids were quietly able to assume real power in Baghdad. The Buyids were defeated in the mid-11th century by the Seljuk Turks, who continued to exert influence over the Abbasids, while publicly pledging allegiance to them. The balance of power in Baghdad remained as such- with the Abbasid in power in name only- until the Mongol invasion in 1258 sacked the city and definitely ended the Abbasid dynasty.

During the Abbasid period an enfranchisement was experienced by the mawali and a shift was made in political conception from that of a primarily Arab empire to one of a Muslim empire and in 930 C.E a requirement was enacted that required all bureaucrats of the empire be Muslim.

Islamic golden age, Shu'ubiyya movement and Persianization process

Islamization was a long process by which Islam adopted by the majority population of Iran. Richard Bulliet's "conversion curve", indicates that only about 10% of Iran converted to Islam during the relatively Arab-centric Umayyad period. Beginning in the Abbasid period, with its mix of Persians as well as Arab rulers the Muslim percentage of the population rose from approximately 40% in the mid-9th century to close to 100% by the end of the 11th century. Seyed Hussein Nasr suggests that the rapid increase in conversion was aided by the Persian nationality of the rulers.

Although Persians adopted the religion of their conquerors, over the centuries they worked to protect and revive their distinctive language and culture, a process known as Persianization. Arabs and Turks participated in this attempt.

Brief History of Persian Empire

In the 9th and 10th centuries, non-Arab subjects of the Ummah created a movement called Shu'ubiyyah in response to the privileged status of Arabs. Most of those behind the movement were Persians, but references to Egyptians, Berbers and Aramaeans are attested. Citing as its basis Islamic notions of equality of races and nations, the movement was primarily concerned with preserving Persian culture and protecting Persian identity, though within a Muslim context.

The Samanid dynasty led the revival of Persian culture; an Event that we could truly call the Persian Renaissance. This was in many ways similar to the European Renaissance that commenced almost seven hundred years later in the fifteen century C.E in Europe! As mentioned in the previous chapter the Arabs had forbidden the use of Persian languages (Pahlavi, and Dari as well as other local dialects and had forced all Iranians to exclusively learn and use Arabic). However, once Jacob Laysea Safar, the Founder of Safarid dynasty, revolted against the Caliphate in Baghdad and received the charter of governorship of a number of Persian eastern territories, he encouraged the poets and writers to start using Persian language. Mohammad Vasif Sistani was, thereafter the first poet commissioned to write all his poems in Persian. Other poets and in particular Rudaki, who was later called "the father of Persian poetry" followed suit and Persian became once again the formal language alongside Arabic for writing and speaking throughout the Iranian territories. This was the start of Persian Renaissance almost two hundred years after the fall of Sassanian Empire. The Samanids also revived many ancient Persian festivals. Their successor the Ghaznavids, who were of non-IranianTurkic origin, also became instrumental in the revival of Persian culture. The Ghaznavids actually facilitated and encouraged gathering of a large number of Persian poets and writers led by the famous Persian poet Onsori, at their Royal Court. The Ghaznavid dynasty was a Persianate Muslim dynasty of Turkic mamluk origin, at their greatest extent ruling large parts of Iran, Afghanistan, much of Transoxiana and the northwest Indian subcontinent from 977 to 1186 C.E after helping to overthrow the Samanids at the instigation of The Caliphate in Baghdad. The dynasty was founded by Sabuktigin upon his succession to rule of the region.

The culmination of the Persianization movement was the Shah-nameh, the national epic of Iran by Ferdowsi, written entirely in Persian. This voluminous work reflects Iran's ancient history, mythology, its unique cultural values, its pre-Islamic Zoroastrian religion, and its sense of nationhood. (This great literary masterpiece will be introduced in the later chapters). According to Bernard Lewis:

"Iran was indeed Islamized, but it was not arabized. Persians remained Persians. And after an interval of silence, Iran re-emerged as a separate, different and distinctive element within Islam, eventually adding a new element even to Islam itself. Culturally, politically, and most remarkable of all even religiously, the Iranian contribution to the new Islamic civilization is of immense importance. The work of Iranians can be seen in every field of cultural endeavor, including Arabic poetry, to which poets of Iranian origin composing their poems in Arabic made a very significant contribution. In a sense, Iranian Islam is a second advent of Islam itself, a new Islam sometimes referred to as Islam-I- Ajam. It was this Persia Islam, rather than the original Arab Islam, that was brought to new areas and new peoples: to the Turks, first in Central Asia and then in Middle East in a country which came to be called Turkey, and of course to India. Ottoman Turks brought a form of Iranian civilization to the walls of Vienna"

The Islamization of Iran was to yield deep changes within the cultural, scientific and political structure of Iran's society: The blossoming of Persian literature, philosophy, medicine and art became major elements of the newly forming Muslim civilization. Inheriting a heritage of thousands of years of civilization, and being at the "crossroads of the major cultural highways", contributed to Persia emerging as what culminated into the so called "Islamic Golden Age" all thanks to ingenuity, creativity, and exceptional talents and work of Persians. During this period, hundreds of Persian scholars and scientists whom Europeans mistakenly labeled Arab because, their books and manuscripts were written in Arabic, vastly contributed to technology, science and medicine, later influencing the rise of European science during the Renaissance.

The Most important scholars of almost all of the Islamic sects and schools of thought were Persian or lived in Iran, including the most notable and reliable Hadith collectors of Shia' t and Sunni like Shaikh Saduq, Shaikh Kulainy, Hakim al-Nishabouri, Imam Muslim and Imam Bukhari, the greatest theologians of Shia't and Sunni like SheikhTusi, Imam Ghazali, Imam Fakhr al-Razi and Al-Zamakhshari, the greatest physicians, astronomers, logicians, mathematicians, philosophers and scientists like Avicenna, and Nasir-al-Din al-Tusi, the greatest Shaykh of Sufism like Rumi, and Abdul-Qadir Gilani.

Brief History of Persian Empire

Persianate states and dynasties (977-1219)

In 977 C.E a Turkic governor of the Samanids, Subuktigin, conquered Ghazna (in present-day Afghanistan) and established a dynasty, The Ghaznavids, that lasted to 1186. The Ghaznavids Empire grew by taking all of the Samanids territories south of the Amu Darya in the last decade of the 10th century, and eventually occupied parts of Eastern Iran, Afghanistan, Pakistan and north-west India.

The Ghaznavids are generally credited with launching Islam into a mainly Hindu India. The invasion of India was undertaken in 1000 AD by the Ghaznavid's ruler, Sultan Mahmud, and continued for several years. It is reported that Mahmud invaded India about twelve times. The dynasty was however, unable to hold power for long, particularly after the death of Mahmud in 1030 C.E. By 1040 the Seljuqs had taken over the Ghaznavid's territories in Iran.

The Seljuqs, who like the Ghaznavids were Persianate and of Turkic origin, slowly conquered Iran over the course of 11th century. The dynasty had its origin in The Turcoman tribal confederation of Central Asia and marked the beginning of Turkic power in the Middle East. They established a Sunni Muslim rule over parts of Central Asia and the Middle East from the 11th to 14th centuries. They sat upon Empire known as Great Seljuq Empire stretched from Anatolia in the west to western Afghanistan in the East and the western borders of (modern-day) China in the north-east; and were the target of the First Crusade. Today they are regarded as the cultural ancestors of the Western Turks, the present –day inhabitants of Turkey and Turkmenistan, and they are remembered as great patrons of Persian culture, art, literature, and language.

The dynasty Founder, Tughril Beg, turned his arm against the Ghaznavids in Khorasan. He moved south and then west, conquering but not wasting the cities in his path. In 1055 the caliph in Baghdad gave Tughril Beg robes, gifts, and the title King of the East. Under Tughril Beg's successor, Malik Shah (1072-1092), Iran enjoyed a cultural and scientific renaissance, largely attributed to his brilliant vizier Nizam al Mulk. These leaders established the observatory where Omar Khayyam did much of his experimentation for a new calendar, and they built religious schools in all the major towns. They brought Abu Hamid Ghazali, one of the greatest Islamic theologians, and other eminent scholars to the Seljuq capital at Baghdad and encouraged and supported their work.

When Malik Shah died in 1092, the empire split as his brother and four sons quarreled over the apportioning of the empire among themselves. In Anatolia, Malik Shah 1 was succeeded by Kilij Arsalan 1 who founded the Sultanate of Rum and in Syria by his brother Tutush 1. In Persia he was succeeded by his son Mahmud 1 whose reign was contested by his other three brothers Barkiyaruq in Iraq, Muhammad1 in Baghdad and Ahmad Sanjar in Khorasan. As seljuq power in Iran weakened, other dynasties began to step up in its place, including a resurgent Abbasid caliphate and the Khwarezmshahs. The Khwarezmid Empire was a Sunni Muslim Persianate dynasty, of East Turkic origin, that ruled in Central Asia. Originally vassals of the Seljuqs, they took advantage of the decline of the Seljuqs to expand into Iran. In 1194 the Khwarezshah Alaad-Din Tekesh defeated the Seljuq sultan Toghrul 111 in battle and the Seljuq Empire in Iran collapsed. Of the former Seljuq Empire, only the Sultanate of Rum in Anatolia remained.

A serious internal threat to the Seljukqs during their reign came from the Nizari Ismailis, a secret sect with headquartes at Alamut Castle between Rasht and Teheran. They controlled the immediate area for more than 150 years and sporadically sent out adherents to strengthen their rule by murdering important officials. Several of the various theories on the etymology of the word assassin derive from these killers.

Parts of northwestern Iran were conquered in the early 13th century C.E by the Kingdom of Georgia, led by Tamar the Great.

Mongol conquest and rule (1219-1370)

The Khwarezmian dynasty only lasted a few decades, until the arrival of the Mongols. Genghis Khan had unified the Mongols, and under him the Mongol Empire quickly expanded in several directions, until by 1218 it bordered Khwarezm. At that time the Khwarezmid Empire was ruled by Ala ad-Din Muhammad (1200-1220). Muhammad, like Genghis was intent on expanding his lands and had gained the submission of most of Iran. He declared himself Shah and demanded formal recognition from the Abbasid caliph Al-Nasir. Hence the caliph rejected his claim, Ala ad-Din Muhammad proclaimed one of his nobles Caliph and unsuccessfully tried to depose Al-Nasir.

Brief History of Persian Empire

The Mongol invasion of Iran began in 1219, after two diplomatic missions to Khwarezm sent by Genghiz Khan had been massacred. During 1220-21 Bukhara, Samarkand, Hearat, Tus and Nishabour were razed, and the whole populations were slaughtered. Khwarezm Shah fled, to die on an Island off the Caspian coast. During the invasion of Transoxiana in 1219, along with the main Mongol force, Genghiz Khan used a Chinese specialist catapult unit in battle; they were used again in 1220 in Transoxiana. The Chinese may have used the catapults to hurl gunpowder bombs, since they already had them by this time

While Genghiz Khan was conquering Transoxiana and Persia, several Chinese who were familiar with gunpowder were serving in Genghiz Khan's army. "Whole regiments" entirely made out of Chinese were used by the Mongols to command bomb hurling trebuchets during the invasion of Iran. Historians have suggested that the Mongol invasion had brought Chinese gunpowder weapons to Central Asia. One of these was the huonchong, a Chinese mortar. Books written around the area afterward depicted gunpowder weapons which resembled those of China.

Destruction under the Mongols

Before his death in 1227CE, Genghiz had reached western Azerbaijan, pillaging and burning cities along the way.
The Mongols invasion was disastrous to the Iranians, although the Mongol invaders were eventually converted to Islam and accepted the culture of Iran, the Mongol destruction of the Islamic heartland marked a major change of direction for the region. Much of the six centuries of Islamic scholarship, culture, and infrastructure was destroyed as the invaders burned libraries, and replaced mosques with Buddhist temples.

The Mongols killed many Iranian civilians. Destruction of qanats (underground water canals), irrigation systems destroyed the pattern of relatively continuous settlement, producing numerous isolated oasis cities in a land where they had previously been rare. A large number of people, particularly males, were killed; between 1220 and 1258, 90% of the total population of Iran may have been killed as a result of mass extermination and famine.

Il-khanate (1256-1335)

Chapter 1

After Genghiz's death, Iran was ruled for almost 300 years by several Mongol commanders. Genghiz's grandson, Hulagu Khan, was tasked with the westward expansion of Mongol dominion. However, by the time he ascended to power the Mongol Empire had already dissolved, dividing into different factions. Arriving with an Army, he established himself in the region and founded the Ilkhanate, a breakaway state of the Mongol Empire, which would rule Iran for the next eighty years and become Persian in the process.

Hulago Khan seized Baghdad in 1258 and put the last Abbasid caliph to death. The westward advance of his forces was stopped by the Mamelukes, however, at the battle of Ain Jalut in Palestine in 1260. Hulagu's campaign against Muslims also enraged Berke, khan of the Golden Horde and a convert to Islam. Hulago and Berke fought each other, demonstrating the weakening unity of the Mongol Empire.

The rule of Hulago's great-grandson, Ghazan (1295-1304), saw the establishment of Islam as the state religion of the Ilkhanate. Ghazan and his famous Iranian vazier, Rashi al-Din, brought Iran a partial brief economic revival. Rashid al-Din actually built a great cultural and theological city called Rashidiyeh with art and medical schools and other facilities of more than 10,000.00 people. The Mongols lowered taxes for artisans, encouraged agriculture, rebuilt and extended irrigation works, and improved the safety of the trade routes. As a result, commerce increased dramatically.

Items from India, China, and Iran passed easily across the Asian steppes, and these contacts culturally enriched Iran. For example, Iranians created a new style of painting based on unique fusion of solid, two-dimensional Mesopotamian painting with the feathery, light brush strokes and other motifs characteristic of China. After Ghazan's nephew Abu Said died in 1335, however, the Ilkhanate lapsed into civil war and was divided between several smaller dynasties- most prominently the Jalayirids, Muzaffarids, Sarbdars, and Kartids.
The mid-14th century Black Death killed about 30% of the country's population.

Sunnism and Shiism in pre-Safavid Iran

Brief History of Persian Empire

Prior to the rise of the Safavid Empire, Sunni Islam was the dominant religion, accounting for around 90% of the population at the time. According to Morteza Motahari the majority of Iranian scholars and masses remained Sunni until the time of Safavids.The domination of Sunnis did not mean Shia'ts was rootless in Iran. The writers of the Four Books of Shia'ts were Iranian, as well as many other great Shia'ts scholars.

The domination of the Sunni creed during the first nine Islamic centuries characterized the religious history of Iran during this period. There were however some exceptions to this general domination which emerged in the form of the Zaydis of Tabarestan, the Buydis, the Kakuyids, the rule of Sultan Mohammed Khoda'bandeh and the Sarbedaran.

Apart from this domination there existed, firstly throughout these nine centuries, Shia inclinations among many Sunnis of this land and, secondly, original Imami Shiism as well as Zaydi Shiism had prevalence in some parts of Iran. During this period, Shia in Iran was nourished from Kufah, Baghdad and later from Najaf and Hillah. Shiism was the dominant sect in Tabaristan, Qum, Kashan, Avaj and Sabzevar. In many other areas merged population of Shia and Sunni also lived together.

During the 10th and 11th centuries, Fatimids sent Ismailis Da'I (missioners) to Iran as well as other Muslim lands. When Ismaillis divided into two sects, Nizaris established their base in Iran. Hassan-e Sabbah conquered fortresses and captured Alamut in 1090 AD. Nizaris used this fortress until a Mongol raid in1256.

After the Mongol raid and fall of the Abbasids, Sunni heierarchies faltered. Not only they did lose the caliphate but also the status of official mazhab (religion). Their loss was the gain of Shia, whose center was not in Iran at that time. Several local Shia dynasties like the Sarbedars were established during this time.

The main change occurred in the beginning of the of the 16th century, When Ismail 1 founded the Safavid dynasty and initiated a religious policy to recognize Shia Islam as the official religion of the Safavid Empire and the fact that modern Iran remains an officially Shi'it state is a direct result of Shah Ismail's actions

Timurid Empire (1370-1507 CE)

Chapter 1

Iran remained divided until the arrival of Timur, an Iranified Turco-Mongol belonging to the Timurid dynasty. Like its predecessors, the Timurid Empire was also part of Persianate world. After establishing a power base in Transoxiana, Timur invaded Iran in 1381and eventually conquered most of it. Timur's campaigns were known for its brutality; many people were slaughtered and several cities were destroyed.

His regime was characterized by tyranny and bloodshed, but also by its inclusion of Iranians in administrative roles and its promotion of architecture and poetry. His successors, the Timurids, maintained a hold on most of Iran until 1452, when they lost the bulk of it to Black Sheep Turkmen. The Black Sheep Turkmen were conquered by the White Sheep under Uzin Hasan in 1468; Uzun Hassan and its successors were the masters of Iran until the rise of the Safavids.

Kara Koyunlu

The Kara koyunlu were Oghuz Turks who ruled over northwestern Iran and surrounding areas from 1374-1468 C.E. The Kara Koyunlu expanded their conquest to Baghdad, however, internal fighting, defeats by the Timurids, rebellions by the Armenians in response to their persecution, and failed struggle with the Ag Qoyunlu led to their eventual demise.

Aq Qoyunlu

Aq Qoyunlu was Oghuz Turkic tribal federation of Sunni Muslims who ruled over most of Iran and large parts of surrounding areas from 1378 to 1501 CE. Aq Qoyunlu emerged when Timur granted them of Diyar Bakr in present-day Turkey. Afterward they struggled with their rival Oghuz Turks, the Kara Koyunlo. While the Aq Qoyunlu was successful in defeating Kara Koyunlu, their struggle with the emerging Safavid dynasty led to their downfall.

Early modern era (1502-1925)

Brief History of Persian Empire

Persia underwent a revival under the Safavid dynasty (1502-1736), the most prominent figure of which was Shah Abbas 1.Some historians credit the Safavid dynasty for founding the modern nation-state of Iran. Iran's contemporary Shia character and significant segments of Iran's current borders take their origin from this era.

The Safavid Empire (1501-1736)

The Safavid dynasty was one of the most significant ruling dynasties of Persia (modern Iran). And "is often considered the beginning of modern Persian history"
They ruled one of the greatest Persian empires after the Muslim conquest of Persia and established the Twelver school of Shi'a Islam as the official religion of their empire, making one of the most important turning points in Muslim History. The safavids ruled from 1501 to 1722 (experiencing a brief restoration from 1729 to 1736) and at their height, they controlled all of modern Iran, Azerbaiejan and Armenia, most of Georgia, the North Caucasus, Iraq, Kuwait and Afghanistan, as well as Turkey, Syria, Pakistan, Turkmenistan and Uzbekistan. Safavid Iran was one of the Islamic "gunpowder empires", along with its neighbors, its archrival and principle enemy the Ottoman Empire, as well as the Mughal Empire.

The Safavid ruling dynasty was founded by Ismail, who styled himself Shah Ismail 1 and practically worshipped by his Qizilba'sh followers. Ismail invaded Shirvan to avenge the death of his father, Shaykh Haydar, who had been killed during his siege of Derbent, in Dagestan. Afterwards he went on a campaign of conquest, and following the capture of Tabriz in July 1501, he enthroned himself as the Shah of Iran, minted coins in this name, and proclaimed Shi'ism the official religion of his domain.

Although initially the masters of Azerbaijan and southern Dagestan only, the Safavids had, in fact, won the struggle for power in Persia which had been going on for nearly a century between various dynasties and political forces following the fragmentation of the Kara Koyunlu and the Aq Qoyunlu. A year after his victory in Tabriz, Ismail proclaimed most of Persia as his domain, and quickly conquered and unified Iran under his rule. Soon afterwards, the new Safavid Empire rapidly conquered regions, nations, and the peoples in all directions, including Armenia, Azerbaijan, parts of Georgia, Mesopotamia (Iraq), Kuwait, Syria, Dagestan, large parts of what is now Afghanistan, parts

Chapter 1

of Turkmenistan, and large chunks of Anatolia, laying the foundation of its multi-ethnics character which would heavily influence the empire itself (most notably the Caucasus and its peoples).

Tahmasp1, the son and successor of Ismail I, carried out multiple invasions in the Caucasus which had been incorporated in the Safavid Empire since Shah Ismail 1 and for many centuries afterwards, and started with the trend of deporting and moving hundreds of thousands of Caucasians, Georgians, and Armenians to Iran's heartlands. Initially only solely put in the royal harems, royal guards, and minor other sections of the Empire. Tahmasp believed he could eventually reduce the power of the Qizilbash by creating and fully integrating a new layer in Iranian society. As Encyclopedia Iranica states; for Tahmasp, the problem circled around the military tribal elite of the empire, the Qizilbash who believed that physical proximity to and control of a member of the immediate Safavid family guaranteed spiritual advantages, political fortune, and material advancement. With this new Caucasian layer in Iranian society, the undisputed might of the Qizelbash (who functioned much like the ghazis of the neighboring Ottoman Empire) would be questioned and fully diminished a society would become fully meritocratic.

Shah Abbas 1 and his successors would significantly expand this policy and plan initiated byTahmasb deporting during his reign alone some 200,000 Georgians, 300,000 Armenians and100,000 -150,000 Caucasians to Iran, completing the foundation of a new layer in Iranian society. With this, and the complete systematic disorganization of the Qizilbash, by his personal orders he eventually succeeded in replacing the power of the Qizilbash, with that of Caucasian ghulams. These new Caucasian elements (the so-called Ghilman "servants") almost always after conversion to Shi'asm depending on given function would be, were unlike the Ghizilbaash, fully loyal only to Shah. The other masses of Caucasians were deployed in all other possible functions and positions available in the empire, as well as in the harem, regular military, craftsmen, farmers, etc. This system of mass usage of Caucasian subjects remained to exist until the fall of Qajar dynasty.

The greatest of the Safavid monarchs, Shah Abbas 1 "The Great" (1587-1629) came to power in 1587 aged 16. Abbas 1 first fought the Uzbeks recapturing Hearat and Mashhad in 1598, which had been lost by his predecessor Mohammad Khodabandeh by the Ottoman-Safavid War (1578-1590). Then he turned against the Ottomans, the archrivals of Safavids recapturing

Brief History of Persian Empire

Baghdad, eastern Iraq and the Caucasian provinces and beyond by 1618. Between 1616 and 1618, following the disobedience of his most loyal Georgian subjects Teimuraz 1 and Luarsab 11, Abbas carried out a punitive campaign in his territories of Georgia, devastating Kakheti and Tbilisi and carrying away 130,000-200,000 Georgian captives towards mainland Iran. His new army which had dramatically been improved with the advent of Robert Shirley and his brothers following the first diplomatic mission to Europe, pitted the first crushing victory over the Safavid's archrivals, the Ottomans in the above mentioned (1603-18) war and would surpass the Ottomans in military strength. He also used his new force to dislodge the Portuguese from Bahrain (1602) and Hormoz (1622) with the aid of the English navy, in the Persian Gulf.

He expanded commercial links with the Dutch East Indies Company and established firm links with the European royal houses, which had been initiated by Ismail 1 earlier on by the Habsburg-Persian alliance. Thus Abbas 1 was able to break dependence on the Ghizilbash for military might and therefore was able to centralize control. The Safavid dynasty had already established itself during Shah Ismail 1, but under Abbas 1 it really became a major power in the world along with its archrival Ottoman Empire, against whom it became able to compete on equal foot. It also started the promotion of tourism in Iran. Under their rule Persian Architecture flourished again and saw many new monuments in various Iranian cities, of which Isfahan is the most notable example.

Except for Shah Abbas the great and Shah Ismail1, Shah Tahmasp 1, and Shah Abbas 11, many of the Safavid rulers were ineffectual, often more interested in their women, alcohol and other leisure activities. The end of Abbas 11's reign in1666 marked the beginning of the end of the Safavid dynasty. Despite falling revenues and military threats, many of the later Shahs had lavish lifestyles. Shah Soltan Hosseyn (1694-1722) in particular was known for his love of wine disinterest in governance.

The declining country was repeatedly raided on its frontiers. Finally Ghilzai Pashtun chieftain named Mir Wais Khan began a rebellion in Kandahar and defeated the Safavid army under the Georgian governor over the region, Gurgin Khan. In 1722 , Peter the Great of neighboring Imperial Russia launched the Russo-Persian War (1722-1723), capturing many of Iran's Caucasian territories, including Derbent, Shaki, Baku, but also Gilan,

Chapter 1

Mazandran and Astrabad. At the midst of all chaos, in the same year 1722 an Afghan army led by Mir Wais's son Mahmud marched across eastern Iran, besieged and took Isfahan. Mahmud proclaimed himself 'Shah of Persia'. Meanwhile, Persia's imperial rivals, the Ottomans and the Russians, took advantage of the chaos in the country to seize more territory for them. By these events, the Safavid dynasty had effectively ended. In 1724,' Conform' the Treaty of Constantinople, the ottomans and the Russians agreed to divide the newly conquered territories of Iran amongst themselves.

Nader Shah and his successors

Iran's territorial integrity was restored by a native Iranian Turkic Afshar warlord from khorasan, Nader Shah; He defeated and banished the Afghans, defeated the Ottomans, reinstalled the Safavids on the throne, and negotiated Russian withdrawal from Iran's Caucasian territories, with the Treaty of Resht and Treaty of Ganja. By 1736, Nader had become so powerful he was able to depose the Safavids and have himself crowned Shah. Nader was one of the last great conquerors of Asia and briefly presided over what was the most powerful empire in the world. To financially support his wars against Persia's archrival, the Ottoman Empire, he fixed his sights on the weak but rich Mughal Empire to the east. In 1739 accompanied by his loyal Caucasian subjects including Erekle 11, he invaded Mughal India, defeated a numerically superior Mughal army in less than three hours, and completely sacked and looted Delhi, bringing back immense wealth to Persia. On his way back, he also conquered all the Uzbek khanates- except for Kokand, and made the Uzbek his vassal's. He also firmly re-established Persian rule over the entire Caucasus, Bahrain, as well as large parts of Anatolia and Mesopotamia. Undefeated for years, his defeat in Dagestan, following guerrilla rebellions by the Lezgins and the assassination attempt on him near Mazanderan is often considered the turning point in Nader's impressive career. To his frustration, the Dagestan's resorted to guerrilla warfare, and Nader with his conventional army could make little headway against them. At the battle of Andalal and the battle of Avaria, Nader's army was crushingly defeated and he lost half of his entire force, as well as forcing him to flee for the mountains. Though Nader managed to take most of Dagestan during his campaign, the effective guerrilla warfare as deployed by the Lezgins, the Avers, and Laks made the Iranian re-conquest of the particular North Caucasian region this time a short lived one. Several years later Nader was forced to withdraw. Around the same time, the assassination attempt was made on him near Mazandran which accelerated the course of history; he slowly grew ill and megalomaniac, blinding his sons who he suspected of the assassination attempts, and showing increasing cruelty against his subjects and officers. In his later years this eventually provoked multiple revolts and, ultimately Nader's assassination in 1747.

Nader's death was followed by a period of anarchy in Iran as rival army commanders fought for power. Nader's own family, the Afsharids, was soon reduced to holding on to a small domain in Khorasan. Many of the Caucasian territories broke away in various Caucasian Khanates. Ottomans regained lost territories in Anatolia and Mesopotamia. Oman and the Uzbek khanates of Bukhara and Khiva regained independence. Ahmad Shah Durrani, one of Nader's officers, founded an independent state which eventually became modern Afghanistan. Erekle II and TeimurazII. Who, in 1744, had been made the kings of Kakheti and Karti respectively by Nader himself for their royal service, capitalized on the eruption of instability, and declared de facto independence. Erekle II assumed control over Kartli after Teimuraz II's death, thus unifying the two as the kingdom of Kartli-Kakheti, becoming the first Georgian ruler in three centuries to preside over a politically unified eastern Georgia, and due to the frantic turn of events in mainland Iran he would be able to remain de facto autonomous through the Zand period. From his capital Shiraz, Karim Khan of the Zand dynasty ruled "an island of relative calm and peace in an otherwise bloody and destructive period, however, the extent of Zand power was confined to contemporary Iran and parts of the Caucasus. Karim Kan's death in 1779 led to yet another civil war in which the Qajar dynasty eventually triumphed and became kings of Iran. During the civil war, Iran permanently lost Basra in 1770 to the Ottomans, which had been captured during the Ottoman-Persian War (1775-76), and Bahrain to Al Khalifa family after Bani Utbah invasion in 1783.

Qajar dynasty (1796-1925)

Agha Mohammad Khan emerged victorious out of the civil war that commenced with the death of the last Zand king. His reign is noted for the reemergence of a centrally led and unified Iran. After the death of Nader Shah and the last of the Zands, most of Iran's Caucasian territories had broken away into various Caucasian Khanates. Agha Mohamad Khan, like the Safavid kings and Nader Shah before him viewed the region as no different as the territories in mainland Iran. Therefore, his first objective after having secured mainland Iran was to reincorporate the Caucasian regions into Iran. Georgia was seen as one of the most integral territories. For Agha Mohammad Khan, the re subjugation and reintegration of Georgia into the Iranian Empire was part of the same process that had brought Shiraz, Isfahan, and Tabriz under his rule. As the Cambridge History of Iran states, its permanent secession was inconceivable and had to be resisted in the same way as one would resist an attempt at the separation of Fars or Gilan. It was therefore natural for Agha Mohammad Khan to perform whatever necessary means in the Caucasus in order to subdue and reincorporate the recently lost regions following Nader Shah's death and the demise of the Zands, including putting down what in Iranian eyes was seen as treason on the part of the valli (viceroy) of Georgia, namely the Georgian King Erekle II (Heraclius II) who was appointed viceroy of Georgia by Nader Shah himself.

Agha Mohammad Khan subsequently demanded that Heraclius II renounce its 1783 treaty with Russia, and to submit again to Persian suzerainty, in return for peace and the security of his kingdom. The Ottomans, Iran's neighboring rival, recognized the latter's rights over Karti and Kakheti for the first time in four centuries. Heraclitus appealed then to his theoretical protector, Empress Catherine II of Russia, pleading for at least 3000 Russian troops, and he was ignored, leaving Georgia to fend off the Persian threat alone. Nevertheless, Heraclitus II still rejected the Khan's ultimatum. As a response, Agha Mohammad Khan invaded the Caucasus region after crossing the Aras River, and, while on his way to Georgia, he re subjugated Iran's territories of the Erivan Khanate, Shirvan, Nakhchivan Khanate, Ganja Khanate, Derbent Khaneh, Baku khanate, Talish Khanate, Shaki Khanate, Karabakh Khanate, which comprise modern day Armenia, Azerbaijan, Dagestan, and Igdir. Having reached Georgia with his large army, he prevailed in the battle of Kartsanisi, which resulted in the capture and sack of Tbilisi, as well as the effective re subjugation of Georgia. Upon his return from his successful campaign inTiblisi and in effective control over Georgia together with 15000 Georgian captives that were moved back to mainland Iran, Agha Mohammad Khan was formally crowned Shah in 1796 in the Mughan Plain, just as his predecessor Nader Shah was about sixty years earlier.

Agha Mohammad Shah was later assassinated in 1797, while preparing a second expedition against Georgia, in Shusha (now part of the republic of Azerbaijan). And the seasoned king Heraclius died early in 1798). The reassertion of Iranian hegemony over Georgia did not last long; in 1799 the Russians marched intoTiblisi. The Russians were already actively occupied

Brief History of Persian Empire

with an expansionist policy towards its neighboring empires to its south, namely the Ottoman Empire and the successive Iranian kingdoms since the late 17th/early 18th century. The next two years following Russian's entrance into Tiblisi was a time of confusion, and the weakened and devastated Georgian kingdom, with its capital half in ruins, was easily absorbed by Russia in 1801. As Iran could not permit to allow the cession of Transcaucasia and Dagestan, which had been an integral part of Iran for centuries, this would lead to the wars of several years later, namely the Russo-Persian Wars of 1804-1813 and 1826-1828. The outcome of these two wars (in the Treaty of Gulistan and the Treaty of Turkmenchay, respectively) proved for the irrevocable forced cession and loss of what is now eastern Georgia, Dagestan, Armenia, and Azerbaijan to Imperial Russia.

The area to the north of Aras, among which the territory of the contemporary republic of Azerbaijan, eastern Georgia, Dagestan, and Armenia were Iranian territory until they were occupied by Russia in the course of the 19th century.

Migration of Caucasian Muslims

Following the official loss of vast territories in the caucuses, major demographic shifts were bound to take place. Following the 1804-1813 War, but also per the 1826-1828 war which ceded the last territories, large migrations, so- called Caucasian Muhajeries, set off to migrate to mainland Iran, Some of these groups included the Ayrums, Qarapapaqs, Circassians, Shia Lezgins, and other transcaucasian Muslims.

After the battle of Ganja of 1804 during the Russo-Persian War (1804-1813), many Thousands of Ayrums and Qarapapaqs were settled in Tabriz. During the remaining parts of the 1804-1813 War, as well as through the 1826-1828 war, a large number of Ayrums and Qarapapaqs that were still remaining in newly conquered Russian territories were settled in and migrated to Solduz (in modern-day Iran's West Azerbaijan province) . As the Cambridge History of Iran states ; "The steady encroachment of Russian troops along the frontier in the Caucasus, General Yermolov's brutal punitive expeditions and weakness of the central government, drove large numbers of Muslims, and even some Georgian Christians, into exile in Iran.

In 1864 until the early 20th century another mass expulsion took place in of Caucasian Muslims as a result of the Russian victory in the Caucasian War. Others simply voluntarily refused to live under Christian Russian rule, and thus departed for Turkey or Iran. These migrations once again, towards Iran, included masses of Caucasian Azerbaiejanis, other Trancaucasian Muslims, as well as many North Caucasian Muslims, Such as Circassians, Shia Lezgins and Laks. Many of these migrants would prove to play pivotal role in further Iranian history, as they formed most of the ranks of the Persian Cossack Brigade, which was established in the late 19th century. The initial ranks of the brigade would be entirely composed of Circassians and other Caucasian Muhajiris. This brigade would prove decisive in the following decades in Qajar history.

Furthermore, the 1828 Treaty of Turkmenchay included the official rights for the Russian Empire to encourage settling of Armenians from Iran in the newly conquered Russian territories. Untill the mid-fourtheenth century Armenians had constituted a majority in Eastern Armenia. At the close of the fourteenth century, after Timure's campains, the Timurid Renaissance flourished, and Islam had become the dominated faith, and Armenians became a minority in Eastern Armenia. After centuries of constant warfare on the Armenian plateau, many Armenians chose to emigrate and settle elsewher. Following Shah AbbasI's massive relocation ofArmenians and Muslims in 1604-05, their numbers dwindled even further.

At the time of Russian invasion of Iran, some 80% of the populations of Iranian Armenians were Muslims (Persians, Turkics, and Kurds) whereas Christian Armenians constituted a minority of about 20%. As a result of theTreaty of Gulistan (1813) and theTreaty of Turkmenchay (1828), Iran was forced to cede Iranian Armenia (which also constituted the present day Armenia) to the Russians. After the Russian administration took hold of Iranian Armenia, the ethnic make up shifted, and thus for the first time in more than four centuries, ethnic Armenians started to form a majority once again in one part of historic Armenia. The new Russian administration encouraged the settling of ethnic Armenians from Iran proper and Ottoman Turky. As a result, by 1832, the number of ethnic Armenians had matched that of Muslims. It would be only after the Crimean war and the Russo-Turkish war of 1877-1878, which brought another influx of Turkish Armenians, that etnic Armenians once again, established a solid majority in Eastern Armenia. Nevertheless, the city of Erivan retained a Muslim majority up to the twentieth century. According to the traveler H.F.B. Lynch, the city was about 50% Armenian and 50% Muslim (Azerbijanis and Persians) in the early 1890s.

Brief History of Persian Empire

Fath Ali Shah's reign saw increasing diplomatic contacts with the West and the beginning of intense European diplomatic rivalries over Iran. His grandson Mohammad Shah who succeeded him in 1834 fell under the Russian influence and made two unsuccessful attempts to capture Hera't. When Mohammad Shah died in 1848 the sucssesion passed to his son Nasse-e-Din, who proved to be the ablest and most successful of the Qajar sovereigns. He founded the first modern hospital in Iran.

Consitutional Revolution and deposition

"The Great Persian Famine is believed to have caused the death of two million people"
A new era in the history of Persia dawned with the Persian Constitutional Revolution against the Shah in the late 19th and early 20th centuries. The Shah managed to remain in power, granting a limited constitution in 1906 (making the country a constitutional monarchy). The first Majles (parliament) was convened on October 7, 1906.
The discovery of oil in 1908 by the British in Khuzestan spawned intense renewed interest in Persia by the British Empire. Control of Persia remained contested between the United Kingdom and Russia, in what became known as The Great Game, and codified in the Anglo-Russian convention of 1907, which divided Persia into spheres of influence regardless of her national sovereignty.
During World War 1, the country was occupied by British, Ottoman and Russian forces but essentially neutral. In 1919, after the Russian Revolution and their withdrawal, Britain attempted to establish a protectorate in Persia which was unsuccessful.
Finally, the Constitutionalist movement of Gilan and the central power vacuum caused by the instability of the Qajar government resulted in the rise of Reza Khan, who was later to become Reza Shah Pahlavi, and the subsequent establishment of Pahlavi dynasty in 1925. In 1921, a military coup established Reza Khan, an officer of the Persian Cossack Brigade, as the dominant figure for the next 20 years. Seyyed Zia'ed-Din Tabatabai was also a leader and important figure in the preparation of the coup. The coup was not actually directed at the Qajar monarchy; according to Encyclopaedia Iranica, it was targeted at officials who were in power and actually had a role in controling the government; the cabinet and others who had a role in governing Persia. In 1925, after being a prime minister for two years, Reza Khan became

Chapter 1

the first Shah of the Pahlavi dynasty following the vote of the Constitutional Parliamen (Majles-e-Moassesan).

Reza Shah (1925-1945)

Reza Shah ruled for almost 16 years until September 16, 1941 C.E. (20 Shahrivar 1320 Shamsi) when he was forced to abdicate by the Anglo-Soviet invasion of Iran. He established an authotarian government that valued nationalism, militarism, secularism, and anti-communism. He introduced many socio-economic reforms, re-organizing the army, created air and naval forces as well as Government administration, and finances.

To his supporters his reign brought "law and order, discipline, central authority, and modern amenities – schools, new cross-country railroad system, city and inter-cities bus services, radios, cinemas, telephones, country-wide infra-structure, and much more. However, his attempts of modernization, have been criticized by his opponents for being "too fast" and superficial.

A number of the new laws and regulations enacted created resentment amongst the clergy.

World War Two-Invasion of Iran

Reza Shah tried to avoid involvement with the UK and the Soviet Union. Though, many of his projects required foreign technical expertise, he avoided awarding contracts to British and Soviet companies because of dissatisfaction during the Qajar dynasty between Persia, the UK, and the Soviets. Although the UK, through its ownership of the Anglo-Iranian Oil Company, controlled all of Iran's oil resources, Reza Shah preferred to obtain technical support and assistance from Germany, France, Italy and other European countries. This created problems for Iran after 1939, when Germany and Britain became enemies in World War II. Reza Shah proclaimed Iran as a neutral country, but Britain insisted that German Engineers and technicians in Iran were spies with missions to sabotage British oil facilities in Southwestern Iran. Britain demanded that Iran expel all German citizens, but Reza Shah refused, claiming this would adversely affect his development projects.

In April1941, the war reached Iran borders, when Rashid Ali, with assistance from Germany and Italy, launched the1941Iraqi coup d'etat, sparking the Anglo-Iraqi war of May, 1941. Germany and Italy quickly sent the pro-Axis forces in Iraq military aid from Syria, but during the period from May to July the British and their allies defeated the pro-axis forces in Iraq and later Syria and Lebanon.

In June 1941, Nazi Germany broke the Molotove-Ribbentrop Pact and invaded the Soviet Union, Iran northern neighbor. The soviets quickly allied themselves with the Allied countries and, in July and August 1941, the British demanded that the Iranian government expel all Germans from Iran. Reza Shah refused to expel the Germans and on 25 August 1941 the British and Soviets launched a surprise invasion and Reza Shah's government quickly surrendered after less than a week of fighting. The invasion's strategic purpose was to secure a supply line to the USSR (later named the Persian Corridor), secure the oil fields, Abadan Refinery (of the Uk-owned Anglo Iranian Oil Company), and limit German influence in Iran. Following the invasion, on 16 September 1941, Reza shah abdicated and went into exile in South Africa where he died after two years.

During the rest of World War II, Iran became a major conduit for British and American aid to the Soviet Union and an Avenue through which over 120,000 Polish refuges and Polish Armed Forces fled the Axis advance. At the 1943 Teheran Conference, the Allied "Big Three" – Joesph Stalin, Frank D. Roosevelt, and Winston Churchill—issued the Teheran Declaration to guarantee the post-war independance and boundaries of Iran. On September 13 1943 the Allies reassured the Iranians that all foreign troops would leave by March 2 1946. At that time, the Tudeh Party of Iran, a communist party that was already infuencial and had members in the parliament too was becoming increasingly militant and was working to bring Iran into Soviet Dominion by first setting up an Intependant communist self rule in Azerbaijan and Kurdistan. This prompted action by the government in Teheran to dispatch armed forces to remove the local communist government in the North as well as occupy and close down the branches of Tudeh headquarters in Teheran and Isfahan. However, the Soviet troops present in the Northern parts of the country, prevented the Iranian forces to enter the aeas. Thus, by November 1945, Azerbaijan had become an autonomous state helped by the Tudeh communist party. This pro-Soviet nominal-government fell, by November 1946, after support from the United States for Iran to reclaim the regions that had declared themselves autonomous.

Chapter 1

At the end of the war Soviet troops remained in Iran and established two puppet states in north-west; namely the People's Government of Azerbaijan and the Republic of Mahabad. This led to the Iran crisis of 1946, one of the first confrontations of the Cold War, which ended after oil concessions were promised to the USSR and Soviet forces withdrawal from Iran proper in May 1946. The two puppet states were soon overthrown and the oil concessions were later revoked.

CHAPTER 2. BASICS OF PERSIA

Persian Language

Persian language predominantly spoken and used officially within Iran, Afghanistan and Tajikistan in three mutually intelligible standard varieties, namely Iranian Persian, Dari Persian (officially named Dari since 1958) and Tajiki Persian (officially named Tajik since the Soviet era). It is also spoken natively in the Tajic variety by a significant population within Uzbekestan, as well as within other regions with a persianate history in the cultural sphere of Greater Iran. It is written officially within Iran and Afghanistan in the Persian alphabet, a derivation of the Arabic script, and within Tajikestan in the Tajik alphabet, a derivation of Cyrillic. "Cyrillic script is a writting system used for various languages across Eurosia and is as a national script in various Slavic, Turkic, Mongolic and Iranic-speaking countries in Estern Europe, Caucasus, Central Asia and Northern Asia."

The Persian language is a continuation of Middle Persian, the official religious and literary language of the Sassanian Empire (224-651 CE), itself a continuation of Old Persian, which was used in the Achaemenid Empire (550-330 BC).It originated in the region of Fars (Persia) in southwestern Iran. Its grammar is similar to many European languages.

Persian also known by its endonym Farsi is a Western Iranian language belonging to the Iranian branch of the Indo-Iranian subdivision of the Indo-European language. It is a pluricentric language.

Throughout history, Persian has been a prestigious cultural language used by many empires in Western Asia, Central Asia, and South Asia. Old Persian written works are attested in Old Persian cuneiform on several inscriptions from between the 6th and the fourth centuries BC, and Middle Persian literature is attested in Aramaic-derived scripts (Pahlavi and Manichean) on inscriptions from the time of the Achaemenian and Parthian Empires for writing, and in books centerd in Zoroastrian and Manichean scriptures from between the 10th century BC to 3rd century CE. These inscriptions contain royal edicts and similar texts composed in a very formal style; they contributed little to the development of literature in Iran. However, in some collateral sources (including the Bible) there are indications that epic literature existed in the oral tradition of reciters at court.

There exist documents written in the Old Iranian languages that have survived for nearly three millennia. The oldest texts are Ga'tha's,16 (or perhaps 17) short hymns written in an archaic form of an old Iranian language called Avestan, named for the Avesta, the holy book of Zoroastrianism. The Ga'tha's have been handed down as part of the Avesta along with several more recent texts. It is generally accepted that they contain the original teachings of the prophet Zoroaster (Zarathustra), who lived in the first half of the 1st millennium BC. His hymns show traces of versification, the precise prosody of which is still imperfectly known. Also important to early Iranian literature are the remenants of the Persian myths preserved in the Avesta, especially in the yashts, which are texts addressed to Iranian deities. The names of several kings and heros who later appear as semihistorical figures in Persian epic poetry are also here mentioned; the myths to which these texts refer were well known to the original audience but are now lost.

Persian Literature

The conquest of the Achaemenian Empire by Alexander about 330 BC caused a radical break in Iranian culture. During the new era, which lasted until the Arab conquest of the seventh century CE, Iran was deeply influenced by Hellenism. Greek and Aramaic became the dominant languages. For almost 500 years the Iranian languages were not used in writing. The oldest preserved documents that use Middle Iranian languages date only from the third century CE. They consist of inscriptions of the Sassanian kings and queens and religious texts of the Manicheans, the followers of the Gnostic prophet Mani (3rd century CE). The most widely used written language was middle Persian, better known as Pahlavi which remained in use with Zoroastrians into Islamic times. Only a few literary works have survived from this period, notably two episodes later incorporated into the Iranian epic as it was recorded by Ferdowsi in the 11th- century Sha'hna'meh; Aya'dga'r-eZareran ("Memorial of Zare'r"), about the establishment of Zoroasterianism, and Ka'rna'mag-Ardeshir, on the founder of the Sasanian dynasty. The myths, legends, and romanticized historical tales of this epic tradition were probably assembled into a continuous story in the early 7th century CE under the last Sassanian king. After the coming of Islam these texts were translated into Arabic prose.

Basics of Persia

Both versions were later lost, but their contents survived in the works of historians writtings in Arabic

Lyrical poetry was an oral tradition of minstrels, even at the royal court, and has left no traces. Texts written in other Iranian Middle languages such as Sogdian and Khotanese and Saka, had no more than a marginal influence on the literature of Islamic period.

The Arab Invasion

The Sassanian Empire that at the beginning of the seventh century (C.E) was still one of the two greatest empires in the Middle East crumbled almost instantaniously when the Bedouins invaded Iran. The conquest was completed about 640 (C.E). The Caliphate that came to be established was an Islamic state ruled by Arabs, but very soon the non-Arabs who had assimilated themselves to the new situation began to participate in the affairs of the Muslim community. The contribution made by the descendents of Sassanian elite, to the political and administrative institutions of the Caliphate increased in the 8th century when Baghdad was founded as the capital of Abbasid dynasty, close to the place where once Sassanian rulers had their Palace. Iranians contributed much to the development of the scholarly traditions of Islam. The linguistic and literary sciences dealt primarily with the Qura'n and with the poetry of the pre-Islamic Arabs, both of which provided the norms for Classical Arabic and for its use in Arabic literature. These sciences included on the one hand, grammar and Lexicography and, on the other, the theories of metrics, rhymes and rhetorics. They also included philological conventions for the collection, arrangement and preservation of texts. Together, these constituted a tradition of dealing with literary texts become a model in all literatures that subsequently emerged in the Islamic world. Among its features was the divan (diwa'n)—the collection of one poet's output in a systematically arranged volume—and several types of anthologies. Tools of this kind were important for the preservation of literature and its distribution to outlying parts of an extensive Empire. They also contributed to the standardization of form and style in poetry.

Described as one of the great literatures of humanity, including Goethe's assessment of it as one of the four main bodies of world literature, Persian literature has its roots in surviving works of Middle Persian and old Persian as it was briefly mentioned in the preceeding chapters; Persian languages. Persian literature has its roots in surviving works of Middle Persian and Old

Chapter 2

Persian, the latter of which date back as far as 522 BC, the date of the earliest surviving Achaemenid inscriptions; the Behistun Inscriptions. The bulk of surviving Persian literature, however, comes from the times following the Muslim conquest of Persia in 650 CE. After the Abbasids came to power (750 CE), the Iranians became the scribes and bureaucrats of the Islamic Caliphate and, increasingly also its writers and poets. The new Persian language and literature arose and flourished in Khorasan and Transoxiana because of political reasons; early Iranian dynasties of post-Islamic Iran such as Tahirids and Samanids being based in Khorasan. Persian poets such as Ferdowsi, Sa'di, Hafez, Attar, Nezami, Rumi and Omar Khayyam are also known in the West and have influenced the literature of many countries.

CHAPTER 3.

PERSIAN LITERATURE OF THE MEDIEVAL PERIOD

While initially overshadowed by Arabic during the Umayyad and early Abbasid caliphates, New Persian soon became a literary language again of the Central Asian and West Asian lands. The rebirth of the language in its new form is often rightfully accredited to Rudaki, Ferdowsi, Unsuri, Daqiqi, and their generation, (Persian Rennaisance), as they used pre-Islamic nationalism as a conduit to revive the language and customs of ancient Iran.

So strong is the Persian inclination to versifying everyday expressions that one can encounter poetry in almost every classical work, whether from Persian literature, science, or methaphysics. In short, the ability to write in verse form was a pre-requisite for any scholar. For example, almost half of Avicenna's medical writings (Cannons of Medicine) are in verse. Works of the early era of Persian poetry are characterized by strong court patronage, an extravagance of panegyrics and what is known as "exalted in style". The tradition of royal patronage began perhaps under the Sassanid era and carried over through the Abbasid and Samanid courts in every major Iranian dynasty. The Qasida was perhaps the most famous form of panegyric used, though quatrains such as those in Omar Khayyam's Ruba'iyyat are also widely popular.

Khorasani style, whose followers were mostly associated with the Greater Khorasan, is characterized by its supercilious diction, dignified tone, and relatively literate language. The chief representatives of this lyricism are Asjadi, Farrukhi Sistani, Unsori, and Manuchehri. Panegyric masters such as Rudaki were known for their love of nature, their verse abounding with evocative descriptions. Through these courts and system of patronage emerged the epic style of poetry, with Ferdowsi's Shahnama standing at the apex. By glorifying the Iranian historical past in heroic and elevated verses, he and other notables such as Daqiqi and Assadi Tusi presented the "Ajam" (none-Arab Iranians) with a source of pride and inspiration that has helped to preserve a sense of identity for the Iranian people over the ages. Ferdowsi set a model to be followed by a host of other poets later on.

Chapter 3

The thirteenth century marks the ascency of the lyric poetry with the consequent development of the ghazal into a major verse form, as well as the rise of mystical and Sufi poetry. This style is often called Araqi (Iraqi) style; (western provinces of Iran were known as The Persian Iraq (Araq-e-Ajam) and is known by its emotional lyric qualities. Rich meters, and the relative simplicity of its language. Emotional romantic poetry was not something new however, as works such as Vis O Ramin by As'ad Gorgani, and Yusof O Zoleikha by Am'aq Bokharaie exemplify. Poets such as Sana'I and Ata'r (who ostensibly inspired Rumi), Khaqani Shervani, Anvari, and Nezami, were highly respected ghazal writers. However, the elite of this school are Rumi, Sa'adi and Hafez Shirazi.

Regarding the tradition of Persian love poetry during the Safavid era, Professor Ehsan Yarshater notes, "As a rule, the beloved is not a woman, but a young man. In the early centuries of Islam, the raids into Central Asia produced many young slaves. Slaves were also bought or received as gifts. They were made to serve as pages at court or in the households of the affluent, or as soldiers and bodyguards. Young men, slaves or not, also served wine at banquets and receptions, and the more gifted among them could play music and maintain a cultivated conversation. It was love toward young pages, soldiers, or novices in trades and professions which was the subject of lyrical introductions to panegyrics from the beginning of Persian poetry, and of the ghazal." During the same Safavid era, many subjects of the Iranian Safavids were patrons of Persian poetry, such as Teimuraz I of Kakheti.

In the didactic genre one can mention Sana'I's Hadiqat-ul-Haqiqah (Garden of Truth) as well as Neza'mi's Makhzan-ul-Asra'r (Treasury of Secrets). Some of Attar's works also belong to this genre as do the major works of Rumi, although some tend to classify these in the lyrical type due to their mystical and emotional qualities. In addition, some tend to group Naser Khosrow's works in this style as well; however true gems of this genre are two books by Sa'adi, a heavyweight of Persian literature, The Bustan and the Gulistan.

After the 15th century, the Indian style of Persian poetry (sometimes also called Isfahani or Safavi style) took over. This style has its roots in the Timurid era and produced the likes of Amir Khosrow Dehlavi, and Bhai Nand Lal Goya.

Prose writings

Medieval Persian Literature

The most significant prose writings of this era are Nezami Aruzi Samarqandi's "Chaha'r Maqa'leh" as well as Zahiriddin Nasr Muhammad Aufi's anecdote compendium " Javami ul-Heka'yat". Shams al-Mo'ali Abol-hasan Ghaboos ibn Woshmgir's famous work, the Qabus Nama (A mirror for Princes), is a highly esteemed Belles-letters work of Persian literature. Also highly regarded is Siyasatnama, by Neza'm al-Mulk, a famous Persian vizir. Kelileh VA Demneh, translated from Indian folk tales, can also be mentioned in this category.It is seen as a collection of adages in Persian literary studies and thus does convey folkloric notions.

Biographers, hagiographis, and historical works

Among the major historical and biographical works in classical Persian, one can mention Abolfazl Beyhaghi's famous Tarikh-e Beihaghi, Lobab ul-Albab of Zahireddin Nasr Muhammad Aufi (which has been regarded as a reliable chronological source by many experts), as well as Ata-Malek Juvayni's famous Tarikh-e Jahangushaay-e Juvaini (which spans the Mongolid and Ilkhanid era of Iran), Atta'r's Tazkerat-ol-Owliya ("Biographies of the Saints") is also a detailed account of Sufi's mystics, which is referenced by many subsequent authors and considered a significant work in mystical hagiography.

Literary criticisms

The oldest surviving work of Persian literary criticism after Islamic conquest of Persia is Muqaddamehe-ye Shahname-ye Abu Mansuri, which was written during the Samanid period. The work deals with the myths and legends of Shahnameh and is considered the oldest surviving example of Persian prose. It also shows an attempt by the authors to evaluate literary works critically.

Storytelling

One Thousand and One Nights is a medieval folk tale collection which tells the story of Schehrezad, a Sassanid queen who must relate a series of stories to her malevolent husband, King Shahriyar to delay her execution. The stories are told over a period of one thousand and one nights. And every night she ends the story with a suspenseful situation, forcing the King to keep her alive for another day. The individual stories were created over several centuries, by many people from a number of different lands.

Chapter 3

The nucleus of the collection is formed by a Pahlavi Sassanid Persian book called Heza'r Afs'anah, a collection of ancient Indian and Persian folk tales. During the reign of the Abbasid Caliph Harun al-Rashid in the eight century, Baghdad had become an important cosmopolitan city. Merchants from Persia, China, India, Africa, and Europe were all found in Baghdad. During this time, many of the stories that were originally folk stories are thought to have been collected orally over many years and later compiled in a single book. The compiler and 9th century translator into Arabic is reputedly the storyteller Abu Abd-ellah Muhammad el-Gahshigar.The frame story of Shahrzad seems to have been added in the 14th century.

Persian Dictionaries

The biggest Persian dictionary is Dehkhoda's (16 volumes) by Ali-Akbar Dehkhoda. It is the largest comprehensive Persian dictionary ever published, comprised more than 27000 pages.It is published by the Tehran University under the supervision of the Dehkhoda Dictionary Institue. It traces the historical development of the Persian language, providing a comprehensive resource to scholars and academic researches, as well as describing usage in its many variations throughout the world. He names two hundred lexicographical works in his dictionary, the earliest, Farhang Oim and Farhang Menakhtay, from the late Sassanid era. The most widely used Persian lexicons in the Middle Ages were those of Abu Hafs Soghdi and Asadi Tusi written in 1092 C.E. Also highly regarded in the contemporary Persian literature lexical corpus are the the works of Dr. Mohammad Moin. The first volume was published in 1963. In 1645 C.E, Christian Ravius completed a Persian-Latin dictionary, printed at Leiden. This was followed by J.Richardson's two-volume Oxford edition (1777) and Gladwin-Malda's (1770 Persian-English Dictionaries, Schaif and S.Peters'Persian-Russian dictionary (1869), and 30 other Persian Lexicographical translatins through the 1950s. Also in the second half of 20th century English –Persian dictionaries of Manouchehr Aryanpour and Soleiman Haim are in wide use in Iran.
The first ever produced Iranian Encyclopeadia, which stands at the Apex of Iranian cultural creations is Encyclopeadia Iranica, a masterpiece in its own right, produced, edited and published by Iranica Encyclopeadia Foundation, supervised and edited by late Professor Ehsan Yarshater (Chief editor in-charge).

CONTEMPORARY PERSIAN LITERATURE

History

In the 19th century, Persian literature experienced dramatic change and entered a new era. The beginning of this change was exemplified by an incident in the mid-19th century at the court of Nassered-Din Shah of Ghajar dynasty, when the reform-minded Prime Minister, Amir Kabir, chastised the poet Habibollah Qa'ani for "lying" in a panegyric qasida written in Kabir's honor. Amir Kabir saw poetry in general and the type of poetry that had developed during the Qajar period as detrimental to "progress" and "modernization" in Iranian society, which he believed was in dire need of change. Such concerns were also expressed by others such as Ali Akhundzadeh, Mirza Agha Khan Kermani, and Mirza Malkom khan. Khan also addressed a need for a change in Persian Poetry in literary terms as well, always linking it to social concerns. Eventually it was not before long that these concerns culminated in the form of certain intellectual movements in Iran that involved the Iranian experience of modernity and its associated art, science, literature, poetry, and political structures that have been changing since the late 19th and 20th centuries, leading to the Persian Constitutional Revolution of 1906-1911, the idea that change in poetry was necessary became widespread. Many argued that Persian poetry should reflect the realities of a country in transition. This idea was propagated by notable figures such as Ali-Akbar Dehkhoda and Abolgha'sem Aref, who challenged the traditional system of Persian poetry in terms of introducing new content and experimentation with rhetoric, lexico-semantics, and structure. Dehkhoda, for instance, used a lesser-known traditional form, the mosamant, to elegize the execution of a revolutionary journalist. Aref employed the ghazal, "the most central genre within lyrical tradition" to write his "Payam-e Azadi" (Message of Freedom). Some researchers argue that the notion of "sociopolitical ramifications of esthetic changes led to the idea of poets "as social leaders trying the limits and possibilities of social change."

An important movement in modern Persian literature centerd on the question of modernization and westernization and whether terms are synonymous when describing the evolution of Persian society. It can be argued that almost all advocates of modernism in Persian literature, from Akhundzadeh, Kermani, and Malkom Khan to Dehkhoda, Aref, Bahar, and Taqi Rafat, were inspired by developments and changes that had occurred in western,

Chapter 3

particularly European literature. Such inspirations did not mean blindly copying western models but rather, adopting aspects of western literature and changing them to fit the needs of Iranian culture.

Following the pioneering works of Ahmad Kasravi, Sadeq Hedayat, Moshfeq Kazemi and many others, the Iranian wave of comparative literature and literary criticism reached a symbolic crest with the emergence of Abdolhossein Zarrinkoob, Shahrokh Meshkoob, Houshang Golshiri and Ebrahim Golestan.

In Afghanistan

Persian literature in Aghanistan has also experienced a dramatic change during the last century. At the beginning of the 20th century, Afghanistan was confronted with economic and social change, which sparked a new approach to literature. In 1911, Mahmud Tarzi, who came back to Afghanistan after years of exile in Turkey and was influential in government circles, started a forthnightly publication named Saraj'ul Akhbar. Sara'j was not the first such publication in the country, but in the field of journalism and literature it launched a new period of change and modernization. Sara'j not only played an important role in journalism, it also gave a new life to literature as a whole and opened the way for poetry to explore new avenues of expression through which personal thoughts took on a more social colour.

In 1930, after months of cultural stagnation, Sara'j founded the Heart literary circle. A year later, another group calling itself the Kabul Literary Circle was founded in the capital. Both groups published regular magazines dedicated to culture and Persian literature. Both especially the Kabul publication, had little success in becoming venues for modern Persian poetry and writing. In time, the Kabul publication turned into a stronghold for traditional writers and poets, and modernism in Dari literature was pushed to the fringes of social and cultural life.

Three of the most prominent classical poets in Afghanistan at the time were Qari Abdulah; Abdul Haq Betab and Khalid ulah Khalili.The first two received the honorary title Malek uk Shoara (King of poets). Khalili, the third and the youngest, was drawn toward the Khorasani style of poetry instead of the usual Hendi style. He was also interested in modern poetry and wrote a few poems in a more modern style with new aspects of thought and meaning. In1939 after two poems by Nima youshij titled "Gharab" and "Ghoghnus" were published, Khalili wrote a poem under the name "Sorude Kuhestan" or "the song of the mountain" in the same rhyming pattern as Nima and sent it to the Kabul Literery Circle. The traditionalists in Kabul refused to publish it because it was not written in the traditional rhyme. They criticized khalili for modernizing his style.

Very gradually new styles found their way into literature and literary circles despite the efforts of traditionalists. The first book of new poems was published in the year1957 (1336 AH), and in 1962 (1341), a collection of modern Persian (Dari) poetry was published in Kabul. The first group to write poems in the new style consisted of Mahmud Farani, Ba'regh Shafi I, Soleyman Layegh, Soheil Ayeneh and a few others. Later, Vasef Bakhtari, Asadullah Habib and Latif Nazemi, and others joined the group. Each had his own share in modernizing Persian poetry in Afghanistan. Other notable figures include Leila Sarahat Roshani, Sayed Elan Bahar and Parwin Pazvak. Poets like Mayakovski, Yase Nien and Lahouti (an Iranian poet living in exile in Russia) exerted a special influence on the Persian poets in Afghanistan. The influence of Iranians (Farrokht Yazdi and Ahmad Shamlou) on the newly established Afghan prose and poetry, especially in the second half of the 20th century, must also be taken into consideration. Prominent writers from Afghanistan like Asef Soltanzadeh, Reza Ebrahimi, Amene Mohammadi, and Abbas Jafari grew up in Iran and were influenced by Iranian writers and teachers.

In Tajikestan

The new poetry in Tajikestan is mostly concerned with the way of life of people and is revolutionary. From the1950's until the advent of new poetry in France, Asia and Latin America, the impact of the modernization drive was strong. In the 1960's modern Iranian poetry and that of Mahmud Iqbal Lahouri made a profound impression inTajik poetry. This period is probably the richest and most prolific period for the development of themes and forms in Persian poetry inTajikestan. Some Tajic poets were mere imitators, and one can easily see the traits of foreign poets in their work. Only two or three poets were able to digest the foreign poetry and compose original poetry. InTajikestan, the format and pictorial aspects of short stories and novels were taken from Russian and other European literature. Some of Tajikestan's prominent names in Persian literature are Golrokhsar Safi Eva, Mo'men Ghena'at, Farzaneh Khojandi and Layegh Shir-Ali.

Chapter 3

Persian Contemporary Play writers

Bahram Beyzai- Akbar Ra'adi-Gholam-Hossein Sa'edi-
Esmaiil Khalaj-Ali Nassirian-Mirza-Agha Nassirian-
Mirza Agha Tabrizi-Bijan Mofid.

Literary criticism

This is the study, evaluation, and interpretation of literature. Modern literary criticism is often influenced by literary theory, which is the philosophical discussion of literatur's goals and methods. Though the two activities are closely related, literary critics are not always, and have not always been, theorists. In this particular field some of the outstanding literary critics are considered to have been:

Abdolhossein Zarrinkoob was a scholar of Iranian history and literature, Persian culture and history and an outstanding critic and author. Saeed Nafisi analysed and edited several critical works. He is welknown for his work on Rudaki and Sufi literature.

Professor Ehsan Yarshater, in addition to his extensive and valuable contributions to the development of Persian cultural heritage in ancient Iranian languages, literature and histor, took the giant step, starting in the years of 1960's and continuing into the present time, to implement the monumental task of compiling, editing and publishing for the first time in Iran's history, "The Encyclopeadia Iranica" in English in order to introduce and share with the world at large, among many other things, Iran's rich cultural and literary heritage.

Parviz Natel-Khanlari and Gholamhossein Yousefi, who belong to Nafisi's generation, were also involved in modern literature and critical writings. Natel-Khanlari is distinguished by the simplicity of his style. He did not follow the traditionalists, nor did he advocate the new trend. Instead, his particular approach accommodated the entire spectrum of creativity and expression in Persian literature. Ahmad Kasravi, an experienced authority on literature and history, attacked the writers and poets whose works were at the service of unjust and corrupt authorities and burocrats. He prematurely lost his life in this fight.

Medieval Persian Literature

Contemporary Persian literary criticism reached its maturity after Sadegh Hedayat, Ebrahim Golestan, Houshang Golshiri, and Abdolhossein Zarrinkoub:

Among these figures, Zarrinkoob held academic positions and had a reputation not only among the intelligentsia but also in academia. Besides his significant contribution to the maturity of Persian language and literature, Zarrinkoob boosted comparative literature and Persian literary criticism. Zarrinkoub's Serr e Ney is a critical and comparative analysis of Rumi's Masnavi. In turn, Shahrokh Meshkoob worked on Ferdowsi's Shahnamah, using the principles of modern literary criticism.

Mohhamad Taghi Bahar's main contribution to this field is his book called "Sabk Shenasi (Stylistics). It is a pioneering work on the practice of Persian literary historiography and the emergence and development of Persian literature as a distinct institution in the early part of the 20th century. It contends that the exemplary status of Sabk-shenasi rests on the recognition of its disciplinary or institutional achievements. It further contends that, rather than a text on Persian 'stylistics,' Sabk-shenasy is a vast history of Persian literary prose, and, as such, is a significant intervention in Persian literary historiography.

Jalal Homaei, Badiozzaman Forouzanfar and his student Mohammad Reza Shafiei-kadkany, are other notable figures who have edited a number of prominent literary works. Critical analysis of Jami's work has been carried out by Ala Khan Afsahzad. His classic book won the prestigious award of Iran's year Best book in the year 2000.

Classical Persian Poetry in modern times

A few notable classical poets have arisen since the 19th century, among whom Mohammad Taghi Bahar and Parvin Etesami have been most celebrated. Mohammad Taghi Bahar had the title of "king of poets given to him byMozafar ed-Din Shah and a significant role in the emergence and development of Persian Literature as a distinct institution in the early parts of the 20th century. The theme of his poems was the social and political situation in Iran.

Parvin Etesami may be called the greatest Persian woman poet writing in the classical style. One of her remarkable series, called Mast VA Hoshyar (The

Chapter 3

Drunk and the Sober), won admiration from many of those involved in romantic poetry.

Modern Persian poetry

Nima Yushij is considerd the father of modern Persian poetry, introducing many techniques and forms to differentiate the modern from the old. Nevertheless, the credit for popularizing this new literary form within a country and culture solidly based on a thousand years of classical poetry goes to his few desciples such as Ahmad Shamlou, who adopted Nima's methods and tried new techniques of modern poetry.

What Nima founded in contemporary poetry, his successor Ahmad Shamlou continued.

The Sepid poem (which translates to white poem), which draws its sources from this poet, avoided the contemporary rules which had entered the Nimai' school of poetry and adopted a more free structure. This also allowed a more direct relationship between the poet and his or her emotional roots. In previous poetry, the qualities of the poet's vision as well as of the subject could only be expressed in The transformation brought about by Nima who freed Persian poetry from the fetters of prosodic measures, was a turning point in a long literary tradition. It broadened the perception and thinking of the poets that came after him. Nima offered a different understanding of the principles of classical poetry. His artistry was not confined to removing the need for a fixed –length hemistich and dispensing with the tradition of rhyming but focused on a broader structure and function based on a contemporary understanding of human and social existence. His aim in renovating poetry was to commit it to a "natural identity" and to achieve a modern discipline in the mind and linguistic performance of the poet.

Nima held that the formal technique dominating classical poetry interfered with its vitality, vigor and progress. Although he accepted some of its aesthetic properties and extended them to his poetry, he never ceased to widen its poetic experience by emphasizing the "natural order" of this art.
general terms and were subsumed by the formal limitations imposed on poetic expression.

Medieval Persian Literature

Nima's poetry transgressed these limitations. It relied on the natural function inherent within poetry itself to portray the poet's solidarity with life and the wide world surrounding him or her in specific and unambiguous details and scenes. Sepid poetry continues the poetic vision as Nima expressed it and avoids the contrived rules imposed on its creation. However, its most distinctive difference with Nima's poetry is to move away from the rhymes it employed. Nima paid attention to an overall harmonious rhyming and created many experimental examples to achieve this end.

Ahmad Shamlou discovered the inner characteristics of poetry and its manifestation in the literary creations of classical masters as well as the Nimai's experience. He offered an individual approach. By distancing himself from the obligations imposed by older poetry and some of the limitations that had entered the Nimai's rules, the poem is written in more "natural" words and incorporates a prose-like process without losing its poetic distinction. Sepid poetry is a developing branch of Nima's poetry built upon Nima Youshij's innovations. Nima thought any change in the construction and tools of a poet's expression is conditioned on his or her knowledge of the world and a revolutionized oulook. Sepid poetry could not take root outside this teaching and its application.

According to Simin Behbahani, Sepid poetry did not receive general acceptance before Bijan jalali's works. He is considerd the founder of Sepid poetry according to Behbahani. She herself used the "Char Pareh" style of Nima, and subsequently turned to ghazal, a free flowing poetry style similar to the Western sonnet. Simin contributed to a historic development in the form of ghazal, as she added theatrical subjects, and daily events and conversation into her poetry. She has expanded the range of traditional Persian verse forms and produced some of the most significant works of Persian literature in the 20th century.

A reluctant follower of Nima Yushij, Mehdi Akhavan Salees has established a bridge between the Khorasani and Nima Schools. The critics consider Mehdi Akhavan Sales as one of the best contemporary Persian poets. He is one of the pioneers of free verse (new style poetry) in Persian literature, particularly of modern style epics. It was his ambition, for a long time, to introduce a fresh style to Persian poetry.

Chapter 3

Forough Farrokhzad is important in the literary history of Iran for three reasons: First, she was among the first generation to embrace the new style of poetry pioneered by Nima during the late 1920's, which demanded that poets experiment with rhyme, imagery, and the individual voice. Second, she was the first modern Iranian woman to graphically articulate private sexual landscapes from a woman's perspective. Finally, she transcended her own literary role and experimented with acting, painting, and documentary film making.

Fereydoon Moshiri is best known as a concillator of classical Persian poetry with the New Poetry initiated by Nima Youshij. One of the major contributions of Moshiri's poetry, according to some observers, is the broadening of the social and geographical scope of modern Persian literature.

A poet of the last generation before the Islamic Revolution worthy of mention is Mohammad Reza Shafiei-Kadkany (M.Sereshk). Though he is from Khorasan and sways between allegiance to Nima and Akhavan Sales, in his poetry he shows the influences of Hafez and Mowlavi. He uses simple lyrical language and is mostly inspired by the political atmosphere. He is the most successful of those poets who in the past four decades have tried hard to find a synthesis between the two models of Ahmad Shamlou and Nima Youshij.

In the twenty first century, a new generation of Iranian poets continues to work in the New Poetry style and now attracts an international audience thanks to efforts to translate their works. Editions Bruno Doucey published a selection of forty-eight poems by Garus Abdolmalekian entitled Our Fists under the Table (2012), translated into French by Farideh Rava. Other notable names are poet and publisher Babak Abzari and emerging young poet Milad Khanmirzaei.

THE INFLUENCE OF PERSIAN LITERATURE ON WORLD LITERATURE: SUFI LITERATURE

William Shakespeare referred to Iran as the "land of Sophie" Some of the Persia's best-loved medieval poets were Sufis, and their poetry was, and is, widely read by Sufis from Morocco to Indonesia. Rumi, in particular is

Medieval Persian Literature

renowned both as a poet and as the founder of a widespread Sufi order. The themes and styles of this devotional poetry have been widely imitated by many Sufi poets. Many notable texts in Persian mystic literature are not poems, yet highly read and regarded. Among those are Kimiya-yi sa'adat, Asrar al-Tawhid and Kashf- al- Mahjoob.

Beginning in the early 16th century, Persian traditions had a large impact on the Georgian ruling elites, which in turn resulted in Persian influence on Georgian art, architecture and literature. This cultural influence lasted until the arrival of the Russians.
Jamshid Ginashvili remarks on the connection of Georgian culture with that of the Persian literary work Shahnameh:

The names of many Shahnama heroes such as Rostam, Themine, Sa'm or Zaal are found in 11th and 12th-century Georgian literature. They are indirect evidence for an Old Georgian translation of the Shahnama that is no longer extant. The Shahnama was translated, not only to satisfy the literary and aesthetic needs of readers and listeners, but also to inspire the young with the spirit of heroism and Georgian patriotism. Georgian ideology, customs, and world view often informed these translations because they were oriented toward Georgian poetic culture. Conversely, Georgians consider these translations works of their native literature. Georgian versions of the Shahnama are quite popular, and the stories of Rostam and Sohrab, or Bijan and Manizha became part of Georgian folklore. Farmanfarmaian a top literary critic and scholar wrote in the Journal of Persionate Studies:

"Distinguished scholars of Persian such as Gvakharia and Todau are well aware that the inspiration derived from the Persian classics of the ninth to the twelfth centuries produced a 'cultural synthesis' which saw, in the earliest stages of written secular literature in Georgia, the resumption of literary contacts with Iran, "much stronger than before". Ferdowsi's Shahnama was a never-ending source of inspiration, not only for high literature, but for folklore as well, "Almost every page of Georgian literary works and chronicles contain the names of Iranian heroes borrowed from Shahnama". Ferdowsi, together with Nezami, may have left the most enduring imprint on Georgian literature.

Asia Minor

Chapter 3

Despite that Asia Minor (or Anatolia) had been ruled various times prior to the Middle Ages by various Persian-speaking dynasties originating in Iran, the language lost its traditional foothold there with the demise of the Sassanian Empire. Centuries later however, the precise and usage in the region would be strongly revived. A branch of Seljuk's, the Sultanate of Rum, took Persian language, art and letters to Anatolia. They adopted Persian language as the official language of the empire. The Ottomans, which can "roughly" be seen as their eventual successors, took this over. Persian was the official language of the empire. The educated and noble class of the Ottoman Empire all spoke Persian, such as sultan Salim I, despite being Safavid Iran's archrival and one who strongly opposed Shia Islam. It was a major literary language in the empire. Some of the noted Persian literature works during the Ottoman rule are Idris Bdisti's Hasht Behesht (Eight Paradises), which begun in 1504 and covered the reign of the first eight Ottoman rulers, and the Salim-Namah, a glorification of Salim I. After a period of several centuries, Ottoman Turkish (which was highly persianised itself) had developed towards a fully accepted language of literature, which was even able to satisfy the demands of a scientific presentation. However, the number of Persian and Arabic loanwords contained in those works increased at times up to 88%. The Ottomans produced thousands of Persian literary works throughout their century long lifespan.

Areas once under Ghaznavid or Mughal rule: South Asia

With the emergence of the Ghaznavids and their successors such as the Ghurids, Timurids and Mughal Empire, Persian culture and its literature gradually moved into South Asia too. In general, from its earliest days, Persian literature and language was imported into the subcontinent by culturally Persianised Turkic and Afghan dynasties. Persian became the language of nobility, literary circles, and the royal Mughal courts for hundreds of years. In the early 19th century, Hindustani replaced it.

Under the Mughal Empire during the 16th century, the official language of the Indian subcontinent became Persian. In 1832 the British army required South Asian countries to begin conducting business in English. Persian literature in fact flourished in these regions while post-Safavid Iranian literature stagnated. Dehkhoda and other scholars of the 20th century, for example, largely based their works on the detailed lexicography produced in India, using compilations such as Ghazi Khan Badr Muhammad Dehlavi's A'dat al-Fuzala, Ibrahim

Medieval Persian Literature

Ghavamuddin Farughi's Farhang-e Ibrahimi, and particularly Muhammad Padshah's Farhang-e Anandraj.

PERSIAN LITERATURE IN THE WEST

Persian literature was little known in the West before the 18-19th century. It became much better known following the publication of several translations from the works of late medieval Persian poets, and inspired works by various Western poets and writers.

German literature

In 1819 Goethe published his West-ostlicher Divan, a collection of lyrical poems inspired by a German translation of Hafez.

The German essayist and Philosopher Niycheh was the author of the book, "Thus Spoke Zarathustra (1883-1885), referring to the ancient Persian prophet Zoroaster (1700 BCE)

English literature

A selection from Ferdowosi's Shahnameh (935-1020) was published in 1832 by James Atkinson, a physician employed by the British east India Company.

A portion of this abridgment was later versified by the British poet Mathew Arnold in his 1853 Rustam and Sohrab.

The American poet Ralph Waldo Emerson was another admirer of Persian poetry. He published several essays in 1876 that discuss Persian poetry: Letters and Social Aims, from the Persian gghazals of Hafiz.

Perhaps the most popular Persian poet of the 19th and 20th centuries in England was Omar Khayyam (1048-1123). His Rubaiyat was freely translated by Edward Fitzgerald in 1859. Omar Khayyam is esteemed more as a scientist than a poet in his native Persia, but in Fitzgerald's rendering, he became one of the most quoted poets in English. Khayyam's line, "A loaf of bread, a jug of wine, and thou", is known to many who could not say who wrote it, or where:

Ah, would there were a loaf of bread as fare,	گر دست دهد ز مغز گندم نانی
A joint of lamb, a jug of vintage rare,	وز می دو منی ز گوسفندی رانی
	وانگه من و تو نشسته در ویرانی

Chapter 3

And you and I in wilderness encamped-
No Sultan's pleasure could with ours
compare

عیشی بود آن نه حد هر سلطانی

The Persian poet and mystic Rumi (1207-1273) (known as Molana in Iran, Afghanistan and Tajikestan and as Mevlana in Turkey) has attracted a large following in the late 20th and early 21st centuries. Popularizing translations by Coleman Barks have presented Rumi as a New Age sage. There are also a number of more literary translations by such scholars such as A.J.Arbery. The classical poems (Hafez, Sa'di, Khayyam, Rumi, Nezami and Ferdowsi) are now widely known in English and can be read in various translations. Other works of Persian literature are mostly not translated and little known.

Swedish literature

During the last century, numerous works of classical Persian literature have been translated into Swedish by Baron Eric Hamelin. He translated works by, among others, Farided-Din Attar, Rumi, Ferdowsi, Omar Khayyam, Sa'di and Sanna'i influenced the writings of the Swedish mystic Emanuel Swedenborg, who was especially attracted to the religious or Sufi aspects of classical Persian poetry. His translations have had a great impact on numerous modern Swedish writers, among them Karl Weinberg, Wlly Kyrklund and Gunnar Ekelof. More recently classical authors such as Hafez, Rumi, Araqi and Nezami, have been rendered into Swedish by the Iranist Ashk Dahlen, who has published several essays on the development of Persian literature. Excerpts from Ferdowsi's Shahnameh have also been translated into Swedish prose by Namdar Nasser and Anja Malmberg.

Italian literature

During the last century, numerous works of classical and modern Persian literature have been translated into Italian by Alessandro Bausani (Nezami, Rumi, Iqbal, Khayyam), Carlo Saccone ('Attar, Sana'i, Hafez, Nasser-Khosrow, Nezami, Ahmad Ghazali, Ansari of Her'at, Sa'di, Ayene'), Angelo Piemontese(Amir Khosrow Dehlavi), Pio Flippani-Roncono (Nasser-Khosrow, Sa'di), Ricardo Zipoli (Kay Ka'us, Bidil), Maurizio Pistoso (Neza'mol-Mulk), Giorgio Vercellin (Neza'mi 'Aruzi), Giovanni Maria D'Erme (Ubeyd Zakani,Hafez), (Sergio Foti (Suhrawardi, Rumi, Jami), Rita Bargigli (Sa'di, Farrukhi, Manuchehri,Unsuri), Nahid Norozi

Medieval Persian Literature

(Sohrab Sepehri, Khawju of Kerman, Ahmad Shamlou), Faezeh Mardani (Forough Farokhzad, Abbas Kiarostami). A complete translation of Ferdowsi's Shahnameh was made by Italo Pizzi in the 19th century.

Contemporary Novel and short story writers in Iran

During the period after the end of the 1st World War and the beginning of the 2nd World War, talented Persian writers inspired by the works of mostly the European novelists of the 18th and 19th centuries begun the task of writing Novels. The most well-known ones include:

Mohammad-Ali Jamalzadeh, Sa'deghHedayat, Sadegh Chubak, Gholam-Hossein Sa'edi, Jala'lAl-e-Ahmad, Simin Da'neshvar, Bozorg Alavi,Ebrahim Golestan, Houshang Golshiri, Reza Baraheni.

CHAPTER 4:

EARLY WRITERS OF PERSIAN POETRY BEGINNING WITH THE RULE OF SAFARID DYNASTY ABOUT 250 (C.E)

Mohammad Vasif Saistani, First Persian writer & poet
post Arab invasion

The stories that have been written about the life and works of the early Persian writers after the Arab invasion of Iran are somewhat contradictory and the details even sometimes hard to believe, however there is no doubt that such poets did exist and made serious attempts to start writing using the ancient Persian language known as Farsi Dari, a dialect mostly used in the eastern parts of the pre-Arab Persian empire. The oldest of such stories have been narrated in a book; 'History of Sistan" (Tarikh Sisttan) whose writer or writers are not known but the first or oldest part of the book indicates that it was written in the 10th or early part of the 11th century(C.E). There are other books too that contain such information but they all date back to the early years of the 13th century (C.E).

The author of the 'History of Sistan" has indicated that "Jacob Layse Safar, governor of Khorasan who was directed by the Abasi caliph to take 'Har'at', Sistan, Kabul, Kerman, and Fars from Mohammade-ben-Taher was being eulogized by poets praising his victories in Arabic. Jacob who was displeased at hearing eulogies written in Arabic, a language that he could not understand or pretended that he did not understand, retorted and said: "Something that can not be understood why it must be said". Mohammad Vasif who was present there, soon after, attempted to compose in Farsi and other writers followed suit. Since the overthrow of the Sassanian dynasty by the Arabs and their conquest of Persian Empire no Persian writer had ever attempted to write poetry or prose in Farsi up to that time. All writings were done in Arabic.
Once Jacob Safar conquered the city of Her'at and killed Zanbil and Ammar Khareji, he was given the governorship of Kerman and Fars too.

Early Persian Poets

Mohammad Vasif then wrote this piece in Farsi praising Jacob's victory:

O'Chief, all chiefs of other territories are subservient to you	ای امیری که امیران جهان خاصه و عام
	بنده و چاکر و سگ بند و غلام
By the Divine destiny, those territories are rightfully yours.	ازلی خطی در لوح که ملکی بدهید
	به ابی یوسف یعقوب بن لیث همام

Mohammad Vasif Sistani was Jacob's chief of staff throughout his life. He survived him by a few years until probably 918-919 (C.E) and kept writing poetry even after Jacob's death.

Mohammad vasif was one of the first Persian poets who used the original Persian Rhyms and poetic measures (which are somewhat close to Arabic prosody) in the composition of his poetry. Vasif's later elegies show a significant improvement over his first ones, which were rather primitive and low quality. The following is an elegy which was written by him in the year 905(C.E.)

Man's effort is afforded him by God's grace, This was the work of destiny and not your fault,	کوشش بنده سبب از بخش است کار قضا بود وترا عیب نیست
To be or not to be is determined by God, Helpless God's creatures have no say in this.	بود و نبود از صفت ایزد است بنده درمانده بیچاره کیست
Creatures are destined to Decline and Decadence	اول مخلوق چه باشد زوال کار جهان اول وآخر یکیست
God's word, you read: perseverance belongs to him. Believe in what He has said, and accept.	قول خداوند بخوان فاستقم معتقدی شو وبر آن بر به ایست

Chapter 4

During the years of 918-919 certain events took place which caused Taher and Jacob II the grandchildren of Jacob Lays Safar great distress afterwards. Mohammad Vasif wrote a poem lamenting the loss of their kingdom:

The country had become unparrareled with any other, Amro had become its ruler,	مملکتی بود شده بی قیاس عمرو بر آن ملک شده بود راس
From the border of India to the borders of China and Turk, From the border of Zanzibar to the borders of Rum and Gas	از حد هند تا به حد چین وترک ازحدزنگ تا به حد روم وگاس
The Head fell and bad luck caused gold turn copper! Alas! That the kingdom of Jacob fell,	راس ذنب گشت وبشد مملکت زرزده شد زنحوست نحاس دولت یعقوب دریغابرفت
Leaving behind tormented souls! O', Sorrow came and joy passed, My heart filled constantly with fear.	ماند عقوبت به عقب برحواس ای غما کامد وشادی گذشت بود دلم دایم ازاین پرهراس
All that we do, we receive back, Fate may not be avoided! ,	
People turned all Orang-otang, The Orang-otang all turned people. Fatherland was not facetious about its glorious past, Light does not extract from darkness,	هرچه بکردیم بخواهیم دید سود ندارد زقضا احتراض
Great effort by Jacob was needed, To bring Ayas out of Jeda. [Ayas was an Arab elder who served Jacob and his son Amro].	ناس شدند نسناس آنگه همه آن همه نسناس گشتند ناس
	ملک ابا هزل نکرد انتساب نورزظلمت نکند اقتباس

Early Persian Poets

جهد وجد یعقوب باید همی

تاکه زجده بدر آید" ایاس"

During this period there were other poets who wrote poetry in Persian. Not much information about their life or many of their poetry is available. These are:

Hanzaleh Ba'dgheisi,
Mahmood Varagh Heravi
Firooz Mashreghi
Abu Salik Gorgani

All four of them lived in the late 8th and 9th centuries (C.E.).These poets are considered to have been amongst the first composers of the Persian verse. One of the most characteristic features of this period is an abundance of poets. Perhaps the main reason for this abundance could be the tremendous attention accorded to poetry by the royal courts, because the courts used to bestow upon the poets financial awards and handsome gifts, the instances of which are given in the narratives like the one about Rudaki who is said to have been so rich that whenever he moved seventy camels had to be used to transport his household. The Samanid court gains more importance than the other governments in that it did to expand and develop Persian literature. The Samanid kings, who considered themselves to be of Iranian stock, attached great importance to the Persian language and literature. With this view in mind, they encouraged the translation of Iranian epics, commentaries and historical books from the Arabic into Farsi, and the emirs (princes) like Naser ibn Ahmad and Nuh ibn Mansur themselves took to the supervision of this task. Their viziers like the Bal'ami family were persons of literary and scholarly attainments. Shahid Balkhi, Daqiqi and Kasa'yyi, with the exception of Rudaki, were among the celebrated poets of the 9th century. On the other hand not only Bukh'ra', but Sistan, Qaznayn, Gurgan, Nishabour, Ray and Samarghand were also seats of literature; this is an indication that literature must have burgoned more in the Eastern regions and Khorasan than in other areas. Also poets such as Mukhallidi Gurgani, Daylami Ghazvini, and Khusravi Sarakhsi were connected to the Ziyarid court. Shams al- Ma'a'lli

Chapter 4

Qabus ibn Voshmgir, the most famous king of this dynasty, also wrote poetry in Persian, and was obviously aware of the principles of criticism considering the Qabus-nameh his most celebrated work. Poets such as Bakhtiyari Ahwazi Mantiqi Razi, Badi al-Zam'an Hamad'ani were residing in the central region of the Buyid court.

In the 8th and 9th centuries (C.E), in addition to poets attached to the courts, there were a group of poets and writers who had no relations with the court including Abu Nasr Farabi, Abu Abdullah Khafif of Shiraz, Abu Sai'd Abu al-Khayr, Abu al-Qasim Bashar, Yasin and Ba'ba'Taher Hamadani.
This shows that the mystical poets gradually emerged in the 9th and 10th centuries; of the literary characteristics of this period is the expression of mystical meanings in the form of quatrains. From the point of view of structure, however, qasida (ode) and mathnavi were more in vogue during this period and with the advent of Ferdowsi in the 10th century, the epic literature reached its perfect consummation.

Hanzaleh B'adgheisi

Historians have reported that Hanzaleh B'adgheisi was a contemporarian of Taheriyan dunasty. Nezami Aruzi has reported that Ahmad Al-Khajestani has seen this verse in B'adgheisi's divan (collection of poems). Reza gholi Khan Hedayat has identified that Hanzaleh was living in the 8th century (C.E) and has died in the year 841(C.E). More accurate reports have confirmed that he lived in the first half of the 9th century.The poetries that are claimed to have been written by Hanzeleh carry more similarity to the works of the 9th century writers than those of the 8th century.

"If greatness is to be found in the lion's mouth,
"Go, face the danger and fetch it out of its mouth,

مهتری گربکام شیردراست
شو خطر کن زکام شیر بجوی

"If greatness, glory, affluence, and dignity, is desired,
"Death may have to be faced the way heroes do"

یا بزرگی وعزوحشمت وجاه
بجوی

یا چومردانت مرگ روباروی

Early Persian Poets

Mahmood Varagh Heravi

Historian, Reza Gholi Khan Hedayat has reported that this poet was a contemporary of Taherid and Safari dynasties. The only story that exists about his life is that he owned a beautiful slave and theTaheri ruler desired her and went to the poets' home and offered him two bags of gold for the slave girl. When he realized that the two were deeply in love with each other, changed his mind, gave them the bags of gold and left the house.

The entire collection of this poet's works is lost except the following verse:

"Darling I shall not let go of you if it costs my life,
Thou, to me, are more valuable than my life
"

گرانی در بها ارزانت ندهم

گرفتستم به جان دامان وصلت

نهم جان از کف و دامانت ندهم

You are what keep me alive,
I shall let go of my life, before I let go of you!"

Firooz Mashreghi

Historians have reported that he lived during the reign of Amro ebn-Leys. 887-909 (C.E.) He died in the year 905 (C.E.). None of his poetry have survived.

Abu Salik Gorgani

same time as Firooz Mashreghi classified his name as one of the great masters who came the great poets of Khouple of verses orasan and before him. The Historian and biographer Aufi has reported him to have been a contemporarian of Amro-ebn Layse. (Son of Jacob Leys, {the founder of Safarid dynasty}. He therefore must have lived during the followings are cwritten by him:. Manoochehri the famous poet has said that Abu Salik was one of

"If you shed your blood on the ground,

خون خود را گر بریزی بر زمین

"It's better than loosing your honor and respect.

به که آب روی ریزی در کنار

"Idle-worshiper is preferable to folk-worshiper,
"Listen to good advice, learn and implement!"

بت پرستنده به از مردم پرست
پند گیر و کار بند و گوش دار

Abu Zaraeh Moamari Jorjani (Gorgani)

Abu Zaraeh was a contemporary of Rudaki, who is credited to have been the father of Persion poetry after the invasion of Iran by the Arabs. Rudaki's life and poetry will be discussed in a later chapter. About the life and poetry of Abuzerae, we know very little. However it is said that one of the rulers of Khorasan complemented him by comparing him with Rudaki saying" It has been said that you write poetry like Rudaki does to which his answer was: "I write better than he does" He then composed these three verses:

"If my wealth is nowhere near that of Rudaki,
Do not be surprised if my words are no less than his,

اگر به دولت با رودکی نمی مانم
عجب مکن سخن از رودکی نه کم دانم

If he discovered the World with his blind eyes,
I can not go blind for the sake of discovering the World,

اگر بکوری چشم او بیافت گیتی را
ز بهر گیتی من کور بود نتوانم

One thousandth of what other kings gave him,
Did you give me! Thousand times more be heard from me"

هزار یک ز آن کو یافت عطای ملوک
به من دهی سخن آید هزار چندانم

Early Persian Poets

His date of birth is not known, nor his date of death. It appears that he was employed as a poet in the Samanid's court, which must have been after the death of Rudaki.

Some scattered verses satirizing his rivals have been found in various literary dictionaries. His poetries appear to indicate that he had lived a hard life with many heart wrenching problems. Following are some of his poetry:

"Where there would be money, the world I can overthrow
Where there would be speech, the iron I can turn to wax,
Should wind blow, with wind I can blow,
With cup and harp, or with Cuiras and Chain,

آنجا که درم باید دنیا براندازم
وانجا که سخن باید چون موم کنم آهن
چون باد همی گردد با باد همی گردم
گه با قدح وبربط گه با زره با جوشن

Abu Taher Ben-Mohammad Khosravani 10th century C,E, Persian poet

He was a poet from the era of Samanid dynasty in Khorasan. It is said that Ferdowsi has guaranteed (tazmin) in one of his poems this verse of Khosravani:

"I lament now the loss of my youth,
When I remember this hemistich by Bu Taher Khosravani,

I remember the absurdity of my youth,
My youth! Alas, Alas!

بیاد جوانی کنون مویه دارم
برآن بیت بو طاهر خسروانی

جوانی به بیهودگی یاد دارم
دریغا جوانی دریغا جوانی

This verse is an indication that Khosravani must have been living during the latter years of the second half of the 10th century. Aufi the famous historian and biographer mentions that Khosravani was a peer amongst the poets of his time and that he enjoyed a comfortable life at the court of the Samanids.

Chapter 4

Khosravani's musical odes were extremely popular. Sadly few of his poetries have survived the passage of time to reach us. Even this few is sufficient evidence of his great mastery in the composition of love-poems. The following is a section of one:

"My eyes are overcome with tears, your face I can not see,
Speak I can't for there is so much clamour,
Your face has the shine of the sun! The sun is dull! In comparison.
Your lips have the color of ruby! The ruby is rock in comparison

رخت دید نتوانم از آب چشم
سخن گفت نتوانم از بس غرنگ
رخ تست خورشید و خورشید خاک
لب تست یاقوت و یاقوت سنگ

Not the like of Khosravani, nor
the like of you,
Have Idol, Barahman, Hereme or the Ganges seen!

نه چون خسروانی نه چون توبتا
بت و برهمن دید مشکوی گنگ

Ferdowsi, was a great admirer of Khosravani, and has quoted a number of Khosravanie's poems in "Shahnameh".

Alas! Your delay in making peace,
Alas! Your haste in making war

فغان زان درنگت به هنگام وصل
فغان زان شتابت به هنگام جنگ

Your haste delays my rest,
So I rush to die because of it,

درنگم براحت همه زان شتاب
شتابم بمردن همه زان شتاب

Your love has never been without separation, Your separation and love, clasped have always been,

نبودست عشق تو بی هجر هیچ
بیکدیگر اندر زدستند چنگ

Separation is the whale and sea is the love,
Whale, for ever has had his home at sea.

نهنگی است هجران ودریاست عشق
بدریا بود جاودانه نهنگ

My eyes are overcome with tears. Your face I cannot see.
Speak I cannot, there is so much clamor!

Your face has the shine of the Sun.The sun
is dull in comparison.

رخت دید نتوانم از آب چشم

سخن گفت نتوانم از بس غرنگ

Your lips have the color of ruby!
The ruby is dull in comparison

لب توست یا قوت ویاقوت سنگ

.

Not the like of Khosravani, nor the like of
you,
Has Idole, Barhaman, Herem, Ganges
seen.

نه چون خسروانی نه چون توربتا

بت وبرهمن دید مشکوی وگنگ

The contents of Khosravani's div'an gives reader the impression that the poet
like Rudaki has been a pleasure loving, happy and joyfull person with no
worry or anxiety who, with his songs, attracts lovers to himself. The following
is a very popular poem that he has written in the last moments of his life:

"I found four groups of people to be
feebler than me!
 For no benefit ever came my way from
their:

چهارگونه کس از من به عجز
بنشستند
کز این چهاربه من ذره ای شفا
نرسید

Medicine, prayars, fortune telling and
talismans,
These were the physicians, asetics,
astrologers and magicians.

طبیب وزاهد واخترشناس
وافسونگر
به داروی وبه دعای وبه طالع
وتعویذ

It is important to note that Khosravanie's broad-mindedness was against the
superstitions of the time and not intentded against the traditional Splendour.
He had great respect for visions of the enlightened and beneficient people and
shared their views deeply. The following poem expresses his views in this
regard:

Greed and avidity I washed off from me, Since then, doors no longer remain closed to me.	تا پاک کردم از دل زنگار حرص و طمع زی هر دری که روی نهم در فراز نیست
He, who is void of greed, finds dignity, value and gain. He, who is void of avidity, his is honor, dignity and respect.	جاه است و قدر و منفعه آن را که طمع نی عز است و صدر مرتبه آن را که آز نیست

Clearly, criticism and reproach of the court poets are evident from these lines; the panegyrists whose greed and avidity seem to be their entire motivation in writing poetry. The underlying message found great application in the writings of the other poets of the 10th and 11th centuries. The following famous verses of Khosravani are inspired by similar verses written earlier by Rudaki:

I am astonished by the old folks, That they dye their beards black,	عجب آید مرا ز مردم پیر که همی ریش را خضاب کنند
They do not escape mortality doing that, Ending up torturing selves is all they accomplish	به خضاب از اجل همی نرهند خویشتن را همی عذاب کنند

Abul Moayed Balkhi, 10th century (C.E) poet and writer

This great poet and writer of the early 10th century lived during the rule of the Samanid dynasty. He is known to have composed a great deal of outstanding literary work in both poetry and prose. His most famous work was compiled in to one single book; a great number of Mythological stories relating to ancient and prehistoric times of two legendary Iranian dynasties; Pishdadian and Kianian. The book was called "Shahnameh Abumansoori" which was later versified and augmented by Ferdowsi to form the basis for his great book: "Shahnameh Ferdowsi". Abul Moayed Balkhi is also said to have been the first poet to have versified the ancient love-story of "Joseph

& Zoleikha". However this very important book has not reached our time other than one of its many stories i.e, "Garsha'spna'meh". Abul Moayede's Shahname kown as "Shahnameh Abu Manoori" contains a great number of legends relating to ancient and prehistoric Iran, its heroes and its peoples in prticular the kings and ruling dynasties. This great classical masterpiece has always been considered to have been the "Mother book", upon which all later versions of Shahnames been based.

Abu Shokoor Balkhi, 9th-early-10th century (C.E)

The exact date of the birth of this Samanid period poet is not known. He was; however a contemporarian of Rudaki and Ferdowsi i.e, he lived during the last years of Rudaki's life and early years of Ferdowsi's. Abu shakoor has written few verses in which both Rudaki's and Ferdowsi's influence is evident.
Abu Shakoor as it is obvious from his name was born in the city of Balkh. It is very little known of his early life, but it is known that some time in his young days he emigrated from Balkh to Bukhara where he seemed to have been living a rather lonely life before he established ties with the court of the Samanid king, Nooh-ebn-Samani. He composed a rather long elegy:"Afarin-nameh (Letter of Creation) which he completed in the year 958 (C.E). This book that earned him great fame has been lost over the passage of time and no copy of it exist to-day.

.Professor Saiid Nafisi was able to collect from a number of biographiies and history books about five hundred distiches of misceleneous poetries to show that Abu-Shakoor has written other works too besides the "Afarin-name" which of course represents his most important composition. The following verses which must have inspired Ferdowsi to write a similar poem seem to have come from his "afarin-nameh":

Your enemy shall never afford you kindness. The enemy resembles a tree of bitter nature	به دشمن برت مهربانی مباد که دشمن درختی است تلخ از نهاد
The tree of bitter nature, Even if you feed it sweet nourishment,	درختی که تلخش بود گوهرا اگرچرب وشیرین دهی مرورا
It shall, still, bear bitter fruit. It will not produce sweet fruit	همان میوه تلخت آرد پدید ازوچرب وشیرین نخواهی مزید

Chapter 4

If you be given suger by the enemy,
Suspect it to be poison, never eat it.

ز دشمن گر ایدونکه یابی شکر

گمان بر که ز هرست هرگز مخور

It appears that the following distich, which in fact attaches great importance to acquiring knowledge, comes from the same work i.e, "Afarin-nameh:

Acquire knowledge in order to have a good life,
Do not burn yourself the way of the butterflies.

بیاموز تا بد مباشدت روز

چو پروانه مر خویشتن را مسوز

But, at the same time he admits that knowledge does not provide answers to all our questions:

"All the knowledge that I acquired,
Made me only aware of my ignorance"

تا بدانجا رسید دانش من

که بدانم همی که نادانم

Here are some more verses from the "Afarin-nameh" collection of poetry emphasising the importance and significance of proper speech and merits of proper conversation:

"Although talk is a precious thing
It can become base if uttered by ignoble.

سخن گرچه باشد گرانمایه تر

فرومایه گردد ز کم پایه تر

Talk if uttered magnanimously,
It will find a place in the legends.

Talk that serves no useful purpose but loss and harm,
It should not be uttered.

سخن کز دهان بزرگان رود

چو نیکی بود داستانی شود

نگین بدخشی بر انگشتری

It has been said that talk,
 Cuts like diamonds and sharp swords do.

Talk brings down homes and thrones,
It can cause a snake to come out from its
hole.

Talk can be poison, antitoxin, burning or
soothing,
Talk can be bitter or sweet, remedy or
pain.

Talk that comes out from unauaspicious
mouth,
Is like a snake that comes out of its hole.

Stay away from such talk,
For closer you are, it can sting you easier.

Here is another example of Abu Shakoor's
great respect and admiration for
knowledge

ز کهتر به کمتر خرد مشتری

سخن کاندرو سود نه جز زیان
نباید که رانده شود بر زبان

شنیدم که باشد زبان سخن
چو الماس بران و تیغ کهن

سخن بفکند منبر و دار را
ز سوراخ بیرون کشد مار را

سخن زهر و پاد زهر و گرمست
و سرد
سخن تلخ و شیرین و درمان و درد

سخن کز دهان ناهمایون جهد
چو ماریست کز خانه بیرون جهد

نگه دار خود را از او چون سزد
که نزدیک تر را سبکتر گزد

Try hard to become learned man
fast'
You shall exalt should you become
learned one.

The exalted one is not necessarily
the learned one,
But the learned one becomes the
exalted one,

بدان کوش تا زود دانا شوی
چو دانا شوی زود والا شوی

نه داناتر آنکس که والاتر است

You shall not see the kings on the throne,

نبینی ز شاهان که بر تختگاه

Asking advice from the learned ones,
Although they stay in power long and late,

ز دانندگان باز جویند راه
اگر چه بمانند دیر و دراز

They always have a need for the learnedones.
You guard the treasure from the enemies

بدانا بودشان همیشه نیاز
نگهبان گنجی تو از دشمنان

And knowledge guards you for ever more.
Knowledge turns man virtuous,

و دانش نگهبان تو جاودان
به دانش شود مرد پرهیزکار

Thus said the intelligent wise man!
Also that knowledge gives you refuge if in hardship,
And shows you the Way, should you go wrong!

چنین گفت آن بخرد هوشیار
که دانش ز تنگی پناه آورد
چو بیراه گردی براه آورد

Abu-Shakoor must have written other mathnavies, besides the "Afarin-nameh".This may be concluded from the existence of verses written by him and scattered in a number of dictionaries. These verses must have come from two other separate collections of poetries by him and usually contain advice, exortations, and sermons.

The Devil has caused you great regret,
For the loss of wealth you have suffered,
Your bubble talk and fight,
Stupfies and belittles you

دیو بگرفته مر ترا بفسوس
تو خوری بر زیان مال افسوس
همه دعوی کنی و خایی ژاژ
در همه کارها حقیری و ها ژ

Here is another of Abu Shakoor' poetry. It is probably part of a longer qasida. However only two destiches have survived the ravage of time:

O longing for so long for your love has weakened me,
Suffering the pain of separation has caused my stuture bent,

O I have washed my hands from your slyness and deceit
Is there anyone who resembls you in character and nature?

ای گشته من از غم فراوان توپست
شد قامت من ز درد هجران توشست

ای شسته من از فریب ودستان تودست
خود هیچ کسی بسیرت وسان تو هست؟

Manjik Tirmizi, 10th century Persian poet

With the emergence of the Ghaznavid dynasty, that indisputably succeeded the Samanid dynasty, Persian literature flourished considerably in the eastern region and Khurasan. The immesurable wealth the Ghaznavid kings had secured from India induced them to confer lavish gifts upon the poets and writers; hence the emporium of panegyric and praise was in full fruition. The idea is not that only the attention the Ghaznavids paid to poets and poetry was the main reason for the development of literature in the 9th and 10th century, but that the Samanids had laid the foundation of literature and Farsi Dari on firm ground in the second century, and the attention the samanids paid to Persian literature helped advance the literature of the 9th century, namely, during the Ghaznavids period.

Capturing the western parts of India and establishing links with those parts, the Ghaznavids introduced Persian literature to a new region, which is known as the Indian region or the Indian subcontinent. The poets such as Mas'ud S'ad Salman, of whom we shall speak later, belonged to this region. He composed verses in praise of Lahore and India. The celebrated poets of the 9th and 10th centuries include Bahrami Sarakhsi, Zaynabi, A'lavi, Asjidi, Ghazayeri, Labibi, Manijik Tirmizi, Asadi, Unsuri, Ferdowsi, Manuchehri, Abul-Faraj Runi, Mas'ud S'ad, Abu Hanifa, Iskafi, Ayughi etc. Prominent among the characteristics of all these poets are their use of tangible poetic metaphors and their objective view of things.

Chapter 4

Abulhassan Minjik Tirmizi a native of the city of Tirmiz, which is located on the banks of the river Jeyhoon (A'moon darya'). The poet used this verse to make mention of his name:

"O King, your crown, shines like that of the Moon and the Venus!	ای آنکه زتاج تو بتابد مه و زهره
How long this indigent Menjik is to dewel in this cell	تا کی بود این مسکین منجیک به حجره

Menjik is one of the celebrated poets of the second half of the 10 century. He was a poet in the court of Choghanian following the famous poet, Daghighi. He has written plegyrics in tribute to Amir Abul Mozafa Choghani. Famous biographer and historian, Hedayat has stated that Menjik has also written plegyrics in tribute to the Samanid and Ghaznavid rulers. However there are no such poetries in existence at present time. His plegyrics only relate to the two Choghani amirs.

Menjik was a powerful, eloquent, and witty poet and writer. The poems that have been written by him and have reached our time are testimony to his extraordinary literary talent. His vocabulary is expressive with profound sense of reality and use of eloquent and rare metaphores. Menjik's divan (collection of poetries) was popular in Iran in the 11th century. And was used and enjoyed by poetry lovers and scholars. Nasser Khosrow, great writer, poet and philosopher has mentioned him in his diaries. Menjiks' literary talent, appears not only in his plegyries, odes and other kinds of verse, but shows itself in witty and satirical poems that he has written and is actually quite clever. Hedayat has commented on his satire saying"No one was safe from his sarcasm or his satire "

His poems can be found scattered in the literary miscellanies, biographies and dictionaries. Books like Labab-al-B'ab, Haft Eghlim, Assadie's Persian Dictionary, Majma-ol-Fosaha and other treaties and books of poetry. Here are a few examples:

"Take a look at a twin colored rose,
It looks like a pearl beneath a plain
Carnelian,
Or a lover and the beloved in private,
Lay cheek to cheek.

نیکوگل دورنگ را نگاه کن
دراست بزیر عقیق ساده

یا عاشق ومعشوق روز خلوت
رخساره بر رخساره نهاده

"O, you have swum the sea of wisdom!
You are conscious of all the life's good and
Bad

ای بدریای عقل کرده شنا
وزبدونیک روزگار آگاه

How can you allow your pure nature
becomes veiled!
How can you allow your pink face turn
black!

چون کنی طبع پاک خویش پلید
چه کنی روی سرخ خویش سیاه

Dip your bread into the tears of your own
eyes,
Do not seek milk from any mean person's
door

نان فرو زن به آب دیده خویش
وزدر هیچ سفله شیر مخواه

"O' Your body is softer than the finest silk
from Armenia,
Yourself is purer than the pre spring rain
drops

ای خوبتر زپیکر دیبای ارمنی
ای پاکتر زقطره باران بهمنی

The fragrance of your hair spreads musk in
the air.
The country side lights up wherever your
face shows up,

آنجا که موی تو همه برزن بزیر
مشگ

وان جا که روی تو همه کشور
بروشنی

Don't glance at the moon, for out of
jeolosy it will become dull.

منگر به ماه نورش تیره شود
زرشگ

In the eyes of your lover you are the new
spring;

مگذر به باغ سرو سهی پاک بشکنی
خرم بهار خواند عاشق ترا که تو
لاله رخ وبنفشه خط ویاسمن تنی

Your cheeks resemble roses, brows violet
and body jasmine

My heart is in agony with the pain of
separation;
Such good defence is patience against the
pain of separation".

ما را جگربتیرفراق توخسته شد
ای صبربرفراق بتان نیک جوشنی

Asjodi, 11th century Persian poet

Little is known about the life of this famous poet and peligyrist who was part
of the retinue of the poets living at the court of Sultan Mahmood Ghaznavi.
His date of birth is not known. He wrote a along and fervent qasida (elegy)
when Sultan Mahmood conquered the Sumanat temple in India.

Here is the opening verse of that elegy

When the king of the kings invaded the
Soomenat,
His action set standard for miracles a new.

تا شاه خسروان سفر سومنات کرد
کردار خویش را علم معجزات
کرد

This elegy was written by Asjodi in the year 1038 which was the year of Sultan
Mahmood's invasion of Sumanat. Asjodi's poems are found scattered in
books like Labab-olAlbab, Majmaol-Fosaha', Assadie's Dictionary and
Farhang Jahangiry.Here are examples of his poetry:

It is dawn and the musk-diffusing breeze is
passing by,
Seize the moment; it is pasing your
beloved's alley! Wake up, there is no time
to sleep, life is passing you by!,
Breath and smell the breeze, before the
caravan leaves!

صبح است و صبا مشگ فشان
میگذرد
دریاب که از کوی فلان میگذرد

برخیز چه خسبی که جهان
میگذرد
بویی بستان که کاروان میگذرد

CHAPTER 5.

REBIRTH OF THE PERSIAN CULTURE AFTER THE ARAB INVASION, "THE PERSIAN RENAISSANCE"

Beginning with the early years of the fifteen century (C.E), a major Event took place in the continent of Europe that left its permanent mark on the civilization of the western world. Rebirth or as commonly known "Renaissance", altered the course of the history in many ways, in particular cultural values of the nations, setting them free from the bondage of the Dark Ages, (C.E. seventh century to C.E fifteen century) during the long period that the Christian church strongly imposed its doctrines and controls upon the people's everyday conduct of life, human mind, and values, in particular the cultural goals and aspirations.

In the two hundred years that followed the Dark Ages major steps were taken by the scholars, and libertarians to revive the works of art, the literary ,scientific, philosophical, and, musical creations some of which dating back to the grand Greek and Roman civilizations, as well as those of the ,Middle Eastern, Islamic, Persian, and Oriental countries, and to incorporate them into the new scientific, architectural, educational, artistic, and literary creations of the newly born European countries, that were springing out of the Serfdoms of old Europe, from Russia in the east and all the way to the British Isles in the west, bordering the Atlantic.

Italians were at the forefront of this great "Movement". Dante, and Peter Ark, the two poets of the fourteenth century, Giovanni Boccaccio, writer of the mythological stories, promoted , and encouraged study of the classical readings, and ancient literary texts. Gradually the flame of knowledge that was lighted up by the Italians spread to other parts of Europe. Polish astronomer, Nichols Cupric, and Italian scientist, Galileo, founded the basics of the modern science. Leonardo Deviancy and Michael Angelo created the greatest works of art in painting, sculptor and architecture in classical styles. In Germany, France, and England great writers and poets such as Van Hogan, Jeffery Chaucer, John Culet, Edmond Spencer, William Shakespeare, Francis

Bacon, and many others created great literary works in writing , poetry, prose, philosophy, playwriting, and more, majority of which were deeply inspired by the newly discovered and adopted classical creations of Greeks and Romans of ancient times, thus laying the foundation for advancement and progress towards building the new western culture and civilization in the centuries to come.

Seven hundred years before the birth of the European "Renaissance", Iran witnessed the rebirth of its post- Islamic culture, beginning with the rise of Safarid dynasty spearheaded by a brave Iranian patriot, Jacob Laice Safari from the province of Sistan in the eastern parts of Iran bordering India. A number of Iranian poets and scholars headed by Rudaki were at the forefronts of this movement. These were, Rabeea Ghozdari, the first Iranian female poet, Mohammad Vasif Sistani, the first Iranian male poet, Abu moayed Balkhi, Abolhassan Shahid Balkhi, Ammareh Marvazi, Kassai Marvazi, and continuing through with many others, reaching its pinnacle with Hakim Ablghassem Ferdowssi with his masterpiece "The Shahnameh Ferdowsi". These great writers and poets over a period of almost 200 years wrote their poetry in "Farsi Dari" and attempted to recover the lost treasures of the ancient Persian classical works in painting, art, music, and poetry. This resulted in the reincarnation of "Farsi Dari" and the extensive use of the language by almost everyone in the Iranian communities. The basic structure of the language had been saved, although a great number of Arabic vocabulary had found its way in to it as the result of the presence of Arabs on the country's national and social scene over a lengthy period of time since the invasion. The new" Farsi", was now more diversified, richer in the use of vocabulary, and its power of expression greatly enhanced.

Safarid dynasty was superseded some hundred and twenty years later by Samanid dynasty during whose reign Persian culture and Farsi language flourished: "The Renaissance of Persian culture and language", started to witness its greater days. The Samanid monarchs were the descendants of the pre Arab Sassanian era with great love and devotion for the cultural values of ancient Iran. They went out of their way to support and encourage the poets, writers, and scholars of the new Times. The cultural movement expanded to include classical Persian music, Persian mythology, patriotic, epical melodies and folk songs. Additionally a number of old Persian manuscripts that had survived during the Arabs burning down of the libraries, and had later been translated in to Arabic, were now translated back in to Farsi. In the centuries that followed great literary masterpieces were written in the new Farsi language both in prose and poetry by the poets and writers of the new movement giving rise to one of world's greatest and richest cultural treasures ever created by any one nation in the history of the world. Rudaki as mentioned before played a major role in the process of starting up the Renaissance of the Persian culture, and further energizing it by his extensive literary contribution such as his poetry collection containing few hundred thousand verses, in addition to the translation from Arabic to Persian poetry, of the famous masterpiece,"the Kelileh & Demneh, a collection of poems called "the epoch of the sun", and a very old story from the Orient, by the name of "Sindbad and the deceit of the woman". Rudaki's artistic contribution to music was also a major factor in the development of new Persian music based on the old musical creations of the Sassanian era, as well as invention of couple of musical instruments. Rudaki was also a great philosopher, thinker, and a man of unparallel wisdom that left behind great words of advice, and guidance to educate and enlighten people mostly in the way that Socrates and Plato, the Greek philosophers, had done during the ancient times. Finally it must be emphasized that Rudaki's poetry and style inspired and led the way for many of the poets and writers during the Iranian Renaissance movement in the next two hundred years.

Rudaki Samarghandi (Father Of Persian Poetry) 9th century poet

Abu Abdelah Jafar entitled Rudaki was born in the village of Rudak, a suburb of Samarkand, in the province of Tajikistan, that at the time was a part of what was known as Greater Khorasan, in the Iranian plateau, under the rule of the "Samanid" dynasty. His exact date of birth is not known, but it is said to have been born sometime in the early years of the 9th century. His outstanding literary and musical talent manifested itself from an early age in the form of writing popular musical compositions for harp, composing melodies, singing and playing harp. Abu Nasr Samani, the ruling monarch, soon heard of his extraordinary skills and invited him to his Royal court where he served for many years. This new assignment brought him much fame and fortune. It is said by a number of historians that he composed more than a million verses of poetry. However the more accurate counts indicate that he has at least written one hundred and twenty thousand. Rudaki also translated the famous tales of "Kelile & Demneh" from Arabic to Farsi, however, almost none of that treasure exists to day. Professor Saied Nafisi was able to collect about six hundred of his verses.

Rudaki's major contribution to the evolution and development of new Persian poetry of the 9th century, was that he laid out the foundation upon which almost all poets of later years could build their poetical framework by using mostly the style, form and vocabularies of "Farsi Dari", the ancient Iranian language used, before the Arab's invasion of Iran. This in fact was the stepping stone for the rebirth of the Old Persian culture and language. His musical genius made the same contribution to the rebirth of ancient Iranian music dating back to the era of the Sassanian dynasty.

Rudaki was a very skilful poet, he wrote thousands of poems in a variety of styles comprising of lyrics, odes and quatrains all in a masterly fashion maintaining such a high standard of eloquence that caused the admiration and respect of all his contemporaries as well as the future generations of masters. He drew major support from the kings and the royal families of the ruling Samanid dynasty who strongly supported the efforts of all talented poets, writers, artists, and in general all scholars of the time who in one way or other were trying to contribute to the revival of the Persian language, works of art, and music, and to put an end to the domination and influence of Arabs who under the cover of Islamic faith were attempting to wipe out the culture and language of all nations living under their rule throughout the Islamic Empire. Samanid monarchs paid great attention to education, and went out of their way to compile and create libraries where people could benefit from the treasures of knowledge available at that time. Rudaki under the rule of Samanid dynasty gathered great wealth, and lived a very comfortable life. His mastery of language (Farsi Dari) as well as his poetic skills enabled him to translate a number of literary texts from Arabic to Farsi. Here is a piece translated by him from the Book of Kalileh & Demneh, arranged in Persian poetry.

All persons up and down the world Will not be able to do without knowledge,	تا جهان بود از سر مردم فراز کس نبود از راه دانش بی نیاز
Wise persons at all times, in hundred different ways	مردمان بخرد اندر هر زمان گنج دانش را به صد گونه زبان
Gathered and honored the treasures of knowledge,	گرد کردند وگرامی داشتند تا تا به سنگ اندر همی بنگاشتند

And cut those treasures on to stone for the
benefit of posterity,

دانش اندر دل چراغ روشن است

Believing knowledge to be the light of
Man's mind,
Protecting him as cuirass does against all
evil.

وز همه بد بر تن تو جوشن است

Other famous poets of the time of Samanid dynasty are Shahid Balkhi,
Amareh Marvazi, Abu Shakur Balkhi, and Kassai Marvazi. However none of
them compare to Rudaki in literary talent, skill, and output, neither their level
of contribution to the development of Persian poetry after the Arab invasion.
Shahid Balkhi was a close friend of Rudaki, and when he passed away, Rudaki
wrote:

Caravan of Shahid departed before ours,
Consider ours gone too

کاروان شهید رفت از پیش
وان ما رفته گیر و می اندیش

Body count now one less,
But wisdom count, a thousand less.

از شمار دو چشم یک تن کم
وز شمار خرد هزاران بیش

Rudaki has composed his poetry in the "Khorasani style". This is the oldest
style used by early Persian poets of 9th to 13th century, majority of whom lived
in the province of Greater Khorasan. This style is known for its simplicity, ease
of acceptance, and transparency. Rudaki's poetry is clean, void of complex
metaphors, allegory, and hard to grasp poetical allusions. This in fact is a
common characteristic of the poetry of all poets of the Samanid era.

It has been reported by some historians that Rudaki was born blind. This has
been the subject of much debate and controversy, in almost one thousand years
since the death of the poet. The overwhelming evidence, however, is that such
a belief is not completely accurate and that the poet lost his vision in the later
years of his life due to other reasons. The fact that he was not born blind is
evident from his exact descriptions of surrounding scenery, colors, details and
events which would be impossible for a born blind person to be aware of. His
poetry provides us with indisputable evidence:

I saw a bird near the city of Sarakhs,
It had raised its song to the clouds,

پوپک دیدم به حوالی سرخس
بانگ بر برده به ابر اندرا

I saw a colorful chador (veil) on it,
So many colors on its chador,

چادرکی رنگین دیدم بر او
رنگ بسی بر آن چادرا

Further evidence is clearly seen in his very famous poem in which he proudly describes his own teeth:

Pearl and coral pulled onto a white line of silver,
Stars and the droplets of rain at dawn,

مرا بسوخت و فرو ریخت هرچه
دندان بود
نبود دندان لابل چراغ تابان بود

All wore off and fell off, not one left,
Bad luck, as bad luck as the planet Saturn,

سپید سیم رده بود ودر و مرجان
بود
ستاره سحری بود و قطره باران
بود

Let me tell you, it was not luck nor was it long life,
It was the will of God,

کنون نماند یکی ز ان همه بسود و
بریخت
چه نحس بود همانا که نحس کیوان
بود

نه نحس کیوان بود ونه روزگار
دراز
چه بود؟ منت بگویم قضای یزدان
بود

O' Beautiful! You are looking at Rudaki now,
Not at the time, when he was in Khorasan.

تو رودکی را ای ماهرو کنون
بینی
در آن زمانه ندیدی که در

Rebirth of Persian Culture

خراسان بود

From the description given in his own poems, it is reasonable to assume that he was not born blind, but lost his eye sight later in life. Professor Saied Nafissi, who has done extensive research in to the life and works of Rudaki, has concluded that Rudaki was blinded by Esmailieh loyalists after, Amir Nasr the Samanid king, was defeated by them; reason being that Rudaki was a close friend of the King. This may also be considered a possible reason as to why, of the enormous volume of poems written by Rudaki, only a handful have survived, in particular his masterpiece, the versification in Farsi of the famous book of Kalileh and Demneh. Rudaki's closeness to the court of Samanids is most evident from the story of the departure of Amir Nasr, from Bukhara his capital, on a summer vacation:

It is said that as summer days drew to end, the king continued prolonging his trip and not wanting to return to Bukhara, while his entourage were anxious to go back home to their families, and no one had the courage to bring up the matter to the king's attention. In the mean time, some one, came up with the idea to ask Rudaki for help as people were aware of his close relationship with the monarch. Rudaki agreed to help. He wrote a poem, composed music for it, and presented it to the king, who was so deeply affected by it that, at once decided to return to Bukhara

The J'u-yi- Muliyan we call to mind, We long for those dear friends long left behind.	<div dir="rtl">بوی جوی مولیان آید همی یاد یار مهربان آید همی</div>
The sands of Oxus, toilsome though they are, Beneath my feet were soft as silk to me,	<div dir="rtl">ریگ آمون ودرشتی های او زیر پایم پرنیان آید همی</div>
Glad at the friend's return, The Oxus deep,	
Up to our girths in laughing waves shall leap.	<div dir="rtl">ای بخارا شاد باش و دیر زی میر زی تو شادمان آید همی</div>
Long live Bukhara! Be thou of good cheer,	

Joyous towards thee hasteth our Amir,

میر ماه است و بخارا آسمان
ماه سوی آسمان آید همی

The Moon's the prince, Bukhara is the sky;
O sky, the Moon shall light thee by and by!
Bukhara is the mead, the Cypress he;
Receive at last, O mead, the Cypress.

آب جیحون از نشاط روی دوست
خنگ ما را تا میان آید همی

میر سرو است و بخارا بوستان
سرو سوی بوستان آید همی

Rudaki was the first Persian poet that extensively utilized quatrains in the composition of poems. It should be remembered that in those days almost all folk songs and sonnets were in the form of quatrains, and Rudaki whilst mainly in the service of the royals and aristocrats, still had great love and loyalty for the ordinary people, their music, and songs. This may explain the reason behind constructing so many quatrains in his poetry

Life taught me a noble and free lesson,
If you look at life, it is nothing but, a lesson

زمانه پندی آزادوار داد مرا
زمانه چون نگری سر به سر همه پند است

Life taught me not to be sad that other's days are happy,
There are so many others who wish they had your days.

بروز نیک کسان گفت تا تو غم نخوری
بسا کسان که به روز تو آرزومند است

It is also apparent, that the last years of his life were not very happy ones; as there are many of his poems, specially the quatrains, that carry the same sad tones. These must have been the times when he had, apparently, lost favor with the ruling monarchy, lost his wealth and worse than that his vision. Here is another quatrain with the similar sad tone.

Many occasions, I was drunk and happy in this house,

بسا که مست در این خانه بودم و شادان

As my rank was higher than the Princes, and the Royalties,

چنانکه جاه من افزون بد از امیر و ملوک

Now I am the same, the house the same, and the town the same,

کنون همانم وخانه همان و شهر همان

Will you not tell me why happiness has turned in to sorrow!

مرا نگویی چرا شدست شادی سوگ

As it was previously indicated, Rudaki during the course of his life wrote a great number of poems, but almost all of this precious literary treasure has been lost. Professor Saied Nafisi was able to identify and collect only 804 verses from almost 120,000 that are believed to have been written by Rudaki. This collection is comprised of 360 odes, 64 quatrains, 224 musical odes, 154 couplets. He also, at the direction of Amir Nasr, translated the book of Kelileh and Demneh from Arabic to Persian verse (Farsi Dari).

It is said that two other stories, "Epoch of Sun", and "Sindbad and Deceit of the woman" were also versified by Rudaki. The former was a very popular legend in the Orient.
Rudaki was considered a great master, who led the way for all the other great poets of the Ghaznavi era, such as Farrokhi, Manoochehri, Ghazaeri Razi, coming after him. Those poets were all inspired, in one way or other, by him.

Verses by Rudaki:

There is no happiness in this world,
Better than meeting a friend.
****
There is no bitterness bitterer to the heart, than separation from a close friend.

Chapter 5

****
Knowledge in the heart is a bright light,
That shields your body from every evil.
****

Whoever does not learn from daily experiences?
Will neither learn from any instructor?
****

No ordinary teacher will ever teach,
Who, passage of time failed to teach.

Rudaki extensively pondered over the meaning and purpose of Creation, in particular Life and Death as two inevitabilities, and expressed such ideas in a number of his poems. Many years later, Omar Khayam seemingly inspired by him, used them to compose many of his own quatrains on similar basis. One quatrain by Rudaki, in particular, gives us an insight into his flight of fancy as he was gripping with the inevitability of death.

You shall sleep inside tomb,	زیر خاک اندرونت باید خفت
Although now you sleep in silk,	گرچه اکنونت خواب بر دیباست
We are all prey in this world my boy	جمله صید این جهانیم ای پسر
We are same as goldfinch, death as raven,	ما چو صعوه مرگ بر سان زاغان
Every flower withers sooner than late,	هر گلی پژمرده گردد زود نه دیر
Death will crash everyone the same as in the Oil press.	مرگ بفشرد همه را زیر غان

Rudaki, above all, was a folk writer and this is, in particular, manifest in his choice of words in the composition of musical poetry, the minimal use of Arabic words in poetry, giving advice and guidance to people, in general, and staying close to people's heart beat in the composition of music and poetry. To sum it up one should classify him as a patriotic folk writer. Although he had great mastery of Arabic language, which is apparent in the literary dictionary of Arabic-Farsi that was compiled by him, contrary to most aristocrats of mid Asian countries, he never considered nor put Arabic language or Arabic culture superior to that of Iranian's.

Rebirth of Persian Culture

Without a shadow of doubt, Rudaki is one of the most powerful and proficient Iranian poets. His natural poetic gift, and his mastery of the Persian language, combined with his great musical talent in musical composition and performance captivated all his audience during his entire life. As it was previously said he played harp beautifully, had a great voice, and the two when combined with his tender loving lyrics penetrated the heart and soul of young and old.

Rudaki died in the year 942 or 943 (C.E), and was buried in his home town, the village of Bonaj, a suburb of Rudak, City of Samarghand, in the province of Greater Khorassan, presently inThe Republic of Tajikestan.

Bayazid Bastami, 9th Century (C.E) Gnostic & poet

Bayazid Bastami, one of the greatest Gnostics of the 9th century known as Sultan-al-Arefan, was born sometime during the early part of the 8th century between the years of 738-748 during the rule of Omavian dynasty, some of the most cruel and corrupt Arab rulers after the advent of Islam.

His birth place was the city of Bastam in the province of khorasan in the north east of Iran. His family a devout Muslim well known for their strong faith and religious beliefs were descendants of pre-Islam Zoroastrians of ancient Iran, who had converted to Islam after the invasion of Arabs. Little is known of the details of the early years of his life. Historians and Gnostics such as Sahlaki, Imam Mohammad Ghazali, Sohrevardi, and Attar Neishabouri, have all reported contradicting details and stories about his life. However they all share the opinion that Bayazid was a Gnostic of great stature and rank, well known and highly respected during the entire span of the history of Sufism in Iran. He was known by a number of special titles such as Sultan-al-Arefin, Borhan-al-Movahedin, Morad-al Salekin, Borhan-al-Mohagheghin, and Morshed-al-Salekin. Except a few years that he spent to travel in other parts of Iran, as well as Arabian peninsula, Syria and Iraq, in order to associate with other Sufis, and Gnostics to benefit from their knowledge and experience, almost all his life was spent exclusively at his birthplace the city of Bastam, in the service of the poor and needy, personal meditation and worship of the Divine. Hypocritical ascetics who could not tolerate the purity of his soul and heart or the sincerity of his service to the community instigated the naïve and simple hearted citizens to, several times, revolt against him, accusing him of heresy and conspire to throw him out of town in to exile. When he was being thrown out, he would ask what crime have I committed? He would be told you are a heretic, to which he would reply, "how lucky would be the people in the city where there is only one heretic, and that one is me!"

To accuse a person such as me of blasphemy is idle talk,	کفر چو منی گزاف آسان نبود
No other man's faith can be stronger than mine,	محکم تر از ایمان من ایمان نبود
One blasphemer in this world and that is me!?	در دهر یکی وآن چومن هم کافر
Then there exists no one Muslim in this world!	پس در همه دهر یک مسلمان نبود
I can not have but scorn for those, Who would think of me as a Lord and Master!	چو مولام خوانند وصدروکبیر نمایند مردم به چشمم حقیر

Although as said before, the details of the life of this great Iranian Gnostic is unclear, and contradictory, but what remains of his teachings in Gnosticism is neither incomplete nor contradictory. It is quite clear that he was a great man who was able to explain, for the first time, the sophist's revelations and inspirations that come to them during the periods of ecstasy, and unconsciousness. This has been the main reason behind the rebellion of the devout clerics against him and them pursuing action to instigate the residents of the city of Bastam to call for his exile.

Bayazid led a life of asceticism and renounced all worldly pleasures in order to be one with the absolute. Bayazid became known as the first "intoxicated "Sufi. According to his peers he was both a devout Moslem and a dangerous heretic. His belief in the ancient Persian idea of "unity of existence" angered the Islamic clerics in his town: "Whoever dissolves himself in God and grasps the truth he himself becomes the truth as he will become the representative of

Rebirth of Persian Culture

God in himself and thus finds himself within himself" or,"Moses desired to see God; I do not desire to see God; he desires to see me."
Bayazid was one of the most extraordinary and indeed rare human beings of all times, quite unique, for his views on universal freedom, superior Gnosticism and humanism. Naser khosrow Ghobadiani, great poet and thinker of the 8th century attempts to describe Bayazid's basic Gnostic concept in the following poem:

Invisible can only be sighted by the sight of the mind, Invisible, cannot be seen with the physical eye, Invisible can be seen by man, who is free, He, who sees the visible, will not see the "Invisible"	به چشم نهان بین نهان جهان را که چشم عیان بین نبیند نهان را نهان در جهان چیست؟ آزاده مردم نبینی نهان را به بینی عیان را

Sanaie Ghaznavi, the famous Iranian poet and Sufi of the 8th century praises Bayazid in the following poem:

It takes days, for the world, to perhaps one night,	روزها باید که تا گردون گردان یک شبی
Bring a lover to his beloved, or a lonely man to his home,	عاشقی را وصل بخشد یا غریبی را وطن
It takes weeks for a bundle of wool from the back of a goat,	هفته ها باید که تا یک مشت پشم از پشت میش
To be made in to a cloak for a clergy, or bridle for a horse,	زاهدی را خرقه گردد یا حماری را رسن
It takes months for a cotton seed in the soil, To be made into a towel for a woman or a shroud for a martyr,	ماهها باید که تا یک پنبه دانه زا آب و گل شاهدی را حوله گردد یا شهیدی را کفن
It takes years for an even highly talented child,	

To become a learned man or an outstanding poet,

It takes ages for granite to turn, under the heat of the sun,
Ruby in Badakhshan or agate in Yemen,

It takes centuries, and only by the grace of God, that Men,
Like Bayazid, or Oveis walk this Earth in Khorasan, or in Gharan.

سالها باید که تا یک کودکی از ذات طبع

عالمی دانا شود یا شاعری شیرین سخن

عمر ها باید که تا یک سنگ خاره ز آفتاب

در بدخشان لعل گردد یا عقیق اندر یمن

قرنها باید که تا از لطف حق پیدا شود

بایزیدی در خراسان یا اویسی در قرن

Most significant in Bayazid's belief and Gnostic teachings were his love and respect for human beings of all race and creed. In this regard notice should be taken of some quotes from his sermons:

Bayazid was questioned by one of his disciples on the requirement for being a true Dervish. He said:
A true Dervish searches deep in his heart to find a treasure, wherein he finds a Gem, called Love. He, who finds that, is a true Dervish.
He was asked what should be the work of people and Sufis.
He replied: It will be that their hearts will always be with God, and want not but God, and do well for people, and be their care giver.
He was asked who loves and obeys God.
He replied: the person who is as generous as the sea, as compassionate as the sun, and as humble as the earth.

Attar Neishabouri, the great poet and Gnostic, in his book "Tazkeratol Olia", narrates a story about Bayazid:

"It is said that Bayazid left to go on a pilgrimage to Mecca. He had not gone but a short distance, when he returned. People asked him what happened. You had never before, changed your mind about a mission. He said, on the way I came across a man who asked me where I am going? I said I am on pilgrimage to Mecca. He asked how much money do I have?. I said 200 Dinars. He said

give it to me that I have a family of 10 to feed. This is your pilgrimage. I gave him the money and returned home
.

Bayazid was the first Iranian Gnostic who daringly put forward the concept of Monism or Pantheism, which is unity of Man and God. Although, harshly criticized and mistreated by the Muslim clergy, for promoting such ideas which were considered heresy, his fate did not turn out to be as violent as his followers in the next two hundred years such as Mansoor Halaj Shirazi, Einolghozat Hamadani, Sohrevardi, and other great Gnostics who were violently put to death for making similar proclamations. Four hundred years after the death of Bayazid great Iranian Gnostic and poet, Mowlana Jalaeldin Balkhi, "Rumi" deeply inspired by the message contained in that story of Bayazid, appreciates it in a beautiful Lyric of his own in the "Divan of Shams Tabrizi":

Circumambulate the "Kaaba" of the heart,
if thou hast a heart.
Heart is the "Kaaba" of the Divine, why
conceited by stone!
Lord commanded circumambulation of
"Kaaba",
As a way of showing kindness and
compassion,
If you go on pilgrimage to "Mecca"
barefooted a thousand times,
It will not please The Lord should thou
break a man's heart,

Give away your wealth and make some
needy person happy,
That, will light up your tomb one dark
night,

You may bring a thousand bags of gold to
The Lord.
Lord will say: you want to bring us
something! Bring us" Heart",

طواف کعبه دل کن اگر دلی
داری
دل است کعبه معنی تو گل چه
پنداری
طواف کعبه صورت حقت بدان
فرمود

که تا بواسطه آن دلی بدست آری

هزار بار پیاده طواف کعبه
کنی
قبول حق نشود گر دلی بیازاری

بده تو ملکت و مال و دلی بدست
آور
که دل ضیا دهدت در لحد شب
تاری

هزار بدره زر گر بری به
حضرت حق
حقت گوید:"دل آر اگر بما آری"

Do not hold in contempt "The Heart," even though is contempt, "The Heart" is dear to us even when it has been contempted,
Helping a needy and torn apart heart,
Pleases the Lord better than going on pilgrimage to Mecca,
The torn apart Heart holds the key to the Lord's treasures,
For most treasures are buried in the "Ruins",
If happiness and fortune is desired by you,
You are to seek" Heart" and avoid insolence,

If you get lucky and be bestowed favor of "The Heart"
Then sources of wisdom will stream out of your heart,
Words of immortality will flow out of your mouth,
Your breath will be medicine for the sick like that of Jesus,
"Khamoosh", words cannot explain the secrets of the "Heart".
Even if it may have at its disposal, hundreds of words

مدار خوار دلی را اگرچه خوار بود

که بس عزیز است دل در آن خواری

عمارت دل بیچاره دو صد پاره

ز حج و عمره به آید به حضرت باری

کنوز گنج الهی دل خراب بود

که در خرابه بود دفن گنج بسیاری

اگر سلامت و مطلوب گشت مطلوبت

شوی تو طالب دلها وکبر بگذاری

چو هم عنان تو گردد عنایت دلها

شود منابع حکمت ز قلب تو جاری

روان شود ز لسانت چو سیل آب حیات

دمت بود چو مسیحا دوای بیماری

"خموش" وصف دل اندر بیان نمی گنجد

اگر بهر سر مویی دو صد زبان داری

Bayazid's personality looms large on the horizon of early Persian Gnosticisms. Few Gnostics have impressed and perplexed their contemporaries and successive generations as much as him. Strange mystical experiences and a profound faith in God have been attributed to him. His theosophical locutions as well as his paradoxes reached, another although somewhat different mystic; Joneid Baghdadi, the leader of Baghdad school, who held that Bayazid had not reached the final stop in the Seeker's path to Transience.

Numerous attempts have been made by researchers in Europe to explain Bayazid's enigmatic personality and utterances. The best of these studies is the short and penetrating one done by Helmut Ritter and R.C .Zackery where he stresses the possibility of Indian influences upon Bayazid. However this seems doubtful at best.

As said before Bayazid was the first powerful, sharp, clear-sighted, and brave Iranian Gnostic who fought against the superstitious and superficial public beliefs, and fearlessly professed the Pantheistic ideas and doctrines eloquently and beautifully, both in words as well as by his actions, thus founding a new school of Gnosticism, which was in later years followed by self sacrificing and great Gnostics such as Hossein Halaj Shirazi, Sheikh Abolhassan Kharaghani, Sheikh Abu saeid Abolkheir, Einolghozat Hamadani, Mohi al-Din Arabi, and finally, Shams Tabrizi, and Rumi who elevated it to its highest level, and perfection.

Bayazid's basic Gnostic belief, was inspired by the idea of the unity of 'Devine' that everything in the universe emanates from God, and that our existence and that of God is intertwined, and is one ''انالحق''. This idea was in fact proclaimed by Bayazid towards the end of 8th century nearly one hundred years before it was adopted by the other famous Iranian Gnostic, Mansour Halaj Shirazi. Bayazid's exact words were '' سبحان ما اعظم شانی'', meaning "praise me! How sublime is my rank". Thus Bayazid should really be considered the forerunner of the Pantheistic doctrine and ideas during the Islamic Sufi movement. It should also be said that this group of Gnostics were the ones with deep conviction in the sanctity of human values, and respect for freedom of thought and belief all inspired by the pre-Islamic, ancient Iranian philosophy and doctrine of "Illumination"or Enlightenment"

Bayazid's nephew, who transmitted some of Bayazids words, once asked him about his renunciation. Bayazid commented by saying that renunciation has no value, adding: I was three days in renunciation, by the fourth day I had

Chapter 5

finished it. First day I renounced this world, on the second day I renounced the other world, the third day I renounced everything save God; on the fourth day, and nothing was left but God. I reached a desperate longing. Then I heard a voice calling: O'Bayazid, you are strong enough to endure with me alone. I said:" that is exactly what I want" then the voice said: you have found, you have found.

The usual classification of the stages of love dates back to early times. Bayazid spoke of the fourth fold nature of love: There are four stages: one from you, that to obey Him, one for Him and that is you recollecting Him, and one between the both of you and that is love. Sufis have often tried to describe the state of true love in poetic forms. Bayazid saw the spring like quality of love: "I walked in the steppe, it had rained love, and the soil was moist just as the foot of man walks in a rose garden, thus my feet walked in love"

Jalaledin Mohammad Balkhi (Rumi), became deeply inspired by the Gnostic doctrine and spiritual revelations of Bayazid conveyed to him by Shams Tabrizi during the almost three years of association with him in Quinea. This led to Rumi's complete transformation from an ordinary teacher and Islamic theologian into one of the most outstanding Gnostics and poets of the last eight hundred years. We shall discuss this further and in more details in the chapter that is allocated to the life and poetry of Rumi in this book.

Bayazid was an extremely generous man when it would come to help the poor and needy. He would also encourage and persuade his disciples, and followers to follow suit. It is said of him that one day a wealthy man in the city of Bastam asked him a question:

What is the mandatory rate for giving alms to the poor according to the Islamic law?
Bayazid asked the man:
Rate for me or rate for you?
The man said,
Is there a difference?
Bayazid said, yes; the rate for you according to the Islamic law is, 5 Dirham for each 100 Dirham, however as far as mine is concerned; every thing that I possess belongs to the poor.

Rebirth of Persian Culture

It is to be noted that Bayazid's profession, in addition to teaching and guiding people and acting as spiritual leader, was cattle breeding and agriculture. The above conversation is a clear indication of the high degree of humanity and generosity that existed within the spirit of this great and outstanding Gnostic.

Bayazid was also a great writer and originator of Persian classical rhymed prose; his writings had inspired a number of writers and poets of the generations after him, in particular Kha'je Abdolah Ansari, who was greatly inspired by him in composing fervent prayers in the form of hymns, as well as Sa'di, and others.

Your beauty far exceeds my sense of vision to see, Your secrets far exceed my ability to perceive,	حسن تو فزون است ز بینایی من راز تو برون است زدانایی من
My loneliness ends with your love, My ability fails me, when it comes to describing you	در عشق تو انتهاست تنهایی من دروصف تو عجز است توانایی من

Hakim Abolghasem Ferdowsi, 10th Century (C.E) Persian epic poet

Hakim Abolghasem Ferdowsi, greatest Iranian epic poet was born in the year 951, in the village of Baj, suburb of the city of Toos in the province of what was then known as the Greater Khorasan. He died there in the year 1033 at the age of 80, or as reported by some biographers sometime in between the age of 85 to 90. He was buried in a corner of his garden, since some zealot clergies in Toos would not allow his body to be buried in the town's public cemetery claimed by them as having been reserved for the devout Moslems only! We do not know much about the details of his life specially the early years and the stories that have been written and reached our hands are often somewhat contradictory. This is, however, certain that he was born in a family of Landowners (Dahaghin), and spent most of his life farming the lands that he had inherited. He completed his basic education in the city of Toos, and some years later studied Gnosticism, history, philosophy and poetry with two masters; Sheikh Mahmood Toosi and Sheikh Abubaker Toosi. Nezami Aroozi a distinguished writer and historian who attempted to do a biography of Ferdowsi almost 100 years after the death of the poet, writes that Ferdowsi was a land owner, making a comfortable living, however during the 35 years that he dedicated his life to the task of compiling his literary masterpiece; The Shahnameh, "Book of the kings" he, inevitably, neglected his estate, and as the result became very poor during the last several years of his life. His hearing, his vision and his health, in general deteriorated and worst of all he lost his 35 years old son too. The piece in Shahnameh where he eulogizes his son has a sad and painful tone.

It is said that in his young days due to strong and fervent patriotic sentiments that he carried towards his homeland and the deep despise of the Arab domination of Iran he joined an underground movement called "Shoubeieh". These were a group of landowners and freedom lovers who were struggling against the foreign invaders and interested deeply in upholding cultural and human values, in an attempt to revive the ancient Persian culture and language. In the course of his association with the group he was able to learn "Pahlavi dialect", which was the language used at the royal court of Sassanian dynasty and by the people of higher class and echelon, as well as in the writing of books and manuscripts, and was almost out of use, under the rule of Arabs, who were attempting to replace it by Arabic. This new skill helped Ferdowsi to access ancient texts that helped him tremendously, when he came to prepare for the great job of versifying "The Shahnameh". The main body of the subject matter for the book; the mythology, already existed in the form of a prose, "Shahnameh Abumansoori" that "Daghighi", another prominent Persian poet; had previously started to compose. However, with only a thousand couplets written, he came to a sudden and violent death in the hands of his slave servant and work was left unfinished.

Ferdowsi now in his early 50's embarked on a monumental task that when was finished after 35 years of arduous work, turned out to be a true and unique Epic masterpiece that surpassed , by far, the other ancient Epic; Homer's Iliad and Odyssey.

The true nature of Ferdowsi's relationship with Sultan Mahmood Ghaznavi is not very clear and it is narrated in different forms and shapes. It is of course possible that Ferdowsi, was at first considering dedicating The Shahnameh to

Rebirth of Persian Culture

Sultan Mahmood in order to get greater support and recognition for the book, but this was definitely not his motivation behind spending over thirty years of his life to creat it. His love for and loyalty to the homeland to preserve and reincarnate her national language and historical heritage must have been the driving force behind the accomplishment of this task. The supposedly monetary reward was neither important to a man like Ferdowsi, nor enough reason to make him spend those many years of his life to complete the task.

Upon completion of the book Ferdowsi set out for Ghazni to present it personally to the king whose royal court was occupide with a large number of poets competing to win favors from the king in the hope of benefiting from his generous rewards; thus an air of jealousy loomed over the entire Court. Sultan Mahmood was a fervent Sunni Muslim with contempt and dislike towards Shiite Muslims that Ferdowsi was one. Making the situation even worse was the unfortunate replacement of the king's Prime Minister Esferyani with a man by the name of Meimandi who deeply despised Iranians and the Farsi language and wanted everything to be written in Arabic. The previous Prime Minister Esferaieni, had been a staunch supporter of Ferdowsi and with him gone, rivals found an opportunity to confuse the Kings' mind who showed Ferdowsi a cold shoulder. The poet bitterly disappointed with the treatment he got from the King returned to Toos, and later travelled to the northern province of Mazanderan to seek refuge at the court of Sepahbad Shahreyar, descendant to the great kings of Sassanian dynasty who had ruled Iran before the invasion of Arabs. There, he presented the book to Sepahbad and offered to dedicate it to him. In addition he wrote a satire in contempt of Sultan Mahmood which contained a hundred verses. Sepahbad, who feared the wrath of Mahmood for Ferdowsi, refused to accept the dedication and offered to buy the satire from Ferdowsi paying him one thousand Dinars in gold for it. Six verses of the satire have survived:

They said: "This bard of over-fluent song, Hath loved the prophet and" Ali for long" Yea, when I sing my love for them, I could Protect from harm a thousand Mahmood,	مرا غمز کردند کان پر سخن بمهر نبی و علی شد کهن اگر مهرشان من حکایت کنم چو محمود را صدحمایت کنم
But can we hope for any noble thing! From a slave's son, e'en was his sire a King?	و پرستار زاده نیاید بکار گر چند باشد پدر شهریار

Chapter 5

از این در سخن چند رانم همی
چو دریا کرانه ندانم همی

For had this King aught of nobility
High-throned in honor should I seated be,

بنیکی نبد شاه را دستگاه
وگرنه مرابرنشاندی بگاه

But since his sires were not of gentle birth
He hates to hear me praising name of worth.

چواندر تبارش بزرگی نبود
ندانست نام بزرگان شنود

The effects of Ferdowsi's love and admiration for Iran and its glorious and great history must be considered not only in the transmision of the culture, morals, customs and literature of ancient Iran to Islamic Persia but also in the spread of Persian as the national language and the preservation of Iranian national identity which was being threatened as the result of Arab conquest of Iran. As said before, the movement had already began before Ferdowsi's time with the national struggle started with"Sheobieh", a band of Iranian intellectuals fighting to re-establish Iranian cultural values of the pre Arab invasion of the old Empire as well as other nationalistic groups – finaly bearing fruit through Ferdowsi's efforts. As such Iran is deeply indebted to Ferdowsi, both as regards its historical continuity and its national and cultural identity.

In discussing Ferdowsi's achievement one must consider, on the one hand, the totality of the Shahnameh as a whole, and on the other hand his artistry as a storyteller. Throughout the entire Shahnameh a balance is masterfully maintained between words and meaning, on the one hand, and passion and thought, on the other. Ferdowsi's poetic genius is creating a lofty dynamic epic language that is brief but to the point and free from complexity which greatly contributes to the strengths of his style.

The most important figures of speech in the Shahnameh include: hyperbola paronomasia, comparisons (similes and metaphors), representative images, proverbial expressions, parables, and moral and ethical advice. The most important passages of Shahnameh are descriptions of war, the beauty, nobility and purity or on the contrary the evil, infernal and wicked of the people, and the beauty of nature.

Rebirth of Persian Culture

In a historical context Shahnameh represents a documentation of ancient and almost forgotten events and chapters of the pre-historic Iranian mythology as well as more recent history going back as early as the times of Ashkanian and Sassanian dynasties (250 BC) and later events leading to the fall of the Persian empire in the hands of Arabs. It must of course be said that the stories relating to such Events were collected and compiled by others before Ferdowsi, and what Ferdowsi did which by itself is of paramount importance, is that he narrated them in poetic, enchanting and enjoyable to read dialect of Farsi Dari, the national language of Iranians as well as any other Persian speaking nations enabling and encouraging them to read or at least listen to, when read by professional narrators, thus keeping the history as well as the language of the Iranian nation alive, saving it from oblivion. It is important to remember that had it not been for Ferdowsi and other prominent writers such as Rudaki, Daghighi, Farrokhi Sistani, Shahid Balkhi, Kasaii Marvazi, Rabea Ghozdari, just to name a few, Persian language, would have not survived the constant persecution and prohibition of Arab invaders who were consistently pressing for the abolishment of Farsi and replacing it with Arabic, maintaining that Arabic is holy, being the language that Holy Kuran has been written in, and therefore should be the language to be spoken and written by all Muslims. This policy which was implemented throughout the Islamic Empire forced nations to abandon their local and national languages and gradually replacing it by Arabic, the result being that most nations in the Islamic Empire such as Egyptians, Syrians, North Africans, and others lost their ancestral languages, except Iranians who preserved it to this date. Shahnameh has been translated and published in to English, French, German, Italian, Dutch, Goojrati, Turkish, Arabic, and Russian.

It is to be emphasized that Shahnameh is not just an epic masterpiece; it is at the same time a treasure that is rich in philosophical and intellectual discussions and discourse, moral, ethical, and educational teachings and points of view. In this regard it is comparable with two other literary masterpieces; "Boostan", and "Golestan" by great Iranian poet and writer of the 13th century Sadi Shirazi.

A study of the Shahnameh, gives us a literary excuse for exploring how culture moves across space and time, becoming part of the global common heritage. Aside from its utmost literary importance, Shahnameh which is written in almost pure Persian had been pivotal for reviving the Persian language subsequent to the long standing influence of Arabic.The book reflects Iran's history, cultural values, its ancient religion (Zoroastrianism), and its profound sense of nationhood.

Ferdowsi completed the shahnameh at the point in time when Iranian's national independence had been compromised. While there are memorable heroes and heroines of the classical type in this work; ongoing hero is Iran itself.

The book is of paramount importance to all Iranians, but also to all Persian speakers throughout the world, including Afghanistan and Tajikistan, to other Persian speakers of Central Asia, as well as, in India, Pakistan, and as far as China. In short, as mentioned a study of Shahnameh gives us a literary excuse for exploring how culture moves across space and time, becoming part of the global heritage.

Shahnameh recounts the history of Iran beginning with the creation of the world and the introduction of art and civilization (fire, cooking, metallurgy, law) to the Arians and ends with the Arab conquest of Persia. The work is not precisely chronological, but there is a general movement through time. Some characters live for hundreds of years (as do characters in the Bible), but most have normal life spans. There are many Shahs and kingdoms who come and go as heroes and villains but the lasting hero is Iran itself and a succession of sunrises and sunsets, no two exactly alike, yet illustrative of the passage of time.

Father time, a Saturn- like image, is a reminder of the tragedy of death and loss, yet the next sunrise comes, bringing with it the hope of a new day. In the first cycle of creation evil is external (Devil). In the second cycle we see the beginning of family hatred, bad behavior, and evil permeating human nature. Shah Fereydoon's two eldest sons have greed and hatred towards their younger brother and thinking their father favors him, they murder him. The murdered prince's son avenges the death, and all are immersed in the cycle of murder and revenge, blood and more blood.

In the third cycle we encounter a series of flawed shahs. There is a Phaedra-like story of Shah Keykavoos, his wife Sudabeh, and her passion and rejection by her stepson, Seyavash.

In the next cycle all players are unsympathetic and selfish and evil. This epic is darker over all other epics most of which have some sort of resolution and catharsis. This tone is reflective of perhaps two things, perhaps the conquest of Persians by the Arabs and the reflection of the last days of Zoroastrianism.The old religion had been fraught with heresies, and somehow Zoroaster's optimistic view of Man's ability to choose had become life denying and negative of this world. There is an enormous amount of bad luck and bad faith here.

It is only in the characterizations of the work's many figures both male and female that Zoroaster's original view of the human condition comes through. Zoroaster emphasized human free will. We find Ferdowsi's entire characters highly complex. Nobody is an archetype or a puppet. The best characters have bad flaws, and the worst have moments of humanity.

Shahnameh and Its Impact on Modern Persian

After Ferdowsi's Shahnameh a number of other similar works surfaced over centuries within the cultural sphere of the Persian language. Without exception, all such work was based in style and method on Ferdowsi's Shahnameh, but none of them could quite achieve the same popularity.

Some experts believe the main reason the modern Persian language is more or less same as that of the time of Ferdowsi 1000 years ago is due to the existence of works like Shahnameh which have had lasting and profound cultural and linguistic influence. In other words Shahnameh Ferdowsi has been one of the main pillars upon which modern Persian language has been standing and surviving throughout these long and tumult'ous years.

Shahnameh is one of the few original epics in the world. Many peoples of the world have their own epic stories; more often than not; the original theme of these epics are borrowed from others, usually from a neighboring culture. This is not the case with Shahnameh, which is based on original Iranic stories.

Shahnameh has 62 stories, 990 chapters, and 60,000 rhyming couplets, making it more than seven times of Homer's Iliad, and more than twelve times of German Neibelunglwith. There have been a number of English translations, almost all abridged. In 1925 the brothers Arthur and Edmund Warner published a complete version in 9 volumes, now out of print.

The Mythical Age

After opening in praise of God and wisdom, Shahnameh gives an account of the creation of the world, of man, as believed by Sassanians. This introduction is followed by the story of first man Keyoumars, who also became the first king after a period of mountain deweling. His grandson Houshang, son of Seyamak accidentally discovered fire and established Sadeh feast in its honor.

Chapter 5

Stories of Tahmuras, Jamshid, Zahak and Kaveh, Fereydoon and his three sons, Salm, Toor and Iraj, and his grandson Manouchehr are explained in this section. This portion of Shahnameh is relatively short amounting to some 2100 verses or four percent of the book. It narrates the events with simplicity, predictability and swiftness of a historical work. Naturally the strength and charm of Ferdowsi's poetry have done much to make the story of this period attractive and lively.

The heroic age

Almost two thirds of Shahnameh is devoted to the age of heroes extending from the Manouchehr's age to the conquest of Alexander of Maccedonia. The main feature of this age is the role played by the Sagzi (sakas) Sistani heros who appear as the backbone of Persian Empire. Garshasp is briefly mentioned with his son Nariman, whose own son Sam acted as the leading paladin for Manouchehr while reigning in his own right in Sistan. His successors were his son Zal and his son Rostam, the bravest of the brave and then Faramarz.

The Feudal society in which they lived is depicted admirably in the Shahnameh with accuracy and lavishness. Indeed the Master's descriptions are so vivid and impressive that the reader feels himself participating in the events or closely viewing them. The tone is significantly epic and moving, while the language is extremely rich and varied.

Amongst the stories described in this section is the romance of Zal and Rudabeh, the seven stages or (labores) of Rostam, Rostam and Sohrab, Seyavash and Sudabeh, Rostam and Akvan-e- Div, the romance of Bijan and Manijeh, the wars with Afrasiab, Daqiqi's account of the story of Gushtasp and Arjasp, Rostam and Esfandyar.

It is noteworthy to mention that the story of Rostam and Sohrab is only attested to in Shahnameh and as usual begins with a lyrical prelude. Here Ferdowsi is in the Zenith of his poetic and has become a true master of storytelling. The thousand or so verses of this tragedy comprise one of the most moving tales of world's literature.

Historical Age

A brief mention of Ashkanian dynasty follows the history of Alexander and precedes that of Ardeshir 1, the founder of Sassanid dynasty. After this the history of the Sassanids is related with greater accuracy. The fall of the Sassanid dynasty and the conquest of Arabs are narrated romantically and in a most moving poetic language. Here the reader can easily see Ferdowsi lamenting over this catastrophe and over what he calls "the army of darkness". According to Ferdowsi the final edition of Shahnameh consists of sixty thousand distiches but this is a rounded figure, most of the relatively reliable manuscripts have preserved a little over fifty thousand distiches. Nezami Aruzi has reported that the final version of Shahnameh sent to the court of Sultan Mahmood Ghaznavi was prepared in seven volumes.

The Shahnameh's message

Shahname's style is of a superb poet. His epic language is so rich, moving and lavish that it truly enchants the reader. Personal touches in Shahnameh prevents it from falling in to a dry reproduction of historical narrative, no history has been so eagerly read, so profoundly believed and so ardently treasured in Iran, as has the Shahnameh of Ferdowsi. If a history were ever to influence its readers, the Shahnameh has done and still does in its finest way. Where many "Tajic and religious leaders failed, Ferdowsi succeeded.

Thus, to this extent, the master is so righteously confident of its endurance and immortality over the ages, that he versifies in the following exhilarating magical couplets:

Prosperous buildings get ruined, By rainfall and exposure to the sun,	بناهای آباد گردد خراب زباران و از تابش آفتاب
Ergo, I founded a high tower of verse, That shall not be damaged by sun or rain,	پی افکندم از نظم کاخی بلند که از باد و باران نیابد گزند
I shall therefore not die, and will live henceforth, For I have disseminated the seeds of discourse.	نمیرم از این پس که من زنده ام که تخم سخن را پراکنده ام

Ferdowsi, did not expect his readers to pass over the historical events in his book indifferently, but wants them to pounder over the reasons for the rise and fall of individuals and nations carefully and to learn from the past to improve the present and to better shape the future.

Chapter 5

The Shahnameh stresses that since the world is transient, since everyone is merely a passerby, one is wise to avoid cruelty, lying, avarice and other acts of evil; instead one should strive for justice, truth, order and other virtues which bring happiness, ease and honor.

The single message that the Shahnameh tries to convey is the idea that the history of the Sassanid Empire was a complete and immutable whole; it started with Keyoumars and ended with his fiftieth scion and successor Yazdgerd the 3rd, six thousand years historical legend of Iran. The task of Ferdowsi was to prevent future generations from losing their connection with this history.

The opening lines of the celebrated Episode of Rustam and Suhrab which is generally reckoned one of the finest passages in the Shahnameh.

The story of Suhrab and Rustam now hear:

Other tales thou have heard: to this also give ear.	سخنهای این داستان شد ببین زسهراب ورستم سرایم سخن
A story it is to bring tears to the eyes, And wrath against Rustam will rise.	اگر تند بادی براید ز کنج بخاک افکند نارسیده ترنج
If forth from its ambush should rush the fierce blast, And down in the dust the young orange should cast,	ستمکاره خوانیمش اردادگر هنرمند دانیمش ار بی هنر اگر مرگ دادست بیداد چیست
Then call we it just, or unkind and unfair,	زداد این همه بانگ وفریاد چیست از این راز جان تو آگاه نیست
And say we that virtue or rudeness is there?	بدین پرده اندر ترا راه نیست همه تا در آز رفته فراز
When, then, is injustice, if justice be death? Naught knoweth thy soul of this mystery pale;	بکس بر نشد این در راز باز برفتن مگر بهتر آیدش جای
No path shall conduct thee beyond the dark veil,	چو آرام یابد به دیگر سرای دم مرگ چون آتش هولناک
	ندارد ز برنا و فرتوت باک در این جای رفتن نه جای درنگ

All follow their ways to this hungering door,

A door which once shut, shall release them no more!

Yet perhaps thou shall win, when from hence thou shall
Roam the other abode to a happier home.

If death's clutch did not daily fresh victims enfold,

Our world would be choked with the young and the old.

Is it strange if the flame of the ravenous fire?
Once kindled, should lead to a holocaust dire?

Nay, its burning outbursteth holdeth, once grant it a hold,
As tender twigs spring from some root strong but old.

Death's breath doth resemble such pitiless fire,
Consuming both alike the son and the sire.

Even the young in the joy of their living must pause,
For, apart from old age, Death has many a cause.

Should Death bid thee fare to thy long home with speed?
And constrain thee to mount on pale destiny's steed,

بر اسپ فنا گر کشد مرگ تنگ
چنان دان که دادست وبیداد نیست

چو داد آمدش جای فریاد نیست
جوانی و پیری بنزدیک مرگ

یکی دان چو اندر بدن نیست برگ
دل از نور ایمان گر آکنده ای

ترا خامشی به که تو بنده ای
برین کار یزدان ترا راز نیست
اگر جانت با دیو انباز نیست

به گیتی در ان کوش چون بگذری
سرانجام نیکی برخود بری

کنون رزم سهراب رانم نخست
ازان کین که اوبا پدر چون بجست

Chapter 5

Think not that for Justice Injustice is sent,
And if Justice then wherefore beware and
lament?

In Destiny's sight Youth and Age are as
one;
Thus know if ye want not Religion undone.

If thy heart is fulfilled with Faith's light,
then I trow

That silence is best, for God's servant art
thou.

Be thy business to supplicate, worship,
obey,

And order thine acts for the last Judgement
Day.

In thy heart and thy soul hath the demon
no lot,

Then to fathom this secret of God's sought
thou not.

Seek now in this world of religion a share;
That alone will support thee when hence
thou shall fare.

Now harken: the story of Suhrab I will tell,
And the strife that'twixt him and his father
befell."

It is sometimes assterted that Shahnameh contains practically no Arabic
words. This is incorrect: Ferdowssi avoided their use as far as possible in his
Epic, because he felt it to be unsuitable to the subject of his poem, but even in

his time many Arabic words had become so firmly imbeded in the language that it was impossible to avoid their use. The twenty one verses translated above comprise about 250 words, of which nine ('ajab, tarab, sabab, qada, ajal, khalal, n'ur, iman, and islam,) are pure Arabic, and one (hawl nak) half Arabic; and this is about the usual proportion, namely, 4 or 5 percent.

Passing now to Ferdowsi's remaining poetical works, we come next to his mathnavi on the romance of Joseph and Zulaykha, greatly expanded and idealized from its original basis, has always been a favorite subject with the romantic poets of Persia and Turkey, however Ferdowsi was not the first Persian poet to handle it, Abu Moayed Balkhi and Bakhtiyari of Ahwaz having both, according to one manuscript authority, already made it the subject of a poem.These two earlier versions are otherwise quite unknown to us ,while our knowledge of Ferdowsi's version, which luckily has survived the vicissitudes of time, is largely due to Dr. Ethee's and a number of tireless efforts by others. Though the book is but rarely met with in the East, a sufficient number of manuscripts (seven at least) exist in the great public libraries of England and France.

The value of Ferdowsi's lyric poems, have been generally underrated. Here is a rendering of the lines cited by famous historian, Awfi. In this poem, Ferdowsi here introduces his verse as a tazmin to the lyric by Khusrawani:

"Much toil did I suffer, much writing I pondered,
Books written in Arabian and Persian of old;
For sixty two years many arts did I study:
What gain do they bring me in glory or gold?
Save regret for the past and remorse for its failings
Of the days of my youth every token hath fled,
And I mourn for it now with sour weeping and wailings,
In the words Khusrawani Bu Tahir hath said:

بیاد جوانی کنون مویه دارم
بر آن بیت بوطاهر خسروانی

جوانی به بیهودگی یاد دارم
دریغا جوانی دریغا جوانی

Chapter 5

"My youth as a vision of childhood in
sooth,
I remember: alas and alas for my youth!"

Manuchehri Damghani, 11th Century Poet

Manuchehri is one of the outstanding Persian poets of the 11th century. He
was also member of the group of early Persian writers and scholars who has
been given credit for playing an important role in the movement which lead
to the renaissance of the new Persian culture after the Arab invasion of Iran.
Manuchehri was an eloquent poet whose special talent was manifested in
writing long and delightful qasidas (elegies) describing natural sceneries and
praising the ruling monarchs at whose courts he served; The Ziari king
Manuchehre ibn Qabus, and Sultan Masood Ghaznavi. For his poetry he has
also borrowed themes from pre-Islamic Arab poets. These include description
of the desert, the camel, as well as tribal life and tribal raids. Joy is one of the
important themes in Persian poetry that is distinctly expressed in
Manouchehrie's poems. He was a cheerful, pleasure-seeking, realistic poet;
he created a world full of happiness in his poems mainly by relying on visual
effects of nature, description of different celebrations, birds, flowers, various
seasons etc. Contrary to the works of other poets of the tenth and eleventh
centuries whose works were mostly collected and compiled during their life
time or shortly thereafter, Manuchehrie's "diva'n" (collection of poetry) was
compiled couple of centuries after his death. Therefore one cannot be sure that
all the poems that are included in the'divan' are in fact his, and have reached
us with no additions or changes to the content by others. Still there is no doubt
about his extraordinary poetical skill which can easily be seen by reading his
poetry. He intertwines his knowledge of theology, medicine, astronomy with
the social, political, and often even personal issues of the time. The inclusion
of exotic subjects, and his insistence in accommodating the names of almost
all the Persian and Arab poets who have lived before him, makes some of his
verses difficult to read or underestand. Often a lack of knowledge of Arabic
and, indeed, of the scientific jargon he uses, places those poems beyond the
reach of the casual reader but, in general, his poetry is simple and delightful
to read. As was previously indicated Manuchehri started his career as a poet

in the court of the Ziarid dynasty of Tabarestan. The dynasty was started by Taher Zolyaminein, the first semi independent Iranian rulers after the invasion of the country by the Arabs almost three hundred years earlier. He wrote a number of elegies praising the Ziari ruler and later the Ghaznavi rulers, Sultan Mahmood and Sultan Masood. Manuchehri gained special rank at the court of Sultan Masood serving under the court's poet laureate Onsori, whom he praised.

Manuchehri was a powerful writer and a remarkable scholar with great knowledge in the field of Persian poetry. He created a new form of poem; mosammat. This is a short form of poetry in which the first three to five hemistiches rhyme while the last hemistich introduces a new rhyme. This particular style was used by him in the composition of a large number of his poems. Thus he could be credited to have been the inventor of mossamat in Persian poetry which has been extensively used by many other Persian poets after him. He is generally said to have borne the sobriquet of "Shast galle", a term variously interpreted, but generally as meaning "sixty herds" in allusion to his wealth. However, other researches exist like the one in "R'ahatal-Sudur", indicating that "sixty herds" was the title given to two other Persian poets of later centuries with similar names to wit, Abu-Najm Ahmad Minucheri, and Shamsed-Din Ahmad Minucheheri.

Manuchehri, as reported by biographer Aligholi Hedayat has written a total of about 30,000 verses in qasida, ruba'is, and elegy, but what is available presently comprises of fifty seven qasidas, (odes), eleven mosammats, twenty qit'as (stanza), few rob'ais (quatrains), and several unfinished qasidas. His diva'n (complete works) was published in Teheran in1952, and a translation in French in Paris in1888.

Dolatshah Samarghandi has indicated that Manuchehri was born in the city of Balkh, in the latter years of the 11th century, however, there seems to be no doubt that he was a native of the city of Damghan and this has been confirmed by him in one of his poems: He was a poet at the court of Sultan Masood Ghaznavi and well liked and revered by the King.

Not much is known about the early years of his life, but this we know that he completed his early education in Damghan, learning Persian, Arabic, theology, poetry, history, medicine and astronomy as was customery at that time.. He started his career as a poet in the court of Ale-ziar of Daylam in

Mazanderan. He adopted the pen-name Manuchehri because of his attachment to the court of Falak-al-Ma'ani Manuchehr-ben-Shams-ol-Ma'ali Qabus-ebn-Voshmgir, one of the kings of the Al-Ziar dynasty. Sultan Masood Ghaznvi during his trip to invade Gorgan and Mazanderan invited him to join him there. Manuchehri states in one of his poetries that he travelled on foot all the way from Rey to Estrabad to be with the King:

"Thou knowst that I am residing at the court of the king, Until his return from the 'Sarie's garden of tulips	دانی که من مقیم بر درگه شهنشه تا بازگشت سلطان از لاله زار ساری
I traversed barefooted these plains and mountains, My feet got injured, my eyes went dark!	این دشت ها بریدم وین کوه ها پیاده دو پای با جراحت دو دیده گشته تاری
All in hope of the audience, with the king Thus luck comes my way, making my day, bright like a spring day."	بامید آنکه روزی خواند ملک بپیشم بختم شود مساعد روزم شود بهاری

Manuchehri's special talents, coupled with extensive knowledge in literature, history philosophy, theology etc, and his popularity with the King prompted the envy and jealousy of the rest of the poets residing at the royal court. As it was mentioned before; he was a naturalist, and has composed poetry describing the natural phenomenaes such as the four seasons, scenes from the nature and in particular flowers which he has used them as Methaphors and Similes. One example is the use of Judas tree with its beautiful purple flowers. Manuchehri has used this tree at poetry lines in Methaphoere and Similis. Places such as beloved, bird, ring, embryo etc.

Manuchehri has written poetry in different styles. Here is one of his famous musamats describing autumn:

Rise and wrap yourself in silk botched now that it's autumn	خیزید وخز آرید که هنگام خزان است

Rebirth of Persian Culture

A chill wind blows from the direction of Kharazm

باد خنک از جانب خوارزم روان است

Look at the wine leaves on the branches of vines.
They seem like tatters from a dyer's smock.

آن برگ رزان بین که بر آن شاخ رزان است
گویی بمثل پیرهن رنگرزان است

The dehghan bites his knuckle in amazement
That in garden and meadow no rose or Pomegranate blossom remains.

دهقان به تعجب سرانگشت گزان است
کاندر چمن و باغ نه گل ماند و نه گلنار

Like at the citron and wonder at its appearance
Its breasts firm and full and pendant,
Yellow and white, its whiteness increasing,

بنگر بترنج ای عجبی دارکه چونست
پستانی سختست و درازست ونگونست

All yellow without but white within
No silvery within, but without gold like dinars,
And its silver interior is stuffed with royal pearls'

زردست و سپیدست و سپیدیش فزونست
زردیش برونست و سپیدیش درونست

And that apple likes a smooth-turned ball of white suger
That has been dipped three hundred times in yellow dye,

چون سیم درونست و چو دینار برونست
آکنده بدان سیم بود لولوشهوار

On its cheek some small spots of coral,
And onits tail a green saddlecloth of emerald hue-

وان سیب چو مخروط یکی گوی تبرزد
در معصفری آب زده باری سیصد

In the stomach are two or three tiny domed chambers,
In each sleeps a Negro child, as black as pitch.

برگرد رخش بر نقطی چند زبسد
وندردم او سبز جلیلی ززمرد

Chapter 5

At dawn, when the dehghan leaves his house,
He neither hesitates nor stands at gaze,
He approaches the vineyard and opens the gate,
To see how his daughters the vines are, and what they are about

Not one of his daughters turns a virginal face to him
All are pregnant and all infirm.
He says, "My little daughters, what happened to you?

Who has seen your veiled cheeks?
Who has drawn the curtain of your rooms aside?
Who has torn your God-given veil of Hymen?

Who has come here since I left the house?
Turn to your actions and try to explain them!

"I will tell you how I will punish you.
First I will separate you each from each.

I will take you from the garden to prison, and I will
Delay in coming.

Once I have reached you I will not hesitate
I will crash your bodies under foot,
For you deserve no better than this"

For three measured months he mentions not them

وانـدر شکمش خردک خردک دو سه گنبد
زنگی بچه ای خفته بهریک در چون غار

دهقان به سحرگاهان کز خانه بیاید
نه هیچ بیارامد و نه هیچ بپاید
نزدیک رز آید در رز را بگشاید
تا دختر رز را چه بکارست و چه شاید

یک دختر دوشیزه بدو رخ ننماید
الا همه آبستن والا همه بیمار

گوید که شما دخترکان را چه رسیده ست
رخسار شما پردگیانرا که بدیده ست

وزخانه شما پرده گیانرا که کشیده ست
وین پرده ایزد بشما بر که دریده ست

تا من بشدم خانه در اینجا چه رسیده
گردید به کردار و بکوشید به گفتار

من نیز مکافات شما بازنمایم
اندام شما یک بیک از هم بگشایم

ازباغ بزندان برم و دیر بیایم
چون آمد می نزد شما دیرنپایم

اندام شما زیر لگد خرد بسایم

He knows he will not be blamed for their
blood

زیرا که شما را بجز این نیست
سزوار

Then one day he rises up lightly, happy,
laghing and gay,
He comes to the prison and removes the
door's seal.

سه ماه شمرده نبرد نام ونشا نتان
داند که بدان خون نبود مرد گرفتار

When he looks smiling in upon the prison
and the Imprisoned,
A hundred lamps and candles fall upon his
teeth and lips.

یکروز سبک خیزد شاد و خوش
وخندان
پیش آید وبردارد مهر از در وبندان

Roses in abundance, he sees, and in
abundance jasmine
Flowers,
Such as no one has seen in a rose garden
or a field of Jasmine

چون در نگرد باز به زندانی
وزندان
صد شمع وچراغ اوفتدش برلب
ودندان

I will never quit your company
And I will hold you dearer than my eyes –
heart and soul

گل بیند چندان و سمن بیند چندان
چندانکه به گلزار ندیدست
وسمنزار

I wll rain red rosewater on your brow,
And pass you around in a crysralline cup

از مجلستان هرگز بیرون نگذارم
وزجان ودل ودیده گرامی تردارم

I will recompose you well
And treat you with complete justice.

برفرق شما آب گل سوری به بارم
با جام چوآبی بهم اندربگسارم

The dehghan then brings in a large cup
And holds it for a moment in his palm,

من خوب مکافات شما بازگزارم
من حق شما بازگزارم به بتاوار

Its [silver] color paints moons on his
Two cheeks
And the aloes and balsam of its scent
pierces his brain

آنگاه یکی ساتگنی باده برآرد
دهقان وزمانی به کف دست بدارد

He says this dark wine will be indigestible,

بردورخ اورنگش ماهی بنگارد
عود وبلسان بویش در مغزبکارد

Unless it is drunk to the just and elect
Shah.

گوید که مرا این می مشکین
نگوارد
الا که خورم یاد شهی عادل
ومختار

Abolhassan Shahid Balkhi, 9th century poet and philosopher

Abolhassan Shahid Balkh is one of the greatest poets and philosophers of the 9th century. He was a contemporary of Rudaki, and Mohammad Zakaria Razi. He lived during the reign of the Samanid dynasty. He died in the year 947 (C.E) just a few years before the passing away of Rudaki. Here is the famous elegy that Rudaki wrote on the occasion of his death.

Procession of "Shahid" left ahead of us,   کاروان شهید رفت از پیش
Consider our's gone too,   وان ما رفته گیرومی اندیش

Body count, we are short one,   از شمار دو چشم یک تن کم
Wisdom wise we are short a thousand!   وزشمارخرد هزاران بیش

Shahid Balkhi was not only an outstanding poet but he was a great philosopher, theologian and Sufi. He was involved in philosophical discussions with the prominent Iranian scientist and philosopher Mohammad Zakaria Razi, the discoverer of alcohol. Shahid Balkhi was a keen promoter of knowledge and learning amongst the common people during a time when Iranians were struggling to free themselves from the centurie's old domination of Arab rule. He was extremely sad and disappointed to notice people's indifference towards education and knowledge and their contempt for the learned individuals, scholars and intellectuals. Here is a poem in which he expresses his immense grief and sadness:

"If grief gave out smoke like fire does,   اگر غم را چوآتش دود بودی

Rebirth of Persian Culture

The entire world would be dark for ever,

جهان تاریک بودی جاودانه

If you search the world over,
You shall not find one wise person.

در این گیتی سر اسر گر بگردید
خرد مندی نیابی جاودانه

Knowledge and wealth are like narcisses and rose,
The two will not grow and flower together.

دانش وخواسته است نرگس وگل
که نرویند ونشکفند بهم

He who has knowledge, has no wealth,
He who has wealth has no knowledge.

هرکه را دانش است خواسته نیست
هرکه را خواسته است دانش نیست

Shahid Balkhi was revered by all the scholars, poets and gnostics of his time. He was born in the city of Balkh which is to-day part of the republic of Afghanestan. Very little is known about his life, and only few pieces of his poetry have survived. He has written a number of eulogies in praise of natural sceneries, feelings of love, sentiments and similar. Here is a piece expressing such sentiments:

"Cloud weeps the same as the lovers do,
Garden laughs same as the beloved does,

ابر همی گرید چون عاشقان
باغ همی خندد معشوق وار

Thunder roars the same way as I,
Lament at the early hours of dawn.

رعد همی نالد ماند من
چونک بنالم به سحرگاه زار

This piece is part of a spring serenade which is interwoven masterly with expressions of love and grief.
Shahid also seems to have been carrying bitterness against certain individuals, personalities and rich of the time has vented such feelings in satirical poems that are pointed and sharp causing some European critics such as "Darmesteter" to compare him with the French poet Charles Baudelaire.

Generations of poets and critics who came after Shahid Balkhi have all greatly admired his poetry. However a number of the rich and mighty who were the target of his satire and critism did not particularly care for his writings. Professor Saiid Nafisi who has extensively researched Shahid's work has said that Shahid not only was a great poet of his time, but also a scholar and an outstanding learned man as well as a distinguished caliographer. As it was mentioned before he had neumerous discussions with Hakim Ra'zi on the subject of methaphisics, philosophy and divinity. This in itself can be considered enough evidence towards his degree of knowledge that has made Ra'zi getting involved with him in intellectual discussions.

Shahid is said to have also composed poetry in Arabic and has eulogized Samanid ruler Nasre Samani and his minister Mohammad Jeyhani.

Fakhreddin As'ad Gorgani, 11th century poet

Fakhreddin As'ad Gorgani was the famous Persian poet of the 11th century. His date of birth is not accurately known, but the evidence seems to indicate that he was born in one of the early years of the 11th century in the city of Gorgan, and thus his title; Gorgani.

Attempts to versify the ancient stories in Persian literature started to become popular at the beginning of the 11th century (C.E), and As'ad Gorgani was in fact one of these poets. Other famous Persian poets who embarked on this venture to versify the romantic love stories of the ancient times were Onsori the poet lauriete of the royal court of Sultan Mahmood. Gorgani attempted to versify the old stories of "Vamegh va Azra" and "Sorkh Bot va Kheng Bot". Abureyhan Byrooni did a versified translation of two other ancient stories: "The story of "Ormozdyar & Mehryar "and "The story of Dazeme & Geramidokht" from Persian into Arabic. Another poet, a contemporary of Sultan Mahmood, by the name of Eyvaghi versified the old story of "Vargheh va Golshah". Fakhreddin Gorgani attempted to do a versified translation of "Vis & Ramin" from Pahlavi into Persian. This story seems to have originated from the period of Sasanian. The versified translation turned out to be such a popular and well-liked masterpiece that started a new trend for this kind of work and influenced other poets like Nezami Ganjavi and others in the 12th century and beyond to undertake similar tasks. Nezami in particular versified a number of such love stories: Khosrow & Shirin, Leili & Majnoon, Story of Alexander, and the story of Bahram, the Sassani emperor. It is generaly believed that the story of Vis & Ramin by Fakhreddin As'ad Gorgani must have been a source of inspiration for Nezami.

Rebirth of Persian Culture

Fakhreddin As'ad was an extremely talented and proficient writer and a great scholar. He lived during the reign of Sultan Abutaleb Toghrol Saljooghi. He was admitted into his royal court and was part of his entourage during his various campaigns:

ÓAbuTaleb great king of kings.
The most supreme commander of the world

ابوطالب شهنشاه معظم
خداوند خداوندان عالم

He is the king with great determination
He has afforded all persons rank and riches.

ملک طغرل بک آن خورشید همت
بهرکس زورسیده عزونعمت

He who is named same name as "Mohammad"
He was confirmd to become victorious same as he was.

هرآوراکاوست همنام محمد
چواومنصورشد چون اوموید

The poet continuously travelled with Sultan Toghrol and recorded the details of his victories as Toghrol waged wars aginst the various Kharazm rulers, and other ones in Khorasan, Tabarestan, Gorgan, Rey, Kerman, Moosel, Ahvaz, as well as meeting with the Roman Ceasers, and The Khalif in Baghdad. He finally spent seven months with Toghrol in Isfahan. He wrote these lines complaining about not be able to get a decent sleep there:

"From every corner throughout the Land,
News of victory the messengers him constantly brought,

ازآطراف ولایت هرزمانی
بفتحی آوررندش مژدگانی

From the constant clamour of the horns and the drums,
Seven months, sleepless, I went in Isfahan"

زبانگ طبل وبوق مژده خواهان
نخفتم هفت مه اندر صفاهان

The poem, in fact indicates that he accompanied the king during his seven months stay in Isfahan. However when the king finally departs the city for battle to take the city of Hamadan, Fakhreddin gets permission to stay behind with the new governor of Isfahan, Amid Abolfathe Mozafar Neishabouri.

"The king alighted in the mountain, The mountain became green and fresh like a garden.	فرود آمد شهنشه در کهستان کهستان گشت خرم چون گلستان
The day that followed, he departed the mountain, Travelling non-stop, he alighted to land in Tehran Behind in Isfahan, I stayed, to do the things that I had to do,	روان گشت از کهستان روز دیگر بکوهستان تهران رفت یکسر مرا اندر صفاهان بود کاری در آن کارم همی شد روزگاری
Long time there, passed me, to finish what I was there to do This was the reason why I stayed behind in Isfahan.	بماندم زین سبب اندر صفاهان نرفتم در رکاب شاه شاهان

Following a series of meetings between Fakhreddin As'ad Gorgani and Abulfath Mozafar the governor of Isfahan, one day the governor mentioned the ancient story of Vis & Ramin, and suggested to Gorgani that it would be good if he attempted to versify the story. The poet undertook the commission and within six months the versification of the story was completed and he presented it to the governor at the Mehregan festival. It appears that the poem must have finished before the death of Toghrol as no mention is made in it about any other kings that succeeded Toghrol. The book ends with these verses in which points to the fact that the poet in fact had died at a young age:

O' master of words, once you have read this book, Ask God Almighty to forgive my sins,	چون این نامه بخوانی ای سخن دان گناه من بخواه از پاک یزدان
Pray and say, bless this youn man's soul, That has versified this beautiful story.	بگوی رب بیامرز این جوان را که گفتست این نگارین داستان را

As it was briefly mentioned the story of Vis & Ramin is one of the ancient Persian stories. The author of the book, 'Mojmal-al Tavarikh (A Compendium of Stories & Historical Events), states that the story originates from the period of the Sassanid emperor, Shahpoor the 1st. The story is known to have been in existence during the reign of Shahpoor, However there are other researches that indicate the story is much older and has originated from the Arasid (Parthian) period. The story was popular amongst Iranians even before Fakhreddin As'ad attempted to versify it. The oldest mention of it has been noted in the poetries of Abunava's a famous Iranian poet from the time of Haroon-al-Rashid the Abasid caliph. The story was never translated from Pahlavi into Arabic after the Arab invasion, but those Persians who were familiar with Pahlavi knew about it and used to read it in different parts of Iran. The versified text which was done by Fakhreddin Gorgani greatly helped the story to survive through centuries to reach our time. Here is a piece from the versified version of Vis & Ramin by Fakhreddin As'ad Gorgani:

"The World has us ambushed by day and night! The same way that a panther has a deer ambushed	جهان بر ما کمین دارد شب و روز تو پنداری که ما آهو و اویوز
The pasture, constantly we gallop, Not ever knowing what came to the one that parted us.	همی گردیم تازان در چراگاه ز حال آنکه از ما شد نه آگاه
Constantly we boast of knowledge! Even a goat, Would know better did he possess such knowledge!	همی گوییم دانایيم و گربز بود دانا چنین حیران و عاجز
Not we know where we have come from, Not we know where we are going to!	ندانیم از کجا بود آمدنمان ویا زیدرکجا باشد شد نمان
Two peaceful worlds there exist! One is the mortal world, the other immortal.	دو آرامست ما را دو جهانی یکی فانی و دیگر جاودانی
Our hopes we have put into the mortal one, The other, we hardly ponder about!	بدین آرام فانی بسته امید نیندیشیم از آن آرام جاوید

Through this door, we see that we shall surely pass,
But, our eyes we do not believe,

همی بینیم کاین در بر گذاریم
ولیکن دیده را باور نداریم

How ignorant and dishevelled we are
Not to believe in or desire immortality over Mortality,

چه نادانیم و چه آشفته راییم
که از فانی به باقی نه گراییم

In a house that we are but a single time,
Infinite provisions we are seeking to make.

سرابی را که در وی یک زمانیم
در وجویای ساز جاودانیم

The world is a prison and its prisoner's content we are,
Yet we do not seek companionship of God!

جهان بندست و دربند خرسند
نجوییم آشنایی با خداوند

The God that gave us the two worlds
,Mortal, and the immortal He gave us,

خداوندی که ما را دو جهان داد
یکی فانی ودیگر جاودان داد

Blessed is the one, who chooses him for a friend,
And by obeying him he wins himself value and valour.

خنک آن کس که او را یار گیرد
ز فرمان بردنی مقدار گیرد

Blessed is the one, who comes to good end,
Blessed is the one, who
leaves of himself goodname

خنک آن کش بود فرجام نیکو
خنک آن کش بود هم نام نیکو

If we search news of those who departed,,
Others will search for the news of us tomorrow.

چو ما از رفتگان گیریم اخبار
ز ما فردا خبر گیرند ناچار

We that were news searchers will ourselves become'news
We that were story tellers will ourselves become stories.

خبر گردیم و ما بوده خبر جوی

سمرگردیم وخود بوده سمرگوی

Hakim Omar Khayam Neishabouri,9th century scientist and poet

Hakim Omar Khayam Neishabouri was one of the most remarkable men in the entire scientific and literary sphere of 9th century Persia. His special talents were applied to mathematics, astronomy, philosophy and least of all to poetry. Writing poetry was not his main occupation, rather something to relax him because of his preoccupation with more arduous scientific research in mathematics, astronomy, and philosophy and relating problem solving exercises. He was both fascinated and deeply perplexed by the secrets of Universe and Creation:

This circle inside which we arrive and we depart,
Hast no beginning nor ending,

No one has a clue as to its secrets,
Nor anyone knows where one comes from or goes to.

در دایره ای که آمد و رفتن ماست
او را نه بدایت نه نهایت پیداست

کس می نزند دمی در این معنی راز
کین آمدن از کجاورفتن به کجاست

His title (Takhalos) or poetical name (Khayam) signifies a Tentmaker, and he is said to have at one time exercised that trade, perhaps before Nezamolmolk's generosity raised him to independence. Many Persian poets similarly derive their names from their occupations, thus we have, Attar, a perfume maker, Assar, an oil presser etc. Omar himself alludes to his name in the following whimsical lines:

"Khayam, who stitched the tents of science,
Has fallen in grief's furnace and been suddenly burned,

The shears of fate have cut the tent ropes of his life.
And the broker of Hope has sold him for nothing!"

Chapter 5

The story behind Khayam's acquaintance with Nezamolmolk is a fascinating one: At a young age Khayam gets to be sent to a private school to benefit from the teachings of one of the greatest wise men of Khorasan, Imam Mowaffak of Neishabour. A man highly honored and revered by all scholars of the time. It was commonly believed that the pupils, who attend the teachings and guidance of this master, usually attain high positions in their communities later in life. At this school, Khayam came to know another pupil who grew up to become the first minister to Malekshah Saljugh, the ruling monarch. Years later this very powerful and highly influential minister Khaje Nezamolmolk met with Khayam again, received him warmly, rendered him support, provided him with a generous annual pension of 1200 misghals of gold, built him an observatory in Neishabour and introduced him to Sultan Malekshah Suljugh. Sultan was so highly impressed by Khayam, assigned him to a team comprised of 8 other scientists with the task of calculating a new calendar which was later named after the monarch, and is known as Jalali calendar (تقویم جلالی)

Khayam thus lived in Neishabour the rest of his life busied himself with more scientific research especially in astronomy and mathematics, wherein he attained to a very high preeminence. Under the Sultanate of Malekshah he would get invited to the city of Marve for audience with the king, who always greatly praised him for his proficiency in science and showered him with favors. The calendar reform which won great recognition for Khayam, resulted in "Jalali era"- a computation of time which surpasses the Julian, and approaches the accuracy of the Gregorian style. Khayam is also the author of some astronomical tables, entitled "Ziji-Malekshahi", which was first published in Europe by the French, and an Arabic Treaties of his on Algebra.

Though the sultan "shower's Favors upon him," Omar's Epicurean audacity of Thought and Speech caused him to be regarded askance in his own time and country. He is to have been especially hated and dreaded by the Sufis, whose practice he ridiculed, and whose Faith amounted to little more than his own, when striped of the mysticism and formal recognition of Islamism under which Omar would not hide. Their poets, including Hafez, who are (with exception of Ferdowsi) the most considerable in Persia borrowed largely indeed, of Omar's material, but turning it to a mystical use more convenient to themselves and the people they addressed; a People quite as quick of doubt as of belief, as keen of Bodily sense as of Intellectual, and delighting in a cloudy composition of both in which they could float luxuriously between

Rebirth of Persian Culture

Heaven and Earth, this world and the next on the wings of poetical expression, that might serve indifferently for either. Khayam was too honest of Heart as well of Head for this. Having failed (however mistakenly) of finding any Providence but Destiny, and any world but this, he set about making the most of it preferring rather to sooth the Soul through Senses into acquiescence with things as he saw them, than to perplex it with vain disquietude after what they might be. It has been seen, however, that his worldly ambition was not exorbitant; and he very likely takes a humorous or perverse pleasure in exalting the gratification of sense above that of intellect, in which he must have taken great delight although it failed to answer the questions in which he, in common with all men, was most vitally interested.

For whatever reason, however, Khayam as before said, was never popular in his own country up to the last one hundred years or so, and certainly not before the coming of the new Age of Enlightenment in Iran which only begun to take shape during the early years of the nineteenth century.

The Europeans got acquainted with the poetry of Omar Khayam mainly by the way of a poetic translation of a number of his quatrains rendered and published by English poet, Gerald Fitzgerald. Other translations by a number of translators followed soon, but the English version by Fitzgerald still remains as the most popular. It was not long before Omar Khayam became a best seller throughout the world. It is said that one day a man walked in to a book shop in London, asked the bookseller what book sells the most in England. The bookseller replied, Holy Bible. The customer then asked what book sells more next to Holy Bible. The bookseller replied, Rubbaiyat of Omar Khayam.

Although Fitzgerald as said before, played a major role in popularizing the poetry and philosophy of Omar Khayam in Europe, one could confidently say that the timing was also right for the introduction of Khayam and his poetry to European Community. Europe as a whole was just beginning to emerge from centuries of theocratic rule and domination by the Catholic Church. Free societies were taking shape, and liberal values were being advocated and adhered to everywhere. The Renaissance was in full swing promoting new concepts, ideas and thoughts in art, science, education and literature. The Europeans now after centuries of censorship were able to talk, read and write freely and be acquainted with new input from writers, poets, thinkers, philosophers and scientists. It was during this new period that Khayam's poetry was introduced and although received condemnation by the Catholic Church, but received overwhelming acceptance from people in general. Omar Khayam through the translation of his poetry by Fitzgerald opened a new gateway to the literary treasures of the Orient for Europeans who, up to that time, had no access to them. Here is a selection from Omar Khayams's poetry as translated by Fitzgerald:

As far as possible taunt not the drinkers, Build not upon the foundation of hypocrisy and idle tales, Pride not yourself in your not drinking, You do a hundred things that are as low as a slave next to that.	گر می نخوری طعنه مزن مستان را بنیاد مکن تو حیله و دستان را تو غره بدان مشو که می مینخوری صد لقمه خوری که می غلامست آنرا
Come, my love, and for the sake of my heart, Resolve my problem with your beautiful presence,	برخیز و بیا بتا برای دل ما حل کن به جمال خویشتن مشگل ما
Bring us a jug of wine, let's drink it together, Before so many jugs are fashioned out of our clay	یک کوزه شراب تا بهم نوش کنیم زان پیش که کوزه ها کنند از گل ما
To day you have no hold on tomorrow, And the thought of tomorrow is naught but sadness,	امروز ترا دسترس فردا نیست و اندیشه فردات بجز سودا نیست
Waste not this breath if your heart be no mad, For you know not the price of the rest of your life,	ضایع مکن این دم ار دلت شیدا نیست کاین باقی عمر را بها پیدا نیست
And we, that now make merry in the room, They left, and summer dresses in new bloom,	ابر آمد و باز برسر سبزه گریست بی باده ارغوان نمیباید زیست

Rebirth of Persian Culture

We must be beneath the Couch of Earth,
Descend, ourselves to make a Couch for whom?

این سبزه که امروز تماشاگه ماست
تا سبزه ما تماشاگه کیست

To the face of the rose the New Year's breeze is pleasant,
On the background of the meadow a beautiful face is pleasant,

بر چهره گل نسیم نوروز خوشست
در صحن چمن روی دل افروز خوشست

Of bygone yesterday nothing you may say is pleasant,
Be merry speak not of yesterday, today is pleasant!

از دی که گذشت هرچه گویی خوش نیست
خوش باش و زدی و زدی مگو که امروز خوشست

Whether at Naishapur or Babylon,
Whether the Cup with sweet or bitter run,

چون عمربسر رسد چه شیرین وچه تلخ
پیمانه که پر شود چه بغداد وچه بلخ

The Wine of Life keeps oozing drop by drop,
The Leaves of Life keep falling one by one.

می نوش که بعداز من وتو ماه بسی
از سلخ بغره آید از غره به سلخ

And this delightful grass whose tender green,
Fledges the river's lip on which we lean.

هر سبزه که بر کنار جویی رسته است
گویی ز لب فرشته خویی رسته است

Ah, lean upon it lightly for who knows,
From what once lovely lip it springs unseen.

پا برسر سبزه تا بخواری ننهی
کان سبزه زخاک لاله رویی رسته است

The revelations of the devout and the learned,
Who rose before us, and as prophet turnd!

آنانکه محیط فضل وآداب شدند
در جمع کمال شمع اصحاب شدند

Are all but stories, which awoke from Sleep!

ره زین شب تاریک نبردند برون
گفتند فسانه ای ودر خواب شدند.

Chapter 5

They told their comrades and to sleep they returned.

Those who became obsolete and those who are new, Each one of them has walked a pace his own way, This worldly possession remains not with one for ever, Others came and left and the new ones shall come and shall leave.	آنها که کهن شدند واینها که نواند هرکس بمراد خویش تک تک بدوند این کهنه جهان بکس نماند باقی رفتند ورویم ودیگرآیند و روند
Alas, that spring should vanish with the Rose, That Youth's sweet- scented Manuscript should close,	افسوس که نامه جوانی طی شد وان تازه بهار زندگانی دی شد
That Nightingale that in tree branches sang, Ah, whence, and whither flown again, who knows?	آن مرغ طرب که نام اوبود شباب افسوس ندانم که کی آمد کی شد
One moment in annihilation, One moment, out of the well of Life to taste,	این قافله عمر عجب میگذرد دریاب د می که با طرب میگذرد
The Stars are setting and the Caravan, Starts for the Down of Nothing-Oh, make haste!	ساقی غم فردای حریفان چه خوری پیش آر پیاله را که شب میگذرد

.
Omar khayam is truly a legendary thinker and a great innovator who's original, and controversial philosophical ideas have fascinated people all around the world starting with his appearance on the literary and scientific scene of the tenth century Iran as well as the entire Middle-East and centuries later in Europe during the Movement of Renaissance.

Khayam, besides his poetry, is well known as a Mathematician and Astronomer first and foremost in his homeland for his influential Treatise on

Rebirth of Persian Culture

Demonstration of Problems of Algebra (1070), which laid down the principles of algebra, part of the body of the Persian Mathematics. that was eventually transmitted to Europe. In particular he derived general methods for solving cubic equations and even some higher orders.

In "The Treaties" he wrote on the triangular array of binomial coefficients known as Pascal's Triangles. His other major paper was on the subject of the' Explanations of the Difficulties of the Postulates of Euclid. An important part of the book deals with the Euclid's famous Parallel Postulate, and his criticism that eventually made its way to Europe may have contributed to the eventual development of non- Euclidean geometry.

Omar Khayam created important works on geometry, specifically on the theory of proportions. In this paper Khayam talks about his intention to eventually giving full solution to the cubical equations:" If the opportunity arises, and I can succeed, I shall give all these fourteen forms with all their branches and cases and how to distinguish whatever is possible and whatever is impossible so that a paper containing elements which are greatly useful in this art will be prepared.

As a mathematician Khayam has made fundamental contribution to the philosophy of mathematics especially in the context of Persian mathematics and Persian philosophy in which other Persian philosophers and mathematicians such as Avicenna and Abureyhan Byrooni and Tussi are associated.
There are at least three basic mathematical concepts of strong philosophical dimensions that are associated with Khayam:
Mathematical Order: From where does this order issue? And why does it correspond to the world of nature? His answer is in one of his philosophical" Treaties on being". Khayam's answer is that" The Divine origin of all existence not only emanates "wojud" being by virtue of which all things gain realty. But it is the source of order which is inseparable from the very act of existence.

The significance of axioms in geometry and the necessity for the mathematician to rely upon philosophy and hence the importance of the relation of any particular science to prime philosophy. This is the philosophical background to khayam's total rejection of any attempt to "prove" the parallel postulate, and hence his refusal to bring motion in to the attempt to prove this postulate, because Khayam associated motion with the world of matter, and wanted to keep it away from the world of purely intelligible and immaterial world of geometry.

Clear distinction made by Khayam, on the basis of the work by earlier Persian philosophers such as Avecina, between natural bodies and mathematical bodies. The first is defined as a body that is in the category of substance and that it stands by itself. And hence a subject of natural sciences, while the second, called "Volume", is of the category of accidents "attributes" that do not subsist by themselves in the external world and hence is the concern of mathematics. Khayam was very careful to respect the boundaries of each discipline.

Poetry:

It has been reported by some biographers that Khayam has written over 900 quatrains, but more accurate and recent research done by distinguished researchers have indicated that only 560 of those could actually be attributed to him. A most distinguished Iranian author and scholar, Mohammad ali Foroughi has certified that even that last number has been grossly exaggerated and that only 56 of the total number is truly written by Omar Khayam. As indicated before, Omar Khayam was first introduced to the western world through a poetic translation of the Rubaiyat of Omar Khayam presented by English poet Fitzgerald. Other translations do exist but the most famous is that of Fitzgerald. Since that time Rubaiyat (meaning quatrains) of Omar Khayam have been translated in to many other languages, making Khayam one of the most widely read poets of all times in almost every country in the world. Many of those translations have been made directly from Persian, and are more literal than those done by Fitzgerald:

A French orientalist named Franz Toussaint was so dissatisfied by the translation done by Fitzgerald and some other translations done into other languages using the translation by Fitzgerald, that he did his own translation of Rubaiyat directly from Persian, trying to express the spirit of verses rather than just to versify them. His translation was continuously published between the years of 1929 to 1969, and many translations were made into other languages from it.

Behold the robe of the rosebud has been torn by the Zephyr
The nightingale has been enchanted by the beauty of the rose,
Rest in the shade of the rosebush, for such rose,
Will year after year come alive, but we shall be buried

بنگر ز صبا دامن گل چاک شده
بلبل ز جمال گل طربناک شد

در سایه گل نشین که بسیار این گل
در خاک فروریزد و ما خاک شده

There was a door, to which I found no key,
There was a veil past which I might not see,

اسرار ازل را نه تودانی ونه من
وین حرف معما نه توخوانی ونه من

Some little talk awhile of me and Thee,
There seemed-and then no more of Thee and me.

هست از پس پرده گفتگوی من وتو
چون پرده برافتد نه تومانی ونه من

Get up and forget the cares of the ephemeral world,
Enjoy yourself and spend your brief moment with joy,

برخیز ومخور غم جهان گذران
بنشین ودمی به شادمانی گذران

For if the world was to be faithful to any would not have had your turn before others.

در طبع جهان اگر وفایی بودی
نوبت بتوخود نیامدی از دگران

O! Friend, come, let not worry about tomorrow,
Let make the most of the moments of life,

ای دوست بیا تا غم فردا نخوریم
وین یکدم عمر را غنیمت شمریم

When, tomorrow, we cross over to the Other Side!
We shall be same as those of seven thousand years back!

فردا که از این دیر کهن درگذریم
با هفت هزارساگان سربسریم

Chapter 5

Khaghani Shervani, 12th Century Poet

Afzaledin Badil (Ibrahim) known as khaghani, a title he was given at the behest of Manuchehr Shirvanshah during his service at the Royal court of the king, was born in the year 1142 in the city of Shervan, a suburb of the province of Azerbaijan. Khaghani died in the city of Tabriz, at the relatively young age of 68, grief stricken by the death of his daughter and his young wife, in the year 1210.

Khaghani is one of the most outstanding Iranian poets mostly known for his beautiful, sophisticated, and profound elegies. Elegy is a type of poetry which can comprise of between 20 to up to 70 or 80 or more couplets or verses narrating a particular topic, such as a historical or social event, in memorial, celebrating a birthday, coronation, death of an important personality like the heads of states, a loved one, or victory in a battle etc. Some of Khaganies elegies like the famous "Eivane Madaen", (The Portals of Madaen), are true masterpieces of Persian poetry. The complete collection of Khaghani's poetical works covers a wide range of Persian poetry including elegies in which he was a true master of, quatrains, lyrics, and couplets, each and every one arranged beautifully in eloquent fashion and style. It is sad that his great works have not been extensively read and enjoyed by Iranians, and are not known in the western world with the exception of France, due to unavailability of translation in other languages.

Khaghani, was born in to a family of artisans, his father was a carpenter, and his mother a descendant of Christians (originaly from ancient Roman Empire) who had immigrated to Iran decades before, and converted to Islam. Khaghani lost his father at an early age, and was brought up and educated by his uncle, Kafi-ed-Din Shervani, who taught him literary sciences, poetry, history, philosophy, Methaphisics, Medicine, and Astronomy. He was admitted to the court of Shervanshah in the city of Ganja, where he became a disciple of Abolala' Ganjavi, a prominent poet and scholar, to whose teachings Khaghani owes flourishment of his poetical talents. This great man introduced Khaghani to the Monarch who conferred upon him the title of "Khaghani" by which he became known afterwards. He also gave Khaghani his daughter in marriage, a mark of favor which caused some annoyance to another of his pupils, the young poet; Falaki of Shirvan. Shortly after this, however, Abul-Ala, being annoyed, apparently, at certain signs of growing arrogance on Khaghani's part, addressed to him the following insulting verses:

"My dear khaghani, skilful though you are
In verse, one little hints I give you free:

Mock not with satire any older poet;
Perhaps it is your sire, though you don't know it".

Khaghani, furious, demanded an apology and explanations, whereupon Abu-Ala renewed his attack in the following lines:

O Afthalud-Din, if the truth I should tell thee,
By thy soul, with thy conduct I am terribly pained;

They call you in Shirvan 'the son of a joiner;
The name of Khaghani through me has thou gained
,
Much good have I wrought thee, I trained thee and taught thee,
Enriched thee, and gave thee my daughter to wife
;
Why wilt thou neglect me, and fail to respect me,
Who called thee my Master, my son, and my Life?

How often this slander wilt lay to my credit?
Black slander, of which I no memory keep?

What matter if I or another one said it?
What matter if thou wert awake or sleep?

To this Khaghani replied with a satire of inconceivable coarseness. Not content with accusing his former friend and master of the vilest crimes, Khaghani does not hesitate to bring against him incomparably more dangerous than any suspicion of moral delinquency, declaring roundly that he is a follower of Hassan Sabah and a confederate of the Assassins of Alamut. Khaghani, after this incident, left his native town and joined the court of the then reigning monarch, Shirvanshah Akhtisan Manouchehr, who had transferred his capital to Baku. At the court, however, things did not go too well for Khaghani, for Shirvanshah appears to have been exacting, suspicious, and hard to please. Khagani later on even came under suspicion of having been disrespectful to the monarch and ordered to be hung, but his life was spared subsequently by the monarch as a result of him apologizing. In all Khaghani served as a court poet in the Royal courts of Shervanshah, and his son and heir to the throne, king Akhtisan for almost forty years.

Khaghani left Ganja around the year 1172 on a pilgrimage to visit and enjoy the audience of the prominent poets, laureates and scholars of Khorasan, in particular, the various Rulers of that vast province. Khorasan was in fact the cradle of Persian poetry after the invasion of Arabs, at the advent of Persian Renaissance Movement. When he arrived in the province of Rey, he became very ill, and was not able to continue with his trip. Regretfully, he had to return to Shirvan. Somtimes later after he recovered from his illness, this verse by him describes his intent to leave his trip unfinished and return home to Shirvan:

Since I have no permission to proceed to Khorasan I will even turn back; I will not endure the affliction of Rey	چون نیست رخصه سوی خراسان شدن مرا هم بازپس شوم نکشم من بلای ری
If leave be granted me to go back to Tabriz, I will give thanks for the favor of the king of Rey.	گر بازپس رفتنم سوی تبریز اجازت است شکرانه گویم از کرم پادشاه ری

After his return to Tabriz, around the year 1172 to 1174, Khaghani embarked on a new adventure: A second pilgrimage to Mecca, around the year 1173-1174. On this trip, he started writing his other master piece, the mathnavi of "Tohfat al Araghain",(Gift from the two Araghs) one being Arak province in Iran, and the second referring to what is known to day as Iraq, (Messapotemia), the land bordered by Tigris and Euphrates rivers. This poem is divided in to five discourses, of which the first consists mainly of doxologies, the second is for the most part autobiographical, the third describes Hamadan, Iraq, and Baghdad, the fourth Mecca, and the fifth, and last, Al- Madina. Here is one verse from one of Khaghani's finest elegies that describes the journey:

Here are the confines of the desert: advance upon it:
And draw from its fragrant breeze healing for the spirit!

سرحدات بادیه است روان باش برسرش
تریاک روح کن ز ی سموم معتبرش

On the way back from this trip, he was received by some of the most important rulers of the time including Sultan Mohamad-ebn-Saljoughi, Jamal-eldin-Mohamad Isfahani, and Abasi caliph, Almoghtaza-be-Amrelah, who even offered him the position of the Secretary to Caliph should he decide to stay in Baghdad, the job that he refused. During this trip he also composed a number of beautiful elegies, the most popular of which amongst Iranians is the "Eivane Madaen" (The Portals at Madain)., when he visited the ancient ruins of the capital of Sassanian Empire, and overcame with a deep grief over what had happened to the glorious metropolis that once was the envy of the entire world.

O'Heart that heeds warnings, open your eyes and,
Consider the "Portals at Maddain" a lesson to be learned,

ای دل عبرت بین از دیده نظرکن هان
ایوان مداین را آیینه عبرت دان

From the banks of Tigris, walk the path to Madain,
Let the stream of your tears wet the soof Madain,
The Tigris sheds tears, tears not! Stream laden with blood,
Bitter tears that fall from lashes warm as drops of fire…..

یک ره ز لب دجله منزل به مداین کن وز دیده دوم دجله بر خاک مداین ران

خود دجله چنان گرید صد دجله خون گویی کزگرمی خونابش آتش چکداز مژگان....

Khaghani had also the opportunity to visit Isfahan, where an unpleasant situation similar to what had happened to Anvari in Balkh, occurred. He was first well received, but a satirical on the people of Isfahan composed by his student Mojir-ed-Din of Baylaqan, somewhat damaged his popularity causing the anger of the great Isfahani poet Jamal-ed-Din Abdulrazzagh Isfahani to come out with a most abusive reply. In order to free himself from his student's indiscretion and restore the Isfahanis to good humor, Khaghani composed a

Chapter 5

long and celebrated quasida in praise of that city and its inhabitants, in the course of which he says, after describing the tributes of praise which he had already paid it:-

"All this I did without hope of recompense, not for good,
Not hoping to receive crow or gold from the bounty of Isfahan.

That stone-smitten (rajim), devil who stole my eloquence
Rebelled against me if he dared to satirize Isfahan.

He will not rise with a white face in the resseruction,
because he strove to blacken the neck of Isfahan!

Why the people of Isfahan speak ill of me?
What fault have I committed in respect to people of Isfahan?"

When Khaghani retuned home to Shirvan, whether on account of his greatly increased self- esteem (a quality in which he was at no time deficient), or he was accused by his detractors of seeking another patron, incurred the displeasure of Akhtisan Shirvanshah, and was imprisoned by him in the fortress of Shabiran, where he wrote his celebrated "Habsiyeh" or prison poem. As to the length of the imprisonment and his subsequent adventures, until his return to Tabriz, we have scanty information. The "Habsiyeh" contains some of his most powerful and eloquent language. On his release from the prison, the relationship with Akhtisan improved and he was able to obtain permission to retire to Tabriz. It was in Tabriz that after a relatively short time, real tragedy struck: first, his young son Rashid-ed-Din died, and before long his daughter passed away, followed finally by the death of his beloved wife. These tragedies completely devastated him, causing him to write some sorrowful elegies in lamentation for the unexpected death of his wife and children. Deeply overcome by grief, as mentioned before, he died at an early age of 68, and was buried in the cemetery called "Maghbara-tal-Shoara", cemetery of poets, in the city of Tabriz, the province of Azerbaijan.

Khaghani was a close friend of the other Persian great, the famous poet and philosopher, Nezami Ganjavi, who praying to die before Khaghani wrote this memorable poem:

Rebirth of Persian Culture

I prayed that Khaghani be the one to lament my death,
Alas that, it is I to have to lament the death of Khaghani.

همی گفتم که خاقانی
دریغاگوی من باشد
دریغامن شدم آخر
دریغاگوی خاقانی

The complete works, diva'n, written by Khaghani, is very extensive and forms a valuable treasure of Persian poetry. It comprises of :400 odes (غزل), 200 elegies (قصیده), 340 quatrains, (رباعی), a number of strophe-poem (ترجیع بند)" totaling 900 verses, and composite-ties " (ترکیب بند)" totaling 400 verses. There are also a total of over 2000 verses of miscellaneous poetry.

Khaghani's poems include chapters containing his opposition to social injustice, oppression, and promoting reason, intellectual and moral values. Few of the last elegies he wrote while in Tabriz and before dying contain sad and sorrowful lamentations on the death of his son, daughter, and wife.

Jan Rypka praises Khaghani for his intellect, a poet with a great heart, who fled from the outer world to the inner one. A personality who did not conform to type, and a Master of language, all this places him in the front ranks of Persian literature.

Quatrains by Khaghani:

The bird that sings the song of pain is Love,
The messenger who knows the words of unseen is Love,

مرغی که نوای درد راند عشق است
پیکی که زبان غیب داند عشق است

The Existence that calls you to non Existence is love,
That which redeems you from self is Love.

هستی که به نیستیت خواند عشق است
وانچ ازکه ترا باز ستاند عشق است

Do you know what I gained in this world? Nothing,
And what was my gain from the days of my Life? Nothing,

دانی ز جهان چه طرف
بربستم هیچ
وز حاصل ایام چه در دستم هیچ

شمع خرد ام ولی چو بنشستم هیچ

Chapter 5

I am the Candle of wisdom, but once extinct, nothing,
  I am the Cup of Jamshid, but once broken, Nothing.

آن جام جم ام ولی
چو بشکستم هیچ

Hakim Nezami Ganjavi, 11ᵗʰ century poet & gnostic

Hakim Jallal- ed-Din Mohammad Elias –ebn-Yousuf known as Nezami, a true star in the domain of eleventh century Persian poetry, was born in the city of Ganji, presently located in the Republic of Azerbaijan. Some historians have mentioned town of Ghom 150 kilometer south of Teheran, as being his birthplace. Some of his poetry in fact bears evidence as to the truth of this report. The poet however grew up in Ganji and spent his entire life there. He only made a short trip, at the invitation of Ghazal Arsalan, to a nearby city where he was received with full honors. Because Nezami was not a court poet he does not appear in the annals of the dynasties, which list the details of the life of poets and writers. He had a far higher conception of the poet's aims and duty than the countless panegyrists and court-poets of whom Anvari and some others are the type, and that, as tradition and internal evidence both show, he despised panegyric and stayed away from the Royal Courts, though he so far adhered to the prevailing fashion of his time as to dedicate his poems to contemporary rulers.

Consequently the details of his life are not very well known. His father, Yousuf, died when the poet was very young. His mother was of a noble Kurdish family, and did not survive long after the death of her husband. An uncle is believed to have taken care of the poet after the death of his father and mother. Nezami's brother also achieved considerable reputation as a poet. A copy of a book containing his qasidas (elegies) still exists in the British Museum.

Nezami seems to have been married three times, and had a son who was 14 when Nezami started writing the tragedy of "Leili & Majnoon ". His first wife, A'fa'gh was a slave girl gifted to him by Fakhr- ed-Din Bahramshah, the ruler of Darband. This woman, who bore him his first son, was the love of his life. Her death, which happened at the completion of his first masterpiece,

Rebirth of Persian Culture

Khosrow & Shirin, and later on the death of his son were the two greatest tragedies in Nezami's life. His two other wives also died before him.

Nezami Ganjavi is one of five pillars of Persian literature in all times, others being Ferdowsi, Mowlavi, Saadi, and Hafez. Like Saadi, and Hafez he ranks the highest in writing odes, and lyrical poems. Nezami brought a colloquial and realistic style to Persian epic poetry and he is an acknowledged master of romantic mathnavi. In this regard only Ferdowsi and Mowlavi are considered to be of equal stature. Nezami is well liked and widely read not only in his own country, Iran, but also throughout the former Soviet Republics such as Tajikistan, Afghanistan, Kurdistan, and Azerbaijan.

Nezami also ranks one of the highest in literary sciences, Arabic language and literature, physical and metaphysical sciences, and philosophy. At times during his life time he also taught these subjects. Nezami was considered a leader and pontiff in Gnosticism, and although, a devout Moslem, he never hesitated to make his views known wherever differed with the basic Islamic laws.

Nezami was a man of pure character with high moral principles. His language was clean and completely void of profanities. He was genuinely pious, yet singularly devoid of fanaticism and intolerance; self respecting and independent, yet gentle and unostentatious; a loving father and husband; and according to his explicit declaration in Sikandar-name, a rigorous abstainer from wine. In a word he may justly be described as combining lofty genius and blameless character in a degree unequalled by any other Persian poet whose life has been the subject of careful and critical study. Amongst his contemporary poets and writers, Nezami communicated and maintained friendly and cordial relationship with Khaghani. His love and affection for him was to such a degree, that he would wish for himself to die before Khaghani.

A particular verse in one of his poetries clearly reflect :

I prayed that Khaghani be the one to lament my death,	همی گفتم که خاقانی دریغا گوی من باشد دریغا من شدم آخر دریغا
Alas, that I had to be the one to have to lament Khaghani's.	گوی خاقانی

Chapter 5

Nezami died in the city of Ganje in the year 1221 at the relatively young age of 68. His tomb, which over time, had turned into ruins was rebuilt by the local government of the Republic of Azerbaijan and is visited by thousands of poetry lovers from countries far and near.

Nezami is reported by Doulatshah Samarghandi to have written, besides his Khamseh (Quintet) known as "The five Treasures", a collection of miscellaneous poetry comprising of 20,000 verses, but a great number of these have been lost and not reached our hands. "The Five Treasures": the Makhzan-al- Asrar (Treasury of Mysteries) written about C.E. 1183, second, the romantic mathnavi of Khosrow & Shirin in C.E. 1193, third, the romantic mathnavi of Leili & Majnoon in C.E. 1206, fourth, the romantic mathnavi of Alexander of Maccedonia, C.E. 1209, fifth and the last, the mathnavi of Haft Paykar, or "Seven Effigies", in 1217. Nezami adhered to the prevailing fashion of his time as to dedicate his poems to contemporary rulers. Thus the Makhzan-al-Asrar is dedicated to Ildigiz, the ruler of Azerbaijan,; Khusrow & Shirin to his two sons and successors, Muhhamad and Qezzel Arsalan, as well as to the last Seljuq ruler in Iran, Toqrol Beyk Arsalan, Leili & Majnoon, to Akhtisan Manuchehr, King of Shirvan, the Eskandar Nameh, to Azzod-ed-Din Masood, the Ruler of Mosoul.

The first mathnavi, from the "Five Treasures"; Makhzanol Asrar (Treasury of Mystries) is comprised of 2260 verses. this mathnavi which was the first of the five to have been written by Nezami was completed when he was forty years old. The book which is in twenty chapters comprises mainly of esoteric subjects such as philosophy, wisdom, sermons in theology, moral, religious, and ethical topics, social principles of justice, equity, and humanity. Nezami faithfully attempts to guide his fellow men in to the path of Divinity, purity, life of chastity, and spiritual resurrection, pulling them away from acts of evil and misconduct.

The second mathnavi, "khosrow & Shirin", a romance in 6500 verses narrates the love story of Sassani Emperor, Khosrow Parviz, and Shirin the princess of Armenia. The poem has its origin in the stories of the time of Sassanid dynasty, one millennium or so before the time of Nezami. The story was handed down from generation to generation, undergoing changes until it reached Nezami in its present form. Here is a passage from that story describing the tragic death of Farhad, the third player in the ring of the star crossed lovers' misfortune which brought about the tragic death of all three of them.

When Farhad heard this message, with a groan From rock-galley he fell like a stone.	چو افتاد این سخن درگوش فرهاد ز طاق کوه چون کوهی در افتاد
So deep a sigh he heaved that thou wouldst say A spear had cleft unto his heart its way.	به زاری گفت کآوخ رنج بردم ندیده راحتی در رنج مردم
'Alas, my labor! 'That this bitter cry- 'My gardon still not won, in grief I die!	اگر صد گوسفند آید سراپیش برد گرگ از گله قربان درویش
Alas the wasted labor of my youth! Alas the hope which vain hath proved in truth!	چه خوش گفت آن گلابی با گلستان که هرچت باز باید داد مستان
I tunneled mountain- walls: behold my prize! My labor's wasted: here the hardship lies!	فرورفته به خاک آن سرو چالاک چرا برسر نریزم هر زمان خاک
I, like a fool, red rubies coveted; Lo, worthless pebbles fill my hands instead!	زگلبن ریخته گلبرگ خندان چرا برمن نگردد باغ زندان
What fire is this that thus doth me consume? What flood is this that hurls me to my doom?	پریده از چمن کبک بهاری چرا چون ابر نخروشم به زاری
	فرومرده چراغ عالم افروز چرا روزم نگردد شب بدین روز
The world is void of sun and moon for me: My garden lacks its box and willow-tree.	چراغم مرد بادم سرد از آنست مهم رفت آفتابم زرد از آنست
For the last time my beacon light hath shone; Not Shirine, but the sun from me is gone!	به شیرین در عدم خواهم رسیدن به یک تک تا عدم خواهم دویدن
	صلای درد شیرین در جهان داد زمین بریاد او بوسید وجان داد

Chapter 5

The cruel sphere pities no much-tried
weight;
On no poor luckless wretch doth grace
alight!
Alas for such a sun and such a moon,
Which black eclipse hath swallowed all
too soon!

Before the wolf may pass a hundred sheep,
But on the poor man's lamb 'tis sure to
leap.

O'er my sad heart the fowls and fishes
weep;
For my life's stream doth in to darkness
creep.

Why am I parted from my mistress dear?
Now Shirin is gone why I tarry here?

Without her face should I desire to thrive?
'T would serve me right if I were boned
alive! ....

Felled to the dust, my cypress quick lies
dead:
Shall I remain to cast dust on my head?

My smiling face is fallen from the tree:
The garden is a prison now to me.

My bird of spring is from the meadow
flown,
I, like the thunder- cloud, will weep and
groan.

My world; my kindling lamp is quenched
for eye:
Shall not my day turn in to night to-day?

My lamp is out and chilly strikes the gale:
My moon is darkened and my sun is pale.

Beyond death's portals Shirin shall I greet
So with one leap I hasten death to meet!

Thus to the world his mournful tale he
cried,
For Shirin kissed ground, and kissing died.

The third mathnavi,"Leili & Majnoon" was written by Nezami in the year 1206. It comprises of 4700 verses, and was completed in an amazingly short time of four months. Nezami wrote this at the special request of Shervanshah Akhistan.The monarch wrote to him the following lines:

"O 'Nezami, The magical writer: Now that you have completed the story of Khosrow & Shirin, I want you to accomplish another work of magic that is to write the love story of Majnoon. No one of Arabs or Persians has yet put this story in to poetry. I like to read this story as written by you. You well know that you will be properly compensated for your effort, the way that has been the tradition in our royal family."

The story had been one of Arab origin, and very popular amongst the Bedouins in the Arabian Peninsula. It is the tragic love story of two unfortunate lovers, whose family's feud eventually cost the lives of the young lovers. Here is an excerpt from the story, which describes the Garden of Eden where the two lovers who could never have each other in real life embrace each other in after-life, as seen by Zayd in a dream:

"Now when once more the Night's ambrosial dusk
Upon the skirts of day poured its musk,

In sleep an angle caused him to behold
The heavenly gardens' radiance untold,

Whose wide expanse shadowed by lofty trees,

Chapter 5

heavenly wine and commune mouth to ear,

Now from the goblet the ruby wine they sip;
Now interchange their kisses, lip to lip

Was cheerful as the heart fulfilled of ease.
Each flow' ret in itself a garden seemed;

Each rosy petal like a lantern gleamed.
Each glade reflects, like some sky- scanning eye,

A heavenly mansion from the azure sky,
Like brightest emeralds its grasses grow,

While its effulgence doth no limit know.
Goblet in hand each blossom of the dale

Drinks to the music of nightingale,
 Celestial harps melodious songs upraise,

While cooing ring- doves utter hymns of praise.
Beneath the roses that like sunset gleam,

A coach was set beside a rippling stream.
With fair brocades and fine this coach was spread,

Lustrous and bright as heaven's azure bed.
Thereon were seated, now at last at rest,

The immortal angles of these lovers blessed,
 From head to foot adorned with robes of light

Like hours in heavens mansion's bright,
Amidst eternal spring their souls they cheer

With Now hidden mysteries of love unfold;
And now in close embrace each other hold.

Rebirth of Persian Culture

The next mathnavi is called Bahram nameh, or Haft Peykar (seven effigies), written by Nezami, in the year (C.E) 1217 and contains 5136 verses. This is the story of Bahram Goor, The Sassanid king, going back to the previous millennium, during the rule of the Sassanid Emperors in Iran. In this story, Nezami tells the life story of Bahram from childhood through adolescence up to his coronation and early years of his life as a king. He then tells the story of the seven girls from seven parts of the world, for whom, Bahram orders his architect to build a dome each with a different color. He then goes in search of the seven girls whose pictures he had discovered in a sealed room long time ago and had fallen in love with them. He finds the girls and brings them to his palace and resides each under each of the seven domes. Bahram would then visit each girl one day in a week spending time with them and listening to the stories that the girls would narrate for him. The seven stories that are narrated by the seven girls are constructed by Nezami in a beautiful and romantic fashion, and occupies almost three quarters of the whole book. Bahram preoccupied by spending his time with the seven princesses neglects the affairs of the country and allows his corrupt minister to cause harm and injustice to the people, as well as allowing the treasury to become bankrupt, thus weakening the country and the nation, encouraging the neighboring countries to take advantage of the chaos and start preparing to invade the country. Bahram takes action by firing the corrupt minister and executing him, taking charge of running the affairs of the nation and restoring order and prosperity to his kingdom. Bahram also orders the seven pleasure domes to be converted to Fire-Temples for worship. Having accomplished everything that he had to do, decides to take a break and goes on a hunting trip that he always loved. In the course of hunt, he gives chase to a wild ass following it in to a cave and mysteriously disappearing there never to come out alive.

The "Haft Peykar is considered by many as being Nezami's masterpiece, and one of the most important poetical creations of the whole oriental Indo-European literature. In this masterpiece Nezami illustrates the harmony of the Universe, the affinity of the sacred and profane and the concordance of the ancient and Islamic Iran.

Take not apart the good pearl from the string, from him who is ill-natured flee,	گوهر نیک را ز عقد مریز آنکه بد گوهر است از او بگریز

Chapter 5

An evil nature does act consistently, have you not heard that Nature does not err.

بد گهر با کسی وفا نکند
اصل بد در خطا خطا نکند

The evil-natured man does keep faith with none; the erring nature does not fail to err,

اصل بد با تو چون شود معطی
آن نخواندی که اصل لایخطی

The scorpion since it is bad by nature, to kill it, is good, to let it live is bad,

کژدم از راه آنکه بد گهر است
ماندنش عیب وکشتنش هنر است

Seek knowledge; since through knowledge you affect those doors be opened for you and not closed.

هنر آموز کز هنرمندی
درگشایی کنی نه دربندی

He, who shames not from learning, can draw forth pearls from water and rubies from rock,

هرکه ز آموختن ندارد ننگ
سر بر آرد ز آب وسنگ از لعل

Whilst he to whom no knowledge is assigned - that person, you will find, ashamed to learn.

وانکه دانش نباشدش روزی
ننگ دارد ز دانش اندوزی

How many, keen in mind, slack in effort, sell pottery from lack of pearls (to sell)!

ای بسا تیز طبع کاهل کوش
که شد از کاهلی سفال فروش

How many a dullard, through his being taught becomes the chief judge of, The Seven Climes!

ای بسا کور دل که از تعلیم
گشت قاضی القضات هفت اقلیم

The fifth poem, The Eskandar-nameh which is written in a style proper to epic verse is divided into two distinct parts, of which the first is properly entitled: Eqbal-nameh, or "Book of Alexander's Fortune", while the second one is correctly named the Sharafnameh, "The book of Alexander's Wisdom". The two books consist of close to 10,000 verses, of which two thirds belong to the first part and one third to the second part. The poem narrates the three stages

Rebirth of Persian Culture

in Alexander's life: the first part relates to Alexander' conquest of the world, forming his vast empire, then as a seeker of knowledge to the extent that he gains enough wisdom to acknowledge his own ignorance, and finally as a prophet travelling again around the world from east to west and from north to south to proclaim his own monotheistic creed to the world at large.

The Sharaf-nameh discusses the birth of Alexander to the time that he came to power, his wars against the Africans who came to invade Egypt, his invasion of Persian Empire, his marriage to the daughter of Darius, the king of Persia, conquest of India and China as well as many other foreign lands and concludes with his unsuccessful search for the fountain of immortal life.

The Eqbal-nameh contains a description of Alexander's personal growth into an ideal ruler on a model ultimately derived, through Islamic intermediaries from Plato's Republic. He has debates with Indian and Greek philosophers, and a major part of the book is devoted to the discourses he has had with seven Greek sages. The poet then tells of Alexander's end and the death of the seven sages.Nezami's image of Alexander is of an Iranian knight which as we know; is totally false.

The influence of Nezami on the subsequent development of Persian literature has been enormous and Khamsa "The five Treaures" became a pattern that was emulated in later Persian poetry and also in other Islamic literature. The legacy of Nezami's influence is widely felt in Islamic world and his poetry has influenced the development of Persian, Arabic, Turkish, and Urdu Poetry amongst many other languges. It is widely believed that his stories of Shirin & Farhad and Leili & Majnoon may have inspired even William Shakespeare, in the development of some of his plays.

In Persian miniature, the stories of Nezami alongside with those of Ferdowsie's Shahnameh have the most frequently illustrated literary works. Nezami is also greatly admired for his clarity and originality of style. He composed his poetry in Persian language and a great number of orientalists and world famous great scholars unanimously consider him a significant Persian poet, and hail him as the greatest exponent of epic romantic Persian poetry in Persian literature.
A poem by Nezami:

I went to the tavern last night, but I was not admitted,

Chapter 5

I was bellowing, yet no one was listening to me,

Either none of the wine-sellers were awake,
Or I was a nobody and no one openes the door for a Nobody.

When more or less half of the night had passed,
A shrewd perfect man (rend) raised his head from a booth and showed his face

I asked him to "open the door", he told me, go away, do not talk nonsense!
At this hour no body opens the door for any body,

This is not a mosque where its doors are open any moment,
Where you can come late and move quickly to the first row,

This is the Tavern of Magians and, rends (libertines) dwell here
There are Beauties, candles, wine, sugar, reed, flute and song

Whatever wonders that exists, is present here.
(In this tavern) there are Moslems, Jews, Zoroastrians, Nestorians, and Armenians

You must become a dust upon the feet of everyone in order to reach your (spiritual) goal.

O' Nezami, if you knock the ring at this door day and night
You won't find except smoke from this burning fire.

Farrokhi Sistani, 10th century Persian poet"

| The story of Alexander has aged and become legend | فسانه گشت و کهن شد حدیث اسکندر |
| Bring forth new stories, since the new has a different charm | سخن نو آر که نو راست حلاوتی دیگر |

Farrokhi Sistani is one of the most eloquent poets in the history of Persian literature, in particular in the art of writing elegies which is considered to be his specialty. The exact date of his birth is not known, but we know that he

was born sometime in one of the later years of the 10th century (C.E) in the province of Sistan. Little is known about the earlier years of his life. We only know that he worked mainly as a farmer for one of the landowners of Sistan, and that he learned music, and played harp beautifully. He also had a good voice and learned to compose songs and singing. He developed special skills in writing poetry, but could not gain any success in his own town, and decided to migrate in search of opportunities to establish himself as a poet. Having heard glowing reports of the munificence of the Amir Abu'l Mozafar of Chaghaniyan (a place in Transoxiana, between Titmidth and Qubadian), he set off to try his fortune with this new patron, as he himself says:
"In a caravan for Hilla bound from Sistan I did start,
With fabrics spun within my brain and woven by my heart"
On arriving at his destination, he found that the Amir Abu'l Mozafar, was absent in the country, and has travelled to his "branding-ground', to supervise the branding of his colts and mares. In his absence the poet was received by his steward, the Amir Assad, who being himself a poet at once recognized the merit of the qasida which Farrokhi recited to him, but could hardly believe that the uncouth, ill-dressed Sistani, who was "of the most unprepossessing appearance from head to foot", and his head was crowned "with a huge turban, after the manner of Sagzis, could really be its author, so he said:

"The Amir is at the branding ground, whither I go to wait upon him, and thither I will take thee also, for it is a mighty pleasant spot—
"World within world of verdure wilt thou see full of tents and star-like lamps, and from each tent comes the songs of Rudaki and friends sit together drinking wine and making merry, while before the Amir's pavilion a great fire is kindled, in size like a mountain, where at they brand the colts. And the Amir, goblet in one hand and lasso in the other, drinks wine and gives away horses. Compose, now, a qasida describing this branding ground, so that I may present thee to the Amir".
So that night Farrokhi composed the following qasida, which is reckoned one of his most successful qasidas:

Since the meadow hides its face in satin shot with greens and blues,	چون پرند نیلگون بر روی پوشد مرغزار
And the mountains wrap their brows in silver vales of seven hues,	پرنیان هفت رنگ اندر سر آرد کوهسار

Chapter 5

Earth is teeming like the musk-pod with aromas rich and rare, Foliage bright as parrot's plumage doth the graceful willow wear,	خاک را چون ناف آهو مشگ زاید بی قیاس بید را چون پر طوطی برگ روید بیشمار
Yestere'en the midnight breezes brought the tidings of the spring: Welcome, O you northern gales, for this glad promise which ye bring!	دوش وقت نیمشب بوی بهار آورد باد حبذا باد شمال وخرما بوی بهار
Up its sleeve the wind, misdeemed, pounded musk hath stored away. While the garden fills its lap with shining dolls, as though for play.	باد گویی مشگ سوده دارد اندر آستین باغ گویی لعبتان ساده دارد در کنار
On the branches of syringe, necklaces of pearl we see, Ruby ear-rings of Badakhshan sparkle on the Judas-tree.	ارغوان لعل بدخشی دارد اندر مرسله نسترن لولوی مکنون دارد اندر گوشوار
Since the branches of the rose- bush carmine cups and beakers bore Human-like five-fingered hands reach downwards from the sycamore,	تا رباید جامهای سرخ رنگ از شاخ گل پنجه ها چون دست مردم سر بر او رداز چنار
Gardens all chameleon –coated, branches with chameleon whorls, Pearly lustrous pools around us, clouds above us are raining pearls!	باغ بوقلمون لباس و راغ بوقلمون نمای آب مروارید رنگ و ابر مروارید بار
On the gleaming plain this coat of many colors doth appear Like a coat of honor granted in the Court of our Amir.	راست پنداری که خلعتهای رنگین یافتند باغهای پرنگار از داغگاه شهریار
For our Prince's Camp of branding stirreth in these joyful days,	سبزه اندر سبزه بینی چون سپهر اندر سپهر خیمه اندر خیمه بینی چون حصار اندر حصار

Rebirth of Persian Culture

So that all this age of ours in joyful
wonder stands a-gaze,

Green within the green you see like stars
within the firmament;
Like a fort within a fortress spreads the
army, tent on tent.

Every tent contains a lover resting in his
sweetheart's arms,
Every patch of grass reveals to a friend
a favorite's charms.

Harps are sounding midst the verdure,
minstrels sing their lays divine,
Tents resound with clink of glasses as
the pages pour the wine,

Kisses, claspings from the lovers; coy
reproaches from the fair;
Wine –born slumbers for the sleepers,
while the minstrels wake the air,

Branding fires like the suns ablaze, are
kindled at the spacious gate
Leading to the state-pavilion of our
Prince so fortunate,

Leap the flames like gleaming lances
draped with yellow-lined brocade,
Hotter than a young man's passion,
yellower than gold assayed,
Branding tools like coral branches ruby-
tinted glow a main
In the fire, as in the ripe pomegranate
glows the crimson grain.

Rank on rank the active boys, whose
watchful eyes no slumber know;

سبزه ها با بانگ رود مطربان چرب
دست
خیمه ها با بانگ نوش ساقیان می
گسار

هر کجاخیمه است خفته عاشقی
بادوست مست
هرکجا سبزه است شادان یاری از
دیدار یار

عاشقان بوس وکنار ونیکوان
ناز و عتاب
مطربان رود وسرود ومیکشان خواب
وخمار

روی هامون سبز چون گردون
ناپیداکران
روی صحرا ساده چون دریای ناپیدا
کران

واندر آن گردون ستاره وان ستاره
بی مدار
هرکجا کهسار باشد آن سماری کوه
بر
هر کجا خورشید باشد آن ستاره سایه
دار
معجزه باشد ستاره ساکن وخورشید
پوش

نادره باشد سماری که بر وصحرا
گذار
اندر آن دریا سماری وآن سماری
کوه بر

Steeds which still wait the branding
rank on rank and row on row.

On his horse the river-forder, roams our
genial prince afar,
Ready to his hand the lasso, like a young
Isfandyar.

Like the locks of pretty children see it
how it curls and bends,
Yet be sure its hold is stronger than the
covenant of friends.

Bu'l-Mudhaffar Shah, the upright,
circled by a noble band,
King and conqueror of cities, brave
defender of the land.

Serpent-coiled in skilful hands his
whirling noose and circling line,
On the face and flank and shoulder ever
bears the Royal sign.

But though on one side he brands, gives
he also rich rewards
Leads his poets with a bridle, blinds his
guests as though with cords."

بر در پرده سرای خسرو پیروز بخت
از پی داغ آتشی افروخته خورشید
وار

برکشیده آتشی چون مطرد دیبای
زرد
گرم چون طبع جوان و زرد چون زر
عیار

داغها چون شاخهای بسد یاقوت
رنگ
هر یکی چون ناردانه گشته اندر زیر
نار

ریدکان خواب نادیده مصاف اندر
مصاف
مرکبان داغ ناکرده قطار اندر قطار

خسرو فرخ سیر بر باره دریا گذر
با کمند اندر میان دشت چون
اسفندیار

اژدها کردار پیچان در کف رادش
کمند
چون عصای موسی اندر دست
موسی گشته مار

همچو زلف نیکوان خرد ساله تاب
خورد
همچو عهد دوستان سالخورده
استوار گردن

هر مرکبی چون گردن قمری بطوق
از کمند شهریار شهر گیر شهردار

Rebirth of Persian Culture

هر که را اندر کمند شصت بازی در فگند

گشت داغش بر سر رین و شانه و رویش نگار

هر گه زین سک داغ کرد از سوی دیگر هدیه داد

شاعران را با لگام و زاییران را با افسار...

"When Amir Asad heard this qasida", continues the author of the Chahar Maghale, he was overwhelmed with amazement, for never had the like of it reached his ears. He put aside all his business, mounted Farrukhi on a horse, and set out for the Amir whose presence he entered about sundown, saying 'O Sire, I bring thee a poet the like of him the eye of Time has never seen since Daghighi's face was veiled in death. Then he related what had passed. "so the Amir accorderd Farrukhi an audience, and he, when he had comin, did reverence and the Amir gave him his hand and assigned to him an honorable place, inquiring after his health, treating him with kindness, and inspiring with hopes of favors to come. When the wine had gone round several times, Farrukhi arose and in a sweet and plaintive voice, recited his elegy beginning:

'In a caravan for Hilla bound from Sistan I did start;   با کاروان حله برفتم ز سیستان

With fabrics spun within my brain and woven in my heart'   با حله تنیده ز دل بافته ز جان

When he had finished the Amir himself, something of a poet, expressed his astonishment at this qasida, 'Wait, said Amir Asad, till you see! Farrukhi was silent until the wine had its full effect on Amir; then he rose and recited this qasida on the branding -ground. The Amir was amazed and in his admiration turned to Farrukhi, saying: they have brought in a thousand colts, all with white forheads, fetlocks, and feet. Thou art a cunning rascal, a Sagzi; catch as many as thou can, and they shall be yours. Farrukhi, on whom the wine had now produced its full effect, came out, took his turban from his head, hurled himself into the midst of the herd, and chased a drove of them before him across the plain; but though he caused them to gallop here and there, but could not catch a single one. At last a ruined rest-house situated on the edge of the camping ground came into view and there the colts fled. Farrokhi, being tired out, placed his turban under his head in the porch of the rest-house, and at once fell asleep because of extreme fatigue, and the effect of wine. When the colts were counted, they were forty two in number. The Amir, being informed of this, laughed and said: 'he is a lucky fellow, and will come to great things. Look after him, and look after the colts too. When he awakens, awaken me also. So they obeyed the Prince's orders.

"The next day, after sunrise, Farrukhi arose. The Amir had already risen, and, when he performed his prayers, he gave Farrokhi an audience, treated him with great consideration, and handed over the colts to his attendants. He also ordered Farrukhi to be given a horse and equipments suitable to a man of rank, as well as a tent, three camels, five slaves, wearing apparel, and carpets. So Farrukhi prospered in his service, and enjoyed so that twenty servants girt with silver girdles rode behind him".

Some years later Farrukhi moved to Ghazni the capital city of the rule of Sultan Mahmoodd of Ghaznavi. At this time his fame had reached the distant cities, spreading to the Court of Sultan Mahmood. Sultan received him warmly. At the service of this king Farrukhi prospered, and enjoyed the greatest circumstances. His arrival to the Court of Sultan Mahmood was around the year 931 (C.E). He accompanied Sultan in all of his expeditions, invasions and wars. Forrukhi wrote a large number of elegies describing Mahmood's victories, acting also as his adviser and companion.

Farrukhi was an extremely talented poet. He is without doubt one of the greatest poets and lyrists in the Persian literary history. He is particularly skilful in describing Nature's sceneries, delicate human feelings, and wars, in which he was always in attendance during the reign of Mahmood. His descriptive details were never exaggerating, rather truthful. Farrukhi had also a keen sense of humor which is evident in a number of his poetries, as well as being exceptionally bold, fearless, direct, and honest even in his praise of the persons he liked and admired. He had self educated himself in all branches of knowledge of his time; history, literature, philosophy, and science. He is titled "Hakim" which means sage, in view of his special wisdom and knowledge. He died rather young. His contemporary, Labiby mourned his death writing:

Farrukhi died, Onsori, still alive,
An old man lives, but a young man dies,

A wise, learned man perished; great loss,
A mad man lives; who benefits no one.

گر فروخی بمرد چرا عنصری نمرد

پیری بماند وجوانی بمرد زود

فرزانه ای برفت وزرفتنش هرزیان

دیوانه ای بماند وزماندنش هیچ سود

As was said before, Farrukhi was a skilled musician, and great singer. This made him even more popular with the kings who always received him graciously at their royal courts.

Ohadedin Anvari Abivardi. 12th century poet

Anvari Abivardi is one of the most distinguished poets of the sixth century who played a major role in altering the course and style of Persian poetry: He is mentioned in the following verses having been put in the same supreme class with two other great Masters of Persian poetry of all times i.e Ferdowsi and Saadi

Three rank as prophets in the poetic arena,
An opinion, which is shared by all, (that are experts)

در شعر سه تن پیامبرانند
قولیست که جمله گی براانند

Ferdowsi, Anvari, and Saadi,
No other came after them, (ranking higher)

فردوسی و انوری وسعدی
هرچند که لانبی وبعدی

With regard to the circumstances surrounding his life, we know little, though a careful and thorough study of his poetry casts some light on to the unknown details of his life. We know that he had studied, and had become quite knowledgeable, in Astronomy, Geometry, Music, Metaphysics, Natural Science, and Judicial Astrology, and even declares himself proficient "in every science, pure or applied, known at his time". Famous biographer

Chapter 5

Dolatshah Samarghandi writes that he was born in the village of Abivard in the province of Khavaran and at first wrote under the pen-name of Khavari, which he afterwards changed to Anvari. He had studied in the city of Tus, and lived a meager life, aspiring to become a man of science, however, one day standing by the gates of his college, he saw a man riding a horse, dressed magnificently, and followed by an entourage. He asked who this person is, and was told that he is a poet. Good heavens! He exclaimed!: Am I so poor when the rank of Science is so high, and is he so rich when the grade of Poetry stands so low. From to day onwards I am going to devote my life to poetry which is the lowest of my accomplishments!, and that very night he composed his famous qasida which starts with:'

"If Heart and Hand can rank as sea and mine
It is this Heart and Hand, O Sire, of Thine!"

گر دل و دست بحر و کان باشد
دل و دست خدایگان باشد

Next morning he presented himself at Sultan Sanjar's reception, and, having recited his poem, was asked whether he desired a monitory reward or a position at the Court; to which he replied:

Save at thy threshold in the world no resting place have I;
Except this gate no place is found whereon my head would lie.

به جز آستان توام در جهان پناهی نیست
به سر مرا بجز این درحواله گاهی نیست

Sultan Sanjar, having heard this, ordered him an allowance and took him with himself to Marve, his State Capital. Anvari was given special place in the court of Sultan Sanjar of Seljuk, where he accompanied the king in all his expeditions. His literary powers are considerable and his exercise in irony and ridicule make pungent reading. He was expert in astrology and astronomy, and considered superior to his contemporaries in logic, music, theology, mathematics and all other intellectual pursuits. It appears that his patrons after

Rebirth of Persian Culture

Sultan Sanjar had failed to value his services as highly as he did himself, and he considered his rewards inadequate. Either that fact or the jealousy of his rivals caused him to renounce the writing of eulogies and ghazals although it is difficult to determine at what point in his life this took place. Doubtless his satires created him enemies.

An incident happened while still at the service of Sultan Sanjar that took a toll upon his reputation, and prestige, when the seven planets were at one period in the Sign of the Balance, Anvari predicted that on that day a great windstorm will happen that will destroy all buildings and uproot all trees. Many people for the fear of this storm dug deep cellars to seek refuge from the impending calamity, but when the day arrived the air was so calm that not a branch on the trees shook. This caused great disappointment, by people, in Anvari some of whom had gone in to great length to protect themselves against the storm. Anvari's great reputation as a scientist /astrologer was naturally undermined causing him great distress. On this Farid-e-Kateb, wrote the following poem to criticize him, and his prediction:

"Said Anvari, 'Such fearful gales shall blow As houses, may even hills, shall overthrow,	گفت انوری که از سبب بادهای سخت ویران شود عمارت وکه نیز برسری
The day proved breathless; Anvari, Iween you And Aeolus must settle it between you!	در روز حکم او نوزیدست هیچ باد یا مرسل الریاح تو دانی وانوری

At present no accurate data exists regarding the exact date of Anvari's birth or his death, but it is probable that his death must have taken place between the C.E 1203 and 1209.

Anvari's most celebrated qasida is thought by many critics to be the "The Tears of Khorasan; on account of its historic interest, its human feeling, and its expressive tones:

"O' morning breeze, should you blow over Samarghand? Carry the letter of the inhabitants of Khorasan to the Sultan"	بر سمرقند اگر بگذری ای باد سحر نامه اهل خراسان به بر خاقان بر

Chapter 5

Anvari is believed to have spent the last few years of his life at Balkh, where he retired after the loss of prestige which he suffered as the consequence of the failure of the astrological prediction to which it was previously pointed out. Here again the misfortune struck him, for there appeared a satire on the people of Balkh entitled "Kharnameh", or "Book of Asses" of which, though it was really written by the other famous "Suzani", Anwari was wrongly accused to have had written it. According to other accounts the offending poem was a fragment of five verses characterizing the four chief cities of Khurasan (Balkh, Marve, Nishahbour, and Hera't), composed by Futuhi at the instigation of Suzani and deliberately ascribed by him to Anvari, in which Balkh is described as a town "filled with rogues and libertines" and destitute of a single man of sense. In any case Anvari was roughly handled by the people of Balkh, who, furious at what they considered an unprovoked outrage, paraded him through the streets with a woman's headdress on his head, and would have gone further had they not been dissuaded and pacified by some of the poet's influential poets such as Nezame-ed-Din Ahmad the professor, to whom the poet bewails his adventure and offers his thanks in a qasida of a hundred verses, beginning with:

| "O Muslims, alas for the tyranny of hoop-like heaven,
And the treachery of Mercury, the ill-intent of the Moon, and the guile of Jupiter, | ای مسلمانان فغان از جور چرخ چنبری
وز نفاق تیر و قصد ماه و کید مشتری ... |

The action of the beneficent water on my palate is fire,
The state of the quite earth in my abode is tempestuous!

With the boat of my life heaven ever deals in [one of] two ways,
Urging it onward in time of gladness, anchoring it in time of grief....."

A literal translation of the original three verses is indicated:

Rebirth of Persian Culture

This qasida, is the original of the piece called"Palinodia" from the "Song of the Reed" by the late Professor E. H. Palmer a rendering so free that it can at most be described as a paraphrase, of which the first two verses, corresponding to the first three distiches of the original, are as follows:
"Ah! The spheres are incessantly rolling,
And the archer is shifting his ground,

And the moon is for ever patrolling,
And Jupiter going his round.

The water that tastes to another,
Refreshing and cool on the lip,

Is as fire that no efforts can smother,
In the cup which I sip.

"The dust that all quiet is laying
When others recline on the ground,

Around me in volumes is flying,
Like a desert where whirlwinds abound;
And Fate, in the ship of my being,
In happiness hurries me past,

But if ever from sorrow I am fleeing,
It anchors me fast."

Perhaps the most celebrated of all Anvari's poems ,at any rate in Europe, is that first translated into English verse by Captain William Kirkpatrick, under the title of The Tears of Khorassan," in 1785, and again by professor palmer in his Song of the Reed.
"This poem," says Kirkpatrick," is one of the most beautiful in the Persian language. The sentiments are throughout natural, and frequently sublime; the images for the most part are striking and just; the diction is at once nervous and elegant, animated and chaste; and the verification although not everywhere equally smooth and flowing, seems notwithstanding, to be happily adapted to the subject, the measure being, as I believe, the most slow and solemn that is used in Persian poetry."

"O morning breeze, if thou pass by Samarqand,
Bear to the Prince (khaqan) the letter of the people of Khorassan,

A letter whose opening is grief of body and affliction of soul,
A letter whose close is sorrow of spirit and burning of heart,

A letter in whose lines the sighs of the miserable are manifest,
A letter in whose folds the blood of the martyrs is concealed,

The characters of its script dry as the bosoms of the oppressed,
The lines of its address moist from the eyes of the sorrowful;

Whereby the auditory channel is wounded at the time of hearing,
Whereby the pupil of the eye is turned to blood at the time of looking!

O'er the great ones of the age the small are lords,
O'er the nobles of the world the mean are chiefs;

At the doors of the ignoble the well-born stand sad and bewildered,
In the hands of libertines the virtuous are captive and constrained.

Thou see no man glad save at the door of Death,

به سمرقند اگر بگذری ای باد سحر
نامه اهل خراسان به بر خاقان بر

نامه ای مطلع آن رنج تن وآفت جان
نامه ای مقطع آن درد دل وسوز جگر

نامه ای بررقمش آه عزیزان پیدا
نامه ای درشکنش خون عزیزان مضمر

نقش تحریرش از سینه مظلومان خشگ
سطر عنوانش از دیده محرومان تر

خون شود مردمک دیده از اووقت نظر

بربزرگان زمانه شده خردان سالار
بر کریمان جهان گشته لیمان مهتر

بردر دونان احرار حزین وحیران
در کف رندان ابرار اسیر و مضطر

شاد الا به در مرگ نبینی مردم
بکر جز در شکم مام نیابی دختر

Thou see no girl a maiden save in her mother's womb.

The main mosque of each city for their beasts
Is a resting place, whereof neither door nor roof is visible?

مسجد جامع هر شهر ستور انشانرا
پایگاهی شده نه سقفش پیدا و نه در

Nowhere [it is true] do they read the khutba in the name of Ghuzz,
For in all khorassan there is neither preacher nor pulpit"

خطبه دیگر نکنند به نام غز زانک
درخراسان نه خطیب است نه منبر

This qasida was written by Anvari to describe the calamity that fell upon the people of Khorasan following the invasion of the Tribe of Guzz, who ransacked the entire province and all its big and small cities. It is a rather long poem consisting of almost 90 verses. It has a considerable historical interest, as a graphic description of the deplorable ravages wrought in what was previously one of the most flourishing parts of Persia by the barbarous Turcoman tribe of Guzz, about the end of the year 1170 C.E. This tribe, whose pasture -grounds, lay around about Khatlan, a dependency of Balkh, paid a yearly tribute of 24000 sheep to the kitchen of King Sanjar. The harshness and greed of his steward (khansalar) having lead to disputes and bloodshed, Qumaj, the Governor of Balkh, wrote to Sanjar to complain of the growing power and insolence of the Guzz, and asking to be commissioner (Shahneh) over them, promising to, speedily reduce them to obedience, and to raise their tribute to 30,000 sheep. Qumaj however failed to make good his promise, for he was defeated by them and driven out of their territories and his son was also killed. Thereupon, Sanjar was persuaded by his nobles to take action against the enemy, and to reject the apologies and indemnity of 100,000. Dinars and 1000 Turkish slaves which the frightened Guzz now offered. When he drew near their camp they came out to meet him as suppliants, accompanied by their women and children, praying for forgiveness, and offering seven mounds of silver from each household. Again Sanjar was prevented by his Amirs, from listening to their proposals; battle ensued and the Guzz now desperate, fought with such fury that they utterly routed Sanjar's army, took him prisoner, and brought him captive to Merve, his own capital,

Chapter 5

which they looted for three days, torturing the unfortunate inhabitants to make them disclose their hidden treasures. Thence reinforced by three times their number of disbanded soldiers and other rogues, they pushed on to Nishahbour, where meeting with some resistance, in which several of their number were killed, they wrought so terrible massacre in the Great Mosque that "the slain could not be seen for the blood wherein they lay. "They also burnt the Mutarriz Mosque, a building large enough to hold 20,000 persons and by the light of a great fire that they burnt, continued their ravages. They camped outside the city, visiting it daily to kill, torture, plunder, and destroy. Amongst the victims of their cruelty, who numbered several thousands were many eminent and godly men, as well as nobles, and intellectuals. So complete was the destruction of this once flourishing city that, says the author of the unique history of Seljuks dynasty entitled Rahatu's-sudoor, Mu'izzi in a poem:

"Where once my charmer might be found in garden fair with friends around,
The owls and vultures now abound, the foxes, wolves, and jackals stray;
Where stood the cups and bowls, the fleet wild-ass now tramples with its feet
;In place of fruit and flute so sweet now crows and ravens wing their way,
So utterly the dark-blue Sphere has swept away those traces dear,
That no explorer now, I fear, could guess where once I wooed my may."

Throughout all Khurasan, with the exception of Hera't, which successfully held out against them, the Guzz acted in the same way and for two years Sanjar was captive in their hands. Then at last he succeeded, by bribing some of the Guzz chiefs in arranging his escape from Balhk to Merve, where he began to collect an army; but grief at the destruction and desolation of his domains brought about an illness which proved to be fatal in C. E 1174. He was buried in Merve.

Anvari's poems were collected in a div'an and contain panegyrics, eulogies, satires and others. The Cambridge History of Iran calls Anvari one of the greatest figures in the literary history of Iran. His poetry, despite their beauty, often requires much help with interpretation, as they were often complex and difficult to understand. Anvari's panegyric in praise of Sultan Sanjar won him, royal favor with the king and his two successors to the throne, and went on to live a nice living at their court. However as said before when his prophesy about the disaster did not come true, he was forced in to a life of scholarly service, eventually taking his own life.

Faridu'din Attar Neishabouri, 12th century Persian poet and mystic

Faridu'din Attar ranks as one of the highest in the vast arena of Persian mystics, poets, writers and lyricists. He was born sometime in between the year C.E 1152-1159 in the small village of Kadkan a suburb of the city of Neishabour. There exists much controversy regarding his exact date of birth. Also there exists little information regarding the early years of his life and education. It has been reported that his father owned a perfume, and medicine store in the village of Shadyakh, and his son followed in the same steps, as was the tradition in those days. The name Attar means a man who deals in or sells perfume. (Attr) means perfume. It seems almost certain that Attar spent the early years of his life and even some years after having studied history, philosophy, literature etc, in that store, while conducting his business of selling perfume and tending to the sick who visited the store to buy medicine to cure their ailments. He makes a reference to his practice of medicine in that store, in one of his books; Khosrow nameh:

O' Master of the virtual world, Who occupied yourself day and night with Medicine?	به من گفت ای به معنی عالم افروز چنین مشغول طب گشتی شب وروز

And again in his other book,"Mosibatnameh", he writes:

"Mosibat nameh" that contains the agonies of the world, "Elahiname" (the Book of Divine) that contains the secrets of the world,	مصیبت نامه که اندوه جهانست الهی نامه که اسرار نهانست
These, both, I started in the medicine shop,	به داروخانه کردم هردو آغاز چگونه زود رستم زین وآن باز
Where, I daily, felted the pulse of 500 persons, Thus how quickly I saved myself from them all.	به داروخانه پانصد شخص بودند که در هرروز نبضم می نمودند

Chapter 5

It is understood from these verses that Attar was not, after all, too enthusiastic about managing the medicine store which must have been inherited from his father, eventually gave it up and, embarked on a series of soul searching journeys to other countries visiting Baghdad, a flourishing Metropolis with culture, science, music, and art, Basra, Kufa, Medina, Mecca, Damasqus, Kharazm, and countries such as Turkistan, Tajikistan, and India visiting with Sufi Shaykhs, and eventually returning home to teach and promote sophism.

It is not quite clear by whom, Attar was initiated in to sophism, but it is widely said that this happened in the hand of Majd-Din Baghdadi, a disciple of the great Sufi, Najm-e-Din Kobra. No doubt the seeds of Gnosticism must have been planted in him from childhood by his father and later during the time that he was engaged in the profession of medicine at his shop, by reading and engaging in meditation and spiritual exploration and self discovery. For thirty nine years he busied himself in collecting the verses and sayings of sufi saints, and never in his life , he tells us, did he engage his poetic talent in panegyric. He was later greatly admired by Mowlavi, whom he had deeply inspired, and influenced. Mowlavi wrote of him

Attar was the spirit and Sanaii, his eyes twin And in time thereafter, came we in their train,	عطا ر روح بودوسنایی دوچشم او ما از پی سنایی و عطار آمدیم
Attar completed the tour of the seven cities of love, We are yet tangled up in the first alley.	هفت شهر عشق را عطار گشت ما هنوز اندر خم یک کوچه ایم

The thoughts depicted in Attar's works reflect the whole movement of Sufi evolution. The starting point is that the body bound soul awaits its release and return to its source in the other world. This can be experienced during the present life in mystic union attainable through inward purification. In explaining his thought Attar uses material not only from specific Sufi sources, but also from older ascetic legacies. Although his heroes, for the most parts are Sufis and ascetics, he also introduces stories from historical chronicles, collected anecdotes and all types of highly esteemed literature. His talent for perception of deeper meanings beyond outward appearances enables him to turn details of everyday life in to illustrations of his thoughts. The idiosyncrasy of 'Attar's presentation invalidates his works as sources of the historical persons whom he introduces on hagiology and phenomenology of Sufism. However, his works have immense value.

Judging from Attar's writings he approached the available Aristotelian heritage with contempt and skepticism and dislike. Interestingly he did not want to reveal the secrets of Nature. This is particularly remarkable in the case of medicine, which fell within the scope of his professional expertise as a pharmacist. He obviously had no motive to share his knowledge in the manner customary among court panegyrists, whose type of poetry he despised and never practiced. Such knowledge is only brought in to his works in contexts where the theme of a story touches on a branch of natural sciences.

Attar has produced in his life time a great number of works, including his divan,"The collection of his lyrics" all of superior beauty and quality, various books written on the subject of Mysticism, the most famous of all is Mantegh-o-Tayr "Speech of the birds". This is an allegorical poem of something over 4600 couplets. Its subject is the quest of the birds for the mythical Simurgh, the birds typifying the Sufi pilgrims, and the Simurgh God "the Truth". The book begins with the usual doxologies, including the praise of God, of the Prophet, and of the four Caliphs, the latter clearly showing that at this period Shaykh Attar was a convinced Sunni. The narrative portion of the poem begins at verse 593, and is comprised in 45 "Discourses" (Maghala), and a "Conclusion" (Khatameh). It opens with the account of the assembling of the birds, some thirteen species. They decide that for the successful pursuit of their quest they must put themselves under the guidance of a leader, and proceed to elect to this position the Hoopoe (Hudhud), so celebrated amongst the Muslims for the part which it played as Solomon's emissary to Bilqis, The Qeen of Sheba. The Hoopoe harangues them in a long discourse, which concludes with following account of the first Manifestation of the mysterious Simurgh,

"When first the Simurgh, radiant in the night,	ابتدای کار سیمرغ ای عجب
Passed over the land of China in its flight,	جلوه گر بگذشت بر چین نیمه شب
	در میان چین فتاد از وی پری

Chapter 5

A feather from its wing on China soil	لاجرم پرشور شد هرکشوری
Fell and the world in tumult did embroil, Each one did strife that feather to portray;	هرکسی نقشی از آن پر برگرفت هرکه دید آن نقش کاری درگرفت
Who saw these sketches, fell to work straightaway. In China's Picture-hall that feather is: "Seek knowledge even in China", points to this.	آن پر اکنون در نگارستان چین است اطلبو العلم ولو بالچین از اینست
Had not mankind the feather's portrait seen, Such strife throughout the world would never have been,	گر نگشتی نقش بر او عیان این همه غوغا نبودی در جهان
	این همه آثار از فر اوست جمله آن نمودار نقش پر اوست

Its praise has neither end nor origin:
Unto what end its praise shall we begin?

No sooner, however , has the quest been decided upon that the birds "begin with one accord to make excuse" The nightingale pleads its love for the rose; the parrot for its beauty in a cage; the peacock affects diffidence of its worthiness because of its connection with Adam's expulsion from Paradise; the duck cannot dispense with the water; the partridge is too much attached to the mountains, the heron to the lagoons, and the owl to the ruins which these birds respectively frequent; the Homa loves its power of conferring royalty; the falcon will not relinquish its place of honor on the King's hand; while the wagtail pleads its weakness. All these excuses, typical of the excuses made by men for not pursuing the things of Spirit, are answered in turn by the wise hoopoe, which illustrates its arguments by a series of anecdotes.

The hoopoe next describes to the other birds the perilous road which they must traverse to arrive at the Simurgh's presence, and relates to them the long story of Shaykh Sanaan, who fell in love with a Christian girl, and was constrained by his love and her tyranny to feed swine, thus exposing himself to the censure of all his former friends and disciples. The birds then decide to set out under the guidance of the hoopoe to look for the Symurgh, but they shortly begin again to make excuses or raise difficulties, which the hoopoe answers, illustrating his replies by numerous anecdotes. The objections of twenty two birds, with the hoopoe's answers to each, are given in detail. The remaining birds they continue their quest, and, passing in succession through the seven valleys of search, Love , Knowledge, Independence, Unification, Amazement, Destitution, and Annihilation, ultimately, purged of all self and purified by their trials, find the Simurgh, and in finding it find themselves. The passage that describes this is so curious, and so well illustrates the Sufi conception of "Annihilation in God" (Fana fi'ellah):

Through trouble and shame the souls of these birds were reduced to utter Annihilation, while their bodies became dust.

Being thus utterly purified of all, they all received Life from the Light of the (Devine) Presence.

Once again they became servants with souls renewed; once again in another way were they overwhelmed with astonishment.

Their ancient deeds, sins and omissions were cleansed away and annihilated from their bosoms.

The Sun of propinquity shone forth from them; the souls of all of them were illuminated by its rays.

Through the reflection of the faces of these thirty birds (si murgh) of the world they then beheld the countenance of the Simurgh.

When they looked, that was the Simurgh: without doubt that Simurgh was those thirty birds (si murgh).

All were bewildered with amazement, not knowing they were this or that.

They perceived themselves to be naught else but Simurgh,

while, the Simurgh was naught else than the thirty birds (simurgh).

When they looked towards the simurgh, it was indeed Simurgh which was there.

Chapter 5

While, when they looked towards themselves, they were si murgh (thirty birds), and that was Simurgh;

And if they looked at both together, both were the Simurgh, neither more nor less.

This one was that, and that one this; the like of this has no one heard in the world.

All of them were plunged in amazement, and continued thinking without thought.

Since they understood naught of any matter, without speech they made enquiry of that Presence.

They besought the disclosure of this deep mystery, and demanded the solution of "we-ness" and thou-ness".

Without speech came the answer from the Presence, saying: This sun-like Presence is a mirror.

Whosoever enters it sees him in it; in it he sees body and soul, soul and body.

Since you came hither thirty birds (Si murgh), you appeared as thirty in this Mirror.

Should forty or fifty birds come, they too would discover themselves.

Though many more had been added to your number, ye yourselves see, and it is yourself you have looked on.

Here is the version in Farsi of Atar's conception of "Annihilation in God" from his famous Mantegh-al-Tayr or "Speech of the Birds":

سرنگون گشتند در خون جگر	زین سخن مرغان وادی سر به سر
نیست بر بازوی مشتی ناتوان	جمله دانستند کین شیوه گمان

زین سخن شد جان ایشان بیقرار   هم در آن منزل بسی مردند زار

وین همه مرغان همه آن جایگاه   سرنهادند از سر حسرت به راه

سالها رفتند در شیب و فراز   صرف شد در راهشان عمری دراز

آنچه ایشان را در این ره رخ نمود   کی تواند شرح آن پاسخ نمود

گر تو هم روزی فروآیی به را   عقبه آن ره کنی یک یک نگاه

باز دانی آنچه ایشان کرده اند   روشنت گردد که چون خون خورده اند

آخرالامر از میان آن سپاه   کم رهی ره برد تا آن پیشگاه

زان همه مرغ اندکی آنجا رسید   از هزاران کس یکی آنجا رسید

باز بعضی غرقه دریا شدند   باز بعضی محو ونا پیدا شدند

باز بعضی برسر کوه بلند   تشنه جان دادند در گرم و گزند

باز بعضی را از تف آفتاب   گشت پرها سوخته دلها کباب

باز بعضی را پلنگ و شیر راه   کرد یکدم به رسوایی تباه

باز بعضی نیز غایب ماندند   در کف ذات المخالب ماندند

باز بعضی در بیابان خشگ لب   تشنه از گرما بمردند از تعب

باز بعضی ز آرزوی دانه ای   خویش را کشتند چون دیوانه ای

باز بعضی سخت رنجور آمدند   باز پس ماندند و مهجور آمدند

باز بعضی در عجایب های راه   باز استادند هم در جایگاه

باز بعضی در تماشای طرب   تن فرودادند فارغ از طرب

عاقبت از صدهزاران تایکی   بیش نرسیدند آنجا اندکی

عالمی پر مرغ میبردند راه   بیش نرسیدند سی آن جایگاه

سی تن بی بال و پر رنجور و سست   دل شکسته جان شده تن نادرست

حضرتی دیدند بی وصف و صفت   برتر از ادراک عقل و معرفت

برق استغنا همی افروختی   صد جهان در یک زمان میسوختی

صدهزاران آفتاب معتبر   صدهزاران ماه و انجم بیشتر

همچو ذره پای کوبان آمده	جمع میدیدند حیران آمده
ذره ای محو است پیش این آفتاب	جمله گفتندای عجب چون آفتاب
ای دریغا رنج برده ما براه	کی بدید آییم ما این جایگاه
نیست زان دست اینکه ما پنداشتیم	دل بکل ازخویشتن برداشتیم
همچومرغ نیم بسمل ملندند	آن همه مرغان چوبیدل ماندند
تا بر آمد روزگاری نیز هم	محومیبودند وناچیز هم
چاوش عزت برآمد ناگهی	آخرازپیشان عالی درگهی
بال وپر نه جان شده درتن گداز	دید سی مرغ خرف را مانده باز
نه تهی شان مانده نه پرمانده	پای تا سردرتحیرمانده
در چنین منزلگه ازبهرچه اید	گفت هان ای قوم ازشهرکه اید
یا کجا بودست آرام شما	چیست ای بی حاصلان نام شما
با چه کار آیند مشتی ناتوان	یا شمارا کس چه گوید در جهان
تا بود سیمرغ ما را پادشاه	جمله گفتند آمدیم این جایگاه
بی دلان وبیقراران ره ایم	ما همه سرگشتگان این رهیم
از هزاران سی به درگاه آمدیم	مدتی شد تا در این راه آمدیم
تا بود مارا دراین حضرت حضور	برامیدی آمدیم ازراه دور
آخرازلطفی کند درمانگاه	کی پسندد پادشاه آن رنج ما
همچو در خون دل آغشتگان	گفت آن چاوش کای سرگشتگان
اوست مطلق پادشاه جاودان	گرشما باشید وگرنه درجهان
هست موری بردراین پادشاه	صد هزاران عالم پرازسپاه
بازپس گردید ای مشتی حقیر	از شما آخر چه خیزد جززحیرت
کان زمان چون مرده جاوید شد	زان سخن هریک چنان نومید شد
گردهد مارا بخواری سربراه	جمله گفتند این معظم پادشاه
وربود خواری ازعز نبود	زوکسی را خواری هرگزنبود

There is much controversy about the date that Attar died, much the same way that there is about the date of his birth. However according to what has been reported by historians such as Doulatshah Samarghandi, Hedayat and Djami, he died in the year 1249 C.E in the hand of a Mongol. Similar controversy exists about the way that it happened. An unconfirmed story goes to say that during the invasion of Khorassan by the Mongols, he got arrested by a Mongolian, who was going to kill him. A passerby told the Mongol; do not kill this old man, I will buy him from you for the price of one thousand Dinar. Attar turned to the Mongol and said: do not sell me at this price as others will buy me at a higher price. Couple of hours later another person offered two bags of hey for him. Attar said to the Mongol: take the offer that I am not worth more than this. This enraged the Mongol so much that he turned around and pierced his dagger in to Attar's heart and killed him.

Attar is known to have written a total of seventeen books besides his Divan which contains around 22000 verses, although some must have been attributed to him as they lack conformity with his general beliefs and style. A study of Rumi's Mathnavi reveals that he was greatly inspired by Attar and has adopted a number of stories and fables from the collection of Attar's writings.

The some of seventeen books which are said to have been written by Attar are: Lessan-ol-Gheyb, (The Mystic Tongue), Elahi-nameh (the Book of Divine), Asrar-nameh (the book of secrets), Oshtor-name (The book of Camel), Bolbol-nameh (The Book of Nightingale), Pand-nameh (The book of Advice), javaher-name (The book of Jewel), and few others. Mantegh-o-Teyr being considered to be his masterpiece. This book contains over 4500 verses, and contains stories about Joseph, Sultan Mahmood Ghaznavi, Sultan Sanjar, Nizam-ol-molk, some mystics such as Sheikh Sanan, Abu said Mahneh and others as well as mystical narratives narrated by a group of birds.

Nasser Khosrow Ghobadiani. 1th century Persian poet

Nasser Khosrow Ghobadiani is one of the most distinguished philosophers and poets in the history of Persian culture. His wide and varied scope of knowledge extended from poetry to philosophy, science, religion, history, and covering all branches of human knowledge of his time. He travelled extensively, compiling the memoires of his travel meticulously and in great

Chapter 5

detail such that no one before him had ever done in such fashion and accuracy. He was later on given the title of "Hojat", meaning "His Eminnence" by the rulers of Egypt, the Fatemiyeh dynasty.

Nasser Khosrow was born in the year 1016 (C.E.) about a thousand years ago in the village of Qobadian, a suberb of the old city of Balkh, and died in the village of Yumgan a suburb of the province of Badakhshan. He lived a long life of adventure ranging from being a close courtier in the courts of monarchs to living a life of exile in the mountainous regions of Badakhshan under extreme and harsh conditions in poverty and destitute. The prosperity enjoyed by him during the early years of his life was due to his vast and profound knowledge in various fields, i.e. Philosophy, Gnosticism, Poetry, Writing, Mathematics, Geography, and other branches of knowledge available in his time. The poverty and misery suffered by him during the last years of his life was due to his extreme beliefs in Shiite and attempts to convert people to that sect in a society which was predominantly Sunni, Hannafi, and Rafezzi, the three other sects of Islam. He ended up dying in poverty in exile far from family and home.

His adventurous life started with him spending the early years of his youth studying the fields of knowledge at various schools, which continued even to the rather late age of forty, away from fanatical and strong religious beliefs, and keeping himself occupied with science, and philosophy of Greek times, medicine, music, arithmetic, geometry astronomy, poetry, eulogies in praise of kings at royal courts, drinking occasionally and in general immersed in life's worldly pleasures. He had gathered considerable wealth. In his diaries there are reports of having visited the royal courts of king Mahmood, and his son king Massood.

Around the age of forty for reasons unknown, he underwent a remarkable spiritual transformation, turned away from material interests to the extent of refusing to write lyrics and love-poems, and in search for exaltation and Gnostic Truth embarked on a series of journeys, travelling as far east as borders of China, westward as far as shores of Mediterranean, and south to north Africa. His literary skills enabled him to write a meticulous and accurate report of his journeys, and compile them into what is known as "Nasser Khosrow's diaries" which exists to day and is considered a very important historical document.

Rebirth of Persian Culture

Nasser Khosrow's vast knowledge in all fields of science, literature, history, philosophy, astronomy, etc gained and enriched by his years of travel through many countries, his discourse and discussions with distinguished , and knowledgeable men during long years of travel, were all compiled in a number of books, most of which have survived to our time and form a significant treasure which give us access to the scientific and literary works of great men before him, covering works by Greek scientists, and philosophers of ancient time to other great men of knowledge throughout history up to his time.

 It is said that he embarked on his long trip to see the world following a dream that he had in the year 1059 (C.E.). He first travelled to Arabia on pilgrimage to Mecca, accompanied by his brother and a slave from India. This lasted seven years before his return to Balkh. During this long trip he toured Iran, from extreme north to the south and east to west, then to Armenia, countries in Asia Minor, Damascus, Tripoli, all the cities in Syria, Palestine, Arabia, Egypt, Tunisia, and Sudan. During this trip, he spent three years in Egypt which was under the rule of Fatimid Caliphs. It was there that he converted to Fatimid and Ismailia sect of Islam. He was noted by the Fatimid Rulers, because of his expertise, in almost, every field of human knowledge, and was commissioned by them to return to Khorassan, where most people were Sunnis, and to attempt to convert them to Shiite. He was also given the title of "Proof", (Hujjat), which means religious Leader and Ambassador. The details of his trips are contained in his diaries. Here is an excerpt from the Diaries on Egypt:

"While I was there, he says, in the year C.E.1061, a son was born to the King, and he ordered the public rejoicings. The city and bazaars were decorated in such wise that, should I describe it, some men would probably decline to believe me or credit it. The shops of the cloth – sellers, money-changers, etc., were so filled with precious things, gold, jewels, money, stuffs, gold embroidery, and satin garments, that there was no place for one to sit down. And all felt secure in the justice of the King, and had no fear of myrmidons or spies, by reason of their confidence in him that he will oppress no one and covet no one's wealth."

"There I saw wealth belonging to private individuals, which, should I speak about it or describe it, would seem incredible to the people of Persia; for I could not estimate or compute their wealth, while the well-being which I saw there I have seen in no other place. I saw there, for example, a Christian who was one of the richest men in Cairo, so that it was said to be impossible to compute his ships, wealth, and estates. Now one year, owing to the failure of Nile, grain waxed dear; and the King's Prime Minister sent for this Christian and said: The year is not good, and the King's heart is oppressed on account of his subjects. How much corn can you give me either for cash or on loan? ' by the blessing of the King and his minister; replied the Christian, 'I have ready so much corn that I could supply Cairo with bread for six years,' Now at this time there were assuredly in Cairo so many inhabitants that those of Nishahbour, at the highest computation, would equal that one fifth of them, and whoever can judge of quantities will know how wealthy one must be to possess corn to this amount, and how great must be the security of the subjects and the justice of the sovereign in order that such conditions and such fortunes may be possible in their days , so that neither doth the king wrong or oppress any man, nor does the subject hide or conceal anything."

The long trip covered a distance of 13220 kilometers. His Diaries end with a promise that his next trip will be going eastward. Nasser 's intention in this long journey was search for "Truth", and getting answers to many questions that he had, and not just touring the lands of near and far. Every town, or every country that he visited , his first and foremost task was to find the learned Men and to sit in intellectual discussions with them, in an effort to find answer to his questions. These learned Men often included the Gnostics, philosophers, scientists, astronomers, physicians, and frequently religious leaders which included Sunnis, Shiites, Jews, Ma'navies, Indians, etc.

Nasser Khosrow was 50 years old, when at the conclusion of his trip to Egypt, he returned to Balkh with a mandate given to him by the Fatima Rulers to try to convert Sunnis into Shiites. This commission resulted in the unfortunate exile of the poet later on. When he returned to Balkh, he completed his famous book " Zad-al-Mosaferin", (a gift from the trip) in the year 1075 C.E. and started with his mission to propagate the new Ismaiili religion (A sect of Shiite) amongst the Sunni population in Greater Khorassan. In this new endeavor he faced fierce opposition and hostility by the Sunnis, and the chief clergy of Balkh issued a death sentence on him. He fled Balkh and after wandering from place to place, and in hiding, he went to Mazanderan in the hope of finding refuge with the Shiite rulers there. Ferdowssi, we should recall, had also tried to find refuge there too. Naser Khosrow, eventually, as was said before, found refuge in the small mountainous city of Yumgan in the mountains of Badakhshan, where he spent as a hermit the last decades of his life, gathering a considerable number of devotes who have handed down his doctrines to succeeding generations.

In the following verses he points out to his exile in Mazanderan and Yumgan:

"Although I am originally of Khorassan, after [enjoying] spiritual leadership, authority and supremacy,

گرچه مرا اصل خراسانی است از پس پیری و مهی وسری

Love for the Family and House of the Prophet have made me a dweller in Yamgan and Mazanderan.

دوستی و عزت خانه رسول کرد مرا یمگی و مازندری

His Divan contains poetry alluding to the harsh conditions of his life in exile and his outcry against the rulers of Khorassan, whom he considers responsible for his misery and deprivation as well as loss of contact with his family. When in Yumgan, he also learned that the Sunni people in Balkh, had ransacked his home and his garden, and burnt it down. The incident was during the reign of Abu-Suleiman Chogribeick, father of King Alparsalan, who later established the Seljuk dynasty. Here is part of a famous Ghassidah (elegy), he wrote addressing the people of Khorassan:

"Bear from me to Khurasan, Zephyr, a kindly word,
To its scholars and men of learning, not to the witless herd,

سلام کن ز من ای باد مرخراسان را
مراهل فضل وخرد را نه عام ونادان را

And having faithfully carried the message I bid thee bear,
Bring me news of their doings, and tell me how they fare,

خبر بیار از ایشان به من چو داده بودی
ز حال من به حقیقت خبر مر ایشان را

I, who was once as the cypress, now upon Fortune's wheel
Am broken and bent, you may tell them; for thus does fortune deal.

بگویشان که جهان من چو چنبر کرد به مکر خویش خودانست کارکیهان را

Let not her specious promise you to destruction lure:

نگرکه تان نکند غره عهد و پیمانش

Chapter 5

Never was her covenant faithful; never was her pact secure."	که او وفا نکند هیچ عهد و پیمانش

The task undertaken by Naser Khosrow was a difficult and dangerous one because there were few Ismaiili Shiites at the time in Khorassan, facing a great number of highly prejudiced, vindictive and wild adversaries enjoying great power and influence. Punishment for inviting people to convert to Ismaiili brand of Shiites would be exile, torture and even death. Naser Khosrow arrived in Yumgan at the age of 60, where he lived for twenty five years. He finally died there in poverty and destitute in 1103 C.E. He is buried in the Yumgan valley. His tomb was visited by many during the later years. To this date, there are still some Ismaiili Shiites living in those areas.

His works:
1) divan (collection of poetry) which amongst his other works contains most of the lyrical poems that were composed in his retirement and their chief topics are an enthusiastic praise of Imam Ali, his descendants, and Al-Mustanir in particular, along with passionate outcries against Khorassan and its rulers, who had driven him from his home. It also explores his immense satisfaction for the quiet solitude of Yumgan, and his utter despondency again in seeing himself despised by his former associates and excluded from participation in the glorious contest of life. Scattered through all these alternating outbursts of hope and despair, there are lessons of morality, solemn warnings against the tricks and perfidy of the world. The vanity of all earthly splendors. The greatness, the folly and injustice of men, and the hypocrisy, frivolity and viciousness of fashionable and princely Courts. He criticizes the poets like Onsori who have occupied themselves with constantly praising despotic rulers like Sultan Mahmood of Gaznavi, in their poetry and eulogizing them constantly in their poetries

Safarnameh (the travel diaries) is Naser Khosrwo's most famous work. He visited a great number of cities throughout Middle-east, Asia Minor, and North Africa, some of which have already been mentioned. The trip took almost seven years. He wrote extensively and in great details about places of interest, visits with scientists, rulers, philosophers, learned men of all class and creed, the population of the cities, as well as their surface areas, and memories with great accuracy.

Naser Khosrow's other works are: Gushayesh va Rahayesh, a philosophical text translated in to English under the title of "Knowledge & Liberation" also, "Roshanai-nameh" and Saadat-nameh (Book of Felicity). Other important works by Naser Khosrow are "Zadolmosaferin" (The gift from a trip), and a book on Mathematics.

Here is a piece from his "Divan":
"Were the turns of the wheel of Fortune proportioned to worth alone?
Over the vault of the Lunar Heaven would have been my abode and throne.

But no! For the worth of wisdom is lightly esteemed in sooth,
By fickle Fate and Fortune, as my father warned me in youth.

Yet knowledge is more than farms, and estates, rank. And gold;
Thus my dauntless spirit, whispering, me consoled;

With a heart more brightly illuminated than the moon can ever be
What was a throne of glory over the sphere of the Moon to thee?

To meet the foreman's falchion and fate's close-serried field
Enough for me are Wisdom and Faith as defense and shield.

Sana'i Of Ghazna, 11th century Persian poet & Gnostic

Sana'i of Ghaznai whose proper name Abu'l-Majd Majdud b.Adam is the first of the three most distinguished mystical poets and mathnavi-writers of all times. The second being Shaykh Faride-d Din 'Attar, and the third Mowlana Jalalu'd-Din Mowlavi, known in the western world as "Rumi", who, though by far the greatest, had the humility to write:

"Attar was the Spirit, and Sana'i its two eyes;
We come after Sana'i and 'Attar"

عطار روح بود وسنایی دو چشم او
ما از پی سنایی و عطار آمدیم

Sana'i was born in the city of Ghazni in to-day's Afghanistan in the year 1084 (C.E). Without a shadow of doubt it can be said that Sanaii must have been one of the greatest mystical poets of all times, and the person much admired and loved by Mowlavi to the extent that caused him to remember Sanai in the poem outlined above. His famous book, "Hadighatol-Haghighat" (Garden of Truth) has always been considered a classic handbook for the mystics since it was first written. Mowlavi was greatly inspired by him and deeply respected him as a mentor, and a man who had shone a light on the dark and complex road to union with God so called "The Path". Further more these two men shared a common path to reach the ultimate goal i.e. both underwent a major mid-life transformation before walking "The Path".

Sana'i, had actually started his career as a lyrical poet, and served mainly in the courts of the ruling monarchs as a eulogist and panegyrist, enjoying all that came his way of the worldly pleasures and not at all involved with mystical and spiritual values. However, during the mid years of his life he underwent a transformation, pulling him away from his earlier life style, and somehow was guided in to the "Gnostic Path". It is said that the transformation was initiated by a visit to a legendary mystic by the name of "Laykhar". Remembering Sanai's visits and friendship with other prominent poets, mystics and scholars who were in abundance in those days, and scattered throughout the greater Khorasan, it is plausible to assume that he had somehow already become attracted to the ideas and Doctrines of Sophism and Gnosticism. Sanai had spent a few years of his youth in the cities such as Balkh, Sarakhs, Hera't, and Neishabour. When in Balkh he also went on a pilgrimage to Mecca. There is a mention of this trip in one of his eulogies:

Time has now come that we should embark out with other Men, Leave our abode to go on a flight to "Saturn"!	گاه آن آمد که با مردان سوی میدان شویم یک ره از ایوان برون آییم و بر کیوان شویم

Then later on when he becomes home sick laments bitterly:

Missing Balkh while in Iraq, Alighted storm of fire in our heart	از فراق شهر بلخ اندر عراق از چشم دل گاه در آتش بودیم وگه در طوفان شویم

Rebirth of Persian Culture

After returning from Mecca, he resided in Balkh during which time he wrote his book "Karnameh Balkh" (Report of Balkh). He then went to Sarakhs, Merve and Neishabour. About the year 1140 (C.E) he went back to Ghazni. It was finally at this time that his transformation in to a full fledged mystic reached its pinnacle of perfection. His poetry reflects this new state of mind and purity of spirit containing some of the most beautiful Gnostic expressions of Divine love and submission.

Sanai was a great admirer of early 8th century mystic Bayazeed of Bastam. In this eulogy he shows his profound love and admiration for this one of the great founders of mysticism and Divine enlightenment:

Days are needed ere a handful of the wool from back of a sheep, Can provide the ass's halter, or the hermit's gabardine,	روزها باید که تا گردون گردان یک شبی عاشقی را وصل بخشد یا غریبی را وطن
Months are needed ere, by earth and water fed, the cotton-seed, Can provide the martyr's shroud, or clothe the fair raiment fine	هفته ها باید که یک مشت پشم از پشت میش زاهدی را خرقه گردد یا حماری را رسن
Lives are needed, ere by Nature's kindly fostering, the child, Can become a famous poet, or a scholar ripe and fine	ماه ها باید که تا یک پنبه دانه ز آب وگل شاهدی را حوله گردد یا شهیدی را کفن
Years are needed ere the sunshine, working on the primal rock, Yemen's blood-stone or Badakhshan's rubies can incarnadine.	سالها باید که تا یک کودکی از ذات طبع عالمی دانا شود یا شاعری شیرین سخن
Ages needs must pass before a Bu'-Wafa or an Uways Can arise from Adam's loins to glorify the Might Divine."	عمرها باید که تا یک سنگ خاره ز آفتاب در بدخشان لعل گردد یا عقیق اندر یمن

Chapter 5

قرن ها باید که تا از لطف حق پیدا
شود
بایزیدی در خراسان یا اویسی در
قرن

Sanai was one of the founders of a style in Persian poetry known as "Khorasani style". Some of the greatest Persian poets of sixth, seventh, and eight centuries have arranged their poetries in this particular style. His words are meticulously and beautifully chosen and are arranged in the lines of a poetry that flows smoothly full of profound feelings of love and ecstasy to convey to the reader a sense of exaltation reaching the farthest corners of Universe to extend into eternity. His eulogies, other than some which are in praise of monarchs and rulers are profound and overwhelming and based on stories and fables that always contain messages applicable to the common everyday life experiences and always with praise, submission, and Divine love.

Sanai's work, so far as it has come down to us, consists of seven mathnavies and a divan the former the Hadiqat'l-Haqiqat ("Garden of Truth") is the only one which is mostly known and celebrated ; the other six, : Tariqu't-Tahqiq ("Path of Verification"), Gharib-nama (Book of the stranger"), Sayrul-ebad ela'-Ma'dd ("Pilgrimage of [God's[servants to the Hereafter), Kar-nama Balkh (Report of "Balkh"), 'Eshgh- nama ("Book of Love, and Aghl-nama ("Book of Reason"), are very rare other than the "Sayrul- ebad" which has been published in Iran frequently. Sanai's divan has also been published frequently and is available. In all, perhaps some twelve thousand bayts distributed amongst the qasidas, tarji-bands, tarkib-bands, ghazals, and quatrains which compose the whole. The Hadiqa is much the most frequently met with of all Sanii's work.

The Hadiqa, dedicated to Bahramshah, Sultan of Ghazni,is moral and ethical rather than a purely mystical poem of about eleven thousand verses, divided in to ten books, the first in praise of God, the second in praise of prophet, the third on reason, the fourth on the excellence of knowledge, the fifth on carelessness, the sixth on the Heavens, and zodiacal Signs, the seventh on Philosophy, the eight on Love, the ninth on poet's own condition and circumstances, and the tenth in praise of Bahramshah, Sultan of Ghazni. The poem is written in a halting and not very attractive metre, and far inferior to the mathnavi of Jallaled-Din Mowlavi. The following parable, illustrating the impossibility that man should be able to form more than a partial and distorted conception of God, may be taken as, on the whole, a favorable specimen:-

About the company of blind men and the characteristics of the elephant:

Not far from Ghur once stood a city tall Whose denizens were sightless one and all?	بود شهری بزرگ در حد غور وندران شهر بودند مردمان کور
A certain Sultan once, when passing nigh, Had pitched his camp upon the plain hard by,	پادشاهی در آن مکان بگذشت لشگر آورد وخیمه زد بر دشت
Wherein to prove his splendor, rank and state, Was kept an elephant most huge and great.	داشت پیلی بزرگ با هیبت از پی جاه وحشمت وصولت
Then in the townsmen's minds arose desire, To know the nature of this creature dire.	مردمان را ز بهر دیدن پیل آرزو خواست زان چنان تهویل
Blind delegates by blind electorate Were therefore chosen to investigate	چند کور را از میان آن کوران بر پیل آمدند از آن عوران
The beast, and each, by feeling trunk or limb, Strove to acquire an image clear of him.	تا بدانند شکل و هیبت پی هر یکی تازیان در آن تعجیل
Thus each conceived a visionary whole, And to the phantom clung hear and soul.	آمدند وبدست میسودند زانکه از چشم بی بصر بودند
When to the city the were come again, The eager townsmen flocked to them a main.	هر یکی را به لمس بر عضوی اطلاع افتاد بر جزوی
	هریکی صورت محالی بست دل وجان در پی خیالی بست
	چون بر اهل شهر باز شدند برشان دیگران فراز شدند

Each one of them-wrong and misguided all-
Was eager his impression to recall,

Asked to describe the creature's size and shape,
They spoke while round about them, all agape,

Stamping impatiently, their comrades swarm
To hear about the monster's shape and form,

Now for his knowledge each inquiring weight
Must trust to touch, being devoid of sight,

So he who'd only felt the creature's ear,
On being asked, "How does its heart appear?

"Mighty and terrible; at once replied,
"Like a carpet, hard and flat and wide!'

Then he who on his trunk had laid his hand
Broke in:" Nay: nay! I better understand

It's like a water-pipe, I tell you true,
Hollow, yet deadly and destructive too,

While he who'd had but leisure to explore
The sturdy limbs that the great beast upbore,

Exclaimed, 'No, no! To all men be it known
It's like a column tapered to cone!'

آرزو کرد هر یکی ز ایشان
آنچنان گمرهان و بد کیشان

صورت و شکل پیل پرسیدند
وانچه گفتند جمله بشنیدند

آنکه دستش به گوش پیل رسید
دیگری حال پیل از او پرسید

گفت شکلی ست سهمناک عظیم
پهن و صعب و فراخ همچو گلیم

وانکه دستش رسید زی خرطوم
گفت گشتست مر مرا معلوم

راست چون ناودان میانه تهیست
سهمناک است و مایه تبهیست

وانکه را بود زیپیل ملموسش
دست و پای سطبر بر بوسش

گفت شکلش چنانکه مظبوط است
راست راست همچون عمود
مخلوط است

هر یکی دیده جزیی از اجزا
همگان را فتاده ظن خطا

هیچ دل را ز کل آگه نیست
علم با هیچ کور همراه نیست

جملگی را خیال های محال
کرده مانند غنفره به جوال

از خدایی خلایق آگه نیست

Each had but known one part, and no man all;　　　　　　　　عفلا را در این سخن ره نیست
Hence in to deadly error each did fall.

No way to know the all man's heart can find;
Can knowledge ever accompany the blind?

Fancies and phantoms vain as these, alack!
What else can you expect from a fool in the sack?

Naught of Almighty God can creatures learn,
Nor even the wise the wise such mysteries discern."

The divan contains poetry of a far higher order than the Hadiqa; so much higher that one might almost be tempted to doubt whether the same author composed both, were it not for the unquestionable fact that seldom Persian poets excel in all forms of verse.

"Boast not dervish-hood when you still possess   worldly riches; (that is, the treasure of poverty for God's sake)

Neither rogue –like deck thy visage, nor like craven-heart repine.
Either woman-like adopt the toilet tricks of paint and scent,

Or like men approach the field, and cast the ball across the line, (Allusion is here made to the game of polo)

All that thou see, beyond thy lusts is heaven; clasp it to they soul

All that thou find short of God's is an idol; break it,   crash it fine!

Dance when you like the headman's carpet heart and soul lie beneath thy feet

Clap thy hands when earth and heaven in thy grasp thou dost confine!

From the bowers of meditation raise thy head that thou may see

Those who still, though slain, are living, rank in rank and line on line,

Wondrous is the zeal of faith, wherein, like candle, waxing faint,

By removal of thy head thy radiance doth brighter shine.

 For the Jew in this
arena fearless casts himself amain,

برگ بی برگی نداری لاف درویشی مزن
رخ چو عیاران نداری جان چو نامردان مکن

یا برو همچون زنان رنگی وبویی پیش گیر
یا چومردان اندر آی وگوی در میدان فکن

هر چه بینی جز هوا آن دین بود برجان نشان
هر چه یابی جز خدا ان بت بود در هم شکن

چون دل وجان زیر پایت نطع شد پا بکوب
چون دو کون اندردودستت جمع شد دستی بزن

سربرآر از گلشن تحقیق تا در کوی دین
کشتگان زنده بینی انجمن در انجمن

درد دین خود بولعجب دردیست کاندروی چوشمع
چون شوی بیمار بهترگردی از گردن زدن

اندر این میدان که خودرا می در اندازد جهود
وندر این مجلس که خودرا می بسوزد برهمن

And the Brahmin in this temple burns its idol at the shrine.

اینت بی همت شگرفی کو برون نآید زجان

وانت بی دولت سواری کو برون نآید زتن

هرخسی از رنگ گفتاری بدین ره کی رسد

درد باید عمر سوز و مرد باید گام زن

The following short ghazal is also by Sanaii:

"That heart that stands aloof from pain and woe
No seal or signature of love can show:

هر دل که قرین غم نباشد
از عشق در او خبر نباشد

Thy love, and Thy love I chose, and as for wealth,
If wealth be not my portion, be it so!

من عشق تو اختیار کردم
شاید زدرم در او خبر نباشد

For wealth, I wean, pertains to the world;
Never can the world and love together go!

زیرا که درم از این جهانست
جانان و جهان زهم نباشد

با دیدن رویت ای نگارین
گویی که غمست غم نباشد

So long as thou do dwell within my heart!
Never can my heart become the thrall of woe."

تا در دل من نشسته باشی
هرگز دل من دژم نباشد

پیوسته در آن بود سنایی
تا جز به تو متهم نباشد

And here is another specimen of Sanaii's lyrical verse:

Darling, my heart I gave to thee- good-night! I go

ترا دل دادم ای دلبر شبت خوش باد من رفتم

Thou know my heartfelt sympathy- good-night! I go,	تودانی با دل غمخور شبت خوش بادمن رفت
Should I behold thee never again it's right it's right I clasp this Hour of Parting tight- good night! I go	اگر وصلت بگشت از من روا دارم روا دارم بیردی نور روز و شب بدان زلف ورخ زیبا
With raven trees and visage clear, Enchantress dear, Hast made my daylight dark and drear; good-night!	زهی جادوز هی دلبر شبت خوش باد من رفتم به چهره اصل ایمانی به زلفان مایه کفری
O Light of faith thy face, thy hair, Like Doubt's Despair Both this and that yield	ز جور هر دو آفت گر شبت خوش باد من رفتم
torment rare- Good night! I go	میان آتش و آبم از این معنی مرا بینی
Therefore 'twixt Fire and water me Thou thus dost see Lips parched and dry, tear-raining eye: Good night! I Go.	لبان خشگ و چشم تر شبت خوش بادمن رفتم
I was content my love just with news of you , Was this too much to ask for? Good night!I go	بدان راضی شدم جانا که از حالم خبر پرسی از این آخر بود کمتر شبت خوش باد من رفتم

These specimens selected at random show grace, beauty and originality; and there are probably few unexplored treasures of Persian poetry that would yield to the diligent reader a richer store of gems:

Avicenna, The 10th Century (C.E)
Persian Scientist, philosopher & poet

Rebirth of Persian Culture

Aviceena was the most outstanding scientist, philosopher and physician that Iran has produced in the past one thousand years. He was a towering pillar who reached the peak of advancement for his time and centuries that came after him, in theoretical as well as practical sciences: Medicine, mathematics, astronomy, philosophy, poetry and even music. Aviceena wrote more than 450 books which formed, throughout history and up to late nineteenth century, a valuable part of the treasure of human knowledge.

Avicenna was born in the year 992 (C.E) in the village of Afshineh, a suburb of the city of Bokhara. He was named Hussein and was nicknamed "Ibn-Sina", some years later. He appeared at a time when Europe was tangled up in the religious fanaticism and bigotry of the dark ages. Holy Bible was the only book most Europeans, if not all were permitted to read, and that was in Latin. Almost all population lived as Serfs inside the Serfdom territories as peasants with no schooling whatsoever. During these dark times hawkers, barbers and peddlers knew more about medicine than the doctors who graduated the London school of Medicine. The church branded the healers and anybody who tried to cure diseases as magicians and would bring them to the Courts of Inquisition. Punishment would be burnt alive or smothered in the river. During those times attending schools was considered a sin, and going to the Islamic educational institutions of the east was punishable by hanging. The Catholic Church owned the body and soul of the parishioners and considered interfering in the health related issues of people a sinful act.

Eleventh century (C.E), was one of several centuries of the so called Dark Ages in the life of the peoples in the continent of Europe, and it was during this period that Avicenna shines on the horizon of Iranian scientific and cultural scene. Avicenna made valuable contributions to the advancement of science, medicine, and almost every field of human knowledge of his time. George Sartor considers him the most remarkable scientist in the East, and most famous. His two masterpieces, "Cannon of Medicine, an overview of all aspects of medicine that became a standard textbook at many medieval universities in Europe and remained in use as late as 1650, and "The Book of Healing", a vast scientific and philosophical Encyclopedia, are most well known of all of his works through the world. Of all 450 works that he has written in mathematics, medicine, philosophy, astronomy, alchemy, geography, psychology, Islamic theology, Greek philosophy, logic, geology, and poetry only about 220 exist.

Chapter 5

Avicenna created an extensive collection of work during what is commonly known as the Islamic Golden Age, in which the translations of Greco-Roman, Persian, and Indian texts were studied extensively. Greco-Roman (Mid-and Neo-platonic, and Aristotelian) texts by the Kindi school were commented, redacted and developed substantially by Islamic intellectuals who also built upon Persian and Indian mathematical system, astronomy, algebra, trigonometry and medicine. The Samanid dynasty in the eastern part of Persia, Greater Khorasan and central Asia as well as the Buyid dynasty in the western part of Persia and Iraq provided a thriving atmosphere for scholarly and cultural development. Under the Samanids, Bukhara rivaled Baghdad as a cultural capital of the Islamic world. Avicenna, Razi and Farabi had provided methodology and knowledge in medicine and philosophy. Other prominent scholars of the time with whom Avicenna had meetings and discussions were Rayhan Birooni, Abu Nasr Iraqui and Abu Sahl Masihi, amongst others.

During the few centuries known as The Dark Ages in Europe, the people in those countries were made to believe that the Earth was flat, were not allowed to read books other than Holy Bible, and that only in Latin. The continent of Americas was not yet discovered, schooling and learning were forbidden, the countries in the east of the Mediterranean and extending as far east as central Asia, were flourishing with advancement of knowledge in all fields of human intellect. Great scientists, philosophers, poets and writers were surfacing through out the lands and provinces were mainly under the rule of Abbasian calliphs, but internally independent; mainly Samanids, Ghaznvis, and Seljuqes. It was during this time that as it was said before Avicenna was born in the province known then as Greater Khorasan.

The 11th century genius was only ten years old when he had already memorized literary and scientific texts, including Koran. He had learned philosophy, logic, geometry, history, and theology. He started learning Medicine when he was fourteen. He was not yet eighteen, when he was called to the Samanid court to attend to an illness that the Samanid king was suffering from, and other physicians had failed to cure.

It is sad, and regretful, but worth remembering that this brilliant scientist has been introduced to the world throughout centuries, as an "Arab", while everyone knew that he was born in Greater Khorasan, he spoke Farsi dari, and none of the members of his family were "Arab". His true nationality was falsified because, Persian Empire, at the time, had been invaded by Arabs, and also because he spoke, read and wrote Arabic fluently. The same falsification of national identity was done to all Iranian scientists, and intellectuals such as Razi, Farabi, Birooni, Ghazali, Kharazmi, even poets, and philosophers as well as many others, such as Mowlavi (Rumi). It should be pointed out that Avicenna lived his life almost entirely in Iranian cities like Neishabour, Rey, Isfahan, and Hamadan where he he has been buried..

Here is part of this so called"Arab" autobiography written in his ow words, and in fluent Farsi:
"My father, Abdollah, was from the people of Balkh, (A city in Khorasan). He moved to Bokhara during the reign of Noah, son of King Mansoor. The Samanid. Bokhara was at that time one of Iranian largest cities. My father was employed by the Royal Samanid court, in a clerical position and was assigned to the town of Afshaneh near the city of Bokhara. It was there that my father married my mother. My mother's name was Setareh. I was born in the year 992 (C.E). My parents named me Hussein. Some time later my father moved to Bokhara where they put me under the care of teachers to be taught Koran, and literal arts. I was ten years old when I became proficient in Koran, and literature. My teachers were amazed at my learning abilities.

It was at this time that a man by the name of Abdollah came to Bokhara. He was a learned man; he knew a lot about the various branches of knowledge of his time. My father hired him to be my in-house tutor. When Natel arrived at our house, I had already had another teacher by the name of Ismaiil Zahed, who was teaching me Jurisprudence, and I was considered his best student. I had already excelled in the technique of "Debating" which was very popular amongst the learned intellectuals of that time. Natel taught me Logic, and Geometry, and because he found me to be a very smart boy, he recommended to my father that he should not allow me to follow a carrier other than in science, and encouraged me to do the same. I persisted in getting the best education possible, and I would excel in any thing that he would teach me. In some instances I would improve over him too. When Natel left Bokhara,I continued my studies in Theology and Natural sciences. Before long I became interested in Medicine. I read and reviewed the writings of physicians of older times. I did not find Medicine to be particularly a hard science and made great progress in it fast. I had become so successful in it that great physicians of my time would come to me for guidance, help, and to learn. While I would attend to the needs of my patients, I would continue to study other sciences. I spent a great deal of time studying philosophy almost day and night. Later on I devoted my time to Theology, and started to read Aristotle's book on

Chapter 5

Metaphysics, but was not able to understand it. I read it a second time, and continued to read it forty times. By then I had it memorized completely, but still could not understand it. I was beginning to despair, saying to myself that there is no hope of success in this subject. One afternoon I was passing through the Booksellers Bazzar. A man was passing me by with a book in his hand offering it for sale. He persuaded me to buy it. "Metaphysics", by Abu Nasr Farabi. I bought the book. When I reached my home, I sat to read it. Because I had already memorized all that was there to learn about "Metaphysics", reading that book helped me to understand all the difficulties that I had with that subject; understand everything that I could not understand before.

This was the year 1009 (C.E) and I was 17 at this time. When I was 18, Noah, son of king Mansoor, became ill. The physicians were unable to cure his illness, and because I had made a name for myself at the time as a physician, they invited me to the royal court and asked permission from Noah to allow me to try and cure his illness. I attended to his illness and cured him. Noah permitted me to use his library where I found many books there that most people had never even heard of them. This helped a great deal, I benefited tremendously. Some time later my father passed away and that changed my life entirely. I left Bokhara and went to the city of Gorganaj in Kharazm. There I was welcomed and was received warmly by the Governor. I had also the opportunity to write a few books there. Previously when I was in Bokhara, I had written a few books too. At this time the world around us underwent adverse changes. I left and travelled hopelessly from city to city until finally was able to settle in Gorgan. I stayed there for sometime and completed writing a few more books."

Avicenna suffered great ups and downs during the course of his life. From holding Cabinet position to imprisonment, from holding high positions in the government to exile and being forced to travel the deserts aimlessly in search of hiding. He had experienced it all during a short life span of 58. Abu-Obeid Jozani one of the most outstanding scientists of that time who was a student of Avicenna and also a close friend accompanied him in all his travels. He narrates, in his memoires, that his mentor and teacher at one time travelled to the city of Rey in the foothills of Alborz Mountains to the court of Majdol-Doleh Dailami who was suffering from Melancholy to cure him of his illness. After that Avicenna travelled to the city of Ghazvin and from there to the city of Hammadan, where he was appointed a Minister in the cabinet of Shamsol-Doleh the governor general of Hammadan. It was during this time that

Rebirth of Persian Culture

Avicenna compiled his two famous masterpieces: the "Jurisprudence" in Medicine and "The Book of Healing" in Philosophy, Logic, Mathematics, and Natural Sciences. After the death of Shamsol-Doleh, because Avicenna refused to accept the position of Minister in the cabinet which was offered to him by Shamsol-Doleh's son, he was imprisoned on the false charges that he had collaborated with Alaol-Doleh the governor general of Isfahan. While he was in prison he compiled and wrote three books and after four and a half months, when released from jail, escaped Hammadan dressed as a wandering Dervish and traveled to Isfahan where he was warmly received by Alaol-Doleh and continued in his service as his advisor and companion.

While in Isfahan he wrote many other books and completed his masterpiece "The Book of Healing". In the year 1050 (C.E.) during a trip to Hammadan, accompanying his Master, Alaol-Doleh, he became ill with colic, and died in that city and was buried there. Avicenna did also write poetry, many in Arabic as well as 70 to 80 verses in Farsi, although probably not all were actually his. Here is one famous Quatrain by him;

Up from Earth's Center through the Seventh Gate, I rose and, on the throne of Saturn sate,	از قعر گل سیاه تا اوج زحل کردم همه مشگلات گیتی را حل
And many knots unraveled by the Road, But not the Master- knot of Human Fate.	بیرون جستم ز مکر هر قید وحیل هر بند گشاده شدمگر بند اجل

It is claimed by some researchers that this quatrain is written by Omar Khayam and not by Avicenna.

As it was said before Avicenna had also written a number of poetries in Arabic. The most remarkable and beautiful of all his poetries in Arabic is "Human Soul". A careful examination of this quatrain gives the reader an impression that Mowlavi (Rumi) might have been inspired by contents of this quatrain in his epilogue to "Divan Mathnavi, where he writes:

Though plainly cometh my wail, It is never bared to my mortal ken; As soul from body has no veil,	"تن ز جان و جان ز تن مستور نیست

Chapter 5

Yet is the soul unseen of men." لیک کس را دید جان دستور
نیست"

Here is an English translation of Avicenna's famous poem in Arabic "The Human Soul":

It descended upon thee from out of the regions above,
That exalted, ineffable, glorious, heavenly dove,

It was concealed from the eyes of all those who its nature would ken,
Yet it wears not a veil, and is ever apparent to men,

Unwilling it sought thee, and joined thee, and yet, though it grieve,
It is like to be still more unwilling thy body to leave

It resisted and struggled, and would not be tamed in haste,
Yet it joined thee, and slowly grew used to this desolate waste,

Till, forgotten at length, as I wean, were its haunts and its troth,
In the heavenly gardens and groves, which to leave it was loath,

Until, when it entered the D of its downward Descent,
And to earth, to the C of its centre, unwillingly went,

The (I) of Infirmity smote it, and lo, it was hurled,
Midst the sign-posts and ruined abodes of this desolate world,

It weeps, when it thinks of his home and the peace it possessed,
With tears welling from his eyes without posing or rest,

And with plaintive mourning it broods like one bereft,
Over such trace of his home as the fourfold wind have left,

Thick nets detain it, and strong is the cage whereby,
It is held from seeking the lofty and spacious sky,

Until, when the hour of its homeward flight draws near,
And it is time for it to return to its ampler sphere,

Rebirth of Persian Culture

It carols with joy, for the veil is raised, and it spies,
Such things as it cannot be witnessed by waking eyes,

On a lofty height, doth it warble its songs of praise?
(For even the lowliest being doth knowledge raise),
And so it returns, aware of all hidden things,

In the universe, while no stain to its garment clings
Now why from its perch so high was it cast like this

To the lowest Nadir's gloomy and drear abyss
Was it God who cast it forth for some purpose wise?

Concealed from the keenest seeker's inquiring eyes,
Then is its descent a discipline wise but stern,

That the things that it hath not heard it thus may learn,
So it is she, whom Fate doth plunder, until her star,

Like a gleam of lightning which over the meadows shone,
And, as though it never had been, in a moment.

Avicenna wrote extensively on early Islamic philosophy, especially the subjects of logic, ethics, and metaphysics, including treaties named "Logic & Metaphysics". Most of his work was written in Arabic, then the language of science in Middle-East; thus the false identity given him: "An Arab", by which he has unfortunately been recognized even by Europeans throughout the centuries.

Avicenna also wrote a lot of his work in Persian. Of linguistic significance even to this day are a few books that he wrote in pure Persian, including his autobiography where he clearly tells us where he was born, lived his childhood, got his education, posts and ranks that he held, etc. Also in particular "The Daneshnameh Ala" a book in philosophy written for and dedicated to Alaol-Doleh, the governor of Isfahan, in central Iran, whom he served for a few years. Avicenna's commentaries on Aristotle often were critical of the Greek philosopher. In the medieval Islamic World due to Avicenna's successful reconciliation between Aristotelian and Neopolitanian philosophies, Avicenna eventually became the leading school of Islamic philosophy by the 12th century, with Avicenna becoming a central authority on philosophy. Avicenna was also influential in medieval Europe, particularly his doctrines on the nature of the soul and his existence-essence distinction, along with the debate and censure that they raised in scholastic Europe. This was particularly the case in Paris, where Avicenneanism was later proscribed in 1210. Nevertheless, his psychology and theory of knowledge influenced William of Auvergne, Bishop of Paris and Albertus Magnus, while his metaphysics had an impact on the thought of Thomas Aquinas.

Abulghassem Hassan Ahmad (Onsori), 10th century Persian (C.E) poet

Onsori is one of the most prominent poets and writers of the 10th century. He was the poet laureate at the royal court of Sultan Mahmood Ghaznavi, heading a long retinue of famous poets in the king's court. He acted also as a confidant and advisor to the monarch and was well liked and admired by him. Little is known of his life. His Divan does not contain a large number of poems, but although few in number but extremely high in quality. He must have been born in mid 10th century (C.E) because, as narrated by Labibi, his contemporarian, at the time of the invasion of the famous Temple of Sumenat in India by Sultan Mahmood, he was in his senior years.

Dolatshah Samarghandi has written a short biography of this outstanding poet:

"His merits and talent are plainer than the sun. He was the chief of the poets of Sultan Mahmood's time, and possessed many virtues beyond the gift of song, so that by some he is styled,The Sage (Hakim). It is said that four hundred eminent poets were in constant attendance on Sultan Mahmud.
Of all those Master Onsori was the chief and leader, whose disciples they acknowledged themselves. At the Sultan's court he combined the functions of poet and favorite courtier, and was constantly celebrating in verse the wars and powers of the King. In a long panegyric of some hundred and eighty couplets he has recorded in meter all the Sultan's wars, battles and conquests. Finally Sultan bestowed on him letters-patent investing him with Laureateship in his dominions, and commanded that wherever, throughout his empire, there might be a poet or writer of elegance, he should submit his productions to "Onsori", who, after examining its merits and defects, should submit it to the Royal Presence. So Onsori's daily receptions became the goal of all poets, and

thereby there accrued to him much influence and wealth. Ferdowsi, in his epic, The Shahnameh, bestows on him an eloquent encomium, as will be set forth in its proper place; though God knows whether it is true!"

This last saving clause applies to a great deal of Dowlatshah's information, which is more circumstantial than correct in many cases. As a sample of Onsori's verse he chooses a panegyric (qasida), of the kind known as "Question and Answer" (sualu jawab), of which, since it serves to give an idea of his verse it is attached here. This poem is in praise of Sultan Mahmood's brother, the Amir Nasr Suboktakin, Governor of Khurasan:

"To each inquiry which my wit could frame last night, from those fresh lips an answer came,

Said I, 'One may not see thee save at night;
'When else,Said she, 'would'st see the Moon's clear light?

Said I, 'The sun doth fear thy radiant face;
Said she, 'When thou art here, sleep comes apace!

Said I, 'With hues of night stain not the day!'
Said she, stain not with blood thy cheeks, I pray!'

Said I, 'This hair of thine right fragrant is! '
Said she, 'Why not? 'Tis purest ambergris!'

Said I, 'Who caused thy cheeks like fire to shine? '
Said she, 'That one who grilled that heart of thine.'

Said I, 'Mine eyes I cannot turn from thee!'
'Who from the mihrab turns from thee?'

Said I, 'Thy love torments me! Grant me grace! '
Said she, 'In torment is the lover's place!'

Said I, 'Where lies my way to rest and peace?'
'Serve our young prince,'said she. 'Without cease!'

Said I, 'Mir Nasr, our Faith's support and stay?'

Chapter 5

Said she, 'That same, whom despot kings obey!

Said I,' what share is his of wit and worth? ,
'Nay, 'she replied, 'our knowledge they transcend! ,

Said I, who are his messengers of war? ,
Said she, 'the spears that are near, the darts afar,

Said I, Because of age is he sore in sooth? ,
Said she, 'Yes, more than we live we need youth!,

Said I, 'him been seen before?'
Said she, 'Not even in the books of yore,

Said I, 'What do you say of his hand?' Said she,
'Like a mirage that seems beside the sea!

Said I, 'He harkens to the beggar's cries;
Said she, 'With gold and garments he replies,

Said I, 'What's left for men of gentle birth?
'Honor, 'she answered, 'rank, and power, and worth!'

'What deems thou his arrows? Questioned I:
'Meteors and shooting stars, she made reply

Said I, His sword and he who stirs its ire?
'This quicksilver, said she, 'and that the fire!

Said I, Lies aught beyond his mandate's calls?
Said she, 'If aught, what into ruin falls,

Said I, 'How false his foes! She answered, yes,
More false than false Musalman are they!

'What lands, 'said I, 'are left, were mine the might,
Were his, 'said she, 'what's left, can never be right.

Said I, 'Then does his bounty cause no stint?

Said she, 'of time, in cloth-mill and in mint,

Said I, 'what nobler is than all beside-'
'-Hath God vouchsafed to him; my friend replied,

Said I, 'this spacious realm where holds the King?
Said she, 'Beneath his stirrups and his ring.

Said I, 'From praising him I will not rest,
Said I, 'Long life, and Fortune ever young

Ba'ba' Taher Oryan of Hamadan, 11th Century
Persian Poet & Gnostic

Ba'ba' Taher Oryan is one of the best known and most popular poets in the history of Persian literature in particular amongst the native Iranians. His poetry which is written in a dialect of Persian (Folk Songs, and melodies) has been extremely popular throught Iran by almost all Iranian generations. He is most famous for his du-bayti (double distiches), exhibiting in melodious and flowing language sincerity and spirituality with profound philosophical undertones. His poetry is also of paramount importance because incorporates a large number of local dialects and vocabulary used by ethnic Persians scattered throughout the country in far off villages and tribesmen.

Little is known about Ba'ba's early years of life. Even his exact date of birth is not known by certainty. He probably spent a major portion of his life in Hamadan, and must have travelled extensively throughout the country and lived amongst local people and in particular various tribesmen. His byname, Oryan (the naked) suggests that he was also a Gnostic. This fact is particularly evident from the Gnostic intones inherent in most of his poetries. A number of biographers have testified that Ba'ba' was indeed a man of purity, faith, strong moral virtues, and spiritual devotion.

The following story mentioned in 'Ra'hat-ol-Sodoor" bears testimony to his character, beliefs and high moral principles as well as the great respect that he enjoyed amongst the Iranian nation all the way up the social higher archey including the ruling Monarch Toghrol Beig. Story goes to tell that the Monarch arrived in Hamadan, during one of his visits to that city, enroute, he noticed three elders. These three were the elders of (The Sufis), Ba'b'a Ta'her,

Chapter 5

Ba'ba' Jafar, and Sheikh Hamsha'. Now there is by the gate of Hamada'n a little mountain called Khadir, and there they were standing. The Sultan's eyes fell upon them; he halted the vanguard of his army, alighted, approached, and kissed their hands. Ba'ba' Taher, who was somewhat unimpressed by the entourage said to him, O Turk, what wilth thou do with God's people?' 'Whatever thou bidest me; replied the Sultan. 'Do [rather] that which God biddest thee; replied Ba'ba'; '"Veryly God enjoieth Justice and Well-doing." The Sultan wept and said, 'I will do so.' Ba'ba' took his hand and said, dost thou accept this from me?' 'Yes,'replied the Sultan. Baba' had on his finger the top of a broken ibrigh (pitcher) with which he he had for years performed his ablusions. This he took off and placed on the Sultan's finger, saying: 'Thus do I place on thy hand the empire of the world; be thou just!' The Sultan used to keep this amongst his smulets, and, when a battle was impending, used to put it on his finger. Such was his pure faith and sincere belief; for in the Moslem religion there was none more devout or watchful than he."

The meeting here described probably took place abou1069 (C.E) or 1072 (C.E) so that we may safely reject the date 1032 (C.E) assigned to Ba'ba' Taher's death by Reza-gholi khan Hedayat in the Riyazul-Arefin. The anecdote cited above is quite in character both with the little we know of Ba'ba' Ta'her from other sources, and with the consideration and respect still shown by the highest and noblest in the Islamic countries to dervishes with a reputation for sanctity.

Ba'ba' Taher poems are recited to the present day all over Iran accompanied by Setar, three stringed viol or lute. Their origin and style are very old and probably come from the pre-islam era of Sassanian dynasty or even older.They are basically folk songs and melodies in Pahlavi, Kurdi, luri and Hamadani dialects that were re-encarnated by Ba'ba' Taher, in his continual search for Persion ancient melodies and songs.The quatrains of B'ba' Taher have a more amorous and mystical connotations rather than philosophical. His do-bayties are a type of Persian quatrains, which some scholars regard as having affinities with mid-Pahlavi verses. Classical Persian music is based on Persian poetry and Ba'ba' Ta'her's poems are the weight that carries a major portion of this music. His poetry is the basis for Dastgahe-Shoor and in particular Dashtestani, Choopani and Deylaman. Also attributed to him is a work by the name; Kalamat-Ghesar, a collection of nearly 400 apphorisms in Arabic, which has been the subject of commentaries, one allegedly by Ein ol-Ghozat Hamadani. One example of such a saying is when Ba'ba' tie knowledge with gnosis: Knowledge is the guide to gnosis, and when gnosis has come the vision of knowledge lapses and there remains only the movements of knowledge to gnosis; "knowledge is the crown of the gnostic, and gnostic the crown of knowledge"; whoever witnesses what is decreed by the God remains motionless and powerless.

Here are a number of Do-Beyties (short quatrains by B'aBa'Taher):

Beneath the tyranny of eyes and heart I cry, For all that the eyes see the heart stores up I will fashion me a pointed sword of steel Put out mine eyes, and so set free my heart.	ز دست دیده و دل هر دو فریاد که هر چه دیده بیند دل کند یاد بسازم خنجری نیشش ز فولاد زنم بر دیده تا دل گردد آز
O Lord! This heart of mine afflicts me sore, I weep this heart of mine both day and night, Often I grieve but for my grief; O Some-one Rid me of this heart that I may be free.	خداوندا ز بس زارم از این دل شو و روزام در آزارم از این دل ز بس نالیدم از نالیدنم کس ز موبستون که بیزارم از این دل
When Trees to grow beyond their boundries dare, They cause the Gardners much anxious care, Down to their very roots they must be pruned, Though Pearls and Rubies are the fruits they bear.	هر اون باغی که وارش سربدربی مدامش باغبان خونین جگربی بباید کندنش از بیخ و از بن اگر بارش همه لعل و گهربی

Here is sample poetry in original Pahlavi/Persian:

who am I, and of what company,
How long shall tears of blood thus blind mine
eyes?
When other refuge fails,I will turn to thee,
And if Thou fails me, wither shall I go?

خداوندا که بوشم با که بوشم
مژه با اشگ خونین تا که بوشم
همم کز در برانن سوته آیم
تو کم از در برانی واکه بوشم

"I am that sea and have come into a bowel,
I am that dot and have come in to a letter,
In every thousand one straight- as-alef (alef-
qadd) appears,
I am that straight one, for I came in a
thousand.

من آن بحرم که در ظرف آمدستم
من آن نقطه که در حرف آمدستم

"Art thou a lion or a leopard, O Heart, O
heart?
That thou warres ever with me, O heart,O
heart
Fall thou into my hands, I will spill thy blood,
To see what color it is O' heart, O' heart"

مگرشیرو پلنگی ای دل ای دل
به مو دایم به جنگی ای دل ای دل
اگردستم فتی خونت بریزم
بوینم تا چه رنگی ای دل ای دل

"Black is my lot, my fortune is overturned
Ruined are my fortunes, for my luck is
brought low,
A thorn, a thistle I, on the mountain of Love,
For my heart's sake, drown it in blood O
Lord!"

سیه بختم که بختم سرنگون بی
توه روژم که روژم واژگون بی
شدم خاروخس کوه محبت
زدست دل که یارب غرق خون بی

My heart is dainty as a drinking cup
I fear for it whenever I have a sigh;
It is not strange my tears are as blood,
I am a tree whose roots are set in blood

دلی نازک بسان شیشه ام بی
اگرآهی کشم اندیشه ام بی
سرشگم گربودخونین عجب نیست
موآن دارم که درخون ریشه ام بی

"My beautiful thou hast my heart and soul,
Thou hast my inner and my outer self,
I know not why I am so very sad,
I only know that thou hold'st the remedy

نگارینا دل و جونم ته دیری همه
پیدا و پنهونم ته دیری ندونم مو که
این درد از که دیری
همی دونم که درمونم ته دیری

"Thy tangled curls are scattered o'er thy face,

مسلسل زلف بر روریته دیری

Rebirth of Persian Culture

Mingling the roses with hyacinths;
But part as under those entangled strands,
On every hair thou'it find there hangs a heart.

گل و سنبل بهم آویته دیری
پریشون چون کری آن تار زلفون
به هر تاری دلی آویته دیری

"Briar and thorn beset thy way, o Heart,
Beyond the Dome of Heaven is thy road,
If thy are able, the thy very skin,
Cast off from thee, and lighten thus thy load."

دلا راه تو پر خاک و خسک بی
گذرگاه تو بر اوج فلک بی
گر از دستت برآیو پوست از تن
بیفکن تا که بارت کمترک بی

"O heart of stone, thou burnst not for me,
That stone burns not, is not indeed so strange
But I will burn till I inflame thy heart.
For fresh-cut logs are difficult to burn alone"

دلت ای سنگدل بر ما نسوجه
عجب نبود اگر خارا نسوجه
بسوجم تا بسوجونم دلت را
در آتش چوب تر تنها نسوجه

"When thou art away, mine eyes o'er
flows with tears,
Baren is the tree of hope when thou' rt
away,
Without thee, night and day, in a solitary
corner,
I sit till life itself come to an end

بی تو اشگم از مژگان تر آیو
بی تو نخل امیدم بی برآیو
بی تو در کنج تنها شو و روز
نشینم تا که عمرم بر سر آیو

"Without you in the garden, Lord, may no
flower bloom?
Or blooming, may none taste its sweet
perfume,
So, when my heart expand when thou are not
nigh,
T was vain! My heart's grief nought could
turn to joy
"What blundering Moth in the entire World
like me?
What madman like me in the Universe?
The very Serpents and the Ants have nests,
But I-poor wretch-no ruin shelters me.

به گلشن بی تو گل هرگز مرویا
وگر رویا کسش هرگز مبویا
بی شادی بی تو هرکس لو گشایه
لوش از خون دل هرگز مشویا

چومو یک سونه دل پروانه ای نه
جهان را همچومو دیوانه ای نه
همه مارون و مورون لانه دیرن
من بیچاره را ویرانه ای نه

Chapter 5

Baba Taher is buried in Hamadan. His tomb is located near the northern entrance of the city in the north west of Iran. The structure which is surrounded by shrubs, flowers and tall trees consists of twelve external towers which enclose the main tower housing the tomb.

Sheykh Abu Said Abolkheir, 10th century Persian poet and mystic

Abu Saiid is one Iran's most famous and admired mystic poets. He was born in the village of Mahineh, a suberb of the city of Abivard of Greater Khorasan in the year 979 (C.E) and passed away in the year 1062 (C.E) at his birthplace where he is buried. His early years of education were in the cities of Marv and Sarakhs. His father was a herbalist and physician with great interest in Sufism. He held frequent Sufi gatherings at his home at which the young Saiid got his early inspiration and became deeply attracted to the doctrine of Sufism. He then travelled to Neishabour where he remained for a few years and frequently travelled to other cities where he met the prominent Sufi Sheykhs and spent time with famous teachers such as Sheykh Abulfazl Sarakhsi and Abulabas Amoli getting his Sufi training. He practiced Sufism in his home town of Mihane. As was said before he spent few years in Neishabour before returning To Mihane to commence teaching and practice Sufism at his own Khaneghah (Sufi center). During his trips throughout Khorasan he angered a number of Sufi leaders who were in direct opposition from his views, however it was not long before they all came to accept him and with such acceptance the opposition died down and Abu-Saiid established himself as one of the most revered and admired Sufis of all times with many followers throughout the vast land of the greater Khorassan.

His mysticism is a typical example of Khorasani school of Sufism. He extracted the essence of the teachings of the past Sufis of this school and to some extent other schools too and expressed them in a simpler and deeper sense without the use of philosophy. He held a great reverence for other Sufis before him like Bayazid Bastami, Mansoor Halaj, and in particular Abul Hassan Kharaghani, whom he visited and was greatly impressed and influenced by him.

Abu-Saiid has been described by Eth'e who has done extensive research on him as the first master of theosophical verse, the first to popularize the quatrain as a vehicle of religious, mystic, and philosophic thought and to make it" the focus of all mystic-pantheistic enlightenments and irradiations," and the first "to give the presentations and forms of the Sufi doctrine those fantastic and gorgeous hues which thenceforth remained typical of this kind of poetry"

Love came and flew like blood in my veins,	دوست آمد وشد چوخونم اندر رگ وپوست
Emptied me of myself and filled me with the "Beloved"	تا کرد مرا تهی وپرکرد زدوست
Each part of my being "It" conquered	اجزای وجودم همگی دوست گرفت
Now a mere name is left of me and the rest is" Beloved".	نامیست زمن برمن وباقی همه دوست

Abu-Saiid was a contemporary of Aviceena and is said to have come into personal relations with him. When they separated after their first meeting, according to the popular story, the mystic said ,"What I see he knows," while the philosopher said, "What I know he sees". But Eth'e has shown that (as, indeed, was to be expected) they were on important points of belief (e.g., the efficacy of faith without works) in direct antagonism.

Abu-saiid is credited with pre-eminent importance in the history of Persian Mysticism-an importance hardly recognized even by his own countrymen, who, following the well-known saying of their greatest theosophical writer Jalaled-Din Mowlavi (Rumi), commonly reckon Sana'I and Atta'r, both of whom were subsequent to Abu-Said, as the first and second of their three arch-mystagogues. Dr.Eth'e has amply shown in the selection of Abu-Said's quatrains which he published, all the characteristics of Persian mystical thought and diction now for the first time present themselves in a combination which has ever since remained typical of Persian, Turkish, and Indian Sufi poets. The following selection should clearly and amply demonstrate this

"O Thou whose visage makes our world so fair,	ای روی تومهر عالم آرای همه وصل توشب وروزتمنای هم

Whose union, night and day, is all man's prayer?
Are kinder unto others? Woe is me!
But woe to them if my anguish they share!

گر با دگران به زمنی وای به من
وربا همه کس هم چومنی وای همه

"In search of martyrdom the ghazis go
To fight Faith's battles; do they then not know
That martyred lover's higher rank, as slain
By hand of Friend, and not by hand of foe

قاضی بره شهادت اندررگ وپوست
غافل که شهید عشق عاقلتر از اوست
فردای قیامت این بدان کی ماند
کان کشته دشمنست و این کشته دوست

"Let no one of Thy boundless Grace despair;
Your own elect shall ever upward fare;
The mote, if once illuminated by Thy sun,
The brightness of a thousand suns shall share

از لطف تو هیچ بنده مقبول نشد
مقبول تو جز مقبل جاوید نشد
مهرت بکدام ذره پیوست دمی
کان ذره به از هزار خورشید نشد

١

"Till Mosque and college fall beneath Ruin's ban,
And Doubt and Faith be interchanged in man,
How can the order of the Qalandars (Dervish),
Prevail, and rise up one true Musulman?

تا مدرسه ومناره ویران نشود
این کارقلندری به سامان نشود
تا ایمان وکفر ایمان نشود
یک بنده حقیقتا مسلمان نشود

"Sir, blame me not if I drink, or spend
My life in strife of Wine and Love
When sober, I with rivals sit; but when
Beside myself, I am beside the friend."

منع مکن ای خواجه اگر می نوشم
در عاشقی وباده پرستی کوشم
تا هوشیارم نشسته با اغیارم
چون بی هوشم با یار هم آغوشم

"When I at length your love's Embrace shall claim
To glance at Paradise I'd deem it shame,
While to a Thee-less Heaven were I called,
Such Heaven and Hell to me would seem the same

درد وزخم ار زلف تودر چنگ آید
از حال بهشتیان مرا ننگ آید
وربی توبه صحرای بهشتم خوانند

صحرای بهشت بر دلم تنگ آید

"Brahmin, before that cheek rose-tinted bow
Of fourteen-year-old beauty, for I vow
That, failing eyes God-seeing, to adore
Fire is more fit than to adore a cow!"

ای بر همن آن عذار چون لاله برست
رخسار نگار چهارده ساله برست
گر چشم خدای بین نداری باری
خورشید پرست شونه گوساله پرست

The verses above illustrate most of the salient peuliarities of Sufi thought and diction. There is the fundamental conception of God as not only Almighty and All-good, but as the sole source of Being and Beauty, and, indeed, the one Beauty and the one Being, "in whom is submerged whatever becomes non-apparent, and by whose light whatever is apparent is made manifest."Closely connected with this is the symbolic language so characteristic of these, and, indeed, of nearly all mystics, to whom God is essentially" The friend, The Beloved. "And "The Darling"; the ecstasy of mediating on Him "The Wine" and "the Intoxication"; His self-revelations and Occultation, "The Face" and "The Night-black Tresses," and so forth. There is also the exaltation of the Subjective and Ideal over the Objective and Formal, and the spiritualization of religious obligations and formulae, which has already been noticed amongst the Isma'illis from whom, though otherwise strongly divergent, the Sufis probably borrowed it. Last, but not least, is the broad tolerance which sees Truth in greater or less measure in all Creeds; recognizes that "the Ways unto God are as the number of the souls of men" and, with the later Hadiidh, declares that "any shrine is better than self-worship"

Innumerable sayings and anecdotes of Abu Saiid are recorded by his diligent biographers. A very few examples of these must suffice. Being once asked to define Sufism, he said, "To lay aside what thou has in thy head (such as desires and ambitions), and to give away what thou has in thy hand and not to flinch from whatever that befalls thee". "The veil between God and His servant,"he observed in another occasion, "is neither earth nor heaven, nor the Throne nor the Footstool; thy selfhood and illusions are the veil, and when thou remove these thou has attained unto God." They described to him how one holy man could walk on the water, how another could fly in the air, and how a third in the twinkling of an eye transport oneself from one city to another. "The frog can swim and the swallow skim the water," he replied; "the crow and the fly can traverse the air, and the Devil can pass in a moment from East to West. These things are of no great account; he is a man who dwells amongst mankind, buys and sells, marries, and associates with his fellow-creatures, yet is never for a single moment forgetful of God".

It is said that one of Abu Saiid's favorite verses part of an Arabic poem was this:
"I would answer thy voice should thou call me, though over my body lay Heavy the earth of the grave-yard, and my bones were crumbled away".

To conclude, AbuSaiid's main focus of teaching is "liberation from self" which he considers to be the only obstacle in reaching God and to which he attributes all personal and social misfortunes. His biography indicates that he would never I or We, but instead they. This idea of selflessness appears as "Fotovat" which has a meaning very near to chivalry in his ethical teachings and as "Mallamat", a kind of selflessness before the Beloved which he considers a sign of perfect love in his strictly mystical teachings.

Both of these concepts in a certain sense are spiritual forms of warrior ethics. Despite their apparent simplicity he believed that their implementation require the grace of God and the guidance of a Sufi Sheikh or spiritual guide, and is impossible through personal efforts alone. His picture as portrayed in various Sufi writings is a particularly joyful one of continuous ecstasy. Other prominent Sufis such as Attar have mentioned him as their spiritual guide.

Abu Saiid had a great love for poetry to such an extent that he had requested the following verses be read at his funeral instead of verses from Holy Koran:

What   sweeter   than   this   in   the   world,
Friend met friend and the lover joined his Beloved,

That   was   all   sorrow,   this   is   all   joy,
Those were all words, this is reality.

Sheykh Moslehed-Din Saadi Shirazi, 11th Century Poet and Writer

The exceptionally rich treasure of Persian poetry glows with some of the most amazing and dazzling jewels. However one stands alone in a class by itself. The poet ,writer and thinker whose work is so different from any other writer in the more than twelve hundred years of Persian literature since its revival in the 9th and 10th centuries (C.E) during a time which one can rightly name the "Renaissance of Persian culture" after the Arab invasion of Iran. This truly shining star is Saadi Shirazi, who was born in Shiraz around 1324 (C.E). Sa'di is the most well-known Persian poet in the western world coming only second to the other famous poet Omar Kayam whose poetry was translated and published by Gerald Fitzgerald in Europe in the seventeen century.

When the United Nations Headquarters was established in Geneva Switzerland and moved to New York in later years a quotation by Saadi was recognized as the "most appropriate and fitting" to be engraved in the main hall of the building:

Of one Essence is the human race, Thus lay has the Creation put the Base!	بنی آدم اعضای یک پیکرند که در آفرینش ز یک گوهرند
One Limb impacted is sufficient, For all others to feel the Mace.	چو عضوی به درد آورد روزگار دگر عضو ها را نماند قرار
The Unconcerned with Other human's Plight, Are but Brutes with Human Face	تو کز محنت دیگران بی غمی نشاید که نامت نهند آدمی

The world thus honors Sa'di for his call that truly and uniquely breaks all barriers.

Chapter 5

Sa'di was born in Shiraz around the year 1324 (C.E). He came from a family who were mostly highly educated and well respected, descendents of outstanding socialites in Shiraz.

Little we know of Sa'di's early years of life other than the fact the he lost his father when he was very young and was brought up by an uncle of his mother. He describes this tragedy in a poem:

Protect thou the orphan whose father is dead; Brush the mud from his dress; ward all hurt from his head.	پدرمرده را سایه برسرفکن غبارش بیفشان وخارش بکن
Thou know not how hard his condition must be; When the root has been cut, is there life in the tree?	نه دانی چه بودش فرومانده سخت؟ بود تازه بی بیخ هرگز درخت؟
Cares not and kiss not a child of your own, When an orphan is present who is neglected and lonesome.	چو بینی یتیمی سرافکنده پیش مده بوسه بر روی فرزند خویش
If an orphan sheds tears, who his grief will assuage? If his temper should fail him, who cares for his rage?	یتیم ار بگرید که نازش خرد؟ وگر خشم گیرد که بارش برد؟
O see that he weeps not, for surely God's throne Doth quake at the orphan's most pitiful moan!	الا تا نگرید که عرش عظیم بلرزد همی چون بگرید یتیم
With infinite pity, with tender care, Wipe the tears from his eyes, brush dust from his hair.	برحمت بکن آبش ازدیده پاک به شفقت بیافشانش ازدیده خاک
No shield of parental protection his head, No shelters; be thou his protector instead!	اگر سایه خود برفت از سرش تو در سایه خویشتن پرورش

Rebirth of Persian Culture

When the arms of a father my neck could
enfold,

Then, was I crowned
like a monarch with gold.

من انگه سر تاجور داشتم
که سر در کنار پدر داشتم

If even a fly should upon me alight
Not one heart but many were filled with
affright,

اگر بر وجودم نشستی مگس
پریشان شدی خاطر چند کس

While now should men make me a captive
and thrall,
No friend would assist me or come to my
call.

کنون دشمنان گر برندم اسیر
نباشد کس از دوستانم نصیر

The sorrows of orphans full well can I
share,
Since I tasted in childhood the orphan's
despair"

مرا باشد از درد طفلان خبر
که در طفلی از سر برفتم پدر

After the death of Sa'di's father, Massoud-Ebn Masaleh Farsi was trusted with
the guardianship of Saadi who arranged for him to complete his elementary
education in Shiraz and then sent him to Baghdad to continue his higher
education at the famous Nezamiyeh College established years before by Khaje
Nezam-ol Molk, the then prime minister of Malekshah Saljughi. During his
stay in Baghdad, Saadi met and spent time with the famous Iranian Mystic
and philosopher Sheykh Shahabe-Din Sohrevardi. Some of Saadi's writings
reflect the views of Sohrevardi and clearly indicating that he was influenced
and impressed by the Sheykh's deep piety and unselfish love of his fellow-
men. There is a piece of poetry which points to this relationship:

My spiritual leader
"Shahab
Gave me two advice while sailing on
water,

مرا شیخ دانای مرشد شهاب
دو اندرز فرمود بر روی آب

First; when with the crowed, do not be a
pessimist,

یکی آنکه در جمع بدبین مباش
دگر آنکه در نفس خود بین مباش

Chapter 5

Second; in spirit, do not be self-conceited,

He who suffers much in service of God, Shall always be respected as a "Noble One",	به آزادمردی ستودش کسی که در راه حق رنج بردی بسی
My hopes and trust are in God, For it is a mistake to do otherwise.	امیدی که دارم به فضل خداست که بر سعی خودتکیه کردن خطاست

During this time he also profited by the teachings and instructions of another eminent man Shamsu'd-Din Abu'l-faraj ibnu'l-Jawzi.

Sa'di's trip to Baghdad marks the beginning of the first three periods in his life, viz., the first period lasting until he was about 25 years old. Yet even during this period he made, as from a story in book 5 of "Golestan", the long journey to Kashghar. Even then as we learn from this story his fame had preceded him to this remote outpost in the north-east Asia, a fact notable not merely as showing that he had succeeded in establishing his reputation at the early age of twenty six.

The second period commenced with the unsettled conditions following the Mongol's invasion of Iran, which led him to leave Shiraz after his return there from Baghdad to wander abroad through Anatolia, Egypt, Syria and Iraq. To his departure from Shiraz he alludes in the following verses in the Preface to the Golastan:

"O knowest thou not why, an outcast and exile, In lands of the stranger a refuge I sought?	وجودم به تنگ آمد از جور تنگی شدم در سفر روزگاری درنگی
Disarranged was the world like the hair of a Negro When I fled from the Turks and the terror they frought,	برون جستم از تنگ ترکان چو دیدم جهان درهم افتاده چون موی زنگی
Though outwardly human, no wolf could surpass them In bloodthirsty rage or in sharpness of claw;	چو باز آمدم کشور آسوده دیدم ز گرگان بدر رفته آن تیز چنگی خط ماهرویان چومشگ تتاری سرزلف خوبان چودرج فرنگی

Though within was a man with the mien of an angel,
Without was a host of the lions of war,

At peace was the land when again I beheld it;
Even lions and leopards were wild but the name.

Like that was my country what time I forsook it,
Fulfilled with confusion and terror and shame:

Like this in the time of 'Bu Bar the Ata'baak
I found it when back from my exile I came."

به نام ایزد آباد و پرناز و نعمت
پلنگان رها کرده خوی پلنگی

درون مردمی چون ملک نیک
محضر   برون لشگری چون
هژبران جنگی

چنان بود در عهد اول که دیدی
جهانی پر آشوب و تشویش وتنگی

چنین شد در ایام سلطان عادل
اتابک ابوبکر سعدابن زنگی

Sa'di also refers in his writings to India and central Asia as it was mentioned earlier. In his travels Saadi sat in remote tea-houses late at night and exchanged views with merchants, farmers, preachers, wayferers, thieves, and Sufi mendicants as well as survivers of the Mongol holocaust. For twenty years or more he continued the same schedule of preaching, advising, learning, honing his sermons, and publishing them into gems illuminating the wisdom and foibles of his people. At one point he joined a group of Sufis who had fought arduous battles against the Crusaders. When he was captured at Acre (Tripoli) he spent seven years in captivity and was put to work as slave digging trenches outside the fortress. He was later released when one of the Mamlukes paid ransom for Muslim prisoners being held in Crusader dungeons

Sa'di visited Jerusalem and then set out on pilgrimage to Mecca and Medina. It is believed that he may have also visited Oman and other lands in the south of Arabian Penninsula. He finally returns to Persia via Azarbayejan, visited Isfahan, and Khorasan and eventually traveled to India visiting with the Vazir (Minister) in Gujarat and visited the large temple of Somanath, from where he flees due to an unpleasant encounter with the Brahmans. The story goes to tell that while at the temple he engaged himslf in the investigation of the mechanism of a wonder –working Hindoo idol. He was discovered by the custodian who tried to run away from him. Saadi pursued him and in a struggle that ensued, pushed the custodian into a well and killed him. He then ran away and manged to save his life. Sa'di narrates this story in the chapter eight of his book, "Boostan":

"The door of the Temple I fastened one night, Then ran like a scorpion left and right;	در دیر محکم به بستم شبی دویدم چپ وراست چون عقربی
Next the platform above and below to explore I began, till a gold-broidered curtain I saw,	نگه کردم از زیر تخت و زبر یکی پرده دیدم مکلل به زر
And behind it a priest of the fire-cult did stand With the end of a string firmly in his hand,	پس پرده مطرانی آذرپرست مجاور سر ریسمانی بدست
As iron to David grew piant as wax, So to me were made patent his tricks and his tracks,	به فوری در آن حال معلوم شد چو داود کاهن بر او موم شد
And I knew that 'twas he who was pulling the string, When the Idol's arm, in the Temple did swing.	که ناچار چون در کشد ریسمان برآرد صنم دست فریاد خوان
When the Brahman beheld me, most deep was his shame, For 'tis shame to be caught at so shabby a game,	برهمن شد از روی من شرمسار که شنعت بود بخیه بر روی کار
He fled before me, but I did pursue And into a well him head-foemost I threw,	بتازید و من در پیش تاختم نگونش به چاهی در انداختم
For I knew that, if he should effect his escape, I should find myself soon in some perilous scrape,	که دانستم ارزنده آن برهمن بماند کند سعی در خون من

And that he would most gladly use poison or steel
Lest I his nefarious deed should reveal.

پسندد که از من بر آید دمار
مبادا که سرش کنم آشکار

You too, should you chance to discover such trick,
Make away with the trickster; don't spare him! Be quick!

چو از کار مفسد خبر یافتی
ز دستش بر آور چو در یافتی

For, if you should suffer the scoundrel to live,
Be sure that to you he no quarter will give,

که گر زنده اش مانی آن بی هنر
نخواهد ترا زندگانی دگر

And that though on your threshold his head should be bowed,
He will cut off your head, if the chance be allowed.

اگر سر به خدمت نهد بر درت
اگر دست یابد به برد سرت

Then track not the charlatan's tortuous way,
Or else, having tracked him, smith swiftly and slat!

فریبنده را پای در پی منه
چو رفتی و دیدی امانش مده

So I finished the rogue, notwithstanding his wails,
With stones; for dead men, as you know, tell no tales"

تمامش بکشتم به سنگ آن خبیث
که از مرده دیگر نیاید حدیث.

After almost thirty years wandering through strange lands, Sa'di finally returned to Shiraz in the year 1277 (C.E) and finished writing his book "Boostan". He is quoted to have said "This is the gift from my trips to my country-men. This marks the beginning of the third period in his life. Shiraz was now under the rule of Attabak Sa'd-ebn-Zangi enjoying peace, tranquility and prosperity after years of wars, bloodshed and insecurity. Saadi was warmly welcomed to the city and well received by the ruler, took his pename "Sa'di" from the ruler's name and dedicated his book "Boostan" to him. In the years that followed he composed a number of panagyrics as a sign of gratitude to the ruler's name.

Sa'di died in Shiraz sometime between the years of 1312 to 1317 C.E. He was buried there and his Moselium has been visited by millions over the years.

Sa;di is the third of the great poets of the Persian literary history after the Arab invasion of Iran, as rightly portrayed by one of his contemporaries;

Amongst poets, three are considered to be the "Prophets"! This is the "Opinion" shared by everyone. Ferdowsi, Anvari, and Saadi, No other prophet ever came after.	در شعر سه تن پیامبر انند قولیست که جملگی بر آنند فردوسی وانوری وسعدی هرچند که لانبی بعدی

No Persian writer enjoys to this day not only in his own country, but wherever his language is cultivated, a wider celebrity or a greater reputation. As mentioned earlier his "Golestan" and his "boostan: are generaly the first classics to which the students of Persia are introduced, while his Ghazals, or his odes, enjoy popularity second only to those of his fellow-townsman Hafez. He is a poet of quite a different type from Ferdowsi and Mowlavi, and represents on the whole the astute, pious, half worldly side of Persian character, as the other two represent the passionately devout and mystical. Mysticism was so much in the air, and its phraselogy was-as it still is- so much a part of ordinary speech, that its traces in Sa'di's writings are neither few nor uncertain; but in the main it may be said without hesitation that worldly wisdom rather than mysticism is his chief characteristic, and that the the Golestan in particular is one of the most Macchiavellian works in the Persia language. Pious sentiments and aspirations, indeed, abound; but they are, as a rule, eminently practical, almost devoid of that visionary quality which is so characteristic of the essentially mystical writers.

Sa'di's works:
Sa'di's works cover a wide and varied range in both poetry and prose. He has applied his remarkable and exceptional genius to carve out an almost complete Encyclopeadia of Persian culture and ethics ranging in topics from philosophy, history, mysticism, humanities, moralities; advice, council and guiance to everyone inclusive of kings, rulers, clergies, dervishes, and ordinary common people. Codes of conduct, justice, liberality and fairness, modesty, contentment, faith, love, and life experiences covering human's life

from birth to death, reflections on the beheaviour of dervishers, their ecstatic practices and the kings. Throughout his works, as becomes appropriate and necessary, Saadi demonstrates a profound awareness of the absurdity of human existence.

As it was indicated, Saadi's most celebrated and popular works are the two books; Boostan (The Orchard) and Golestan (The flower Garden). Boostan is composed entirely in verse (epic metre) while Golestan, a combination of prose and verse. The former comprises of tales, anectotes, some authobiography and personal experiences, advice and council in the form of short stories. Besides these his "Kolliyat" or collected works comprise Arabic and Persian qassidas (Elegies), Ghazals (odes), and in short covers almost all types and classes of Persian poetry. Indeed, the real charm and attraction of Saadi and the secret of his popularity lies not only in his consistency but in catholicity; in his works is matter for every taste, the highest to the lowest, the most refined to the most coarse and variety abound. His writings are a microcosm of the East, alike in its best and most ignoble aspects, and it is not without good reason that wherever the Persian language is remembered or is studied, they are and they have been for seven and a half centuries, the first books placed in the learners'hands.

For western students the Boostan and Golestan have a special attraction; but Saadi is also rememberd as a great panygerist and lyrist, the author of a numer of masterly general odes portraying human experience, and also of particular odes such as the lament on the fall of Baghdad after the Mongol invasion. His lyrics are to be found in Ghazaliyat ("Lyrics") and his Odes in Qasida ("Odes"). He is also known for a numer of works in Arabic. The peculiar blend of human kindness and cynicism, humanity and resignation displayed in Saadi's works, together with a tendency to avoid the hard dilemma, make him , to many, the most typical and lovable writer in the world of Iranian culture. Here is an example of Sa'di's delightful lyrics (Ghazal)

"Precious are these heartburning sighs, for lo This was or that, they keep the days to go,	دوست میدارم من این نالیدن دلسوزرا تا بهرنوعی که باشد بگذرانم روزرا
All night I wait for one whose dawn-like face	شب همه شب انتظار صبح رویی میرود

Lends fresh radiance to the morning's grace,

کان صباحت نیست این صبح جهان افروز را

My friend's sweet face if I again might see,
I'd thank my lucky star eternally.

وه که گرم بازبینم چهر مهر افزای او
تا قیامت شکر گویم طالع پیروز را

Shall I then fear man's blame? The brave man's heart,
Serves as his shield to counter slander's dart.

گرمن ازسنگ ملامت روی برپیچم زنم
جان سپر کردند مردان ناوک دلدوز را

Who wins success has many a failure to bear,
The New Year's Day is reached through the winter's cold.

کامجویان را ز ناکامی چشیدن چاره نیست
برزمستان صبر باید طالع نوروز را

For Layla many a prudent lover yearns,
But Majnoon wins her, who his harvest burns.

عاقلان خوشه چین از سرلیلی غافلند
این کرامت نیست جز مجنون خرمن سوز را

I am thy slave: pursue some wilder game:
No tether's needed for the bird that's tame,

عاشقان دین ودنیا بازرا خاصیتی است
کان نباشد زاهدان مال وجاه اندوز را

Strength is his, who casts both worlds aside,
This is to wrldly anchorites denied,

دیگری را در کمند آور که ما خود بنده ایم
ریسمان درپای حاجت نیست دست آموز را

To-morrow is not: yesterday is spent:
To-day, O Saadi, take thy heart's content.

سعدیا دی رفت و فردا همچنان موجود نیست
درمیان این وآن فرصت شمار امروز را

Sa'di distinguished between the spiritual and practical or mundane aspects of life. In his Boostan, for example Sa'di uses the mundane world as a spring board to propel himself beyond the earthly realms. The images in Boostan are delicate and soothing. In the Golestan, on the other hand, mundane Sa'di lowers the spiritual to touch the heart of his fellow wayfarers. Here the images are graphic and thanks to Sa'dies dexterity, remains concrete in the readers mind. Realistically, too, there is a ring of truth in the division.The Shaikh preaching in the Khaneghah expriences a totally different world than a merchant passing through a town. The unique thing about Sa'di is that he embodies both the Sufi Shaikh and the travelling merchant. They are as he himself puts it, two almond kernels in the same shell. Sa'di's prose style, described as "simple but impossible to imitate" flows quite naturall and effortlessly. Its simplicity however is grounded in a semantic web consisting of synonymy, homophony, and oxymoron buttressed by internal rhythm and external rhyme. Here is another one of Sa'dis'delightful Ghazals (ode) in which he pays a charming tribute to the city of Shiraz, and as such is greatly loved and admired by the natives of that great city.

"O Fortune suffers me not to clasp my sweetheart to my breast, Nor lets me forget my exile long in a kiss on her sweet lips pressed,	رها نمی کند ایام در کنار منش که داد خود بستانم به بوسه از دهنش
The noose wherewith she is won't to snare her victims far and wide, I will steal away, that so one day I may lure her to my side,	همان کمند بگیرم که سید خاطر خلق بدان همی کند و درکشم به خویشتنم
Yet I shall not dare caress her hair with a hand that is over-bold, For snared therein, like birds in a gin, are the hearts of lovers untold,	ولیک دست نیارم زدن در آن سر زلف که مبلغی دل خلقست زیر هر شکنش
A slave am I to that gracious form, which, as I picture it, Is clothed in grace with a measuring rod, as tailors a garment fit.	غلام قامت آن لعبتم که بر قد او بریده اند لطافت چو جامه بر بدنش

O cypress-tree, with silver limbs, this color and scent of thine, Have shamed the scent of the myrtle plant and the bloom of the eglantine,	زرنگ وبوی توای سروقد سیم اندام برفت رونق نسرین باغ و نسترنش
Judge with thine eyes, and set thy foot in the garden fair and free, And tread the jasmine under thy foot, and the flowers of the Fudas tree.	یکی به لطف نظرپای درگلستان نه که پایمال کنی ارغوان و یاسمنش
O joyous and gay is the New Year's Day, and in Shiraz most of all; Even the stranger forgets his home, and becomes its willing thrall.	خوشا تفرج نوروز خاصه درشیراز که برکند دل مرد مسافراز وطنش
O'er the the garden's Egypt, Joseph-like, the fair red rose is the king, And the Zephyr, e'en to the heart of the town, doth the scent of his raiment bring.	عزیزمصرچمن شد جمال یوسف گل شگفت نیست گراز غیرتتوبرگلذار بگرید ابرو بخندد شکوفه برچمنش
O wonders not if in time of spring thou dost rouse such jealousy, That the cloud doth weep while the flowers smile, and all on the account of thee!	دراین روش که تویی گربه مرده برگذری عجب نباشد اگرنعره آید ازکفنش
If o'er the dead thy feet should tread, those feet so fair and fleet, No wonder it were if thou should'st hear a voice from his winding –sheet.	
Distruction is banned from this our land in the time of our lord the King, Save that I am distructed with love of thee, ad men with the songs I sing".	نماند فتنه درایام شاه جزسعدی که برجمال توفتنه است وخلق برسخنش

There is also another Ghazal in which Sa'di vaguely points to a danger which threatens his reputation for wisdom and prudence built up in fifty years, through love, for his patron "Saheb-Divan" written apparently before his departure from Shiraz for Baghdad:

"My soul is weary of Shiraz, utterly sick and sad, If you seek for news of my doing, you will have to ask at Baghdad,	دلم از صحبت شیراز بکلی بگرفت وقت آنست که پرسی خبر از بغدادم
I have no doubt that the Premier there will give me the help I need;	هیچ شک نیست که فریاد من آنجا برسد عجب از صاحب دیوان نرسد فریادم
Sa'di that the love of one's native land is a true tradition is clear! But I canot afford to die of want because my birth was here."	سعدیا حب وطن گرچه حدیثی است صحیح نتوان مرد به سختی که من اینجا زادم

It has been customary and fairly common practice amongst Persian poets, especially of former years, to insert a stich of another well known or well respected poet in one or more verses of their own. This tradition is known as (Tazmin). Hafez, the other great Persian poet, whose life and poetry will be included in the later chapters (He lived almost a hundred years after Saadi) and was greatly inspired by Saadi has adopted a number of stiches from Saadi's poetries to use for this purpose in his own:

"Thou didst speak me ill and I am content: God pardon thee, thou didst speak well; A bitter answer befits a ruby lip which feeds on sugar!"	بدم گفتی و خرسندم عفاک الله نکو گفتی جواب تلخ میزیبد لب لعل شکرخارا

Sa'di has the first hemistich of this verse in his book Tayabat. The hemistich with which it is here joined means:

"Thou didst call me a dog, and I am acquiesced: God reward thee,Thou didst confer on me a favor.

بدم گفتی و خرسندم عفاک الله نکو گفتی

سگم خواندی و خرسندم جزاک الله کرم کردی

In his book, "Badayeh", Saadi says:

"One can mention no defect in thy beauty save this,
That love comes not forth from that nature and disposition

جز این قدر نتوان گفت در جمال تو عیب

که مهربانی از آن طبع و خو نمی آید

Hafez has taken the first hemistich of that verse, and joined it with this hemistich of his own:

"That the beauty-spot of love and fidelity is not on that fair face."

که خال مهر و وفا نیست روی زیبا را

In his book "Tayebat" Sa'di says:

"Life without a friend has no great attraction;
My head is enveloped in smoke [of the heart, i.e., sighs] by reason of this hidden fire"

ذوقی چنان ندارد بی دوست زندگانی

دودم به سر برآمد زین آتش نهانی

Hafez has taken the first hemistich of this and has supplemented it by the "complete anagram"of itself:

Without friend, life has no great attraction.

بی دوست زندگانی ذوقی چنان ندارد

Rebirth of Persian Culture

Mowlana Jalaled-Din Muhammad (Mowlavi), 13th century Persian Gnostic & Poet

Jalaled-Din Muhammad better known by his later title of Mawlana ("our Master") Jalaled-Din-e-Rumi (i.e., "of Rum," or Asia Minor, where the greatest part, over 50 years, was spent), is without doubt the most eminent Sufi poet and renouned Gnostic that Persia has produced, while his mystical master piece Mathnavi deserves to rank amongst the great poems of all time. He was born at Balkh a city in the province then called the greater Khorasan in 30 September, 1207 C.E. The family to which our poet belonged had been settled in Balkh for several generations; it was highly respected and, according to his biographers, had produced a notable succession of jurists and devines. So far as can be ascertained, its history begins with his great- grandfather, who claimed descent from Arab stock, and from no less a person than Abu Bakr, the first Caliph of Islam.

His father Baha 'al-Din, was a man of great learning and piety, an eloquent preacher and distinguished professor.Unfortunately not content with the way he and other religious leaders were being treated by the ruling monarch Mohammad Kharazmshah as well as the king's ever increasing fear of the extent of Bah' al-Din's influence and popularity with people and last but not least the perpetuating rumors of an imminent attack on the land by the Mongol tribes, convinced Baha 'al-Din that it is prudent to seek refuge elsewhere by migrating westwards in the company of his family and friends and to join a caravan of pilgrims on pilgrimage to Mecca in Arabian peninsula. At this time Jalal'al-Din was only twelve years old. They passed through the city of Neishabour, according to a well-known story, and visited the famous Sufi, Shaikh Farid al-Din Attar who received them warmly. In the course of this visit Attar became highly impressed by the young Jalal al- Din took the boy in his arms and gave him his blessing and a copy of his book "Asrar-Nameh (book of mysteries), predicting his greatness, and told his father "value this son!, it will not be long before he lights fire in the hearts and souls of the world's devotees.

From Neishabour they went to Baghdad; where they received the news of the Massacre and destruction of Balkh by Jingiz Khan; then to Mecca, Damascus,

Chapter 5

and Malatiyya (Melitene), where they remained four years, and thence to Laranda (now Qaraman), about forty miles south east of Qouniya (Iconium), where they abode seven years. Here Jalal al-Din married a lady named Gawhar Khatoon, daughter of Lala Sharaf al-Din of Samarqand about 1246 C.E. She bore him two sons; Baha' al-Din Sultan Valad and 'Ala' al-Din.

Soon afterwards the family settled in Qonia, the capital of the Seljuq prince, 'Ala'al-Din Kaiqubad, where Baha'al-Din resumed his professional activity as an eminent theologian, a teacher and preacher, venerated by his students and highly esteemed by the reigning monarch, to whom he acted as a spiritual guide. He died in February 1231, and Jala'l succeeded to the vacant chair. One or two years later, Burh'anal-Din Mohaqaq of Tirmiz, a former student of Bah'al-Din at Balkh, arrived in Qounia. Under his influence, it is said, Jal'l al-Din, now in his twenty fifth years, became imbued with enthusiasm for the discipline and doctrine of the Sufis who sought to unite themselves with God. During the next decade he went for a time to Aleppo and Damascus, and was instructed by Burhan al-Din in the mystic lore of "The Path".

He devoted himself to the imitation of his Pir (sufi master) and passed through all the stages of mystical life until, on the death of Burh'n al-Din, a few years later, he in turn assumed the rank of Shaikh and thus took the first step, though probably unpremeditated, towards forming a fraternity of the desiples amongst whom his ardent personality was in ever increasing numbers.

Although the fame of his erudition and the brilliancy of his eloquence brought eager desciples from every quarter to his sermons and lectures—he had a class of 400—the positive sciences could not, he felt, satisfy the soul's infinite longing for freedom and rest. He embraced accordingly the panteisthic doctrines which had already taken root in the barren soil of Islam, and sown boadcast over the Islamic Empire by a long series of wandering saints, sprang up and blossomed with oriental luxuriance.

The remainder of his life, as described by by his son in (valadnameh), falls into three periods, each of which is marked by a mystical intimacy of the closest kind with a "Perfect Man," i.e. one of the saints in whom Divine attributes are mirrored, so that the lover, seeing himself by the light of God, realize that him and his beloved, are not two, but one.These experiences lie at the very center of Rumi's theosophy and directly or indirectly inspire all his poetry. In handling the verse narrative of a mystic's son who was himself a mystic it is prudent to make ample allowance for the element of allegory; yet it would be rash to reject the whole story as pious fiction seeing that at the date when it was written many persons were living who could say whether it was or, it was not, a recognizable picture of things which they themselves had witnessed.

Mowlavi at the young age of 36 was at the peak of his career. He was highly respected as a Theologian and Orator. He was also aTeacher, a Jurist, a Pier with a large number of followers and a Councilor and spiritual Guide to the ruling monarch, Sultan Qayqobad Seljuk. On the 28th of November 1244, a wondering dervish, known to posterity by the name of Shams al-Din of Tabriz arrived in Qoniya, and took residence in a small chamber in the Bazar of cotton merchants in the center of the city. A "weird figure wrapped in coarse black felt who suddenly out of nowhere flits across the stage for a moment and disappears mysteriouly and tragically couple of years later". This strange personage was, as discovered later, the son of that Jal'lu'd-Din "Naw Musalman" whose zeal for Islam and aversion from the tenets of the Assassins (Group of Ismailits founded by Hassan Sabbah), whose pontiff he was supposed to be, had earned by his extensive and flighty wanderings the nickname of Paranda ("the Flier "). He has been described as of an "exceedingly aggressive and domineering manner," and a "most disgusting cynic". Nicholson has best summed up his characteristics in the following words; "He was comparatively illiterate, but his tremendous spiritual enthusiasm for God, based on the conviction that he was a chosen organ and mouthpiece of Diety, cast a spell over all who entered the enchanted circle of his power. In this respect, as in many others, for example, in his strong passion for poverty, and his violent death, Shams-e-Tabrizi curiosly resembles Socratis; both imposed themselves upon men of genious, who gave their crude ideas artistic expression; both proclaim the futility of external knowledge, the need for illumination, the value of love; but wild raptures and arrogant defiance of every human law can ill atone for the lack of that 'sweet reasonableness' and moral grandure which distinguish the sage from the devotees."

Jal'l-al-Din found in the stranger that perfect image of the Divine Beloved which he had long been seeking. He took him away to his house, and for a year or two they remained inseparable. Sultan Valad likens his father's all-absorbing communion with this "hidden saint"to the celebrated journey of Moses in company with Khadir, the Sage whom Sufis regard as the supreme

Chapter 5

hierophant and guide of travelers on the way to God. Meanwhile the Mowlavi's disciples, entirely cut off from their Master's teachings and conversation and bitterly resenting his continued devotion to Sham-al-Din alone, assailed the intruder with abuse and threats of violence. At last Shams fled to Damascus, but was brought back, in triumph by Sultan Valad, whom Jalal'al-Din, deeply agitated by the loss of his bosom friend, had sent in search of him. Thereupon the deciples "repented" and were forgiven. But the tongues of his jealous traducers soon wagged again, and presently, perhaps in 1247, the man of mystry vanished without leaving a trace behind. Sultan Valad vividly describes the passionate and uncontrollable emotion which overwhelmed his father at this time.

"Never for a moment did he cease from listening to music (Sama'), and dancing.
He had been a mufti: he became a poet;
He had been an ascetic: he became intoxicated by Love.
It was not the wine of the grape; the illuminated soul drinks only the wine of Light".

Here Sultan Valad alludes to the Diwa'n-Shams-e Tabriz (Lyrics of Shams of Tabriz), an immense collection of mystical odes composed by Jal'l al-Din in name of Shamsal-Din and dedicated to the memory of his alter ego. The first verse does not confirm, but may have suggested, the statement of some authorities that grief for the loss of Shams-e Tabriz caused Jal'l al-Din to institute the characteristic Mowlavi religious dance with its plaintive reed-flute accompaniment. The tall, drab-coloured felt hat and wide cloak still worn by members of the Mowlavi Dervish order, as well as the peculiar gyrations which have earned for them amongst Europeans the name of "Dancing Dervishes" are said by Aflaki (one of Mowlavie's biographers) to have been instituted at this time by Jalal al'-Din in memory of his lost friend. In the same biography Aflaki mentions also other reasons for the introduction of the chanting and dancing practiced by his desciples.

The next episode in Mowlavi's spiritual life is a fainter repetition of the last. For many years after the disappearance of Shams he devoted himself to Sala'h al-Din Zarkub, who as his deputy (khalifah) was charged with the duty of instructing the Mowlavi acolytes. They showed their resentment in no uncertain manner, and the ringleaders only gave in when they had been virtually excommunicated.

Rebirth of Persian Culture

On the death of Salah a'l –Din the poets's enthusiasm found a new and abundant source of inspiration in another disciple, Husa'm al-Din Hassan, whose name he has mystically associated with his great work, the celebrated Masnavi. He calls Masnavi "the book of Husam al-Din" and likens himself to a flute on the lips of Husa'mal-Din, pouring forth "the wailful music that he made." During the last ten years of the poet's life this last beloved follower acted as his Khalifah, and upon his death in November 1273, succeeded him as the Head of Mowlavi Order, a dignity he held until 1284, when Sultan Valad took his place.

The biography of Mowlavi as outlined above is a first hand account of his life given in verse by his son. There are other biographys in prose written by Aflaki and others that ad little to this one or are some what unreliable.

Mowlavi's literary output, as stupendous in magnitude as it is sublime, consists of:
The great mystical Mathnavi, comprising of six books, contains according to Aflaki's statement 26,660 couplets. The date that the first book begun to be written is unknown but the second book was begun in C.E.1263, two years after the completion of the first book. It was interrupted due to the death of the wife of Husam'al-Din. It is almost certain that the first book was started a long time after the disappearance of Shams, but it remaind incomplete in book six as a result of the death of Mowlavi in the year C.E. 1273. Its composition, therefore, probably extended over a period of some ten years. Each book except the first begins with an exhortation to Husa'm al-Din who is likewise spoken of in the Arabic preface of book one as having inspired that portion also. As he became Mowlavi's assistant and companion after the death of Sala'hed-Din in 1258, C.E., it is probable that the Mathnavi was begun after this period.

The Divan-e Shams-e Tabriz consists of a very large collection of mystical, and lyrical poems "odes" perhaps as many as 2500. As Nicholson points out, implied by Dowlatshah they were chiefly composed during the absence of Shams-Tabrizi at Damascus, while, Reza Gholi Khan Hedayat regards them rather as having been written in memorium; but Nicolson's own view, which is probably correct, is;"that part of diva'n was composed while Shams-Tabrizi was still living, but probably the bulk of it belongs to a later period".

Chapter 5

The Ruba'iya't or quatrains, of which may be about 1600 are authentic. Mowlavi is also the author of a treatise in prose, entitled Fihi ma' fih, which runs to three thousand bayts and is addressed for the most part to Mu'in al-Din, the Parvaneh of Rum, Maja'lese- saba' (seven lectures) which is composed before meeting Shams, and Maka'tib which contains of his letters written to people. These are all published.

The forms in which he clothes his religious philosophy had been fashioned before him by two great Sufi poets, Sana'ii of Ghaznah and Farid al-Din Attar of Neishabour. Though he makes no secret of his debt to them both, expressing his admiration and respect for them:

Attar was the Soul and Sanaii, his two eyes,	عطار روح بود و سنایی دو چشم
We are the posterity of them both,	او
	ما از پی سنایی و عطار آمدیم

However, his flight takes a wider range, his materials are richer and more varied, and his method of handling the subject is so original that it may justly be described as "a new style." It is a style of great subtlety and complexity, hard to analyze; yet its greatest features are simple and can not be doubted. In the Masnavi, where it is fully developed, it gives the reader an exhilarating sense of largeness and freedom by its disregard for logical cohesion, defiance of conventions, bold use of the language of common life, and abundance of images drawn from homely things and incidents familiar to everyone. The poem resembles a trackless ocean: there are no boundaries; no lines of demarcation between the literal "husk" and the "kernel" of doctrine in which its inner sense is conveyed and abundantly explained. The effortless fusion of text and interpretation shows how completely, in aesthetics as in every other domain, the philosophy of Mowlavi is inspired by the monistic idea. "The Masnavi", he says "is the shop for Unity (wahdat); anything that you see there except the one "God" is an idol." Ranging over the battlefield of existence, he finds its conflicts and discords playing the parts assigned to them in the universal harmony which only mystics can realize.

Mathnavi is commonly said in Persia that it is "The Quran in Farsi", while its author describes it, in the Arabic Preface to book one, as containing "the Roots of the Roots of the Roots of the Religion, and the discovery of the Mysteries of Reunion and Sure Knowledge" "It is," he continues, "the supreme Science of God, the most resplendent Law of God, and the most evident proof of God. The likes of its Light is 'as a lantern wherein is a lamp' shining with an effulgence brighter than the Morning. It is the Paradize of the Heart, abounding in fountains and foliage; of which fountains is one called by the Pilgrims of this Path Salsabil, but by the possessors of {Supernatural} Stations and God-given powers 'good as a station'and Best as a noon-day halting – place. Therein shall the righteous eat and drink, and therein shall the virtuous rejoice and be glad. Like the Nile of Egypt, it is a drink for the patient, but a sorrow to the House of Pharaoh and the unbelievers: even as God saith, 'Thereby He leadth many astray, and thereby He guideth many right: but He misleadth not thereby any save the wicked,"

It contains a great number of rambling anectotes of the most various character, some sublime and dignified, and others though few not as dignified with mystical and theosophical digressions, often of the most abstrusive character, in sharp contrast with the narrative portions, which, though presenting some pecularities of diction, are as a rule couched in very simple and plain language. The book is further remarkable as it begins abruptly, without any doxology, with the well-known and beautiful passage the opening canto of the Mathnavi "The song of the reed":

Listen to the reed how it tells a tale, Complaining of separation,	بشنو از نی چون حکایت میکند از جدایی ها شکایت میکند
Saying,"Ever since I was parted from the reed-bed from the reed-bed, my lament hath caused man and woman to moan.	کزنیستان تا مرا ببریده اند از نفیرم مرد و زن نالیده اند
I want a bosom torn by by severerence, That I may unfold (to such a one) the pain of love desire.	سینه خواهم شرحه شرحه از فراق تا بگویم شرح درد اشتیاق
Everyone who is left far from his source, Wishes back the time when he was unite with it.	هرکسی کو دور ماند از اصل خویش بازجوید روزگار وصل خویش
In every company I uttered my wailful notes,	

I consorted with the happy and with them that rejoice.	من به هرجمعیتی نالان شدم جفت بد حالان وخوشحالان شدم
Everyone became my friend from his own opinion; None sought out my secrets from my within.	هرکسی از ظن خود شد یارمن ازدرون من نجست اسرار من
My secret is not far from my plaint, But ear and eye lack the light (whereby it shoud be apprehended)	سر من ازناله من دور نیست لیک چشم وگوش را آن نورنیست
Body is not veiled from soul, Yet none is permitted to see the soul.	تن زجان وجان زتن مستورنیست لیک کس را دید جان دستورنیست
This noise of the reed is fire, it is not wind: Whose hath not this fire, may he be nought!	آتش است این بانگ نای ونیست باد هرکه این آتش ندارد نیست باد
'Tis the fire of Love that is in the reed, 'Iis the fervour of love that is in the wine.	آتش عشق است کاندرنی فتاد جوشش عشق است کاندرمی فتاد
The reed is the comrade of everone, who has been parted from a friend, Its strains pierced our hearts.	نی حریف هرکه ازیاری برید پرده هایش پرده های ما برید
Who ever saw a poison and antidote like the reed? Who ever saw a sympathizer and a longing lover like the reed?	همچونی زهری وتریاقی که دید همچونی دمسازومشتاقی که دید
The reed tells of the Way full of blood, And recounts stories of the passion of Majnoon. Only to the senseless is this sense confided: The tongue has no customer save the ear.	نی حدیث راه ون میکند قصه های عشق مجنون میکند

Rebirth of Persian Culture

In our woe the days (of life) have become untimely:
Our days travel hand in hand with burning griefs.

محرم این هوش جز بیهوش نیست
مرزبان را مشتری چون گوش نیست

If our days are gone, let them go!
'Tis no matter. Do Thou remain, for one is holy as Thou art?

در غم ما روزها بیگاه شد
روزها با سوزها همراه شد

Whoever is not a fish becomes sated with His water;
Whoever is without daily bread finds the day long.

روزها گر رفت گو رو باک نیست
تو بمان ای آنکه چون تو پاک نیست

None that is raw understands the state of the ripe;
Therefore my words must be brief.Farewell!

هرکه جز ماهی ز آبش سیر شد
هرکه بی روزیست روزش دیر شد

If thou pour the sea into a pitcher,
How much will it hold? One day's need!

درنیابد حال پخته هیچ خام
پس سخن کوتاه باید والسلام

The Picher, the eye of the covetous, never becomes full:
The oyster-shell is not filled with pearls until it is contented.

گر بریزی بحر را در کوزه ای
چند گنجد قسمت یک روزه ای

He (alone) whose garment is rent by a (mighty) love,
Is purged of covetness and all defects.

کوزه چشم حریصان چر نشد
تا صدف قانع نشد پر در نشد

Hail, O Love that bringest us good gain.
Thou that art the physician of all our ills

هرکه را جامه ز عشقی چاک شد
او ز حرص و جمله عیبی پاک شد

The remedy of our pride and vainglory,
Our Plato and our Galen!

شادباش ای عشق خوش سودای ما

Through love the earthy body soared to the skies:

ای طبیب جمله علت های ما

Chapter 5

The mountain began to dance and became
nimble.

Was I joined to the lip of one in accord
with me?
I too, like the reed, would tell all that may
be told;

- (But) whoever is parted from one, who
speaks his language,
Becomes dumb, though he has a hundred
songs.

When the rose is gone and the garden
faded,
Thou wilt hear no more nightingale's
story.

The beloved is all and the lover (but) a
vale;
The Beloved living and the lover a dead
thing.

When Love hath no care for him,
He is left as a bird without wings, alas for
him then!

How should I have conciousness (of
aught) before or behind?
When the light of my Beloved is not before
me and behind.

Love wills that this Word should be shown
forth:
If the mirror does not reflect, how is that?

Dost thou know why the mirror (of thy
soul) reflects nothing?

ای دوای نخوت وناموس ما
ای تو افلاطون وجالینوس ما

جسم خاک از عشق برافلاک شد
کوه در رقص آمد و چالاک شد

با لب دمساز خود گر جفتمی
همچونی من گفتنی ها گفتمی

هرکه او از همزبانی شدجدا
بی زبان شد گرچه دارد صد نوا

چون که گل رفت وگلستان درگذشت
نشنوی زین پس ز بلبل سرگذشت

جمله معشوق است وعاشق پرده ای
زنده معشوق است وعاشق مرده ای

چون نباشدعشق را پروای او
اوچو مرغی ماند بی پروای او

من چگونه هوش دارم پیش وپس
چون نباشد نوریارم پیش وپس

عشق خواهد کین سخن بیرون رود
آینه غماز نبود چون بود

Rebirth of Persian Culture

Because the rust is not cleared from its face.

آینه دانی چرا
غماز نیست
چون که زنگار از رخش
ممتاز نیست

These are some of the themes underlying Mowlavi's poetry. He is not their original author, they may be regarded as having been gradually evolved by the long succession of Sufi thinkers from the nineth century (C.E.), onwards, then gathered together and finally formulated by the famous Andalusian mystic, Ibn-'Arabi (1165-1240 C.E.). Ibn Arabi has every right to be the father of Islamic pantheism. He devoted clossal powers of intellect and imagination to constructing a system which, though it lacks order and connection, covers the whole ground in detail and perhaps, all things considered, is the most imposing monument of mystical speculation the world has ever seen. While it is evident that Mowlavi borrowed some part of his terminology and ideas from his elder contemporary, who himself traveled in Ru'm and lies buried in Damascus, the amount of the debt has inevitably been exaggerated by later commentators whose minds are filled with forms of thought alien to the Masnavi, but familiar to readers of Ibn al-Arabi's Fusus al-Hekam (Bezels of Wisdom) and al-Futuhat al Makkiyah (Meccan Revelations). The Andalusian always writes with a fixed philosophical purpose, which may be defined as a logical development of a single all-embracing concept, and much of thought expresses itself in a dialectic bristling with technicalities. Mowlavi has no such aim; his mysticism is not "doctoral" in the Catholic sense but "experimental." He appeals to the heart not to the head, scorns the logic of the schools, and nowhere does he embody in philosophical language even the elements of a system.

The Masnavi for the most part shows Mowlavi as the perfect spiritual guide engaged in making others perfect furnishing novice and adapt alike with matter suitable to their needs. Assuming the general monistic theory to be well known to his readers, he gives them a panoramic view of the Sufi gnosis (direct intuition of God.) and kindles their enthusiasm by depicting the rapture of those who "break through to the Oneness" and sees all mysteries revealed.

While Mathnavi is generally instructional in character, though it also has entertaining passages, as befits a book intended for the enlightenment of all sorts of disciples, the diwa'n of Shams Tabrizi and, on a much smaller scale,

Chapter 5

the Ruba'iyat are personal and emotional in appeal..Lyrics and quatrains alike have everywhere the authentic ring of spiritual inspiration, while in image, style and language they often approximate very closely to the Mathnavi. In some of these poems the mystic's passion is so exuberant, his imagination so overflowing, that we can catch glimpses of the very madness of Devine experience. Yet the powerful intellect of Mowlana the man never quite capitulates to the enthusiasm of Mowlana the mystic; at the last moment there is a sudden drawback, a cosciousness that certain matters are too secret and too holy to be communicated in words. It is not surprising to read that these poems, chanted (as many of them were doubtless composed) in the spiritual séance of the Mowlavi's, roused the hearers to an almost uncontrollable fervor.

Music and often dance were the inseparable format and foundation of Mowlavi's poetry. His words often pored out in a state of mental and spiritual ecstacy and trance while singing and dancing. One could say that he felt the musical rythemes first and then assigned words to them. It is a style of music by itself. His poems were spoken with music; the work was the work of opening the heart. Here is one that he spoke as part of that work:

"One night, a man was crying: Alah, Alah,
His lips grew sweet with praising, until a
cynic said so,

I have heard you calling out,
But have you ever gotten any response?

The man had no answer for that.
He quit praying and fell in to a confused
sleep; when he dreamed,

He saw hether the guy of sous in thick
green foliage.
Why did you stop praising? He asked.

Because I never heard back anything.
This longing you express is the return
message,

Rebirth of Persian Culture

The grief you cry out from within draws
you towards union,
Your pure sadness that once felt is the
secret cup,

Listen to the moan of a dog for his master.
That winning is the connection,

There are love dogs no one knows the
names of,
 if you like to be one of them.

One night a man was crying,
one night a woman was crying: Alah,
Alah, Alah.

Mowlavi's extreme devotion to God and love of Him is completely and clearly manifest throughout the almost 60,000 verses of poetry written beautifully and eloquently in his two masterpieces, The Diva'n of Shams Tabrizi, and the six books of Mathnavi, as well as his other works in poetry and prose that were mentioned before. His profound, intense and firey love and yearning for the"Beloved"and continuos desire to unite with Him is clearly reflected throughout his work. This passion is so intense that at times, it seems is pushing him to the borders of insanity; in fact he often equates and compares this burning love with the state of insanity. In a beautiful piece written which is titled "In the arms of love" arranged in the form of question and answer, this love and desire manifests itself ever so clearly:

"He said: who is at my door?
I said: "your humble servant"

He said "what business do you have?
I said "To greet you my Lord"

He said" how long will you journey on?
I said "until you stop me"

He said"how long will you boil in the fire?

Chapter 5

I said "until I am pure"This is my oath of love"

For the sake of love'
"I gave up wealth and position"

He said "you have pleaded your case, but you have no witness".
The pallor of my face is my proof;

He said"your witness has no credibility; your eyes are too wet to see"
I said,"by the splendour of your justice my eyes are clean and faultless.

He said"what do you seek?
I said "to have you as my constant friend"

He said what do you want from me?
I said"your abundant grace"

He said who was your companion on the journey?
I said "the thought of you O'King"

He said "what called you here?"
I said the "the fragrance of your wine"

He said "what brings you the most fulfillments?"
I said"The company of the Emperor"

He said "what do you find there?"
I said "a hundred miracles"

He said"why is the palace deserted?"
I said"they all fear the thief'

He said"who is the thief'

I said "the one who keeps me from you"
He said"where is their safety?"

I said "in service and reunification"
He said"what is there to renounce?"

I said"the hope of salvation"
He said"where is their calamity?"

I said in the presence of your love"
He said"how do you benefit from this life?"

I said "by keeping true to myself"
"Now it is time for silence".

If I told you about his true essence, you would fly from yourself and be gone, and neither door, nor roof could hold you back.

Mowlavis' world revolves around Divine Love which he considers to have been God's reason for the creation of Man in His own image. This Divine love eternally reverbrates throughout the infinite Universe, and can only be felt by gnostics who have exalted themselves to higher levels of spiritual unconciouness and somehow connected with the "Source". Man's inner soul connects with God through Divine love and therefore his actions on Earth should be guided by this love. Love of God and love of fellow humans.
In Mowlavi's belief love is the healer of all ailments. Love is behind every Man's triumph and is the engine that drives Man's genius to creat beauty. In a larger sense, love creats, nourishes and maintains the colossal and unimaginable system that is called "Universe". Universe would not have been possible without Divine Love. In Mathnavi he hails this Love:
  Hail, O'love that bringst us good gain

Thou that art the physician of all our ills. The remedy of our pride and vainglory; our Plato and our Galan.	شادباش اعشق خوش سودای ما
	ای طبیب جمله علت های
	ای دوای نخوت و ناموس ما
Through Love the earthly body soared to heavens	ای تو افلاطون وجالینوس ما
The mountain began to dance and became nimble.	جسم خاک از عشق بر افلاک شد
	کوه در رقص آمد و چالاک شد

Chapter 5

Dr Johnson the great English writer and thinker writes about Mowlavi, saying:"He makes plain to the pilgrims the secrets of the way to Unity and enveils the Mystries of the path to the Eternal Truth".

The great message of Mowlavi as of all mystic poets is centered on love. He has always sung of love and announces that it is love which is dominant in every being or thing that originated from God who created the world for the manifestation of His love. Mowlavi cheers of love for God saying:

His love is manifest and the beloved is hidden, The friend is outside and his splendor is in the world'	عشق او پیدا ومعشوقش نهان یار بیرون فتنه او در جهان

The philosophy of Mowlavi, like that of all Sufis is based upon the conception that not only "Being" but beauty and goodness belong exclusively to God, although they are manifested in thousand mirrors in the phenomenal world. Everything in the Universe emanates from "Him" and eventually returns to "Him" saying:

The Beloved is all and the Lover only a veil' The Beloved living and the lover a dead thing.	جمله معشوقست و عاشق مرده ای زنده معشوقست وعاشق مرده ای

Mowlavi describes the miracles of love in Mathnavi:

"Miracle of Love"

Love, turns bitterness, into sweetness, Love, turns copper, into gold,	از محبت تلخها شیرین شود از محبت مسها زرین شود
Love, makes dregs, clear, Love, turns, pains, a healing	از محبت درد ها صافی شود از محبت درد ها شافی شود
Love, revives, the dead, Love, turns, thorns, into flower,	از محبت مرده زنده میکنند از محبت شاه بنده می شود

Love, turns misery into fortune,
Love, turns gallows, a throne,

Love, transforms prison, into a rose garden,
Love, lites the home,

Love, turns thorn into a lily,
Without love, wax turns into steel,

Love, turns fire into light,
Love. transforms devil into an angle

Without love, garden becomes hell,
Love. turns sorrow into joy,

Love, transforms monsters to shepperds,
Love. turns sting into pleasure,

Love. transforms lion to mouse,
Love, turns sickness, into health,

Love, turns fury to mercy,
Love, brings dead back to life,

Love, brings dead back to life
Love, turns a king into a servant,

از محبت خارها گل میشود
وز محبت سرکه ها مل میشود

از محبت دار تختی میشود
وز محبت بار بختی میشود

از محبت سجن گلشن میشود
وز محبت خانه روشن میشود

از محبت خار سوسن میشود
بی محبت موم آهن میشود

از محبت نار نوری میشود
وز محبت دیو حوری میشود

از محبت سنگ روغن میشود
بی محبت روضه گلخن میشود

از محبت حزن شادی میشود
وز محبت غول هادی میشود

از محبت نیش نوشی میشود
وز محبت شیر موشی میشود

از محبت سقم صحت میشود
وز محبت قهر رحمت میشود

از محبت مرده زنده میشود
وز محبت شاه بنده میشود

He further goes on to glorify love and its bounless power comparing it to the vastvess of ocean and the peak of the heighst mountain emphasizing that power of love is miraculously behind all Man's achievements and triumphs saying:

Chapter 5

| Love cannot be contained in talking and hearing, | درنگنجد عشق درگفت و شنود |
| Love is an ocean with no bottom in sight, | عشق دریاییست قعرش ناپدید |

| The drops in that ocean cannot be counted, | قطره های بحر را نتوان شمرد |
| The seven seas are even miniscule, in comparison, | هفت دریا پیش آن بحر است خرد |

| Love boils the ocean like a kettle, | عشق جوشد بحر را ماند دیگ |
| Love crumbles the mountain into pebbles, | عشق ساید کوه را ماند ریگ |

| Love explodes a hundred cracks in the heavens' | عشق بشکافد فلک را صد شکاف |
| Love shakes the Earth by its might. | عشق لرزاند زمین را از گزاف |

In Mowlavi the Persian mystical genius found its supreme expression. Viewing the vast landscape of Sufi poetry, we see him standing out as a sublime mountain-peak; the many other poets before and after him are but foot-hills in comparison. The influence of his example, his thought and his language is powerfully felt through all the succeeding centuries; every Sufi after him capable of reading Persian has acknowledged his unchallengable leadership.

The following is a passage from the Mathnavi taken from the story of the "Jewish Vazir"

Nightly the souls of men thou lettest fly From out the trap wherein they captive lie,	شب ز زندان بی خبر زندانیان نه غم واندیشه و سود و زیان
Nightly from out its cage each soul doth wing Its upward way, no longer slave or king.	نه خیال این فلان و آن فلان حال عارف این بود بی خواب هم
Heedless by night the captive of his faith, Heedless by night the Sultan of his State.	گفت ایزد هم رقود زین مر خفته ا ز احوال دنیا روز و شب

Gone thought of gain or loss, gone grief
and woe;
No thought of this, or that, or So-and-so.

Such, even when awake, the Gnostic's
plight;
God saith: 'They sleep':
    recoil not in affright!

Asleep from worldly things by night and
day,
Like to the pen moved by
God's hand are they.

Who in the writing fails the Hand to see?
Thinks that the Pen is in its movements
free.

Some trace of this the Gnostic doth
display:
Even common men in sleep are caught
away.

Into the Why-less Plains the spirit goes,
The while the body and the mind repose,

Then with a whistle dost thou them recall,
And once again in toil and moil they fall;

For when once more the morning light
doth break;
And the Gold Eagle of the Sky doth shake.

Its wings, then Isra'fil-like from that born
The 'Cleaver of the Dawn' bids them
return.

The disembodied souls He doth recall,

چون قلم در پنجه تقلیب رب
آنکه او پنجه نبیند در رقم
فعل پندارد به جنبش از رقم
شمه ای از حال عارف وانمود
عقل را هم حال حسی در ربود
رفته در صحرای بی چون جانشان
روحشان آسوده و ابدانشان
وز صفیری باز دامن درکشی
جمله را در داد و داور درکشی
چونک نور صبحدم سربرزند
. کرکس گردون زرین پرزند
فالق الاصباح اسرافیل وار
جمله را در صورت آرد زان دیار
روحهای منبسط را تن کند
هر تنی را باز آبستن کند
اسپ جانها را کند عاری ززین
سرالنوم اخ الموتست این
لیک بهر آنک روز آیند باز
برنهد بر پایشان بند دراز
تا که روزش واکشد زان مرغزار
وز چراگاه آردش در زیربار
کاش چون اصحاب کهف این روح را
حفظ کردی یا چوکشتی نوح را
تا از این طوفان بیداری و هوش

And makes their bodies pregnant one and all.
Yet for a while each night the spirit's steed
Is from the harness of the body freed:

'Sleep is Death's brother': come, this riddle rede!
But lest at day-break they should lag behind,

Each soul He doth with a long tether bind,
That from those groves and plains He may revoke

Those errant spirits to their daily yoke.
O would that, like the 'Seven Sleepers; we
As in the Ark of Noah kept might be,

That mind, and eye, and ear might cease from stress
Of this fierce Flood of waking consciousness!

How many 'Seven sleepers' by thy side,
Before thee, round about thee, do abide!

Each in his care the Loved One's whisper hears:
What boots it? Seal'ed is thine eyes and ears!

وا رهیدی این ضمیر وچشم وگوش
ای بسی اصحاب کهف اندرجهان
پهلوی توپیش هست این زمان

یاربااوغار با اواندر
سرود
مهربرچشمست وبرگوشت چه
سود

Here is another of Mowlavi's beautiful and exhilarating odes from the Divan of Shams-Tabrizi which clearly indicates how Mowlavi has freed himself from all worldly dependencies and has sweared alligence to no one and nothing but the "Divine Love"

"Lo, for I to myself am unknown now in God's name what must I do?

چه تدبیر ای مسلمانان که من خود را نمیدانم

I adore not the Cross or the Crescent; I am not a Giaour or a Jew.

نه ترسا نه یهودم من نه گبرونه مسلمانم

East nor West, land nor sea is my home, I have kin nor with angle nor gnome,

نه شرقیم نه غربییم نه بری ام نه بحری ام
نه از کان طبیعت نه از افلاک گردانم

I am wrought not of fire nor of foam, am I shaped neither of dust nor of dew.

نه از هندم نه از چینم نه از بلغار و سقسینم

Not in this world nor that world I dwell, not in Paradize neither in Hell;

نه از ملک عراقینم نه از خاک خراسانم
نه از خاکم نه از بادم نه از آتش نه از بادم

Not from Eden and Ridwa'n I fell, not from Adam my lineage I drew,

نه از عرشم نه از فرشم نه از کونم نه از کانم

In a place beyond uttermost Place, in a tract without shadow of trace,

نه از دنیا نه از عقبی نه از جنت نه از دوزخ
نه از آدم نه از حوا نه از فردوس و رضوانم

Soul and body transcending I live in the soul of my "Beloved" anew!"

مکانم لا مکان باشد نشانم بی نشان باشد
نه تن باشد نه جان باشد که من از جان جانانم

After the sudden disappearance of Shamse-Tabrizi, Mowlavi's life underwent a tragic and sad change. He deeply missed his dear old friend and this sadness is reflected in his poetry almost throughout his first Master-piece, the "Divan of Shams-Tabrizi". Here is a beautiful piece from the Divan heralding the Devotees to prepare for the final journey to unite with the "Beloved":

Chapter 5

"Up, O ye lovers, and away! 'Tis time to leave the world for aye.

Hark, loud and clear from heaven the drum of parting calls--let none delay!

The cameleer hath raised amain, made ready all the camel-train,

And quittance now desires to gain; why sleep ye, travelers, I pray?

Behind us and before there swells the din of parting and of bells;

To shoreless Space each moment sails a disembodied spirit away.

From yonder starry lights and through those curtain-awnings darkly blue

Mysterious figures float in view, all strange things display.

From this orb, wheeling round its pole, a wonderous
slumber o'er thee stole:

O weary life that weighest naught, O sleep that on my soul dost weigh!

O hear, towards thy heart's love wend, and O friend, fly toward the Friend,

Be wakeful, watchman, to the end: draws seemingly nowatchman may."

" ای عاشقان ای عاشقان هنگام
کوچ است از جهان
در گوش جانم میرسد طبل رحیل
از آسمان

نک ساربان برخاسته قطار ها
آراسته
از ما حلالی خواسته چه خفته اید
ای کاروان

این بانگها از پیش و پس بانگ
رحیل است و جرس
هر لحظه ای نفس و نفس سر میکشد
در لامکان

زین شمع های سرنگون زین پرده
های نیلگون
خلقی عجب آید برون تا عیب ها
گردد عیان

زین چرخ دولابی تو را آمد گران
خوابی تورا
فریاد از این عمر سبک زنهار از این
خواب گران

ای دل سوی دلدار شو ای یار
سوی یار شو
ای پاسبان بیدار شو خفته نشاید
پاسبان

Fakhr e-Din Araghi. Seventh century Persian poet & mystic

Fakhre'd-Din Ibrahim Hamadani known by his nom de guerre (Takhalos), of "Araghi", was born in the year 1232 (C.E) in the village of Komejan a suberb of the city of Hamadan and died in the year 1310 (C.E) in the city of Damascus. He came from a family of learned and intellectuals. He was sent to elementary school at the age of five. He soon proved to be an extremely talented and smart young boy. Nine months after having been admitted to the school he was able to read Holy Kuran by heart. He possessed a beautiful voice and was able to sing theams from Kuran delightfully .At the young age of seventeen he had learned History, philosophy, Juriceprudence, Arabic as well as whatever of literary sciences that were available at his time. He continued his higher education at "Shahrestan high school", where he was also given a teaching position. Reference has been made to his life and works by a number of biographers notably Jami in the Nafahahatul-Uns and by Husayn Mirza Bayaghra in the Majalisu'l Ushagh; but in the absence of contemporary testimony the particulars there given must be received with a certain reserve, while his writings, almost entirely of a mystical and erotic character, little or nothing is to be gleaned as to his personal adventures. He is the typical "ghalandar' (wandering dervish), heedless of his reputation, and seeing in every beautiful face or object a reflection, as in a mirror, of the Eternal Beauty. "Love," as one of his biographers says, "Was predominant in his nature," and hence his ghazals have an erotic character which has exposed him to very harsh strictures on the part of some European critics. My personal opinion is that he may have been somehow misunderstood. Similar criticisms were also made of some of his ghazals by some dervishes in India when arrived there later, to which I shall point out in the following discussion of his life-story. In the meantime, here is one of Araghi's beautiful ghazals:

"The wine wherewith the cup they first filled high,
Was borrowed from the Saghi' languorous eye

نخستین باده کاندر جام کردند
ز چشم مست ساقی وام کردند

چو با خود یافتند اهل طرب را
شراب بیخودی در جام کردند

Since self-possessed the revelers they found
The draught of selflessness they handed round.

The loved on's wine-red lips supplied the cup:
They named it 'Lover's wine,' and drank it up.

So many a hearts it robs of its repose.
For good and bad a place within our hall

They found, and with one cup confounded all.
They cast the ball of beauty on the field,

And at one charge compelled both worlds to yield
The drunken revellers from one eye and lip

The almond gather and the sugar sip.
But that sweet lip, desired of all, most fair,

Marketh harsh words the helpless lover'share
They loosen and set free their locks of jet

That they therewith for hearts a snare may set.
A hundred messages their glances dart;

Their eyebrows signal secrets to the heart.
They speak in confidence and silence claim,

And then their secrets to the world proclaim.

لب میگون جانان جام د ر داد
شراب عاشقانش نام کردند

سر زلف بتان آرام نگرفت
زبس دلها که بی آرام کردند

بمجلس نیک و بد را جای دادند
بجامی کار خاص و عام کردند

چو گوی حسن در میدان فکندند
بیک جولان دو عالم رام کردند

ز بهر نقل مستان از لب وچشم
مهیا شکر و بادام کردند

از آن لب کآرزوی جمله دلهاست
نصیب بی دلان دشنام کردند

دلی را تا بدست آرند هردم
سر زلفین خود را دام کردند

به غمزه صد سخن گفتند با جان
بدل زابرو دو صد پیغام کردند

نهان با محرمی رازی بگفتند
جهانی را از آن اعلام کردند

به عالم هرکجا درد و غمی بود
بهم کردند وعشقش نام کردند

چو خود کردند راز خویشتن فاش
عراقی را چرا بد نام کردند

Where'er in the entire world is grief and
gall

They mix them up, the mixture 'Love' they
call.

Why should they seek to hurt 'Aragh's
fame?
Since them themselves their secrets thus
proclaim?"

Araghi's course of life and destiny took a sharp turn when one day, sitting in
the classroom with his pupils surrounding him, a small group of Ghalandars
(wandering dervishes) arrived at the school and started a 'Sama'and singing
in sweet voice this 'ghazal'

"We removed ourselves from the Mosque to the pot house, And said"fairwell" to ascetism and position of authority.	ما رخت ز مسجد به خرابات کشیدیم خط بر ورق زهد و مقامات کشیدیم
We joined the line of "Lovers" in the alley of Tavern-keepers, Took the"Cup", at the pot house, from the libertins' hands.	در کوی مغان در صف عشاق نشستیم جام از کف رندان خرابات کشیدیم
So that our heart may claim its dignity, now that, We are flying the flag of our State in the heavens.	گر دل بزند کوس شرف شایدازاین پس چون رایت دولت به سماوات کشیدیم
The ascetism and position of authority, we bid "farewll" to, As they burdend us with much fatigue and toil."	از زهد و مقامات گذشتیم که بسیار کاس تعب از زهد و مقامات کشیدیم

Chapter 5

The Sema' of the dervishes accompanied by their beautiful chanting of those exhilarating love songs intoxicated Araghi so deeply that he descended from his seat, threw away his turban and cloak and joined them in Sema'. Some time later the wandering dervishes left Hamadan. Araghi could not bear the pain of seeing them go, he ran after them and joined their rank on their trip to Isfahan. Eventually they ended in India. Araghi settled in the city of Mult'an and became a disciple of Shaikh Baha'u'd-Din Zakariyy'a of who he says in one of his poems:

"If thou shouldst ask of the world 'Who is the guide of men?'	پرسی اگر از جهان کیست امام الانام
Thou wilt hear from heaven no other answer than 'Zakariya".	نشنوی از آسمان جز زکریا جواب

After a while Shaikh Zakaraiya become deeply impressed with Araghi's aptitude and special talents, clothed him in his own khirghe "dervishes-cloak" and subsequently gave him in marriage his daughter, who afterwards bore him a son named Kabir ed-Din.

Twenty five years passed, and Shaikh Baha' u'd-Din died, naming Araghi as his successor. The other dervishes, purely out of gealousy disapproved of his nomination, and complained to King of Araghi's antinomianatism. He feard his life and thereupon left India and visited Mecca and Al-Medina in Arabia and from there he travelled to Asia Minor. He met Mowlavi with who he became frienly.Also while in Qonya (Iconium) he attended the lectures of the famous Shaikh Sadre'd-Din of Qonya on the discussion of the Fusu's of Shaikh Muhiyyu'd-Din ibnu'l-Arabi, and composed his most celebrated prose work, The Lama'a'at ("Flashes" or "Effulgences"), which was submitted to the Shaikh and won his approval. The powerful nobleman Mu'in'ed-Din the Parvaneh was Araghi's admirer and disciple and built for him, it is said, a khanaghah or monastry at Tuqa't, besides showing him other favors. Now seemingly everything was going right for him. However it was not meant to be. His proteg'e, Parvaneh, fell under the suspicion of the Mongol ruler, Abagha khan and accused of secretly aiding the Egyptions in the war against the Mongols. He ordered that Parvaneh and his family of 35 be slaughtered, and their bodies be eaten by the Mongols as this was their tradition. It is said that he himself also participated in this act of canabalism.

Rebirth of Persian Culture

Fearing for his life, Araghi escaped Ru'm and went to Egypt where he was received warmly by the Egyption ruler. He lived in that country for a few years at Salehiye khanghah and then moved to Damascus, where he also got an equally good reception, and there, after six months' stay, he was joined by his son Kabire'd-Din from India. Reunion unfortunately did not last too long. Soon after Araghi became ill and died five days later in the year 1310 (C.E). He was buried in the Salihiyya' Cemetery at Damuscus, beside the great mystic Shaykh Muhiyyed-Din ibna'l-A'rabi, who had predeceased him by 50 years, and whose influence in Persia, still prevalent even in our days, was largely due to Araghi and others of the same school. In his death bed Araghi was murmering these verses:

At the beginning when everyone's fate was sealed,That fate was not detemined as per our liking.	در سابقه چون قرار عالم دادند جانا که نه بر مراد آدم دادند
Whatever that was set for each of us on that day, We shall get no more than or no less.	زان قاعده وقرار کانروز فتاد نه بیش به کس دهند نه کم دادند

The following poem from Araghi's diva'n may serve besides that already given, as typical of his style:

"From head to toe thou art gracious, pleasant, and sweet, O Love! Thee to prefer to life it were right and meet, O Love!	سر به سر لطفی و جانی ای پسر خوشتر از جان چیست آنی ای پسر
To thee doth aspire the heart's desire of all, O Love! A hunter of hearts art thou to hold us in thrall, O Love!	میل دلها جمله سوی روی تست وه که شیرین دلستانی ای پسر
To mine eyes appear thy features fair and dear, O Love! Awake or sleep like a crystal stream so clear, O Love!	زان به چشم من درآیی هرزمان کز صفا آب روانی ای پسر از می حسن ارچه سر مستی مکن با حریفان سر گرانی ای پسر

Though Beauty's wine doth incarnadine
thy cheek, O Love!
Bear with thy comrades, nor do causless
quarrels seek, O Love!

They melt in air, hope's promises false and
fair, O Love!
Excuses, I ween, you'll find enough and to
spare, O Love!

Kisses sip from thine lips own fair lip, and
behold, O Love!
The Water of Life with its savour so sweet
and so cold, O Love!

In the dust hard by thy path I die at the
door, O, Love!
That a draught of wine on this dust of mine
thou mayst pour, O Love!

Jewels of speech on all and each thou dost
hurl, O Love!
So that every soul in its ear may wear a
pearl, O Love!

None do I see in grace like thee, and I am
sure, O Love!
Thou art soul incarnate and spirit essential
and pure, O Love!

In mine eyes and heart thou hast thy part
and share, O Love!
Never a moment on earth from North to
South, O Love!

May Araghi aspire to have his desire of thy
mouth, O Love!

وعده امید اگرچه کج بود
از بهانه در نمانی ای پسر

بر لب خود بوسه ده وانگه ببین
ذوق آب زندگانی ای پسر

زان شدم خاک درت کز جام می
جرعه ای برمن فشانی ای پسر

گوش جانها پر گهر شد بسکه تو
از سخن در میفشانی ای پسر

از لطیفی می نماند کس به تو
زان یقینم شد که جانی ای پسر

در دل و چشمم ز حسن و لطف تو
آشکارا و نهانی ای پسر

نیست در عالم عراقی را دمی
بر لب تو کامرانی ای پسر

Rebirth of Persian Culture

Araghi was an accomplished Gnostic and a proficient, well rounded and eloquent poet. He was a follower of Shaikh Shaha'b ed-Din Sohrevardi and Muhiyye'd ed-Din ibne' Ara'bi. He lived during the height of the revival of Islamic spirituality. He is known by many Sufis as a commentator on Sufi teachings. Aragh is also considered to have reached an exalted station of spiritual realization within the Sufi tradition. As indicated before he was both a member of the school of Persian Sufi poetry but also has been identified with the Ibn Arabian School of Sufism. Araghi was also a Gnostic who often spoke in the language of love. For him as well as many other Sufis, love was a realized knowledge.

Araghi's odes are exiliratingly beautiful. Here is one example of many:

"Save love of thee a soul in me I cannot see, I cannot see; An object for my love save thee I cannot find, I cannot find.	مرا جز عشق تو جانی نمی بینم نمی بینم دلم را جز تو جانانی نمی بینم نمی بینم
Repose or patience in my mind, I cannot find, I cannot find, While gracious glance or friendship free I cannot see I cannot see	بخود صبری و آرامی نمی بینم نمی بینم ز تو لطفی و احسانی نمی بینم نمی بینم
Show in thy face some sign of grace, since for the pain wherewith I am slain Except thy face a remedy I cannot see, I cannot see.	زروی لطف بنما رو که دردی را که من دارم بجز روی تو درمانی نمی بینم نمی بینم
If thou wouldst see me, speed thy feet, for parted from thy presence sweet, Continued life on earth for me I cannot see, I cannot see.	بیا گر خواهیم دیدن که دور از روی خوب تو بقای خویش چندانی نمی بینم نمی بینم
O friend stretchout a hand to save, for I am fallen in a wave Of which the crest, if crest there be, I cannot see, I cannot see.	بگیر ای یار دست من که در گردابی افتادم

Chapter 5

With gracious care and kindly air come hither and my state repair; Some pathway to Araghi teach whereby thy gateway he may reach,	که آنرا هیچ پایانی نمی بینم نمی بینم زروی لطف و دلداری بیا سامان کارم کن
For vagrant so bemused as he I cannot see, I cannot see." A better state, apart from thee, I canot see I cannot see.	که خود را بی تو سامانی نمی بینم نمی بینم عراقی را بدر گاهت رهی بنما که در عالم چو او سرگشته حیرانی نمی بینم نمی بینم.

Araghi's"collection of poems" containing about 5000 verses of odes, qasideh,"paneygerics", tarkibband , "composite- tie", tarji'band "Strophe-poem", taraneh, "melodi", and mathnavi "couplets". Besides his lyric poetry, Araghi composed a mathnavi poem entitled the 'Oshaagh-nameh, or "Book of Lovers" which contains 1063 verses. This book which is also known as, Dah nameh "Ten letters" comprises of 10 chapters and is fashioned in a similar style to Sannai's Hadighatul- Haghighat "Garden of Truth". It contains a series of mystic discussions accompanied by stories and allegories.

The other work by Araghi is his famous book in prose similar to the writing style of the famous Sufi and Theologian Ahmad Ghazali. The book is called Lama'at" Flashes" or "Effulgences", a mystical treatis inspired by the teachings of Muhiyyed-Din ibn''l-Arabi.

The Lama'at is a comparatively small book, containing, perhaps, between 7000 and 8000 words, and though written in prose, includes numeous pieces of verse.The many –sided and talented poet and mystic of the fourteenth century, Abdolrahman Jami of whom we will be speaking in the later chapters, wrote a commentary on it, entitled Ashaatol-Lamaat "Rays of the Flashes" , in the preface to which he says that he began by being prejudiced against the work and the authore, but, being requested by one of his spiritual guides to study and collate the text, he found it to consist of "graceful phrases and charming suggestions, verse and prose combined together and subtlties in Arabic and Persian intermingled, wherein the signs of [human] knowledge and [superhuman] gnosis were apparent, and the lights of rapture and ecstasy manifest, so that it would awaken the sleeper, cause him who was awakened to apprehend secret mysteries, kindle the fire of Love, and put in motion the chain of Longing." The book is divided into 28 "Flashes" (Lam'a't), probably in correspondences with the number of letteres in the Arabic alphabet. Here is a specimen from the opening pages of the first Lam'a, the prose portion in English:

"Praise be to God who illuminated the countenance of His Friend with the Effulgence of Beauty, so that it gleamed withlight; and made visible therein the limits of Perfection, and rejoiced therein with joy; and raised him up by His hand and chose him out while Adam was not yet a thing mentioned, nor had the Pen written, nor the Tablet been inscribed. [His Friend, who was theTreasure-house of the treasures of Being, the Key of the Store-houses of Bounty, the Qibla of Desire and the Desired One, the Possessor of the Standard of Praise and the Laudable Station, the tongue of whose high degree declares:]

'Though in outward form I seem one of Dam's progeny,
Yet the underlying truth claims for me paternity'.

Here is one of Araghi's typical nostalgic odes from his famous 'La'mat':

'Although in form of Adam's race,'said he,
'Higher by far than his is my degree.

My beauty mirrored in a glass I see,
And the enire world a picture seems of me.
Creation's Sun is I: doth it amaze
If each created atom me displays?

The holy Spirits make my Essence plain,
And human forms my attributes retain.

The boundless sea's a sprinkling of my grace;
The radiant light's a reflex of my face.

گفتا بصورت اگرچه زاولاد آدمم
ازروی مرتبه بهمه حال برترم

چون بنگرم درآینه عکس جمال خویش
گردد همه جهان بحقیقت مصورم

خورشید آسمان ظهورم عجب مدار
ذرات کاینات اگر گشت مظهرم

ارواح قدس چیست نمودار معنیم
اشباح انس چیست نگهدار پیکرم

بحر محیط رشحهاز فیض فایضم

From Throne to Footstool all is but a mote Which in the radiance of my Sun doth float? The Veil of my Attributes aside is hurled, And my bright Essence brightens the entire world.	نور بسیط لمه ای از نور از هرم از عرش تا به فرش همه ذره ای بود در نور آفتاب ضمیر منورم
The stream which Khidr's ebb of life did stop Was a single drop of my Kawthar-stream?	روشن شود ز روشنی ذات من جهان گر پرده صفات خود از هم فرودرم
That breath wherewith Christ loosed the thralls of Death, Was but a blast of my soul-saving breath?	آبی که خضر گشت از و زنده جاودان آن آب چیست قطره ای از حوض کوثرم
My essence all the Names doth manifest; I am of Names the greatest and the best!	آن دم کزو مسیح همی مرده زنده کرد یک نفخه بود از نفس روحپرورم
Araghi glorifies and defines the Divine love crying out:	فی الجمله مظهر همه اسماست ذات من
Exalted high is Love o'er men's ambition, And o'er ideas of union or partition; For when a thing transcends all thought and mention 'Tis freed from likeness and from comprehension.	بل اسم اعظمم بحقیقت چو بنگرم

It is veiled by the Veil of glory and isolated in its perfection. Its attributes are the veils of its Essence and implicit in that Essence. Its Splendour is the Lover of its beauty, which is involved in that Splendour. For ever it makes love to itself, and concerns itself not with aught else. Every moment it casts aside the Veil from the face of some loved one, and every instant it raises a new song in the way of loverhood.

Within the Veil Love sings its air: Where is the lover to hear it, where?	عشق در پرده می نوازد ساز عاشقی کو که بشنود آواز

Each moment it chants a different lay And ever some melody fresh doth play,	هر نفس نغمه دگر سازد هرزمان زخمه ای کند آغاز
The entire Universe echoes its song; Who hath heard such an anthem long?	همه عالم صدای نغمه اوست که شنید اینچنین صدای دراز
Its secret out from the world doth leap; How can an Echo its secret keep?	راز او از جهان برون افتاد خود صدا کی نگاهدارد راز
I tell no tales, but loud and clear From the tong of each atom its secret hears.	سراو از زبان هر ذره خود تو بشنو که من نیم غماز

Every moment with every tongue it tells its secret to its own ear; every instant with all its ears it hears its speech from its own tongue; every minute with all its eyes it flashes its beauty on its own vision; every second in every aspect it presents its being to its own notice.It speaks with me through speaking and through speechless;Through lowered eyelashes and glancing eyes.Knowest thou what it whispersin my ears?

I am Love, for which in these worlds there is found not a place; The 'Phoenix am I of the west, who hath never a trace.	عشقم که دردوکون مکانم پدید نیست عنقای مغربم که نشانم پدید نیست
By my glance and my eyebrow the world I have captured, I trow, Heed not that I do not possess either arrow or bow.	زابروو غمزه هردو جهان صید کرده ام منگر بدان که تیروکمانم پدید نیست
Revealed in the face of each atom am I, like the sun; So apparent am I that my form is apparent to none.	چون آفتاب دررخ هرزره ظاهرم از غایت ظهور عیانم پدید نیست
I speak with all tongues, and with every ear do I hear	گویم به هرزبان وبهر گوش بشنوم

Though, strange as it seems, I have neither a tongue nor an ear.	وین طرفه ترکه که گوش وزبانم به دید نیست
I am all that exists in all worlds, so 'tis patent and clear Neither that in this world nor that, have I rival or peer.	چون هرچه هست در همه عالم همه منم مانند در دو عالم از آنم به دید نیست

The following is a translation of the "Forward "from Araghi's Lama'a't (Flashes):

Know that in each 'Flash' of these 'Flashes' some hint is given of that Reality which transcends differentiation, whether you call it Love or Attraction, since there is no dearth of words; and some suggestion is made as to the manner of its progress in diverse conditions and cycles, of its journey through the degrees of dissociation and establishment, of its manifestation in the form of ideas and realities, of its emergence in the garb of Beloved and Lover, and finally of the absorption of the Lover in the Beloved formally, of the inclusion of the Beloved in the Lover ideally, and of the comprehension of both together in the Majesty of its Unity. There divergences are reconciled, ruptures are made whole, the Light is concealed within the Light, and the Manifestation lies latent within the Manifestation, while from behind the pavilions of Glory is cried:

O, is not all save God hollow and vain?

The identity [of each] disappears [in the other], leaving neither sign nor trace, and they merge in God, the One, the All-compelling.

First Flash,

"Setting forth the pre-existence of Love to both Beloved and Lover, and the manner of their production by it, which takes place in the first Differentiation; and setting forth that wherein each stands in need of the other?"The derivation of both Lover and Beloved is from Love, which, in its Abode of Glory, is exempt from differentiation, and in the Sanctuary of its own Identity is sanctified from inwardness and outwardness. Yea, in order to display its perfection, in such way as is identical with its Essence and [equally] identical with its Attributes, it shows itself to itself in the Mirror of Loverhood and Belovedness, and reveals its Beauty to its own Contemplation by means of Seer and the Vision. Thus the names of Loverhood and Beloved-ness appeared, and the description of the Seeker and the Quest became manifest. It showed the Outward to the Inmost, and the Voice of Loverhood arose: It showed the Inmost to the Outward, and the name of Belovedness was made plain.

No atom doth exist apart from it, that Essence single: 'Tis when itself it doth reveal that first those 'others, mingle.	یک عین متفق که جز او ذره ای نبود چون گشت ظاهر این همه اغیار آمده
O Thou, whose ouward seeming Lover is, Beloved thine Essence, Who hitherto e'er saw the Object Sought seel its own presence?	ای ظاهر تو عاشق و معشوق باطنت مطلوب را که دید طلبکار آمده

Love, by way of Belovedness, became the Mirror of the Beauty of Lovehood, so that therein it might behold its own Essence, and by way of Loverhood the Mirror of Belovedness, so that therein it might contemplate its own name and attributes. Although but one object is beheld by the Eye of Contemplation, yet when one face appears in two mirrors, assuredly in each mirror a different face appears.

O how can 'Otherness 'appear when whatsoe'r existeth here? In essence is that Other One becoming to our vision clear?	غیری چگونه روی نماید چو هر چه هست عین دگر یکیست پدیدار آمده ست

It was mentioned earlier that Araghi has also tried his hand in composing Tarji'-band (strophe-poem). Here is the first strophe of a very fine one:

"Cups are those a-flashing with wine, Or suns through the clouds a-gleaming?	اکووس تلالات بمدام ام شموس تهللت بغمام
So clear is the wine and the glass so fine That the two seem are none but one.	از صفای می و لطافت جام در هم آمیخت رنگ جام و مدام
The glass is all and the wine is naught, Or the glass is naught and the wine is all;	همه جامست و نیست گویی می

Since the air the rays of the sun hath caught
The light combines with night's dark pall,

  For the night hath made a truce with the day;
And thereby is ordered the world's array.

If thou know'st not which is day, which night,
Or which is goblet and which is wine,

By wine and cup divine aright
The Water of Life and its secret sign:

  Like night and day thou mayst e'en assume?
  Certain knowledge and doubt's dark gloom
If these comparisons clear not up
All these problems low and high,

Seek for the world –reflecting cup
That thou mayst see with reason's eye

That all that is, is He indeed,
Soul and beloved, sweetheart, heart and creed, all it's He.

یامدامست ونیست گویی جام

تاهوارنگ آفتاب گرفت

هرد و یکسان شدند نوروضلام

روزوشب باهم آشتی کردند
کار عالم ازآن گرفت نظام

گرندانی که این چه روز وشب است یا کدامست جام و باده کدام

سر آب حیات در عالم
چون می وجام فهم کن تومدام

انکشاف حجا ب علم یقین
چون شب وروز فرض کن وسلام

ور نشد زین بیان ترا روشن
جمله آغاز کار تا انجام

جام گیتی نمای را بطلب
تاببینی به چشم عقل تمام

که همه اوست هرچه هست یقین
جان وجانان ودلبر ودل ودین

Rebirth of Persian Culture

Shaykh Mahmood Shabastari, is one of the most respected and admired Iranian Gnostics of the 14th century (C.E). His masterpiece, "The secrets of Rose Garden" (Golshan-e-Ra'z) has established a special rank for itself amongst the writings of Persian Gnostics since it was first introduced in the early years of the 14th century.

Shabastari was born in the village of Shabastar, a suberb of the city of Tabriz in the province of Azerbayejan in the year 1309 (C.E). He completed his elementary and higher education in Tabriz and was a pupil and follower of Shaikh Baha'ed-Din Yaghoob (Jacob) Tabrizi. He travelled extensively and attended the teaching and guidance sessions by other prominent sufies. Before long and at an early age in his short lived life he attracted the attention and respect of many Sufi intellectuals and leaders due to his profound knowledge in the science of Theosuphism, sharpness of mind and remarkable intellect. His dscendents are known as "Khajegan" (Eunuch) or men of distinction. His trips to a number of places eventually brought him to Kerman, where his descendents are known to be living there even up to present time and are known by the same title. He lived during a time that Iran had been ravaged by the Mongole invasion, but he seems to have lived a relatively uneventful life, though very short at or near Tabriz. He died at the young age of 33, about the year 1342 (C.E) and is buried in the village of Shabastar next to the tomb of his teacher and mentor Shaikh Baha'ed-Din. He was by no means a voluminous writer, but his Golshan-e-Ra'z, which is a mathnavi and contains about one thousand couplets, as was mentioned before is one of the best and most compendious manuals of the mystical doctrines of the Sufis, and even at the present day enjoys a high reputation. It has been edited with a translation, Introduction, and valuable notes, by professor E.Whinfield, who gives in his Introduction the few particulars known about the author and the history of the poem. The poem was composed, as the poet himself informs us, in 1332 (C.E) in reply to a series of fifteen questions on mystical doctrine propounded by an enquirer from Khora'sa'n named Amir Hossein Herravi the famous Sufi. It has been said that when the questions were addressed at the gathering of the Sufi followers headed by Shaikh Baha'ed-Din, he turned to Shaikh Shabastari who was also present there to come up with the answers. Shabastari obliged at once, by answering the questions in poetic verses, and gradually building them up to create the "Golshan-Raz". The work was completed in the year 1339 (C.E.) and Shabastari is quoted to have said that this was the first time that he ever started writing any poetry.

Chapter 5

The fifteen questions which are included in the poem are briefly as follows:

As to the nature of thought
Why is thought sometime a sin, sometimes a duty, and what sort of thought is incumbent on the mystic?
What am "I"? What is meant by "travelling into one's self?"
What is meant by the "Pilgrim"? and what by "the Perfect Man"?
Who is the Gnostic (Aref) who attains to the Secret of Unity?
"If knower and Known are one pure Essence, What are the inspirations in this handful of dust?"
"To what Point belongs the expression, 'I am the Truth?
"Why call them a creature 'united'? How can he achieve 'travelling' and 'journey'?
"What is the union of 'Necessary' and 'Contingent'? What are 'near and 'far,' more' and less?
What is that sea whose shore is speech? What is that pearl which is found in the depths?"
What is that Part which is greater than it's whole? What is the way to find that Part?
How are the Eternal and Temporal separate? Is this one the World and the other God?
What means the mystic by those [allegorical] expressions of his?
What does he indicate by "eye"and "lip"?
What does he intend by "cheek", "curl" "down" and "mole"?
(Who is in 'Stations' and 'States'.)"?
"What meaning attaches to 'Wine,' 'Torch' and'Beauty'?
What is assumed in being a haunter of Taverns?
"Idoles, girdles and Christianity in this course
Is all infidelity; if not, say what are they?"

The book contains not only the answers to these questions, but a number of incidental illustrations, parables and digressions, and is on the whole one of the best manuals of Sufi Theosophy which exists especially when taken in conjunction with the excellent commentary of Abdul-Razza'gh al-Lahiji.
Here is', as an example, Question 10 together with the Answer and illustration from the Golshan-e-Raz'
Question 10

چه بحر است آنکه نطقش ساحل آمد   ز قعر او چه گوهر حاصل آمد

Answer 10

"The sea is being; speech its shore;
the shellWords and its pearls Heart's wisdom

Each wave a thousand royal pearls doth pour of
Text, tradition and prophetic lore.

Each moment thence a thousand waves are tossed,
Yet never a drop therefrom is lost.

Knowledge is gathered from that sea profound:
Its pearls enveloped are in words and sound.
Ideas and mysteries descending here
Need some similitude to make them clear"

یکی دریاست هستی نطق ساحل
صدف حرف و جواهر دانش دل

به هر موجی هزاران درشهوار
برون ریزد ز نص ونقل واخبار

هزاران موج خیزد هردم از وی
نگردد قطره ای هرگز کم ازوی

وجود علم از آن دریای ژرف است
غلاف در اوازصوت وحرف است

معانی چون کند اینجا تنزل
ضرورت باشد آن را از تمثل

Illustration.

"In April'month, thus was it told to me?
The oysters upward float in'Umma'n sea'

Up from the depths unto the Ocean's brim
Ascending open-mouthed they shoreward's swim.

Mist from the sea arise and veil the land,
And then in rain dissolve by God's command.

Into each oyster-mouth a raindrop creeps:
The shell doth close, and sinketh to the deeps.

تمثیل در بیان صورت و معنی

شنیدم من که اندر ماه نیسان
صدف بالا رود از قعر عمان

زشیب قعر بحر آید برافراز
به روی بحر بنشیند دهن باز

بخاری مرتفع گردد زدریا
فروبارد به امرحق تعالی

چکاند در دهانش قطره ای چند
شود بسته دهان او به صد بند

A pearl is formed from every drop of rain.
Into the depths himself the Diver hurls,

رود تا قعر دریا با دلی پر
شود آن قطره باران یکی در

And to the shore brings back the lustrous pearls.
Being's the sea: the shore our human frames:

به قعر اندر رود غواص دریا
از آن آرد برون لولوی لالا

Wisdom is the diver in this mighty deep,
Who'neath his cloak a hundred pearls doth keep.

تن تو ساحل و هستی چو دریاست
بخارش فیض و باران علم اسماست

The Heart's the vase wherein is Wisdom found:
Heart's widom's shell the letters, words and sound

خرد غواص آن بحر عظیم است
که اورا صد جواهر درگلیم است

دل آمد علم را مانند یک ظرف
صدف با علم دل صوت است با حرف

The moving breath like lightning doth appear,
And thence words fall upon the hearer's ear.

نفس گردد روان چون برق لامع
رسد زو حرفها با گوش سامع

Break, then, the shell: bring forth the royal pearl:
The kernel Keep: the husk on ash-heap hurl.

صدف بشکن برون کن در شهوار
بیفکن پوست مغز بردار

Lexicon, grammar, and philolog
All these mere accidents of letters are.

لغت با اشتقاق و نحو با صرف
همی گردد همه پیراهن حرف

Whoe'er on things like these his life doth spend
Doth waste his life without an aim or end.

هر آنکو جمله عمر خود در این کرد
به هرزه صرف عمر نازنین کرد

Shaykh Mahmood Shabastari, besides his masterpiece; Golshane-Raz is the author of three other books:"Mera't al-Mohagheghin", "Haghol-Yaghin (certain Truth) and the Resa'la-i-Shahed ("Tract of the witness"). He also translated from Arabic to Farsi, Menhaj ol-Abedin of Ahmad Ghazali.

Rebirth of Persian Culture

Haghol-Yaghin is comprised of eight chapters, corresponding with the eight Gates of Paradise, and dealing with the following subjects:

1- The Manifestation of the Divine Essence.
2-The Manifestation of the Devine Attributes, and the Station of Knowledge.
3- The Manifestation of the Degrees thereof, and the explanation of the origin.
4- On the necessity of the Divine Unity.
5- On Contingent Being and Plurality.
6- On Differentiation of movement, and the continual renovation of Differentiations
7- On the Philosophy of Obligation, compulsion, predestination and conduct
8- Explaining the Ruturn and the Resurrection, and Annihilation and Permanence.

Jamaled-Din Muhammad Salman Saveji, 14th century poet & gnostic

Salman Saveji (of Saveh) was one of the most distinguished poets of the 14th century. He was well respected and greatly admired by the great poets of his time, Hafez for one, who wrote the following verse, as a sign of respect, admiring him:

| "Dost thou know who the chief of the scholars of this Age is? In the way of truth and certainty, not in the way of doubt and falsehood | سرآمد فضلای زمانه دانی کیست زراه صدق ویقین نی زراه کذب وگمان |
| That monarch of the accomplished and king of the realm of verse That ornament of Church and State (Jamaled-Din), the Master of the World Salman" | شهنشه فضلا پادشاه ملک سخن جمال ملت ودین خواجه جهان سلمان |

Such tribute paid to Salman specially coming from Hafez who himself is credited to be one of the world's greatest poets and lyrists, bears testimony to the high rank of Salman as a distinguished poet.

Chapter 5

Despite his disinclination of panegyric and flattery, even description of his peers, Hafez has tended to such a description of Salman. The cause of this must be searched in hidden features in Salman's poetry and character, valuable points of view as well as pure properties which are found in his works. Doing this requires application of research and precise methods of scrutinizing about various and neumerous poetry of this great poet. It should further be said that Salman lived at a time (14th century) when Persian poetry had reached its zenith in brilliance and greatness with the advent of poets such as Mowlavi and Saadi and many others in the 13th century, followed by great masters such as Hafez, Obeid Zakani, Khajoo of Kerman, Khosrow Dehlavi, Mozafar Heravi, Kamal Khojandi, Salman and others. It should also be noted that most of Hafez's contemporary poets were over shadowed by him as no one could truly match the exceptional beauty of the poetry of Hafez or share his overwhelming reputation.

Maleko-l Shoara (The chif poet of the royal court), title given to him when admitted to the court of Ilkhani kings commonly known as Salman Saveji was born in the city of Saveh around the year 1331(C.E). In the later years he accompanied his father to the city of Baghdad and took up residence there. Dolatshah Samarghandi historian and biographer has written this brief about him:

"Salman was a wealthy man in the city of Saveh. His family were highly respected and revered by the monarchs and the members of the royal court. His father Khaje Alaed-Din Mohammad Savejy was a great scholar and writer. Salman himself was a distinguished man of letters and very famous as a poet and scholar."

Salman was first and foremost a panageryst. He was also a brilliant lyrist. He is credited with having been a true and enlightened Gnostic, well respected and liked in the circles of the Sufis. In the beginning Salman joined the court of Khajeh Ghyased-Din Mohamad and Sultan Abusaiid Bahador khan. During this time he wrote a great number of panageries praising these monarchs. He later joined the Court of Ilkhnian as the chief poet following the death of Sultan Abusaiid, and the murder of Khajeh ghyased-Din. It was at the court of Ilkhani monarchs that he was also given the responsibility of tutoring the young Ilkhani prince, the heir to the throne, by his mother Queen Delshad Khatoon. The prince got a thourough education under the tutorship of Salman and became quite proficient in literary arts; especially Persian poetry and prose and turned out as a prominent scholar. He later ascended to the throne as Sultan Oveis Ilkhani, but his life was cut short by an illness and died very young. Salman was devastated when his patron Sultan Oveys suddenly died. One of his most celebrated quasidas was written to commemorate the death of the young monarch.

"O Heaven, go gently! It is no slight thing that thou hast done, Thou hast made desolate the land of Persia by the death of the king,	ای فلک آهسته روکاری نه آسان کرده ای ملک ایران را بمرگ شاه ویران کرده ای
Have caused the fall to earth of the Heaven to earth, turning it to dust.	آسمانی را فرود آورده ای از اوج خویش
To be truthful, this is no small matter! You have robbed every Musalman of, His blood, livelihood, and estate.!	برزمین افکنده ای با خاک یکسان کرده ای نیست کاری مختصرگر با حقیقت میروی قصد خون ومال وعرض هرمسلمان کرده ای

Salman, enjoyed great respect and attention at the royal court, and became a very rich man. Sultan Oveis before his death endowed him a great estate in the suberbs of Saveh where he was planning to retire there later on. This retirement, however never materialized and he was made to reside permanently at the royal court and always in attendance to the royal family. When in later years of his life Sultan Hossein Jalayer ascended the throne, he lost favour with the new monarch and spent the last years of his life in misery and poverty, eventually dying in the year 1400.

Shibli Numani another historian and writer offers a somewhat different story of the last years of Salman's life, indicating that to be based on one of Salman's own qyasidas. In this poem he says that for nearly forty years he has celebrated his Royal patron's praises in the East and in the West; that he is now old and feeble, lame, and weak of sight, and wishes to retire from Court and spend the remainder of his days in praying for the King; that having been the master of the realm of poets, he desires to become the servant of the poor;

that he has no doubt that the King will continue his allowance, but that he would like its source and amount to be definetly fixed; and finally that he owes considerable sums of mney which he cannot pay, and prays the King, to discharge these debts for him. In reply the King is said to have written two couplets on the poet's versified petion, in the first of which he orders his allowance to be continued as heretofore, while in the second he assigns him the revenues of the village of Irin near the province of Ray.

Shibli Numani concludes his notice of Salman with a fairly detailed and wholely favourable appreciation of his skill in the different forms of verse. His skill is mainly apparent in his qasidas, which are remarkable for grace and fluency of language and for a felicity of diction possessed by none of the earlier poets, and peculiar to those of this middle period, between which two groups Salmon makes the transition. Shibli gives the following example to illustrate his assertion:

"Thy mouth smiled, and produced a jar of suger, Thy lip spoke and revealed glistening pearls,	خنده ای ز دد هنت تنگ شکر پیدا کرد سخنی گفت لبت لولوی تر پیدا کرد
Thy waist was undiscoverable, but thy girdle Deftly clasped it round, and revealed it in gold.	بود نایافت میان تو ولیکن کمرت چست بر بست میان را و به زر پیدا کرد
Cast aside the veil from thy waist, for those black tresses Have affected the fairness of thy cheeks"	پرده از چهره بر انداز که آن زلف سیاه در سپیدی عذار تو اثر پیدا کرد
"The freeze of Nowruz brings the aroma of the beautiful rose, And brings the dusk of the musk of Tartary from the borders of the desert,	باد نوروز نسیم گل رعنا آورد گرد مشگ ختن از دامن صحرا آورد شاخ را باغ به نقش دم طاوس نگاشت غنچه را باد بشکل سر ببغا آورد

The garden has decked branch with the patterns of a peacock's tail;
The wind has fashioned the bud into the likeness of a parrot's head.

لاله از دامن کوه آتش موسی بنمود
شاخ بیرون ز گریبان ید بیضا آورد

The [red] anemone hath displayed from the mountain- slopes the fire of Moses;
The branch hath brought forth 'White Hand' from its bosom,

از پی خسرو گل بلبل شیرین گفتار
نغمه باربد و صوت نکیسا آورد

The sweet-voiced nightingale, for the [delectation of the] Rose-Prince,
Hath contributed the strains of Ba'rbad and the songs of Nakisa.

سرور ا باد صبا منصب بالا بخشید
لاله را لطف هوا خلعت والابخشید

The zephyr breeze hath conferred high rank on the cypress;
The sweetness of the air hath endowed the anemone with a noble robe"

As it was briefly mentioned earlier, Salman owed his popularity at the Royal Court to the favors bestowed on him by Queen Delshad Khatun who appointed him to be the tutor of the future king, Prince Owyce who during his short life favored Salman over almost anybody else, showering him with gifts and showng him great kindness and respect. Salman remembers these special favors in this verse, as well as in other pieces that he wrote during his attendance at the Court.

"Through the auspicious fortune of this House,
I have captured the world with the sword of my tongue,

من از یمن اقبال این خاندان
گرفتم جهان را بتیغ زبان

To-day from East to the West,
I am more famous than the Sun"

من از خاوران تا در باختر
ز خورشیدم امروز مشهورتر

Shaykh Uways who had succeeded to the throne, when he was quite young, reigned nearly twenty years, and to him a great number of Salman's qasidas are addressed, while anecdotes given by Dolatshah showed the intimacy which prevailed between the two. This Prince is said by Dowlatshah to have been of such striking beauty that when he rode out the people of Baghdad used to flock into the streets to gaze upon a countenance which seemed to reincarnate the legendry comeliness of Joseph. When overtaken by untimely death he is said to have composed the following fine verses:

"From the spirit- world one day to the realms of Body and Sense did I roam!; I sojourned here for a few days, and now I am going home.	ز دار الملک جان روزی به شهرستان تن رفتم غریبی بودم اینجا چند روزی با وطن رفتم
The servant was I of a mighty Lord, and I fled from my Liege and Lord, Whom now in shame I am going to meet with a winding sheet and a sword	غلام خواجه بودم گریزان گشته از خواجه در آخر پیش او شرمنده با تیغ و کفن رف ,
Comrades of mine, I leave you now to joys that I may not share, And that you may enjoy this banquate long is my parting hope and prayer!	الا ای همنشینان من محروم از این دنیا شما را عیش خوش بادا در این خانه که من رفتم

As is usually the case with panagyrists, many of Salman's qasidas refer to definite historical events, and can therefore be dated. One of such qasidas was written, as mentioned before, to commemorate the death of Shaikh Oways. Another was written on the occasion of the flight of Shaikh Hassan-e- Bozorg to Baghdad, with this opening:

"It is the time of morning, and the brink of Tigris and the freath of spring, O, boy, bring the wine boat to the estuary of Baghdad"	وقت صبحست و لب دجله و انفاس بهار ای پسر کشتی می تا شط بغداد بیار

There were two others written to celebrate a victory of Shah Shuja in Azerbayjan. The second of them which won that Prince's high approval, begins:

"When I began to describe the beauty of her face,

"

My opening verse caused the' Sun' to rise!"

سخن بوصف رخش چون
ز خاطرم سرزد
ز مطلع سخنم آفتاب
سرزد

And it was after hearing it that Shah Shoja' observed:

"We had heard the fame of three notable persons in this country, and found them differing in their circumstances.

Salman exceeded all that was said in his praise; Yusuf Shah the ministrel agreed with his reputation; and Shaikh Kajahani fell short of his".

As already mentioned Salman probably died in 1400 a year or two after the composition of two of the qasidas mentioned above, so that he evidently continued to write poetry until the end of his long life, and did not as stated by Dowlatshah, actually retire into seclusion, though he implies his desire and intention of so doing in an interesting poem cited by Shibli Numani in his "Shearol Ajam".

Shibli in the same biography of Salman gives examples of Salman's skill in inventing those graceful and subtle concepts in which the poets of the middle and later periods take pride. The following specimens may suffice:

"The cornelian of thy lip placed the coin of life in a casket of pearls;
It was a precious stuff, so it put it in a hidden place.

Thy lips put a ruby lock on the lid of that casket;
Thy mole, which was of ambergris, set a seal upon it.

A subtle thought, finer than a hair, suddenly came
Into the heart of the girdle, and named it waist"

در درج در عقیق لبت نقد جان
نهاد
جنس نفیس بود بجایی نهان نهاد

قفلی زلعل بردر آن درج زد لبت
خالت ز عنبرآمد ومهری بر آن نهاد

باریک ترزمو کمرت را دقیقه z
ای ناگاه دردل آمد و اسمش میان
نهاد

"Henceforth make your rosary from the knots of the Magian's tresses. Henceforth take as your 'mehrab' the arch of the idols' (fair ones) eyebrows.	بعدازاین ازگره زلف مغان کن تسبیح بعدازاین ازخم ابروی بتان کن محراب
Arise joyous like the bubbles from the rose-red wine, and base no hopes, On this bubblelike revolving dome (sky)"	خوش برآهمچوحباب ازمی گلگون ومنه هیچ بنیاد براین گنبدگردون چوحباب
"For some while the revolution of this circle parted us from one another, Like the (points of a) compass, but at last brought us together [once more].	مدتی گردش این دایره ما را ازهم همچو پرگارجدا کرد وبهم بازآورد
"The zephyr found the rose-bud laughing before thy mouth, And smoth it so sharply in the mouth that its mouth was flled with blood."	غنچه را پیش دهان توصباخندان یافت آنچنان بردهنش زدکه دهان پرخون شد
"I will not set my foot one hair's breadth outside this circle, Even though they should split me like a compass into two halves"	پاازاین دایره بیرون ننهم یک سرمو گرسراپای چوپرگارکنندم بدو نیم

Hafez of Shiraz (Salman's contemporary, and admirer), has a parallel verse from which it appears that the circle formed by the down on the cheeks is intended here:

He, who fell in love head to foot over you, Willth not escape the Circle so long as he lives.	هرکه را با خط سبزت سرسودا باشد

I was given a "black" horse, not another color.

پای از این دایره بیرون ننهد تا باشد

Oh, yes. Beyond the" black", exists no other color.

اسپ سیه بدادم رنگ دگر ندادند

آری پس از سیاهی رنگ دگر نباشد

Other points in Salman's poetry noted by Shibli Numani are his skill in the successful manipulation of difficult rymes and awkward refrains. Thus he has long qasidas in which each verse ends with such words as 'dast" ("hand"), 'pay' ("foot"), "ru" ("face"), 'bar sar' ("on the head"), preceeded by the ryming word, yet which maintain an easy and natural flow of words and ideas. Shibli Numani next deals with the poets "fragments" (moghatta'at), or occasional verses, which as usual with this class of verse, are connected with various incidents in life, and therefore have a more personal note than the odes (ghazaliyat) and elegies (qasaied), but which are unfortunately ommited from the Bombay lithographed edition.

On one occasion the King gave Salman a black horse, which he did not like and wished to exchange for one of another color, but the Master of the Horses apparently would not permit this. Thereupon he wrote as follows to his patron:

"O King, thou didst promise me a horse; No further discussion is possible about the word of kings.

شاها مرا به اسبی موعود کرده بودی
در قول پادشاهان قیلی دگر نباشد

They gave me an old black horse, and I am of the opinion that no more aged black is to be found in the world.

اسبی سیاه و پیرم دادند و من بر آنم
کاندر جهان سیاهی ز آن پیرتر نباشد

I gave back that horse so that I might get another.
In such wise that none should have knowledge of this secret"

آن اسپ بازدادم تا دیگری ستانم
در صورتیکه کس را زین سرخبر نباشد

Chapter 5

In another fragment Salman excuses his absence from the Court on the plea that his eyes are bad, and that though the dust of the king's threshold is a collyrium, yet the evil eye must be kept far from him.

Finally Shibli Nomani speaks of the innovations introduced by Salman, and specialy by his skillful use of the figure called Iham or 'ambiguity'. The general conclusion seems to be that Salman deserves to be ranked amongst the great panagyrists and qasida-writers; that he was an ingenious, skilfull, and to certain extent original poet, but that he lacks the fire, passion, and conviction which make a poet great and famous beyond the limits of his own time and country the way that other shining stars in the domain of Persian poetry such as Saadi and Hafez proved to be.

Nezamed-Din Obeyd-e-Zakani 14th century Persian poet and satirist

Obayd-e-Zakani is, perhaps, the most remarkable parodist and satirical writer produced by Persia, and though like most Persian, Arabian, and Turkish satirists, his language is frequently coarse his "Akhlaghol-Ashra'f, or "Ethics of the Aristocracy" is a fine piece of irony, while some of his serious poems (which have been too much ignored by most of his biographers) are of singular beauty. It is generally believed that all in all Obayd was able to establish himself as one of the most prominant writers in the realm of Persian literature and in particular his satirical abilities that are second to none amongst the satirists of all times.

Obayed is believed to have been born somtime between the years of 1312 and 1317(C.E), in the village of Zakan a suberb of Qazvin. We know very little about the early years of his life other than, he was an extremely sharp, smart and intelligent child, with an astonishing sense of humor, very talented, with powers of repartee, and critical of influencial and rich people. In the years that followed he became a man of learning and talent, one of the masters of style and sound taste, Although some reckon him as one of the ribald writers, it is only fair to state that, though jests, ribaldry and satire occur in his poems, he deserves to rank as something more than a mere satirist, being, indeed, conspicuous amongst the older poets for his grace and wit, and in these respects approached by few. He was particularly skilful in incorporating in his poems and investing with a ludicrous sense the serious verses of other poets, an achievement in which he left no ground unturned. His own poems, on the other hand, are incomparable in fluency of diction, sweetness and distinction, and are unrivalled in grace and subtlety. Before long he established himself as one of the most accomplished men of letters and learning of his time, acquiring proficiency in every art, and compiling books and treatises thereon.

At that time the Turks in Persia had left no prohibited or vicious act undone, and the character of the Persian people, by reason of association and intercourse with them, had become so changed and corrupted that Ubayed disgusted at the contemplation thereof, sought by every means to make known and bring home to them the true condition of affairs. Therefore, as an example of the corrupt morals of the age and its people, he composed the treatis known as the 'Ethics of the Aristocracy' (Akhlaghul-Ashr'af), which was not intended as mere ribaldry, but as a satire containing serious reflections and wise warnings. So likewise, in order to depict the level of intelligence and degree of knowledge of the leading men of Qazvin, each one of whom was a mass of stupidity and ignorance, he included in his 'joyous Treatis' (Resaleh Delgosh'a) many anecdotes of which each contains a lesson for persons of discernment. As a measure of his accomplishments, experience, learning and worldly wisdom, his 'Tract of a hundred Counsels, (Rersaleh Sad Pand) and his 'Definitions' (T'arifat) are a sufficient proof. Morover, even those who speak as a mere ribald satirist admit that he composed a treatis on Rhetoric (Elm-e Ma''ani bay'an) which he desired to present to the King. The courtiers and favourites, however, told him that the King had no need of such rubbish. Then he composed a fine panegyric, which he desired to recite, but they informed him that His Majesty did not like to be mocked with the lies, exaggerations and fulsome flattery of poets. Thereupon 'Ubayed' said, in that case I too will pursue the path of impudence, so that by this means I may obtain access to the King's most intimate society, and may become one of his courtiers and favourites', which he accordingly did. Then he began recklessly to utter the most shameless sayings and the most unseemly and extravagant jests, whereby he obtained innumerable gifts and presents, while none dared to oppose or contend with him. Thus Obeyed-e-Zakani a serious writer, a moralist and a panegyrist was compelled by circumstances to becom a ribald satirist.

The most striking feature of the serious poems of Obeyed is the constant references to Fars and its capital city Shiraz which evidently held the affection of the poet far more than his native city of Qazvin.

Chapter 5

"It is said that after Obayed had despaired of entering the King's assembly, he extemporized the following quatrain:

"In arts and learning be not skilled like me,
Or by the great like me despised thou'll be,
Wouldst earn applause from this base age of thine?
Beg shamelessly, play lute and libertine!"

در علم و هنر مشو چو من صاحب فن
تا نزد عزیزان نشوی خوار چو من
خواهی که شوی پسند ارباب زمان
کنگ آور و کنگری کن و کنگر زن

"One of his acqaintances, hearing this, expressed astonishment that one so talented and accomplished could abandon learning and culture in favor of ribaldry and lewed utterances. To him Obayed sent the following verse"

"Keep clear of leaerning, Sir, if so you may,
Lest you should lose your pittance for the day,

Play the Buffoon and learn the fiddler's skill;
On great and small you then may work your will"

ای خواجه مکن تا بتوانی طلب علم
کاندر طلب راتب هر روزه بمانی

رو مسخرگی پیشه کن و مطربی آموز
تا داد خود از مهتر و کهتر بستانی

Obayd-e-Zakani has written an extensive number of serious poems and panegyrics, as well as the "Book of Lovers" (Oshagh-nameh) and "Book of Omens" (Fal-nameh).The last contains the largest selection of poetry, including panegyrics on Shaikh Abu Ishagh, Sultan Uways, and other important personalities. Among these one of the pretty ones is the following:

"Once again a passion has entered my head; again my hear inclines in a certain direction,

He is of Royal birth, I am of the dust; he is a king, I am portionless,

افتاد بازم در سر هوایی
دل باز دارد میلی بجایی

او شهریاری من خاکساری
او پادشاهی من بی نوایی

One tall of stature, with locks like lassoes, an outocrat descended from Sultan Hossain,

بالا بلندی گیسو کمندی
سلطان حسینی فرمان روایی

One with eyebrows like bows and slender waist, one unkind, fair and deceitful,

ابرو کمانی نازک میانی
نا مهربانی شنگی دغایی

Such a charmer of hearts, such a graceful cypress-tree, such a shower of oats and seller of barley (the one who makes promises, but never keeps),

زین دلنوازی زین سرونازی
زین جوفروشی گندم نمایی

Without him the sun gives no light; without him the world has no lustre,

بی او نبخشد خورشید نوری
بی او ندارد عالم صفایی

Wherever his ruby-lips smiles, there suger is of no account.

هرجا که لعلش درخنده آید
شکر نیارد آنجا بهایی

Everywhere the heart holds with his vision pleasant speech and sweet discourse

هرجای دارد دل با خیالش
خوش گفتگویی خوش ماجرایی

Thou wouldst say that I come to the house of a physicion, that perhaps I may procure a remedy for my heart.

گویی بیایم جای طبیبی
باشد که سازم دل را دوایی

Everyone else complains of a foe. Our complaint however is of a friend.

دارد شکایت هرکس زدشمن
ما را شکایت از آشنایی

Should the eyes of "Obayd not look their full upon him, then his eyes do not regard any other misfortune!"

چشم عبید ارسیرش نبیند
دیگر نبیند چشمش بلایی

Another fine manuscript of Obayd-e-Zakani, comprises 111 pages, and contains besides the poems, serious and flippant, the "Book of Lovers"

Chapter 5

(Oshagh n'ameh), in verse and partly in dialect; the "Ethics of the Aristocracy" (Akhlaghul-Ashra'f), the (Book of the Beard" (Rish-n'ameh), and the "Ten-Chapters" (Dah-Fasl). The most striking feature of the serious poems is the constant references to the province of F'ars, and its capital. Here are some quotes:

"By the auspicious justice of that King who is gracious to his servants, The region of Shiraz has become an earthly paradise."	ببین معدلت پادشاه بنده نواز بهشت روی زمین است خطه شیراز

So again he says:

By the favour of the Creator the Kingdom of P'ars hath become, Pleasanter than the Courts of Paradise and gayer than the spring"	شد ملک پارس باز بتایید کردگار خوشتر ز صحن جنت وخرمتر از بهار

And again he says:

"The victrious standard of the King who is so gracious to his servants, Hath reached with glee and happiness the region of Shir'az;	رسید رایت منصور شاه بنده نواز بخرمی وسعادت بخطه شیراز
Shaikh Abu Isha'q that world-conquerer of youthful fortune, our liege lord, Who slayeth opponents and maketh the fortune of his loyal supporters"	جهانگشای جوانبخت شیخ ابواسحق خدایگان مخالف کش موافق ساز

The following verse again, is strongly reminiscent of, and was probably inspired by, a very well-known verse of Sa'di occurring in a poem:

The gentle breeze of Mosalla and the stream of Rokn'b'ad cause the stranger to forget his own native land.

نسیم باد مصلی و آب رکن آباد
غریب را وطن خویش می برد
از یاد

The following verse occurring in a poem in which Obayd bids farewell to Shiraz affords further testimony of his attachment to that place:

"I leave the region of Shiraz, being in peril of my life;
Alas, how full of anguish is my heart at this inevitable departure"

رفتم از خطه شیراز و بجان
در خطرم
وه کز این رفتن ناچار چه خونین
جگرم

As in the case of Hafez so also in Obyd's divan we find one disparaging allusion to the port of Hormoz (Ormuz) in the Persian Gulf which would seem to have been written during Hafez's brief visit to that port city on his journey to India at the invitation of the ruler of Beng'al. This trip of course never materialized as Hafez getting scared of the incoming storm, disembarked from the ship and returned home to Shiraz.

"I am thus cast away in Hormoz in grief and sorrow,
Isolated from the companionship of friends and patrons"

در هرمزم افتاده چنین با غم
و درد
از صحبت دوستان و مخدومان
فرد

Amongst the Persian poets and satirists of the old times Obayd stands almost alone in style and subject matter. As one particular example his "Ethics of Aristocracy" is most valuable for the light it throws on the corrupt morals of his age, and it was really written with serious purpose to awaken his countrymen to the sad and deplorable deterioration in public and private life which had taken place in Persia during the Mongole ascendancy.
Here are some verses from this book:

"Whether or no a prophet comes, be thou virtuous in conduct,

نبی آید وگرنه تو نکوسیرت
باش

Chapter 5

For him whose conduct is virtuous will not go to Hell"	که به دوزخ نرود مردم پاکیزه سرشت

"Of whatever creed thou art, be a well-doer and giver, For infidelity combined with good character is better than Islam	بهر مذهب که باشی باش نیکوکار و بخشنده که کفر و نیکخویی به از اسلام و بدخویی

"He who is familiar with the essence of friendship, Will know whence our goods are obtained"	کس که ز شهر آشنایی است داند که متاع ما کجایی است

"Perchance somewhere and somewhen some man of heart May utter a prayer on behalf of this poor soul"	مگر صاحبدلی روزی به جایی کند در کار این مسکین دعایی

After these preliminary remarks the poet proceeds to discuss in turn each of the seven virtues already enumerated, beginning in each case with the "obsolete view" which is exactly modeled on what is set forth at greater length in such well-known treatis on Ethics as the earlier Akhl'agh-e-Naseri or the later Akhl'agh-e-Jala'li or Akhl'agh-e-Mohseni, and then passing on to the "adopted" view of his contemporaries. These verses are selected from the contents of the first chapter:

"Here ever Certainty entered, Doubt departed"	بهر کجا که درآمد یقین گمان برخواست

He to whom they give receives his gift even here,	آن را که داده اند همینجاش داده اند و انرا که نیست وعده بفرداش داده اند

, And he who has nothing [here] is put off with promises for "tomorrow" (promises of a future life)

"O Final Outcome of the Seven and Four, Who by the "Four and Seven" art vexed sore. (The Seven Planets and Four Elements called the "Seven Celestial Fathers"and the "Four Mundane Mothers")

ای آنکه نتیجه چهار و هفتی
وز هفت وچهار دایم اندرتفتی

Drink wine! A thousand times I have said this to you-
When once thou art gone, thou shall return no more!"

می خور که هزاربار بیشت گفتم
باز آمدنت نیست چو رفتی رفتی

"No mansions lie beyond this earth and sea;
No reason dwells outside of me and thee;
That nothing which is deemed by some men All,
O, pass it by;'it's but vain phantasy!"

زین سقف برون رواق ودهلیزی
نیست
جز بامن وتو عقلی وتمیزی نیست
ناچیز که وهم کرده کآن چیزی
هست
خوش بگذر ازاین خیال چیزی
نیست

(And it is for this reason that in their eyes attacks on men's lives, property and honor seem insignificant and of small account.)

'To such one draught of wine in hue like fire
Outweighs the blood of brethrens or of Sire'

براو یک جرعه می همرنگ آذر
گرامی تر زخون صد برادر

Another work by Obayd is the "Book of the Beard" (Rish-nameh) is a fantastic dialogue between "Ubayd-Zakani and the beard considered as the destroyer of youthful beauty.

The "Hundred Counsels"(Sad Pand) was composed in 1372 (C.E), and as its name implies, comprises a hundred aphorisms, some serious, such as :

Chapter 5

"O dear friends, make the most of life"
"Do not defer until to-morrow the pleasure of to-day"
"Profit by the present, for life will not return a second time"
And some ironical and ribald, such as; "So far as you are able, refrain from speaking the truth, so that you may not be a bore to other people, and that they may not be vexed with you without due cause"
"Do not believe the words of pious and learned men, lest you go astray and fall into Hell"
"Do not take lodgings in a street there is a minaret, so that you may be safe from the annoyance of cacophonous mo'adhins"
"Despise not ribaldry, nor regard satirists with the eye of scorn"

The "Joyous Treatis" (Res'al-e-Delgasha) is a collection of short Arabic and Persian stories mostly of ribald character, preceded by a short preface.

The book of "Mouse & Cat" comprising of 174 verses has been considered a classic amongst the people of Persia throughout the ages. It opens with a description of:

the voracious, keen-eyed,"lion-hunting" cat, with eyes like amber and sharp claws, feet like a scorpion, a forehead like an eagle, a belly like a drum, a breast of ermine, eyebrows like bows, and sharp teeth :	ز قضای فلک یک گربه بود چون اژدها به کرمانا گربه دوربین و شیرشکار کهربا چشم وتیزمژگانا پای کژدم عقاب پیشانی شکمش طبل و سینه اش قاقم ابروش قوس وتیزدندانا

۱

This cat being in need of a meal goes to a wine tavern and conceals itself behind a wine- jar. Presently a mouse appears, leaps on the edge of one of the jars, and begins to drink the wine, until filled with the arrogance engendered by alcohol, and ignorant of the proximity of its formidable foe, it begins to boast its powers, saying:

"where is the cat, that I may ring its neck and bear its head to the market place? In the day of my munificence at the time of	گفت کو گربه تا سرش بکنم سراو را برم به میدانا

conferring benefits I would distribute the heads of a hundred cats! Cats are but as dogs in my sight, were I meet them in the open field!"

سر صد گربه را ببخشم من
گاه بخشش به روز احسانا
گربه در پیش من چوسگ باشد
گر شود رو برو بمیدانا

Suddenly the cat leaps out upon it, seizes it, and cries, "O miserable mouse, how wilt thou save thy life?"

ناگهان جست وموش را بگرفت
گفت موشک کجا بری جانا

The mouse effectively sobered now, adopts a tone of piteous entreaty, saying,"I am thy slave; pardon me these sins! If I ate dirt (i.e. talked nonsense) I was drunk, and drunkards eat much dirt! I am your slave, your devoted slave...."

موش گفتا که من غلام توام
عفو کن برمن این گناها نا
مست بودم اگرگهی خوردم
گه فراوان خورند مستانا
من غلامم غلام حلقه بگوش
طوق بر گردنم غلامانا

The cat, however, pays no heed to the mouse's supplications, kills and eats it, and then goes to the mosque to pray and repent of its mouse-eating....

گربه آن موش را بکشت وبخورد
سوی مسجد بشد خرامانا
دست ورو را بشست ومسح کشید
ورد حق را بخواند ودیانا
بارالها که توبه کردم من
ندرم موش را به دندانا
گربه میکرد توبه در مسجد
یا کریم و قدیم وسبحانا
کار من توبه است واستغفار
ای خداوندگار رحمانا
بهراین خون ناحق ای خلاق
من تصدق دهم دوصد من نانا
تو ببخشی گناهم ای غفار
از گنه گشته ام پشیمانا
در مکروفریب بازنمود
تا بحدی که گشت گریانا

Chapter 5

Another mouse which was hiding in the pulpit of the mosque hears these edifying utterances and hastens to hear the good news of the cat's repentance to the other mice, saying, in a verse which has become proverbial and is alluded to by Hafez:

"Good tidings, for the cat has become devout; an ascetic, a true believer, a Muslim!"

مژدگانی بده که گربه عابد شد
زاهد ومومن ومسلمان شد

The mice thereupon decide to express their satisfaction by sending to the cat a deputation of seven mice bearing suitable presents of wine, raosted meats, sweets, nuts, fruits and sherbets. The cat invites them to approach, and then seizes five of them, one in its mouth, and one in each of its four paws, while the two survivers escape and carry the sad news of the cat's unchanged nature to the other mice. After a week's mourning for their lost comrades, the mice, 330,000 in number, under the command of their king, march out to do battle with the cats. After a fierce battle, the cats are defeated, and the chief offender, taken captive, is brought before the king of the mice, who condemns it to die on the gibbet, but at the end the cat breaks away from the captors, and kills the king of the mice, and scatters or slays his followers. The poem ends:

This strange and wonderful story is a momento of 'Obeyde-Zakani'

هست این قصه عجیب و غریب
یادگار عبید زاکانا

There are a few stories relating to the life and adventures of Obayd-e-Zakani. The following one is quite interesting:

It is said that Salma'n-S'avaji, other great Persian poet, Z'akni's contemporary, wrote these verses satirizing 'Obayd-e-Zakani whom he had never met but was familiar with his satirical writings:

"Obayd-e-Zakani, the rhymester, whose damnable satirist pen,
Hath made him accursed before God and obnoxious to men;
He is an ignorant oaf from the country, and not a Qazwini at all;
Though him, and that not without reason, "Qazwini" they call.

جهنمی هجا گو عبید زاکانی
مقرر است به بیدولتی وبی دینی
اگرچه نیست زقزوین وروستازاده است
ولیک میشود اندر حدیث قزوینی

As soon as Obayd-e-Zakani heard this verse, he at once set out for Baghdad, on his arrival there, he found Salm'an surrounded with great pomp and circumstance, on the banks of river Tigiris, occupied with pleasure and diversion and the society of the learned and accomplished men. When by some means he succeeded in entering the circle, Salm'an had just composed his hemistich descriptive of Tigris and asked the bystanders to complete:

'With drunken frenzy and fury fierce this

دجله را امسال رفتاری عجب
مستانه است

year the Tigris flows'-

Thereupon Obeyd-e-Zakani, extemporized the following complementary hemistich:

'With its foaming lips and its feet in chains, you might suppose it is mad.

پای در زنجیروکف
برلب مگردیوانه
است

Salm'an was delighted, and enquired where he came from? He replied 'From Qazwin.' In the course of ensuing conversation Salm'an asked him whether his name was known or any of his verse familiar in Qazwin, or not. Obayd-e-Zakani replied, 'the following fragment of your poem is very well known:

"A frequenter of taverns is I, and a lover of wine,
Besotted with drink and desire at the Magian's shrine,
Like a wine-jar from shoulder to shoulder is I carried,
Going from one hand to another like goblet or glass"

من خراباتیم وباده پرست
درخرابات مغان عاشق ومست
می کشندم چو سبودوش بدوش
می برندم چوقدح دست بدست

"Now although Salm'an is an accomplished poet, added Obayd-e-Zakani, and these verses may perhaps be truly ascribed to him, yet in my opinion they were most probably composed by his wife. (The implication is, of course, that his wife was a woman of loose morals and bad character.)

Salm'an perceived from this witty speech that this was none other than Obayd himself, apologized for his satire, received him warmly and whilst Obayd was in Baghdad fell short of no service which he could render him. And Obayd used often to say to him'O Salm'an you got lucky in that you quickly made your peace with me, and so escaped from the malice of my tongue.

Dolatshah Samanghandi has indicated that Obayed got his higher education in Shiraz during the time of Shah Abu-Eshagh and before long he became to be considered a high ranking and well respected scholar, writer, poet, and quite unique as a satirist in the literary community. Upon the completion of his education in Shiraz, he returned to his birth place the city of Qazvin and took a job as a teacher and a Juge.

 Few years later he moved to Baghdad for a while and then finally returned to Shiraz where he took permanent residence until his death in 1394 (C.E). Some have reported that he died in Shiraz, while others have quoted Isfahan as the place where he died. As to his tomb, no one seems to have any knowledge of its whereabouts.

Mowlana Obayed was born about forty years after the death of Sa'di. He was a contemporary of Hafez, but there is no knowledge available about these two great men of having ever connected with each other and neither of them has mentioned the name of the other in their writings.

In prose, Obayed has followed the style of Sa'di, and has been deeply inspired by the great Master. Sa'di's eloquence is clearly evident in all the works written by Obayed; the only difference being that Obayed's style in prose is slightly simpler than that of Sa'di's. Obayed was also quite proficient in Arabic and has composed great works in both poetry and prose in that language.

Majde Hamgar, 13th century Persian poet

Majde Hamgar is one of the greatest Persian poets and scholars of the 13th century (C.E.). He was a contemporary of Mowlana Jalal-e-Din Mowlavi, and Iran's greatest lyrist Sa'adi of Shiraz. Despite the outstanding quality of his poetry he could not attain the same widespread fame and recognition enjoyed by the two above mentioned poets as his work was naturally eclipsed by the works of those two.

Rebirth of Persian Culture

It is only fair to say that although he wrote outstandingly high quality poetry, but from the point of quality and quantity his work does not match those of Mowlavi's and Sa'di's.

Majde Hamgar was born in the year 1229 (C.E) in the city of Yazd, but he refers to himself in several places as Majd-e-Parsi, perhaps because he spent a great part of his adult life in Shiraz, capital city of the Pars province. His father Ahmad-e-Hamgar of Yazd, was one of the prominent scholars of his time, and according to Majd's repeated claims their illustrious lineage could be traced to King Anushiravan of the ancient Sassanian dynasty, and was on this account a somewhat priviledged person at the courts that he frequently visited. To this genealogy the poet alludes in his following verses as are mentioned in the book; Majma'u'l-Fusah'a:

"My virtues all a cruel age hath made for me a bane;
My youthful blood the aged Sphere hath shed in grief and pain.

بر من زمانه کرد هنرها همه وبا ل
وزغم بریخت خون جوانیم چرخ زال

The envious Mercury hath plucked the pen from out my hand,
The arching Heaven hath drawn a bow to smite me where I stand.

کلکم ز دست بستد تیر حسود شکل
برمن کمان کشید سپهر کمان مثا ل

O Sphere, what is it that you want of me, a poor, and barefotted one?
O Time, what is that you seek from me, a bird with broken wing?

چرخا چه خواهی ازمن عور برهنه پای
دهر اچه خواهی ازمن زار شکسته بال

Make of the falcon's eyes a dish to satisfy the owl;
Make of the lion's thighs

از چشم باز پخته کن لقمه های بوم

the food for which the jackals prowl.

وزران شیر ساخته کن طعمه شغال

In no wise like the noisy drum will I his blows bewail,
Although his lashes on my back descend as falls the flail.

از زخم او چو طبل ننالم به هیچ روی
ورخود زپشت من بمثل برکشد دوال

O foot of troubl's elephant, prey thee more
gently press!
O hand of this ignoble Sphere, increase
my dire distress!

Through tribulations bravely borne my
heart hath grown brighter,
As mirrors gain by polishing in radiancy
and light.

What time the rosebush from the dust doth
raise its floweing head,
The sapling of my luck (what luck!) hath
withered and is dead.

My fault is this that I am not from some
base seed upgrown:
My crime is this that noble is the pedigree
I own.

The sons of Sa's'an, not Tigin, my
ancestors I call;
I am of the race of Kisr'a, not the
household of In'al.

My verse is sweet and exquisite as union
with the fair;
My pen in picture-painting hath the gifts
of fancy rare.

No eye has seen an impulse mean impede
my bounty's flow.
The ear of no petitioner hath heard the
answer 'No!

When youth is gone, from out the heart all
love of play is cast;

ای پای پیل فتنه مرا نرم
تربکوب
ای دست چرخ سفله مرا سخت
تربمال

از مالشی که یافت دلم روشنی
گرفت
روشن شود هرآینه آیینه از صفال

وقتی چنین که شاخ گل از خاک
بردمید
طالع نگرکه بخت مرا خشک شد
نهال

عیبم همین که نیستم از نطفه
حرام
جرمم همین که زاده ام از نسبت
حلال

هستیم ز نسل ساسان نه ز تخمه
تکین
هستیم ز صلب کسری نه ز دوده
ینال

شعری به خوش مذاقی چون
چاشنی
وصل کلکی بنقشبندی چو صورت
خیال

And luster fadeth from the sun which hath the zenith passed"

زرفتی ندیده چشم کس ازمن بوقت جود

لاناشنوده گوش کس ازمن گه سوال

دل را نشاط لهو نباشدپس ازشباب

خورشید را فروغ نباشد پس از زوال

Majd- Hamgar spent the first part of his life studying literature, calligraphy, prose composition and poetry, and then went to Shiraz and joined the royal court of the Salgurid At'abecks. He gained the title of Malek-ol-Shoara' (poet-laureate) of the At'abek Mozaffar-el-Din Abu Baker-ebn.S'ad Zangi, and composed qasidas praising this ruler and his son, S'ad-ebn-Abu Baker who was an enthusiastic patron of poets. In 1272 (C.E), just ten days after succeeding his father, S'ad himself died of dropsy. His son Mohammad Zangi took his place, but he also died within couple of years. In 1277, the rule of the Salgurid At'abeks in Fars came to an end, an event which Majd often bemoans in his poetry:

Where is it gone the Kingdom of Sulgurid; the pride of the Kingdoms of S'asa'n and S'am'an!

کجاست مملکت سلغری که غیرت بود

براو ممالک ساسان ودولت سامان

The Kingdom got so deeply uprooted, That even its shadow can hardly be visioned in a dream!

چنان زبیخ درآمد درخت آن دولت که در خیال نیابد بخواب سایه آن

No trace can be found from all those good acts, No mention is made of all those good works.

نماند زان همه کرداربوی واثر نماند زان همه آثارخوب نشان

There remains no castles, no treasures, roots or off- springs, There remains no throne, banquets or audience,

نه قلعه ماند ونه گنج ونه اصل ماندونه نسل نه تخت ماندونه تاج ونه بارماندونه خوان

Chapter 5

No more, roar of the drums is heard from the corridors, or vestibule,
No more flutes are heard playing in the squares.

خروش کوس نمی خیزد ازدر دهلیز
فغان نای نمی آید از سرمیدان

I need to have a thousand eyes to shed tears,
Over the fall of those good-natured and descent Kings.

هزارچشم بباید مرا که خون گرید
برآن شهان نکوسیرت نکوسامان

The fall of the Sulgurid government in F'ars caused the poet great distress, and although the new Mongoli ruler went to visit him and offered him protection and livelihood, he declined the offer and set out for Kerman which was under the rule of Qaraketa'is. There, for a while he lived under the protection of the Qaraketa'I rulers and eulogized them during his stay there. Soon after he decided to return to Shiraz, and after suffering much hardship, finally connected with the important and powerful family of Joveini's, and went to live in Isfahan in the court of Shams-ed-Din Mohammad Jovini, prime minister to Mongol emperor A'ba'a'gha'Khan. This kind and scolarly ruler took him under his protection and provided a very comfortable life. He even offered him the governorship of Musul (a city to the north of Baghdad). He became friends also with the brother of Shams-ed-Din, Att-ol-Molk Joveini and travelled to Baghdad to visit him. These two great men clearly appreciated the extraordinary literary talent of the poet, as they themselves were both scholars of Persian literature. During the last years of his life luck turned away from the Joveini family, they lost the favor of the Mongol ruler, and their entire family was rutelessly slaughtered by the savage Mongol. Now the poet who had once before had witnessed the fall of his protectors, the Salgurid dynasty, became extremely sad and distraught. He lamented the death of the Joveini brothers and the family in this eulogy:

On the demise of "Shams", blood was seen dripping from the 'Aurora',
The 'Moon' tore up its face and the 'Venus' cut its tress,

دررفتن شمس ازشفق خون بچکید
مه چهره بکند وزهره گیسو بدرید

Night clad itself in black to mourn, and Morning,

Rebirth of Persian Culture

Let out a cold breath, and rended its collar.

شب جامه سیه کرد از این ماتم
وصبح
برزد نفس سرد وگریبان به درید

Dolatshah Samarghandi reports that S'adi, the poet of Shiraz cried reading this quatrain, praised Majde-Hamgar and prayed for him.

Majde-Din's quatrains unlike the quatrains of 'Umar Khayam, Abusaiid Abolkhayr, and other masters of this style of verse deal less with mystical and philiosophical ideas than with concrete things and persons. Some are merely abusive epigrams, such as the following:

"Born of a mother of accursed womb
From ganja's town of Abkhaz thou didst come,

آن مادرشوم فرج چون زاد ترا
از گنجه به ابخاز فرستاد ترا

Where that dog-training swinchered nurse of thine
Fed thee on dog's milk and the blood of swine"

وان دایه خوک خوار سگبان به غذا
شیر سگ وخون خوک میداد ترا

"O heaven never turn aside my reins from wandering;
Give me my bread from Sarandib (Ceylon), my water from Sar'ab,

ای چرخ عنانم از سفر هیچ متاب
نانم زسرندیب ده آبم زسر

Grant me each evening (sh'am) a loaf of bread from Bami'an,
And give me every morning (b'am) a draught of water from Sh'am (Damascus).

هرشام زبامیان دهم قرصی نان
هربام زشام ده مرا شربتی آب

In the two following quatrains he laments his advancing age:

"Fiery and fluent, once my heart did hurl,
Spontaneous verses forth, each verse a pearl;

آن شد که دلم زطبع چون آتش وآب

Then Love, Desire and Youth were mine. These three Not e'en in dreams I now can hope to see!"	می ریخت بدیمه هایی چون در خوشاب عشقی وجوانیی وکام دل بود وین هرسه دگربار ه نبینم در خواب
"This foot of mine no more the srirrup suits; For me no more are spurs and riding-boots. Oppressed by aches and age, there now remains No foot for stirrup and no hand for reins."	این پای مرا که نیست پروای رکاب نه روی رکوب ماند ونه رای رکاب زین سان که بتنگ آمدم ازپیری وضعف نه دست عنان دارم ونه پای رکاب
"Compared to you a pig is a pretty sight; Beside thy face an ape's the heart's delight. Thy temper's uglier than e'en thy face, Compared to it thy face is fair and bright."	ای دیدن خوک پیش دیدار تو خوب با چهر ه توبوزینه معشوق قلوب ازروی توخوی توبسی زشت تر است با زشتی خوی توزهی روی تو خوب

The following is addressed to his sweetheart:

"No means have I by thee to pitch my tent, Nor money in thy street to rent a home; My ears and eyes serve only to this end, To hear thy voice and on thee gaze intent."	نه برگ که خیمه ای زنم پهلویت نه سیم که خانه ای خرم در کویت من دیده وگوش را بدان میخواهم تا بشنوم آواز وببینم رویت

Majd-Din Hamgar was a great admirer of Emami Ahari another of his contemporary poets. He created uproar amongst the literary society of his time, when he was asked by Mu'enu'd-Din the Parwa'na, Malek Eftekhar'e'd-Din, Rasadi, and the S'aheb-Diwa'an Shamse'd-Din enquiring his opinion as to the respective merits of himself, Sa'di Shirazi and Em'ami Ahari, a poet of not such rank and standing compared to Sa'di .His reply was as follows:

'Though I in song am like the tuneful birds,	ما گرچه بنطق طوطی ای خوش نفسیم
Fly-like I sip the sweets of Sa'di's words;	بر شکر گفته های سعدی مگسیم
Yet all agree that in the arts of speech	در شیوه شاعری باجماع امر
Sa'di and I can ne'er Immami reach."	هرگز من وسعدی به امامی نرسیم

To this Emmami replied in the following complementary quatrain:

"Though throned in power in eloquence's fane,	در صدر بلاغت ارچه با دست رسم
And, Christ-like, raising song to life again,	در علم نظم ارچه مسیحا نفسم
Ne-er to the dust of Majd-e-Hamgar's door,	دانم که بخاک در دستور جهان
That Sabh'an of the Age, can I attain."	سبحان زمانه مجد همگر نرسم
(Sabh'n, a famous Arab poet from ancient times).	

Saadi, on the other hand, vented his spleen;

"Who e'er attaineth no position high?	هرکس که به پایگاه سامی نرسد
His hopes are foiled by evil destiny.	از بخت بد وسیاه کامی نرسد
Since Hamgar flees from all who pray or preach,	همگر چو بعمر خود نکرد دست نیاز
No wonder he 'can ne'r Em'mi reach	آری چه عجب گربه امامی نرسد

(Em'am also is the title for religious leader).

The following is one of the prettiest poems of Em'mi:

"We celebrate the New Years' Feast but once in all the year	یک روز بود عید به یک بار به یک سال

A Feast perpetual to me affords thy presence dear.

همواره مرا عید ز دیدار تو هموار

One day the roses hang
in clusters thick upon tree;
A never –failing crop of roses yield thy cheeks to me.

یک روز بشاخ اندر پر بار بود گل
روی تو مرا هست همیشه گل پربار

One day I gather violets by the bunch in gardens fair,
But violets by the sheaf are yielded by thy fragrant hair.

یک روز بنفشه برم از باغ بدسته
زلفین توپیوسته بنفشه است بخروار

The wild narcissus for a single week the field adorns;
The bright narcissus of thine eyes outlasts three hundred morns.

یک هفته پدیدار بود نرگس دشتی
آن نرگس چشم تو همه ساله پدیدار

The wild narcissus must its freshness lose or vigil keep;
To thy narcissus-eyes no difference waking makes or sleep

نرگس نبود تازه که بیدار نباشد
تازه است سیه نرگس تو خفته وبیدار

Fragrant and fair the garden jasmine is in days of spring,
But round thy hyacinths the jasmine-scent doth ever cling,

باشند سمن زاران بهنگام بهاران
برسنبل تو هست شب وروز بهاران

(hyacinth is a poetical metaphor for hair).

Nay, surely from thy curls the hyacinths their perfume stole,
These are the druggist's stock-in-trade and that food for the soul.

از جعد سیاه تو رسد فیض به سنبل
کین مایه جان آمد وآن مایه عطار

Those from a ground of silver (the fair,
silver-like skin) spring, and these from
heaps of stone;
Those crown a cypress-form, while these
adorn some upland lone".

There is a garden-cypress which remains
ever green,
Yet by thy cypress-stature it appears
uncouth and mean."

این را وطن از سیم شد آنرا وطن
از سنگ
این از برسروسهی آن از برکهسا

سروست که درباغ همه ساله بود
سبز
با قد توآن سروبود کوژونگونسار

Poetical interrogations amongst the poets of the sort mentiond above seem to
have been the fashion at that time. Another example is when certain people of
the city of Kashan addressed a similar versified question as to the respective
merits of the poets Anvari and Zahir of F'ary'ab to Majde-Din Hamgar, and
Em'mi. In that case both he and Em'mi preferred Anvari to Zahir, a judgement
in which nearly all competent critics will concur. Majde-Din's claim to prefer
Em'ami's poetry not only to his own but to S'adi's, on the other hand, cannot
be taken seriously, and must have been prompted by some personal motive
such as a desire to please Em'ami or to annoy S'adi. All Persian writers who
have noticed this matter at all have expressed amazement at the view which
Majd-e-Din Hamgar saw fit to advance; for in truth Em'ami's poetry, so far
as we can judge from the specimens given by Dowlatshah and in the 'Atash-
Kadeh and the Majmaol-Fusah'a, has no special distinction or originality,
while S'adi's claim to be reckoned among the half-dozen greatest poets of his
country has never been disputed.

Majd-Hamgar was recognized both by his contemporaries and later
biographers as being one of the greatest poets of his generation. His poetry
reveals the influence of the poets of the 12th century Khorasan. In every verse
form, whether qasida, gazal or rob'ai, his poetry is characterized by the use of
simple language to express delicate and subtle thoughts. His div'an contains
some 3000 verses of poetry in total.

Majde-Din Hamgar as it is suggested by some of his poetry lived a long life
of over 80. After the fall of his patrons the Joveini family he went to Isfahan,

settled to a lonely life which was overburdend by adverse poverty and hardship. He stopped writing poetry. The exact date of his death is not known.

Amir Khosrow Dehlavi, 13th century Persian poet & Sufi

Amir Khosrow Dehlavi, is one of the most distinguished Persian-writing poets born in India, a truly great and revered Sufi, whose father Amir Seifed-Din Mahmood immigrated to India following the Mongole invasion of Balkh a city in the territories known as "greater Khorasa'n. " Amir Seifed-Din settled in Patali, and it was there that Khosrow was born in 1253. In an early age he displayed poetical talent and was encouraged by his maternal grandfather Emaded-Din who put him uder the care of a master in poet; Shehab-ed-Din Mahmera Bada'uni a panegyric and poet. In later years Khosrow joined the service of Sultan Balban's family, accompanied his son to Bengaland later on to Multan. The prince was killed in a war with Mongols and Khosrow was taken a prisoner. After getting freed he returned to Delhi. He then joined the service of Sultan Jalaled-Din Khalji, and upon his assassination, continued with Al'ed-Din Khalji, as a court poet.

Amir Khosrow's special literary and artistic talents enabled him to achieve mastery in many fields in particular music and poetry. He turned out to be one of the greatest lyric writers in the Indian sub-continent. Although his specialty was lyrics, he was also an outstanding writer of prose and was able to emulate all styles of poetry which had developed in Iran. He has shown special mastery in writing qasida and mathnavi. He made great contribution to the development of Ghazals of outstanding quality in India opening the way for many future generations of Indian Persian poetry writers, who earnestly followed his pattern and style. At the young age of 19, he compiled his first diva'n, and rightfully named it (Tohfatel-Seghar (gift of Youth) followed by another diva'n, naming it Wastel-haya't.(middle of life). When he was around 35 to 40 years old, collected another diva'n and named it Ghorrat al-kamal', which also contains his own autobiography in prose. In 1318 Khosrow collected another diva'n naming it Baghiya-ye naghiya, and finally followed by the Nehayat al-kamal.

Amir Kosrow's knowledge of Arabic, Persian, Turkish, and Hindi enabled him to produce exotic puns, wordplays, and stunning literary tricks so that W. Berthels with full right speaks of his "powdered style".

Rebirth of Persian Culture

This particularly is visible not only in his lyrics and panegyrics but also in his numerous epics. Between 1298 and 1301 he wrote with great ease an imitation of Nezami's Khamsa, which comprises: Matla'al-anwar, Majnoon o Leyla', Shirin o Khosrow, Ayenai-ye Sekandari, and Hasht behesht .The work was often illustrated in later times, but in spite of its artistery lacks the flavor of Neza'mi's work. More important is Amir Khosrow's contribution to a new genre of poetry, the historical epic. In 1289 he poetically elaborated the meeting of Bogra Khan with his estranged son Keyghoba'd in Oudh (Qera' al-sa'dayn). Two years later he described four major victories of Jala'l-Din Khalji in Meftah al-fotuh (part of Gorrat al-kama'l). Perhaps the most famous epic of this group is Dowalra'ni Khazer Khan, the Ashiqa, which tells the love story of Khezr (Khazer) Khan,Ala'-ed-Din Khalaj's son, and a Rajput princess and was enlarged after Khezr Kha'n's tragic end in Gwalior (1315). In !318 the poet produced a particularly artistic work, Noh sepehr, where the nine spheres are represented in nine different meters; its descriptions of Indian culture, customs, languages, and festivals are an excellent source for our knowledge of medieval India, though all of Khosrow's work bear traces of Indian influence, whether in form (e.g., the "rain song") or vocabulary. In 1320 the Toghlogh-na'ma was written to celebrate Ghia-sed-Din Toghlogh's achievements. Amir Khosrow also composed remarkable prose works. The Khaza'en al-fotooh sometimes referred to as Tarikhe-alaie describes Ala'ed-Din Khalaje's conquest as well as other works.

Amir Khosrow is praised as having invented Hindustani music; he may have done so, but none of his works in this field has been preserved. In any case the musical flow of some of his gazal's has made them the favorites of musicians up to our time. He is also credited with poetry in Hindi, but discussions about the authenticity of the fragments ascribed to him continues. He uses Hindi with perfect ease and plays with them; the riddles and conundrums under his name may well be his. He is noted for versatility and his remarkable rhetorical skill. He had a keen eye and ear, as is understood from his description of the peculiarities of his homeland.

Besides being an elegant courtier, Amir Khosrow was also interested in Sufism; from 1272 onward he was attached to Nez'am-al –Din Awlia', the great Cheshti saint of Delhi, who lovingly called him Torkala'h. He devoted a number of poems to Nezam-el-Din, though otherwise a Sufi flavor is difficult to detect in his writings. A small collection, Afzal al-fawa'ed is said to contain sayings of Nezamal-din collected by Amir Khosrow.

Chapter 5

Amir Khosro died shortly after his maser and was buried close to him; his tomb in its present shape was finished in 1605 and is still visited by large numbers of people. In honor of his 700th anniversary (a number chosen casually), India, Pakistan and the USSR convened national and international congresses.Here is one short extract from Amir Khosrow's Layla' wa Majnun in which he mourns, with a remarkable touch of feeling, the death of his mother and younger brother , both of whom died in 1298-9. The poet's love for his other sister, which is in strong contrast with his lack of appreciation of his daughter, is one of the most attractive features of his character.

"A double radiance left my star this year: Gone are my mother and brother dear.	امسال دو نور ز اخترم رفت هم مادر و هم برادرم رفت
My two full moons have set and ceased to shine In one short week through this ill luck of mine	یک هفته ز بخت خفته من گم شد دو مه دو هفته من
My double tortures! I am racked of Fate, By double blow doth Heaven me prostrate.	بخت از دو شکنجه داد پیچم چرخ از دو طپانچه کرد هیچم
Double my mourning, double my despair; Alas that I this double grief must bear!	ماتم د و شد و غمم د و افتاد فریاد که ماتمم د و افتا د
Two brands for one like me is it not a shame? One fire is enough to set a stack in flame,	حیف است دو داغ چون منی را یک شعله بس است خرمنی را
One breast a double burden should not bear, One head of headaches cannot hold a pair.	یک سینه دو بار بر نگیرد یک سر دو خیار بر نگیرد
Beneath the dust my mother lies dead; Is it strange if I cast dust upon my head?	چون مادر من بزیر خاکست گر خاک بسر کنم چه با کست

Where are you mother mine, in what strange place? Can't you not, mother, show me your dear face?	ای مادر من کجایی آخر روی از چه نمی نیایی آخر
From heart of earth come smiling forth once more, And take compassion on my weeping sore!	خندان ز دل زمین برون آی بر گریه زار من ببخشای
Wherever in days gone by your feet did fall That place to me does Paradise recall,	هر جا که ز پای تو غباریست ما را ز بهشت یادگاریست
Your being was the guardian of my soul, The strong support that, kept me safe and whole!	ذات تو که حفظ جان من بود پشت من و پشتبان من بود
Whenever those lips of yours to speech were stirred Ever to my advantage was your word.	روزی که لب تو در سخن بود پند تو صلاح کار من بود
To-day your silence makes its dumb appeal, And lo, my lips are closed as with a seal!"	امروز منم بمهر پیوند خاموشی تو همی دهد پند

Pur-I-Baha'-Yi-Ja'mi 13th century Persian poet

Pur Baha Ja'mi was born into a family of administrators who had seen better times and who instilled a pervasive sense of injustice in the resulting biting and vindictive satirist. He was a native of Ja'm in Khorasa'n and his youth was spent in Hera't. Since the time of the tenth century Sa'ma'nids, his family had held positions of local influence in the province as judges (gha'zi) and scholars, though during the poets' life time the post of qa'zi in his family's particular case had become a titular adornment carrying little if any legal or political clout. In an anecode addressed to Nassir- ed-Din Tusi the poet admits to his own unsuitability for the post of Judge but pleads for a relative, Saheb-ed-Din, to be appointed deputy governor of (na'eb) Ja'm. He claimed that the family's decline had been brought about by the arrival of a newcomer from Ba'karz, Qa'zi Emad-ed-Din who had been able to assume the role of governor.

It is this same Ema'd-ed-Din Ma'lini who earns the invective and ridicule in Pur Baha's often Rebelaisian verse, his mathnavi, in particular ,where six verses are devoted to this arch-enemy, whom he labeled Ema'd-Lang (the Lame Ema'd, "Inauspicious, like an owl. Hungry like a raven; thief like a magpie; ill-omened like crow; like a crane , all neck and legs; a bat, all talons and claws. In other verses and poems Emad-ed-Din's reputation is made to pay a high price for usurping the poet's ancestral position as the governor of Ja'm; Pur Baha' even suggested that the governor's harem was open to paying guests. The poet felt free to malign and slander the officials and specially the clergy in a similar fashion generally employing coarse language and imagery to emphasize his point.

An interest in literature was evident from his youth, and two poets, Mawla'na' Rokn-ed-Din Qoba'I and Seied Heravi, exerted an influence during these early years in Hera't. While in Khora'san as a panegyrist poet he made an impression at the court with the governor who at the time enjoyed the favor of of the Young Il-Khanid prince, Argun Kha'n and who had matrimonial links with the powerful Joveyni brothers. The governor Ezz-ed-Din Ta'her Farymadi who was married to the daughter of Bah'-ed-Din Joveyni, and his son Wajih-ed-Din Zangi appreciated his stinging satire and presumably approved of its content. During this period, the poet acted as panegyrist (maddah) for a number of high Ilkhanid officials who served inder Abaqa Kha'n (r.1265-82), and his experience served him well. When he moved west, to Isfahan and Tabriz, the targets of his satire were often those whom he continued to perceive as having usurped the position of his family.

After leaving Khorasan' the poet is known to have spent most of his time in Tabriz, Isfahan, and Baghda'd, where he achieved particular fame as a panegyrist for the Joveyni family, most noticeably for the historian and governor of Baghda'd, Ala'-ed-Din Ata' Malk, the prime minister, Sa'heb Diva'n Shams-ed-Din Mohammad and the notorious governor of Isfahan and son of Shams-ed-Din Baha'-ed-in. Pur Baha' was also favored by the extremely influencial, Nasir-ed-Din Tusi, to whom he would allude in his work. However Pur Baha' was not writing in a vacuum, and the transformed

Rebirth of Persian Culture

empire emerging from the divisive civil war of 1260 was culturally vibrant and dynamic.

The Toluid Mongols in the east and west oversaw a shared cultural renaissance, which was surprisingly liberal in many respects, and the Yua'n elite indulged a taste for satire equally bitting in as that found at the Ill-kKhanid court, as one example can demonstrate. With religious figures and tax collectors the target of the satirist's pens in the western branch of the Toluid Empire, in the east in the popular Yu'an opera, the revered army found Yuan the butt of disdainful mockery. Mongol generals prided themselves in their mastery of military tactics with a pomposity readily open to ridicule: "Complete is my mastery of the Seven Stratagems and the Four Manoeuvres; the Four Manoeuvres, they are the Heavenly Manoeuvre, the earthly Manoeuvre, the Manly Manoeuvre, the Horse Manoeuvre"

Since Por Baha' was so closely identified with Joveini famiy, it is likely that he suffered a similar fate to his illustrious patrons and that if he did not lose his life he most certainly would have lost his fortune. Tact was not a trait associated with the poet, and he was vicious with those who challenged or threatened his interests or those of his patrons. As noted above a distinctive characteristic of the poet was to combine praise and vitriol in the same work, lauding his patron while later insulting someone who had crossed him. He concluded most of his odes (qasida) with the following words."in praise (madh) of so-and so and in mockery(hajv) of so-and-so,". When Majd-al-Molk, a member of of the powerful Qazvini family and rival and enemy of the Joveini brothers, finally lost the fight against his hated foes and met a particularly gruesome fate, Pur Baha' was there, ready with a clever ditty. "He {Majd-al-Molk} wanted his hand to reach as far as Iraq; his grasp couldn't reach but his hand did arrive. Aware that Maj-al-Molk had always hoped to extend his grip on power and influence as far as Baghdad, the poets' whimsical words refer to the fact that Majd-al-Molk was sliced up in the course of his execution and his body parts were sent to various parts of the kingdom.Pur Baha' enjoyed the irony of Majd-al-Molk's hand achieving his ambition but presumably not the rest of his body or mind.

What is particularly noteworthy in Pur Baha's work is his use of Mongolian and Turkish idioms many of which are rarely found in other literary works of the time. Though, his usage is highly stylized in works such as" Mongol ode" (qasid-ye-mogholia) also use of the names of the rulers who had done good works for the benefit of the common people. An example of that is the poem accounting for the earthquake in Neishabour where he refers to the good-works of Abaqa Khan and describes him as the "Nushiravan of our time, Abaqa, the lord of the world, the sovereign of the earth, the world conqueror. The two following poems by Pur Baha' written in the grand style cultivated by court poets and filled with elaborate word-plays and far- fetched metaphors, are chiefly interesting because they can be exactly dated. The first refers to the destruction of Neishabour by an earthquake in 1267-8, and the second to its restoration in 1270-71 by the order of Abaqa Kha'n.

"Through the shakes and knocks of the earthquake shocks it is upside down and awry, So that beneath the Fish is Arcturus sunk, while the Fish is raised to thr sky.	ززخم زلزله زیر وز بر شده است چنان زیر سمک شده است سمک فراز
That fury and force have run their course, and its buildings are over-thrown, And raven and ruined are whole and part, and the parts asunder strewn.	بجور وقهر بر انداختش زبن بنیاد بکل وجزفرو ریختش زهم اجزا
Not in worship, I wean, are its chapels seen with spires on the ground low lying. While the minarets stoop or bend in a loop, but not at the bedesmen's crying.	نهاده سربزمین بی سجود مقصوره مناره قامت خود بی رکوع کرده دوتا
The libraries are upside down, and the colleges all forsaken, And the Friday mosque in ruin is laid, and the pulpits are shattered and shaken.	کتابخانه نگون رسم مدرسه مدروس خراب مسجد آدینه منبر اندر وا
Yet do not suppose that this ruin arose from the town's ill destiny, But ask me if thou fain wouldst see the wherefore of this and the why.	گمان مبرکه زنقصان او بد این نکبت زمن بپرس اگر نیست باورت که چرا
It was Because the Lord had such high regard for this old and famous place	چو حق عنایت بسیار داشت در حق او

That he turned his gaze on its fashions and
ways with eyes of favore and grace

نظر فکند بر احوال او بچشم رضا

And such was the awe which His glance
inspired, and His Light's effulgent rays
That with shaking feet to earth it fell for fear
of that awful blaze.

چو هیبت نظر و پرتو تجلی او
بر اوفتاد ز هیبت در اوفتاد زپا

For did not the Mountain of Sinai once fall
down and crumble away
Where Moses stood, and the Face of God to
behold with his eyes did pray?"

نه از تجلی او کوه طور پاره شدست
کلیم چون بدعا خواست از خدای لقا

The buildings of Nishabour Time had striven
to displace
And Ruin wide from every side had thither
turned its face'

چوکهنه بودو قدیمی بنای نیشابور
نهاد روی سوی او خرابی از هرجا

God willed that men should once again its
buildings strive to raise
In the reign of just Abaqa',the Nushirwa'n of
our days.

خدای خواست که بازش ز نو بنا سازند
بعهد دولت نوشیروان عهد اباقا

Of all the world the Lord is he, of all the earth
the king,
Foe-binder, world-subduer he, all kingdoms
conquering.

خدایگان جهان پادشاه روی زمین
جهانگشای عدوبند شاه شهرگشا

It happened in the year six-hundred and three-
score and nine
That from its ruins rose again this city famed
and fine.

بسال ششصد و شصت نه اتفاق افتاد
بنا نهادن این شهر شهره زیبا

Venus and Soul in Tarurus, Ramada'n ending
soon;
In Gemini stood mercury, In Pisces stood the
Moon.

اواخر رمضان آفتاب و زهره بثور

قمر بحوت و عطارد نشسته درجوزا

May this new town's foundation to thee a blessing bring,
And every desert in the reign bear towns flourishing!

بنا نهادن شهر نوت مبارک باد

بعهد دولت تو شهرباد هر صحرا

By thy good luck Nishabour old is now grown young again.
Like to some ag'ed dotard who his boyhood doth regain.

بدولت تو نشاپور کهنه نوشد باز

بسان پیرخرف گشته کوشود برنا

Three things, I pray, may last for aye, while earth doth roll along;
The Khwa'ja's life, the city's luck, and Pur-i-Baha's song.

سه چیز باد وبماناد هر سه تا به ابد

بقای خواجه دگر شعر پور بها .

Pur Baha'was a poet very closely associated with administration apparatus (diva'n) and with the Joveini brothers in particular. His present fame rests in many ways in his diatribes against the harsh taxation system imposed on the country by the ruling Il-kha'nid regim.

Another poem uncharacteristically free from satire or attack summarises the poet's personal views on life.It may have been written after his fall from grace, when he saw the cruel face of fate finally beckoning; but if he is the author, he reveals a carefully hidden side to his personality. He explains his view on life in this untypically bucolic verse, a view probably popular at the Persian courts in the 13 century. The opening verses claim that he never intended nor knowingly given any distress or grievance to anyone, a dubious claim from one famed for his barbed pen and vitriolic phrase. He continues in images reminiscent of an earlier poet:

"I am content to sit quietly in a corner,
Free from sorrow and exempt frome blame and quarrel;

I am fond of a few small things in the
world,
A cheerful place, new clothes, a pleasant
smell,

A good face, a few books of wisdom, and
a backgammon board,
A true friend, a sound of strings, a cup of
wine,
A pot of meat, a hot loaf, and a draught
of cold water.

No one collection contains all Pur Baha's work, and his verses remain
scattered.
However, the job of identifying his work is made easier by the very
idiosyncratic style that he employs in almost all his work. Even though his
one long mathnavi,
The "Ka'rna'me-ye awqaf" appear under another authors name on the earliest
extant manuscript, the style, content, and personal references clearly indicate
it as belonging to Pur Baha's divan. His work appears in anthologies,
biographical dictionaries, and historical chronicles, among them
Dowlatsha'h's collection of Persian verse, which contains the so called
Mongol ode.
The largest collection of Pur Bah's work can be found in the Ketab-e Pur
Baha' dated 1619-20, which was compiled on the instruction of the Qotbsa'his
of Yaydarabad.

Homa'm-ed-Din Tabrizi 14th century Persian poet & Gnostic

Kha'je Homam-ed-Din Ala' Tabrizi who had selected "Homam" for his pen
name was one the eminent poets and Gnostics who lived in Iran during the
rule of the Mongole Ilkhani dynasty and at the peak of the savage destruction
brough to this country by the invaders. The exact birth place of Homam is not
known but it is almost certain that he was born in the year 1314 or 15.
Homa'm, it is said that he was either a student or associate of Khaje Nasired-
Din Toosi. Or Ghotbed-Din Shirazi

Chapter 5

Almost all of his poetical works is of extremely high quality and comprise of a variety of styles such as Rubaie, ghazals, q' atta, quatrains, qasidas and mathnavies. However ghazal was his specialty and that is for which he is famous. In writing ghazal he has adopted the style of Sa'di. It is reported by Dowlatsha'h Samarghandi that the two met once in Tabriz during a trip made by Sa'di to meet with Kha'je Shams-ed-Din Saheb-Divan Joveini.

Homa'm rose to political and intellectual circles in Tabriz and was close to the Joveini family. He was a friend and boon companion of Shamsed-Din Divan Joveini brother of Ata' Malek Joveini, and accompanied him on an administrative journey to Anatolia. This friendship further reflected by the fact that the Sa'heb-Diva'n endowed the Kha'negha'h that Homa'm had founded with an income of 1,ooo.oo dinars per year, that Shamsed-Din mentions Homa'm in the farewell letter to his friends shortly before his execution and that Homa'm dedicated his mathnavi "Sohbat-na'me to Shamsed-Din's son Sharafed-Din Ha'run Joveini. In passing it should be said that the cruel and unjustified execution of Shamsed-Din and other members of his family was the most shameful crime added to millions of other crimes and atrocities and destruction committed by the savage lawless Mongol barbarians during the invasion of Iran and the rest of the nations of the world where ever that they set foot and in particular, the subsequent rule over Iran and other lands lasting over more than 200 years.

With regard to other travels, Homa'm mentions a journey to Baghdad in a qasida dedicated possibly to Rashided-Din Fazloll'h, in an unpublished tazkera (biography) states that Hom'm made the pilgrimage to Mecca, although there is no further evidence to confirm this.
Homa'm left one prose piece, a commendation (taghriz) of R ashid-ed-Din's "Esha'r't,", contained in his diva'n, in the library of the University of Teheran. The most important of Homa'm's literary works is his diva'n of 3,944 verses, which includes some of his most beautiful ghazals. His divan of which two manuscripts are being kept, one in the library of Paris and the second one in Punjab university library was collected shortly after his death by the order of Rashid-ed-Din Fazlolla'h. As mentioned before writing gazal was in particular one area of poetry in which he truly excelled. As noted before, in the composition of ghazal, he followed Sadi's style and tone. Many are written in the form of answers to a particular ghazal of Sa'di. Later in his life he was called by many "the S'di of Azerbayejan". Some people have actually gone the length to say that Homa'm was in fact jealous of Sa'di!, this, however

should surprise no one ; because when it comes to ghazl no one can match the beauty and extraordinary power and influence of Sa'di, none other than perhaps Hafez of Shiraz. Homa'm in general surpassed many of his contemporaries in the composition of poetry and prose of the highest quality, both in Persian and Arabic. Among Homa'm's gazals are a bilingual poem (molamma) in standard Persian and a Central Iranian dialect similar to that found in the quatrains of Ba'ba' Taher.

Among the mathnavis in Homa'ms diva'n are two worthy of special attention. one is the meter and style of San'I's Hadighat al –haghigha and focuses on similar themes (diva'n, pp.225-56), the other, "Sohbat-na'meh," is a disquisition on love dedicated to Sharaf-ed-Din Ha'run Joveini, son of Shams-ed-Din Sa'heb-Diva'n, and includes four interpolated gazals in the same meter as the main poem (diva'n, pp.259-81).

Just as Homa'm's poetry was influenced by earlier poets such as Sana'I, Anwari, and Sa'di, his poetry in turn was admired by later poets such as Obeyd Za'kani, who included two gazal's of Homa'm'sin his "Osha'gh- nameh, Ha'fez, who interpolated two bayts of Homa'm's in his gazals, and Kam'l of Khojand, who used a mesra' from Homa'm in a qeta''.

 Homa'm was a powerful orator and public speaker who deeply impressed and influenced his audience and public. He was a Sufi who had achieved a high rank in the Sufi way, and was greatly admired, loved and respected by his devotees and students. He acted as a guide to the followers of the Sufie's so called "The Path"and loved by all. Homa'm is said to have met Sa'di during a trip that was made by Sa'di while passing through the city of Tabriz. Homa'm was also, according to Juwayni's Ta'rikh-e-Jaha'n-gosha, edited by Mirza' Muhammad, was one of the panegyrists of Sa'heb-divan Joveyni and was extremely saddened and heartbroken when the whole Joveyni family were slaughtered by the order of the Mongole ruler Abagha'. The following specimens of his verse (which is said to have been greatly influenced by that of Sa'di) are taken from Haft "Eghlim"

"On the day of life's surrender I shall die desiring Thee:	در آن نفس که بمیرم در آرزوی تو باشم
I shall yield my soul craving of thy street the dust to be	بدان امید دهم جان که خاک کوی تو باشم

Chapter 5

On the Resurrection Morning, when I raise
my head from sleep,
I shall rise desiring Thee, and forth to seek
for Thee shall creep,

بوقت صبح قیامت چو سر ز خواب
برآرم
به آرزوی تو خیزم به جست
وجوی تو باشم

I will smell not blossoms of Eden, nor of
heavenly gardens speak,
Nor, desiring thee alone, shall I Celestial
Houris seek."

حدیث روضه نگویم گل بهشت
نبویم
بسوی حور نپویم در آرزوی تو
باشم

"When the parting from country and
friends to my vision appears
The stages I tread are fulfilled with the
flood of my tears.

وداع یار و دیارم چو بگذرد بخیال
شود منازلم از آب دیده مالا مال

In parting one moment, one breath like ten
centuries seems:
How weary the days and the weeks and the
months and the years!"

فراق را نفسی چون هزار سال بود
ببین که چون گذرد روز و هفته
و مه سال

That day of parting seemed the Day of
Doom:
How was it if our friendship had been less?
Make much, then, of your friends while
they are here,
For this false sphere is fraught with
faithlessness."

قیامت دیدم آن روز جدایی
چه بودی گر نبودی آشنایی
غنیمت دان حضور دوستان را
که دوران مینماید بیوفایی

"Last night to tell my tale I did prepare
Unto my Friend, and forth from every hair
Flowed speech, unfinished was my song;
Blame not the night, the tale was over-
long!"

شد دوش بر یار حکایت آغاز
از هر بن مویم برآمد آواز
شب رفت و حدیث ما بپایان نرسید
شب را چه گنه قصه ما بود دراز

Awhaded-Din Kermani 13th century Persian poet & Gnostic

Sheikh Abu Hamid Awhaed-Din Kirmani known as Ohadi Kermani was, a personal friend or disciple of the great Sheikh Mohiyed-Din ibne al-Arabi, and had met that, not much known about, Shamsed-Din Tabrizi, the inspirer of Jalalal-Din Mowlavi's Mathnavi and the diva'n of Shams Tabrizi. He was also acquainted, as some assert, with Awhadi Maraghei and with Araghi himself, who in his heedlessness of appearances and passionate admiration of beauty, he somewhat resembles Sheikh Shahabed-Din, who, for chronological reasons, cannot be the famous Suhravardi, strongly disapproved of him, called him a "heretical inventor", and refused to admit him to his presence, on hearing which Awhaded-Din recited the following:

"
I mind not that bad names thou dost me call I am glad that thou shouldst mention me at all."

Ja'mi apologizes for him for "contemplating the Truth through the medium of its Manifestations in Phenomena, and beholding Absolute Beauty in finite forms," and adds that, being asked by Shams-Tabrizi what he was doing, he replied, "I am contemplating the Moon in a bowl of water," meaning the Beauty of the Creator in the beauty of the creature; to which Shams-Tabrizi replied , "Unless you are afflicted with a carbuncle on the back of your neck why do you not look at the Moon in the sky?" Similarly Mawlana Jalaled-Din Rumi, being told that Awhaded-Din sought the society of the beautiful, but with purity of purpose, exclaimed, "Would rather that his desires had been carnal, and that he had outgrown them!" Awhaded-Din expresses his own point of view in the following quatrain:

"Therefore mine eyes insistent gaze on forms	زآن مینگرم بچشم سر در صورت
Because the Idea itself displays in forms:	زیرا که زمعنیست اثر در صورت
We live in forms; this World's the formal World:	این عالم صورتست وما در صوریم
	معنی نتوان دید مگر در صورت

Chapter 5

The Idea we thus must needs appraise in forms"

Apart from a few quatrains cited in Nafaha'tal-Unse of Ja'mi and other biographical works Awhaded-din seems to have left little except a mathnavi poem entitled "The Lamp of Spirits""Mesbahul-Arwa'h" from which long extracts are given in the "Majmaol -Fusaha;" and the following eight couplets in the Nafahatal-Uns.

"While the hand moves, the shadow moves too:
What else, indeed, can the poor shadow do?

تا جنبش دست هست مادام
سایه متحرک است ناکام

It's but the hand that
makes the shadow fall,
The shadow, then, no substance has at all.

چون سایه ز دست یافت مایه
پس نیست خود اندر اصل سایه

To call 'existent' what no Being has,
Save through another, is not wisdom's path.

چیزی که وجود او بخود نیست
هستیش نهادن از خرد نیست

Absolute Being only wise men call
Being, and naught save God exists at all

هست است ولیک هست مطلق
نزدیک حکیم نیست جز حق

That which existent but through God became
Is NOT in truth, but only IS in name.

هستی که بحق قوام دارد
او نیست ولیک نام دارد

And yet the Artist loves His work, it's clear
There is none but He, so be thou of good cheer.

بر نقش خود است فتنه نقاش
کس نیست در این میان توخوش باش
١

Himself at once the Truth does hear and tell

خود گفت حقیقت وخود اشنید
وان روی که خود نبود خود دید

The Face He shows He does perceive as
well,

پس باد یقین که نیست والله

Know, then, by Allah, for certainty
That nothing else existence has save He."

موجود حقیقتی جز الله

Awhadi Maraghai 13th century Persian poet & gnostic

He was a disciple of Awhaded-Din Kermani, also called Isfaha'ni because his father was originally from the city of Isfahan. Awhadi was born in 1274. He lived during the reign of Abu Saiid Baha'dor Khan the ninth Mongol Illkhan of Iran. He spent a portion of his life in Isfahan. He selected Awhadi as his pen name because of his devotion as said before to Sheikh Awhad-ed-din Kerma'ni.

Awhadi died in 1337. His chief poem was an imitation of Hadigha of Sana'ii entitled Ja'm-e-Jam (the "Cup of Jamshid also known as the "World-displaying Glass"), of which copious extracts are given by the biographers. Dawlatsha'h followed by the 'Haft Eghlim', states that this poem was so popular that within a month of its production four hundred copies of it were made and sold at good price, but adds that in his time (1487) it was seldom met with and little read. This seems to have been the only mathnavi poem he wrote, but his diva'n estimated by the other biographer Reza'-gholi Khan, the author of Majmaol-Fosaha', to contain seven to eight thousand verses, including qasidas, quatrains, ghazals, tarjibands, and roba'is of which a selection is given by the biographers. Most of the ghasidas are in praise of Abu Said and his vizier Gia'sed-din Mohammad (son of Rashided-din Fazlola'h). Most of the other poems are on mystic, ethical, and religious subjects. Awhadi is at his best in his martias (elegies) and his ghazals, where his style prefigures that of Ha'fez. Awhadi died in Maragheh and his tomb is still in place. The following is an example of his style: (part of a qasida taken from the' Haft Eghlim')

How long wilt pride in beard and turban
take?

چند زین ریش و جبه ودستار
دوست آن گیرودست بدار

That Friend adopt as friend: all else
forsake.

With stir and movement fill thy heart with
pain
The soul in rest and quiet strength doth
gain.

درد دل کن بجنبش وحرکت
قوت جان سازدر سکون وقرار

All scent and hue of self do thou efface,
That HE may clasp thee tight in HIS
embrace.

رنگ وبوی خودازمیان برگیر
تا ترا تنگ درکشد بکنار

تا نگردی شکسته کی بینی
بدرستی جمال آن رخسار

Till thou art contrite vainly shall thou
seek?
In truth the beauty of that lovely cheek.

آنچه گوید اگر توانی کرد
هرچه گویی توان کند ناچار

If thou cannot do what he enjoins on thee
He will do what thou do ask assuredly.

He is keen enough: all else forsake
forthwith:
When will thou free yourself from kin and
kith?

خویشت اوبس زدیگران بگذر
چون مجرد شوی زخویش وتبار

Ask of thyself, when from thyself set free,
God-vexer, where and who thy God may
be?

چون زخود رسته ای زخود بر
که خدا کیست ای خدا آزار

Who is it in thee who speak of 'us' and
'me'?
Who fixed the evil and the good for thee?

ازتو این ما ومن که میگوید   با تو
این نیک و بد که داد قرار

If there are others 'others' prithee point
them out:
Art thou alone? Then wherefore 'others'
flout?

گرکسی دیگر است بازش جوی
ور تویی چیست زحمت اغیار

To be united is not to see:

هست فرقی میان دیدن ووصل
نیست زرقی مرا در این گفتار

Rebirth of Persian Culture

In this my speech is no hypocrisy.

Were sight and union one in fact and deed,
The eye on looking at the thorn would bleed.

وصل و دیدار گر یکی بودی
دیده خونین شدی ز دیدن خار

A cup he gives thee: spill not, drink it up!
Hold fast when I bestow another cup!

ساغری داده ات مریز و بنوش
دیگری میدهم بگیر و بدار

One is the Master's Face: pluralities
From Mirror and from Mirror-holder rise.

جز یکی نیست صورت خواجه
کسرت از آیینه است و آینه دار

One the King's portrait and the coining-die:
Numbers in gold and silver coinage lie.

سکه شاه و نقش سکه یکیست
عدد از درهم است از دینار

One sap supplies the flower which does adorn
The rose-bush and the sharp and cruel thorn.

از یکی آب نقش می بند د
برسر گلبنن ار گلست و ارخار

Orange and fire alike their hue drive.
From that life-giving sun they thrive.

از یکی آفتاب گیرد رنگ
خواه نارنج گوی و خواهی نار

A thousand circles issue from the point
What time the compass doth enlarge its joint.

نقطه ای را هزار دایره است
گرقدم بیشتر نهد پرگار

The world entire reveals His Vision bright:
Seek it, O' ye who are endowed with sight:

همه عالم نشان صورت اوست
باز جویید یا اولو الابصار

All things His praises hymn in voices still,
Sand in the plain and rocks upon hill".

همه تسبیح او همی گویند
ریگ در دشت و سنگ بر کهسار

Chapter 5

"The following fragment is possessed of some beauty, but is imitated from one of Sa'di's

'Think o thou who does inherit, yet didn't labor never, Who was he whose wealth was yours, and who art thou, the heir?	آی رنج ناکشیده که میراث میخوری بنگر که کیستی تو ومال که میری
He amassed but did not spend it, so it was left behind: Use it well, that when thou flit away, others good may find.	او جمع کرد چون نمی خوردازاوبماند دریاب کز توباز بماند چوبگذری
Gold a goblin is and woman for the neck a chain: Chained and goblin-haunter's he who greatly loves the twain.	زر غول مرد باشد وزن غل گردنش در غل و غول باشی تا با زن وزری
Over-anxious for thy offspring be not, for the Lord Knows better than the servant, how to guard his ward!	فرزند بنده است خدا راغمش مخور تو آن نه ای که به ز خدا بنده پروری
Dally not with lust and passion, which do curses bring, Curses that thou shall not escape with Flying Ja'fa'rs wing	گرد هوا مگرد که گردد وبال تو گر خود ببال جعفر طیار می پری
Thy lust and thy craving are a sea of strife: Can you not swim? Wherefore venture in the waves thy life?	دریای فتنه این هوس وآرزوی تست در موج او مرو چو نداری شناوری
Washing of the coat and turban naught can profit you: Wash thy hands of worldly longings; this is washing true!	این شست و شوی جبه ودستار تا بکی دست از جهان بشوی که این است گاذری

On the evil wrought by others never wilt thou dwell
If upon the deeds thou doest thou should not ponder well.

Truth there lacks not in the sayings Awhadi doth say:
It's who hearkens to his counsel wins to Fortune's way!

The following ode is another favorable specimen of Awhadi's
Work:

"Many a spring shall autumn follow when thou art passed away?
Many an evening, many a morning, many a night and day

To the world thy heart incline not, though it seems fair;
Deem it not a faithful friend who for its friends does care.

Thou to-day who like a scorpion everyone do sting,
Snakes shall be thy tomb's companions, shame to thee shall bring.

Comfort some afflicted spirit; that is worth thy while;
Else to vex thy fellows 'spirits easy, is and vile

Look not on earth's humble dwellers with a glance so proud;
Knowing not what Knight is hidden midst the dusty cloud."

هرگز نباشدت ببد دیگران نظر
در فعل خویشتن تو اگر نیک بنگری

گفتار اوحدی نبود بی حقیقتی
قولش قبول کن که به اقبال ره بری

بسکه بعد ازتو خزانی و بهاری باشد
شام وصبح آید ولیلی و نهاری باشد

دل نگهدار که بر شاهد دنیا ننهی
کین نه یاریست که او را غم یاری باشد

تو که امروز چوکژدم همه را نیش زنی
مونس گور تو ننگ است که ماری باشد

یک دل سوخته بنواز که کاریست عظیم
ورنه آزار دل خلق چه کاری باشد

خاکساران جهان را بحقارت منگر
تو چه دانی که در این گرد سواری باشد

The following fragment must conclude the
citations from Awhadi:

"These suppliant suitors hold in slight esteem; Hold thou their vows as frailer than a dream.	زنهار خوارگان را زنهار خوار مدار پیوند عهدشان همه نا استوار دار
Honors which meanness wins for thy name Regard, if honor touches thee, as shame.	فخری که از وسیلت دونی رسد بتو گر نام وننگ داری از آن فخر عار دار
When Fortune's cup into your hands does pass Think of the headache as you raise the glass.	چون جام دولتت بکف دست برنهند در کاسه نخست نظر بر خمار دار
Like ill-bred camel seems thy restive soul; Put on the leading-rein or lose control!"	بد مهر بختی است سراسیمه نفس تو اورا که با توگفت چنین بی مهار دار

Amir Fakhr-ed-Din Mahmud Ebn Yamin 14th century Persian poet

He was born in 1286 in Faryumad, a center of culture in western Khorasan, into a family of landed gentry; he died in1368. According to his own prose preface to his diva'n, Ebn Yamin's original book of poems was looted in the battle which occurred between Malek Moezz-ed-Din Hoseyn the Kart and Wajih-ed-Din Masud, the second Sarbeda'r leader, in 1342. All extant manuscripts are, therefore, based on a second compilation.

Here is the fragment {in which Ebn Yamin refers to this event} :

"It fell into the hands of spoilers, and thereafter no trace of it was found"

بچنگال غارتگران اوفتاد
وزان پس کسی زو نشانی نیافت

Ebn Yamin sent the following fragment which he had composed from Sabzewa'r to Malek Moezz-ed-Din Hoseyn:

"If Heaven by a trick, snatched my diva'n out of my hands,
Thanks are to God! He who made the diva'n is still with me!

گر بدستان بستد از دستم فلک دیوان من
آنکه او میساخت دیوان شکر یزدان با منست

And if Fate plucked from me a string of pearls fit for a king,
Yet I grieve not at its loss, since the remedy is with me.

ور ربود از من زمانه سلک درشاهوار
لیکن از درد ش نیندیشم چو درمان با منست

And if the wind tore a flower from a branch of the rose-bush of my talent,
A garden full of anemones, eglantine and basil is still with me.

ور ز شاخ گلبن فضلم گلی بربود باد
گلشنی پر لاله و نسرین و ریحان با منست

And if one of my shells of brilliant pearls was emptied,
I still have a mind filled with pearls like the sea of Umma'n.

ور تهی شد یک صدف از لولو لالا مرا
پر زگوهر خاطری چون بحر عمان با منست

What matters if a few drops of the sputtering of my pen are lost?
There still remains with me a talent bountiful as the April cloud!

قطره ای چند از رشاش کلکم ارگم شد چه شد
خاطر فیاض همچون ابر نیسان با منست

If the sweet water of my verse has been cast to the wind like dust
It matters little, for with me is the Fountain of the Water O life.

آب شعر عذب من چون خاک اگر بر بادرفت
سهل باشد چشمه سار آب حیوان با منست

And though y' heart is grieved at the loss of my diva'n,

گرچه آمد دل به درد از گشتن دیوان تلف

Chapter 5

Why should I grieve at this, since my pearl-producing genius remains?

And if the praise of the King of the World is, like the fame of his justice,
Spread throughout the earth, the praise-producing talent is mine!

Although I could compile another diva'n, yet
My life work is wasted, and regret for this remains with me.

If this vile age is unkind to me, what matter?
If the favors of the King of the Age, are mine?

That just Prince Moezz-ed-Din, whose virtue cries,
'Whatever of glory can enter the Phenomenal World is mine'

The chief of the favors which in all circumstances
The King of the Age doth show me amongst all my peers

Is this, that by his favor one of noble rank says to me?
'Rejoice, O Ebn-Yamin, for the constituent parts of the diva'n are in my possession!

Life has passed: may he continue successful until Eternity,

ز آن چه غم دارم چو طبع گوهر افشان با منست

ور ثنای شاه عالم همچو صیت عدل او
منتشر شد در جهان طبع ثنا خوان با منست

گرچه دیوان دگر ترتیب دانم کرد لیک
حاصل عمرم هبا شد انده آن با منست

بی عنایت گر بود گردون دون با باک من چه
چون عنایتهای شاهنشاه دوران با منست

خسرو عالم معز الدین که گوید قدر او
کز جلالت آنچه می گنجد در امکان با منست

معظم چاکر نوازیها که اندر کل حال
شهریار عهد را از جمله اقران با منست

آن بود کز لطف او گوید مرا آزاده ای
شاد باش ابن یمین که اجزای دیوان با منست

عمر شد در کامرانی تا ابد باد و بود
ورد من چاکر دعای شاه تا جان با منست

And may the daily portion of me his servant prayers for the King so long as life remains with me!

"

Seek as they might his diva'n was not to be found, so he made as he alluded in the above verse, made a {fresh} compilation from the anthologies of the Masters {of this art}, and from what each {amateur of verse} remembered by heart, and from what he himself subsequently composed:"

'So that my verses, scattered like the Seven Thrones,	کاشعار پراکنده چو هفت اورنگم
Might be again co-ordinate like the Pleiades"	ماننده پروین به نظام آید باز

Almost all of Ebn Yamin's biographers and hagiographer , from Dolatsha'h to Basta'ni Ra'd, have drawn on the brief prose preface to his diva'n and on his poems, wherein an exceptionally large number of references of the poet's own life and circumstances can be found, in order to sketch his biography and extol by his virtues .

They all portray Ebn Yamin as a man of moral virtues and a master composer of qet'a (fragment), a poetic genre resembling the ghazal pattern. Began in a provincial setting, Ebn Amine's life was an eventful one and culminated in close involvement in the power struggles of Khorasan in the 14th century and in long residence at several courts, most prominently at that Malek Hoseyn the Kart in Herat as mostawfi (State comptroller). Eventually, in old age it led to a longed-for return to Faryumad, the poet's birthplace, and a peaceful death there.

Chapter 5

Ebn Yamin had an eclectic style and a variety of thematic influences. His poetry epitomizes the major characteristics of the late Khorasan school of Persian poetry, both in generic divisions and stylistic features. His diva'n includes almost all the major genres made current by that school, as well as many minor ones like chista'n (puzzle-poem), the epigram, the chronogram, and various occasional and commemorative poems. About 100 short molamma (bilingual poems in Arabic and Persian) fragments as well as poems in Arabic accompanied by their verse translation in Persian are also recorded in his div'n. Following medieval tazkereh writers, several contemporary literary historians and critics have mentioned Ebn yamin's mastery in composition of qeta, a poem of a philosophical , ethical, or meditative character and an arena where "the poet often tells of his own personal experiences". This genre, having risen to importance in the later period of Khorasani school, occupies over half of Ebn Yamin's diva'n, the quality of the poetic utterance varies greatly, inhibiting categorical judgement.

Stylistically, Ebn Yamin's poetry reflects the main features of the Khora'sani school characterized in the main by relatively simple expressive devices, a pronounced rhythm, and a straight forward syntax. At the same time, diverse syntactic complexities and preponderance of a lexicon of Arabic derivation already herald the presence of certain stylistic features from the so called Eraqi school of Persian poetry. In addition to the stock themes and motifs employed in the panegyric qasida and love lyrics, Ebn Yamin's verse compositions aim at propagating human endeavor and industry, warning against excesses of all kinds, and providing observations on the passage of time and onslaught of old age, death, and the afterlife.

Ebn Yamin died on Jan, 1368. The poet is said to have uttered this quatrain a little time before his death.

"Regard not Ebn Yamin's heart of woe See how from out this transient world I go.	منگر که دل ابن یمین پرخون شد بنگر که از این جهان فانی چون شد
Qura'n in hand and smiling, forth I wend With Death's dread messenger to seek the Friend.	مصحف بکف و چشم بر ه روی بدوست با پیک اجل خنده زنان بیرون شد

The following fine verses on the evolution of the soul are amongst the best and most celebrated of Ebn Yamin's poems:

"From the void of Non-Existence to this dwelling-house of clay
I came, and rose from stone to plant; but that hath passed away!

زدم از کتم عدم خیمه به صحرای وجود

Thereafter, through the working of the Spirit's toil and strife,
I gained, but soon abandoned, some lowly form of life; that too hath passed away!

وز جمادی بنباتی سفری کردم ورفت

In a human breast, no longer a mere unheeding brute,
This tiny drop of Being to a pearl I did transmute:
That too passed away!

بعد ازینم کشش طبع به حیوانی بود

At the Holy Temple next did I foregather with the throng
Of Angels, compassed it about, and gazed upon it long:
That too hath passed away!

چون رسیدم به وی ازوی گذری کردم ورفت

Forsaking Ebn Yamin, and from this too soaring free,
I abandoned all beside Him, so that naught was left but HE;
All else hath passed away!

بعد از این درصدف سینه انسان بصفا

قطره هستی خود را گهری کردم ورفت

با ملایک پس از آن صومعه هستی را

گرد بر گشتم ونیکو نظری کردم ورفت

بعد از آن ره سوی اوبردم وبی ابن یمین

همه او گشتم وترک دگری کردم ورفت

The same ideas have been equally well expressed, however, by the great mystical poet Jala'ed-Din Mowlavi (Rumi), who lived a century earlier, in a very well-known passage of the mathnavi which runs as follows:

I died from mineral and plant became
Died from plant, and took a sentient frame;

از جمادی مردم ونامی شدم
مردم از نامی بحیوان سرزدم

Died from the beast, and donned a human dress;
When by my dying did I ever grow less?

مردم از حیوانی و آدم شدم

Another time from manhood I must die
To soar, with Angel-pinions through the sky.
'Midst Angels also I must lose my place,
Since 'Everything shall perish save His Face'

پس چه ترسم کی ز مردن کم شدم

حمله دیگر بمیرم از بشر
تا برآرم با ملایک بال و پر

آز ملک هم بایدم جستن ز نو
کل شی هالک الا وجهه

Let me be naught! The harp-strings tell me plain
That 'unto Him do we return again!"

پس عدم گردم عدم چون ارغنون
" گویدم کانا الاهه راجعون

{Tennyson says, similarly in 'Locksley Hall':
"Love took up the harp of Life, and smote on all the chords with might;
Smote the chord of self, that, trembling, pass's in music out of sight"}

Here is another fragment:

"Only for one of reasons twain the wise
Possession of this varied world the prize:

ز برای دو چیز جوید و بس
مرد عاقل جهان پر فن را

Either to benefit their friends thereby,
Or else to trample down some enemy,

یا از و سودمند گردد دو
یا کند پایمال دشمن را

But he who seeks wealth upon this earth,
And knows not wherein its worth's consists?

وانکه میجوید و نمی داند
که غرض چیست مال جستن را

Is as the gleaner, who with toil doth bind
His sheaf, then casts the harvest to the wind.

چیده باشد بمسکنت خوشه
داده ز آن پس به باد خرمن را

Naught but a weary soul and aching back
Accrue to those who understanding lacks."

غیر جان کندن و ز خستن چیست

Rebirth of Persian Culture

حاصلی ناشناس کودن را

۱

The following is typical in Manichean and Malthusian pessimism:

"Knowest thou wherefore the child no gratitude bears
Even to the father who makes him the chief of his heirs?

دانی چه موجب است که فرزند

مننت نگیرد ارچه فراوان دهد عطا

"It was thou,' he seems to say, 'who my peace didst mar
By bringing me into a world, where such miseries are!"

یعنی در این جهان که محل حوادث است

در محنت وجود تو افگنده ای مرا

The next fragment also represents a line of thought common with Ebn Yamin and others of his school:

"That God who on creation's Primal Day
The first foundations of thy soul did lay

خدایی که بنیاد هستیت داد

بروز الست اندر افگند خشت

Who in His Wisdom did for forty morns
Fashion the house of clay thy soul dorns,

گل پیکرت را چهل بامداد

بدست خود از راه حکمت سرشت

Who bade the Pen inscribe upon thy brow
Whatever betided thee from then till now,

قلم را بفرمود تا بر سرت

همه بودنی ها یکا یک نوشت

It ill be seems him on the Judgment-Day
This was well done, and that done ill' to say!

نزیید که گوید ترا روزحشر

که این کار خوبست وآن کار زشت

For he who sows the camel-thorn can never
Expect the aloe-tree to blossom there.
Since, then, the Muslim and Christian stand

چو از خط فرمانش بیرون نیند

چه اصحاب مسجد چه اهل کنشت

خرد را شگفت آید از عدل او

Subject alike to His supreme command,
'Why should He give, in wonder ask the wise,
'To this one Hell, to that one Paradise?

که آنرا دهد دوزخ این را بهشت

"Whoever he be, wherever he may be
A man should strive to guard his honor well;

مرد باید که هرکجا باشد
عزت خویشتن نگه دارد

Conceit and folly he should put aside,
And turn his back on arrogance and pride;

خود پسندی و ابلهی نکند
هرچه کبر و منیست بگذارد

Should so behave that none through him should ever
Endure vexation even as little as a hair;

بطریقی رود که مردم را
سر مویی زخود نرنجاند

None should despise for lack of power or pelf,
And deem each neighbor better than himself;

همه کس راز خویش به داند
هیچ کس را حقیر نشمارد

Then all his energies and wealth should spend
That so perchance, he thus may gain a friend."

سروزر درطلب نهد آنگه
تا مگر دوستی بدست آرد

A corner which no stranger can explore,
Where no one bores you, and you no one bore,

کنجی که در او گنجش اغیار نباشد
برکس زتو و برتو زکس بار نباشد

A sweetheart, lute, and song, a friend or two—
At most a party not exceeding four;

رودی وسرودی وحریفی دوسه یاری
باید که عدد بیشتر از چار نباشد

A harp, a zither, roasted meats and wine,
A cup-bearer who is a friend of yours,

رودی وشرابی وکبابی وربابی
شرط است که ساقی بجز از یار نباشد

Rebirth of Persian Culture

Reason, which doth distinguish good and ill,	عقلست که تمییز کند نیک و بد از هم
Regarding not thy ploy with eyes malign	او نیز در این کار به آن کار نباشد
Whoever doth disparage such affair?	این دولت اگر دست دهد ابن یمین را
Is in the spirit-world devoid of share;	
To Ebn Yamin should such luck accrue?	با هیچ کسی در دو جهان کار نباشد
For no one in this world or that he'd care!"	

The following fragment is practically a paraphrase of some very well-known Arabic verses ascribed to Qa'bus ibn Woshmgir, Prince of Tabarestan (reigned A.D. 976-1012), which are quoted in the story of the Merchant and the jinni in the Arabian Nights:

"Not as I would, O friends, the world doth go:	آی دوستان بکام دلم نیست روزگار
Of men of genius, it is the constant foe.	آری زمانه دشمن اهل هنر بود
Though fickle Fortune trouble me, what then?	سهلست اگر جفا کشم از دور بیوفا
Trouble is the portion of all noble men.	زحمت نصیب مردم والا گهر بود
The sky holds countless stars, of which not one	در آسمان ستاره بود بیشمار لیک
Suffers eclipse except the moon and the sun.	رنج کسوف بر دل شمس و قمر بود
It is custom now that he who wants for wits	رسمیست در زمانه که هر کم بضاعتی
Ever above the man of talent sits	زاهل هنر بمرتبه ها بیشتر بود
As on the sea the dust and rubbish swim	دریا صفت که منصب خاشاک اندر او
While pearls lie sunk in its abysses dim.	بالای عقد گوهر و سلک در او بود

Chapter 5

Kha'ju Kerma'ni 13th century Persian poet

Abu'l-Ata Kama'l-ed-Din known as Kha'ju Kermani, Persian poet and mystic was born in Kerman in a family of high social status in 24 December 1290. The early years of his life were spent in Kerman, where he obtained his basic education although that did not last that long, but he always remembered those short years joyfully and spoke of his native town with longing and affection. During his first trip to Baghdad he remembered it in his following verse:

"Pleasant the fragrant and sweet-scented morning breeze, This over the earth of Kerma'n, late hath passed!	خوشا باد عنبر نسیم سحر که بر خاک کرمانش باشد گذر
Pleasant the days of the sweet Philomel Which in its groves and gardens fair does dwell	خوشا وقت آن مرغ دستان سرای که دارد در آن بوم ماوا وجای
What fault was mine that Heaven did decree? From that pure land I must an exile be?	زمن تا چه آمد که چرخ بلند از آن خاک پاکم بغربت فکند
Wherefore in Baghda'd city must I dwell That tears like Tigris from mine eyes may well?	ببغداد بهر چه سازم وطن که ناید بجز دجله در چشم من

During his younger years he performed the pilgrimage to Mecca and visited Egypt, Syria, Jerusalem, and Iraq. The main purpose for his travelling must have been to complete his education by meeting with scholars in other countries. It was during such trips that he became the disciple of the eminent and pious Sheikh Rukne-ed-Din Ala'ud-Dawleh Semnani. In 1331, while in Baghda'd, he composed his best-known work, the mathnavi Homa' o Homa'yun. Returning to Persian lands in 1335, he tried to find a position as a court poet by dedicating poems to the rulers of his time, such as the 11-Khan Abu Said Baha'dor Khan and A'rpa' Khan, the Mozaffarid Moba'rez-ed-Din, and Abu Esha'gh of the Inju dynasty. He solicited in particular the patronage of veziers and high officials of the state. After a brief sojourn at Isfahan and Kerma'n, he settled permanently in Shira'z

Simultaneously with furthering his career at these courts, Kha'ju cultivated his relationship with pro minent religious scholars and Sufi Sheykhs. In his poetry he eulogized both his secular and spiritual patrons. He stayed for sometime at the Sufi hospice (khanaghah) of Ala'ed-Dowleh Semnani. His initiation into the Morshediya order was guided by Amin-ed-Din of Balya'n, whom he honored as his spiritual mentor (pir) in a panegyric ode (qasida) and in some of his mathnavies.

The later period of Khaju's life in Shiraz coincided with the formative years of Hafez. The influence of the older poet, who was prolific writer of ghazals, is quite evident in the latter's diva'n. They concern both individual motifs and Hafez's "responses" (java'bs) to entire poems of Khaju.

The lyrical poetry of Kha'ju was collected into two diva'ns. The first collection, entitled Sanaye al-kamal ("Products of Perfection") is preceded by an anonymous preface stating that the volume was collected and assembled during the poet's life time to the order of his patron, the vizier Ta'j-ed-Din Ahmad. It contains besides the qasidas, strophic poems, qeta's (occasional verse), and quatrains-two sections with ghazals; one the safarya't, with poems written during journeys and the second, the hazariya't, with poems written in his own habitual abode.

The poems composed after the first collection were assembled in another collection, under the title Bada'ye al-jama'l ("Marvels of beauty"), containing the ghazals under the heading Showqiyat ("poems of love").

Kha'ju was one of the first poets to write a kamsa, a set of five mathnavis, after the model of Neza'mi of Ganja. Although there are obvious similarities with the latter's poems--in particular in the choice of the meters—the subjects treated by Kha'ju are different.

Homa'y o Homa'yu, in 4435 couplets and dated by the chronogram B-D-L is written in the meter of Nezami's Eskandar-nameh (The motaghareb meter) it is dedicated to the Il-khanid Sultan Abu Said Bahador and his vizier, Ghias-ed-Din Mohammad. The poem relates the adventures of the Persian Prince Homa'y, who falls in love with the Chinese princess, Homayun. After a long fight with her father, the Faghfur, he wins both his beloved and the Empire o

Chapter 5

China. The story is situated in the times of the ancient Iranian King Hushang, and contains elements derived from popular tales'

Gol o Nowruz, written in 5312 couplets and in the meter of Neza'mi's Khosrow o Shirin was completed in 1341. This poem is dedicated to the Vizier Ta'j-ed-Din Era'ghi, but also contains eulogies of the renowned early mystics Ba'yazid Basta'mi and Abu Esh'gh of Kazeroon, and the poets personal pir, Amined-Din of Balya'n. The story tells another love story, this time vaguely situated in the time shortly before the advent of Islam. Nowruz, the son of the King of Khora'sa'n and a descendent of Sa'sa'n, travels to the Byzantine Empire seeking the hand of the Greek princess Gol. The intricate plot involves meetings with magicians and sages, and other features of folklore and wisdom literature. In the end the lovers are married according to "the rite of Ahmad"(i.e. according to marriage laws promulgated by the Prophet of Islam). Before his return to Marv (Merv) to succeed to the throne, Nowruz visits a monastery where he receives moral and religious instruction.

Rowza't-al-Anwa'r, in 2037 couplets, was completed in 1342. The founder of the Morshediye and Kha'ju's personal Sheikh are eulogized, but the poem is dedicated to a secular patron, the vizier and Judge Shams-ed-Din Mahmud Sayen. This is among the earliest imitations of Neza'mi's didactical poem Makhzan-al-Asrar, and closely follows the composition of its example, including also a number of illustrative anecdotes. In twenty 'maghala't' the poet deals with requirements for the mystical path and ethics of kingship.

Kama'l-na'ma, in 1884 couplets and dated 1343, is written in the meter of Neza'mi's Haft peykar, but the first part of this poem has more in common with San'l's Seyrol-eba'd, and the second part with Nezami's Makhzanol-Asra'r.The former contains the account of an allegorical journey and the narrator and instigation of Reason. The itinerary leads from a tavern in the cosmos to a realm circumscribed as being "without place or inhabitants". There he meets with Reason who enters upon a discourse on moral and religious topics interspersed with anecdotes about kings and mystics.

Gowhar-na'ma, in 1022 couplets and in the meter of Khosrow o Shirin, is dated 1345. The poem is a panegyric in praise of Baha'-ed-Din Mahmud, the vizier of the Mozaffarids, and his ancestors up to the celebrated Saljuq vizier Nezamal-Molk of Tus (1018-92). The "essential virtue" (gowhar) of each of these forebears is set forth in a discussion between the poet and a fictional moral guide, called pir-edanesh-afruz. A number of ghazals are inserted inside the mathnavi text, a feature characteristic of the epistolary genre of the Dah-namas (insertion of an exchange of ten letters between the paired lovers in a narrative poem), which became very popular in subsequent centuries.

Other works ascribed to Kha'ju, Mafati al-gholub, a selection of poetry, Resa'la al-badiya, on his pilgrimage to Mecca, Resa'lat Sab'al-matani, on the rivalry between Sword and the Pen, Resa'lat mona'zera-ye Shams o Saha'b, on the strife between The Sun and the Clouds.

Kha'ju was undoubtedly a versatile poet of great inventiveness and originality. Bridging the interval between Sa'di and Hafez, he occupies an interesting position in the development of Persian poetry, especially as a poet of the ghazal and as one of the first to complete a quintet of work (khamsa) in the manner of Neza'mi, adding several new features to the inherited scheme. Yet, there is no unanimity about his status as a truly great Persian poet.Brown, judging by a small selection from his ghazals, found that "his verse, while graceful and pleasing lacks any conspicuous distinction or excellence". Yet there are others who, judge him differently by claiming that Kha'ju would have won a more prominent place in literary history had he been more selective in compiling his ghazals. It cannot be denied that he was an important predecessor of Hafez, particularly as far as the blending of secular and mystical motifs in his works is concerned. Many Hafezian phrases, allusions, and metaphors are already in evidence in Khaju's poetry. His style is often idiosyncratic and innovative. He often chooses uncommon rhymes and radifs, and uses the ghazal as a vehicle for panegyrics as well.

"Pass us not by, for our thought is set on thy constancy Our heart on the hope of thy promise, and our soul on thy faith	مگذر ز ما که خاطر ما در وفای تست دل بر امید وعده و جان در وفای تست
If it be thy pleasure to thwart our pleasure, that matters little; Our object in this world and the next is thy pleasure.	سهلست اگر رضای تو ترک رضای ماست مقصود ما ز دنیی و عقبی رضای تست
Hereafter, since we have staked our head in following thee,	زین پس چو سر فدای قفای تو کرده ایم

Drive us not from thy pleasure, for our heart follows after thee,	ما را مران ز پیش که دل در قفای تست
I put my neck under the yoke and bow my head in service: Forgive me, if thou wilt, or slay me; it is for thee to judge.	گردن ببند می نهم و سر بندگی خواهی ببخش وخواه بکش رای رای تست
He who is thy slave becomes freed from all: He who is thy friend becomes stranger to his own kin.	آزاد گشت از همه آنکو غلام تست بیگانه شد ز خویش کسی کآ شنای تست
O thou who art dearer to my heart than the soul which is in the body	ای دردلم عزیزتر از جان که درتنست
That soul which is in my body exists but for thee!	جانی که د ر تنست مرا از برای تست
This sad-hearted victim who aspires to thy love, His rightist oath is by thy heart-entrancing stature.	این خسته دل که دعوی عشق تومیکند سوگند راستش به قد د لربای تست
Kha'ju, who is passing away through thy cruelty and harshness, His heart is still set on thy love and loyalty!"	خواجو که رفت درسرجور وجفای تو جانش هنوز بر سر مهر و وفای تست

Besides odes (ghazals) and mathnavis Kha'wju has several 'tarkib-bands, one or two "fragments" (mughataa't), and a few quatrains, including one about the dove crying "Ku,Ku" ("where, where" are the great ones of yore departed?), generally ascribed to Umar Khayam.

The following mustaza'd is not without grace:

"Is there none to say from me to that Turk of Cathy (Khata?)
If any fault (khata) has been committed

کس نیست که گوید ز من آن ترک خطا را

گر رفت خطایی

Come back, for we hope from thee for ourselves.

باز آی که داریم توقع بتو ما را

با وعده وفایی

Do not cast pepper in the name of me, the heartbroken
On the fire of thy cheek,

منداز بنام من دلسوخته فلفل

بر آتش رخسار

For because of that musky grain of yours have fallen, o friend
In to the snare of misfortune

کافتادم از آن دانه مشگین تویا را

در دام

بلایی

Today I am, like the curve of your eyebrow, in the city
Like unto the crescent moon

امروز منم چون خم ابروی تو در شهر

مانند هلالی

تا دیده ام آن صورت انگشت نما را

انگشت نمایی

(bent with grief and disappointment)
Since the hand of poor indigent me cannot provide
Anything more than 'hoof money'

باز آی که سر در قدمت بازم و جان را

در پای سمندت

چون می ندهت دست من بی سر و پا را

جز نعل بهایی

Is it a rule in your city not to enquire?
Into the condition of poor strangers?

در شهر شما قاعده باشد که نپرسند

احوال غریبان

After all what hurt could befall the realm of thy beauty?
From one, so helpless {as me}?

آخر چه زیان مملکت حسن شم

از بی سر و پایی

How long, O minstrel, wilt thou play out of tune
The 'Lover's Air'

تا چند مخالف زنی ای مطرب خوشگوی

Sooth me, the poor and portion less, for once By a song of substance!	ازپرده عشاق بنواززمانی من بی برگ ونوارا از بانگ نوایی
After all how much longer can I keep hidden? In my heart this grief of separation O Beloved, I am sure that this grief will spread One day some wither.	زین پیش نهان چند توان داشتن آخر در دل غم هجران دانم که سرایت کند این درد نگارا یک روز بجایی
Through regret for thy ruby lip I am in the Darkness of Alexander (this alludes to Alexander's quest for the Water of Life in the Land of Darkness) Like Kha'ju,	درظلمت اسکندرم از حسرت لعلت ماننده خواجو
But what can I do, since the Kingdom of Darius, Is not meet for beggar?	لیکن چه کنم چون نبود ملکت دارا درخورد گدایی

Later in life he became associated with the Morshediyeh order of Sufies which was founded by Sheikh Abu Esha'gh Kazerouni. He died in Shira'z in 1349 where his tomb is still there at a site, called Darvazeh Ghora'n (Qora'n gate) , an old gateway to the city.
During the younger years of his life he travelled to perform pilgrimage in Mecca followed by trips to Egypt, Syria, Jerusalem, and Iraq.

Hafez Shirazi 14th century Persian poet & lyricist

The world confesses that Hafez is the master of Farsi version of type of poetry named Ghazal. Hafez personality and his poems remove the internal frustration from spirits, and the beauty of his words affect human soul. Hafez is a genius that can with his Ghazaliat affect the elite as well as the ordinary, awake sensation, richness, freedom, love, and relief in human beings. He is a worshiper of the delight-full living, and is a qualified performer in showing all the dreams of Mankind. His extraordinary vision and thought has put him equal to the saints. His lyrics are charming and exquisite - The words that are contained in one of the greatest "immortal" masterpieces ever written by any writer in any time and wshall be cherished for ever. His verse resemble a boundless ocean that allow poetry lovers ride the waves of human intellect and harvest its pearls of hopes and dreams to please and satisfy each individual according to his or hers level of taste and sensation. He is a thoughtful and wise man that invites us to think as well. He is a learned man, a true Gnostic with great powers of imagination, thought, deep sensation, and feeling. When the Iranian contemporary great scholar "Ghazvini" was asked; if you were to choose one the greatest poets of the world who justly deserves his statue be erected in the town's main square who would you select; he answered: Hafez Shirazi. Because in his opinion; Hafez is the poet whose poems contain all the literal and spiritual beauties that are ever possible to exist in a poem. The words that have all the characteristics of an inspiring, rhetorical, factual, and melodic speech that could be desired by any reader any time, anywhere. The poet, that can be compared with any of the stars on the stage of the world's poetry. Ghazvini's candidate is undoubtedly Khaje Shams-ed Din Mohammad Hafez Shirazi.

Professor Mohammad Moein in his book, "Sweet words by Hafez asserts: aside from position of the prophets, poets are considered to be the master of existing world, as the citadel of sensitivity of dreams holding the rein of the masses in their hands. Ali Dashti, in his book, "Impressions of Hafez" asserts: The Hafez that has emerged in my mind is not from Shiraz, is not on the planet Earth, is not the son of son, and is not the father of so and so; he is the lord of the territory of ideas, thoughts, and speech – that has created a literary treasure; while his sack and pocket are empty, but should, in reality, be considered to as being one of the true literary masters in the history of world' literature. notwithstanding he lays a brick under his head for a pillow because he was so poor, but magnanimous and gracious enough not to disgrace himself. He is the Master of his unique rhetoric and eloquence. He does not say bitter words to anyone, nor shows sympathy for the unjust.

Haafez, without doubt is the shinning jewel, the pearl of time and place, the shinning star of Persian literature. He is the all time fresh and beautiful flower in the world's poets garden.. He was a man of illumination, freedom, literature and clarity. He was aware of the ideas and beliefs of the people of his time, and at the same time being conscience and highly proud of his national origin, history and culture. Above all Hafez was a poet that had dedicated his life and talents to humanity. He believed in benevolent speech and imagination and tried to stay the course all his life. He was well aware of the pain and sufferings of the people of his time, and his poetry reflects also, his awareness and concerns for the future generations.

The verses contained in his Ghazalz are so innovative, and beautiful, that deeply charms both the Gnostics as well as ordinary people. Dashti continues: O'Hafez you are the pride of not only our generation, but also those of future generations. Hafez is considered to be one of the greatest personalities of the world's literature both in the western hemisphere as well as in the east, yet there is no doubt that only Farsi speaking people appreciate the true charm, depth, and beauty of his poetry.

Gothe one of the greatest German poets asserts: Hafez thy words resemble the eternity, with no beginning and no end , your speech resembles the sky standing on its own; you are that source of emanation of poetry and rejoice that generates waves after waves in continuity. Hafez! Claiming equality with you in rank signifies madness, you are that tall and magnificent vessel with its sails proudly spread, riding the ocean waves of poetical glamour and everlasting beauty, and me in comparison, an insignificant admirer helplessly watching in ecstasy and awe.

Nitche, famous German poet and philosopher asserts: Hafez you have built a tavern of wisdom that is greater than the biggest castle of the world, and in it you have provided a delicate wine of speech that tastes better than drinking the whole world.

FitzGerald, the famous translator of Omar Khayam asserts: the best of Hafez poems are untranslatable, as he is above all in his choice of nice and exquisit words for melody; Words of speech used byHafez and Ommar Khayam are right and flow same as pure water.
And now in the six hundredth year commemoration of Hafez, the famous Iranian poet, the world's voice of omniscient from Shiraz, the International UNESCO organization (United Nation cultural and Scientific Organization) has chosen it : "The year of Hafez".

Persian lyric poet and panegyrist commonly considered the pre-eminent master of ghazal form, was born in Shiraz, probably in one of the years; 1339 to 1348 C.E, and with few marked absences, he seems to have spent the greater part of his life in Shiraz, and for long moving in or near the court-circle of the Muzzaffarid dynasty. He is believed to have died in Shiraz in 1414 or 1415 and his tomb is perhaps that city's best known monument. Though credited with learned works in prose, his fame rests entirely on his diva'n (collection of works). There are few aspects of the life and writing of Hafez that have not given rise, and especially from about 1930 to 1955, to a vigorous scholarly dispute over matters of both interpretation and fact. The reverence, in which he is held, not only in Persia but widely throughout East and West, as the undisputed composer of the world's most sublime and technically exquisite poetry, will doubtless ensure continued concern with these problems, however intractable and ultimately insignificant some of them may seem to be.

Apart from its general historical framework, the presumed facts of Hafez's life were, for long, largely drawn from biographical prefaces, from usual anecdotal "tazkerehname" sources like Dolatshah Smarghandi, or from casual references by writers like "Mirkhand and his grandson. Such material has of course frequently viewed skeptically; but most of it is of its nature difficult to disprove conclusively, and in one or two instances (as in an alleged encounter with Timur, in 1411C.E. research has, only tended to strengthen if not fully to confirm the legend. Informative biographers of Persian poets are a notorious rarity, and it seems unlikely at this late date that any significant new material of an explicitly biographical nature will be discovered relating to Hafez. Though not a new technique, it has recently become fashionable to analyze the poems themselves for new biographical evidence or for some bearing on the material already at hand. The latest, and the most comprehensive and ingenious work of this kind has been done by Ghasem Ghani and by R.Lescot; but the net result so far is somewhat disproportionate to the formidable effort involved. At best, it has now been convincingly demonstrated that the 'divan' bears a much more direct relationship to the milieu of its composition than was suspected in the traditional view. Such methods always have their dangers, particularly where the basic biographical material is itself so slight; in the case of Hafez the problem is exacerbated by the continued lack of a reasonably authentic text. All this being so, it still seems proper to give here the main outlines of the life in more or less traditional form.

Hafez's father, Baha el-Din or Kamal el-Din (some sources refer to his grandfather), is said to have migrated from Isfahan to Shiraz, where he died in the poets infancy, leaving the family in poor circumstances. In a close-knit, flourishing center of Islamic civilization such as Shiraz at that time was, humble beginnings were only a relative handicap; and it is plausibly suggested that Hafez received a thorough education on the usual lines. It was no doubt in youth that he earned the right to use the title hafez (Kuran memorizer) which became his pen-name; his verse bears ample evidence of familiarity with Arabic, with the Islamic sciences and with Persian literature in general. He is reputed to have been among others a baker's apprentice and a manuscript-copyist during these years of adolescence and early manhood; but, to judge in particular by the dedication of certain poems to Kiwam al-Din Hassan, at sometime, Chancellor to Shah Abu Ishaq Indju, he was into his poetic stride as a panegyrist before the age of thirty. An oft-cited poem mentions nostalgically other Shiraz notables of his period, including the ruler himself. Already by his twenties, in the wake of the disintegration of the Il-Khanid order, Hafez had lived through dynastic upheavals in and around Shiraz.

A second phase in the poet's life begins in 1376. with the capture of Shiraz after a protracted struggle between the Indju and Mozaffarid dynasties by Mubarriz al-Din Muhammad. The latter ruled for five years, before being deposed and blinded by his son Djalal al-Din Shah Shuja. These years were apparently period of rigid Sunni observance, hard on Hafez and his fellow-citizens alike; but the poet seems to have recommended himself with some success to Mubarez al-Din's chief minister, Burhan al-Din Fath Allah. The long reign of Shah Shudja (1381-1408), while at no time settled politically, and though far from being a period of continuous prosperity and success for Hafez, coincides with the phase of maturity in composition. It was during these years that his fame spread throughout Persia, as well as westwards into Arabic speaking lands and east-wards to India; it seems, nevertheless, that he declined invitation to remove to distant courts. The Muzaffarid dynasty effectively came to an end at the hand of Timur, in 1411, during the last few years of Haafez's life though random representatives of it, like Shah Shudja al-Din Mansur, seem to have shown the poet sporadic favor to the end.

It is generally believed that Hafez was more or less out of favor with Shah Shudja for a period of some 10 years, during which time is said to have spent a year or two in Isfahan and Yazd. The reason for such a fall has never been fully explained, though it is traditionally related to the poet's allegedly libertine views and behavior. Though thereafter he enjoyed favor from time to time, from the throne and from ministers like Djalal al-Din Turanshah, he seems never fully to have regained his former standing. Yet it should be remembered that there is still no real certainty that what such standing actually signified: certainly there is frequent reference to poverty throughout the poet's life (whether it be regarded as a complaint, a hint or a literary device), and there is no serious suggestion that he held a regular, richly rewarded as "court poet'". At one time he is said to have been a professor of Kuranic exegesis at a Shiraz madrasa (school), but there is doubt as to which of his patrons might have obtained him this preferment and no record of his period of tenure.

Legend credits Hafez with editing his divan in 1392; over twenty years before his death, but no manuscript of this version is known. Less speculative, perhaps, but still unattested by real evidence, is the edition (with a preface of doubtful biographical value) compiled after poet's death by a disciple a certain Muhammad Golandam.

"Where doth thy love's message echo for my rapt soul to rise? This sacred bird from the world's meshes yearns to its goal to rise.	مژده وصل توکوکز سرجان برخیزم طایر قدسم وازبام جهان برخیزم
I swear, wilt Thou Thy servant name me, by all my love sublime I shall rise to a greater far than the mastery Of life and the living, time and the mortal space	بولای توکه گربنده خویشم خوانی ازسر خواجگی کون ومکان برخیزم
Vouchsafe, Lord, command me as an atom from Man's domain to rise.	یا رب ازابر هدایت برسان بارانی پیشتر زانکه چوگردی زمیان برخیزم
Bring minstrels and wine-cup with thee, or at my tomb never sit: Permit me in thy perfume dancing from the grave's pit to rise.	خیزوبالا بنما ای بت شیرین حرکات کزسرجان وجهان دست فشان برخیزم
Though I am old, embrace me closely, be it a single night: May I, made young by thy caresses, at morn have might to rise!	توم‌پندارکه ازخاک سرکوی تو من به جفای فلک وجور زمان برخیزم

Arouse thee! Show thy lofty stature Idol of winning mien:Enable me, as soul-raft Hafez, from Nature's scene to rise.

گرچه پیرم توشبی تنگ درآغوشم گیر

تا سحرگه زکنارتوجوان برخیزم

برسرتربت من با می ومطرب بنشین

تا به بویت زلحد رقص کنان برخیزم

روزمرگم نفسی مهلت دیداربده

تا چوحافظ زلحد رقص کنان برخیزم

Two kings of India also sought to persuade Hafez to visit their courts. One of these was Mahmud Shah Bahmani of the Deccan, a liberal patron of poets, who, through his favorite Mir Fadullah, invited Hafez to his capital, and sent him money for his journey.Hafez spent a considerable portion of this money before leaving Shiraz, and on arriving at Lar on his way to the Persian Gulf met with a destitute friend to whom he gave the remainder. Two Persian merchants, Khajeh Hamadadani and Khaje Kazerouni,who were on their way to India, offered to defray the poet's expenses in return for the pleasure of his company. He went with them as far as the port of Hurmuz, where a ship was waiting to take them to India, but a storm which arose just as he was embarking caused him such lively consternation that, abandoning his intention, he returned to Shiraz and sent to Muhmood Shah the poem beginning:

"Not all the sum of earthly happiness is worth the bowed head of a moment's pain, And If I sell for wine my dervish cloak worth more than what I sell is what I gain!

دمی با غم بسربردن جهان یکسرنمی ارزد

بمی بفروش دلق ما کزین بهترنمی ارزد

The sultan's crown, with priceless jewels set,encircles fear of death and constant dread;
It is a head-dress much desired- and yet, not sure it is worth loosing the head for.

شکوه تاج سلطانی که بیم جان درودرجست

کلاه دلکش است اما بترک جان نمی ارزد

Down in the quarter where they sell red wine my holy carpet scarce would fetch a cup-
How brave a pledge of piety is mine which is not worth a goblet foaming up?

Full easy seemed the sorrow of the sea lightened by hope of gain- hope flew too

fast! A hundred pearls were poor indemnity, not worth the blast".

بکوی میفروشانش بجامی درنمیگیرند
زهی سجاده تقوی که یک ساغر نمی ارزد

رقیبم سرزنشها کرد کزاین باب رخ برتاب
چه افتاد این سر مارا که خاک در نمی ارزد
چه آسان مینمود اول غم دریا ببوی
سود
غلط کردم که این طوفان بصد گوهر نمی ارزد

It has been said that Hafez suffered the loss of a child sometime in the course of his life. This quatrain seems to support that tragic incidence,

"O heart thou hast seen what that clever son
Has experienced within the dome of this many-colored vault:
In place of a silver tablet in his bosom
Fate hath placed a stone tablet on his head."

دلا دیدی که آن فرزانه فرزند
چه دید اندر خم این طاق رنگین
بجای لوح سیمین در کنارش
فلک بر سرنهادش لوح سنگین

A major difference between Hafez and most other Persian panegyrists such as Anwari, Zahir Faryabi and Salman Sawaji, as Mawlawi Shibli Nu'mani well points out, is that Hafez never employs mean and despicable methods to extort money, or recourse to satire when panegyric fails. We have already seen how devoted Hafez was to Shiraz and he never wearies of singing the stream of Ru'knabad and the rose-gardens of Musalla:

Chapter 5

"Bring, cup-bearer, all which is left of thy wine!
In the Garden of Paradise vainly thou' It seek
The lips of the fountain of Ruknabad
And the bowers of Musalla"

بده ساقی می باقی که در جنت نخواهی یافت
کنار آب رکناباد و گلگشت مصلا را

Gertrude Lowthian Bell very skillfully and in the most illuminating manner offers the best comparison of Hafez with his contemporary poet Dante: Some of us will feel that the apparent indifference of Hafez lends to his philosophy a quality which that of Dante does not possess. The Italian is bound down within the limits of his philosophy, his theory of the universe is essentially of his own age, and what to him was so acutely real is, to many of us merely a beautiful or a terrible image. The picture that Hafez draws represents a wider landscape, though the immediate foreground may not be so distinct. It is as if his mental eye, endowed with wonderful acuteness of vision, had penetrated into those provinces of thought which we of a later age were destined to inhabit. We can forgive him for leaving us so indistinct a representation of his own time, and of the life of the individual in it, when we find him formulating ideas as profound as the warning that there is no musician to whose music both the drunk and the sober can dance.

The tomb of Hafez is in a beautiful garden, called after him the "Hafezieh". It was beautified by Abdu'l-Qas'im Babur, the great grandson of Ti'mu'r, when he conquered Shiraz in 1478 (C.E) it was further embellished later on by Karim Khan Zand, one of the best rulers that Persia has ever had, by whom the present tombstone, a slab of fine alabaster, was contributed. The Hafezieh is much honored and much frequented by the people of Shiraz and by visitors to that city, and the poet's grave is surrounded by the graves of many others who have sought proximity to those illustrious ashes, so that his own words have been fulfilled when he said:

"When thou pass by our tomb, seek a blessing, for it shall become a place of pilgrimage for the libertines of the world.

بر سر تربت ما گر گذری همت خواه
که زیارتگه رندان جهان خواهد بود

Rebirth of Persian Culture

A few of Ghazals by Hafez should hopefully bring about a beautiful conclusion to the eulogy of this one of the greatest lyrics that the world has ever embraced:

"My heart has sought the goblet of Jamshid long,
And begged it's secret from the stranger throng,

A pearl beyond the shell of space and being,
It hunted on the shore, lost souls among.

Last night I took my problem to the Magus
And he with vision clear the truth detected.

I saw him happy, laughing, with a goblet
In which a hundred vistas reflected.

He said: That friend who once adorned the gallows-
Revealing heaven's secrets was his fault.

I asked: This cup, when gave you it the Master?
He said: The day he formed the azure vault.

If once again the Holy Ghost assisted,
As Christ did so could others in that fashion.

Said I: what use are loved one's chainlike tresses?
The Magus said: Ah, Hafez there groans passion!

"O cup-bearer there is talk of the cypress, the rose and the anemone,

سالها دل طلب جام جم از ما میکرد
آنچه خود داشت زبیگانه تمنا میکرد

گوهری کزصدف کون ومکان بیرونست
طلب از گمشدگان لب دریا میکرد

بیدلی در همه احوال خدا با او بود
او نمیدیدش وازدور خدایا میکرد

مشگل خویش بر پیر مغان بردم دوش
کو به تایید نظر حل معما میکرد

دیدمش خوشدل وخندان قدح باده بدست
واندر آن آینه صد گونه تماشا میکرد

گفت آن یارکزوگشت سردار بلند
جرمش این بود که اسرار هویدا میکرد

آنکه چون غنچه لبش رازحقیقت بنهفت
ورق خاطر از این نکته محشا میکرد

گفتم این جام جهان بین بتوکی داد حکیم
گفت آنروزکه این گنبد مینا میکرد

And this discussion goes on with 'the three cleansing draughts'

All the parrots of India will crack sugar
Through this Persian candy which is going
to Bengal.

O Hafez, be not heedless of the enthusiasm
of the Court of Sultan Ghiya'thu'd-Din,
For the affair will be furthered by thy
lamentation"

فیض روح القدس ار باز مدد فرماید
دیگران هم بکنند آنچه مسیحا میکرد

گفتمش سلسله زلف بتان از پی چیست
گفت حافظ گله ای از دل شیدا میکرد

ساقی حدیث سرو و گل و لاله میرود
وین بحث با ثلاثه غساله میرود

شکرشکن شوند همه طوطیان هند
زین قند پارسی که به بنگاله میرود

حافظ ز شوق مجلس سلطان غیاث دین
غافل مشو که کار تو از ناله میرود

This world your charm and beauty
overcame,
For yes, the world can yield to concord's
name.

The rose displayed your perfume and your
hue,
And envy stopped the breeze's breath in
shame.

The candle sought to know the Hermit's
secret;
The key, thank God, its tongue could not
proclaim.

Of that great fire which in my heart is hid

حسنت به اتفاق ملاحت جهان گرفت
آری به اتفاق جهان میتوان گرفت

افشای راز خلوتیان خواست کرد شمع
شکر خدا که سر دلش در زبان گرفت

زین آتش نهفته که در سینه منست
خورشید شعله ایست که در آسمان گرفت
آن روز شوق ساغر می خرمنم بسوخت

The heaven-standing sun is but a flame; كآتش ز عكس عارض ساقى در آن گرفت

That day a lust for wine destroyed my harvest,
For which a spark from Saki was to blame.

خواهم شدن به كوى مغان آستين فشان
زین فتنه ها كه دامن آخر زمان گرفت

A compass was I, resting on the rim:
Time pushed me to the center all the same.

بر برگ گل به خون شقایق نوشته اند
كان كس كه پخته شد مى چون ارغوان گرفت

Shaking my sleeve, I would live among the magi,
Since mishaps scraped the apocalypse's hem

حافظ چو آب لطف ز شعر تو میچكد
حاسد چگونه نكته تواند بر آن گرفت

Drink wine, for all who witnessed the world's destruction,
Would blissfully grasp the goblet's heavy stem;

With tulip's blood on rose petal it is written
That he who mellows quaffs the ruby wine'

O Hafez, from your verses grace does ooze:
How, then, to slight them can the envious can choose?

Kamal ed'Din Massoud of Khojand
14th century Persian poet & gnostic

Better known as Kamal Khojandi is one of the outstanding Gnostics and poets of the 14th century. He was born in the city of Kojand of Tajikestan and exact date of his birth is not known but died around the year 1425. Upon completion of his education in Khojand, he left his birthplace of pilgrimage to Mecca. On the way back travelling through Azarbaijan he decided to settle for life in the city of Tabriz. He was patronized and supported by Sultan Hossein Jalayer who, ordered a Khaneghah (Sufie's house of worship) be built fo him inside a garden in "Valian kooh" a suberb of Tabriz. In view of his high rank as a Sufi, he soon became very famous and people of faith gathered around him to benefit from his insight and be educated and guided by him in the so called "The Path". He soon became extremely attached to his new residence that he would not leave it to go and live anywhere else. He wrote:

Ascetic searches for the Paradise,
Kamal found it in "Valiankooh"

Unfortunately after the death of Sultan Oveice, which was followed by the rule of his sons Sultan Hossein and in particular, Sultan Ahmad, and continued fighting that broke out between the various "Jalayeri" commanders on one hand and the attacks by "Mozafari" rulers and Tukish tribes the situation in A'zarbaijan became untenable. In the winter of the year 1409, the Turkman's army attacked A'zarbayjan, plundering and destroying the city of Tabriz which resulted in the death of a large number of civilians. Before long Mankuhe Khan, the new ruler ordered Sheikh Kamal to be moved to the beautiful small city of "Saray" which enjoyed a very moderate climate and relatively safe. Kamal liked his new residence, settled there and felt at home. Soon after in "Saray" he met and made friends with a famous Gnostic, by the name of Khaje Obeid Chachi, whose companionship he enjoyed enormously. After living there for four years he returned to Tabriz where he was warmly received by the residents of the city. It is said that Kamal was jailed for a period of time in the castle of Sang before his final return to Tabriz, where he enjoyed patronage of the ruler, Timur's son "Miranshah" and his old home in "Valiankooh". It is also said that the King ordered that his debts amounting to 1000.Dinnar be paid off as compensation for the fruits that his soldiers had eaten from his garden. The poet finally found peace and lived there until his death which as reported by historian and poet; "Jami" occurred sometime in the year of 1411 or perhaps a little later. It is said that upon his death of all the worldly assets, all that he owned was nothing but a mat that he used to sleep on.

On the poet's tomb was inscribed this verse

"O Kamal! Thou hast gone from the Ka'ba to the door of the Friend: کمال از کعبه رفتی بر در یار

Rebirth of Persian Culture

A thousand blessings on thee! Thou hast gone right manfully!"

هزارت آفرین مردانه رفتی

Sample pieces of Kamal's poems:

"What company, what paradise, what resting-place are here!
Lasting life, the lip of the cup bearer, the brim of the goblet is here!

این چه مجلس چه بهشت این چه مقامست اینجا
عمرباقی لب ساقی لب جامست اینجا

That fortune which fled from all others did not pass by this door;
That joy which escaped all is here a servant!

دولتی کز همه بگریخت از این در نگذشت
شادی کز همه بگریخت غلامست اینجا

When thou enter our joyous abode with sorrow in thy heart,
All say, 'Indulge not in sorrow, for it is forbidden here!

چون درآیی بطربخانه ما با غم دل
همه گویند مخور غم که حرامست اینجا

We are in the roof of heaven: if thou pass by us
Go gently, for here is the glass and the edge of the roof!

ما ببام فلکیم از برما گربروی
برو آهسته که که جام ولب بامست اینجا

In our audience-chamber there is neither seat of honor nor threshold;
Here King and dervish know not which is which!

نیست در مجلس ما پیشگه وصف نعال
شاه ودرویش ندانند کدامست اینجا

Like wood of aloes we are all hotfooted and burning
Save the ice-cold ascetic, who is here raw?

صفت عود همه گرم رو وسوخته ایم
بجز از زاهد افسرده که خامست اینجا

Chapter 5

How often, O Kama'l, wilt thou ask,
'What station is this which thou possess?
Whose station is this?' For here is neither
abode nor lodging!"

چند پرسی چه مقامست کمال این که تراست
این مقامی که نه منزل نه مقامست اینجا

"Moon of mine, the Festival is come:
may it bring thee happiness!
What wilt thou give as a festal-gift to thy
lovers?

مه من عید شد مبارک باد
عیدی عاشقان چه خواهی داد

Thy cheek is at once your Festal- gift and
our Festival:
Without thy cheek may our Festival be
no Festival!

عیدی ما و عید ما رخ تست
عید ما بی رخ تو عید مباد

Thou hast said: 'I will ask after the next
Festival':
Alas! For this promise is of long
standing:

گفته ای پرسم از تو عید دگر
آه کین وعده هم بعید افتاد

Deliver my soul from grief since the
Festival hath come,
For at the Festival they set free captives.

جانم از غم رهان چو عید رسید
عید زندانیان کنند آزاد

The Festival is come: cease to threaten
Kamal;
At the festal season they make glad the
hearts of all!"

عید شد بگذر از و عید کمال
عید سازند خاطر همه شاد

"Thy pain is better than balm, O Friend!
Thy sorrow enlarges the soul, O Friend!

درد تو به از دواست ای دوست
اندوه تو جانفزاست ای دوست

He who begs of thee at thy door
Seeks naught but pain and calamity

دریوزه گر تو از در تو
جز درد و بلا نخواست ای دوست

Notwithstanding that through poverty I have not
Aught which is worthy of your acceptance, O Friend!

I will lay before thee my two bight eyes,
I will say, it is the gaze of sincerity, O Friend!

پیش تو نهم دو چشم روشن
گویم نظر صفاست ای دوست

Thou didst say,"I will slay thee, but this is not right:
Is it right that a friend should slay, O friend?

گفتی کشمت ولی روا نیست
گر دوست کشد رواست ای دوست

Whatever the heart said in praise of thy stature
God brought true (or straight), O friend!

دل هرچه بوصف قامتت گفت
آورد خدای راست ای دوست

Straight have I made this ode to thy stature?
Write, 'It is by Kamal, O Friend!

کردم به قد تو این غزل راست
نویس کمال راست ای دوست

There are two Kam'als famous in the world
One from Isfahan and one from Khojand.

دو کمالند در جهان مشهور
یکی از اصفهان یکی از خجند

This one is incomparable in the ode,
And that one unrivaled in the elegy,

این یکی در غزل عدیم المثل
وان دگر در قصیده بی مانند

Between these two Kama'ls, in a manner of speaking,
There is no more than a few hairs' breadth' difference!"

فی المثل در میان دو کمال
نیست فرقی مگر بمویی چند

"That sufi with his nose cut of
hath nothing for us but helplessness and humility;

بما آن صوفی ببریده بینی
بغیر از عجز و مسکینی ندارد

One cannot accuse him of the fault of self-conceit (khod-bini) For the poor wretch hath not even a nose (khod-bini na-dard)	نشاید جرم خود بینی بروبست که آن بیچاره خودبینی ندارد

The following fragment seems to show that Kam'al's odes were not collected into a div'an until after his death.

"A certain man of discernment said to me, Why is it That Thou hast {composed} poetry, yet hast no Diwa'n? I replied, because like some others, My word is not copious and abundant.'	گفت صاحبدلی بمن که چراست که تراهست شعرودیوان نیست
	گفتم از بهرآنکه چون دگران سخن من پروفراوان نیست
He said, although, thy verse is scanty (in amount) It is not less (in value) than utterances."	گفت هرچند گفته توکمست کمتر از گفته های ایشان نیست

As is so often the case with Persian poets, Kama'l's fragments are much more intimate and personal, and contain more allusions to contemporary events and persons(though for lack of fuller knowledge these allusions must often remain obscure) than his odes ; and for this reason are quoted here to a disproportionate extent.

Mohammad Yousef Maghrebi Tabrizi (Shirin) 14th century poet & gnostic

Maghrebi is a Sufi poet, of the 14th century. His exact date of birth is not known; however, because both Jami and Khand Mir have indicated that he has died in 1371at the age of 69, his birth must have occurred in 1302. His place of birth is written as the village of (Amand) in the suburb of Tabriz. He had been using "Maghrebi as pen name in his poetries. It is said that his spiritual guide was Esmaiil Sisi Semnani. Maghrebi was contemporary of Kama'l Khojandi and were close friends. The historians have reported that

Rebirth of Persian Culture

Mirza Miranshah, Timur's son who was governor of Azerbaijan at first was a Devotee of Maghrebi but later changed to Kama'l Khojandi and this caused a rift between the two of them.

Maghrebi has written poetry both in Persian and Arabic. His Persian poems which comprise of odes (ghazal) quatrains and tarji'-bands have been published a few times. His poems are of a medium quality mostly dealing with Gnostic beliefs and concepts, especially doctrine of Unity of Being (Pantheism), and his inspiration the rupture of vision generally void of charm and beauty of other Persian poets.

As, indicated above his poetries are limited, mainly comprised of (Ghazaliyat) with a few tarjibands and quatrains. They are included in a small diva'n. of 153 small pages, and the total number of verses may be estimated at about 2300. The poems are entirely mystical, and no allusion to the poet's life and times. The following specimens are typical:

"When The Sun of Thy Face appeared, the atoms of the Two
Worlds became manifest.

خورشید رخت چو گشت پیدا
ذرات دو کون شد هویدا

When the Sun of Thy Face cast a shadow, from that shadow Things became apparent.

مهر رخ تو چو سایه افکند
زان سایه پدید گشت اشیا

Every atom, through the Light of the Sun of Thy Countenance, became manifest like the Sun.

هر ذره ز نور مهر رویت
خورشید صفت شد آشکارا

The atom owes its existence to the Sun, while the Sun becomes manifest through the atom.

هم ذره به مهر گشته موجود
هم مهر به ذره گشت پیدا

The Ocean of Being was tossed into waves; it hurled a wave towards the shore.

دریای وجود موج زن شد
موجی به فکند سوی صحرا

That wave sunk and rose in some heart-delighting raiment and form.

آن موج فروشد و برآمد
در کسوت و صورتی دلارا

Like violets the Ideas sprung up like the pleasant down on some fair beauty's face.

بر رسته بنفشه معانی
چون خط خوش نگار رعنا

The anemones of the {Eternal} Realities blossomed; a thousand tall cypresses appeared.

بشکفته شقایق حقایق
بنموده هزار سرو بالا

What were all these? The counterpart of that Wave; and what was that
Wave? (Identical in substance) with the Ocean.

اجزا چه بود مظاهر کل
اشیا چه بود ظلال اسما

اسما چه بود ظهور خورشید
خورشید جمال ذات والا

Every particle which exists is identical with the whole; then is the whole altogether the parts.

What are the parts? The manifestation of the all; what are things? ; The shadows of the Names.

صحرا چه بود زمین امکان
کانست کتاب حق تعالی

What are the Names? ; The revelation of the Sun, the Sun of the Beauty of the Supreme Essence.

ای مغربی این حدیث بگذار
سر دو جهان مکن هویدا

What is the Shore? ; The land of Contingent Being,; which is the book of God Most High.

O Maghrebi, cease this discourse; do not make plain the Mystery of the two worlds!"

"O Thou in whose life-giving Face all the Universe is manifest,
And O Thou Whose Countenance is apparent in the Mirror of the Universe!

ای جمله جهان در رخ جانبخش توپیدا
وی روی تو در آینه کون هویدا

Since the Darling of Thy Beauty looked in the Mirror
And saw the reflection of his face, he became wild and mad (with love).

تا شاهد حسن تو در آیینه نظر کرد
عکس رخ خود دید بشد واله و شیدا

Every instant Thy Countenance displays the beauty of its features
In its own eyes, in a hundred fair vestments.

هرلحظه رخت داد جمال رخ خود را
بردیده خود جلوه بصد کسوت زیبا

It looked forth from lover's eyes
So that it be held Its Beauty in the faces of Idols

ازدیده عشاق برون کرد نگاهی
تا حسن خود از روی بتان کرد تماشا

Thy Face wrought a Mirror for Its self-display,
And called that Mirror, "Adam and Eve"

رویت زپی جلوه گری آینه ای ساخت
آن آینه را نام نهاد آدم و حوا

He beheld the Beauty of His Face in every face through him,
Therefore hath he become the Mirror of all the Names?

حسن رخ خود را بهمه روی در او دید
زان روی شد او آینه جمله اسما

O Thou who's Beauty hath shone forth to your own eyes,
And who hast plainly seen Thy Face in your own eyes,

ای حسن تو بر دیده خود کرده تجلی
در دیده خود دیده عیان چهره خود را

Since Thou art at once the Seer and the Seen, there is none other than Thee:
Wherefore, then, hath all this strife become apparent?

چون ناظرومنظورتویی غیرتو کس نیست
پس از چه سبب گشت پدید این همه غوغا

O Maghrebi, the horizons are filled with clamor,
When my King of Beauty pitches His tent in the Plain!"

ای مغربی آفاق پراز ولوله گردد
سلطان جمالم چوزند خیمه بصحرا

Chapter 5

"O (Thou who art) hidden from both worlds, who is He who is apparent? And O (Thou who art) the essence of the Apparent, who then is the Hidden One?

Who is that One who in a hundred thousand forms is apparent every moment?

And who is that one who in one hundred thousand effulgences shows forth His Beauty every moment?

Thou say, 'I am hidden from the two Worlds':
Who then is He who appears in each and all?

Thou say, 'I am always silent':
Who then is He who speaks in every tongue?

Thou say, 'I stand outside body and soul':
Who then is He who clothes himself in the garment of body and soul?

Thou say, 'I am neither this one nor that one':
Who then is He who is both this one and that one?

O Thou who has withdrawn apart,
I conjure Thee by God tell me who is in the midst?

Who is He whose effulgence shines forth from the beauty and comeliness of the charmers of hearts?

ای از دو جهان نهان عیان کیست
وی عین عیان پس این نهان کیست

آنکس که بصد هزار صورت
هر لحظه همی شود عیان کیست

وآن کس که بصد هزار جلوه
بنمود جمال هر زمان کیست

گویی که نهانم از دو عالم
پیدا شده در یکان یکان کیست

گفتی که همیشه من خموشم
گویا شده پس بهر زبان کیست

گفتی که ز جسم و جان برونم
پوشیده لباس جسم و جان کیست

گفتی که نه اینم و نه آنم
پس آنکه بودهم این همآن کیست

ای آنکه گرفته ای کرانه
بالله تو بگو در این میان کیست

And who is He who has shown His beauty
And who has cast turmoil into the world?

O thou who remains in doubt,
Not knowing certainly who lurks in thy doubt

Be hidden from the eyes of Maghreb'i,
And see who is apparent through his eyes!"

آن کس که کند همی تجلی
از حسن و جمال دلبران کیست

وآن کس که نمود حسن خود را
و آ شوب فکنده در جهان کیست

ای آنکه تو مانده در گمانی
نا کرده یقین که در گمان کیست

از دیده مغربی نهان شو
وز دیده او ببین عیان کیست

"That One who was hidden from us came and became us,
And He who was of us and you became us and you.

The King of the topmost throne of Sovereignty condescended,
And, notwithstanding that there is no King save him, became a beggar.

آنکس که نهان بود زما آمد وما شد
وآن کس که زما بود وشما ما وشما شد

سلطان سر تخت شهی کرد تنزل
با آنکه جز او هیچ شهی نیست گدا شد

He who is exempted from poverty and wealth
Came in the grab of poverty in order to show forth (true) riches.

Who has ever heard aught stranger than this, that one and the same person?
Became both house owner and his own householder?

That pure substance and peerless pearl

آنکس که ز فقر و ز غنا هست منزه
در کسوت فقر از پی اظهار غنا شد

هرگز که شنیدست از این طرفه
که یک کس
هم خانه خویش آمد و هم خانه خدا شد

آن گوهر پاکیزه وآن دریگانه

When it germinated became earth and heaven.

چون جوش بر آورد زمین گشت وسما شد

In to the raiment of 'how-ness' and 'why-ness' one cannot say
How and why that 'how-less' and 'why-less' Charmer of hearts entered.

در کسوت چونی وچرایی نتوان گفت
کان دلبر بیچون وچرا چون وچرا شد

His eyebrow revealed itself from the eyebrows of the beautiful,

بنمود رخ ابروی وی زابروی خوبان

Until it was pointed at by every finger, like the new moon.

تا بر صفت ماه نو انگشت نما شد

In the garden of the Universe, like the straight cypress and the anemone,
He became both red-capped and green-robed.

در گلشن عالم چوسهی سرو چولاله
هم سرخ کلاه آمد وهم سبزه قبا شد

That Sun of the Eternal Sphere shone forth
So that it became Western (Maghrebi) and Eastern, Sun and Light.'

آن مهر سپهر ازلی کرد تجلی
تا مغربی ومشرقی وشمس وضیا شد

"We have escaped from the Monastery, the chapel and the College,
And have settled in the quarter of the Magians with wine and the Beloved.

از خانقه وصومعه ومدرسه رستیم
در کوی مغان با می ومعشوق نشستیم

We have cast aside the prayer-mat and the rosary,
We have girt ourselves with the pagan girdle in the service of the Christian child.

سجاده وتسبیح بیکسوی فکندیم
در خدمت ترسا بچه زنار ببستیم

On the benches (of the Wine–house) we have torn up the dervish cloak of hypocrisy;

در مصطبه ها خرقه سالوس دریدیم
در میکده ها توبه سالوس شکستیم

In the taverns we have broken our hypocritical repentance.

We have escaped from counting the beads of the rosary;
We have sprung forth from the snares of virtue, piety and asceticism.

In the quarter of the Magians we became annihilated from all existence:
Having become annihilated from all existence, we have become all existence.

Hereafter seek not from us any knowledge or culture,
O wise and sensible friend, for we are lovers and intoxicated!

Thanks be to God that from this worship of self
We are wholly delivered, and are now worshippers of wine.

We are drunkards, wastrels, seekers of wine,
And we are most at ease with him who is, like ourselves, drunk and ruined.

Since Maghrebi has removed his baggage from our assembly, and has departed (for he was the barrier in our path), we are free!"

ازدانه تسبیح شمردن برهیدیم

وزدام صلاح و ورع و زهد بجستیم

در کوی مغان نیست شدیم از همه هستی
چون نیست شدیم از همه هستی همه هستیم

زین پس مطلب هیچ زما دانش وفرهنگ
ای عاقل هشیار که ما عاشق ومستیم

المنته له لله که از این نفس پرستی
رستیم به کلی وکنون باده پرستیم

ما مست وخرابیم وطلبکار شرابیم
با آنکه چوما مست وخرابست خوشستیم

تا مغربی از مجلس ما رخت بدر برد
او بود حجاب ره ما رفت برستیم

Shah Nematollah Kermani 14th century Persian poet & gnostic

Chapter 5

Shah Nematollah Kermani was a prominent Sufi and poet of the eight century. He was a contemporary of Ha'fez. He was born in Kerman and lived to an advance age in Kerman. He died there in the year 1456. And was buried in the beautiful village of Ma'han, in the outskirts of Kerman, of which some malicious wit has said:

"Mahan an earthly Paradise would be, I wot right well,	بهشت روی زمین است خطه ماهان
If you could clear its people out and shake them in hell.	بشرط آنکه تکانش دهند در دوزخ

The site of his grave is marked by a fine monastery inhabited by dervishes of the Sha'h Nematollahi order which he founded; for he was a great saint and mystic as well as a poet, and his verses abound in dark apocalyptic sayings concerning the "Mischief of the last days" " (Fetneh Akharoz-Zaman"), the Advent of Mahdi, and other similar matters.

He was born in Allepo, Syria (or around Kerman, Iran according to some historians) in 1352, but spent most of his youth in Iraq. At the age of 24 he visited Mecca, where he resided for seven years, and became one of the chief disciples of Sheikh Abdollah al-Yaffie, a well-known mystical and historical writer, who died in 1390. He studied intensely with his teacher for seven years. Spiritually transformed, he was sent out for a second round of travels; this time as a realized teacher. He temporarily resided near Samarghand, along the great central Asian Silk Road. It was here that he met the conqueror Tamerlane, but in order to avoid conflict, he soon left. His later life was passed in Hearat, Yazd and finally, as already mentioned, at Ma'ha'n near Kerman, where he spent the last 25 years of his life, and where he died in 1456 aged more than a hundred years.

Sheikh Nematollah was and still is the king of dervishes (the title of "Shah" is always prefixed to his name) and the friend of kings. He enjoyed the special favor and respect of Sha'h-rukh, Tamerlane's son and successor while Ahmad Sha'h Bahmani, King of the Deccan, deemed himself fortunate in persuading to come to his court one of his grandsons. Two other grandsons with their father followed him later, while several of Shah Nemtolla'h descendants who remained in Persia intermarried with the Royal Safavi House. He left more than 500 Sufi tracts besides his diva'n of verse, but the latter is his chief work. The diva'n was published in Teheran about 150 years ago, but numerous selections from it are contained in the various biographies and anthologies in which he is mentioned. His fame, however, that of a saint and mystic rather than a poet, and his verse strikes one on the whole as monotonous and mediocre, similar in style and subject matter to that of Maghrebi. His most characteristic poems though few in number, are those couched in the prophetic strain, and these still exercise a certain influence, and are appealed to by other Persians than those who belong to the order of dervishes which he founded.

Here is one of his poems in regard to "Declaration of sundry mysteries and revelations by way of allegories"

"I see the power of Maker;
I see the state of time.

در اظهار بعضی از رموزات
ومكاشفات كنايات بر سبيل:
قدرت كردگار ميبينم
حالت روزگار ميبينم

The state of this year is of another sort;
not like last year and the year before do I see it.

حال امسال صورتی دگراست
نه چوپيراروپارميبينم

These words I speak not from stars;
rather I see them from the Creator

از نجوم این سخن نميگويم
بلكه از كردگار ميبينم

When 'ayn,raandda'l (=274) have passed of the years I see wonderful doings.

عين ورا دال چون گذشت
ازسال
بوالعجب كارو بار ميبينم

In Khurasa'n, Egypt, Syria and Ira'q I see sedition and strife.

در خراسان ومصروشام
وعراق
فتنه و كارزارميبينم

I see the darkness of the tyranny of the land's oppressors boundless and beyond computation.

ظلمت ظلم ظالمان ديار
بيحد وبيشمار ميبينم

I hear a very strange story; I see vexation in the land.

قصه بس عجب ميشنوم
غصه ای در ديار ميبينم

War, strife, mischief and injustice I see on the right and on the left.

Looting, slaughter and many armies I see in the midst and around.

جنگ وآشوب وفتنه وبيداد
از يمين ويسارميبينم

Chapter 5

I see the servant like the master; I see the
master like the servant.

They impress a new superscription on the
face of the gold; It's dirhams of short
weight.

I see the dear friends of every people
grown sorrowful and abased.

Each of the rulers of the Seven Climes I
see involved with another.

I see the face of the moon darkened; I see
the heart of the sun transfixed.

The appointment and dismissal of officials
and agents, each one I see twice repeated.

In Turk and Tajik towards one another I
see enmity and strife.

I see the merchant left friendless on the
road at the hands of the thief.

I see from small and great much cunning,
guile and trickery.

I find the condition of the Indian ruined; I
see the oppressions of Turks and Tartars.

I see the Holy Place fearfully desolated the
abode of a number of evil men.

Some of the trees of the Garden of the
World I see springless and fruitless.

If there be a little security, that too I see
within the borders of the mountains.

غارت وقتل ولشگر بسیار
در میان وکنار میبینم

بنده را خواجه وش همیبینم
خواجه را بنده وار میبینم

سکه نوزنند بر رخ زر
در همش کم عیار میبینم

دوستان عزیز هر قومی
گشته غمخوار وخوار میبینم

هریک از حاکمان هفت اقلیم
دیگری را دچار میبینم

ماه را رو سیاه می بینم
مهر را دل فگار می بینم

نصب وعزل بتکجی وعمال
هریکی را دوبار می بینم

ترک وتاجیک را بهمدیگر
خصمی وگیرودار می بینم

تاجر از دست دزد بی همراه
مانده در رهگذار می بینم

مکروتزویروحیله بسیار
از صغار وکبار می بینم

حال هندو خراب میبابم
جور ترک تتار می بینم

بقعه خیر سخت گشته خراب

جای جمعی شرار می بینم

A companion, contentment and {quiet} corner I now see as most to be desired.

بعضی اشجار بوستان جهان
بی بهارو ثمارمی بینم

Although I see all these sorrows, I see the {final} joy of the sorrowful.

اندکی امن اگربود آنهم
درحد کوهسار می بینم

Grieve not, for in this trouble I see the harvest of union with the Friend.

همدمی وقناعت وکنجی
خالیا اختیار می بینم

After this year and a few more years I see a world like a {fair} picture.

گرچه می بینم این همه غمها
شادی غمگسارمی بینم

I behold this world like Egypt; I see justice as its stronghold.

غم مخوررزانکه من دراین تشویش
خرمن وصل یارمی بینم

My king and his ministers are seven; all of these I see triumphant.

بعدامسال چندسال دگر
عالمی چون نگار می بینم

Such as rebel against my Immaculate Ima'm I see ashamed and disgraced.

این جهان را چومصرمی نگرم
عدل اورا حصارمی بینم

On the palm of the hand of the Cup-bearer of Unity I see the pleasant wine.

هفت باشد وزیروسلطانم
همه را کامیاب می بینم

The friendly foe-destroying warrior I see as the comrade and friend of the friend.

عاصیان ازامام معصومم
خجل وشرمسارمی بینم

I see the swords of those whose hearts are hard as iron rusted, blunt and of no account.

برکف دست ساقی وحدت
باده خوشگوار می بینم

The beauty of the Law and the splendor of Islam, each one I see doubled.

غازی دوستداردشمن کش
همدم ویاریارمی بینم

I see the wolf and the sheep, the lion and the gazelle, dwelling together in the meadow.

I see the treasure of the Chosroes and the coin of Alexander all put to good use.	تیغ آهن دلان زنگ زده کند وبی اعتبار می بینم
I see the roguish Turk drunk, I see his enemy with the headache born of wine.	چون زمستان پنجمین بگذشت ششمش خوش بهار می بینم
I see Nemattolla'h seated in a corner apart from all.	نایب مهدی آشکار شود بلکه من آشکار می بینم
When the fifth winter has passed I see in the sixth a pleasant spring.	پادشاهی تمام دانایی سروری پروقار می بینم
The vicar of the Mahdi will appear, yea I see him plainly.	بندگان جناب حضرت او سربسر تاجدار می بینم
I see the servants His High majesty all wearing crowns.	تا چهل سال ای برادر من دور آن شهریار می بینم
For forty years, O my brothers I see the cycle of that Prince continue.	دور او چون شود بکام تمام پسرش یادگار می بینم
When his cycle ends victoriously, I see his son as a memorial of him.	پادشاهی تمام دانا یی شاه عالی تبار می بینم
I see a king perfect in knowledge, a ruler of noble family.	بعداز او خود امام خواهد بود که جهان را مدار می بینم
After him will be the Ima'm himself, whom I see as the pivot of the world.	میم حا میم دال می خوانم نام آن نامدار می بینم
I read 'M.H.M.D'; I see the name of that famous one.	صورت وسیرتش چوپیغمبر علم وحلمش شعار می بینم
I see his respect and attribute like the prophet:	ید بیضا که باد پاینده بازبا زلفقار می بینم
I see knowledge and clemency as his distinctive Signes.	

I see again 'the White Hand' conjoined with Dhul-Fiqar.

مهدی وقت و عیسی دوران
هر دورا شهسوار می بینم

I see the Mahdi of the time and the Jesus of the age both royally riding forth.

گلشن شرع را همی بویم
گل دین را ببار می بینم

I smell the rose-garden of the Law; I see the flower of Religion in blossom."

These "apocalyptic" poems, though they have attracted most attention in Iran, constitue but a small fraction of the whole. Most of his verses illustrate the doctrine of "Wahdate-wojud" (Pantheism), while a certain proportion use the favorite illustration of the "Point" (Noghteh), of which the circle is only a manifestation; just as the letter 'alef'(الف) is in the world of calligraphy, a manifestation of the diacritical "point" which shares with the mathematical "point" the same title.

"King and beggar are one, are one; foodless and food are one, are one.

پادشاه و گدا یکیست یکیست
بی نوا و نوا یکیست یکیست

In all the world there is naught but one; talk not of two, for God is One

درد مندیم و دورد مینوشیم
دورد و درد و دوا یکیست یکیست

Mirrors a thousand I see, but the face of that Giver of Life is one.

جز یکی نیست در همه عالم
دو مگو چون خدا یکیست یکیست

We are plagued with the plague of one tall and fair, but we the plagued and the plague are one.

آینه صد هزار می بینم
روی آن جانفزا یکیست یکیست

Drop, wave, and sea, and elements four without a doubt in our eyes are one.

مبتلای بلای بالاییم
مبتلا و بلا یکیست یکیست

Nematola'h is one in the entire world: come, seek him out, he is one, is one.

قطره و بحر و موج و جوهر
بیشکی نزد ما یکیست یکیست

Chapter 5

نعمت الاه یکیست در عالم
طلبش کن بیا یکیست یکیست

The Point appeared in the circle and was not; nay, that point produced the circle

نقطه در دایره نمود ونبود
بلکه آن نقطه دایره بنمود

That Point in its revolution becomes a circle in the eyes of him who measured the circle.

نقطه در دور دایره باشد
نزد آن کس که دایره پیمود

Its beginning and end joined together when the Point measured the measured the completion of the circle.

اول وآخرش بهم پیوست
نقطه چون ختم دایره پیمود

When the circle was completed, the compass put its head and feet together and rested.

دایره چون تمام شد پرگار
سر و پا را بهم نهاد آسود

We are all without being, without being; we are without being
and Thou art Existent.

بی وجودیم بیوجود همه
بی وجودیم ما و تو موجود

I call the whole world His dream: I looked again, and lo, His dream was himself.

همه عالم خیال او گفتم
باز دیدم خیال او او بود

Sweeter than the sayings of our Sayyid Nematolla'h has heard no other words."

خوشتر از گفته های سید ما
نعمت الاه دگر سخن نشنود

"Know that the Named is one and the Names a hundred thousand.

یک مسمی دان واسما صد هزار
یک وجود وصد هزارش اعتبار

Its Form is the Glass, and it's meaning the Wine,
Although, both are one substance in our eyes.

صورتش جامست ومعنی می بود
گرچه هر دو نزد ما یک شیی بود

Perceive in two one unit and two units;
Search it out well, for I have told you a good bit.

در دو می دان یک یکی ودو یکی
نیک در یابش که گفتم نیککی

Without His Being the entire world is non-existent,
Of His Being and Bounty the world is a sign.

بی وجود او همه عالم عدم
بر وجود و جود او عالم علم

The world arises from the diffusion of His universal Being;
Whatever that thou see is from His universal Bounty.

عالم از بسط وجود عام اوست
هر چه می بینی ز جود عام اوست

His Ipseity is essential, while our Ipseity
Is but casual: be annihilated, then, from his annihilation!

او یی او ذاتی و ماییی ما
عارضی باشد فنا شو زین فنا

The Ipseity of the world is the veil of the world;
Nay the world itself is the veil of the world.

ماییی عالم نقاب عالم است
بلکه عالم خود حجاب عالم است

This veil is eternal, O my soul,
O my friend of God and O my proof!

جاودانست این حجاب ای جان من
ای خلیل الاه من برهان من

I tell thee the state of the world in its entirety,
So that thou may know the state of the world, and so farewell!

حال عالم با تو می گویم تمام
تا به دانی حال عالم و السلام

The collection of Nemattola'h poems contains approximately some 14000 verses, including a number of quatrains, and from the following verse it would appear that his literary activities continued until he had reached a very advanced age:

"The Living and Eternal {God} hath vouchsafed to this servant ninety and seven years of pleasant life".

نود و هفت سال عمر خوشی
بنده را داد حیی پاینده

Chapter 5

Abdolrahman Jami 15th century Persian poet & gnostic

The golden ages of the evolution of Persian poetry that had started following the appearance of Rudaki who has been metaphorically called "the father of Persian poetry" almost two hundred years after the Arab invasion of Iran, giving rise to a new phase and a new life which we can rightfully call "The renaissance of Persian culture" reaching its climax seven hundred years later, with the appearance of shinning literary stars such as Ferdowsi, Anvari, Nezami, Sa'di, Mowlana Jallal-ed-Din Mohammad Balkhi Mowlavi, also called by some "Rumi", Hafez and many others, begun to slightly but gradually follow a path of decline, although as it was proved later, turned out to have been only a temporary adjustment.

Abdolrahma'n Jami, an outstanding scholar, Sufi, poet and writer was one of the last great writers of that period.

He was born at the small town of Ja'm in the greater Khorasan on November 7, 1414 and died at Hera't on November 1492. His penname "Jami" by which he is known, he selected from the name of his birthplace, the village of Ja'm, where he spent his childhood. His family however, had moved a long time before from "Dasht", a suburb of Isfahan. His father Ahmad Dashti was known by this name because of their origin. He was a prominent member of the community and his house was frequented by the learned and the pious. One of Ja'mi's biographers Ne-za'mi Bakhazri, relates that the renowned Naghsh-bandi Shaikh Kawje Mohammad Parsa' stopped there on his way to Mecca a showing of "special favor to the five year old Abdol-Rahman." Although this story was probably invented to explain Ja'mi's later spiritual affiliation, it does indicate that his father had the learning and wherewithal to provide Ja'mi with his earliest education in Persian and Arabic letters. When Jami entered his teens, he and his father moved to Hera't where he pursued further education in theology, Arabic grammar, and literature. Here the young Ja'mi soon established himself as a brilliant, though somewhat arrogant young scholar, a reputation he consolidated in Samarghand, the principal center of learning in Khora'sa'n in the first half of 15th century. Ja'mi continued his studies in Samarghand and Hera't throughout his twenties, displaying a prodigious memory and powerful intellect in all fields of learning from Hadith study to astronomy and mathematics.

Rebirth of Persian Culture

It was during this period of his life that Ja'mi fled Herat after an unsuccessful love affair and again sought refuge in scholarship in Samarghand. But no sooner had he arrived there than he saw the Naghshbandi Shaikh Sa'd-ed-Din Ka'shghari in a dream. The Sheikh instructed him to leave his studies, go back to Herat, and take up the Sufi path under Sa'd-ed-Din's direction. The close relations between the Naghshbandi order and the Timurid dynasty would decisively shape the rest of Ja'mi's life. It was apparently at about this time and through the influence of Sa'd-ed-Din that Ja'mi was introduced to the royal court; one of his earliest surviving works, Helya-ye holal, dates from 1452 and is dedicated to the Timurid ruler, Abu'l-ghasem Ba'bor. Ja'mi maintained his affiliation with the court in Herat when the Timurid Abu Said Mohammad came to power in 1457 and he dedicated the first recsension of his diva'n to this ruler in 1463. Abu Said's religious advisor and spiritual counselor was in turn, the Naghshbandi Shaikh kha'wje Obayd-Alla'h Ahra'r, and he and J'a'mi would maintain a close and mutually beneficial relationship for most of the next three decades. Khawje Ahra'r filled the spiritual void in Ja'mi's life left by the death of Sad-ed-Din in 1456, and Ja'mi apparently lent Khawje Ahra'r and his order a cultural and scholarly legitimacy while serving as its semi-official representative in Herat. Under the impact of meeting Khawje Ahrar, Ja' mi began his first major poetic work, the first book of Selselat-el zahab (the Chain of Gold.), and wrote the first of the Arabic commentaries (Naghd al-fosus fi sharhe naghs al- fosus, 1459) on the works of the great Andulusian theosopher Ebn al-Arabi, whose ideas played a central role in Naghshbandi teachings. Khawje Ahrar'ar was active primarily in Transoxiana, and he and Ja'mi did not have the face to face relationship typical of the Sufi master-disciple relationship, but Ja'mi did travel north from Herat on several occasions to meet with Kha'wje Ahrar in Samarghand, Merv and Tashkent.

When Sultan Hosayn Ba'yoghara seized power in Herat in1470, Ja'mi was a respected teacher and spiritual leader in the city and had already established close ties with Sultan Hoseyne's powerful advisor and vizir, Alishir Navai. When Ja'mi was setting out to go on pilgrimage to Mecca in 1472, he entrusted Alishir with his personal affairs in his absence, and Sultan Hoseyn equipped Ja'mi;s entourage and provided him with letters of introduction to the local rulers he would encounter on his way. Travelling west through Nishabour, Semanan, and Qazvin, Ja'mi received a warm welcome from Shah Manuchehr, the governor of Hamada'n, to whom he dedicated his famous mystical treatise Lawa'yeha (Flashes). From Hamada'n, Ja'mi proceeded to

Chapter 5

Baghdad, where he resided for six months in 1472-73. When Ja'mi went to visit the shrine city of Karbala, a disgruntled servant capitalized on verses from Selselat-al-Zaha'b that attack religious dissenters (ra'wa'fezi), to stir up the Shiite population of Baghdad against him. Ja'mi was brought before a public assembly in the presence of local authorities to defend himself.. Although he was able to exculpate himself from the charges against him, his bitter feelings against the city and its populace are evident from a ghazal he wrote about the harsh treatment.

"O cup bearer, unseal the wine jar by the shore of the Tigris	بگشای ساقیا به لب شط سر سبوی
And wash my my memory the unpleasantness of the Bghda'dis	وز خاطرم کدورت بغدادیان بشوی
Seal my lips with the wine-cup, for not one of the people of this land Is worth discussion.	مهرم به لب نه از قدح می که هیچکس
Except not faithfulness or generosity from the unworthy ; seek not	ز ابنای این دیار نیرزد بگفت وگوی
For the virtues of men from the disposition of devils."	از ناکسان وفا ومروت طمع مدار
	از طبع دیو خاصیت آدمی مجوی

Nevertheless Ja'mi stopped at the tomb-shrine of Ali b.Abi Taleb in Najaf, and the poem memorializing his visit shows a devotion to the family of the prophet that transcends sectarian differences. After performing the rites of the Ha'jj in May 1473, Ja'mi began his return trip to Khora'san, stopping in Damascus and Aleppo. While in Allepo, he received an invitation from the Ottoman Sultan Mohammad II (Mehmet the Conqueror) to join his court in Istanbul. Not swayed by the money and gifts that accompanied this invitation, Ja'mi moved quickly to avoid these golden shackles and headed to Tabriz and the court of Uzon Hasan. Although he was warmly welcomed by the Aq Qoyunlu ruler, Ja'mi declined his invitation to remain in the city and finally arrived back in Hera't in January 1474. In addition to its religious purposes, Ja'mi's pilgrimage served to enhance his reputation and establish a network of political and scholarly connections that extended across the Persianate world.

Rebirth of Persian Culture

Shortly after his return to Hera't, an event took place that helped consolidate his standing with Sultan Hossein and Alishir. According to Ba'khazri, the sons of Abu Said in Transoxiana regarded Hera'rt as part of their patrimony and planned a campaign against Sultan Hossein. Despite the rumor that his mentor Khawja Ahra'r had given his blessing to this campaign, Ja'mi stood in defense of Sultan Hossein. His position with the court was further strengthened when Alishir joined the Naghshbandi order, with Ja'mi as his spiritual director. For the last fifteen years of Ja'mii's life, he, Sultan Hossein, and Alishir constituted a religious, military, and administrative "triumvirate" governing Khorasan. Despite his status, wealth, and influence, Ja'mi lived simply and unostentatiously in the district of Kiyaba'n- Heart, just outside of the city. Sometime after his return from the pilgrimage, he married the granddaughter of his first spiritual guide. Sa'd-ed-Din Kashghari. Of the four children born of this marriage, only one survived infancy. ja'mi composed a strophic elegy on the death of his second child, Safi-ed-Din Mohammad in1475. His third and surviving son, Ziya-sd-Din Yuosof, was born in 1477 and Ja'mi would eventually write the Baha'resta'n in 1487 and a treatise on Arabic grammar, al-Fawa'ed el-ziyaaiya as manual for his education. Although Ja'mi often complains of the ills of old age, he made a final trip to Samarghand to visit Khawje Ahra'r and as will be seen below, entered his most productive period as a writer and scholar in the 1480s. Two years after mourning the death of his spiritual guide, Khawje Ahra'r, in 1490, Ja'mi died after a brief illness on 9 November 1492.(C.E)

He was over eighty years old and at the time he was the most renowned writer in the Persian speaking world, receiving appreciation and payment for his works from as far away as India and Istanbul. One of the most remarkable geniuses, Persia ever produced. Besides his poetry, which, apart from minor productions, consisted of three diva'ns of lyrical poetry and seven romantic or didactic mathnavies, he wrote a great number of books close to forty six; touching almost every topic of human intellect available throughout years up and including his own time such as lives of the Saints, Mysticism, Arabic grammar, Rhyme, Prosody, Music, acrostics (muamma'), religion and other subjects. In the Tohfa-i-Sa'mi forty six of his works are enumerated. He was held in the highest honor by his contemporaries, not only by his countrymen, but, by distinguished scholars outside the borders of Persia; by Ottoman emperor who vainly tried to induce him to visit his court. He was regarded as so eminent as to be beyond praise and so well known as to need no detailed

Chapter 5

biography. Thus Ba'bur, in his Ba'bur-na'me, after observing that "in exoteric and esoteric learning there was none equal to him in that time, says that he is "too exalted for there to be any need for praising him" and that he only introduces his name " for luck and for blessing." Sa'm Mirza', the son of Sha'h Isma'il the Safavi, places him first in the fifth section (Sahifeh} of his Tuhfa-i-Sa'mi, and says "by reason of the extreme elevation of his genius....there is no need to describe his condition set forth any account of him, since the rays of his virtues have reached from the East to the uttermost parts of the West, while the bountiful table of his excellencies is spread from shore to shore." Dowlatsha'h, who puts him first, before Mir Ali Shir Nava'ie, in the concluding section of his Memoirs, which deals with living contemporary poets, speaks in a similar strain. Mir Ali Shir, besides the brief notice of him at the beginning of his Majalesaton-Nafa'es, has devoted an entire work, the Khamsatol-Mottohayerin (Quintet of the Astonished) to his praises.

Ja'mi's active career as a writer extended over almost fifty years, and he wrote a prolific amount of poetry and prose in both Persian and Arabic. He turned his hand at one time or another to every genre of Persian poetry and penned numerous treaties on a wide range of topics in the humanities and religious sciences.

In its final recension, prepared at the request of Alishir Nava'ie in 1491 Ja'mi's diva'n is divided into three separately titled sections: Fa'tehat al-Shaba'b (Opening of Youth), Wa'sita al-eqd (Middle of the Necklace), and Kh'temat al-haya-tal-haya't (The End of Life). The titles and arrangement, however, are somewhat misleading. Containing more than 9000 verses, the first section is longer than the other two sections combined. A prose introduction preserved in some manuscripts shows Ja'mi first compiled his untitled div'an in 1463 and dedicated it to Sulta'n Abu Said. He later revised this diva'n in 1468 and again in1475, when he added the poems that he had written in on his pilgrimage; a final version of this diva'n was then completed in 1479 , for which he wrote a new introduction dedicating the work to Sultan Hossein Bayghara'.

In his role as Sufi Shaykh, which began in 1453, J'ami expounded a number of teachings regarding following the Sufi path. He created a distinction between two types of Sufies, now referred to as the "prophetic" and the "mystic" spirit. Ja mi is known for his both extreme piety and mysticism. He remained a staunch Sunni on his path towards Sufism and developed images of earthly love and its employment to depict the spiritual passion of the seeker of God. He began to take in Sufism at an earlier age which he received a blessing by a principle associate Kha'je Mohammad Parsa who came through town. From there he saw guidance, as mentioned before, from Sad-al Din Kashgari based on a dream where he was told to take God and become his comparison. He was known for his commitment to God and his desire for separation from the world to become closer to God often causing him to forget social normalities. He believed there were three goals to achieve a great "permanent with God" through ceaselessness and silence, being aware of one's earthly state, and and a constant state of a spiritual guide. Ja'mi wrote about his feeling that God was everywhere and inherenly in everything. He also defined key terms related to Sufism including the meaning of sainthood, the saint, the difference between the Sufii and the one still striving on the path. The seekers of blame, various levels of tawhid, the charismatic feats of the saints. Often times Ja'mi's methodology did not follow the school of ibn Arabi, like in the issue of mutual dependence between God and his creatures. Jami stated "We and Thou are not separate from each other, but we need Thee, whereas Thou dost not need us"

O Thou whose beauty doth appear in all that appears May a thousand holy spirits be Thy sacrifice!	یا من ندا جمالک فی کل ما بدا بادا هزار جان مقدس ترا فدا
Like the flute I make complaint of my separation from Thee every moment, and this is the more strange since I am not parted from thee from a single instant	من نالم از جدایی تو دم به دم چونی وین طرفه تر که از تونیم یک نفس جدا
It is love alone which reveals itself in the two worlds, sometimes through the raiment of the King, and sometimes through the garment of the beggar'	عشق است وبس که در دو جهان جلوه میکند گاه از لباس شاه وگه از کسوت گدا
One sound reaches your ear in two ways; now thou call it 'echo' and now 'Voice,	یک صوت بر دوگونه همی آیدت بگوش گاهی ندا همی نهییش نام وگه صدا
	برخیز ساقیا زکرم جرعه ای بریز

Chapter 5

Arise, o cup bearer, and graciously pour out a draught of that grief dispelling wine for the sorrow-stricken lovers!	بر عاشقان غمزده زان جام غمز دا
Of that special wine which, when it delivers me from myself leaves in the eye of contemplation naught but God.	زان جام خاص کز خودیم چون دهد خلاص
O Ja'mi, the road of guidance to God is naught but Love: {this} we tell you, and 'Peace be upon who follows the right guida	در دیده شهود نماند به جز خدا جامی ره هدی به خدا غیر عشق نیست گفتیم و السلام علی تابع الهدی

J'mi created an all-embracing unity emphasized in a unity with the lover, beloved and the love one, removing the belief that they were separated. J'mi was in many ways influenced by creating an entirely new concept. In his view love for the Prophet Mohhamad was the fundamental stepping stone for starting on the spiritual journey. J'ami served as a master to several followers and to one student who asked to be his pupil who claimed never to have loved anyone. He said, "God and love first, then come to me and I will show you the way. For several generations, J'ami had a group of followers representing his knowledge and impact. J'mi continues to be known not only for his poetry, but his learned and spiritual traditions of the Prsian-speaking world. In analyzing J'ami's work greatest contribution may have been his analysis and discussion of God's mercy towards man, redefining the way previous texts were interpreted. Jami was also deeply inspired by many of his predecessors naming just a few; Bayazid Bastami, Attar Neishabouri, Mowlana Jal'al-ed-Din Mowlavi, Fakhr ed- Din Eraghi, Sana'I, Mansou Hallaj, Nezami, Ba'ba' Taher, Khaje Abdola'h Ansari, Abu-Saied Abol-Kheir, Hafez Shirazi

The following Ghazal is evidently inspired on the well-known ode of Hafez, which has been composed in the same meter and style:

O Breeze of Morning, visit the hills of Nejd for me and kiss them,
For the fragrance of the Friend comes from those pure camping-grounds.

نسیم الصبح زر منی ربی نجد وقبلها
بوی دوست می آید از آن پاکیزه منزلها

When the longing for union increases, what occasion for blame is there if Majnoon follows the litters in the hope of {finding amongst them} Layla's howdah?

چو گردد شوق وصل افزون چه جای طعن اگر مجنون
ببوی هودج لیلی فتد دنبال محملها

My heart is filled with love for the Friend, who is not heedless thereof, for they say 'hearts have a road to hearts.'

دل من پرز مهر یار و او فارغ نبودست آن
که میگویند راهی هست دلها را سوی دلها

Behold, Salma' has arrived from the road, while I am in such case through bodily weakness; take then O comrade, my spirit as a gift from me and accept it.

رسید اینک زره سلمی و من از ضعف تن زینسان
فخد یا صاح روحی تحفته من واقبلها

O cloud-like eye (weeping) do not shed the rain of regret in her path, for it is better than her horse's hoof should be far removed from the plague of such mire.

مریز ای ابر دیده آب حسرت بر سر راهش
که دور اولی سم اسپش از آسیب چنین گلها

In my heart were knotted a hundred difficulties through separation from her; when I saw her form all difficulties were solved forthwith.

مرا از هجر او در دل گره میبود صد مشکل
چو دیدم شکل او فی الحال حل شد جمله مشگلها

Ja'mi suffers vexations from the harshness of this grievous cycle, but fear of the fearsomeness of penitents did not prolong them."

ز جور دور غم فر جام جامی غصه ها دارها
ولکن خوف املال الندامی لم یطولها

Chapter 5

In the garden, sitting by the brook, Holding the wine-cup
  Rise O' cup-bearer, it's sinful not to drink,

Sheikh is drunk in the monastery attending Sama',
I am the same way as he is but only in the tavern.

You put the cup to your lips and I am so drunk,
I can't tell, if it's your ruby lips,on mine, or the one of the cup

I am not the only one in love with you,
Every one else here tells the same story

No blade you need to cut my heart apart,
Lay down the blade!,your amorous glance does the job

طرف باغ و لب و لب جوی و لب جامست اینجا
ساقیا خیز که پرهیز حرامست اینجا

شیخ در صومعه گر مست شد از ذوق سماع
من و میخانه که این حال مدامست اینجا

لب نهادی به لب جام وندانم من مست
که لب لعل تو یا باده کدامست اینجا

بسته زلف سیاه تو نه تنها دل ماست
هرکجا مرغ دلی بسته دامست اینجا

میکشی تیغ که سازی دل ما را به دو نیم
تیغ بگذار که یک غمزه تمام است اینجا

The fair ones are a thousand, but of them all my desire is one: my speech is one, though they cut me into a hundred pieces with the sword.

خوبان هزارو از همه مقصود من یکیست
صد پاره گرکنند به تیغم سخن یکیست

The assembly of the beautiful is a pleasant meeting-place but the Moon whence this assembly derives its luster is one.

خوش مجمعیست انجمن نیکوان ولی
ماهی کزوست رونق این انجمن یکیست

For each pace of her advance we desire a different present, but we fall short {of this our desire}, for the soul in the body is {only} one.

خواهیم بهر هر قدمش تحفه دگر
لیکن مقصریم که جان در بدن یکیست

I have grown so thin that, but for my lamentation and wailing, it would not appear that there was anybody in this shirt.

گشتم چنین ضعیف که بی ناله و فغان
ضاهر نمیشود که در این بدن یکیست

Where the charming ruby {lips} of Shirin are glowing, rubies and pebbles are alike in the eyes of { Farha'd } the sculptor.

آنجا که لعل دلکش شیرین دهد فروغ
یافوت وسنگ در نظر کوهکن یکیست

It was thou of all the fair ones who didst shutter my name and fame;
Yea, of a hundred Abrahams the breaker of idols is but one.

ناموس و نام ما تو شکستی زنیکوان
آری ز صد خلیل همین بت شکن یکیست

O Ja'mi, close thy mouth of speech in this garden, for there the song of nightingale and the shriek of the raven are one!"

جامی در این چمن دهن از گفتگو به بند
کانجا نوای بلبل وصوت زغن یکیست

Chapter 5

Of the great Persian lyrical poets who preceded Ja'mi, the verses sometimes known collectively as the Nay-nama or "Book of the Reed" he has skillfully imitated the style and lucidity developed the idea of the Prologue to Jala'l-ed-Din Mowlavi's {also known as Rumi } great Mystical Mathnavi. In conclusion, it can be justifiably said that Ja'mi was certainly one of the most talented, versatile and prolific poets in the domain of Persian poetry and mysticism.. In

Ja'mi the mystical and pantheistic thought of Persia has most certainly found its most complete and vivid expression; while, though he may have been equaled or even surpassed by others in each of the numerous realm of literature which he cultivated, no other Persian poet or writer has been so successful in so many different fields, and the enthusiastic admiration of his most eminent contemporaries is justified by his prolific and many sided genius.

CHAPTER 6

THE DECLINE OF PERSIAN POETRY DURING THE RULE OF SAFAVID DYNASTY: POETS & WRITERS BETWEEN C.E. 1500 &1600

Ba'ba Faghani Shirazi 16th century Persian poet & gnostic

An outstanding Persian poet in the 15th century & early 16th century, born in Shiraz, he worked as a cutler in his father's shop. For this reason he chose the pen-name Sakka'ki, but later on he used Faghani instead. After the Sultan Ya qub Ba'yondori (A'q Qouunlu) had given him the title ba'ba' (an appellation of leading dervishes and qalandars), he was most widely known as Ba'ba'

Fagha'ni. He left Shiraz when he was thirty years old and went first to Hera't, where his poetry was not well received, then to Tabriz, where he worked for the Sultan Yaqub and his successors until the A'q Qoyunlu regim began to disintegrate. He then returned to Shiraz, but at the time of Shah Esma'il Safavi's rise to power he moved to Khorasa'n, where he lived for a time at Abivard and then at Mashhad. He died in that city at an age of over sixty in 1519 or, according to some accounts in 1516. It is noteworthy to mention that he was highly esteemed in India in particular in the courts of the kings and amongst the majority of Persian speaking people.

In the later years of his life Ba'ba' Faghani repented and as mentioned before retired to the city of Mashhad, so that perhaps this verse of his ceased to be applicable:

"Stained with wine Fagha'ni sank into the earth:
Alas if the Angels should sniff at his shroud!"

آلوده شراب فغانی بخاک رفت
آه ار ملایکش کفن تازه بو کنند

Ba'ba Fagha'ni's diva'n, which has been printed, comprises of qasidas, tarkib-bands, tarji-bands, gazals, and roba'i's. All are pleasing and well-written. In all his qasidas the simplicity of the poet's diction and the fluency and vividness of his rhetoric are impressive. He deserves praise for his attention to these qualities at a time when other poets were imitating abstruse odes of old masters or concocting purely cerebral lyric and narrative pieces. In his ghazals the same fluidity and objectivity are found together with new phrases and compounds, moving expressions of feeling and original themes. This caused his style to be seen as different from that of his contemporaries and to be taken as a new and acceptable model. A literary critic even described him as a "Lesser Ha'fez" His method of ghazal writing, in particular, was widely studied in 16th, 17th, and 18th centuries and is reflected in the work of poets who regarded him as a master. In all fields Ba'ba' Fagha'ni exercised a lasting influence on Persian style in the Safavid period.

Omidi Tehrani 15th century Persian poet

Omidi was one of the most talented poets who lived in Iran during the rule of Safavid dynasty. He was quite well-known and was admitted to the court of

Chapter 7

Shah Esmaiil Safavi the founder of the Safavid dynasty. The monarch was himself a poet and left behind two diva'ns comprised of a number of poems; one in Persian and the other in Turkish.

Omidi was poetry laureate for some length of time at the court, well liked and respected especially by the two top ministers of the Shah. He, in particular, excelled in writing qasidas. His birthplace was the village of Tehran to the north of the city of Rey. The following verse is quite charming and inspiring:

I do not have luck to have you as my friend, To have you to give comfort to my restless soul, To have you with me during the day and in bed at night, Bringing me support throughout the rest of my life.	ان بخت ندارم که تو یارم باشی آسایش جان بیقرارم باشی شب در بروروز در کنارم باشی سرمایه دور روزگارم باشی

His proper name was Arja'sp. Omidi in the early years of his life traveled from Tehran to Shiraz to pursue his higher education goals and benefited and became a student of the celebrated philosopher Jala'l-ed-Din Dawa'ni, who changed his name to Masoud. He, in particular studied medicine and literature under the supervision of Dawa'ni. Omidi's skill was in qasida rather than ghazal; however his chief goal in getting himself educated was not to become a poet. Writing poetry for him was of secondary importance.

Omidi upon returning from Shiraz built a residence and garden in Tehran and named it"Garden of Hope". Qawam-ed-Din Nur- bakhsh, had set his eyes on that garden and demanded that Omidi sell him the property which he refused to. Qawa'm-ed-Din instigated his assassination and Omidy was killed by one of Qawam's desciples. One of Omidies' students by the name of Na'mi composed the following verses and chronogram on his death: The date of his murder was given by Sa'm Mirza as to have been during the year of 1523 and in 1522 as per Ahsanu't-Tawarikh. At the time of his murder he was 65 years old.

"The much-wronged Omidi, wonder of the Age	نادر عصر امیدی مظلوم کو بنا حق شهید شد ناکام

That suddenly and wrongly became
martyr
Appeared to me at night in a dream
and
said,
O thou that are aware of my inward
state,
Write for the date of my murder:"
Alas for my blood unjustly shed,
alas'".

شب به خواب من آمد وفرمود

کای ز حال درون من آگاه

آه از خون ناحق من آه

It was not too long after the incident that the Nur-bakhshi sect jumped to action again, poisoned and murdered Na'mi this faithful disciple of Omidi too. Omidi was 65 years old at the time of his murder.

Omidi during the course of his life had taught and trained famous other poets such as "Afzal Nami Tehrani" and "Heirani Neishabouri". Omidi's son"Kha'je Mohammad Taher Ra'zi" was also a poet as well as his nephew "Kha'je Mohammad Sharif Tehrani" whose son Etemad-Doleh Jah'angiri held a high rank at the court of Jaha'ngir Shah in India and was the grandfather of Noor Jahan Beygom the famous queen of India.

Omidi composed a qasida in praise of "Najm-Thani" minister at the court of Sha'h Esmail Safavi, and his poetry consisted mainly of panegyrics, though he also wrote a Sa'ghi-na'ma ("Book of the Cup-bearer") of the stereotyped form. Manuscripts of his poems are very rare, but there is one in the British Museum, comprising, however, only 17 leaves, and even these few poems were collected long after his death by the command of Sha'h Safi. Mention is however, made of him, in most of the tazkerehs (biographis). The author of the Haft Iqlim, writing more than seventy years after the death of Omidi, his fellow-townman and apparently kinsman, says that in his day the well-known verses of the poet consisted of 17 qasidas, 3 ghazals, a few fragments and quatrains, and the Sa'ghi-na'ma. The A'tash-kada cites 24 verses from the Sa'ghi-nama and 70 verses from his other poems, amongst these are the following, also given in the Majmaol-Fusaha':

"If the college hall should be turned upside down it matters little!

رواق مدرسه گر سرنگون شود سهل است

But may no injury befall the halls of the wine-taverns of Love!

قصور میکده عشق را مباد قصور

The colleges building, high and low, were destroyed, while the taverns continued to flourish just the same.

بنای مدرسه از جنس عالی وسافل
خراب گشت وخرابات همپنان معمور

Come and hear from this drunk, professing God's Unity;
The water flowing inside the tavern carries with it the same virtue as of Sinai's fire.

بیا و نکته توحید بشنو از من مست
که آب میکده دارد خواص آتش طور

I became the devotee of the Peer (the spiritual guide) of the Pot-house and washed away my vanity in the Tavern's water.

مرید پیر خرابات گشتم و شستم
به آب میکده عشق دل از متاع غرور

How joyful will it be should you coquettishly rend open the slit in your dress,
And glance at your beautiful countenance coquettishly!.

خوش آنکه چاک گریبان به ناز بازکنی
نظر بر آن تن نازک کنی وناز کنی

You are chaste and me, a libertine with rent cloak,
Wonder not that I am being shunned by you!

تو پاکدامن و من رند پیرهن چاکم
عجب نباشد اگر از من احتراز کنی

You always pass me by in disdain, while seeing others offering hundred prayers!

چو از برم گذری با هزار استغنا
به دیگری رسی اظهار صد نیاز کنی

You rob me of sleep, and shame me when I watch you prostrate in front of strangers!

به چشم من نکنی خواب وشرم میدارم
که پیش مردم بیگانه پا دراز کنی

You watch and allow other's tree of hope bear fruit,
While let "Omidiie's" hope and desire turn to despair like those of a beggar.

ترنج غبغب اورا نهال گشت بلند
تو دست کوته "امیدی" چرا دراز کنی

Here is another ghazal by Omidi:

"Thou art a half drunk Turk, I am a half-slain bird; thy affair with me is easy, my desire of thee is difficult.

توترک نیم مستی من مرغ نیم بسمل
کارتو از من آسان کام من از تو مشگل

Thou set thy foot in the field, I wash my hands of life; thou cause sweat to drip from my cheek, I pour blood from my heart.

توپا نهی بمیدان من دست شویم از جان
توخوی چکانی ازرخ من خون فشانم ازدل

Behind that traveler in weakness and helplessness I rise up and subside like the dust until the halting-place {is reached}.

دنبال آن مسافر از ضعف وناتوانی
برخیزم و نشینم چون گرد به منزل

When shall the luck be mine to lift him drunken from the saddle?
While that crystal-clear arm embraces my neck like sword belt?

کو بخت آنکه گیرم مستش زخانه زین
وان ساعد بلورین بر گردنم حمایل

Thou bear a dagger and a goblet; the faithful with one accord drink blood beside thee and give their lives before thee.

خنجر کشی و ساغر اهل وفا سراسر
خون خورده در برابر جان داده در مقابل

Now that my scroll of praise is rolled up, hearken to the tale of Ray:
It is a ruin wherein a madman is governor:

مداحیم چوشد طی بشنو حکایت ری
ویرانه ایست در وی دیوانه ایست عاقل

A mad man whom counsel produced no effect; a madman whom chains did not render sensible.	دیوانه ای که تدبیر در وی نکرده تاثیر دیوانه ایست پرفن دیرینه دشمن من
He is a madman full of craft, my old enemy; be not secure of him, and be not heedless of me.	از وی مباش ایمن وز من مباش غافل بر داور سخندان این نکته ایست پنهان
From the arbiter of eloquence this point is hidden, that a distracted mind is not disposed to verse My genius would snatch the ball of verse from the entire sundry, if only the bailiff were not in my house!"	کاندیشه پریشان نبود به نظم مایل طبعم ز هرکه بودی گوی سخن ربودی اما اگر نبودی در خانه ام محصل

Helaly Joghataie 15th century Persian poet

Mawla'na Badr-ed-Din, accomplished Persian poet was born in Astra'ba'd a suburb of the Province of Gorgan in the year 1470 and died 1520 in Hera't. Hela'li spent his early years in his native town, before moving to Hera't in 1491.

In Hera't he became a member of the literary circle of Sulta'n Hossein Ba'yghara. In particular, he became associate of Ali-Shir Nav'ai, who took him under his protection. He performed Ha'jj with Ja'mi and also came to know SA'm Mirza Safavi, well. Though often thought to be a Shi ite, Hela' li was certainly a Sunnite in religious affiliation. Reza Gholi Kha'n says that in Khora'sa'n he was regarded as a Shi it and in Ira'q as a Sunni. He stayed in Hera't during the critical period when the city was claimed by two rising powers, the Safavids and the Uzbecks.

The conquest of Hera't by Uzbek-Khan Obayd-Alla'h, who considered him a Ra'fezi, led to Hela'li's public execution, at the city's public square (Chaha'r-su) in 1529, an act which the sources present as an example of Ubayd's tyranny. The execution was accompanied with the confiscation of all his properties. The reason commonly adduced for his execution, carried out by a certain "Seyf-Allah" was that he was charged with being a Shi-ite.

However, the most likely reason is to be found in certain derogatory verses, originally composed by him against Sha'h Tahma'sp but subsequently directed against "Obayd-Alla khan, which end with Kafer ba'sham agar mosalma'n ba'shi (I am infidel if you are a believer.).

Hela'li is buried in Heara't near Fakhr-ed-Din Ali Hossein-e Ka'shefi, in a modern Mausoleum built to replace the original tomb at the public square where he had been executed. Hella'li had a daughter called Jama'li (Heja'bi), who went on to become an accomplished poet in her own right, renowned for her ghazals'.

Hela'li's literary output is rightly considered as among the most refind and original examples of Persian literature from the first half of the sixteenth century. Although one can detect the formal adherence to classical models, represented not only by Ha'fez but also by other poets such as A'refi, Ja'mi, and Kama'l Khojandi, Hela'li's work, similar to his life, displays a directness and immediacy which is quite unique in his period. His poetry is well-known in central Asia, in particular in Tajikestan, where it is still recited by folk singers.

The diva'n is Hela'li's principle work. It has been edited several times and it has also received critical attention from Sa id Nafisy, who has published, except for The Layla o Majnoon, the best scholarly edition of Hela'li's work. Further editions have been published in Iran and India. The div'an includes numerous ghazals, some ghasidas, Roba iyats and smaller fragments of verse.

Hela'li also wrote three mathnavis, all of which are of uncertain date. The Sha'h o darvish (often called Sha'h o geda) was most likely written between 1499 and 1508. This work was written in response to the charge, leveled by Hela'li's rival, Abd-Alla'h Hatefi, that he was unable to write a mathnavi. It was dedicated to Badi-ol-Zama'n Mirza' and has been generally well received, though Ba'bor found it rather shallow and immoral. This work is predominantly mystical in content, which may account for its popularity, even outside of the Persian-speaking regions. This popularity is attested by the fact that it has often been reproduced in illustrated manuscripts. The Sha'h o darvish has been translated into German by Ethe and one translation into Turkish by Hamidi is reported by Ka'teb Chalabi as well as by Sa id Nafisi.

With regard to the other two mathnavis, the Sefa't al- a'sheghin, (The attributes of Lovers) which is divided into 20 chapters, each describing a human quality, was written as a response to the Makhzan al asra'r by Nezami, probably after 1508.The third mathnavi, Leyla' o Majnoon, is extant in only one late manuscript at the British Museum Library, in contrast to the other two, which are found in numerous manuscripts. Ivanow has brought attention to the existence also of a treatise on rhyme by Hela'li, entitled Resa'la-ye gha'fiya, which was inspired by Shams- Ghays.Although he is renowned for his writings in Persian, Hela'li did also write some verse in Turkish.

Vashi Ba'fghi 16th century Persian poet

Kamal'-ed-Din Vahshi Ba'fghi, Persian poet of Safavid period, was born in the town of Bafgh situated south east of the city of Yazd in 1583 where he received his earlier training in poetry from his elder brother Mora'di and the local luminary Sharaf-ed-Din Ali of Bafgh.He continued his education in the provincial capital of Yazd before moving to kashan, the great center of literary activity in the early Safavid period.He was working as a schoolteacher when his poetry first attracted the attention of the regional governor.Vahshi seems to have been welcomed on the scene by many local poets who were tired of laurels showered on Mohtashem Kashani, and he quickly became embroiled in the bouts of poetic fleeting that were a prominent feature of the literary culture of the time, exchanging invectives with rivals, such as Fahmi Kashani and Ghazanfar of Koranja'r. His panegyrics (qasidas) in honor of Tahma'sp 1 probably also date from this stage of his career. From Kashan he travelled to other cities of western Iran Such as Ara'k and Bandar Aba's before making his way back to Yazd.

Vahshi was free from the wanderlust that would posses Persian poets over the next fifty years and he spent the remaider of his life in Yazd and nearby palace-town of Taft. Although he sometimes complains of his poverty, he seems to have enjoyed a fairly prominent as the foremost poet at the court of the hereditary rulers of the region, Ghiyas-ed-Din Mir (-e) Mira'n and his son Khalil-Alla'h, who were descendants of the Sufi Sheykh Sha'h Ne'-mat-Alla' Wali and in laws of the Safavid royal house.Vahshi had also dedicated praise poems to the governors of Kerma'n (in particular Bekta'sh Beyg Afsha'r) and wrote two short chronograms on the enthronement of Esma'il II. Vahshi seems to have been retiring by nature, and there is no evidence that he ever married. According to his eventual literary executor, Ohadi of Balya'n, Vahshi died of a strong dose of drink in Yazd in 1583 at the age of 52. He was buried in this city. Although tombs built in his honor have regularly fallen victim to political upheaval. Awhadi gathered some 9000 verses of Vahshi's poetry after his death, and this diva'n contains poems of all the classical genres.

 Vahshi's qasidas include not only panegyrics to the patrons mentioned above, but also several devotional poems in honor of Shi'ite Ima'ms. The qeta' genre served Vahshi primarily as a vehicle for panegyric and other occasional themes. Invective, praise, and architectural description also provide for some ten short untitled poems in rhymed couplets. But it is in various strophic forms, the ghazal and his longer mathnavis (poems in couplet form), that Vahshi most distinguishes himself'. His sole tarji-band (stanzic poem with a refrain) is an extended celebration of mystical intoxication with the full-verse refrain: ma' gushe- neshinan-e khara'ba't elastim / ta bu-ye meyi hast dar in meykadeh mastim, (We are recluses in the premordial tavern / while there is even a scent of wine in this wine-shop, we are drunk) By Fakhre-el- Zama'ni in his "Tazkera-ye Meykhaneh and set an important precedent in the new genre of the sa'ghina'me (wine server's song), which was followed by many later poets like Naziri Nishabouri a few years later. Vahshi used the stansaic poems (tarkib band) effectively as a medium for personal eulogy in poems lamenting the death of his brother, his teacher Sharaf-ed-Din Ali, and his student Qasem Beyg qaesmi Afsha'r, in the masamatat translated by Brown, the five-line strophes take on a ballad-like quality, as the speaker tells how his attentions to a young and inexperienced male lover eventually emboldened him to seek out lovers on his own: This poem ends with the speaker washing his hands of the relationship, and such a note of confident willingness is often found in Vahshi's ghazals as well. This attitude, so different from the long-suffering self-effacement typical of the classical Persian ghazals: Here is the poem:

"O friends hearken to the account of my distraction!.	دوستان شرح پریشانی من گوش کنید
Hearken to the tale of my hidden sorrow!.	داستان غم پنهانی من گوش کنید
Hearken to the story of my disordered state!;	قصه بی سر وسامانی من گوش کنید
Hearken to my description of my bewilderment!.	گفت وگوی من وحیرانی من گوش کنید

How long shall I hide the account of this grievous story! I	شرح این قصه جانسوز نهفتن تا کی
Burn!, I burn!. How long shall I refrain from telling the secrets?	سوختم سوختم این راز نگفتن تا کی
For a while I and my heart dwelt in a certain street:	روزگاری من و دل ساکن کویی بودیم
The street of a certain quarrelsome beauty.	ساکن کوی بت عربده جویی بودیم
We had staked Faith and heart on one dissolute countenance;	دین و دل باخته ویرانه رویی بودیم
We were fettered in the chains of one chain-like tress.	بسته سلسله سلسله مویی بودیم
In that chain was none bound save me and my heart;	کس در آن سلسله غیر از من و دلبند نبود
Of all that exist, not one was captive then.	یک گرفتار از این جمله که هستنند نبود
Her bewitching narcissus-eyes had not then all these love-sick victims;	نرگس غمزه زنش این همه بیمار نداشت
Her curling hyacinthine locks held then no prisoner;	سنبل پر شکنش این همه دلدار نداشت
she had not then so brisk a business and so many customers.	این همه مشتری وگرمی بازار نداشت

She was a Joseph {in beauty} but found no purchaser.	یوسفی بود ولی هیچ خریدار نداشت
I was the first to become a purchaser;	اول آنکس که خریدار شدم من بودم
It was I who caused the briskness of her market.	باعث گرمی بازار شدم من بودم
My love was the cause of her beauty and comeliness;	عشق من شد سبب خوبی و رعنایی او
My shame gave fame to her beauty;	داد رسوایی من شهرت زیبایی او
So widely did I everywhere describe her charms that	بسکه کردم همه جا شرح دلارایی او
The whole city was filled with tumult of the spectators.	شهر پر گشت ز غوغای تماشایی او
Now she has many distracted lovers,	این زمان عاشق سرگشته فراوان دارد
How should she think or care for poor distracted me?.	کی سر وبرگ من بی سروسامان دارد
Since it is so, it is better that we should pursue some other aim,	چون چنین است پی کار دگر باشم به
That we should become the nightingales of some other rose-cheeked beauty,	مرغ خوش نغمه بازار دگر باشم به عندلیب گل رخسار دگر باشم به
That for a few days we should follow some other charmer.	چند روزی پی دلدار دگر باشم به

Where some fresh is young raised whose eloquent nightingale I may become, and	نوگلی کو که شوم بلبل دستان سازش
whom I may {thus} distinguish amongst the youthful beauties of the garden?.	سازم از تازه جوانان چمن ممتازش
Although the fancy for thy face has passed away from Vahshi's mind,	گرچه از خاطر وحشی هوس روی تو رفت
And the desire for thy charming figure has departed from his heart,	وز دلش آرزوی قامت دلجوی تو رفت
And one vexed in heart hath departed in vexation from thy street,	شد دل آزرده واز کوی تو رفت
And with a heart full of complaints hath departed from the displeasure of thy countenance,	با دل پرگله از ناخوشی روی تو رفت
God forbid that I should forget thy constancy,	حاش الله که وفای تو فراموش کنم
Or should listen to man's councels of expediency!.	سخن مصلحت امیز کسان گوش کنم

Themes similar to the one in this particular however, do appear in the shortest of Vahshi's mathnavis, Kholde-barin ("The highest heaven"). This poem follows the structure and meter of Neza'mi's Makhzan-al-asra'r and, at less than 600 verses may be finished. Vahshi also wrote two narrative romances in rhymed couplets. Na'zer o Manzur tells the tale of the passionate relationship of the prince of China, Munzur, with the son of the king's vizier, Na'zer. To avoid scandal the vizier packs his son off to Egypt when his ardor for Manzur causes him to misbehave in school. When Na'zer reveals his secret love in a letter, however, Prince Manzur set off in pursuit, and after many adventures and exploits, the two are reunited in Egypt, where Manzur marries the princess of the country, becomes king, and appoints Na'zer as his prime Minister.

Decline of Persian Poetry 1700-1800

Some 500 verses long and completed in 1588-89, this poem has received little critical attention, but offers an ingenious re-combination of the older motifs, and its story of mutual platonic passion of two men is somewhat unusual in the tradition of Persian narrative romance

Like Na'zer o Manzur, Vahshi's Farh'd o Shirin, is also written in the meter of Neza'mi's Khosrow o Shirin, but draws more directly on its model for its narrative material. Vahshi focuses on one episode of Nezami's story; the tragic affair between the sculptor, engineer, architect Farha'd Kuhkan (mountain cutter) and the Arminian princess, Shirin. Although the work was left unfinished at the time of Vahshi's death, with the introduction and barely 500 verses of the story completed. Farhd oShirin has been recognized as the poets masterpiece from the time of its first appearance until today. Nearly a hundred manuscripts of the work have been cataloged around the world. In a systematic comparison of Nezami's and Vahshi's treatment of Farha'd, Parviz Khanlari has argued that Vahshi elevated the character of Farhad into a symbol of the proud strong minded artist whose life and work are driven by the same creative passion. At the beginning of the tale, Vahshi famously identifies his own experience explicitly with that of his hero:

"I am Farhad, and that sweetly smiling girl Shirin, For whom, like the mountain-cutter, I must chip away my life.	منم فرهاد و شیرین آن شکرخند کز آن چون کوهکن جان بایدم کند

Two poets of Shiraz, Wesa'l and Saber, took on the task of completing Vahshi's poem in the 19th century.

Unlike other poets of the Safavid period Vahshi has continuously enjoyed positive critical reception from his own day to the present. His poetry has little of the allusive or metaphorical complexity found in either his model Nezami or in the "fresh style" poets of the following generations. Perhaps the greatest master of the plain style of the maktab-e woqu, Vahshi's artistry lies in his ability to turn the rhythms and language of every day speech into a precise and elegant medium for capturing a wide range of emotions from a bitter sense of betrayal to helpless yearning. In this regard, Vahshi's styles like that of his predecessor Saadi has been described as sahl o mom tane' –a style whose apparent simplicity belies an inimitable and almost translucent immediacy.

Chapter 7

Orfi Shirazi 16ᵗʰ century Persian poet

Orfi whose proper name was Jama'lud-Din Muhammad was born in Shira'z, in 1555 and died in La'hore in 1591. He was educated in Shiraz and flourished at a very young age in the circles of the great poets and writers of that city. He soon established himself as an outstanding poet rubbing shoulder with great poets of the time such as Mir Mahmud Tarhi, Qeydi of Shira'z, Ghyra'ti of Shira'z as well as few others. His talents were recognized by Mohtashem of Ka'sha'ni, and corresponded with Vahshi of Ba'fgh. Like many of his contemporaries, soon decided to migrate to India and join many distinguished Persian poets who had followed suit in search of fame and fortune that was abundantly available to men of talent in the courts of the Mughal kings of India.

After arriving in the Deccan, he proved his talent in the literary centers, attached himself to Fayzi, but due to his extreme arrogance, soon fell out with him. Fayzi was the leading poet at the court of Akbar Shah whom Fayzi introduced Orfi to. He also introduced Orfi to Masih-ed-Din Hakim Gilani, who supported and patronized Orfi until his death. At a later date Orfi joined the court of Mughal statesman Abdul-Rahim Kh'an Kh'na'n, and last but not least, he became a favorite poet of Akbar Shah, whom he accompanied on his seasonal retreat to Kashmir in 1588. Unfortunately his shining glory did not last for long and he died of dysentery at a very young age of 35 in La'hore. Some three years later his remains were disinterred and reburied in Najaf (Iraq)

In spite of his opportunities and undoubted talents, Orfi's intolerable conceit and arrogance prevented him from being popular, and made him many enemies. Rez gholoi kha'n Hedayat, biographer accords him but a brief notice in Majma'u'l-Fusaha' and observes that "the style of his poems is not admired by the people of this age". Criticism and disparagement are, indeed, courted by a poet who could write:

| "Wherefore did Saadi glory in a handful of the earth of Shira'z | نازش سعدی بمشت خاک شیراز از چه بود |
| If he did not know that it would be my birthplace and abode? | گر نمی دانست باشد مولد وماوای من |

Decline of Persian Poetry 1700-1800

Nor is this an isolated example of his conceit, for in like fashion he vaunts his superiority to Anwari, Abul Faraj, Khaghani, and other great Persian poets, and his unamiable practice may have conducted to his unpopularity amongst his compatriots, who did not readily tolerate this disparagement of the national heroes. The poet himself as mentioned was fully aware and admits that his arrogance made him unpopular, as appears from following poem, wherein he complains of the hypocritical sympathy of the so called "friends" who came to visit him when he was confined to bed by a severe illness:

"My body hath fallen into this state and my eloquent friends Stand like pulpits round my bed and pillow.	تن اوفتاد در این حال و دوستان فصیح بدور بالش و بستر استاده چون منبر
One draws his hand through his beard and cocks his neck, saying	یکی بریش کشد دست وکج کند گردن
O life of thy father! To whom is fortune constant?	که روزگار وفا با که کرد جان پدر
One should not set one's heart on ignoble rank and wealth: Where is the Empire of Jamshid and the name of Alexander?	بجاه و مال فرو مایه دل نباید بست کجاست دولت جمشید ونام اسکندر
Another, with soft voice and sad speech, begins, drawing his sleeve across his moist eyes:	یکی بنرمی آوازو گفتگوی حزین کند شروع وکشد آستین به دیده
O my life! All have this road, by which must they depart:	که جان من همه را این رهست و باید رفت
We are all travelers on the road, and time bears forward the riders	تمام راه روا نیم و دهر راکب بر
Another adorning his speech with smooth words says: O thou whose death is the date of the revolution of news	یکی بچرب زبانی سخن طرازشود که ای وفات تو تاریخ انفلاب خبر

	فراهم آی وپریشان مدار دل زنهار
Collect thyself, and beware, let thy heart be troubled, for I will with single purpose collect thy verse and prose.	که نثرونظم تومن جمع میکنم یکسر
	پس از نوشتن وتصحیح میکنم انشا
After copying it and correcting it, I will compose an introduction like a casket of pearls in support of thy claims;	بمدعای تو دیباچه چو درج گهر چنانچه هستی
An index of learning and culture such as thou art, a compendium of good qualities and talents such as thou art;	فهرست دانش وفرهنگ چنانچه هستی مجموعه صفات وهنر
I will pour forth, applying myself both to verse and prose, although it is not within the power of me to enumerate thy perfections!	بنظم ونثر در آویزم و فرو ریزم اگر چه حصر کمال تونیست حد بشر
May God see what wrath I will pour on the heads of these miserable hypocrites!	خدای عز وجل صحتم دهد بینی که این منافقکان را چه آورم بر سر

Despite dying young, Orfi had a great impact on his contemporaries through the force of both his personality and his poetry. Perhaps because he was disfigured by smallpox in his teens, Orfi was hypersensitive, quick to take offence and respond to any taunt with a ready wit and a sharp tongue. In an oft-quoted anecdote Orfi finds his sponsor, Fayzi, holding a puppy one day and asks the name of the" young master." When Fayzi answers "Orfi" Orfi replies, "Mobarak bashad," both, offering his congratulations on the new pet and suggesting that Fayzi ought to name it after his father, Sheykh Moba'rak. Even his most sympathetic biographer, Abdol-ba'ghi Nah'vandi, remarks on Orfi's on open disregard for the standard protocol and etiquette of the Mughal court. His poetic braggadocio (fakhr) knew few limits, and he declared his poetry to be not only superior to his contemporarians, but also unrivaled by the greatest poets of the past. Some Tazkerehs have even suggested that his premature demise could have been due to this egotism. Not surprisingly, Orfi offended many of his fellow poets, like Naziri of Nisha'bour, his rival at the court of Kha'n-Kha'nan includes a blistering condemnation of Orfi's arrogance in one of his qasidas.However exaggerated Orfi's lofty estimation of his own talents, were not unfounded.

His poetry enjoyed great popularity in his life time throughout Persian-speaking world, and F.J.W.Gibb remarks on Orffi's formative influence on Ottoman-Turkish poetry as well. Both Awhadi and Naha'vandi identify Orfi as the "inventor of the" Tarz-eta'za" (the fresh style). Although no single poet can justly be given credit for the emergence of the "fresh" or "Indian" style (which would dominate Persian poetry for the next two centuries).

Orfi did play a crucial role in the move away from the colloquial diction and realist aesthetics of the makktab-waqu and toward a new evaluation of conceptual subtlety and imagistic complexity. Among Orfi's works, his qasidas have met with special critical acclaim. Though a few of these are addressed to Orfi's early Safavid patrons (Shah Esmaiil II, and Pari-Kha'nom), most date from his career in India and are dedicated to Abul-Fath of Gila'n, Abd-el Rahim Kh''nkh'na'n, prince Salim and Akbar. His style in the qasida has been praised for its measured, yet fluent diction, continuity of theme over extended passages, the coinage of new metaphorical compounds, and innovative comparisons.

These last two features in particular are also evident in Orfii's other genres. His mastery of the qasida has perhaps unjustly overshadowed his ghazals, which at their best demonstrate a powerful command of language and subtlety of thought and imagery. As might be expected from a poet who grew up with maktab-woque, his amatory lyrics are characterized by a discriminating insight into the psychology and negotiations of the love relationship. Orphi's real strength however is in his handling of philosophical and Gnostic themes, and Dak'wati Qaraguzlu has noted the attitude of critical doubt and antinomianism that often informs Orfi's qasidas. Here, he shows his debt to his compatriot of Shira''z, Hafez, one of the few earlier poets whom Orfi praised without reservation and whose gazals, along with those of another fellow poet from Shira'z Baba Faghani, were among his favorite models for response poems. Orfi's diva'n also contains few tarkib bands and tarji bands and several dozen qatas, mostly themes, as well as a couple of hundred roba'is.

Chapter 7

Orfi began work on a khamsa on the model of Nez'ami but he died before bringing even one of the five projected mathnawis to completion. He finished a little over 1400 verses of Majma- al-afka'r (in the meter of Makhzan-al-asra'r), which consists of ethical and didactic tales in a sufi mode. Only four hundred verse of the introductory sections of his Farha'd o Shirin survive. Besides other scattered rhymed couplets. Urfi finished a complete sa'qi-nama, a genre much in vogue at the time. In terms of form, his most unusual work is a satire on contemporary poets, a hybrid between mathnavi and tarji-band. Orfi's interest in Sufism is again apparent in his short prose work entitled Resa'la-nafsiya,"Treatise on the Ego-Self. Finally, samples of his personal correspondence and other prose jottings have been gleaned from manuscripts, miscellanies and some copies of his diva'n.

The contemporary historian Abd-al-Gha'der Bad'uni reports that"there is no street or bazaar where booksellers do not stand with copies of the diva'ns of Orfi and Hoseyn Tanai prominently on display and Orfi's popularity is attested by the more than one hundred manuscripts of his works that are preserved to-day. However he died before being able to see a final definitive compilation of his diva'n. He did prepare a first collection of his own works in1588, but also bemoaned the loss of a manuscript of some six thousand verses that he had lent to a friend, Shortly before his death, he turned his uncollected works and papers over to the library of Abd-al-Rahim Ka;n-Ka'na'n. These were eventually arranged and edited by the poet Sera'je-Isfahani and were published with an introduction by Abd-alBa'qi of Neha'vand in 1615. Further complicating the situation, another compilar Mohammad Nazem of Tabriz dubiously claimed that he caught Sera'j fleeing the Ka'n-e K'na'n's court with the autograph copy of Orfi's works which Na'zem recovered and used as his basis of his own recension of the diva'n. With justifiable skepticism, Mohammad Ali has questioned the authenticity of many of the ghazals in these later versions of the diva'n; his judgment, however is based on literary quality, and not on philosophical grounds, and has been effectively rebutted by Golchin-Ma a'ni and Mohammad al-Haq Ansa'ri. Ansari has untangled the complicated transmission of Orfi's works and has now published the results of a lifetime research in a definitive scholarly edition of Orfi's "Kolliya't", based nearly on forty sources and containing a full critical apparatus. Ansa'ri's edition should provide the basis of future critical inquiry into the work of this controversial and talented poet, who played a critical role in the later development of classical Persian poetry.

Decline of Persian Poetry 1700-1800

Ta'leb Amoli 17th century Persian poet

Seyyed Mohammad Ta'leb A'moli, Persian poet of the early 17th century was born in the city of Amol in Mazandera'n in 1580 and died in India in 1626. Extraordinary talented poet, embarked on his literary career in his late teens, composing praise poems to notables in his native Ma'zandera'n and ghazals (lyrics) under the penname A'shub.

Beginning a lifetime of constant travel, he soon sought to further his career in the major literary centers of Persia. In Kasha'n his maternal uncle held a prominent position as court physician to Sha'h Tahma'sb I, and Ta'leb began a life-long friendship with his cousin and fellow-poet Hakim Rokn-ed Din Masih. During a brief stay in Isfa'ha'n, Taleb wrote two ghasidas (panegirycs) in honor of Shah Abba's I; when these failed to win him entry into the Safavid court, he moved to Merv, where he found a patron in the provincial governor Bekt'sh Khan Osta'jlu around 1606. Under the pretext of attending to family affairs, he left Khora'sa'n in 1608, but rather than returning to Ma'zander'an, he joined the emigration of Persian merchants, administrators, and scholars toward the lucrative new markets of Mughal India.

"Ta'leb leave the flower of this meadow Leave it or you shall otherwise regret it	طالب گل این چمن ببستان بگذار بگذار که میشوی پریشان بگذار
No one carries a Hindu with himself to India Leave this black (i.e. bad) luck of yours behind in Persia"	هندو نبرد تحفه کسی جانب هند بخت سیه خویش به ایران بگذار

Ta'leb spent the next couple of years wandering between Molta'n and Agra' before joining the literary circle of Mirza' Ghazi Tarka'n in Qandeha'r. This young and brilliant military commander was himself a capable poet under the penname Waqa'ri and under the direction of the poet Morshed of Boroujerd, his court became an important transit station for the traffic of literary talent between India and Persia. After Mirza' gha'zi's premature death in 1612 at the age of only twenty five, Ta'leb again spent several years roaming about

Chapter 7

Northern India. During his first appearance before Jaha'ngir, Ta'leb was left speechless by awe and the opium that he had taken beforehand to calm his nerves, but he gradually worked his way back to the imperial court through his service with Mughal generals such as Chin Gholich Kha'n in Sura't and Firuz Jang in Gujra't. However, it was a chance meetung in L'hore with Sha'pur of Teheran, and an introduction to his Uncle Kha'je Ghias-ed-Din Mohammad Etema'd-doleh, that opened Ta'leb's path to the empror's inner circle. With the support of this influencial administrator, Ta'leb entered Jaha'ngir's service about 1616 and was appointed to the post of poet laureate in1619. He was far from modest, for he boasts before he reached his twentieth year he had mastered seven sciences:

"My foot is on the second step of the zenith of the decades,
And behold, the number of my accomplishments exceeds thousands.

پا بر دومین پایه اوج عشرتم
واینک عدد فن ام از آلاف زیادست

In mathematics, astronomy, logic, and philosophy I enjoy a proficiency which is conspicuous amongst mankind.

بر هندسه ومنطق وهیت وحکمت
دستی است مرا کش ید
بیضا ز عبادست

When all these are traversed the savory knowledge of the Truth, which is the Master of the Sciences, is added to the sum total.

وین جمله چو طی شد نمکین علم حقیقت
کاستاد علوم است برین جمله مزاد است

In the concatenated description of my writing this is enough, that every dot from my pen is the hearts core of men of letters.

در سلسله وصف خط این بس که ز کلکم
هر نقطه سویدای دل اهل سواد است

For the next several years Taleb accompanied Shah Jahangir on his frequent journeys through his domains. However, the poet apparently sufered from a mental infirmity during the final years of his life, and the circumstances of his death are unclear. When he died in 1626, he left two young daughters orphans.

Decline of Persian Poetry 1700-1800

They were adopted by his elder sister Sati-alNesa', with whom he shared a deep affection throughout his life and after a long separation she had come from Persia to Agra to see him, Before his death he had sought leave of absence from the Emperor Jaha'ngir in the following verses:

"O Master, Patron of the humble! I have a representation {to make} in eloquent language.

صاحبا ذره پروررا عرضی
بزبان سخن ورست مرا
۱

I have an old and sympathetic sister, who
entertains for me a mother's love'

پیر همشیره ایست غم خوارم
که به او مهر مادر است مرا

Fourteen years or more have passed since my eyes were parted from the sight of her face

چهارده سال بلکه بیش گذشت
کز نظر دور منظر است مرا

I was removed from her service in Iraq, and this sin is a grievous fault of mine.

دور گشتم ز خدمتش بعراق
وین گنه جرم منکر است مرا

She could not bear to remain far from me, for she is as a mother to me.

که به مادر برابر است مرا

Lo, she hath come to Agra, and in longing for her my heart flutters like a pigeon.

آمد اینک به آگره و زشوق
دل طپان چون کبوتر است مرا

My heart craves after her: What can I do? Yearning impels me on the road.

می کند دل بسوی او آهنگ
چه کنم شوق رهبر ست مرا

If leave should be granted to visit her,
it would be worth a world to me.

گر شود رخصت زیارت او
به جهانی برابر است مرا

Chapter 7

By most reports Taleb was an amiable man who avoided the bitter personal rivalries that often flared among the poets of Mughal India. His contemporary Fakhr-al-Zama'ni of Qazvin reports that the poet was "good-natured and affable', and Awhadi of Balya'ni, who met Taleb in both Isfahan and Ajmer, praises his "joyous" and industrious temperament. Such personal qualities help explain the ease with which Ta'leb moved between patrons and his prolificacy. Although it is uncertain when his works were first collected, full manuscript of his diva'n (collected poems) date from only a few years after his death, and many contain well over 20,000 verses. His short mathnawi, "Ghaza' va Ghadar" (one of several works by his name written during the period) tells the fantasy tale of a shipwrecked sailor marooned with a beautiful woman on a desert island. His other two works in rhymed couplets, also less than 500 verses long were written for special occasions; one to request leave from Bekta'sh Kha'n in Merv and the other to celebrate an outdoor banquet held by Jah'ngir. Over seventy qasidas and dozens of short qeta's (topical or occasional poems) provide a full and fascinating record of his professional life as courtier and panegyrist. Like other poets rose in Safavid Persia, Ta'leb also dedicated a number of devotional poems to the Shi' ite Immamas. His strophic poems appear to date from early in his career and cover a range of similar topics. However, by far the greatest portion of his diva'n consists of ghazals some 1750 in number and it is these lyric poems that are largely the basis of his later critical reception.

Though most contemporaries gave fulsome praise to Ta'leb's originality and creativity, a dissenting voice seems to have had the greatest impact on modern scholarship. Monir of La'hore who died in 1644 reports Taleb and asking him about an obscure verse from the notoriously difficult 12th century poet Kha'ghani, when Monir laughed out loud at the poet's absurd explication, Ta'leb rejoined, "In India, they only study such verses, while I can write them with my toenails". Not surprisingly, Taleb is a prime target of Monir's attack on the "fresh style" of contemporary poetry in his Ka'rnama; though Alikha'n A'rzu mounted a vigorous defense of Ta'leb a century later, this anecdote was given new life in an early 18th century collective biography of poets (tazkera); Makhzanal-gha'raeb, and found its way into modern criticism through Shebli-No' mani and Ta'leb's editor, Ta'heri Sheha'b.

Ta'leb enjoys the dubious distinction of being a "natural genius" whose technical acumen sometimes failed to match the exuberance of his imagination. Even sympathetic modern biographers (Safa'and Sharafi) feel obliged to include a sampling of the poet's "incomprehensible" verses; the broader and more representative selection from Ta'leb's ghazals by Ghahrama'n and Abd al-Rashid Khaja give a far more positive impression of the poet's range and capability.

Ta'leb played a cruicial role in the transformation of Persian poetic style at the beginning of the seventeenth century. His work gave free rein to the tendency toward conceptualism (khaya'l pardazi) in the "fresh style" (later known as the Indian style) that had begun to emerge a generation earlier in the poetry of Naziri and Orfi. Like them, Ta'leb showed his debt to the past by responding to poems predecessors such as Khagha'ni in the qasida and Saadi, Amir Khosrow, and Ha'fez in the ghazal; at the same time, he gives a new vitality to conventional images and common idioms by exploring their full figurative implications, a procedure Ta'leb himself revealingly dubs his tarz-e este a'ra (metaphorical style).

His elaboration of two unobtrusive metaphors of everyday speech offers a small indication as to how his imagination works. In the verse: Kha'naya sharia't khara'b ast ke arba'b-e sala'h/ dar ema'ratgari-ye gonbad dasta'rand (The house of religions laws is in ruins, for the lordly pious /are busy constructing the domse of their turbans). Ta'leb revives the dead metaphor of" the house of religious law" in a single long noun phrase that exposes the spiritual ruin behind a sartorial faca'de of clerical ostentation. Paradox, simile, and a neologistic compound all contribute to spinning new meaning from "the thread of life", a tired clich'e in both Persian and English: gereh-zani-st zolf-e 'arusa'n reshte-ye'omram/ze bas peyvand-e ja'n bogsasto man bar yek degar bastam ('Like brides coiffures, the tread of my life is a bed of knots/ so often my soul's bond come apart and I have tied it back together.). The festive union of marriage provides both a model for and a contrast to the speaker's exhausted frustration, a visual and tactile image giving form to an emotional state. Such was the verve inventiveness, and profusion of Ta'lebs similes and metaphors that the great master - poet of the later 17th century, Sa'eb of Tabriz, praises his poetry without reserve and proudly takes his place as Ta'leb's heir and successor.

Naziri Neishabouri 16th century Persian poet & gnostic

Naziri Neishabouri was born in Neishabour in 1560 and having spent about thirty years of his life in India, he died in Gojra't in1612. Naziri left

Neishabour as a young man after the death of his father. Though he traveled to western Persia as a merchant, he was already an accomplished poet when he met the literary biographer Tagh-ed-Din Ka'shi in 1584 in Kasha'n, where Naziri sharpened his skills exchanging verses with experienced poets of the city, such as Ha'tam, Shagha' and Reza'i. Shortly after this meeting, Naziri migrated to India, where he became the first Persian born poet to join the court of the great Mugha'l statesman and literary patron Abdol-Rahim Kh'an-Khana'n. Over the next decade, Naziri established himself as the master poet, composing many panegyrics in honor of the Kha'n and often enjoyed his legendary largess. Through him Naziri was introduced to the Imperial family, though he did not enter the inner circle of Akbar's literary establishment. Abdol-Rahima Kha'n provided him with money to make pilgrimage to Mecca In 1593-94 in response to a qasida beginning:

"Through genius I cannot contain myself, like the Magian wine in the jar,	ز هنر بخود نگنجم چو به خم می مغانی
The very garments are rent on my body when my ideas ferment.	بدرد لباس بر تن چو بجوشدم معانی
Through thy beneficence I experienced all the pleasures of this world;	همه عیش این جهانی بعنایت تو دیدم
What wonder if through thee {also} I should obtain provision for the other world?"	چه عجب اگر بیابم ز تو زاد آنجهانی

When Naziri was waylaid by Bedouin brigands, he called on the aid of Akbar's foster brother, Mohammad- Aziz A'zam Ka'n, who also happened to be in Heja'z at this time and whose conquest of the citadel of Juna Naziri had earlier celebrated.

When Naziri returned to India, he settled in Gujra't distancing himself from his first patron, as his wealth and fame created other opportunities.

Decline of Persian Poetry 1700-1800

In Gujra't, Naziri prospered in agriculture and commercial enterprises and became a wealthy man. He remained in demand as a poet, and wrote panegirycs not only for his previous patron, but also for Prince Mura'd and Jaha'ngir, who called Naziri to Agra in 1610. As a member of the urban elite Naziri built a mansion and contributed to the support of the poor. He became a literary patron for new poets from Persia. Though his poetry occasionally used metaphors typical of the emerging "Shiva- ye-tazeh" (fresh style), he avoided the bolder experiments of his contemporaries. His poems continued in the maktab-woqu', or "realist" school" of poetics, characteristic of Safavid Persia in the 16th century, which avoided sufistic symbolism. He wrote:
"I am neither intoxicated by power and riches, nor am I defeated by poverty and starvation. Neither have I the aspiration to be drunk by a drop; nor am I so greedy as to be demolished by starving .I am the Absolute inspiration and wine can neither elevate nor depress me."

Naziri died sometime around 1613 in Ahmadabad and was buried in a mosque he had built near his home.

Naziri was a powerful and aggressive player in the highly competitive literary world of early Mughal India. Even in his earliest poem to Akbar, he criticizes the plague of no-talent pretenders at the monarch's court. He attacked Orfi, his rival, for the attention of Kha'n-Kha'nan, as the "acme of ignorance and stupidity". In one of his ghazals, he recommends that Sufi of Mazandera'n be hung with his own clerical robe. On the other hand, he displayed great generosity to poets who showed proper deference to his position. He promoted the careers of many younger poets such asTajlily of Ka'sha'n and Na'dem of Gilan and was a deserving object of their praise. Nazziri's appeal on behalf of Gaki of Assadabadi ironically cost this poet his life by reminding Akbar that he was still alive in prison. Naziri was orthodox in matters of religion. He disparages Akbar's ecumenical Din-e elahi in a panegyric to Prince Mora'd. His responses to Ba'ba'Faghani indicate his leeriness of the ecstatic and visionary aspects of Sufism and suggest his preference for a religiosity repose and equanimity. A tarkib-band (a strophe poem in which each stanza ends with a different verse and rhyme, in twelve stanzas), one dedicated to each of the twelve Imams, leaves no doubt in Naziri's Shi'it affiliation.Toward the end of his life, Naziri took up the study of Arabic, hadith and Kuranic exegesis.

Chapter 7

A year or so before his death, Naziri compiled a divan of some 12,000 verses and had it deliverd to Abd-ol-Rahim's library for preservation. Though Nazari never attempted mathnavi, his qasidas provide a lively chronicle of his life. The tarkib- band and tarji- band are his preferred for elegy and his poems mourning the death of his family members, of Prince Morad, and of his fellow poets Tana' and Anisi are among the finest examples of the genre in the period. His reputation, however, is based primarily on ghazals. As suggested by his pen name, Naziri was an assiduous practitioner of nazira-gu'ie (writing a reply to an earlier poem utilizing the same meter and rhyme scheme). He modeled his qasidas after the work of Anvari and Kha'ghani, in the ghazal, he shows a preference too for the works of Saadi , Ba'ba' Fagha'ni, and above all Ha'fez. More than most poets of age, Naziri felt the literary achievements of the past to be a burden rather than a resource. Naziri was well respected by his contemporaries and later readers, even the great proponent of the so called "literary return" (Baz-gasht- adbi), Azar Bigdeli who treats most Safavid-Mughal poets with undisguised disdain, praises Naziri as "a truly incompatible poet". Compared to other poets of his age Naziri was painsticking in his adherence to earlier standards of poetic diction, and his language is distinguished by a fluent, unusual clarity. Based on a comparison of parallel poems by Naziri and Orfi (written in response to ghazals by Fagha'ni) it has been mostly concluded that Naziri is a tradition-bound conservative poet. Following is a few specimens of his poems:

"The weakness of thy body has usurped strength from everyone;"
"Thy ache has afflicted every bone"
"No one is beyond the pain of thy chastisement"
"Everyone's life is in union with thine."
Who is Naziri, just a destitute and the companion of mendicants!
 One who does not present his request before Jamshid!
 Nor does pay heed to Da'ra'.
"Just as strong winds of autumn makes
The tree leaves fall, similarly thy love"
Makes the capital sins disappear.
I am the one for whom the narrow
Confines of the heart are like cheerful garden
The blister on my hand is the cup in which,
 I see the world reflected.
Falling of an old wall is for its becoming new;
No one is after my inhabitation except death.

Though Nazir's poetry occasionally utilizes the conceptualistic metaphors characteristic of the emerging Shiva-ye tazah ('fresh style"), for the most part, he shuns the bold, risky experimentation of his contemporaries. Some of his ghazals propound an ethically oriented, circumspect mysticism. But Naziri's greatest strength may lie in his amatory lyrics. Many of these poems reveal his training in the 'maktab-ewoqu', the 'realist school' of poetics that emerged in Safavid Persia in the sixteenth century and that turned away from Sufi symbology to depict the encounters of flesh-and-blood lovers, their evasions, ploys, delights, and disappointments. In the following verses (a response to Baba' Faghani), the speaker seems at once an active participant and a detached observer:

How sweet it is for two to open their hearts as one To speak of the past, to linger over complaints	چه خوشست از دو یکدل سر حرف باز کردن سخن گذشته گفتن گله را دراز کردن
To catch now a glimpse of love through hidden yearning And then to spy coy beckoning behind apparent reproach	گهی از نیاز پنهان نظری به مهر دیدن گهی از عتاب ظاهر نگهی به ناز کردن
To erase bit by bit traces of bickering from one another's heart To concoct banter to improvise excuses.	اثر عتاب بردن ز دل هم اندک اندک به بدیهه آفریدن به بهانه ساز کردن

The meeting between two former lovers and the unresolved tensions between them is concisely and deftly portrayed in series of short, well-balanced phrases. In this regard, Naziri is perhaps better regarded as a culmination of the poetics of the 'maktab-woqu' than as a forerunner of the literary trends that would shape Persian poetry over the next two centuries.

Abu Taleb Kalim Kashani 16th century Persian poet & Gnostic

Chapter 7

He was born in Hamada'n in 1581 but soon moved to Ka'shan and thus his pen-name Kashani. He studied in Ka'sha'n and Shiraz (some people also call him "Shirazi"), before travelling to India, and settling in Daccan. There he became friends with Shahnawa'z Kha'n of Shia'z, a court official to Ebra'him A'delshah, the ruler of Bija'r. His first trip to India did not bring him the success he desired, and he was imprisoned for a while due to charges of being a spy. In 1619 he returned to Iran, placing high hopes of Iranian patrons, He settled for two years in Isfahan, but won neither fame nor adequate success. In 1621 he became nostalgic for India (where he was genuinely fond of) and returned. Until 1628 he was in Agra in the service of Mir Jomla of Shahresta'n, who himself was a poet with the pen-name of Ruh- al-Amin. He addressed Ruh-al-Amin in several panegyrics. In 1628 due to writing some eulogies of Abu-al-Hassan A'saf Khan, he became a member of the court of Shah jaha'n. He impressed Shah Jahan so much that in 1632 he bestowed upon him the title of (Malek al-Shoara'); poet laureate. He was formally commissioned by Shah Jahan himself to compose a poem immortalizing the emperor's realm. Kalim dedicated the last years of his literary activity to composing a mathnavi entitled Shah-na'ma, at times also referred to with the titled Zafar-na'ma-ye-Sha'h-jaha'ni in 15000 lines. This work narrates the most important events from Sha'h jaha'n's birth up to the first ten years of his reign. To-day still unpublished, this work was never actually completed and its value is rather historical than poetic. Kalim resided in Kashmir while completing this work and fell in love with the beauties of the region, where its climate was beneficial to his health. He lived there until the end of his life and was buried there. Kalim was contemporary with many other poets such as Salim Teherani, Qodsi Mashhadi, Taleb Amol and S'eb Isfahanii (Tabrizi). He revered these poets and was a friend of them. Kalim was a man of genial disposition, free from jealousy, and consequently popular with his fellow poets, of whom Sa'eb Esfahani and Mir masum were his special friends, so that Sa'eb says:

"Except Sa'ib, the epigrammatic Ma'sum, and Kalim,	بغیر صایب و معصوم نکته سنج وکلیم
Who else of all the poets are kind to one another?"	دگر که ز اهل سخن مهربان یکدگرند

Decline of Persian Poetry 1700-1800

When the poet Malek of Qum died, Abu Ta'leb composed the following verses giving the date of his death:

"Malik", that king of the realm of ideas, whose name is stamped on the coin of poetry,	ملک آن پادشاه ملک معنی که نامش سکه نقد سخن بود
So enlarged the horizons of this realm of ideas that the frontiers of his domains extended from Qum to the Deccan"	چنان آفاق گیر از ملک معنی که حد ملکش از قم تا دکن بود بجستم سال تاریخش ز ایام بگفتا او سر اهل سخن بود

In passing it is worth noting that most of the Persian poets who went to India to seek a fortune, or at least a livelihood, according to Shibli in "Sherul-Ajam"(poetry of the Persians), had nothing but evil to say of the country, but Kalim speaks of it with appreciation:

"One can call it the second Paradise, in this sense, that	توان بهشت دوم گفتنش باین معنی که هر که رفت ازین بوستان پشیمان شد
whoever quits this garden departs with regret."	

On one occasion the Sulta'n of Turkey wrote a letter to the Emperor Sha'h Jah'n reproaching him with arrogance in calling himself by this title, which means "King of the World,'" when he was in reality only king of India. Kalim justified his patron in the following verse;

"Since both Hind (India) and Jaha'n (world) are numerically identical,	هند و جهان زروی عدد هردو چون یکیست شه را خطاب شاه جهانی مبرهن است

Chapter 7

The right of the king to be called 'King of the World,' {and not merely 'King of India'is demonstrated."

Shibli discusses Kalim's merits very fully, and cites many of his verses to illustrate them. He includes amongst them especially novelty of topics (مضمون آفرینی), original conceits (خیال بندی) and aptness of illustration (مثالیه). In this last respect, illustrated by the following amongst other verses, kalim resembled the more famous 'Sa'eb':

"Fate sets an ambush against our luck: The thief always pursues the sleeper"	روزگار اندر کمین بخت ماست دزد دایم در پی خوابیده است
"The heart imagines that it has hidden the secret of love: The lantern imagines that it has hidden the candle."	دل گمان دارد که پوشیده است راز عشق را فانوس پندارد که پنهان کرده است شمع را
""	
He who has been raised up from the dust by fortune, like the rider of the hobby horse,	از خاک برگرفته دوران چو نی سوار
always goes on foot, although he is mounted"	دایم پیاده رفت اگرچه سوار شد
"My desolate state is not mended by my virtues,	از هنر حال خرابم نشد اصلاح پذیر
	همچو دیوانه که از گنج خود آباد نشد

Just like the ruin, which does not prosper through its treasure?"

"The mean does not acquire nobility by proximity to the great:

سفله از قرب بزرگان نکند کسب شرف

The thread does not become precious through its connection with the pearls."

رشته پر قیمت از آمیزش گوهرنشود

"What profits it that I, like the rosary, kissed the hands of all?
After all, no one loosend the knots of my affair.'

دست هرکس را بسان سبحه بوسیدم چه سود
هیچ کس نگشود آخر عقده کار مرا

"Her converse with me is as the association of the wave and the shore,

با من آمیزش او الفت موج است وکنار

Ever with me, yet fleeing from me"

دمبدم با من و پیوسته گریزان از من

"Where there is power, the hand and heart are not able {to use it}

چو هست قدرت دست ودل توانگر نیست

The oyster-shell opens its palm when there is no pearl therein"

صدف گشاده کف است آن زمان که گوهرنیست

(This last verse is very similar tone by Sa'eb which runs)

"Blossoms and fruit are never found together in one place:

شکوفه با ثمر هرگز نگردد جمع دریکجا

It is impossible that teeth and delicacies should exist simultaneously".

محالست آنکه باهم نعمت ودندان شود پیدا

Chapter 7

Kalim's poetical works amount to just over 24,000 lines, comprising around 15,000 couplets in the Sha'h-na'ma and about 9,500 couplets collected in his diva'n. The diva'n contains 36 qasidas (odes),2 tarkib-bands (stanzic or strophic poem), 1 tarji-band (a poem with a refrain), 32 qetas (occasional poem), 33 ta'rikhches (chronograms), 26 short mathawis (rhyming couplets), 590 ghazals (lyrics), and 102 roba'is (quatarains), making a total of 9,823 couplets.

Here is one of his most famous and popular ghazals:

"Old age has come and exuberance of the youth departed!	پیری رسید و موسم طبع جوان گذشت
	ضعف تن از تحمل رطل گران گذشت
The weakness of the body no longer supports the heavy cup.	
	وضع زمانه قابل دیدن دو باره نیست
The way of the world is not worth seeing a second time:	
	رو پس نکرد هرکه ازاین خاکدان گذشت
Whoever passes from this dust-heap looks not back.	
	از دست برد حسن تو برلشگر بهار
Through the triumph of thy beauty over the army of spring	
	یک نیزه خون گل ز سر ارغوان گذشت
The blood of the rose has raised a fathom above the top the Judas-tree.	
	طبعی بهم رسان که بسا زی بعالمی
Acquire such a disposition to get along with the world,	یا همتی که از سر عالم توان گذشت

Or such magnanimitye arise above the world!

در کیش ما تجرد عنقا تمام نیست

According to our creed the detachment of the Angha (phoenix) is not complete,

در فکر نام ماند اگر از نشان گذشت

For though it retains no sign, it continues to think of name!

If one can'ot travel the world without sight, then how

بی دیده راه اگر نتوان رفت پس چرا

Can one forsake the world when one close eyes to it?

چشم از جهان چوبستی از او میتوان گذشت

The ill repute of Life endured no more but two days;

بد نامی حیات دو روزی نبود بیش

O Kalim, I will tell you how these too passed!

آنهم کلیم با تو بگویم چسان گذشت

One day was spent in attaching the heart to this and that,

یک روز صرف بستن دل شد به این و آن

The second day; in detaching it from this and that!"

روز دگر به کندن دل زین و آن گذشت

Kalim successfully used all the current poetic genres; His qasidas are considered to be very balanced and his mathnavies are pleasant and measured; and he is considered to be one of the masters of this genre. The ghazal was in fact the favorite genre of all the poets of the Indian style in a historic-cultural context in which the qasida was perceived by the contemporary poets to be mannered and unsuitable for experiments in form and content. Kalim's ghazals are fairly regular in length, consisting of an average of nine lines. Although there is very often a radif (word or phrase repeated after the rhyme), it is not very long and only in eleven ghazals does the radif have a noun. Overall his style is characterized by new themes and new concepts, revealing an incisive poetic fantasy and creativity in line with other poets writing in the same style. Shebli describes him as the initiator and master of the mesaliat (the art of illustrative reasoning or argument by illustration or analogy to enhance the context of the phenomena being handled.)

Recognized as having a powerful imagination, he mainly expresses himself in original metaphors, new comparisons, and refined, fantastic etiologies. He is also described as an artist capable of making traditionally non-poetic themes poetic. His accurate descriptions reveal a remarkable eye for detail and acute power of observation. The deliberate focus on creating new meaning (he was in fact dubbed by the critic and biographer Mohammad-Taher Nasra'ba'di, as Khalaqal-ma a'ni-e sa'ni", second creator of meanings", after the 13th century poet Kamal-al-Din Esma'il) was often stressed by poet himself, who claimed that it was unacceptable for him to use an image he had already elaborated, which he called stealing. In a certain sense, his decidedly poetic output (compared to the diva'n of his contemporaries) confirms this quest for new themes rather that re-elaboration of well-known contents. According to critics, however, this experimentation is never to the detriment of sincere expression and the profundity of his existential thought. His cultural as well as emotional integration in the Indian context is highlighted by his frequent use of Hindi words as well as by several poems expressing his fondness of that country.

Kalim's poetry has been both praised and criticized for a variety of reason. He has been reproached for a certain formal carelessness, an occasional lack of syntactical rigor, the use of words outside the poetic register, a degree of redundancy in some word and phrases, and the presence of contradictory statements and consequent conceptual incoherence. Besides, some of his new analogies are seen as being excessively contrived. Although the assessment of his poetry was always conditioned by a comparison with the works of S'eb-Tabrizi 'Esfaha'n', (the critics concur in judging Sa'eb works to be superior), all the tazkerehs express positive opinion on his work (except for Azar Bigdeli; A'tashgada-ye-Azar, whose aversion to the poets of Indian style is well-known), and the critics acknowledge his significant, and original contribution to the development of the Indian style.

Finally here are some more of his poetry:

'He who has reached {the goal} shuts his lips on 'why?' and 'wherefore?'
Camels' bell stops ringing once the destination has been reached!

واصل ز حرف چون و چرا بسته است لب
چون ره تمام گشت جرس بی زبان شود

"If thou art satisfied with thy portion, the more or less of the world is the same.
When the thirsty man requires but one draught, the pitcher and the ocean are alike

گر به قسمت قانعی بیش و کم دنیا یکیست
تشنه چون یک جرعه خواهد کوزه و دریا یکیست

"We are without knowledge of the beginning and of the end of this world:
The first and last {pages} of this ancient book have fallen out"

ما ز آغاز و ز انجام جهان بیخبریم
اول و آخر این کهنه کتاب افتاده است

"He who becomes acquainted with the mysteries of the world soon departs:
Whoever does his work brilliantly leaves school.

زود رفت آنکه ز اسرار جهان آگه شد
از دبستان برود هرکه سبق روشن کرد

Sa'eb Tabrizi (Esfahani) 16th century Persian poet

Mirza Mohammad Ali S'aeb Tabrizi one of the greatest Persian poets of the seventeenth century was born in Tabriz in 1578. He was a master of a form of classical Arabic and Persian lyric poetry characterized by rhymed couplets, known as the ghazal. Besides writing in Persian, Sa'eb was known to have written 17 ghazals and molammas in Azeri.
Saeb was born in Tabriz, and educated in Isfahan. Later in life rather disappointed with the way that poets and writers were being treated in Persia during the rule of Safavid dynasty, he decided to follow the example of a

number of other Persian poets who had migrated to India, and moved to that country in 1626. He was soon received into the court of Shah Jahan. He stayed for a short time there, and then moved to Kabul and Kashmir returning home after several years. After his return, the emperor of Persia, Shah Abba's the second bestowed upon him the title "poet laurite"

Sa'ebs reputation is based primarily on some 300,000 couplets that it is said he has written, including his epic poem Qandahar-nama ("The campaign against Qandahar"). (The city of Qandahar in to-days Afghanistan was in Sa'ebs lifetime a long standing bone of contention between the Mughal rulers of India and the Safavid' rulers of Persia- Both of whom were at different times the patrons of the poet- until definitely given over to Persian rule as a result of the Mughal-Safavid War of 1649-53)

Sa'eb had only spent two to three years in India before his father almost seventy years old followed him to India to induce him to return home, for which journey he sought permission from his patron Zafar Kha'n in the following verses:

"More than six years have passed since the passage of the steed of my resolve from Isfahan to India took place.	شش سال پیش رفت که از اصفهان بهند افتاده است توسن عزم مرا گذار
The bold attraction of my longing has brought him weeping from Isfaha'n to Agra and Lahore.	آورده است جذبه گستاخ شوق او از اصفهان به آگره ولاهورش اشکبار
I your servant have an aged father seventy years old, who has countless claims upon me by reason of educating me.	هفتاد ساله والده پیوست بنده را تربیت بود به منش حق بی شمار
Before he comes from Agra to the flourishing land of the Deccan with reins looser than the restless torent,	زآن پیشتر کز آگره به معموره د کن آید عنان گسسته تر از سیل بی قرار
And eagerly traverses this far road with bent body and feeble form,	این راه دور را ز سر شوق طی کند با قامت خمیده و با پیکر نزار

دارم امید رخصتی از آستان تو
ای آستانت کعبه امید روزگار

I hope for permission from thy
threshold, O thou whose threshold is
the Ka'ba of the age's hopes.

مقصود او ز آمد نش بردن منست
لب را به حرف رخصت من کن گهرنثار

His object in coming is to take me
hence, therefore cause thy lips to
scatter pearls {of speech} by
{uttering} the word of permission,

با جبهه گشاده تر از آفتاب صبح
دست دعا به بدرقه راه من بر آر

And, with a forehead more open
than the morning sun, raise dy hand
in prayer to speed me on my way."

Sa'ebs seven- year residence in India helped to establish his reputation as the
foremost poet of the age, and he spent the rest of his life in Isfaha'n, travelling
only to visit other cities in Persia.

He apparently enjoyed cordial, if not especially close relations with the
Safavid court. His diva'n contains panegyrics dedicated to Sha'h Safi, and
Shah Abba's II who appointed him to the post of poet laureate. However,
Sa'eb did not take residence in the palace, and a story circulating in Isfahan a
few years after his death tells how he had himself excused from the royal
retinue during an excursion to Ma'zandera'n. On the other hand, his reputed
falling out with Sha'h Soleyma'n seems to be no more than a biographer's
embellishment on the opening verse of his coronation ode. In any case, it is
unlikely that Sa'eb depended on royal patronage for his livelihood. He could
find a ready public audience for his ghazals in Isfa'ha'n's coffee shops and a
more elite clientele in the homes of well-to- do merchants and courtiers. Like
many people in Safavid Persia, he was a moderate and occasionally guilt-
ridden user of intoxicants such as wine, coffee, and tobacco throughout his
life. Saeb family's wealth assured him of a financial independence rare among
medieval Persian poets. Sa'eb's home was one of the grandest in the entire
city of Isfahan and the poet employed his own private calligrapher, A'ref of

Chapter 7

Tabriz, to transcribe copies of his diva'n. In his later years, Sa'eb appears to have retired from public life, receiving only a limited number of his students and literary admirers from throughout the Persian speaking world. He was buried in a garden near the Masjed-Lonba'n in Isfaha'n. His tomb, together with his son and grandson was discovered in 1930's. All evidence including inscription on his tomb point to the year of his death to had been in 1676.

Among the merits ascribed to Sa'eb by Shibli is an appreciation of Indian poets rare with the Persians. Shibli quotes thirteen verses in which Sa'eb cites with approval, by way of tazmin or "insertion" the words of Fayzi, Malek, Ta'leb-i-A'moli, Nawa'I, Awhadi, Showghi, Fathi, Sha'pur, Muti, Awji, Adham, Hadhigh and Raghim. In the following verses he deprecates the jealousy which too often characterizes the rival singers:

Happy that company who are intoxicated with each other's spee ch Through the fermentation of thought, are each other's red wines!	خوش آن گروه که مست بیان یک دگرند ز جوش فکر می ارغوان یک دگرند
They do not break on the stone {of criticism} one another's pearls {i.e.verses}, but rather strive to give currency to the wares of one another's shops.	نمی زنند به سنگ شکست گوهر هم پی رواج متاع دکان یک دگرند
They pelt one another with tender-hued roses, with fresh ideas they become the flowers of one another gardens.	زنند بر سر هم گل ز مصرع رنگین ز فکر تازه گل بوستان یک دگرند
When they shape their poetry it is with blades like diamonds, and when their genius tends to become blunted they are each other's whetstones.	سخن تراش چو گردند تیغ الماس اند زند چو طبع به کندی فسان یک دگرند بغیر صایب ومعصوم نکته سنج دگر که ز اهل سخن مهربان یک دگرند

Sa'eb was a prolific poet, and during the course of a literary career spanning over sixty five years, he compiled one of the largest diva'ns in classical

Decline of Persian Poetry 1700-1800

Persian literature. Although the estimates of the biographers of 120,000.To 200,000. verses are inflated; the most comprehensive edition of the diva'n nevertheless contains some 75,000 lines of poetry.This figure is especially remarkable considering that Sa'eb wrote almost no narrative poetry. He did compose a mathnavi on Shah Abbas II;s conquest of Qandaha'r in 1641, but reports that this work, The Qandahar- or Abba's nama, contains between 35,000 and 135,000 verses are gross exaggerations; no manuscript of the work exceeds 200 lines. Some fifty qasidas and some other short panegyric poems have survived, spanning his career from early poems describing the Ka'ba and the shrine of Najaf to a short chronogram on an architectural restoration carried out by Sha'h Soleima'n in the final year of the poet's life. Dedicated to all of Sa'eb's major patrons in India and Persia, these poems provide crucial documentary evidence not only of the poet's life, but also of Safavid architecture and popular political ideology. However, by far the bulk of Sa'eb's literary output consists of ghazals. In the history of Persian literature only Jala'l-ed-Din Rumi's diva'n-e Shams begins to approach the size and scope of S'aeb's lyric oevre. Qahrama'n's editition of the diva'n contains over 7000 ghazals (including some twenty poems in the Turkish dialect of his native Tabriz), as well as a couple of hundred isolated verses from poems no longer extant in their entirety.

Sa'eb was a great admirer of Hafez, and is also complimentary to his masters Rukna' and Shafa'I; of the later he says:

"Who will care for poetry in Isfaha'n, O Sa'eb? Now that Shafa'I, who's discerning hand was on the pulse of poetry is no more?'	در اصفهان که به درد سخن رسد صایب کنون که نبض شناس سخن شفایی نیست

He puts Naziri not only above himself but above 'Urfi."So far says Shibli," no objection can be made, but it is pity that yielding to popular approbation and fame, he makes himself the panegyrist of Zuhuri and Jal'l-i-Asir......This was the first step in bad taste, which finally established a high road, so that in time people came to bow down before the poetry of Nasir 'Ali, Bi-del, and Shawkat Of Bukhara'.

Chapter 7

'The edifice of wrong-doing was at first small in the world, but whoever came, added thereunto;"

Though Sa'eb tried his hand at all kinds of poetry, it was as said before in the ode (Ghazal) that he excelled. He was a ready wit. One of his students once composed the following absurd hemistich:

"Seek for the bottleless wine from the wineless bottle"
از شیشه بی می می بی بی شیشه طلب کن

Sa'eb immediately capped it with the following:

"Seek for the truth from the heart which is empty of thought."
حق را ز دل خالی از اندیشه طلب کن

On another occasion one of his friends produced the following meaningless hemistich and apparently invited Sa'eb to complete the verse and give it meaning:

دویدن رفتن استادن نشستن خفتن ومردن

Sa'eb immediately prefixed the following hemistich:

بقدر هر سکون راحت بود بنگر تفاوت را

So that the completed verse runs in translation:

"Peace is in proportion to every pause: observe the difference between' to run, to walk, to stand, to lie, and to die."

Sa'eb was a very careful student of the works of his predecessors, both ancient and modern, and he compiled a great anthology of their best verses, of which, according to Shibli, a manuscript exists in Haydar-aba'd in the Deccan, and which appears to have been utilized by Wa'lih of Daghistan and other tazkereh-writers. Shibli, compares Sa'eb to Tamma'm the compiler of the great anthology of Arabic poetry called the Ham'sa, inasmauch as his taste is shown even more in his selective than in his creative powers. Following are a selection of various verses by Sa'eb:

"When poison becomes a habit it ceases to injure; make thy soul gradually acquainted with death."	چو شد زهر عادت مضرت نبخشد بمرگ آشنا کن بتدریج جان را
"The roots of the aged palm- tree, exceeds those of the young one; the old have the greater attachment to the world than young.	ریشه نخل کهنسال از جوان افزون ترست بیشتر دلبستگی باشد به دنیا پیر را
"In this market every head has a different fancy: every one winds his turban in a different fashion"	هر سری دارد در این بازار سودای دگر هر کسی بندد به آیین دگر دستار را
What profit accrues from a perfect guide to those whom Fate hath left empty-handed, for even Khidr brings back Alexander a thirst from the Water of Life?	تهی دستان قسمت را چه سود از رهبر کامل که خضر از آب حیوان تشنه بازآرد سکندر را
"The rosary in the hand, repentance in the lips, and the heart full of sinful longings—sin itself laughs at our repentance!	سبحه بر کف توبه برلب دل پراز شوق گناه معصیت را گریه می آید ز استغفار ما
"The place of a royal pearl should be in a treasury: one should make one's breast the common-place book for chosen verses."	بیاض از سینه باید ساخت شعر انتخابی را در گنجینه میباید مقام گوهر شهوار را

"All this talk of infidelity and
religion finally leads to one place:
The dream is the same dream,
only the interpretations differ."

گفتگوی کفرودین آخر بیکجا میکشد
خواب یک خوابست

اما مختلف تعبیرهاست

The case with which Sa'eb composed poetry gave rise to numerous stories in the tazkereh literature about his ability to complete other's verses on the spur of the moment. They serve to represent Sa'eb's seemingly effortless gift for invention. In a more modern critical idiom, Ghola'm-Hosseyn Yusefi argues that Sa'eb's ability to creat new images and metaphors places him among the outstanding poets in Persian literature and attributes the range of his imagery to the social spread of poetry outside the confines of the court into the realm of everyday urban life. Sa'eb himself uses the phrase" man' a'-ye biga'neh", 'unfamiliar or alien conception,' to refer to the unexpected images, startling similes, and unusual metaphors that flowed from his pen. Poetic inspiration seemd to come to him unbidden through' feys 'or Divine emanation, revealing often unpredictable connections between objects of the material world as manifestations of a cosmic unity of Being.

In some mundane terms, Sa'eb's creative fluency also derived from his prodigious mastery of the earlier tradition. Although we know how little of Sa'eb's training—there are suggestions that he was tutored by Hakim Shafai of Isfa'han or Rokn-ed-Din Masih of Kasha'n—it must have been then, that a highly literary culture could provide. Few poets have been as generous as Sa'eb in acknowledging their debt to their literary peers and predecessors. He mentions some seventy different poets by name in his ghazals, most often at the end of a (jawa'b); response written in homage or emulation of an earlier poem. Most frequently mentioned are Rumi and Ha'fez, but even an examination of his jawa'bs (replies) to a lesser-known poet like Ba'ba Faghani shows how scrupulously and creatively he evaluated and re-created the work of earlier masters. Sa'eb left a record of his reading in his personal anthology of poetry; his" Safina". Shebli No'mani has compared this work to the Hamasa, the great collection of Arabic poetry assembled by Abu Tamma'm, and its treatment of contemporary poets has been discussed by Tarbiat (1932) describes a manuscript of this work in Haydarabad, and other copies are reported to be preserved in the Royal library at the Golestan Palace in Teheran. Publication of this work would provide much information about Sa'eb's taste, circle of associates, and the later reception of the classical tradition.

The adulation of Sa'eb among his contemporaries and later readers is evident throughout the biographical literature. Ta'her Nasra'ba'di writes simply that "the sublimity of his genius and extent of his fame need no description. In India a few years later Sarkhosh writes that" Sa'eb's jewel-like verses have broadcast his fame throughout the world" reporting that the Safavid kings sent copies of his diva'n as gifts to rulers in other parts of Islamic world.
In Persia, however, the late eighteenth century saw the development of the new classical 'bazgasht-e adabi (literary return), which like most new literary movements, found its identity in part by rejecting the values of its immediate predecessors.

In 1779 Azar Bigdeli would accuse Sa'eb of": losing track of the established rules of previous masters" and leading poetry down the path of decline. By the middle of nineteenth century Reza' gholi Khan Hedayat could write simply that Sa'eb wrote in"a strange style that is not now approved". In later years Mohammad Taghi baha'r went as far as succinctly dismissing Sa'eb and his style. However as the 'bazgasht itself came into disrepute with the fall of the Qaja'rs and the rise of modernism, Sa'eb and seventeenth century poetry in general began to be re-evaluated; Sa'eb's return to the canon of classical poetry was officially marked by a conference in Tehern in January 1976 and attended by many of the major literary figures of the day, its proceedings remain as an essential contribution to the critical literature on the poet. Yet even today, Sa'eb remains a controversial figure in Persian literary circles, with both detractors and supports going to extremes of censure and approbation. Sa'eb's success as a self-professed modernist who stretched the limits of poetic expression can perhaps best be measured by the critical passion his work continues to exercise. Here are some more examples of his work and style:

| "The tyrant finds no security against the arrows of the victim's sighs: Groans arise from the heart of the bow before {they arise from} the target." | از تیر آه مظلوم ظالم امان نباشد

پیش از نشانه خیزد از دل فغان کمان را |

"The cure for the unpleasant constitution of the world is to ignore it;
Here he is awake who is plunged in heavy sleep"

چاره ناخوشی وضع جهان بیخبریست
اوست بیدار که در خواب گرانست اینجا

"Blossoms and fruit are never together at a time; it is impossible
That teeth and delicacies should exist simultaneously."

شکوفه با ثمر هرگز نگردد جمع در یکجا
محالست آنکه با هم نعمت ودندان شود پیدا

"Ten doors are opened if one door be shut: the finger is the interpreter of the dumb man's tongue."

ده در گشاده شود اگر بسته شد دری
انگشت ترجمان زبانست لال را

"The simple-minded quickly acquire the color of their companions:
The conversation of the parrot makes the mirror {seem to} speak."

ساده لوحان زود میگیرند رنگ همنشین
صحبت طوطی سخنور میکند آیینه را

"The march of good fortune has backward slips: to retreat one or two paces gives wings to jumper."

گردش اقبال دارد لغزش ادبارها
یک دو خطوه باز رفتن پر دهد وثاب را

"
The wave is ignorant of the true nature of the sea,
How can the Temporal comprehend the Eternal?

موج از حقیقت گهر بحر غافلست
حادث چگونه درک نماید قدیم را

"The touchstone of false friends is the day of need,
By way of proof, ask a loan from friends."

معیار دوستان دغل روز حاجت است
قرضی برسم تجربه از دوستان طلب

"The learned man is a stranger amidst people of the world, Just as the "witness- finger" {i.e. the index-finger} appears strange on the Christian's hand."

در میان اهل دنیا مردم دانا غریب
همچو انگشت شهادت در کف ترسا غریب

"What does it profit thee that all the libraries of the world should be yours? Not knowledge but what thou do put into practice is yours."

چه سود از اینکه کتبخانه جهان از تست
نه علم هرچه عمل میکنی همان از تست

"The life of this transitory world is the expectation of death: to renounce life is to escape from the expectation of annihilation."

هستی دنیای فانی انتظار مردن است
ترک هستی ز انتظار نیستی وارستن است

"O my dear friend! Thou hast more care for wealth than for life: Thy attachment to the turban is greater than to the head."

ترا ز جان غم مال ای عزیز بیشتر است
علاقه تو به دستار بیشتر ز سرست

"Our heart is heedless of the beloved, notwithstanding our complete proximity: The fish lives through the sea, yet heeds not the sea.

با کمال قرب از جانان دل ما غافلست
زنده از دریاست ماهی واز دریا غافلست

"The weeping of the candle is not in mourning for the moth: The dawn is at hand, it is thinking of its own dark night."

گریه شمع از برای ماتم پروانه نیست
صبح نزدیک است درفکر شب تار خودست

"To quit this troubled world is better than to enter it, the rose-bud enters the garden with straitened heart and departs smiling."

رفتن از عالم پرشور به از آمدن است
غنچه دلتنگ به باغ آمد وخندان بر خاست

"If friendship is firmly established between two hearts, they do not need the interchange of news."

اگر میان دو دل هست دوستی بقرار
نمی شوند به آمد شد خبر محتاج

"When a man becomes old, his greed becomes young:
Sleep grows heavy at the time of morning.

آدمی پیر چوشد حرص جوان میگردد
خواب در وقت سحرگاه گران میگردد

"To the seeker after pearls silence is speaking argument, for no breath comes forth from the diver in the sea."

خموشی حجت ناطق بود گویای گوهر را
که از غواص در دریا نفس بیرون نمی آید

"Not one handful of earth is wasted in this tavern: they make it either into a pitcher, a wine-jar, or a wine-cup."

یا سبو یا خم می یا قدح باده کنند
یک کف خاک در این میکده ضایع نشود

In terms of his literary reputation, Sa'eb may have been too prolific and his work too well preserved. Even the best poets' nod, that certain unevenness is inevitable in a literary career of over 60 years and a body of work of over 75,000 verses. Not all of Sa'ebs poetic experiments are equally successful. The literary historian Zabih-ollah Safa' may come closest to offering a measured assessment of Sa'eb's achievement. Remarking that critics have taken objectionable verses as an excuse to denigrate Sa'eb's work as a whole, Safa' maintains that "in reality, Sa'eb is a powerful poet in ghazal, and although he wrote a great deal, his language is seldom open to criticism." Sa'eb's poetry, Safa' continues, "is solid, in accordance with the criteria of eloquence, and full of subtle ideas, delicate thoughts, and graceful images." In conclusion, he notes the "distinctive splendor" that the abundance of social, gnostic, mystical, and social observations gives to Sa'eb's gazalz; It is unlikely that Sa'eb's often- complex poetry will ever be to everyone's taste, but readers are increasingly willing to appreciate it according to its own aims and standards.

Because of the immense fame that Sa'eb enjoyed during his lifetime, his works were frequently copied and are represented in every major collection of Persian manuscripts. Monzavie's bibliographical catalogue cites nearly one hundred and fifty manuscripts of his diva'n in libraries from Persia to India, to Europe and the United Estates, and his list does not include copies in Central Asia or those catalogued over the last fifty years. More important than sheer numbers, however is the fact that many of these manuscripts date from the poet's lifetime and were produced under his own supervision. It should be, however pointed out that it was not until the appearance of Mohammad Ghahreman' s edition that the full extent of Sa'eb's literary production could be accurately assessed. Published in Teheran between 1985 and 1991, Ghahreman's sixty six volume eclectic editions are gathered from over twenty sources and set a new standard of accuracy and comprehensiveness.

CHAPTER 7

THE DECLINE OF PERSIAN POETRY (1700-1800)C.E

From the literary point of view this century is perhaps the most barren in the whole history of Persia, so much so that the only notable poem produced by it is, the celebrated tarji-band of Ha'tef-isfahani, which will follow at the conclusion of this particular historical note.

Presently for the purpose of this brief historical revue, there are two full and authoritative accounts, of this disastrous and tragic period i.e. the invasion of Afghans considered as one of the darkest chapters in the history of Persia, by two men of letters who were personally involved and who have left us a fairly clear and detailed picture of that sad and troubled time. These men were Mohammad Ali Hazin born in 1692, died in 1766 and Luf 'Ali Beg poetically surnamed A'zar, born in 1711, died1781. Both were poets, and the former even a prolific poet, since he composed three or four diva'ns, Their prose writings are even of much more interest and value than their verse.

Mohammad Hazin La'hiji 17th century Persian poet

Hazin La'hiji (originally from the town of La'hijan in the province of Guila'n) was born as he himself tells us, in January 1692 at Isfaha'n and was directly descended in the eighteenth degree from the famous Sheykh Za'hed of Guilan.The family continued to reside in Guila'n, first in Asta'ra' and then at La'hija'n, until the poet's father, Shaikh Abu Ta'leb, at the age of twenty, went to Isfaha'n to pursue his studies, and there married and settled in that city. He died there in 1715 at the age of sixty nine, leaving three sons, of whom Ali Hazin was the eldest. He speaks in the highest terms of his father's character and ability, and quotes a few lines from an elegy which he composed on this mournful occasion. He also mentions that, amongst other final injunctions, his father addressed to him the following remarkable words:

"If you have the choice, make no longer stay in Isfa'ha'n. It was meant that some one of our race should survive." "At that time' " the author continues, "I did not comprehend this part of his address, not till after some years, when the disturbance and ruin of Isfahan took place.

Decline of Persian Poetry 1700-1800

In 1722-3 he began to compile a kind of literary scrap- book or magazine, but it was lost with the rest of his library in the sack of Isfahan by the Afgha'ns a few months later. About the same time or a little earlier he wrote, besides numerous philosophical commentaries, a book on the Horse (Faras-na'ma), published his second Diva'n of poetry, and soon afterwards his third. The Afgha'n invasion and the misery which it caused, especially in Isfa'ha'n, put a stop to Hazin's literary activities for some time.' During the latter days of the siege,'"he says,"I was attacked by severe illness; and my two brothers, my grandmother, and the whole of the dwellers in my house died, so that my mansion was emptied of all but two or three infirm old women–servants, who attended me till my disorder began to abate," Being somewhat recoverd, he escaped from Isfaha'n early in 1722, only a few days before it surrendered to, and was entered byAfgha'ns. During the next ten years he wandered about in different parts of Persia, successively visiting or residing at Khorama'ba'd in Luresta'n, Hamada'n, Neha'vand, Dizful, Shushtar (whence by way of Basra he made the pilgrimage to Mecca and on his return journey he visited Yaman), Kerma'nsha'h, Baghd'ad, and its holy places, Mashhad, Kurdistan, A'zarba'ija'n, Gila'n and Teheran. From Teheran he returned once more to Isfahan to find "that great city, notwithstanding the presence of the King, in utter ruin and desertion. Of all that population and of my friends scarcely any remained". It was the same at Shira'z, wither he made his way six months later." Of all my great friends there,"he says, "the greatest I had in the world, not one remained on foot; and I met with a crowd of children and relatives in the most melancholy condition and without resource" From Shira'z he made his way to La'r, and finally to Bandar- Aba's, intending to go with a European ship to the Hija'z, "because their ships and packets were very spacious and fitted with convenient apartments". He was, however, prevented by illness and poverty. He next returned to Bandar-Aba's in the hope of being able to go thence once again to Baghda'd and the holy city shrines. Finding this impractical owing to Na'der's operations against the Turks, prevailing throughout Persia, he embarked on Feb 14, 1734 to India, where in spite of the dislike which he conceived for that country, he was destined to spend the remaining forty-five years of his life. "To me,"he says: "I do not reckon the time of my residence in this country as a portion of my real life, the beginning of my arrival on the shores of this empire appears as it were the end of my age and vitality.'

Of his subsequent life and travels in India his memoirs tell us comparatively little; though treated as a celebrity, he disliked the country and its people, and wrote satires on them. He was for sometimes patronized by the Mughal court of Mohammad Shah in Delhi, and he hid during Na'der Shah's occupation of capital in 1739. He later engaged in a literary feud with A'rzu (Indian critic and poet) and moved to Agra and Benares, where he died and is buried. Hazin (his pen-name) means "sorrowful "claims to have completed four diva'ns of verse, of which only the fourth survives. All forms are represented, including several mathnavi's, though he excelled in the ghazal, His panegyric qasidas are addressed mainly to the Ima'ms. His poetic diction is generally less elaborate than that of contemporary poets of the sabke-Hendi school, such as Sa'eb, whose work he dismissed. Hazin's prose style is remarkably simple and direct.

After his autobiography, the Tazkerat-al-ahva'l, which has been used by Lockhart and others as a historical source, his second most valuable work is a biographical dictionary of a hundred contemporary poets. Hazin also composed scores of specialized treatise in both Persian and Arabic on a variety of topics, from horses to pearls, most of which are no longer extant. Hazin is emblematic of the urbane, cultivated, and cosmopolitan. A Shiite Muslem of Safavid and post-Safavid Iran who fled a politically dangerous and economically depressed milieu for the courts of Muslim India, there to contribute to the Persianization of the ruling elites. Open-minded and tolerant, he sought out fellow scholars among Christians, Jews, and Sabians, and in return was "equally admired and esteemed by the Muselma'n, Hindoo, and English inhabitants of India

A'zar Bigdeli 18th century Persian poet & biographer

Lotf-Ali Beg Azar Bigdeli better known as Azar Bigdeli, who had selected "Azar" as his pen-name, was an Iranian Anthologist and poet. He is mainly known for his biographical anthology, the "Atashkadeh-ye Azar (Azar's Fire Temple), which he dedicated to Iranian ruler Karim Khan Zand the Persian ruler from 1751 to 1779. Written in Persian, it is considered "the most important Persian anthology of the eighteenth century. As a poet Azar was one of the main supporters of the ba'zgasht-e adabi; the ("literary return") movement.

A'zar's family was descended from the Bigdeli branch of the Turkoman Shamlou tribe. His ancestors and other Shamlou-tribe members moved from Syria to Iran in the fifteenth century (during the last few years of Timur's reign) and settled in Isfahan, where they served the rulers of Iran. Many of Azar's relatives were prominent in the late Safavid era and during the subsequent reign of Na'der Shah (1736-1747) as diplomats and bureaucrats.

Azar was born in Isfahan, the Safavid royal capital, during a time of chaos and instability. In 1722 (the year of his birth), the Safavid state had entered the final stages of collapse and the rebellious Afghans had reached Isfahan. Azar and his family were forced to move to Qom, where they owned property and where he lived for fourteen years. Around 1735 or 1736, his father was appointed governor of Lar and the coastal areas of Fa'rs province and Azar and his family moved to Shira'z (the provincial capital of Fars). In 1737 or 1738, after the death of his father, Azar made pilgrimage to Mecca and then moved to Mashhad, where he enlisted in Nader Shah's army and accompanied his troops to Mazanderan, Azerbaijan, and Persian Iraq. After Nader's death in 1747, Azar served his nephews and successors Adel Shah and Ebrahim Shah, and the Safavid pretenders Ismaiil III and Sulaiman II before retiring to his modest manor in Qom. When Karim Khan Zand (ruled 1751 to 1779) ascended the throne, Azar decided to devote his time to scholarly pursuits and returned to Isfahan. The city was sacked by Ali Morad Khan Bakhtiari in 1750, and Azar reportedly lost about 7000 written verses. In 1774 or 1775 Azar was forced to leave Isfahan again due to the misrule by Zand Governor Mohammad Runani, and he died in 1781.

A'zar is principally known for his anthology. Its chapter titles are based metaphorically on "fire". He completed the book before his death and dedicated it to Karim Khan Zand. Although the work primarily deals with the poets, it also contains information on the history of Iran since the Afghan invasion of 1722, a brief autobiography and a selection of Azar's poems.

When Isfahan was sacked in 1750, a number of Azar's early poems were destroyed. However, he was still a respected poet during his lifetime. Azar's teacher, Mir Sayyed Ali Moshtagh Esfahani who died in 1757 began a "literary return" movement (bazgasht-e adabi) to the stylistic standards of early Persian poetry. The Ateshgadeh, like much other contemporary poetry from Isfahan and Shiraz, was an example of the bazgasht- adabi of which Azar was a leading figure. The movement rejected what was considered excessive "Indian style" (sabk-e Hendi) in Persian poetry and sought, according to late Ehsan Yareshater, "a return to the simpler and more robust poetry of old masters as against the effete and artificial verse into which originated during the Timurid period and was perfected in the courts of Mughal India was called "Indian", it later spread back to Safavid Iran and Ottoman Turkey, where it was prominent in the 17th and (to some degree) the eighteenth centuries.

Azar praises his teacher, SeyedAli Moshtagh Esfahani, in the Atashkadeh:

"After he {Moshtagh} had broken the chain of verse that for years had been in the unworthy grip of the poets of the past, with great and indescribable exertions he repaired it. Having destroyed for contemporary poets the foundation of versifying, he renewed the edifice of poetry built by the eloquent ancients."

De bruin notes that in addition to his diva'n, four extant masnavies have been attributed to Azar: Yousef o Zoleikha (fragments appear in the Atashkadeh); Masnavi-e Azar, a short love poem mirroring Suz-u godaz (Burning and Melting"), a poem by Agha Mohammad Sadegh Tafreshi which was popular in Azar's time; Saqi-na'meh ("Book of the cup-bearer"), and Moghani-nameh "(Book of the Singer)'. Azar may have also written the Ganjinat-ol-haqq ("The Treasury of Truth", a work in the style of Saadi Shirazi's (Golestan) and the Daftar-e noh aseman ("The Book of the nine skies"), an anthology of contemporary poetry. Azar was also influenced by his paternal uncle; Wali Mohammad Khan Bigdeli (died 1763).

A more accessible contemporary account of this period forms the last portion of Azar's Atash-kadeh, which deals with the Persian poets who flourished before the author's time, arranged in alphabetical order under the various towns and countries which gave birth to them, including Tura'n and Hindusta'n. This is followed by an account of sixty of the author's contemporaries, which begins with a brief historical survey of the misfortunes of Persia during the fifty years succeeding the Afgha'n's invasion down to the re-establishment of security and order in the south by Karim Kha'ne- Zand. The author recognizes the absence of poets and men of letters from the literary scene of Persia and ascribes it to the prevalent chaos and misery, "which" he says

" have reached such a point that no one has the heart to read poetry, let alone to compose it." :	تفریق بال و اختلال حال به حدی است که کسی را حال خواندن شعر نیست تا بگفتن شعر چه رسد

To most of these poets the author devotes only a few lines. The longer notices include Mulla' Muhammad M'umin, poetically surnamed Da'I, who died in1743 at the age of ninety ; Mulla' Husayn Rafiq Isfaha'ni ; Sayed Muhammad Shu'la Isfaha'ni ;Sayed Muhammad Sa'diq Tafreshi; Mirz' Ja'far Sa'fi Isfahani ; a young friend of the author's named Sulayma'n, who wrote under the name Saba;hi, and to whose poems he devotes no less than thirteen pages ;Mirza Muhammad Ali Subuh Isfaha'ni ; Aqa Taqi Sahba' of Qum ; Sayed Abdol-baqi Tabib (the physician), Tufa'n-Hazar-jaribi whose death was commemorated by the author in a chronogram giving1776, Aqa' Muhammad Asheq Isfahani, to who he devotes eight pages; and his own younger brother, Ishaq Beg, who wrote under the pen-nam of 'uzhari and died in 1771, according to the chronogram:

بادا در بهشت جاودان اسحق بیگ

Other poets are:Mohammad Ali Beg, Seyed Muhammad Ghalib, Mir seyed Ali Moshtaq Isfahani , Seyed Mohammad Sediq, who besides several mathnavi poems dealing with romances of Leyli & Majnoon, Khusrow & Shirin and Wa'megh & Azra', was engaged on a history of the Zand dynasty. Mirza Nasir and Seyed Ahmad Ha'tef Isfahani, the most famous of most of the above mentioned poets.

Sayed Ahmad Ha'tef Esfahani 18th century poet & gnostic

Hatef Esfaha'ni's exact date of birth is not known, but we know that he was born in one of the early years of the first half of the eighteenth century in Isfahan. His family were from Orduba'd in A'zerba'ijan, who had moved from there to Isfaha'n in Safavid times. He studied the traditional sciences in Isfa'ha'n under Na'ser Tabib Esfahani and the literary and art under Mir Sayyed A'li Moshtaq. He also associated with other important literary figures of the time, including Saba'hi and A'zar Bigdeli. Of the two, the former has highly praised Ha'tef for his Persian and Arabic verses and prose describing him the third after A'sha' and Jarir, and second only to Anwari and Zahir Faryabi. Besides Isfahan Hatef has also lived for a while in Kashan and Qom. Ha'tef died in Qom in the year 1783 and was buried there.

Ha'tef's son Seyed Mohammad Sahab followed in his father's footsteps and became an accomplished poet of the early Qa'ja'r's period. Poems by his daughter Rasha have also been preserved.

Chapter 7

Ha'tef was one of the truly great Persian poets of the 18th century. He had a small but varied poetical output, comprising gazals (lyrics), a few qasidas (panegyric odes), moqatta a't, (occasional pieces), quatrains, and chronograms, i.e. recording the deaths of such literary friends as Moshta'q and Azar, the foundation of buildings, gardens, and other events. He was foremost a poet of ghazals, modeled on the poetry of Saadi and Ha'fez. These are fine compositions, composed in a natural and eloquent style. He is particularly remembered for his tarji-band, a poem in five stanzas (or strophes) with a recurring refrain—a credo in Arabic and Persian affirming Devine unity. In the words of Jan Rypka, this poem "sings of a mystical vision, albeit with all the conventional erotic and wine-house accessories, but in an uncommonly straightforward style, in a lucidly arranged metaphorical language intensified to the highest degree of perfection, free from the euphemisms and obscurities of the foregoing period"

Strophe 1 opens with a complaint from the believer that the way to God is hard and painful. The poet describes his (vision or dream of a) visit to a Zoroastrian service, "s secret gathering bright with the Light of Truth, not with the Flames {of Hell}," and compares the sacred fire with that of burning bush as witnessed by Moses. The celebrants invite him to join in their enjoyment of music, sweets, and wine; the fiery wine overcomes his mental powers, and he swoons into a spiritual experience of the unity of God expressed purely corporeally, through his body and blood: "He is one and there is naught but He:/There is no God save Him alone!"

(Strophe 1)	(بند اول)
"Thou to who both heart and life are a sacrifice and O Thou in whose path both this and that are an offering!	آی فدای تو هم دل و هم جان وی نثار رهت هم این و هم آن
The heart is Thy sacrifice because thou art a charmer of hearts; life is yours offering because Thou art the Life of our lives.	دل فدای تو چون تویی دلبر جان نثار تو چون تویی جانان
	دل رهاندن ز دست تو مشگل جان فشاندن بپای تو آسان

Hard it is to deliver the heart from your hand; easy it is to pour out our life at your feet.

راه وصل تو راه پر آسیب
درد عشق تو درد بی درمان

The road to union with Thee is a road full of hardship; the pain of Thy love is a pain without remedy.

بندگانیم جان و دل بر کف
چشم بر حکم و گوش بر فرمان

We are servants holding our lives and hearts in our hands, with eyes {fixed} on Thy orders and ears {waiting} on Thy command.

گر سر صلح داری اینک دل
ور سر جنگ داری اینک جان

If thou seekest peace, behold our hearts; and if Thou seekest war, behold our lives!

دوش از شور عشق و جذبه شوق
هر طرف می شتافتم حیران

Last night, {impelled} by the madness of love and the impulse of desire,
I was rushing in bewilderment in every direction.

آخر کار شوق دیدارم
سوی دیر مغان کشید عنان

At last desire for the {Beatific} Vision turned my reins towards the temple of the Magians.

چشم بد دور خلوتی دیدم
روشن از نور حق نه از نیران

Far from it be the Evil Eye! I beheld a secret gathering bright with the Light of Truth, not with the Flames of {Hell}.

هر طرف دیدم آتشی کان شب
دید در طور موسی عمران

On very side I beheld that fire which Moses the son of 'Imra'n saw that night on Sinai.

پیری آنجا به آتش افروزی
با ادب گرد پیر مغبچگان

There was an elder {busied} with tending the fire, round about whom respectfully stood the young Magians,

All silver-skinned, and rose-cheeked, all sweet-tongued and narrow-mouthed.

{There were} lute, harp, flute, cymbals and barbiton; candles, desert, roses, wine and basil;

The moon-faced and musky-haired Cup-Bearer the witty and sweet-voiced minstrel

Magian and Magian boy, Fire-priest and High Priest, all with loins girt up for His service.

I, ashamed of my Muhammadanism, stood there concealed in a corner.

The elder enquired, 'who is this?' They answered, "A restless and bewildered lover.

He said 'Give him a cup of pure wine, although he is an unbidden guest

.

The fire-handed and fire-worshiping cup bearer poured into the goblet the burning fire.

همه سیمین عذارو گل رخسار
همه شیرین زبان و تنگ دهان

عود و چنگ ونی ودف وبربط
شمع ونقل وگل ومی وریحان

ساقی ماهروی و مشگین موی
مطرب بذله گوی خوش الحان

مغ و مغ زاده موبد وودستور
خدمتش را تمام بسته میان

من شرمنده از مسلمانی
شدم آنجا به گوشه ای پنهان

پیر پرسید کیست این گفتند
عاشقی بی قرار و سرگردان

گفت جامی دهیدش از می ناب
گرچه ناخوانده باشد این مهمان

ساقی آتش فروزوآتش دست
ریخت در جام آتش سوزان

چون کشیدم نه عقل ماند ونه هوش
سوخت هم کفر از آن وهم ایمان

When I drained it off, neither reason remained nor sense;
Thereby were consumed both Infidelity and Faith.

مست افتادم و در آن مستی
به ز بانی که شرح آن نتوان

I fell down intoxicated, and in that intoxication, in a tongue which one cannot explain,

این سخن می شنیدم از اعضا
همه حتی الورید و الشریان

I heard this speech from {all} my limbs, even from the jugular vein and the carotid artery:

که یکی هست و هیچ نیست جز او
وحده لا الهه الا هو

'He is the One and there is naught but He:
There is no God save Him alone!

Strophe II

In Strophe II he is a helpless lover in lyrical style; he visits a church and protests to his Christian beloved at the slanderous notion of Trinity. "Silk does not become three things if thou call it, Parnian, Harir, and Parand" is there reply, as the refrain of the Devine unity speaks from the peal of the church bell

(Strophe II)

(بند دوم)

"Ó Friend, I will not break my ties with Thee,
even though with a sword they should hew me limb from limb!

از تو ای دوست نگسلم پیوند
گر به تیغم برند بند از بند

الحق ارزان بود ز ما صد جان

Truly a hundred lives were cheap on our part {to win} from Thy mouth a sweet half smile.

وز دهان تو نیم شکر خند

O Father, counsel me not against love for this son of {yours} will not prove susceptible {to counsel}!

ای پدر پند کم ده از عشقم
که نخواهد شد اهل این فرزند

People counsel these {others}: O would that they would counsel me concerning Thy Love!

پند آنان دهندخلق ای کاش
که ز عشق تو میدهندم پند

I know the road to the street of safety, but what can I do? For I am fallen into the snare!

من ره کوی عافیت دانم
چکنم کاوفتاده ام به کمند

In the church I said to a Christian charmer of hearts, O thou in whose net the heart is captive!

در کلیسا به دلبری ترسا
گفتم ای دل به دام تو در بند

'O thou to the warp of whose girdle each hair-tip of mine are separately attached!

ای که دارد بتار زنارت
هر سر موی من جدا پیوند

'How long {wilt thou continue} not to find the way to the Devine Unity? How long wilt thou impose on the One the shame of Trinity?

ره به وحدت نیافتن تا کی
ننگ تثلیث بر یکی تا چند

'How can it be right to name the One True God "Father, "Son," and "Holy Ghost"?

نام حق یگانه چون شاید
که اب و ابن وروح قدس نهی

She parted her sweet lips and said to me, while with sweet laughter she poured sugar from her lips:

لب شیرین گشود وبامن گفت
وز شکرخند ریخت از لب قند

که گر از سر وحدت آگاهی

"If thou art aware of the Secret of the Divine Unity, do not cast on us the stigma of infidelity!

'In three mirrors the Eternal Beauty cast a ray from His effulgent countenance.

تهمت کافری به ما مپسند

در سه آیینه شاهد ازلی
پرتو از روی تابناک افکند

'Silk does not become three things if thou call it Parniyan, Harir and Parand!

سه نگردد بریشم ار اورا
پرنیان خوانی وحریر وپرند

While we were thus speaking, this chant rose up beside us from the church-bell:

ما در این گفتگو که از یکسو
شد ز ناقوس این ترانه بلند

'He is one and there is naught but He:
There is no God save Him alone!

که یکی هست وهیچ نیست جز او
وحدهو لا اله الاهو

In Strophe 3 he seeks out a gathering of drinkers and merrymakers, by convention Zaroastrians but more Hafezian or even Khaya'm-like in their scorn of rationalized religion and devotional decorum. He drinks a cup of their wine, and becomes "free from the pain of understanding and the trouble of sense" and hears the angle Sorus whisper the familiar refrain in his ear.

(Strophe 3)

(بند سوم)
دوش رفتم به کوی باده فروش

Last night I went to the street of the wine-seller,

ز ا آتش عشق دل بجوش وخروش

my heart boiling and seething with the fire of love.

I beheld a bright and beautiful gathering presided over by the wine-selling elder.	مجلسی نغز دیدم وروشن میر آن بزم پیر باده فروش
The attendants standing row on row, the wine drinkers sat shoulder to shoulder.	چاکران ایستاده صف در صف باده خواران نشسته دوش بدوش
The elder sat in the chief seat and the wine drinkers around him, some drunk and some dazed,	پیر در صدر ومیکشان گردش پاره ای مست وپاره ای مدهوش
With chests void of malice and hearts pure, the heart full of talk and the lips silent.	سینه بی کینه ودرون صافی دل پر ازگفتگو ولب خاموش
The eyes of all by the eternal mercy beholding the Truth and their ears hearkening to secrets.	همه را از عنایت ازلی چشم حق بین و گوش راز نیوش
The greeting of this one to that one, 'Wassail l' the response of that one to this one, 'Drink-hale'!	سخن این به آن هداالک پاسخ آن به این که بادت نوش
With ears for the harp and eyes on the goblet, and the desire of the both worlds in their embrace.	گوش بر چنگ وچشم بر ساغر آرزوی دو کون در آغوش
Advancing respectfully, I said' O thou whose heart is the abode of the Angel Surush,	بادب پیش رفتم وگفتم ای ترا دل قرارگاه سروش
'I am an afflicted and needy lover: behold my pain and strive to remedy it!	عاشقم دردمند وحاجتمند درد من بنگر وبه درمان کوش
	پیر خندان به طنز بامن گفت ای ترا پیر عقل حلقه به گوش

Decline of Persian Poetry 1700-1800

The elder, smiling, said to me mockingly: 'O thou to whom the Guide of Reason is a devoted slave!

تو کجا ما کجا ای از شرمت
دختر رز نشسته برقع پوش

Where art thou, and where we are! O thou for shame of whom the daughter of the grape sits with veiled face?

گفتمش سوخت جانم آبی ده
واتش من فرونشان از جوش

I said to him, 'My soul is consumed! Give me a draught of, water, and abate my fire from its vehemence!

دوش میسوختم از این آتش
آه اگر امشبم بود چون دوش

'Last night I was consumed by this fire : alas if my to-night be as my last night

گفت خندان که هین پیاله بگیر
ستدم گفت هان زیاده منوش

He said smiling, Ho! Take the cup!' I took it. He cried, 'Ha! Drink no more!

جرعه ای در کشیدم وگشتم
فارغ از رنج عقل ومحنت هوش

I drained a draught and becamevfree from the the pain of understanding and the trouble of sense.

چون بهوش آمدم یکی دیدم
ما بقی را همه خطوط و نقوش

When I came to my senses I saw for a moment One, and all else mere lines and figures.

ناگهان در صوامع ملکوت
این حد یثم سروش گفت بگوش

Suddenly in the temples of the Angelic World the Suru'sh whispered these words into my ear :

'He is One and there is naught but He :
There is no God save Him alone!'

که یکی هست وهیچ نیست جز او
وحدهولا اله الا هو

Chapter 7

Strophe 4 is a vision of the earthly Paradise beyond the dimensions of time, space, and society where king and beggar are equal, and love-in fact, finding and making love (eshq varzidan) to the one- is the key to bliss
.

(Strophe 4)

Open the eyes of the heart that thou may behold the spirit that thou may see that which is not to be seen.

چشم دل باز کن که جان بینی
آنچه نا دیدنی است آن بینی

If thou will turn thy face towards the Realm of Love thou will see all the horizons a garden of roses.

گر به اقلیم عشق روآری
همه آفاق گلستان بینی

Thou will behold the revolution of the cycle of heaven favorable to all the people of this earth.

بر همه اهل این زمین بمراد
گردش دور آسمان بینی

That which thou see thy heart will desire, and that which thy heart desires thou will see.

آن چه بینی دلت همان خواهد
وانچه خواهد دلت همان بینی

The headless and footless beggar of that place thou will see heavy-headed with the dominion of the world.

بی سروپا گدای آنجا را
سرزملک جهان گران بینی

There also thou will see a bare-footed company with their feet set on the summit of the Guard-stars in heavens.

هم در آن پا برهنه قومی را
پای بر فرق فرقدان بینی

There also thou will see a bare-headed assembly canopied overhead by the throne of God.

هم درآن سربرهنه جمعی را
برسر از عرش سایبان بینی

Each one at the time of ecstasy and song thou will see shaking his sleeves over the two worlds.

گاه وجد و سماع هر یک را
بر دوکون آستین فشان بینی

In the heart of each atom which thou cleaves thou will hold a sun in the midst.

دل هر ذره را که بشکافی
آفتابیش در میان بینی

If thou give whatever that thou have to love, may I be accounted an infidel if thou should suffer a grain of loss

هر چه داری اگر به عشق دهی
کافرم گر جویی زیان بینی

If thou melt your soul in the fire of Love, thou will find Love the Alchemy of Life;

جان گدازی اگر به آتش عشق
عشق را کیمیای جان بینی

Thou will pass beyond the narrow straits of dimensions, and will behold the spacious realms of placelss;

از مضیق حیات در گذری
وسعت ملک لامکان بینی

Thou shall hear what ear has not heard, and shall see what eye has not seen;

آنچه نشنیده گوش آن شنوی
وانچه نادیده چشم آن بینی

Until they shall bring you to a place that of the world and its people thou shall behold one alone.

تا به جایی رسانندت که یکی
از جهان و جهانیان بینی

To that one thou make love with heart and soul, until with the eye of certainty you shall clearly see

با یکی عشق ورزی از دل وجان
تا بعین الیقین عیان بینی

'That He is one and there is naught but He:
There is no God save Him alone!'

که یکی هست و هیچ نیست جز او
وحدهو لا اله الاهو

In Strophe 5 the poet exhorts his listeners to aim high, to search for fulfilmnt through love rather than reason, along the path of mystic.He lists various conventions of mystical-lyrical, some of which he has just used himself, and declares them all to be cryptic keys to an appreciation of the truth summed up in his refrain.

<table>
<tr>
<td>

(Strophe 5)
From door and wall, unveiled, the Friend shines radiant, o ye who have eyes to see!

Thou seek a candle whilst the sun is on high: the day is very bright whilst thou art in darkest night.

If thou wilt but escape from thy darkness thou shall behold the entire universe the dawning-place of all lights.

Like a blind man thou seek guide and staff for this clear and level road.

Open your eyes on the Rose-garden and behold the gleaming of the pure water alike in the rose and the thorn.

From the colorless water {are derived} a hundred thousand colors: behold the tulip and the rose in this garden-ground.

Set thy foot in the passage of search and with love furnish thyself with provision for this journey.

By Love many things will be made easy which in the light of wisdom are very difficult.

</td>
<td>

یار بی پرده از در در دیوار
در تجلی است یا اولو الابصار

شمع جویی وآفتاب بلند
روز بس روشن وتو در شب تار

گر ز ظلمات
خود رهی بینی
همه عالم مشارق انوار

کوروش قاید وعصا طلبی
بهر این راه روشن وهموار

چشم بگشا به گلستان وببین
جلوه آب صاف در گل وخاک

ز آب بیرنگ صد هزاران رنگ
لاله و گل نگر در این گلزار

پا بر اه طلب نه از سر عشق
بهر این راه توشه ای بردار

شود آسان ز عشق کاری چند
که بود پیش عقل بس دشوار

یار گو بالغدو والا صال

</td>
</tr>
</table>

Decline of Persian Poetry 1700-1800

Speak of the Friend in the
mornings and evenings: seek for
the

یارجو بالعشی والابکار

Friend in the gloaming and at
dawn.
Though they tell thee a hundred
times 'Thou shall not see me,'stilll
keep your eyes fixed on the Vision,

صد ر هت لن ترانی ار گویند
باز میدار دیده بر دیدار

Until thou shall reach a place to
which the foot of Fancy and eye of
Thought cannot attain.

تا بجایی رسی که می نرسد
پای اوهام و دیده افکار

Thou shall find the Friend in an
assembly whereunto not even
Gabriel the trusted has access.

بار یابی به محفلی کانجا
جبرییل امین ندارد بار

This is the road this is thy
Provision, this, the Halting-place: if
thou are a roadman, come and
bring!

این ره این توشه تو این منزل
مرد راهی اگر بیا وبیار

And if thou are not equal to the
Road then like the others, talk of
the Friend and scratch the back of
thy head!

ور نه ای مرد راه چون دگران
یار میگویی وپشت سر میخار

O Ha'tif, the meaning of the
Gnostics whom they sometimes
call drunk and sometimes sober,

هاتف ارباب معرفت که گهی
مست خوانند شان و گه هشیار

{When they speak} of the Wine,
the Cup, the Minstrel, the Cup-
bearer, the Magian, the Temple, the
Beauty and the Girdle,

از می و جام ومطرب وساقی
از مغ ودیرو شاهد وزنار

قصد ایشان نهفته اسراریست
که به ایما کنند گاه اضهار

Are those hidden secrets which sometimes declare in cryptic utterance.
If thou should find thy way to their secret thou will discover that even this is the secret of those mysteries,

پی بری گر بر از شان دانی
که همین است سر آن اسرار

'He is one and there is naught but He:
There is no God save Him alone!'

که یکی هست و هیچ نیست جز او
وحدهو لا اله الا هو

CHAPTER 8

THE MOVEMENT OF "LITERARY RETURN" TO CLASSICAL STYLE IN PERSIAN POETRY (BA'Z'GASHT ADABI)

During the last years of the first half of the18th century a group of poetical reformists leading by the great Persian poets from the city of Isfahan the most famous of them; Mohammad Shoeleh Isfahani, Mirza Mohammad Nasir Isfahani, and in particular Mir Ali Moshtagh Isfahani commenced a new movement to do away with the so called predominant "Indian" style which had been in use by almost all Persian and Indian poets from the India's sub-continent.

By all accounts, the effort was as mentioned, initiated and spear-headed by Moshta'gh of whose life little is known except that he was born in the year 1689 and died in 1757. It is also said by the editor of his diva'n that Moshtagh founded a literary society referred to as the Anjoman-e-Adabi-e Moshtagh, and that his close circle of friends were the poets Ha'tef Esfahani, A'zar Bigdeli, A'shegh Esfahani, Saba'hi, and Sahba'Ghomi, all from Esfaha'n. This claim is repeated by other modern critics although there is no early evidence for it. Moshtagh wrote in the 'Eraghi style often in response to particular ghazals of Hafez and Saadi. The pattern that Moshtagh and his circle established was followed for more than a century by poets who turned their back on Indian style.

 An investigation of their technique reveals in general an increased use of literary emulation (esteghbal, which generally consists in adopting the meter and rhyme of the original poem) and of the rhetorical figure tazmin, the direct quotation of a line or half-line from another poet.These rhetorical devices, along with characteristic diction, syntax and imagery, would be the principle used by poets who were trying to imitate the practice of their predecessors. The creative use of the past was common among poets from Rudaki onward. The effects created by the poets of Ba'zgasht were quite different, however, from those produced by earlier poets and it is precisely because of this difference that opinions differ widely on the general quality of the poetry of these poets and writers who were soon joined by a group of young and talented prominent poets; Mohammad Khayat, A'shegh Isfahani, Mohammad Taghi Sahba from Qum, Lotfe-Ali Beig Azar Bigdelli, Seyed H'tef Isfahani, Ha'ji Soleyman Sabahi from Kasha'n, and many others all between the years of 1802 & 1826 .

These poets and writers soon attempted and succeeded to train new group of poetry lovers who soon became some of the most outstanding poets during the reign of Fatah-Ali Shah Gha'ja'r, who himself loved poetry and was soon trained to join the rank of new coming poets. In the meantime there were still a group of others who stayed loyal to the old "Indian" style and kept criticizing the new stylists and would not easily accept and adopt these new-comers.

During the reign of A'gha' Mohamad Kh'an Ghajar a very prominent poet in Isfahan who also happened to be the Governor of the city founded a poetry society which was named after him. : "Nesha't literary society". Gathered in these weekly poetry meetings in his house were almost all of the prominent and famous poets and writers. However it was not too long before Neshat was invited by the Monarch to move to Teheran to become the King's laurite poet and the society lost its most generous and influential member and supporter.

Once the new movement was established the members and the new movement's enthusiasts were eager and pleased to once more adopt and use the old classical style called "Araghi style" .This was the style which had been used for hundreds of years before by great classical Persian poets, such as Manouchehri, Araghi, Onsori, Farrokhi, Hafez, Saadi and others.

While the term bazgasht-adabi refers normally to the writing of poetry, the general effort on the part of the literati to revert to earlier poetic styles that had its effect on prose writing as well. Simple and unadorned prose had continued to be written since the earlier times, and in greater quantities than was the case with poetry. Nevertheless, by the time of Na'der Shah, some genres of courtly prose had become excessively complicated and bombastic, with a multitude of synonyms, repetitions, and obscure words were being used to express what could be said more concisely and elegantly. Unlike poetry, only one model was held up by nineteenth century prose writers as the ideal of eloquent writing, and this was Saadi's Golestan. The mixed genre of molama, with its short anecdotes and verses, is characterized by concise expression and an aphoristic style. This was closer to the ideal of poetry than were the extended

Return to Classical style

and slow-moving narratives of the historians, and the Golesta'n had long been a model of eloquent prose for Persian speakers.

CHAPTER 9

POETS OF THE Q'AJA'R PERIOD

The Qa'jar rule was strong though severe, and in spite of its harshness, was, perhaps, a welcome on the whole to a country which had suffered seventy years of anarchy and civil war. The brief and bloody reign of the eunuch A'qa Muhammad Khan, though practically supreme for eighteen years (CE 1779-1797), he was not crowned until 1796 and was assassinated in the following year, who once more carried the Persian standards into Georgia and captured Tifilis, was followed by the milder administration of his nephew Fath-'Li Sha'h (CE 1797-1834), to whose influence Reza'-quli Kha'n Hedayat, in the Introduction to his 'Majma'ul-Fusaha', ascribes the revival of poetry and the restoration of a better literary taste. He himself wrote verses under the pen-name of Kha'gh'an, and gathered round him a host of poets to whose lives and work several monographs are devoted, such as the "Zinatul-Maddih, the "Anjuman-e-Khaga'n, The "Gulshan-e- Mahmud and 'Safinatu'l-Mahmud, the Nega'restan-e Da'ra', and the Tazkera-eye Mahmud-Sha'hi, One of them , the Gulshan-e Mahmud, contains notices of forty-eight of Fath-'Ali Sha'h's sons who wrote poetry, and at a later date the Royal Family supplied Persia with another verse-making autocrat in Na'sere'Din Sha'h (CE 1848-1896), but these kingly outpourings need detain only those who accept the dictum (Kalamu'l-Muluk Mulu'ku'l Kala'm ("the Words of Kings are the Kings of Words").

These poets of the earlier Qa'ja'r period might very well have been included in the preceding chapter, but for the inordinate length which it has already attained. The only respect in which they differed from their immediate predecessors was in their reversion to earlier models and their repudiation of the school typified by "Urfi, Sa'eb Tabrizi (Isfahani), Shawkat Bu'kha'ra'ie, and their congeners. This fact is established from two opposite quarters. On the one hand Shibli, as we have seen, takes the view that Persian poetry, which began with Rudaki and few others, ended with Sa'eb, and that Gha'a'ni and the moderns did but imitate- the older classical poets, specially Farrukhi and Manuchehri. Reza'-gholi khan takes the same view of the facts, but puts on them a quite different interpretation. According to him, Persian poetry had long been on the decline and at the end of the pre-Q'j'ar period had become thoroughly, decedent, so that the early poets did well to break away from the ideals of their immediate predecessors and revert to earlier models, amongst which he specially mentions the poems of Kha'gha'ni, 'Abdu'l-Wasi'-i-Jabali, Farrukhi, manuchehri, Rudaki, Ghatra'n, Unsuri, Mas'ud-i-Sa'd-i-Salma'n, Sana'I, Jala'led-Din Rumi, Abul-Faraj-i-Runi, Anwari, Asadi, Ferdoowsi, Neza'mi, Saadi, Azraghi, Mukhta'ri, Mu'izzi, La'mi'I, Na'ser-Khosrow and Adib Sabir, all of whom flourished before the Fall of the Caliphate and the Mongol Invasion in the middle of thirteenth century.

Of the later poets Ha'fez was perhaps the only one who retained an undiminished prestige in the eyes of his countrymen, and it is doubtful how far even he served as a model, though this was perhaps because he was inimitable rather than, because, he was out of fashion, like Ja'mi, Urfi and Sa'eb, who lost and never regained the position they had once held in their own country. Henceforth, therefore, the divergence between Turkish and Indian taste on the one hand and Persian taste on the other increases, while the action of the British rulers of India in substituting Urdu for Persian as the court language of that country in 1835-36 and at or about the same time ceaseing to subsidize the publication of Oriental texts, thus inflicting a great injury on Oriental studies, tended still further to cut off India from the intellectual and literary currents of modern Persia.

Saha'b Isfahani 18th century Persian poet

Sayyed Muhammad of Isfahan, poetically surnamed Sah'b, was the son of Sayyed Ahmad Hatef whose biography was previously included. He was the only notable Persian poet of the eighteenth century. Reza'-gholiKha'n says that he was held in high honor by Fath-Ali Shah, for whom he composed, besides numerous panegyrics, a book of memoirs (presumably of poets) entitled Rashahatat-e-Saha'b and that his diva'n comprises only some five thousand verses. The following, censuring the conceit and arrogance of certain poets, are rather interesting:

"Wherein save in good nature lies anyone's 'perfection, and what 'Perfection' can there be to him who has not good nature?	کس را کمال نفس بجز حسن حال چیست وآن را که حسن حال نباشد کمال چیست شعر است هیچ و شاعری از هیچ هیچتر در حیرتم که بر سر هیچ این جدال چیست

Poetry is naught, and the poet's vocation less than naught: I wonder
What is this entire quarrel about nothing!

یک تن نپرسد از پی ترتیب چند لفظ
ای ابلهان بی هنر این قیل و قال چیست

No one will ask about the arrangement of a few words:
O fools! devoid of merit, what is all this talk?

از بهر مصرعی دو که مضمون دیگریست
چند ین خیال جاه وتمنای مال چیست

On account of one or two hemistiches expressing someone else's
Ideas, what are all this thought of position and hope of wealth?

شعر اصلش از خیال بود حسنش از محال
تا از خیال اینهمه فکر محال چیست

The root of poetry is all fantasy, and its beauty lies in the impossible:
What can result from the imagining of all these impossible ideas?

از چند لفظ یاوه نزد لاف برتری
هرکس که یافت شرم چه وانفعال چیست

Whoever has discovered what shame and modesty are will not boast
Of superiority on account of a few silly words.

صد نوع این کمال بر اهل رای و هوش
با حسن ذات عامی نیکو خصال چیست

What are the eyes of men of judgment and sense are a hundred
Sorts of such 'Perfection' compared with the good nature of an ordinary well-disposed man!

گیرم که نظم بحر دروکان گوهر است
با نثر کلک داور دریا نوال چیست

I grant that the Nazm
(arrangement or verse) is an
ocean of pearls, a mine of
precious stones:
But, what is it compared with the
Nasr (prose)
(scattering, or prose) of the pen
of that Lord whose bounty is as
that of the ocean?"

Mijmar of Ardesta'n 19th century Persian poet

Sayyed Husayn-e-Taba'taba'ei with the pen-name Mijmar of Ardesta'n near
Isfahan who earned the title of Mujtahedu'l-Shu'ara', is noticed by Reza'-
gholi Kha'n in all three of his works. He owed his introduction to the Persian
Court to his fellow-townsman and fellow-poet Mirza' Abdul-Waha'b Nesha't,
survived him by eighteen or nineteen years. He appears to have died young,
for Reza'-gholi Khan, after praising his verse, of which but a small collection
was left, says that "had he lived longer, he would probably have attained the
utmost distinction," but even as it is he is one of the five poets of this period
whom Ha'jji Mirza' Yahya' of Dawlata'ba'd placed in the first class. The
others are Furughi, Saba', Nesha't, and Gha'a'ni in the first class; Wisa'l and
Reza'-gholi Kha'n Heddayat in the second; and Wigha'r and Surush in the
third. Copies of his poems are rare, but the British Museum possesses a
manuscript of his Kulliyya't, or collected works.

The two following riddles, the first on the Wind and second on the Pen are
taken from the Tazkereh-e-Delgosha' may serve as specimens of his work.

The Ode of the wind

"

What is that messenger of
auspicious advent and fortunate
presence?

لغزباد
چیست آن پیک مبارک مقدم فرخ
جناب

That is moving every day and night and hastening every year and month?

روزوشب اندر تحرک سال و مه اندر شتاب

That carries musk-pods in his skirt and perfume in his collar,

نافه اش در دامن واندر گریبانش عبیر

Ambergris in his pocket, and pure musk in his sleeve!

عنبرش در جیب و اندرآستینش مشگ ناب

A traveler without food or head, a madman without sense or reason,
A lover with no abode and habitation, a wonderer with no food and no sleep.

رهروی بی پا وسردیوانه ای بی عقل وهوش
عاشقی بی خان ومان آواره ای بیخورد وخواب

None knows for love of whom he is restless; none discovers
Through separation from whom he is so troubled.

کس نمیداند که از عشق که باشد بیقرار
کس نمی یابد که از هجر که دارد اظطراب

Through him water becomes, like the hearts of lovers through the
Tresses of their idols, now wreathed in chains, now twisted and tormented.

آب از او چون دل عشاق از زلف بتان
گاه باشد در سلاسل گه بود در پیچ وتاب

Now the earth dies through him, and again the world lives through him
Like the faculties through old age and like the nature through youth."

مرده گه از او زمین وزنده گه از او جهان
چون قوی از پیری وهمچون طبیعت از شباب

The Ode of the faculty of writing

لغز قلم

"To the rose-bush of the garden of the reasoning faculty

گلبن باغ نفس ناطقه را
من یکی ابر گوهر افشانم

I am a cloud raining down pearls,

Both pouring forth sugar and
diffiusing perfume {like} the
darling's
Lips and the sweetheart's tresses.

همه شکرریز و همه عبیر افشان
لب دلدار و زلف جانانم

In scattering pearls and pouring
forth jewels I am {like} the nature
Of the Minister and the hand of the
King."

در در افشانی و گهر ریزی
طبع دستور و دست سلطانم

Saba' of Ka'sha'n 18th century Persian poet

Fath-'Ali khan of Ka'sha'n, with the pen-name of Saba' was poet-laureate
(Malekol –Shoara') to Fath-Ali Sha'h. Reza'-gholi Khan Hedayat, who has
written about him in all three of his works, says that no poet equal to him had
appeared in Persia for nearly seven hundred years, and that some critics prefer
his Shahansha'h-na'ma to the Sha'hnama of Ferdowsi. He also composed a
Khuda-'na'ma, an Ebrat-na'ma, and a Gulshan-e-Saba', while his diva'n is
said to comprise ten or fifteen thousand verses. He was for a time governor of
Qum and Kasha'n, but latterly devoted himself entirely to the Sha'h's service.
In his youth he was the student of his fellow-townsman the poet Saba'hi, who
was a contemporary of Ha'tef and A'zar, and died, according to the Majmaol-
Fusaha', in 1791. His eldest son Mirza' Husayn Kha'n, poetically surnamed
Andalib ("Nightingale"), succeeded him in the laureateship. His poetry, being
most panegyric, has little attraction and therefore no English translation will
be provided here although it is extraordinarily melodious. The following
extract is from a qasida quoted in the Tazkereh-e-Delgosha':

عیدست و عشرت را بقا بر درگه شه ره
نما
در دم نوای مرحبا بر لب سرود آفرین

عیدست و شاهان جهان گویان بهم در
آستان

برخاست بانگ بارهان بنشست شاه راد
هین

عید است واز نوبت سرا آواز کوس
وبانگ نای
در کاخ هفت اختر صدا در کاس نه
گردون طنین

شهزادگان خورشید فر بر کله پروین
سپر
بر جانشان پا تا بسر در آفرین جان آفرین

برزآسمان شان پایگه بل آسمان شان خاک
ره
دیدار رشگ مهرومه گفتار راز داد ودین

شه را مهین بر آستان با شه سرایان
داستان
گوهرفشان بر آستان چندان که شه
از آستین

فضل وهنر آب وگلش آسان از آن هر
مشگلش
گنج جواهر در دلش گنجور قدرت را
دفین

در پیشگاهی کاسمان بنهاده سر در
آستان
عکسی آز آن باغ جنان فرشی بر آن
عرش برین

شاهنشه فرخنده خو با صدر اعظم راز
گو

گلبرگ رو کافورمو آن پس نگر این پیش
بین

Nesh't Isfaha'ni 18ᵗʰ century Persian poet

Mirza' Abdul-Wahh'b of Isfahan was one of the four most outstanding poets of Q'ja'r period who was in the forefront of the new literary movement known as "Ba'zgashte-Adabi, who were responsible for revolutionizing the predominant poetical style called Hendi (Indian). During the reign of A'gha' Mohammad Kha'n Qa'ja'r Nesha't established in the city of Isfahan a literary society together with a number of other famous poets and he presided over it until he was invited by Fath Ali Sha'h to Tehran and assigned the job of special secretary to the king and was granted the special title of "Motamed-ol-Do'leh". In his capacity as the special assistant to the king he was also part of a team of delegates who travelled to Paris and met The French Emperor Napolean Bonapart. Nesha't died in Tehran at the age of seventy.

Nesha't was greatly celebrated as a calligraphist, as a poet and master of three languages, Arabic, Persian and Turkish. In the course of his lifetime he almost ruind himself by extending his prodigal hospitality and liberality to poets, mystics and men of letters. He excelled in the ghazal, and his best work is entitled Ganjina (the treasury). The following chronogram gives the date of his death as 1828.

از قلب جهان نشاط رفته

"Neshat (Joy) has departed from the
heart of the world"

Mirza' Abu'l-Qasim Qa'im-maqa'm 'put to death in 1835

Two eminent men, father and son, bore this title (of which the literal meaning is exactly equivalent to "liteutenant," in the sense of vicar or deputy). Mirza Isa of Fara'ha'n, called Mirza' Buzurg, who acted as Deputy Prime Minister to Prince A'bba's Mirza' and died in 1831; and his son Mirza' Abul-Qaswm, who on the death of Fath-Ali Sha'h, fell into disgrace, and was put to death by his successor Mohammad Sha'h on June 26, 1835. The latter was, from the literary point of view, the more remarkable, but though he wrote poetry under the name of Thand'I, he is more celebrated as a prose writer. His numerous published letters being regarded by his country-men as models of good style. Many of them are diplomatic documents of some historical importance, e,g. the apology addressed to the Tsar of Russia for the murder of the Minister Grebaiodoff and his staff at Tehran on February 11, 1829, which is here given as a specimen of the Qa'im-maqa'm's much admired style.

The beginning of the record is: In the Name of the All-knowing God, The Living and All-powerful Creator and Provider—that Peerless and Incomparable Being, exempt from every wrong-doing, Who hath set a measure and limit to the recompense of every good and evil deed, and Who, by his far-reaching wisdom, reproves and punishes the doers of evil, and rewards and recompenses the well-doers. And countless blessings upon the spirits of the righteous Prophets and beneficient Leaders"…

اول دفتر بنام ایزد دانا صانع پروردگار حی و توانا وجودی بی مثل ومانند مبرا از هر چون وچند که عادل و عالم است و قاهر هر ظالم. پاداش هر نیک و بدرا اندازه و حد نهاده بحکمت بالغه ی خود بدکاران را زجر وعذاب کند ونیکوکاران را اجر وثواب بخشد ودرود بر روان پیغمبران راست کار وپیشوایان فرخنده کردار باد....

Other poets of the Qaja'r period

It would be easy with the help of the Biographies of poets mentioned above and others of a later period to compile a list of a hundred or two more or less eminent poets of the Q'j'ar period, but it will be sufficient for our purpose to mention ten or a dozen of those who followed the classical tradition. Nor is it necessary to group them according to the reigns in which they flourished, though it will be convenient to arrange them in chronological order.

Of one great family of poets, are the sons and grandsons of Wesa'l (Mirza' Shafi' commonly called Mirza' Kuchek) who died in 1846. He is generally regarded as one of the most eminent of the modern poets and both Reza-

gholikhan Heda'yat who devotes lengthy notices to him in all three of his works, and the poet Bismil, the author of the Tazkera-i-Delghosha' were personally acquainted with him. His proper name was Mirza' Muhammad Shafi'. He was a native of Shiraz. Bismil speaks in the most glowing terms of his skill in calligraphy and music as well as verse, wherein he holds him "incomparable" and praises his lofty character and fidelity in friendship, but describes him "as rather touchy" (andaki zud-ranj), a description illustrated by Reza'ghu'li Kha'n's remark (in the Rawzatu's-Safa') that he was much vexed when the Sha'h, meaning to praise him, told him that he was "prodigal of talents." He is said to have written twelve thousand verses, which include, besides qasidas and ghazals, the Bazm-i- Wesa'l and the continuation and completion of Vahshi Bafghi's Farhad u Shirin described as "far superior to the original." He also translated into Persian Atwd-qu'dh-Dhahab ("Collars of Gold") of Zamakhshari. Bismil, who professes to have read all his poems, only cites the relatively small number of 213 couplets, of which the following are fairly typical, and afford a good instance of what Persian rhetoricians call the "attribution of praise in the form of blame," for the qasida' begins:
"The sea, the land, heaven and the
stars—
Each one of them declares the King
a tyrant—

An opening calculated to cause consternation to courtiers, until it is stated the sea considers itself wronged by his liberality, the mountain because he has scattered its hoarded gold like dust, the stars because they are eclipsed in number and splendor by his hosts, and so forth. As such far-fetched conceits can hardly be made attractive in translation, only a few lines in its original Persian will be quoted here:

هرکس شها زبحروبرو چرخ و اخترست
اقرارمیکنند که خسرو ستمگرست

ز آنها یکیست بحرکه نالد زدست شاه
کابم ازو برفت و کنون خاک برسرست

اندوخته ام تمام بپردخت و خود نگفت

کاین سنگریزه نیست که مرجان و گوهرست

دریا نشست و کوه بر آورد سر که داد
زین شاه جود پیشه مرا دل پر آذرست

بر من هر آنچه رفت بدریا ز شه
نرفت مرجان کجا بپایه ی یاقوت احمرست

لعلی که جست بر افسر شاهان حرام باد
بی آب تر ز افسر شا هانش بردرست

زر مرا ندیدی و آن عزتی که داشت با
خاک ره ز وجود وی اکنون برابرست

این شاه نیست دشمن بحر است و معدنست
این شاه نیست آفت چرخ است و اخترست

Wesa'l's Farha'd u Shirin has been lithographed, and ample selections from his poems are given by Reza'-gholi Kha'n in his Riya'zul-'A'raf'n and Majmaul-Fusafa', which later work also contains an ample introduction of his eldest son Waghar Shirazi who turned out to be an outstanding poet and was presented to Na'sered-Din Sha'h in Tehran in 1857.

The following musammat by Da'vari, describing one of Sha'h's hunting parties:

یک چند جدا از برم آن شوخ پسر بود
ازوی نه نشان بود مرا ونه خبر بود
با موکب منصور همانا بسفربود
از حسرت او آتش شوقم بجگربود

شبهای فراقم ز شب گوربتربود
روزم ز غم هجرسیه ترزشب تار
دوشینه همان ز اول شب ناشده پاسی
زنگی شب افگنده برخ تیره پلاسی
آمد ز در آن دلبربی ترس وهراسی
یکباره ببرد از دل من اندە وتیمار
بربسته میان وزده خنجر بکمربر
مسکین دلم از خنجرتیزش بحذربر

از بس هوس دیدن من داشت بسربر
ازره سوی من آمده با چکمه وشلوار
پرخاک سروزلف ورخ ازگرد سپاهش
خشکیده دو عناب تر از صدمه راهش
از بس نزده شانه بزلفین سیاهش
درهم شده وریخته برگرد کلاهش

چون کاسه خون سرخ شده چشم سیاهش
از صدمه بیخوابی واز زحمت بسیار
یک دسته گل سرخ رهآورد سفرداشت
از سنبل ترنیزیکی دسته به سرداشت

از لعل بدخشانی یک حقه گهرداشت
از حقه عجبترکه یکی تنگ شکرداشت
چون ازدل بیمارمن خسته خبرداشت
درتنگ شکرداشت دوای دل بیمار

گفتم صنما گرچه بسی رنج کشیدی
صد شکرکه شاد آمدی ونیک رسیدی
جان رهی از دست غمان بازخریدی
برگو که در این راه چه کردی وچه دیدی

در موکب منصور چه دیدی وشنیدی
چون بود سرانجام وچه شد عاقبت کار
گفتا که نبودی وندیدی که چه سان بود

نخجیرگه شاه یکی لاله ستان بود

هرگوشه ز خون دجله بغداد روان بود

تا چشم همی کارکند تیر وکمان بود

تا ابر همی جای دهد گرز وسنان بود

نه دشت پدیداربد از لاش و نه کهسار

دلها همه آسوده ز رنج و ز حزن بود

در دشت وبیابان همه گل بود وسمن بود

کبک دری از هرطرفی قهقه زن بود

نخجیرگه از آهو چون دشت ختن بود

اینها همه از بخت شه شیرشکن بود

کاقبال وی افزوده بود بخش بیدار

This poem is simple, sonorous, and graphic; the court page, who has just returned from accompanying the Sha'h on a winter hunting-expedition, and is in so great a hurry to visit his friend the poet that he enters in his riding-breeches and boots (ba chekma wa shalwar), with hair still disordered and full of dust, and eyes bloodshed from the glare of the sun, the hardships of exposure, and lack of sleep, bringing only as a present from the journey (rah-award-e safar) roses and hyacinths (his cheeks and hair), rubies of Badakhsha'n (his lips), and a casket of pearls (his teeth), is a vivid picture; a description of the wholesale slaughters of game instituted by Chingiz Kha'n the Mongol in the thirteenth century as well as any other typical Royal hunting parties elsewhere in other countries in the previous centuries.

Qa'jar period was relatively rich with relatively large number of poets and prose writers exceeding some 300 in numbers, although not all of high literary value. Some of the noted poets of this period are:

Aqa' Mohammad Hasan Zargar (The goldsmith) of Isfahan, who died in 1853 ; Aqa' Mohammad A'sheq Isfahani, a tailor who died at the age of 70, in 1864 Mirza Muhammad "ali Sur'ush of Sedeh, entitled Shamsu'-Shuara'(The sun of the poets) who died in 1868.

Aqa' Mohammad Ali Jayhu'n of Yazd, whose details of life are not known except that his poems are of specially high quality and who, besides writing numerous poems of various types has also written, a prose work entitled Namakda'n (the Salt-cellar) on the model of the Golesta'n of Saa di of Shiraz. His complete works were lithographed at Bombay in 1899, making a volume of 317 pages.

Others who are reckoned amongst the poets were more distinguished in other fields of literature, such as historians Reza-gholi Kha'n Hedda'yat, (born in 1800, died 1871), and Mirza Mohammad Taghi Sepehr of Kasha'n entitled Lesa'n'l-molk (the Tongue of the Kingdom) author of Na'sekhu'l-Tavarikh (Abrogator of Histories), and of another prose work entitled Bara'hinnul-Ajam ("Proofs of the Persians"), {grand father of the contemporary poet Sohrab Sepehri}, And the philosopher Hajii Mula' Ha'di Sabzava'ri, born in 1797, who wrote a small amount of verse under the pen-name of Asra'r ("Secrets"), that died in 1878.

Of the remaining modern representatives of the "Classical School": Gh'a'ni, Furughi and Adibol Mama'lek Faraha'ni are by far the most important, of whom some account will be given here:

Gha'a'ni Shirazi 19th century Persian poet

Gha'a'ni , pen name of Mirza' Haib-Allah Shirazi was born on 20th of October 1808 in Shiraz. He was one of the most prominent poets of Qajar era and a well-known practitioner of the literary return (Ba'zgasht-e adabi) style. A panegyrist who served many patrons, Gha'a'ni was celebrated for the lyricism and melodiousness of his verses, but also heavily criticized, in particular by the modernist poets, for his lack of substance and exaggerated praise of unworthy patrons. His father, Mirza Mohammad Ali "Golshan" was a minor poet in Shiraz. He died when Gha'a'ni was only eleven years old. Gha'a'ni was forced into abject poverty and had to fend for himself. However; he showed an early talent for poetry and took his education into his own hands and entered a madresa (school) in Shiraz. There, by eulogizing the governor of Fa'rs in a few poems, he obtained a stipend sufficient for his basic needs. As he wrote later, "I applied myself so much to my studies that in two years I surpassed my peers to such an extent that everyone who witnessed my progress was amazed; and although I was ugly, I became beautiful in their eyes. The poet's self-consciousness about his appearance, particularly his pockmarked face, was evidently much on his mind, for it is mentioned frequently in his poems.

Chapter 9

Study, in a number of fields and service to an ever more prominent series of patrons, were to characterize the remainder of the poets professional life. Over the next few years, Gha a'ani devoted into mathematics, prosody, and different branches of Islamic sciences while in Shiraz and Isfahan. He also continued to compose poetry and wrote commentaries on the diva'ns of Khaghani and Anvari. In 1823, he came under the protection of the prince Hassan-Ali Mirza' Shoja'-al-Saltaneh, a son of Fath-Ali Sha'h, who had of late come to Shiraz. The prince rendered him many kindnesses, and when Shoja'al-Saltaneh was appointed to the governorship of Khorasan at the end of the same year he took the young poet with him. Gha'a'ni settled in Mashhad, where he delved more deeply into the study of poetry and finding" his luck strong, his purse fat, his riches many, his silver and gold enlarged, and his dirhams and dinars multiplied from ones to thousands" He spent a great deal of money collecting the diva'ns of the classical masters. It was during this period that the poet changed his pen name from Habib to Gha'a'ni in honor of the prince's son, Okota'y-Gha'a'n.

Gha'a'ni accompanied the prince to Yazd and Kerman and also traveled to Gila'n, Ma'zandera'n, and Azerbaija'n, although the dates and circumstances of these journeys are unclear. At some point, apparently after losing his patron who had fallen out of favor with the king after making an unauthorized attack upon Yazd from Kerman, Gha'a'ni gained access to the court of Fath-'Ali Shah where he received a pension and the title " Spiritual Leader of the Poets" (Mojtahed al -Shoara')". After that monarch's death, Gha'a'ni joined the circle of poets in Tehran who celebrated the 1834 enthronement of Mohammad Shah, receiving the title "Hass'a'n of the Persians" (Hass'a'n-al-Ajam, an allusion to Hass'a'n b Sa'bet, a famous Arab poet), popularly regarded as the laureate of the prophet Mohammad) from the king. When Mohammad Shah embarked on his Hera't campaign against the Afghans, Gha' a'ni was among his retenue. But the poet fell ill when the king's cavalcade arrived at Besta'm, and he received permission to return to Tehran. He later commemorated the campaign in a long qasida.

In 1843 or 1844 the poet returned to his hometown of Shiraz, apparently with the intent of settling there permanently. At first he enjoyed peace and tranquility, and found leisure to add English to the other languages with which he was already conversant. But gradually a group of the city's poets turned against him, and after the sympathetic ruler of the city Sa'heb-e Ekhtiya'r, was replaced by Motamedal-dolawla Manuchehr Khan Gorji, who had little

Poets of the Q'aja'r Period

feeling for poetry and delayed paying his salary, Gha'a'ni saw no recourse but to return to Tehran. His return to the capital in 1846 coincided with the death of his friend, the poet Vesa'l Shirazi. He later satirized the people of Fa'rs in a qet'a; (see below). He again won the friendship of the powerful members of the court in Tehran, including the Prince Ali-gholi-Mirza Eteza'd al-Saltana, a great lover of poetry; Mahd-e Olya', mother of Na'ser-ed-Din, the crown prince; as well as the crown prince himself. After the crown prince was enthroned in 1848, he appointed Gh'a a'ni the poet laureate. As official court poet, he was charged with composing topical panegyrics for ceremonial occasions.

His tenure was both short and rocky. The poet ran afoul of Mirza' Taghi Khan Amir-e- Kabir, Naser ed-Din's reform-minded chief minister. In 1849 the latter reduced Gha'a'ni's salary and may even have threatened him bastinado. The punishment apparently occurred after Gh'a'ni recited a poem praising the newly appointed chief minister and criticizing his predecessor Ha'ji Mirza' Agha'si, upon whom he had previously bestowed the most adulatory of titles, including perfect man (Ensa'n-e Kamel), the lord of the two worlds (Kha'je-ye du jaha'n), the manifestation of divine essence (mazhar-e za't-e ba'ri), and the deliverer of the Creator's bounty to the people (resa'nande-ye ruzi-yeh kha'legh be makhloogh).

"In the place of a vile tyrant is seated a just and God-fearing man, In whom pious believers take pride."	بجای ظالمی شقی نشسته عادلی تقی که مومنان متقی کنند افتخار

The beauty of Ga'a;ni's language can naturally only be appreciated by one who can read his poems in the original Persian, which is fortunately easily accessible, as his works have been repeatedly published. Wonderful also is the swing and grace of the poem in praise of the Queen-mother (Mahd-e-'Ulya') beginning:

"Are these violets growing from the ground on the brink of the streams?	بنفشه رسته از زمین بطرف جویبارها
	گسسته حور عیین زلف خویش تارها

Or have the houris {Angels of Paradise} plucked strands from their tresses?

ز سنگ ندیده ای چه سان جهد شرارها

If thou hast not seen how the sparks leap from the rock,

ببرگهای لاله بین میان لاله زارها

Look at the petals of the red anemones in their beds

که چون شراره میجهد ز سنگ کوهسا رها

That leaps forth like sparks from the crags of the mountains"

It seems that Amir-e Kabir, who had in any case little liking for the poetry, took umbrage at the poet's infidelity towards his former patron. Family disputes, financial woes, melancholy, over indulgence in alcohol as well as, apparently opium had a disastrous effect on the poet's health, and he fell seriously ill in 1854. His friend Eteza'd-al-Saltaneh, who witnessed him in the throes of his penultimate illness, reported that the hallucinating poet addressed invisible figures in Persian, Arabic, Turkish, French, and English. He recovered, but not for long. At the final gathering attended by Gha'a'ni, held to celebrate the birthday of 'Ali b. abi Taleb, the poet recited a qasida containing the following verse: "I see the joy of life in death of the body; destroy me with wine…" Listeners rightly worried that the poet was foreshadowing his imminent passing. After falling ill again, Gha'a'ni died in 1854 and was buried in Rayy near the tomb of the twelfth century Qura'nic exegesis Abdul-Fotuh Ra'zi.

Gha'a'ni married twice, both times with disastrous results. His son, Mirza Mohammad Hassan "Sa'mani" also became a court poet, and his poems are often inserted in his father's diva'n. Gha'a'ni evidently had several other children as well, for in one poem calls himself the provider for fourteen family members; and elsewhere, as many as thirty. The turbulence of his home life shows forth vividly in a long letter of supplication written to Na'ser-ed-Din Shah. In it, Gha'a'ni implores the king for financial help and heaps execration upon his wives and mothers-in-law, who, he says, have stripped him of all possessions. The letter, which stands as a superb example of his prose, is quoted in full by Mohammad Jafar Mahjub in his introduction to Gha'a'ni's divan/

Gha'a'ni was remembered by friends as pleasure loving, possessed of a prodigious memory, and so generous in distributing the vast sums of money that came into his hands that he was himself often left impoverished. Gha'a'ni was extremely prompt and proficient in composition that stories of his devisting long and highly accomplished qasidas on the fly are legend. Indeed his enormous poetic output, given the brevity of his life and the melancholy that often afflicted him, is nothing short of astonishing.

Although Gha'a'ni was a prolific writer, only a fraction of his poetry survives, thanks to his lackadaisical attitude toward preserving his works. The 21000 or 22000 verses comprising the most complete edition of of his divan may comprise only one-fifth of his total output; the rest has been lost. notwithstanding these omissions the work is still celebrated in some circles, and has been published repeatedly in Iran and India. The best editions are those based on the manuscript copy compiled by Jal'l-al-Dowla, the Ghajar prince and litterateur in 1857, four years after the poet's death, and known as the "Kalhor" manuscript copy after the calligrapher, Mirza Mohammad Reza' Kalhor, who translated it along with the many qasidas for which Gha'a'ni is best known. His divan also contains mosammats, tarji-bands, gazals, mathnavis, qet'as, and roba'is. At least some of the missing poems are likely to have been additional gazals, since Gha''a'ni reportedly threw many of these poems into the fire one cold winter night after a musicion sang a gazal of Saadi and the drunken poet felt the deficiencies of his own verses in comparison with those of the master.

In addition to poetry, Gha'a'ni also wrote several prose works, although, like his poems, many of these have perished. The most famous extant work is Parisha'n (distracted and disheveled), a collection of more than 100 stories, poems, and maxims, many of them bawdy or satirical, in prose intercepted with verse. Though the poet states in the introduction that the work was modeled after Saa di's Golesta'n, and many critics have accepted this assertion as fact, the scholar Natalia Tornesello convincingly demonstrates that the work bears much closer resemblance in both structure and content to the Resa'le-ye delgosha of Obeyd-e Zakani, to the point that it repeats some stories almost verbatim. Along with mostly cynical counsels to kings and princes, the work presents accounts of the poet's own life, including descriptions of his father's death and his sojourn in Khorasan, and it is often mined for autobiographical material. The poet and scholar Mohammad Tagh Baha'r, in his famous oeuvre on the evolution of Persian prose and stylistics, Sabkshena'si, also speaks of treatises by Gha'a'ni on geometry, magic, and divination which were in his personal collection. Gha'a'ni is thought to have written many others which were never published, or whose existence remain unrecorded.

It is difficult to imagine a Persian poet whose writings has sparked as mixed a critical reception as that of Gha'a'ni. The vitriolic attack on him by some near-contemporary critics is in sharp contrast to the enthusiastic praise of others, who placed him within the ranks of the greatest Persian poets. In many ways, these contradictory responses reveal more about the state of literary criticism in Iran in the 19th and 20th centuries than they do about Gha'a'ni himself. As intellectuals of that period began to assess poetry chiefly according to its reflect and affect on social reform, Gha'a'ni's seemingly slavish pandering to corrupt patrons formed a convenient target for their fire. For example, the politician and litterateur, Ali Dashti, vilified the poet for immersing himself "into a cesspool of flattery to the top of the head", the playwright and social critic Mirza' Fatah-Ali A'khundzadeh called his diva'n "full of ...nonsense", and even Yahya Arianpour, in his judicious and balanced account of the poet, points to some of his failings:"{in praising the least worthy men of the court, and even servants; he brings into play characteristics that no one had ever applied to them before"; and he accuses him of a lack of compassion toward the people of Iran and their sufferings.

 Critics likewise attacked Gh'a'ni's inconstancy and fickleness toward his patrons. Edward G. Browne, for example, tartly noted his tendency to "flatter great men while they are in power, and turn around and rend them as soon as they fall into disgrace". Even when a scholar lauded Gha'a'ni's fluency in one moment, he disparaged his meagerness of content in the next. A'rianpour, for example writes that "notwithstanding Gha'a'ni's power of expression and dexterity in description and metaphors and scene-setting, the majority of his qasidas are poor and insignificant with regard to subject matter"

Beyond his major sins, critics catalogued a host of minor transgressions. One is repetition: description of wine, beautiful boys, the difficulties of travel, spring, fall, night and day appear in his verses with numbing regularity: As Mahjub writes, " The beloved is always arriving tired from the road with a dusty face and disheveled hair. He ponds on the door, Gha'a'ni opens it, embraces him warmly, seats him in the festivities, and serves him wine. The beloved then delivers the glad tidings of the arrival of such –and-such a commander or governor". Another is carelessness, which resulted in errors in grammar, usage, and meter, as well as great inconsistency in the quality of his poetry. The sexual innuendo of many of his poems, as well as the coarseness of his language when speaking about wine-drinking or love-making drew disapproval.

Praise of the poet's work tended to center around the sweetness and lyricism of his language, the wide range of his vocabulary, and his inventiveness. Baha'r, who defended him against the charges of servility by observing that carrying favor with the powerful, was simply the means by which poets earned their keep in that era, spoke of the freshness of Gha'a'ni's style and regarded him as one of the greatest poets of his time. Baha'r likewise maintained that Gha'a'ni was responsible for the invention of a new style (sabk-e Gha'a'ni) reflecting not only the influence of the Khorasani style, known for its dignity and strength, but also the Eraghi style, characterized by its subtlety and use of common expressions- a contention that others vigorously refuted.

Today, the question of whether Gha'a'ni founded a new school no longer burns with the same relevance, and the accusations of pandering no longer delivers the same sting. Read without those screens, his oeuvre reveals many notable poems, some memorable for their explicit homoerotism, others for their stylistic experimentation with diction, and still others for their apparently sincere devotion. One poem noteworthy for its sexual innuendo records Gha'a'ni's coy refusal of a friends advances (Brown, IV, pp.329-30).

Furughi Bastami 19th century Persian poet

Mirza' Abbas, son of A'gha Musa' of Basta'm, who wrote verse first under the pen-name of Meskin and later of Furughi is said to have written some twenty thousand verses and is considered one of the greatest of the Qa'ja'r period. Of the twenty thousand verses, five thousand is placed at the end of the Tehran edition (1884-5) of the works of Gha'a'ni with whom he was so closely associated. Unlike him, however, he seems to have preferred lyric to elegic forms of poetry; at any rate the selections in question consist entirely of ghazals. According to the brief biography prefixed to them he adopted the Sufi doctrine in the extremer forms which it had assumed in ancient times with

Ba'yazid of Basta'm and Hussein ibn Mansur al-Halla'j, and so incurred the suspicion and censure of the orthodox.

Na'sered-Din Sha'h, in the beginning of whose reign he was still flourishing, once sent for him and said. "Men say that like Pharaoh thou does advance the claim ' am your Lord the Supreme, and that thou dost openly pretend to Divinity," " This assertion, "replied Furughi, touching the ground with his forehead, "is sheer calumny….For seventy years I have run hither and thither, and only now have I reached the Shadow of God!" The first three verses from the first ode cited seem to be as good typical as any others. They run as follows:

"When didst thou depart from the heart that I should crave for Thee?	کی رفته ای ز دل که تمنا کنم ترا
When were thou hidden that I should find Thee?	کی بوده ای نهفته که پیدا کنم ترا
Thou hast not disappeared that I should seek Thy presence;	غیبت نکرده ای که شوم طالب حضور
Thou hast not become hidden that I should make Thou appear	پنهان نگشته ای که هویدا کنم ترا
Thou hast come forth with a hundred thousand effulgence;	با صد هزار جلوه برون آمدی که من
That I may contemplate "Thee with a hundred thousand eyes."	با صد هزار دیده تماشا کنم ترا

Adibol-Mamalek Fara'ha'ni 19th century Persian poet & writer

Poets of the Q'aja'r Period

One highly esteemed Persian poet and writer of the late Qa'ja'r period was Mirza'Sa'degh Khan best known by his title Adibol-Mama'lek who was born in 1860 CE and died on 28 February of 1917. He was a descendent in third degree of Mirza' Isa Qa'em-maqam.

In 1889 he was at Tabriz in the service of Amir Neza'm Garrusi in honor of whom he changed his pen-name from Parva'neh to Amiri. In 1893 he followed the Amir Neza'm to Kerma'nshah and Kurdista'n. During the two following years he was employed in the Government Translation Office in Tehran, but in July 1896 he returned with Amir Nezam to A'zerba'yja'n, where he became–master of the Lupmaniayya College at Tabriz, and founded the Adab newspaper, which, as stated above, he afterwards continued in Mashhad and Tehran.

During the years 1900-02 he travelled to the Caucasus and Kha'razm, whence he came to Mashhad, but on March 1903 he returned to Tehran, and for the next two years was the chief contributor to the Ruzna'meyeh Iran Sultani. In 1906 he was joint editor of the Irsha'd at Ba'ku; in 1906 he became chief writer for the Majlis, edited by Mirza'mohammad Sa'deghe-Tabataba'I and he founded the Ir'aq-e-Ajam.

In July 1910 he took part in the capture of Tehran by the Nationalists, and subsequently held the position of President of the High Court of Justice (Raise-Adliyyeh) in Ara'k and Samna'n. He lost his only daughter in 1912.Two years later he was appointed editor of the semi-official newspaper Afta'b ("The Sun"). In 1916-17 he was appointed President of High Court of Justice at Yazd, but soon afterwards he died at Tehran, aged fifty-eight.

The special value and interest of his poems according to his cousin and ultimate friend, Kha'n Malek, lie not only in their admirable and original style, but in their faithful reflection of the varying moods of the Persian people during the fateful years of 1906-1912. In satire it is said that no Persian poet has equalled him since the time of Su'zani of Samarghand, who died in CE 1173. In his pamphelet Kha'n Malek gives the opening verses of all the poems in his possession, with the number of verses in each, and invites those who possess poems lacking in his collection to communicate them to him before December, 1923, when he proposes to publish as complete an edition as possible.

Chapter 9

The Ka'va quote the following verses from one of his poems on the Russian aggressions in Persia, which it compares with the celebrated poems of Saadi on the destruction of the caliphate by the Mongolls, Anwari on the invasion of the Guzz, Turks, and Hafez on Timur's rapacity:

"Since the poor lamb did not forgather with its shepherd, through fear it neither slept nor rested in the plain.	چون بره بیچاره به چوپانش نپیوست از بیم به صحرا در نه خفت ونه نشست
A bear came forth to hunt, and bound its limbs: our lamb became the Prey of that high-handed bear.	خرسی به شکار آمد و بازوش فروبست شد بره ما طعمه آن خرس زبردست
Alas for that new-born and bemused lamb! Alack for that aged and greedy bear!"	افسوس بر آن بره نوزاده ی سرمست فریاد از آن خرس کهن سال شکم خوار

His works include a divan in Arabic and Persian, a collection of Maqa'la't, a rhymed vocabulary, a volumes of travels and several books on Astronomy, Geography, prosody, and other sciences.

CHAPTER 10

CONTEMPORARY PERSIAN POETRY & POETS IN THE 20TH CENTURY

Parvin Etesa'mi 20th century Persian poet

One of the most prominent and outstanding contemporary female poets of Iran, Parvin Etesa'mi was born in the city of Tabriz on 25 Esfand 1285 Shamsi./16 March 1907 to a highly educated and progressive family. Her father Yousef E'tesami, himself a writer, poet and distinguished journalist; a true scholar proficient in Arabic literature, as well as French and Turkish, well-versed in the principles of logic and wisdom, moved the family to Teheran.

Parvin soon after was admitted to the American college in Tehran to get her formal education and was graduated from that school when she had reached the age of seventeen. In the meantime the father, having noticed the child's extraordinary intelligence took her under his own wings teaching her at home poetry, Persian classics in literature, history and Arabic. She was only eight years old when she started writing poetry to the amazement of her father and the distinguished men of letters who came to visit her father at their home. At the age of eleven, she had already mastered the poetry styles of renowned Persian classical poets and writers such as Sanai, Saadi, Rumi, Khayam, Hafez, and Naser khosrow.

In 1924 she graduated with honors from the American college in Tehran. She was given a teaching job at the same school for a period of time. All this really had happened because of the fact that she was a highly gifted child and at the same time benefitted from a remarkable upbringing that her highly educated and enlightened parents had afforded her.

Parvin, from early years of her short life, had got a firm grasp of both Arabic and English. By the time she was 14, she had matured her craft and was composing meaningful poetry. Two of her father's close friends; renowned Iranian poets and writers Ali-Akbar Dehkhoda and Mohammad Taghi Baha'r

Chapter 10

(Malek-ol-Shoara') closely monitored parvin's progress as a poet during their frequent visits to the family home.

Parvin had composed a very special poem to mark her graduation which had touched on women's struggles through historical, social, philosophical, and anthropological themes, titled: "Twig of a Wish" This work clearly demonstrated Parvin's depth of understanding and knowledge of social problems facing women in the then prevailing Iranian society in particular and the third world countries in general. She truly believed that the foundation of any stable and progressive society lays in its ability to educate and empower women. In 1934 she married a distant cousin of her father and moved with him to Kermanshah. The marriage did not last for too long. She divorced from her husband and moved back with her father a short time later. She kept herself busy writing poetry, which soon proved to be one of the most treasured and exceptional collections to have been ever created by a female poet in recent times.

Parvin with her father's assistance and guidance succeeded to publish her first book of poetry (diva'n) in 1935 and 1936. The book won the Ministry of Culture and Science category 3 literature awards. Parvin declined to accept it.The first edition of her diva'n comprising of 156 poems with an introduction by Mohammad Tagh Baha'r. The second edition, edited by her brother Abol-Fath Etesami and including Baha'r's introduction, appeared shortly after her death in 1941. It offered 209 compositions of different lengths in mathnavi, qasida, ghazal, qet'a and stanzaic forms, totaling 5,606 distiches, as well as the original introduction by Baha'r. She is said to have burnt some poems which did not satisfy her taste.

Her father died in 1938 which dealt a serious blow to the life and happiness of this talented and sensitive poet.She became ill soon after with typhoid which was misdiagnosed by her Doctor and prescribed the wrong medicine. She became fatally ill and passed away soon after. She was buried next to her father in the city of Ghom.

Parvin's poetry follows traditional patterns in both form and substance. The protective seclusion of her family life she remained unaffected by, or perhaps unaware of, the ongoing reformistic trends in Persian poetry. In the arrangement of her diva'n there are 42 untitled qasidas, and qeta's, mostly didactic and philosophical reminiscent of the austere tone of Naser-khosrow and Sana'i. There are several other qasida's scattered throughout the collection, particularly in the description of nature that lean heavily on Manuchehri. Parvin did not indulge in lyricism. She by nature and isolated by traditional norms of conduct never expressed inhibited feelings of love and longing. Her diva'n leaves little room for ghazals. Nevertheless several poems including "Arzuha" (longings, Nos.44-48) are perfect examples of lyrics. "Safar-e ashk" (jounney of a tear, no.125) counts among the finest lyrics ever written in Persian)

.

Anecdotes and strife poems, "mona'zera" (dialogue, debate), claim the largest portion of Parvin's diva'n. It is in this genre that her genius unfolds, creating a large number of subtlest examples in Persian Poetry. She composed approximately sixty five mona'zeras and seventy five anecdotes, fables and allegories. Parvin wrote about men and women of different social backgrounds, a wide-ranging array of animals, birds, flowers, trees, cosmic and natural elements, objects of daily life, abstract concepts, all personified and symbolizing her wealth of ideas. Through these figures she holds up a mirror to others showing them the abuses of society and their failure in moral commitment. Likewise, in these debates she eloquently expresses her basic thoughts about life and death, social justice, ethics, education and the supreme importance of knowledge.

Parvin is remarkably silent about major changes and events taking place in Iran during twenty years of her creativity.(1921-41), the only exception being the unveiling of women in 1935, which commemorates approvingly, (no.118). However her diva'n is a faithful mirror of her inner sadness about the plight of masses. Lack of social justice, poverty and the sufferings of the old, the orphan and the sick provoke some of Parvin's moving images. In fairness to the ruling hierarchy during those short years of her life it should be added that her silence could have had its roots in her deep historical and social awareness which convinced her that the present and existing plight of the people has been the result of almost 150 years of Gha'jar's mismanaging, which would naturally take a tremendous amount of time and energy to rectify.

The Orphan's Tear	اشگ یتیم

From every street and roof rose joyous shouts;	روزی گذشت پادشهی از گذرگهی فریاد شوق برسر هرکوی وبام خاست

The king that day was passing through the town

پرسید ز ان میانه یکی کودک یتیم

An orphan boy amidst this speaks his doubts,
What is that sparkle that's atop his crown?

کاین تابناک چیست که بر تاج پادشاست

Someone replied: that is not for us to know,
But it's a priceless thing, that's clear!

آن یک جواب داد چه دانیم ما که چیست

پیداست آنقدر که متاعی پر ارزش است

A crone approached, her twisted back bent low,
She said: that's your heart's blood and my eye's tear!

نزدیک رفت پیرزنی گوژپشت وگفت

این اشگ دیده من و خون دل شماست

We were deceived by shepherd's staff and robe
He is a wolf; for many years he's known the flock
.

ما را به رخت وچوب شبانی فریفته است

این گرگ سالهاست که با گله آشناست

The saint who craves control is but a rogue
A beggar is the king who robs his flock.

آن پارسا که ده خرد وملک رهزن است

آن پادشاه که مال رعیت خورد گداست

Upon the orphan's tears keep fixed your gaze.
Until you see from where comes the jewel's glow,

بر قطره سرشگ یتیمان نظاره کن

تا بنگری که روشنی گوهر از کجاست

How can straight talk help those of crooked ways?
frank words will to most folk deal a blow

Woman in Iran, a poem by Parvin,
translated by Heshmat Moayed
Formerly in Iran, a woman was
considered almost non-Iranian,
All she did was struggling through
dark and distressful days.

Her life was spent in isolation; she
died in isolation,
What was she then if not a prisoner?

None ever lived for centuries in
darkness like she did!

None was sacrificed at the altar of
hypocrisy like she was.

In the courts of justice no witness
was permitted to defend her.

In the school of learning she could
not be admitted.

All her life her cries for justice went
unheeded,

Oppressions of this and other sorts
occurred publicly.

Many men appeared disguised as
her shepherd
Within each a wolf was hiding
instead.

In life's fast arena such was
woman's destiny:

زن در ایران در اسفند
یکهزاروسیصدوچهارده بمناسبت رفع
حجاب سروده شده است

زن در ایران پیش از این گویی که ایرانی
نبود
پیشه اش جزتیره روزی وپریشانی نبود

زندگی و مرگش اندر کنج عزلت
میگذشت

کس چوزن اندر سیاهی قرنها منزل نکرد

کس چوزن در معبد سالوس قربانی نبود

در عدالتخانه انصاف زن شاهد نداشت

در دبستان فضیلت زن دبستانی نبود

دادخواهی های زن میماند عمری بی
جواب

آشکارا بود این بیداد پنهانی نبود

بس کسان را جامه وچوب شبانی بود لیک

To be pushed and shoved into a corner.

در نهاد جمله گرگی بود چوپانی نبود

The light of knowledge was kept from her eyes.
Her ignorance could not be laid to inferiority or sluggishness.

از برای زن بمیدان فراخ زندگی
سرنوشت وقسمتی جز تنگ میدانی نبود

Could a woman weave with no spindle or thread?
Can anyone be a farmer with nothing to sow or to reap?

نور دانش را ز چشم زن نهان میداشتند
این ندانستن ز پستی وگرانجانی نبود

The field of knowledge yielded abundant fruit,
But women never had any share of this abundance.

زن کجا بافنده میشد بی نخ ودوک هنر
خرمن وحاصل نبود آنجا که دهقانی نبود

A woman lived in a cage and died in a cage.
The name of this bird in the rose garden was never mentioned.

میوه های دکه دانش فراوان بود لیک
بهرزن هرگزنصیبی زین فراوانی نبود

Imitation is the desert of women's perdition, the pitfall causing her troubles.
Clever is that woman who never threads
that murky road

در قفس می آرمید ودر قفس میداد جان
در گلستان نام از این مرغ گلستانی نبود

Beauty depends on knowledge, bracelets of emerald
Or Badakhshan rubies do not indicate superiority.

بهرزن تقلید تیه فتنه وچاه بلاست
زیرک آنزن کورهش این راه ظلمانی نبود

All glamour of painted silk cannot match the simple beauty of a tunic.
Honor depends on merit, not on indulgence in vanities.

آب ورنگ از علم میبایست شرط برتری
با زمرد یاره ولعل بدخشانی نبود

جلوه صد پرنیان چون یک قبای ساده نیست

Shoes and clothes are made worthy
by the person who wears them.
One's value does not rise and fall
with high and low prices.

عزت از شایستگی بود از هوسرانی نبود

Simplicity, purity, and abstinence
are the true gems.
Mind gems are not the only brilliant
jewels.

ارزش پوشنده کفش وجامه را ارزنده کرد

قدروپستی از گرانی وبه ارزانی نبود

What is the use of gold, land and
ornaments if the woman is ignorant?
Gold and jewls will not cover up
that blemish.

سادگی وپاکی وپرهیک یک گوهرند

گوهر تابنده تنها گوهر کانی نبود

Only the robe of abstinence can
mask one's faults.
The robe of conceit and passion is
no better than nakedness.

اززروزیور چه سودانجا که نادان است زن

زیوروزر پرده پوش عیب نادانی نبود

A woman who is pure and dignified
can never be humiliated.
That which is pure cannot be
affected by the impurities of
incontinence.

عیبها را جامه پرهیزپوشانده است وبس

جامه عجب وهوی بهترز عریانی نبود

Chastity is a treasure; the woman is
guard, greed the wolf.
Woe if she knows not the rules of
guarding the treasure.

زن سبکساری نبیند تا گرانسنگ است وپاک

پاک را آسیبی ازآلوده دامانی نبود

The Devil never attends the table of
piety as guest.
He knows that that is no place of
feasting.

زن چوگنجوراست وعفت گنج وحرص وآزدزد

وای اگرآگه زآیین نگهبانی نبود

Walk on the straight path, because
on crooked lanes

اهرمن بر سفره تقوی نمیشد میهمان

Chapter 10

You find no provision or guidance, only remorse

ز انکه میدانست کانجا جای مهمانی نبود

Hearts and eyes do not need a veil, the veil of chastity,
A worn-out chador is not the basis of faith in Islam

پا به راه راست باید داشت کاندر راه کج
توشه ای ور هنوردی جز پشیمانی نبود

چشم و دل را پرده میبایست از عفاف
چادر پوسیده بنیاد مسلمانی نبود

This qut'a was written in1314 on the occasion of the unveiling of women

Mommad Tagh Baha'r "Malok-ol-Shoara' 20th century Persian poet & writer

Baha'r's appearance in Iran coincided with the end of the period of social, political and cultural darkness, decline, and decadence which was the direct result of almost 150 years of the despotic rule of Gha'jar'dynasty in Iran. Prosperity, relative calm and national security that had been returned to Iran by Na'der Shah Afshar after the defeat of the Afghan invaders was soon replaced by the establishment in Iran of a cruel, lawless and despotic ruler; Agha Mohammad Khan Ghajar, and the corrupt, lawless, pleasure seeking, irresponsible, and inept dynasty that he had established and left in this country. Two very capable and knowledgable prime ministers; Mirza Abolghasem Farahani and Mohammad Tagi Khan, (Amir Kabir) were orderd murdered by two of these despots; Mohammad Shah and Na'sered-Din Shah. Russian czars took advantage of the weakness of the ruling Fatah Ali Sha'h, invaded and occupied the north, northwest, and northeast territories of Iran forcing the government to give up the sovereignty of seventeen states of the country to Russians. The Turks followed suit and occupied and attached Mesopotamia; part of the western Iranian territories.

Iranians who were by now, deeply frustrated, humiliated and disappointed, to put it mildly, revolted against this inept, corrupt, and despotic rule and forced the ruling monarch to finally give up the power and surrender to a constitutional system of monarchy. The Iranian revolution now blossomed in which Baha'r in his capacity as a journalist and poet played a very effective role.

The Iranian revolution of the 1906-1909 brought about an end to the despotic Gha'jar rule in Iran with the formation of a National Consultative Assembly (Majles). Thus for the first time in the political history of Iran a Constitutional monarchy was established, only to be revoked few years later by Mohammad Ali Shah (Estebda'd Saghir) resulting in a major armed uprising by people against the monarch, giving rise to the re-establishment of parliament and the Constitutional monarchy. Bahar as was said before, in his capacity as a journalist, poet and writer always played a major role in these subsequent efforts and events. He proved himself in later years as an outstanding statesman, literary critic, historian, and a fierce and brave supporter of people's right to rule by the will of majority on the basis of liberal and democratic principles.

Baha'r was born in the city of Mashhad on the 20th of A'zar of 1265 (Shamsi). He completed his studies in Persian, French and Arabic literature and languages as well as history philosophy and Islamic jurisprudence. He had already started writing poetry when he was at the age of ten. Among his later teachers was Adib Nisha'bouri, a traditional poet and scholar in literary sciences who cultivated the style of the ancient poets of Khora'sa'n in the tradition of the ba'zgasht-e adabi.

Baha'r's studies were interrupted at fifteen when his father apprenticed him to his uncle in 1322/1904, and Bah'ar returned to his studies, particularly Arabic which led him to recent books and periodicals from Egypt and eventually drew his attention towards Western ideas of science and progress. Having sent a congratulatory qasid'a to Mozaffar-al-Din Shah on his accession to the throne he was rewarded with his father's title of Maleck-al-Shoara', poet laurite and thus became a government employee at the shrine of Mashhad. For his stipened he wrote and recited poems on official occasions. Already familiar with the ideas of freedom and constitution, he joined constitutionalists in Mashhad at the age of twenty when the constitution was granted in 1324/1906.

Baha'r at the onset of the constitutional Revolution and shortly after decided to resign from the position of Poet Laureateship and joined the revolutionary movement of establishing the parliamentary system of democracy in Iran. He became an active member of the Mashhad branch of Anjoman- Saadat (Prosperity Society) that campaigned for establishment of Parliament of Iran (Majles). He published the semi-covert newspaper Khorasan, Nou-Bahar (New Spring), and Tazeh Bahar (Fresh Spring), both in collaboration with his cousin, Haj Sheykh Ahmad Bahar who acted as the senior editor first in Mashhad and later in Tehran.

Bahar published numerous articles in newspapers in which he passionately exhorted his readers to stand up and bring about the establishment of a functioning parliament. He equally forcefully advocated creation of new and reformed public institutions, a new social and political order and new reforms of expression. After the triumph of the Constitutional Revolution, Baha'r was repeatedly elected as Member of Parliament.

In 1918, when Ahmad Shah Qajar, the seventh and the last ruler of Qajar dynasty, was in power, Baha'r reinvented himself: he ceased all his clerical activities and became an entirely new man. At the same time, together with the writer and poet Saiid Nafisi, the poet and historian, Gholam-Reza Rashid Yasami, the historian Aba's Eqbal Ashtiani, and his talented friend Abdolhosein Teymoortash founded The Literary Association of the Academy (Anjoman-e Adabi-ye Daneshkadeh). The Magazine of the Academy, (Majaleh Daneshkadeh) was the monthly publication of this Association, in which, in addition to works of prose and poetry, other very informative and useful articles were published, under such diverse titles as "Literary Revolution" "How other nations view us" and "The literary History of Iran". In fact, this magazine became Baha'r's vehicle for the publication of the results of his literary researches and introduction of Western Literature to Iranians. The magazine also played a key role in developing and strengthening the present-day form of Persian literature.

Following establishment of Tehran university in 1934 (during the reign of Reza Shah Pahlavi), Baha'r became professor of Persian literature at the Faculty of the literature of this university. In the course of his tenure as Professor, he dedicated most of his time to writing and editing books in Persian literature and history. Notable amongst numerous books written and edited by Baha'r:

Contemporary Persian Poetry

Tarikh Sistan (History of Sistan),Tarikh-Mokhtasar-Ahza'b-Siassi, (A concise history of the political parties)
Sabk-shenasi (Methodology), which concerns the variety of styles and tradition of Persian prose.
Moja'mal-ol-Tava'rikh o Val Ghesal (Concise histories and tales.),
Java'me' ol-hekayat (Anthology of stories).

Baha'r's diva'n in two volumes which is considered by many to be his most important literary and poetic work was published posthumously by his brother Mohammad Malekza'da in Teheran in 1956. Though delicate considerations kept a few poems out of the printed div'an, these two volumes present a complete sweep of the poets' production from his youth to his death-bed. Baha'r's earliest poems are the threnodies for his father, which demonstrates a craft already well learned. His position as poet of the Mashhad shrine led to panegyrics both religious and personal. He owes much to his father's example in his religious poems, while most of his poems are exercises in traditional forms modeled after classical masters. One mossamat in volume 1 of his diva'n page 12 modeled on one by Manuchehri, may be Baha'r's earliest use of a form he exploited later in his political verse. His first important political poem, which won him recognition, was a mostaza'd modeled on one by Shraf Gila'ni and published in the newspaper Khorasan in May-June, 1909. While still in Mashhad, he had to consider the different elements of local society in his public poems, but in Tehran the pressure on him to write formal poems decreased. His poetry now recorded his personal reactions to political events, his style ranging from emulations (esteghba'l) of the old masters to the use of colloquial language.

Baha'r's literary education advanced with his association in the Da'neshkadea group with writers familiar with European languages. Baha'r was able to make Persian versions of their translations from European poetry. These and original poems in a similar vein contributed to the growing number of the poet's "private" poems. At the same time, Baha'r continued to write "public" poetry, attacking many aspects of life and politics as well as political enemies. Such poems reached a climax with the events of 1925, after which the public poems were addressed to the suspicious new monarch, while the private poems became increasingly intimate, restricted to the ears of the poet's immediate circle. Bahar's, experiences in prison and in exile, as a teacher of literature, ere all inspiration for his poetry. The scholarship that were his refuge in the difficult years between 1925 and 1941is manifest to his verse of this period. Reza Shah's abdication is barely mentioned, but other events inspired poems for the rest of his life.Several, including beautiful ghazals, express his pain and isolation during his illness. One qasida, written in his Swiss hospital bed, is an excellent example of Baha'r's use of tradition for contemporary, personal purposes. (diva'n 1, page 774).

Throughout his life, Baha'r wrote poems in all the traditional forms; he experimented a few times with stanza forms of foreign type, but he rejected totally new forms of verse and returned, even at the end of his life, to the old tradition. Yet his subjects, and often his diction, are unmistakably modern.

The Anglo-Russian invasion of 1941 awakened his political conscience. He republished Now-bahar and in 1945 published the first volume history of political parties. In 1945 he was invited to Ba'ku for the 25th anniversary of the establishment of Soviet Azerbaijan and elected to the 14th Majles on his return. In 1945 during the reign of Mohammadd Reza Shah Pahlavi Baha'r served for a short period as the Mininster of Culture and Education in the Cabinet of the Prime Minister Ahmad Ghavam. Earlier in the same year he and Ahmad Ghavam had created the Iran Democratic Party (Hezb-e Demokrat-e Iran).

J'a'leh Gha'em Magha'm Fara'hani 20th century Persian poet

A'lamtaj or Ja'leh, poet and writer, was born in Faraha'n on February 20, 1884, and passed away in Teheran at the age of 63 on September 28, 1947. Her father, Fat'holah Qaem-Magham was the great grandson of Qaem-Magham Farahani, the famous prime minister, writer, and poet of the Qajar dynasty.
Jaleh began schooling when she was five and learned to read and write in Farsi and Arabic.She studied the literary works and poems of famous Persian poets. Jaleh's son Pejzman Bakhtiari tells the story of her father and mothers's unhappy marriage:

When my mother was only sixteen years old, she was forced to marry a 40 years semi-illiterate man by the name of Ali-Morad Khan Mir-panj, (an officer of the Ghajar voluntary army).The marriage was more a political one and a consequence of family's financial problems. My father was only interested in making and saving money. My mother walked from school into the family life and my father was mostly fighting wars and would only come home occasionally. My mother was expecting love, understanding and intimacy but my father was expecting an obedient housewife. The marriage was the result of the "misfortunes of Jaleh's father; Fatholah Qaem Maghami". Jaleh and her husband had totally two different personalities and belonged to different social cultures. The result of the short marriage was a son named Hossein Pejman Bakhtiari, who later became a famous poet.

Pejman describes his parent's marriage as such:"My mother was starting her youth and my father was ending it. My mother was into literature and poetry and my father was spending most of his life fighting wars and conflicts. My mother did not care much for money.and my father did."

When Pejma'n was only one year old, Jaleh decided to take a divorce and moved back to her parent's home. As long as he was alive, he would not allow their son to see her mother. Pejman was able to see her mother finally when he was 27 years old and only after the death of his father. Mother and son then lived together until Jalehs' death in September 1947.

The resulting hardships and bitter challenges including those of her early life and separation from her only child impacted her emotions greatly and have been reflected in her sad poems and writings. Expressions of sadness and bitter feelings have inspired her poetry which had become her only refuge in life. Jaleh was one of the critical and idealistic female poets. When she was 23, the Persian constitutional Revolution took place. During that period of time, the society held conservative views towards women, as well as their activities. This made her portray in her poetry her protesting voice against the submissive role of women in the society. This way, she thought she could help women of her time to attempt to ease the social limitations. Her poetry was concerned about patriarchal society which suppressed women and deprived them of their rights.

She was one of the few first female poets who had the courage to talk about her personal problems. Her poetry was not published for many years. She wrote them for herself and had hidden many of them. Years later her son discovered them and was able to publish them. Her poetry is mostly autobiographical, a reflection of the tragedies and hardships that she had suffered in her personal life. She was aiming to protest against the stereotypes, beliefs, and expectations with regard to defending women's rights. She mostly portrays in her writings women's struggles against gender inequalities. Jaleh was an introspective poet although she mostly lived under melancholic and gloomy conditions. She occupied herselfe with writing and reading. Her main subjects of interest were literature, history, and astronomy.

Iraj Mirza 20ᵗʰ century Persian poet

Prince Iraj Mirza son of prince Gholam-Hossein Mirza, one of the most famous and popular Iranian poets was born on March 1874 in Tabriz and died in Teheran on March 1926. His official royal title was Jala'l-ol-Mama'lek. He was a modernist and his works are associated with the criticism of traditions. He also made translation in verse of literary works written by French and English authors the most important of them, Venus and Adonidus by William Shakespear is considerd to be a masterpiece of classical poetry. His pedigree chart indicates that he was a grandson of Fatah-Ali-Shah Qajar that reigned between the years of 1797 to 1834. His father was the son of Prince Malek Iraj Mirza, son of Fatah-Ali-Shah Qajar. He was a poet lauriate at the Court of Mozafared-Din Mirza, the son of Nasser-ed Din Shah Qajar (the fourth shah of Qajar dynasty who ruled Iran 1848 to 1896.)

It has been said that Iraj Mirza was schooled privately, however reliable sources have reported that he studied at the Tabriz branch of Darol-Fonoon (College of science and technology). At fifteen he was fluent in Persian, French, Arabic and Azerbaijani. He was also familiar with the art of Calligraphy. His handwriting was very artistic and he was and still is considered as one of the famous Colligraphers of Iran.

Iraj got married in 1890 at the age of 16. He lost both his father and his wife at the age of 19. He then took the position of his late father and became the court-poet of Mozaffered-Din Mirza. Soon after the prince ascended to the throne in1896 and was crowned as Mozafaral-Din Shah; Iraj was promoted to the position of Head of poets with (Sadr ol-Shoa'ra') and given the title of Jalal ol-Mamalek.

Few years later, however he left the royal court and joined the Tabriz office of Alikhan Amin ol-Doleh who was the governor of Iranian Azerbaijan. At this time Iraj studied hard to learn French and became very familiar with Russian too.

Contemporary Persian Poetry

When Amino-Doleh was relocated and moved back to Tehran, Iraj also accompanied him. Some time later Iraj left for Europe as a member of a delegation led by Dabir Hozur Ahmad Ghava'm (later Ghavam-ol-Saltaneh). On his return to Persia in 1900, he was appointed the head of the Tabriz chamber of commerce by Nezam-ol-Sultana Mafi and came to Tehran with him in the same year. In 1901 Iraj started to work as a translator at the customs office in Kermanshah and stayed there until 1904. He was then transferred to the Ministry of Education, where he served for five years and founded the ministries' secretarial office. Between 1904 and 1915 he held a number of governmental posts in Tehran, Isfahan, Abadeh, and Anzali before he finally was transferred to Khorasa'n as the deputy director of the financé department in that province. The five years that he spent there proved the most significant and productive periods in his life as a poet. It was during this period that he met the noted poet and literary scholar of the time Adib Nishabouri, to whom he was indebted for the full development of his poetic talent. His famous work, A'ref-nama, a witty poem imbued with homoeroticism in rhymed couples addressed to Abul-Gha'sem Aref Ghazvini also dates from this period.

Two years later, in March 1926, Iraj Mirza died of a heart attack and was buried in the Zahir-ol-Doleh cemetery in Shemiran, a village then north of Teheran. A moving poem he had composed as his own epitaph is inscribed on his modest tomb.

Iraj Mirza has had a strong influence on many later poets. His intimate, idiomatic mode of expression and almost conversational tone initiated an entirely new trend in Persian Poetry, which some critics have referred to as "journalistic style". It was the simplicity of his language that, according to Rashid Ya'sami, caused his poetry to conquer the whole country, and according to Saiid Nafisi, made him "The most sweet-spoken poet of our time". He has been called the Saadi of his time by Mohammad Taghi Baha'r, and complemented in the highest by distinguished poets and literary critics.

Iraj Mirza' is a master of light verse, but behind the apparent levity there is much scathing criticism of the social and political conditions of the country. A frequent theme is the question of the use of veil (heja'b) by women, which effectively barred them from active participation in social affairs. He was writing in the aftermath of the constitutional Revolution, when the country was facing a multitude of new social, political, and cultural challenges. Iraj was an ardent supporter of the revolution in spite of the fact that he was himself a Qa'jar prince with a bloodline from the tyrannical and despotic regime of Qa'ja'r dynasty.

A broad-minded liberal intellectual such as Iraj Mirza could not escape the impact of the Revolution, which, inter alia, had re-invigorated the literary movement that had started in the mid-19th century to address more immediate social and political questions. Many poets and writers (e.g. Dehkhoda', and Ashraf Guilani) used colloquial idioms, even slang, in their serious works, but none with such effortless case as displayed by Iraj Mirza'.

The cultural milieu created by the Constitutional Movment also encouraged poetry to undergo certain changes in terms of diction, form, and vocabulary as well as content. Politics of the day became the focal point of a good deal of poetry produced at this time, as oblique expressions and intricate imagery gave way to direct and robust language, which, even in lyrical poetry, often addressed social issues while criticizing the guardians of the old order. Narrative verses in rhyming couplets (manzuma) gained great popularity, overshadowing other forms. Iraj Mirza composed several pieces in this genre. The best and the most popular among them is a love story titled Zohra o Manuchehr, which is a versified version of an incomplete translation of William Shakespear's Venus and Adonis by Lotf-Ali Suratgar. Others of note are A'ref-nama, Enghela'be-Adabi (Literary revolution), and Sha'h o Ja'm (The king and the cup).

A major characteristic of his poetry is the fact he rarely recognizes any bounds in his diction. He freely and skillfully uses none literary and even obscene terms in his seemingly serious poems, in a way which might shock a casual reader unfamiliar with the thrust and historical background of his work. This feature of his work often provided grounds for authorities to have his diva'n removed from the shelves, while at the same time explaining the' suje de scandale' with which many of his poems were received at publication and their wide circulation and immense popularity. His poetry is rich in linguistic innovations. His application of Arabic morphological rules to Persian words is one of his favorite ploys, creating a scope for satire (e.g; mostmandan "miseable ones", jafang"nonsensical"etc). His diva'n is also rich in the art of simile. His striking sarcasm, pungent and fanged words are pointed at the dishonest clergy, businessmen, merchants and statesmen. In addition, he also composed very nice mathnavi and qa'ta' on the raising and education of children, maternal affection, love and romance.

Contemporary Persian Poetry

Iraj was an enlightened and innovative poet, and tended towards European thought. Despite his famous technical skills, he sometimes used similar cases of rhyme, which is considered by some poetry critics as an intentional rejection of strict traditional poetical rules. Although, Iraj was one of the pioneers of the innovtive movement in Persian poetry, he never thought of abandoning the rules of classical poetry. Some scholars believe that because of the time in which he lived, his depth of literary knowledge and his familiatry with French and other foreign languages, he could also have been one of the masters of free verses if he had wanted to. He is particularly famous for his pederastic and satirical poetry.

Some of his more popular works are Satan (Ebliss), Mother, a letter to A'ref Ghazvini, Woman's picture (Tasvir-e Zan), story of veil (Heja'b) and as mentioned before Shakespear's Zohreh-o-Manoucheh (Venus and Adonis). Briefly in" Mother" the poet describes the childs' affection towards his/her mother and how mother nartures her child from birth onwards. The words that Iraj uses are exquisitely descriptive and beautiful not only in its original Persian but also in the translated version.

The transalation of the story of Zohreh and Manuchehre into Farsi is a famous poetic work. It is based on the ancient Greek tale adopted by Shakespear narrated and written in English. Iraj has used the French version. In this poem, Zohreh (Venus) leaves the Gods and comes to earth in search of love, where she is overcome by the pleasing charm of Manouchehr (Adonis) in his armor. He rejects her advances while Zohreh attempts her first seduction. She goes to great pains to explain the beauty of lovemaking. She finally goes her own way as she returns to Gods. On December 8, 2004 the last Iranian movies launched in France was the story of Zohreh and Manouchehr directed by Mitra Farahani. The film had already participated in the Berlin film festival and several other international events and had attracted many viewers.

Iraj believed that the social status of Iranian women at his time was reminiscent of European women in the Dark ages. Iraj being the enlightened man that he was, could not bear to see the life so intolerable, unbearable and miserable for the courageous, valorous and descent women of Iran.That was why he composed the very powerful and memorable picture of women's day to day lives in Iran. Here is a part of the beautiful narrative of Zohre and Manouchehre (Venus &Adonis) translated and versifed into Farsi by Iraj

Chapter 10

Mirza as well as part of its original version written by William Shakespeare the English poet and dramatist.

The Synopsis of the original play by William Shakespeare

Adonis is a young man renowned for his incredible beauty. However, he is not interested at all in love; he only wants to go hunting. Venus is the godess of love. She falls in love with him, and comes down to earth, where she encounters him setting out on a hunt. She desires him to get off his horse, and speak to her. Adonis does not want to talk to any woman, not even a goddess. So she forces him, and then lies down beside him, gazes at him, and talks of love. She craves a kiss; he wants to leave and go hunting. He manages to get away, and goes to get his horse.

At that moment his horse becomes enamored of another horse, which at first resists, but soon the two animals gallop off together, which keeps Adonis from going hunting. Venus approaches him, and continues to speak to him of love. He listens for a bit, and then turns away scornfully. This pains her and she faints. Afraid he might have killed her. Addonis kneels beside her, strokes and kisses her. Venus recovers and requsts one last kiss, He reluctantly gives in.Venus wants to see him again; Adonis tells her that he cannot tomorrow, bcause he is going to hunt the wild boar. Venus has a vision, and warns him that if he does so, he will be killed by the boar. She then flings herself on him tackling him to the ground. He prises himself loose, and lectures her on the topics of lust verses love. He then leaves; she cries.

The next morning Venus roams the woods searching for Adonis. She hears dogs and the hunters in the distanc. Thinking of her vision that he will be killed by the boar, she is afraid, and hurries to catch up with the hunt. She comes across hunting dogs that are injured. There she finds Adonis, killed by the wild boar. Venus is devasted. Because this loss occurred to the goddess of love, she decrees that love will henceforth be mixed with suspicion, fear, and sadness.Adonis body has grown cold and pale. His blood gives color to the plants all around him. A flower grows from the soil beneath him. It is white and purple, like blood on Adonis's flesh. Venus, bereft, leaves the Earth to hide her sadness where the gods live.

Venus & Adonis-original play by
William Shakespeare '

Even as the sun with purple-
colour'd face
Had taken his last leave of the
weeping morn,
Rose-cheek'd Adonis hied him to
the chase;
Hunting he loved, but love he
laughe'd to scorn;
Sick-thoughted Venus makes amain
unto him,
And like a bold-facedsuitor 'gins to
woo him.

'Thrice-fairer than me,' thus she
began,
'The field's chief flower, sweet
above compare,
Stain to all nymphs, lovelier than a
man,
More white and red than doves or
roses are;
Nature that made thee, with herself
in stride,
Says that the world has ending with
thy life.

'Vouchsafe, thou wonder, to alight
thy steed,
And rein his proud head to the
saddle-bow;
If thou wilt deign this favor, for thy
meed
A thousand honey secrets shalt thou
know;

صبح هنوز سر نزده آفتاب
وانشده چهره نرگس ز خواب
تازه گل آتشی مشگ بوی
شسته ز شبنم به چمن دست و روی
منتظر حوله باد سحر
تا که کند خشگ بدان روی
ماهرخی چشم و چراغ سپاه
صاحب شمشیر و نشان در جمال
بنده مهمیز ظریفش هلال
نجم فلک عاشق سر دوشی اش
زهره طلبکار هم اغوشی اش
نیر و رخشان چو شبه چکمه اش
خفته یکی شیر به هر تخمه اش
دوخته بر دور کلاهش لبه
وان لبه بر شکل مه یک شبه
بافته بر گردن جانها کمند
نام کمندش شده واکسیل بند
کرده منوچهر پدر نام او
تازه تراز شاخ گل اندام او
چشم بمالید و بر آمد ز خواب
با رخ تابنده تراز آفتاب
روز چو روز خوش آدینه بود
در گرو خدمت عادی نبود
خواست به میل دل و وفق مرام
روز خوش خویش رساند به شام
چون ز هوسهای فزون از شمار
هیچ نبودش هوسی جز شکار
اسب طلب کرد و تفنگ و فشنگ
تاخت به صحرا پی نخجیر و رنگ
رفت کند هرچه مرال است و میش
برخی بازوی توانای خویش
از طرفی نیز در آن صبح گاه
زهره مهین دختر خالوی ماه
آلهه عشق و خداوند ناز
آدمیان را به محبت گداز
پیشه وی عاشقی آموختن

Here come and sit, where never
serpent hisses,
And being set, I'll smother thee with
kisses;

'And yet not cloy thy lips with
loathed satiety,
But rather famish them amid their
plenty,
Making the red and pale with fresh
variety,
Ten kisses short as one, one long as
twenty;
A summer's day will seem an hour
but short,
Being wasted in such time-
beguiling sport.'

The precedent of pith and
livelihood,
And trembling in her passion, calls
it balm
Earth's sovereign slave to do a
goddess good:
Being so enraged, desire doth lend
her force
Courageously to pluck him from his
horse.

Over one arm the lusty course's
rein,
Under her other was the tender boy,
Who blush'd and pouted in a dull
disdain,
With leaden appetite, unapt to toy;
She red and hot as coals of glowing
fire,
He red for shame, but frosty in
desire.

خرمن ابنای بشر سوختن
خسته و عاجز شده از کار خویش
واله و آشفته چو افکار خویش
خواست که برخستگی آرد شکست
یک دو سه ساعت کشد از کاردست
سیر کل و گردش باغی کند
تازه ز گل گشت دماغی کند
کند ز برکسوت افلاکیان
کرد به سر مقنعه خاکیان
خویشتن آراست به شکل بشر
سوی زمین کرد ز کیهان گذر
آمد از آرامگه خود فرود
رفت به دان سو که منوچهر بود
و
زیر درختی به لب چشمه سارد

تیر نظر گشت بر او کارگر
کار گرست آری تیر نظر
لرزه بر افتاد در اعصاب او
رنگ پرید از رخ شاداب او
گشت به یک دل نه به صد دل اسیر
در خم فتراک جوان دلیر
رفت که یک باره دهد دل به باد
یاد الوهیت خویش اوفتاد
گفت به خود خلقت عشق از منست
این چه ظعیفی و زبون گشتن است
من که یکی عنصر افلاکیم
از چه زبون پسری خاکیم
آله عشق منم در جهان
از چه به من چیره شود این جوان
من اگر آشفته و شیدا شوم
پیش خدایان همه رسوا شوم
عشق که از پنجه من زاده است
وز شکن زلف من افتاده است
با من اگر دعوی کشتی کند
با دگران پس چه درشتی کند

The studed bridle on a ragged bough
Nimbly she fastens:--O, how quick
is love!—
The steed is stalled up, and even
now
To tie the rider she begins to prove;
Backward she pushed him, as she
would be thrust,
And govern'd him in strength, thou
not in lust.

So soon was she along as he was
down,
Each leaning on their elbows and
their hips;
Now doth she stroke his cheek, now
doth he frown,
And 'gins to chide, but soon she
stops his lips;
And kissing speaks, with lustfull
language broken,
'If thou wilt chide, thy lips shall
never open.'

He burns with bashfull shame: she
with her tears
Doth quench the maiden burning of
his cheeks;
Then with her windy sighs and
golden hairs
To fan and blow them dry sgain she
seeks:
He saith she is immodest, blames
her 'miss;
What follows more she murders
with a kiss

خوابگه عشق بود مشت من
زاده من چون گزد انگشت من
تاری از آن دام که دارم کنم
در ره این تازه جوان افکنم
عشق نهم در وی و زارش کنم
طرفه غزالی است شکارش کنم
دست کشم برگل وبر گوش او
تا بپرد از سر او هوش او
جنبش یک گوشه ابروی من
می کشدش سایه صفت سوی من
من که بشر را بهم انداختم
عاشق ودلداده هم ساختم
خوب توانم که کنم کار خویش
سازمش از عشق گرفتار خویش
گرچه نظامی است غلامش کنم
منصرف از عشق نظامش کنم
این همه را گفت وقوی کرددل
دادبه خود جرات و شد مستقل.
کرد نهان عجزوعیان ناز خویش
هیمنه ای داد به آواز خویش
گفت سلام ای پسرماه وحور
چشم بد ازروی نکوی تو دور
ای زبشر بهتروبگزیده تر
بلکه زمن نیز پسندیده تو
زیر درختی به لب چشمه سار
چشم وی افتاد به چشم سوار
تیر نظر گشت برا.کارگر
کارگرست آری تیر نظر
لرزه برافتاد در اعصاب او
رنگ پرید از رخ شاداب او
گشت به یک دل نه به دل اسیر
در خم فتراک جوان دلیر
رفت که یکباره دهد دل به باد
یاد الوهیت خویش اوفتاد
گفت به خود خلقت عشق از منست
این چه ضعیفی وزبون گشتن است

Even as an empty eagle, sharp by fast,
Tires with beak on feathers, flesh and bone,
Shaking her wings, devouring all in haste,
Till either gorge is stuff'd or prey is gone;
Even as she kissed his brow, his cheek, his chin,
And where she ends she doth anew begin.

Forced to content, but never to obey,
Panting he lies and breatheth in her face;
She feedeth on the steamas on a prey,
And calls it heavenly moisture, air of grace;
Wishing her cheeks were gardens full of flowers,
So they were dew'd wit such distilling showers.

Look, how a bird lies tangled in a nest,
So fasten'd in her arms Adonis lies;
Pure shame and awed resistance made him fret,
Which bred more beauty in his angry eyes?
Rain added to a river that is rank
Perforce will force it overflow the bank.

Still she entreats, and prettily entreats,
For to a pretty ear she tunes her tale;

من که یکی عنصر افلاکیم
این چه ظعیفی و زبون گشتن است
من که یکی عنصر افلاکیم
از چه زبون پسری خاکیم
آله عشق منم در جهان
از چه به من چیره شود این جوان
من اگر آشفته و شیدا شوم
پیش خدایان همه رسوا شوم
عشق که از پنجه من زاده است
وز شکن زلف من افتاده است
با من اگر دعوی کشتی کند
با دگران پس چه درشتی کند
خوابگه عشق بود مشت من
زاده من چون گزد انگشت من
تاری از آن که که دارم کنم
در ره این تازه جوان افکنم
عشق نهم در وی وزارش کنم
طرفه غزالی است شکارش کنم
دست کشم برگل وبر گوش او
تا بپرد از سراو هوش او
جنبش یک گوشه ابروی من
می کشدش سایه صفت سوی من
من که بشر را بهم انداختم
عاشق ودلداده هم ساختم
خوب توانم که کنم کار خویش
سازمش از عشق گرفتار خویش
گرچه نظامی است غلامش کنم
منصرف از عشق نظامش کنم
ی همه را گفت وقوی کرد دل
داد به خود جرات وشد مستقل
کرد نهان عجز وعیان ناز خویش
هیمنه ای داد به آواز خویش
گفت سلام ای پسر ماه وحور
چشم بد ازروی نکوی تو دور
ای زبشر بهتر و بگزیده تر
بلکه ز من نیز پسندیده تر

Still is he sullen, still he lours and frets,
'Twixt crimson shame and anger ashy-pale;
Being red, she loves him best; and being white,
Her best is better'd with a more delight.

Look how he can, she cannot choose but love;
And by her fair immortal hand she swears,
From his soft bosom never toremove,
Till he takes truce wit her contending tears,
Which long have rain'd, making her cheeks all wet;
And one sweet kiss shall pay this countless debt.

Upon this promise did he raise his chin?
Like a dive-dapper peering through a wave,
Who, being looked on, ducks as quickly in;
So offers he to give what she did crave;
But when her lips were ready fo his pay,
He winks, and turns his lips another way.

Never did passenger in summer's heat
More thirst for drink than she for this good turn.

ای گه پس از خلق تو خلاق من
همچو خلایق شده مشتاق تو
ای تو بهین میوه باغ بهی
غنچه سرخ چمن فرهی
چین سرزلف عروس حیات
خال دلارای رخ کاینات
در چمن حسن گل و فاخته
سرخ وسفیدی به رخت تاخته
بسکه تو خلقت شده ای شوخ وشنگ
گشته به خلقت کن تو عرصه تنگ
کزپس تو باز چه رنگ آورد
حسن جهان را به چه قالب برد
بی تو جهان هیچ صفایی نداشت
باغ امید آب وهوایی نداشت
قصد کجا داری ونام تو چیست
در دل این کوه مرام تو چیست
کاش فرود آیی از آن تیز گام
کز لب این چشمه ستانیم کام
در سر این سبزه منوتو بهم
خوش بهم آییم در این صبحدم
مغتنم است این چمن دلفریب
ای شه من پای در آر ازرکیب
شاخ گلی پا به سر سبزه نه
شاخ گل اندر وسط سبزه به
بند کن آن رشته به قربوس زین
جفت بزن از سر زین بر زمین
خواهی اگرپنجه بهم افکنم
وز دو کف دست رکابی کنم
تا تو نهی بر کف من پای خود
گرم کنی در دل من جای خود
یا که بنه پا به سر دوش من
سر بخور از دوش به آغوش من
نرم و سبک روح بیا در برم
تات چو سبزه به زمین گسترم
بوسه شیرین دهمت بی شمار
قصه شیرین کنمت صد هزار

Her help she sees but help her cannot get;
She bathes in water, yet her fire must burn:
'O, pity,' 'gan she cry, 'flint-hearted boy!
'Tis but a kiss I beg; why art thou coy?

I have been woo'd, as I entreat thee now,
Even by the srern and direful god of war,
Whose cinewy neck in battle never did bow
Who conquers where he comes in every jar;
Yet hath he been my captive and my slave,
And begg'd for that which thou unmask'd shalt have.

Over my altars hath he hung his lance,
His batter'd shield, his uncontrolled crest
And for my sake hath had learn'd to sport and dance.
To toy, to wanton, dally, smile and jest,
Scorning his churlish drum and ensign red
Making my arms his field, his tent my bed.

Thus he that overruled   I oversway'd,
Leading him prisoner in a red rose chain:

كوه وبيابان پى آهو مبر
غصه هم چشمى آهو مخور
گرم بود روز دل كوهسار
آهووكا دست بدار از شكار
حيف بود كز اثر آفتاب
كاهد از آن روى چو گل آب وتاب
يا ز دم باد جنايت شمار
بر سر زلفت به نشيند غبار
خواهى اگر با دل خود شور كن
هرچه دلت گفت همان طور كن
اين همه بشنيد منوچهر از او
هيچ نيامد به دل مه از او
روح جوان همچو دلش ساده بود
منصرف از ميل بت وباده بود
گرچه به به قد اندكى افزون نمود
سال وى از شانزده افزون نبود
كشمكش عشق نديده هنوز
لذت مستى نچشيده هنوز
با همه نوش لبى اى عجب
كز مى نوشش نرسيده به لب
بود در او روح سپاهيگرى
مانع دل با ختن و دلبرى
لا جرم از حجب جوابى ندا د
يافت خطايى وخطابى نداد
گويى چسبيده ز شهد زياد
لب به لب آن پسر حور زا د
زهره دگر باره سخن ساز كرد
زمزمه دلبرى آغاز كرد
كاى پسر خوب تعلل مكن
در عمل خير تا مل مكن
مهر مرا اى به تو از من درود
بينى و از اسب نيايى فرود؟
صبح به اين خرمى و اين چمن
با چمن آرا صنمى همچو من
حيف نباشد كه گرانى كنى
صابرى و سخت كمانى كنى

Strong-tmpered steel his stronger
strength obey'd

Yet was he servile to my coy
disdain.

O, be not proud, nor brag not of thy
might,

For mastering her that foil'd the god
of fight!

Touch but my lips with those fair
lips of thine,--

Though mine be not so fair, yet are
they red.—

The kiss shall be thine own as well
as mine.

What seest thou in the ground?hold
up thy head:

Then why not lips on lips, since eyes
in eyes?

Art thou ashamed to kiss? Then
wink again

And I will wink; so shall the day
seem night;

Love keeps his revels where where
they are but twain.

Be bold to play, our sport is not in
sight:

These blue-vein'd violets whereon
we lean

Never can blab,nor know not what
we mean.

The tender spring upon thy tempting
lip

Shows thee unripe; yet mayst thou
well be tasted;

Make use of time, let not advantage
slip;

لب مفشار اینهمه بر یکدگر
رنگ طبیعی ز لب خود مبر
بر لب لعلت چوبیاری فشار
رنگ طبیعی کند از وی فرار
یا برسد سرخی اورا شکست
یا کندش سرخ تر از آنچه هست
آنکه ترا این دهن تنگ داد
وان لب جان پر ور گلرنگ داد
داد که تا بوسه فشانی همی
گه بدهی گه بستانی همی
گاه به ده ثانیه بی بیش وکم
گیری سی بوسه ز من پشت هم
گاه یکی بوسه ببخشی ز خویش
مدتش از مدت سی بوسه بیش
بوسه اول ز لب آید به در
بوسه ثانی کشد از ناف سر
حال ببین میل کدامین تراست
هر دو هم ار میل تو باشد رواست
بازچو ای گفت و جوابی ندید
زور خدایی به تن اندر دمید
دست زد وبند رکابش گرفت
قیشه جان ورگ خوابش گرفت
خو اه نخواه از سر زینش کشید
در بغل خود به زمینش کشید
هردو کشیده سر سبزه دراز
هردو زده تکیه بر آرنج ناز
قد متوازی و محاذی دو قد
گویی که اندازه بگیرند قد
عارض هردو شده گلگون وگرم
این یکی از شهوت وآن یک ز شرم
عشق به آرزم مقابل شده
بر دوطرف مسا له مشگل شده
زهره طناز به انواع ناز
کرد بر او دست تمتع دراز
تکمه به زیر گلویش هر چه بود
با سر انگشت عطوفت گشود

Beauty within itself should not be wasted;
Fair flowers that are not gathere'd in their prime
Rot and consume themselves in little time.

Were I hard-favoured, foul, or wrinkled-old,
Ill nurtured, crooked, churlish, harsh in voice,
O'verworn, despised, rheumatic and cold,
Thick-sighted, barren, lean and lacking juice,
Then mightst thou pause, for then I were not for thee.
But having no defects, why dost abhore me?

'Thou canst not see one wrinkle in my brow;
Mine eyes are grey and bright and quick in turning;
My beauty as the spring doth yearly grow,
My flesh is soft and plump, my marrow burning;
My smooth moist hand, were it with thy felt,
Would in thy palm dissolve, or seem to melt.

'Bid me discourse, I will enchant thine ear,
Or, like a fairy, trip upon the green,
Or, like a nymph. with long dishevell'ed hair,

یافت چو با بی کلهی خوشترش
کج شد وبر داشت کلاه از سرش
دست به دو قسمت فرقش کشید
برقی از آن فرق به قلبش رسید
موی که نرم افتد وتیمار گرم
رفت که بوسد ز رخ فرخش
رنگ منوچهر پرید از رخش
خورد تکان جمله اعضای او
از نوک سر تا به کف پای اوی
گفت که ای دخترک با جمال
تهبیه در نطق توسحر حلال
با چه زبان از تو تقاضا کنم
شر ترا از سر خود وا کنم
گر به یکی بوسه تمام است کار
این لب من از آن لب تو هان بیار!
گر بکشد مهر تو دست از سرم
من سر تسلیم به پیش آورم
گر شوی از من به یکی بوسه سیر
خیز وعلی الاه و بیا وبگیر
عقل چو از عشق شنید این سخن
گفت که : یا جای تو یا جای من
عقل و محبت بهم   آو یختند
خون ز سر وصو رت هم ریختند
چون که یکی خون ز سر عقل ریخت
جست و زمیدان محبت گریخت
گفت برو آن تو وآن یار تو
آن به کف یار تو افسار تو
رو که خدا بر تو مدد کار باد
حافظت از این زن بد کار باد
زهره پی بوسه چو رخصت گرفت
بوسه خود از سر فرصت گرفت
همچو جوانی که شبان گاه مست
کوزه آب خنک آرد به دست
جست وگرفت از عقب او را به بر
کرد دو پا حلقه بر اوچون کمر
داد سرش را به دل سینه جا

Dance on the sands, and tet no
footing seen;
Love is a spirit all compact of fire,
Not gross to sink, but light, and will
aspire.

'Witness this primerose bank
whereon I lie;
These forceless flowers like sturdy
trees support me;
Two strenghless doves will draw me
through the sky,
From morn till night, even where I
list to sport me;
Is love so light, sweet, sweet boy,
and may it be
That thou shouldst think it heavy
unto thee?

'Is thine own heart to thine own face
affected?
Can thy right hand seize love upon
thy left?
Steal thine own freedom and
complain on theft.
Narcissus so himself himself
forsook, and died to kiss his shadow
in the brook.

'torches are made to light, jewels to
wear,
Dainties to taste, fresh beauty for
the use,
Herbs for their smell,and sappy
plants to bear;
Things growing to themselvesare
grow'ths abuse;
Seeds spring from seeds and beauty
breedeth beauty;

به به از آن متکی و متکا
دست به زیر زنخش جای داد
دست دگر بر سر دوشش نهاد
تار دو گیسوش کشیدن گرفت
لب به لبش هشت ومکیدن گرفت
زهره یکی بوسه ز لعلش ربود
بوسه مگو آتش سوزنده بود
بوسه ای از ناف در آمد برون
رفت دگر باره به ناف اندرون
هوش ز هم برده ومدهوش هم
هر دو فتادند در آغوش هم
کوه صدا داد از آن بانگ بوس
نوبتی عشق فرو کوفت کوس
داد یکی ز ان دوکبوتر صفیر
آه که شد کودک ما بوسه گیر !
آن دگری گفت که شادیم شاد
بوسه ده وبوسه ستان شاد باد !
یک وجب از شاخه بجستند باز
بوسه که رد شد بنشستند باز
خود ز شعف بود که ای پر زدند
یا ز اسف دست به هم بر زدند؟

. . . .
گفت برو ! کار ترا ساختم
در ره لاقیدیت انداختم
بار محبت نکشیدی بکش !
زحمت هجران نچشیدی بچش !
چاشنی وصل زدوری بود
مختصری هجر ضروری بود
تا سخط هجر بیابی همی
با دگران سخت نتابی همی
زهره چوبنمود به گردون صعود
باز منوچهر در آن نقطه بود
مست صفت سست شد اعصاب او
برد در آن حال کمی خواب او
از پس یک لحظه ز خمیازه ای
جست ز جا بر صفت تازه ای

Thou wast begot;to get it is thy duty.

'Upon the the earth's increase why
shouldst thou feed,
By law of nature thou art bound to
breed,
That thine may live when thou
thyself art dead;
And so, in spite of death, thou dost
survive,
In that thy lokeness still is left alive.

By this the love-sick queen began to
sweat,
For where they lay the shadow had
forsook them,
And Titan, tired in the mid-day heat,
With burning eye did hotly overlook
them;
Wishing Adonis had his team to
guide,
So he were like him and by
Venus'side.

And nw Adonis, with a lazy spright,
And with a heavy, dark, disliking
eye,
His louring brows o'erwhelming his
fair sight,
Like misty vapours when they blot
the sky,
Souring his cheeks cries 'Fie, no
more of love1
The sun doth burn my face : I must
remove.'

'Ay me,' quoth Venus, 'young, and
so unkind"

چشم چو ز ان خواب گر ان برگشود
غیر منوچهر شب پیش بود
دید کمی کوفتگی در تنش
لیک نشاطی به دل روشنش
گفتی از آن عالم تن در شده
وارد یک عالم دیگر شده
در دل او هست نشاط د گر
دور و بر اوست بساط د گر
جمله اعضای تنش تر شده
قالبش از قلب سبکتر شده
لحظه ای این گونه تصاویر داشت
پس تنش آ سود و عرق واگذاشت
چشم چوبگشود در آن دامنه
دید که جا تر بود و بچه نه
خواست رود دید که دل مانع است
پای هم البته به دل تابع است
عشق شکار از دل او سلب شد
رفت و شکار تیش قلب شد
هیچ نمیکند از آن چشمه دل
جان ودلش گشته بدان متصل
همچو لیمی که سر سبزه ها
گم کند انگشتری پر بها
گویی ماندست در آنجا هنوز
چیزکی از زهره گیتی فروز
بر رخ آن سبزه نیلی فراش
رفته ومانده است بجا جای پاش
از اثر پا که بر آن هشته بود
سبزه چو او داغ به دل گشته بود
می دهد اما به طریقی بدش
سبزه خوابیده نشان از قدش
گفت که گر گیرمش اندر بغل
نقش رخ سبزه پذیرد خلل
این سر و این سینه و این ران او
این اثر پای در افشان او
گر بزنم بوسه بر آن جای پای
سبزه خوابیده بجنبد ز جای

What bare excuses makest thou to
be gone!
I'll sigh celestial breath, whose
gentle wind
Shall cool the heat of this
descending sun :
I will make a shadow for the of my
hairs;
If they burn too, I'll quench them
with my tears.

The sun that shines from heaven
shines but warm
And, lo, I lie between that sun and
thee ;
That heat I have from thence doth
little harm,
Thine eye darts forth that fire that
burneth me;
And were I not immortal, life were
done
Between this heavenly and earthly
sun.

'Art thou obdurate, flinty, hard as
steel,
Nay, more than flint, for stone at
rain relenteth
Art thou a woman's son, and canst
not feel
What 'tis to love? How want of
lovetormenteth?
O, had thy mother borne so hard a
mind,
She had not brought forth thee, but
died unkind.

'What am I, that thou shouldst
contemn me this?

حیف بود دست بر این سبزه سود
به که بماند به همان سان که بود
این گره آنست که او بسته است
بر گره او نتوان برد دست
بسته اورا به چه دل وا کنم
به که بر این سبزه تماشا کنم
آه چه غرقاب مهیبی است عشق!
مهلکه پر ز نهیبی است عشق
غمزه خوبان دل عالم شکست!
شیر دل است آنکه از این غمزه رست

Chapter 10

Or what great danger dwels upon
my suit?
What were thy lips the worse for one
poor kiss?
Speak, fair ; but speak fair words, or
else be mute
Give me one kiss, I 'll give it thee
again,
And one for interest, if thou wilt
have twain.

'Fie, lifeless picture, cold and
senseless stone,
Well-painted idol, image dun and
dead,
Statue contending but the eye alone,
Thing, like a man, but of no
woman's complexion,
For men will kiss even by their own
direction.

This said, impatience chokes her
pleading tongue
And swelling passion doth provoke
a pause;
And now she weeps, and now she
fain would speak;
And now her sobs do her
intendments break.

Sometimes she shakes her head and
then his hand
Now gazeth she on him, now on the
ground;
Sometimesher arms infold him like
a band;
She would, he will not in her arms
be bound;

And when from thence he struggles
to be gone,
She locks her lily fingers one in one.

'Fondling,' she saith, 'since I have
hemm'd thee here
Within the circuit of this ivory pale,
I'll be a park, and thou shalt be my
deer;
Feed where thou wilt, on mountain
or in dale;
Grazeon my lips; and if those hills
be dry,
Stray lower, where the pleasant
fountains lie.

Within this limitis relief enough,
Sweet bottom-grass and high
delightful plain,
Round rising lillocks, brakes
obscure and rough,
To shelter thee from tempest and
from rain
Then be my deer; since I am such a
park;
No dog shall rouse thee, though a
thousand bark.

At this Adonis smiles as in disdain,
That in each cheek appears a pretty
dimple;
Love made those hollows, if himself
were slain, he might be buried in a
tomb so simple;
Foreknowing well, if there he came
to lie,
Why, there Love lived and there he
could not die.

Chapter 10

These lovely caves, these roun
enchanting pits,
Open'd their mouths to swallow
Venus' liking;
Being mad before, how doth she
now for wits?
Struck dead atfirst, what needs a
second striking?
Poor queen of love, in thei own law
forlorn,
To lve a cheek that smiles at thee in
scorn!

Now which way shall she turn?
What shall she say?
Her words are done, her woes are
more increasing;
The time is spent, her her object will
away,
And from her rweinig arms doth
urge releasing.
'Pity,' she cries, 'some favour, some
remorse!'
Away he springs and hasteth to his
horse.

But, lo, from forth a copse that
neighbors by,
A breeding jennet, lusty, young and
proud,
Adonis'trampling   courser   doth
espy,
And forth she rushes, snorts and
neighs aloud;
The strong –neck'd steed, being tied
unto a tree,
Breaketh his rein, and to her straight
goes he.

Imperiously he leaps, he neighs, he
bounds,
And now his woven girths he breaks
asunder;
The bearing earth with his hard hoof
he wounds,
whose hollow womb resounds like
heaven's thunder;
The iron bit he crusheth 'tween his
teeth,
Controlling what he was controlled
with.

His ears up-pricked'd; his braided
hanging mane
Upon his compasse'd crest now
stand on end;
His nostrils drink the air, and forth
again,
As from a furnace, vapours doth he
send;
His eye, which scornfully glisters
like fire,
Shows his hot courage and his high
desire;

Sometime he trots, as if he told the
steps,
With gentle majesty and modest
pride;
Anon he rears upright, curvets and
leaps,
As who should say 'Lo, thus my
strength is tried,

And this I do to captivate the eye
Of the fair breeder that is standing
by.'....

Chapter 10

....

Continue reading "Venus and Adonis" in Google.

Nima' Yushij 20th century Persian poet (Founder of the new style Persian poetry)

Nima Ushij (Ali Esfandiari) was born in 1897 at the village of Yush in Mazanderan. His family was originaly from Tabarestan with some roots from her mothere's side going back to Georgia. He grew up in the village of Yush. As a boy he visited many local summer and winter camps and mingled with shepherds and itinerant workers. Images of life around the campfire, especially those emerging from the sheperds' simple and entertaining stories about village and tribal conflicts impressed him greatly. These images etched in the young poet' memory waited until his power of diction developed sufficiently to release them.

Nima's early education took place in maktab khane (private school). He was a truant student and the mullah (the teacher) often had to seek him out in the streets, drag him to school, and punish him. At the age of twelve, Nima was taken to Teheran and registered at the St.Louis school which was run by the French missionary in Tehran. The atmosphere at this Roman Catholic school did not change Nima's ways and beheavior, but the instructions of one thoughtful teacher did. Nezam vafa, a major poet himself took the budding poet under his wing and nurtured his poetic talent.

Instruction at the Catholic school was in direct contrast to instruction at the Maktab khana. Similarly, living among the urban people was at variance with life among the tribal and rural peoples of the north. In addition both these lifestyles differed greatly from the description of the lifestyles about which he had read in his books or listened to in classroom. Although it did not change his attachments to tradition, the difference set fire to young Nima's imagination. In other words, even though Nima continued to write poetry in the tradition of Saadi and Hafez for quite sometime his expressin was being affected gradually and steadily. Eventually, the impact of the new empowered the tendency of tradition and led Nima down a new path. Consequently, Nima began to replace the familiar devices that enhanced free flow of concepts. "Ay Shab" (O Night) and "Afsaneh" (Myth) belong to this transitional period in the poet's life.

In general, Nima reformed the rhythm and allowed the length of the line to be determined by the depth of the thought being expressed rather than by the conventional Persian meters that had dictated the length of a bayt (verse) since the early days of Persian poetry. Furthermore, he emphasized current issues, especially nuances of oppression and suffering, at the expence of the beloved's moon face or the ever- growing conflict between the lovers, the beloved, and the

rival. In other words, Nima realized that while some readers were enthused by the charms of the lover

and the coquettish ways of the beloved, the majority preferred heroes with whom they could identify. Nima actually wrote quite a few poems in the traditional Persian poetry style and as critiqued by Abdolali Dastgheib, showed his ability well. However he felt the old ways limit his freedom to express his deep feelings or important issues faced by society. This led him to break free from the old classical styles of Persian poetry and create a whole new style for modern
poetry.

Along the Riverbank

Along the river bank wanders the old turtle
The day is a sunny day.

The old turtle is basking in the warm lap of the sun,
Sleep at ease
Along the riverbank.

Along the riverbank there's only me
Tired from the pain of desire,

Chapter 10

Awaiting my sun.
But my eyes
 cannot see it for an instant.

My sun
Has hidden its face from me in the distant waters.
For me everything is clear everywhere
In my standing,
In my hurrying ,
Only my sun is not clear
Along the riverbank.

In the Cold Winter Night

The furnace of the sun too
Burns not like the hot hearth of my
lamp,

And no lamp is luminous as mine
Neither has it frozen like the cold
moon shines above.
I lit my lamp when my neighbor was
walking in a dark night,
And it was a cold winter night,
The wind encircled the pine,
Amid silent heaps
She was lost from me, separated
from this narrow lane,
And still the story is remembered,
And on my lips these words lingered
'Who lights? Who burns?
Of my lamp

Who saves this tale of the heart?
 In the cold winter night
The furnace of the sun too
Burns not like the hearth

Hey People

Hey you over there
Who are sitting on the shore, happy
and laughing,
Someone is dying in the water,
Somone is constantly struggling

در شب سرد زمستانی

کوره خورشید هم چون کوره گرم چراغ
من نمی سوزد

و به مانند چراغ من
نه می افروزد چراغی هیچ
نه فروبسته به یخ ماهی که از بالا می
افروزد
من چراغم را در آمد رفتن همسایه
افروختم در یکشب تاریک
و شب سرد زمستان بود
باد میپیچید با کاج
در میان کومه ها خاموش
گم شد او از من جدا زین جاده باریک.
و هنوز هم قصه بر یاد است
وین سخن آویزه لب :
" که می افروزد؟ که میسوزد
چه کسی این قصه را در دل من می
انددوزد؟"
در شب سرد زمستانی
کوره خورشید هم چون کوره گرم چراغ
من نمی سوزد

آی آدمها

آی ادمها که بر ساحل نشسته شاد و
خندانید یک نفر در آب دارد می سپارد
جان
یک نفر دارد که دست و پای دایم می زند
روی این دریای تند وتیره و سنگین که
می دانید.
آن زمان که مست هستید از خیال دست
یابیدن به دشمن
آن زمان که پیش خود بیهوده پندارید

Chapter 10

On this angry, heavy, dark, familiar
sea.
When you are drunk
With the thought of getting your
hands on your enemy,
When you think in vain
That you have given a hand to a
weak person
To produce a better weak person,
When you tighten your belts, when?
When shall I tell you?

That someone in the water
Is sacrificing in vain?
Hey you over there
Who are sitting happy and laughing,
Someone is dying in the water
Someone is constantly struggling,
On this angry, heavy, dark familiar
sea.
When you are drunk
With the thought of getting your
hands on your enemy,
When you think in vain
That you have given a hand to weak
person,
When you tighten your belts, when,
When shall I tell you?
That someone in the water
Is sacrificing in vain?
Hey you over there
Who are sitting pleasantly on the
shore,!
Bread on your tables, clothes on
your back
Someone is calling you from the
water,
He beats the heavy wave with his
tired hand,

که گرفتسدید دست ناتوانی را
تا توانایی بهتر را پدید آرید
آن زمان که تنگ میبندید
بر کمر هاتان کمر بند.
در چه هنگامی بگویم من ؟
یک نفر در آب دارد میکند جان قربان !
آی آدمها که بر ساحل بساط دلگشا دارید !
نان به سفره جامه تان بر تن
یک نفر در آب می خواند شما را.
موج سنگین را به دست خسته می کوبد
باز می دارد دهان با چشم از وحشت دریده
سایه هاتان را ز راه دور دیده
آب را بلعیده در گود کبود و هر زمان بی تابیش افزون
می کند زین آبها بیرون
گاه سر گاه پا
آی آدمها
او ز راه دور این کهنه جهان را باز من پاید
می زند فریاد و امید کمک دارد
آی آدمها که روی ساحل آرام در کار تماشایید !
موج می کوبد به روی ساحل خاموش
پخش میگردد چنان مستی به جای افتاده.
بس مدهوش
می رود نعره زنان. وین بانگ باز از دور می آید
--"ای آدمها"....
و صدای باد هر دم دلگدازتر
در صدای بانگ باد از دورها
از میان آبهای دور و نزدیک
باز در گوش این نداها:

His mouth agape, eyes torn wide
with terror,
He has seen your shadows from a
far,
Has sowallen water from the deep
blue sea.
Each moment his impatience grows
He rises from these waters
A foot at times,

At times his head....
Hey you are there
He still has his eyes on this old
world from afar,
He is shouting and he hopes for
help,
Hey you there
Who are watching calmly from the
shore!
The waves beat on the silent shore,
Like a drunk fallen in his head,
unconscience
Receeds with a roar and this call
comes from afar again...
Hey you over there...
And the sound of the wind
More heart rending by the moment,
And his voice weaker in the sound
of the wind,
From waters near and far
Again this call is heard:
Hey, you overthere.....

Moon light

می تراود مهتاب
می درخشد شبتاب
نیست یکدم شکند خواب به چشم کس
ولیک

The moon beams
The glowworm glows
Sleep is seldom ruined, but

غم ای خفته چند

خواب در چشم ترم میشکند

نگران با من استاده سحر

صبح میخواهد از من

کز مبارک دم او آورم این قوم به جان

باخته را بلکه خبر

در جگر لیکن خاری

از ره این سفرم میشکند.

نازک آرای تن ساق گلی

که به جانش کشتم

و به جان دادمش آب

ای دریغا! به برم میشکند

دستها می سایم تا دری بگشایم

برعبت می پایم

که به در کس آید

در و دیوار بهم ریخته شان برسرم میشکند

می تراود مهتاب

می درخشد شبتاب

مانده پای آبله از راه دراز

بر دم دهکده مردی تنها

کوله بارش بردوش

دست او بر درمی گوید با خود:

غم این خفته چند

خواب در چشم ترم میشکند

Worry over this heedless lot
Ruins sleep in my tearful eyes.
Dawn stands worried at my side
Morning urges me to announce
Its arrival to the lot.
Alas a thorn inside,
Stops me in my tracks.
A delicate rose stem
Which I planted with my hands
And watered with my life
Its thorn break inside me.
I fumbled about to open my door
Uselessly expecting someone to meet

A jumble of walls and doors
Crambles over my head.
The moon beams
The glow-worm glows
Blisters make a distant road
Standing before the village
A lonely man
Knapsack on his back, hand on the knocker, murmurs
Worry over this lot
Ruins sleep in my tearful eyes.

It is night;

A Night of deep darkness,
On the branch of the old fig tree
A frog croaks without cease,
Predicting a storm,a deluge,
And I am drowned in fear.

Contemporary Persian Poetry

It is night,

And with night the world seems
Like a corps in the grave;
And in fear I say to myself;
"what if torrential rain fall
everywhere"?
"what if the rain does not stop
Until the earth sinks into water
Like a small boat?"

In this night of awful darkness

Who can say in what state we will
be,
When dawn breaks?
Will the morning light make
The frightening face of the storm
Disappear?.

Furthermore, Nima enhanced his images with personifications that were very different from the "frozen" imagery of the moon, the rose garden, and the tavern to name a few. His unconventional poetic diction took poetry out of the rituals of the court and placed it squarely among the masses. The natural speech of the masses necessarily added local color and flavor to his compositions. Lastly, and by far Nima's most dramatic element was the application of symbolism. His use of the symbols was different from the masters in that he based the structural integrity of his creations on the steady development of the symbols incorporated. In this sense, Nima's poetry could be read as a dialogue among two or three symbolic references building up into a cohesive semantic unit. In the past only Hafez had attempted such creations in his Sufic ghazals. The basic device he employed, however, was thematic, rather than symbolic unity. Symbolism although the avenue to the resolution of the most enigmatic of his ghazals, plays a secondary role in the structural make up of the composition.

The venues in which Nima published his works are noteworth. In the early years when the press was controlled by the powers that be, Nima's poetry, deemed below the established norm, was not allowed publication. For this reason, many of Nima's early poems did not reach the public until the 1930's. After the fall of Reza Shah, Nima became a member of the editorial board of the "Music" magazine. Working with Sadegh Hedayat, he published his work at his own expense. "The Pale story "and "The soldier's family."

The closing of "Music"magazine coincided with the formation of the Tudeh Party and the appearance of a number of leftist publications. Radical in nature, Nima was attracted to the papers and published many of his groundbreaking compositions in them.

Aref Qazvini 20th century Persian poet & reformist

Aref Qazvini as his name so indicates was born in Qazvin in 1882. He learnt the elementary sciences in Qazvin. But he had no expertise in panegyric and was attracted to live in Tehran which was only at a distance of 100 kilometer away to the east. Aref was a multi-talented bright youngman. A skilfull poet and musician with a great voice. These assets helped him greatly to find his way up to the important persons in the high ranks of the government, and the royal court. The Shah had him enrolled in the ranks of the royal valets. He found this distastefull and finally managed to obtain release. In private life, A'ref became a rogue, a heavy drinker, and a profligate, a condition aggravated by the failure of his marriage. In his last years he became withdrawn and suspicious and was described by some who met him as ill-natured and hot-tempered. A bronchial disorder which finally prevented him from singing added to his despair. Another incident that adversely affected his life was the rift in his long time friendship with Iraj Mirza during a trip to khorasan, ending up with the writing and publication of A'ref-nama by Iraj. Later on Aref moaned and complained that what Iraj did to him with his A'ref-nama was the most devastating blow to his life that finally caused his back to break. Despite his fame and the success of his concerts especially those at the Tehran Grand Hotel which yielded him a substantial income, he spent most of his life, in particular, the last years in such misery that he longed for an early death.

A'ref devoted his art to the people and used poetry as an effective means of expressing political ideas and stirring emotions. A whole-hearted supporter of the constitutionalists, he left Iran for Turkey with other militants in 1916 and stayed at Istanbul for sometime. A single qasida is all that survives before this journey. A few years later he joined Colonel Mohammad Taghi Khan Pesya'n who had rebelled in Khorasan in 1921. When Pesya'n died in a clash with Zafara'nlu Kurds, he mourned his death in several poems including a famous Tasnif. He also supported Sarda'r-e Sepah, the future Reza' Shah, in his call for abolishing the Qaja'r monarchy and the establishment of a republican state.

Aref's poetry totals about 150 gazals, tasnif, qeta'a, and mathnavi forms. He sometimes wrote melodius verses in literary style, but elsewhere he introduced slang that accorded well with the subject and mood; thus Malek-ol Shoara' Ba har described him as a "poet of common people". A fine calligrapher, he studied and copied the poetry of Saadi and Ha'fez. His most impressive and important works are his tasnifa't (song lyrics), which he composed in response to the political events of the day and sang to large and enthusiastic audiences. The tasnif had sunk to banality in wording and content, but he was able to impart a poetic quality to it. He had little knowledge of formal music but possessed an extraordinary keen ear; he was both a good judge of music and an original composer. Despite his boasts of mastery, he owed his fame mainly to the mood of the time and the revolutionary content of his poems. His authobiogrophy and some letters are preserved. He eventually went, or according to one source was banished To Hamada'n where he spent his remaining years in solitude and poverty. He died on 21 January 1934 and was buried in the courtyard of the Ebn Sina' mausoleum.

When constitutional era started, Aref was among the first poets who got involved in the revolutionary movement and applied his poetic and intellectual talents to this important historical event. Constututional Revolution was realized in 1905 and the charter was signed by Mozafar-ed-Din Shah. All revolutions bring about their own particular literature followed by their own tailor made evolutions to suit their own specific goals and aspirations. The authocracy of Qajar had evolved with almost 150 years of despotic rule, and deeply influenced by the colonial style rule of foreign powers. This produced its own particular Constitutional poetry that was the best form of a sympathetic historical necessity which featured mainly in the field of the content governing anti-authocratic and anti-colonial struggles applying its own specific methods. As will be seen later, the poets and thinkers in this period were inevitably depended on western achievements requiring rule of law, freedom, opposition to veil etc in their anti-colonial struggles.

Chapter 10

Aref was also one of the poets that were affected during the Constitutional era by the western civilization. Feeling of patriotism, and love to see Iran regain its ancient glory, dislike of and hatered towards the enemies of the mother land, deep nationalistic feelings and even entertaining the ideas of anti-colonial struggles to promote complete independence from foreign influence and meddling in the countrie's internal affairs that in those times were almost norm rather than exception. Such ideas were in those days the biggest source of inspiration for poets, especially Aref. This feature has a special manifestation in his diva'n, including:

The chicken's moaning is for
nothing but for homeland
The conduct of the chicken caught
in cage is the same as mine.
O fellow men make a thought about
their freedom
If not their condition will be the
same as mine
The volition I want from the wind at
dawn
To send news to my close friend
who is ignorant
Those who were zealous in the way
of their Land
Iran was settled again by their
blood, viva Iran.

A'ref always considered all of Iran as his home and that is why he never wanted to build a house for himself, because he thought this would be a kind of parochialism and desired Iran's entire landscape to flourish. For him the homeland was not merely a terrestrial range or part of geography but the symbol and manifestation of his ancestor's history and culture. His ancestor's blood was meddled with it and had made it sacrosanct.

A'ref's social and revolutionary concerns perpetuated from the early periods in his life to the time of his death. He was accompanied always with those who had inclinations towards social movements, uprising and transformation inspired by their feelings of sensationalism and credulity.

From the early days of the
Consitutional Revolution, Aref was
in tune with revolution and
libertianism.
For the martyr's blood to secure
freedom
Behold how the blood of Siavash
was raised by
Aref praised and promoted the
revolutionary ideals in his various
poems and ballads:
Down with the oppression of Zahak
(the legendry oppressor)
Up with Kaveh (the legendry hero
who revolted against Zahak)

Fereydoon Moshiri 20ᵗʰ century Persian poet

Fereydoon Moshiri was born in September 1926 in the city of Tehran. His family was known to have a legacy of poetry. His grandfather Javad khan Motamen-ol mamalek was a famous poet during the reign of Na'ser-ed Din Shah Ghaja'r. Fereydoon's father and mother were both intellectuals, well read and loved poetry. Fereydoon's elementary education was done in Mashhad, however the family returned to Tehran where he was able to finish his further education at Dar-ol-Fonoon high school. Fereydoon upon graduation got a job at the Ministry of Post and Telegraph and Telephone, where he served until retirement. Father and mother in the meantime nurtured and encouraged their son's interest in poetry and that was his first introduction to the exciting world of Persian literature.Throughout these years his early poems started to appear in progressive journals and magazines inTehran. This was the beginning of an outstanding literary career that continued for more than thirty years.

In 1954 he married Eghbal Akhavan then an art student at the University of Tehran. Before he was a poet, Fereydoon was a journalist and his occupation helped him to get acquainted with the distinguished literary scholars of Persian language and literature such as Ala'meh Dehkhoda, Dr Moin and Ibrahim Pourdavood.

Fereydoon began to compose verse at an early age. His first poem was published in Irane-ma' a periodical that published such noted poets as Mohammad Hoseyn Shahryar and Nima' Yushij and other prominent contemporary poets and writers. Moshiri received his diploma in 1965 and enrolled at the then Faculty of Literature of Teheran University, but due to apparently financial problems he never completed the course of study, switching to journalism instead. Finally he abandoned this field as well.

Notable among the magazines that Moshiri worked with were Sepid O siah, a literary and cultural magazine, and Sokhan, the monthly journal of Iranian studies founded in 1943 by Parviz Natel Khanlari. His most important contributions were as editor -in-chief, from 1953 to 1972, to the cultural pages of Roshanfekr, a weekly journal founded by Rahmat Mostafavi in 1953. During this period he was responsible for introducing many promising young poets to the public, the most notable among them were Forugh Farokhzad and Manuchehre Atashi. He is survived by two children, Baha'r and Ba'bak.

In1962 Moshiri was appointed a member of Radio Iran's Council of Writers, and in 1971 he joined the production unit of Radio Iran's Musical Council. In 1978 Moshiri retired from the Ministry of Post, Telegraph, and Telephone. In 1997 Moshiry travelled abroad and participated in nights of poetry reading in four cities in Germany, including Frankfurt and Berlin, and a number of American cities, including Los Angeles, Dallas, New York, and Miami.The events drew the warm applause of the audience. In 2005, five years after his death on 23 November 2000, a selection of his unpublished works appeared in two volumes, Az darichea-ye-mah (From the moon's window) and Navai hamahang-e baran (A song tuned to rain). Both collections almost like all collections that he published during his lifetime, include poems in Nimaie verse, as well as in classical and new traditionalist verse.

Moshirie's poetry is an invitation to kindness, humanity, and love, and he is considered among the most widely read Iranian poets of his generation. His poems of fragments thereof have often been set to music. Moshirie's early poems are usually romantic in imagery and tone. The majority of verses in Teshna-ye tufa'n are on the agonies of unrequited love or laments on the fickleness of the beloved. His next two collections, Gonaha-Darya' and Abr-o kucha, which includes one of his most celebrated poems, also deal largely with affairs of the heart.

The Alley

On a moonlit night once again
Through the alley, I wandered, without you.

My body, an eye gazing in search of you,
My soul, a cup teeming with anticipation
Of seeing you,
Now, I became the mad lover, a new!

Deep in my soul's treasure- chest,
A flower, your memory, gleaming.
The garden of a thousand memories, smiling,
The scent of a thousand memories, beaming

That night, I recalled,
Through the alley, we wondered, side by side.
Wings wide- open, in cherished solitude, soaring.

For a time, by the brook, resting

You, all the world's secrets in your black eyes,

I, by your glances, mesmerized.

Clear skies, quiet night,
Faith smiling, time tame

بی تو مهتاب شبی باز از آن کوچه گذشتم

همه تن چشم شدم خیره به دنبال تو گشتم
شوق دیدار تو لبریز شد از جام وجودم
شدم آن عاشق دیوانه که بودم

در نهانخانه جانم گل یاد تو درخشید
باغ صد خاطره خندید
عطر صد خاطره پیچید

یادم آمد که شبی با هم از آن کوچه گذشتیم
پر گشودیم و در آن خلوت دلخواسته گشتیم

ساعتی بر لب آن جوی نشستیم.

تو همه راز جهان ریخته در چشم سیاهت

من همه محو تماشای نگاهت

آسمان صاف وشب آرام

بخت خندان وزمان رام

Moonlight, grapes pouring down into the water.
Tree branches, fingers reaching up to the moon.

خوشه ماه فروریخته در آب
شاخه ها دست برآورده به مهتاب

The night, the meadow, flowers and rocks,
Silently charmed by the nightingale's song.

شب و صحرا و گل وسنگ
همه دل داده به آواز شباهنگ

Your words of warning, I recalled,
Avoid this love!

یادم آید تو به من گفتی :"از این عشق حذر کن !

Behold this brook for a while!
Water mirrors timid love.

لحظه ای چند بر این آب نظر کن !
آب آیینه عشق گذران است

Today, you care for a glance of your lover,
But, tomorrow, your heart will belong to another.

تو که امروز نگاهت به نگاهی نگران است !
باش فردا که دلت با دگران است !

Leave this town for a while.
Forget this love!

تا فراموش کنی چندی از این شهر سفر کن !"

How would I avoid this love!

با تو گفتم : - "حذر از عشق ؟ ندانم سفر از پیش

I do not know how! I cannot!

تو هرگز نتوانم

That first day, my heart became a bird of desire.
Like a dove, I perched on your roof,

روز اول که دل من به تمنای تو پر زد
چون کبوتر لب بام تو نشستم

Rocks, you threw at me,
I did not fly away.
I did not fall apart.

تو به من سنگ زدی ! من نه رمیدم نه گسستم."

A prairie deer is I, you the hunter.
Round your traps I wandered and wandered,
For to be captured by you, to surrender!

باز گفتم که: تو صیادی ومن آهوی دشتم
تا به دام تو در افتم همه جا گشتم و گشتم

How would I avoid this love!
I do not know, I said.
How would I leave your side, I cannot
From a branch, a leaf, falling,
A bitter moan, an owl flying,
Tears in your eyes, gleaming,
Moon, at your love, beaming!

حذر از عشق ندانم!
سفر از پیش تو هرگز نتوانم نتوانم !"

برگی از شاخه فرو ریخت !
مرغ شب ناله تلخی زد وبگریخت !
اشگ در چشم تو غلتید
ماه بر عشق توخندید !

You fell silent, I recall.

Covered by a blanket of gloom,

I did not fly away.
I did not fall apart.

یادم آید که دگر از توجوابی نشنیدم .
پای در دامن اندوه کشیدم.
نگسستم نرمیدم....

Many a night have passed in melancholy darkness
You have abandoned your tormented lover.

رفت در ظلمت غم آن شب وشبهای دگر هم !
نه گرفتی دگر از عاشق آزرده خبر هم

You would not set foot in that alley again!
Oh, but how, but how!
Through the alley, I wondered, without you.

نه کنی دیگر از آن کوچه گذر هم....!
بی تو اما به چه حالی من از آن کوچه گذشتم....

While with the passage of time Moshiri no longer composed as much amorous verse, erotic love remains, an area of interest, and romantic poetry continues, to the very end, to appear in all of his collections—a characteristic for which Moshiri's poem are often criticized.

Chapter 10

References to natural elements, birds and flowers, sea and sky, wind and rain, the sun and moon—abound in Moshirie's poems.
His nature poems, although not fully bereft of urban settings and imageries more often depict idyllic settings. He has written extensively in admiration of spring and its manifestations:

Lucky those Half-opened Buds
خوش به حال غنچه های نیمه باز

The scent of rain, the scent of greens, the scent of soil,	بوی باران بوی سبزه بوی خاک
Washed boughs rained on, clean	شاخه های شسته باران خورده پاک
Blue sky and white cloud,	آسمان آبی و ابر سپید
The green leaves of willow	برگ های سبز بید
The perfume of narcissus, dance of the winds,	عطر نرگس رقص باد
The passing song of joyfull swallows,	نغمه شاد پرستو های شاد
The intimate sanctum of intoxicated birds….	خلوت گرم کبوتر های مست
Warm seclusion of drunken sparrows,	نرم نرمک میرسد اینک بهار
Gently, gently arrives the spring,	خوش به حال روزگار
Lucky world!	

Ira'nema, Iran-e Javdan ma	ایران ما ایران جاودان ما
The meaning of my life is to be with you…	معنای زنده بودن من با تو بودن است
That moment which without you passes, let there not be.	آن لحظه ای که بی تو سراید مرا مباد
The significance of my death,	مفهوم مرگ من
In honoring you, beside you,	در راه سرفرازی تو در کنار تو
Is the significance of my life!	مفهوم زندگی است
The meaning of love too,	معنای عشق نیز
In my destiny,	در سرنوشت من
	با تو همیشه با تو برای تو زیستن.

With you, always with you, for you
to live.

Although classical schemes have never been absent from Moshiri's poetry corpus, the majority of his popular or most celebrated poems are composed in Nimaic meters. Examples include "Ja'm agar beshkast" and" Kuche" (Abr o kuche), and "jadu-ye bi Asar". Moshiri never tried his hand in free verse, or at least he never published any.

While many of poems chronicle life's trava'ils, the dignity he gives to the pains of existence and his accepting outlook on life have a notable presence in his work. In this manner Moshiri affirms life and advocates optimism, without denying the difficulties of existence.

Although long poems, occasionally longer than demanded by the poem's content, are not in Moshiri's collections, many of his poems, often written in short or relatively short classical schemes such as roba'I or ghazal, benefit from brevity. Moshiri's language is relatively straightforward, both in the expressions employed and in his turn of phrase. His poems are generally devoid of obscure or obtuse references and do not convey other meanings than that which first meets the eye.

To have a mother…	مادر داشتن…
Removing the sky's crown from its summit, Wearing that crown eternally..	تاج از فرق فلک برداشتن جاودان آن تاج بر سر داشتن
Gaining entry to the paradise of desire,	در بهشت آرزو ره یافتن هر نفس شهدی به ساغر داشتن
Raising nectar-filled goblets with each breath.	
Days spent in plenty and pleasure, Nights spent embrasing a beauty.	روز در انواع نعمت ها وناز شب بتی چون ماه در بر داشتن
At dawn, from atop the world, like sunlight,	صبح از بام جهان چون آفتاب

Illuminating the face of the universe.	روی گیتی را منور داشتن
At dusk, like the dream-maker moon, Charming heavens and stars.	شامگه چون ماه رویا آفرین ناز بر افلاک و اختر داشتن
Like the morning breeze in"the sky's green meadow" Fluttering wings alongside the doves.	چون صبا در مزرع سبز فلک بال در بال کبوتر داشتن
Attaining the nobility and splendor of Solomon, Gaining the glory and grandure of Alexander.	حشمت و جاه سلیمان یافتن شوکت و فر سکندر داشتن
Forever living at the pinacle of power, Seizing the realm of existence.	تا ابد در اوج قدرت زیستن ملک هستی را مسخر داشتن
I'll bestow all upon you, For what delights me more, even if for a moment, It is the pleasure of having a mother!	بر تو ارزانی که ما را خوشتر است لذت یک لحظه مادر داشتن

Translated by: Faranak Moshiri.

The clarity of Moshiri's syntax and the grammatically correct phrases and sentences he employs, the beautiful and easily accessible imageries of his poems, and the sustained balance between the old and new poetry by which his work is recognized, have earned him the praise of scholars of Persian literature. On the other hand, his detractors among literary critics, especially those not inclined toward classical poetry, are not few. Some criticize the emotional overtone of his work as skin-deep and lacking in intellect, and others find fault with the didactic overtone of his poems, the position he takes between the traditionalists and the modernists, and his reluctance to experiment with new forms.

Contemporary Persian Poetry

The relative absence of politically charged imagery in Moshiri's poems has led some to criticize him for lacking social sensitivity and perspective. It should be noted, however, that Moshiri's last two collections Az Dariche-ye mah and Nava'i hama'hang-e baran published after his death, do include many poems, charged with social motifs and ideas. In some of these poems, he even places a finger on specific socio-political problems and joins the ranks of many dissidents in expressing a deep concern over the suppression of ideas and the nation's political inequities.

A breeze from the land of peace	نسیمی از دیار آشتی
Indeed, if someday someone asks me "During your time on earth, what did you do?"	باری اگر روزی کسی از من بپرسد "چندی که در روی زمین بودی چه کردی؟"
I will open my book of verse before him, I will hold my head up, laughing, crying	من میگشایم پیش رویش دفترم را گریان و خندان بر می افرازم سرم را
I will say that this seed is "newly sown" It needs time to come to fruition and bloom.	آنگاه میگویم که :بذری نوفشانده است تا بشکفد تا بر دهد بسیار مانده است
Under this vast cerulean sky, With all my might, in every song,	در زیر این نیلی سپهر بی کرانه چندان که یارا داشتم در هر ترانه
I evoked the revered name of love. Perhaps, by this weary voice, An oblivious someone was awakened, Somewhere in the four corners of this world! I praised kindness, I battled against wickedness.	نام بلند عشق راتکرار کردم با این صدای خسته شاید خفته ای را در چارسوی این جهان بیدار کردم
	من مهربانی را ستودم من با بدی پیکار کردم

I suffered the "wilting of a single stem of flower",
I grieved the "death of a caged canary,"

"پژمردن یک شاخه گل"را رنج بردم
"مرگ قناری را در قفس" غصه خوردم

And, for people's sorrow,
I died a hundred times a night.
I am not ashamed if at times,
When one ought to have screamed from deep within,
With Jesus-like patience,
I kept my silene.

وز غصه مردم شبی صد بار مردم
شرمنده از خود نیستم گر چون مسیحا
آنجا که فریاد از جگر باید کشیدن
من با صبوری بر جگر دندان فشردم

If I were to arm myself with a sword,
To fight against the ignoranc,

اما اگر پیکار با نابخردان را
شمشیر باید می گرفتم

Blame me not for taking the road to love.

بر من نگیری من به راه مهر رفتم

A sword in hand implies,
A man may meet his demise.

در چشم من شمشیر در مشت
یعنی کسی را میتوان کشت

We were passing through a bleak road,
Where the darkness of ignorance was devastating!

در راه باریکی که از آن میگذشتم
تاریکی بی دانشی بیداد میکرد

My belief in humanity was my torch!
The sword was in devil's hand!
Words were my only weapon in this battlefield!

ایمان به انسان شبچراغ راه من بود
شمشیر دست اهرمن بود
تنها سلاح من در این میدان سخن بود

Many endless nights, I did not sleep,
To re-tell humanitie's message from man to man,
In the thorny land of animosity,

شب های بی پایان نخفتم
پیغام انسان را به انسان بازگفتم
حرفم نسیمی از دیار آشتی

My words were a freeze from the
land of peace.

بود

But, perhaps, they should've been a
mighty windstorm,To uproot all this
wickedness.

Translated by: Farank Moshiri.

Moshirie's literary career, unlike those of many of his contemporarians, did
not change shape and content in parallel with the dominant social and political
ideas and trends, and instead it followed a smooth path marked by his concern
over the dehumanizing materialism of modern times, the ravages of war, and
the increased aggression and hatered in the world (Ashgi dar gozargah tarikh,
Kuche, Bah'r ra' ba'var kon and Az dia're-ashena'ie.)
His call to stay true to humanistic and moral values, gives him a signature
voice in modern Persian poetry.

Sohra'b Sepehri 20th century Persian poet & painter

Sohrab was born in Qom on October 1928, a very talented artist and a gifted
poet, He rose to stardom with the publication of the The Water's Footfall
which was subsequently followed by the Traveler and the Green Volume.
Sepehri is so popular with the Iranians that he is usually known by his first
name "Sohra'b" as if he is a friend everyone knows and understands. Sohra'b
travelled beyond the normal trajectory of everyday meanings. He translated
speech into a language hitherto unknown to Iranians. A pioneer poet, he
utilized western forms and reconstructed the normal way of poetry. His use of
new forms in poetry makes him complicated to understand.Yet, readers find
themselves so attached to him and his poetry that there remains no room for
boredom. Readers are so immersed in his poetry that they sometimes forget
the world of realities and experience a fresh recognition of man and the whole
universe.

 With the exception of the first few months of Sohra'b's life, his family lived
in Kashan. His father worked at the local office of the Ministry of Post and
Telegraph and Telephone. Sepehri's grandfather Mirza' Mohammad Taghi
Kha'n Lessan ol-Molk Sepehr was the noted 19th century historian and

scholar, the author of Na'sekhol-Tavarikh. During the first few years of his life Sohrab lived with his family in their ancestral home; a large and beautiful home surrounded by orchards and gardens full of flowers and a refreshing small stream giving the residence a refreshing and pleasant atmosphere which was eched in Sohrab' childhood memory for as long as he lived and was later recounted in his posthumously published book, Ota'ghe-A'bi (the blue room). Sohrab's early schooling was done in Kasha'n where he started painting and reading literary articles leading to writing his first short poem at the age of ten. He completed his high school education in Kasha'n and when the large family house that was home to Sohrab with all the happy memories of his childhood was sold, he moved to Teheran to attend the Teacher's training school .Upon graduation in 1945, he returned to ka'shan and got a job as a school teacher where he met the poet Abba's Keymanesh who got him seriously involved with writing poetry and that changed for ever Sohra'b's life. His early introduction into Persian poetry was the poetries of Sa'eb Tabrizi and Bidel who profoundly influenced his poetic work. In summer of 1947 he published his first book of poetry titled Dar ken'-a'r'e a'ra'mga'h-e eshgh (Along the love's resting place) followed by Memories of Youth, remembering his childhood years in Ka'shan. Around the same time he met the poet and painter Manuchehr Sheyba'ni who introduced him to the works of Vincent van Gogh and poetry of Nima'youshij, both of whome deeply influenced his style of writing poetry and painting.

At this time he quit his job in Kasha'n and moved toTehran and enrolled at the Faculty of Fine Arts of Teheran University, where he graduated with honors. Sohra'b's first poem influenced by the Nima's style entitled "Bima'r" (the paient) was published in September 1948 in the journal Jaha'-e now in Teheran.

In fall 1951, Sepehri published his first collection of Nimaic poetry titled Marge-rang (the death of color).The early 1950's has marked the beginning of his friendship and acquaintance with other notable poets and painters, many of them would become important figures in the Persian modernism in their own right, namely Forugh Farokhza'd, Marco Gregorian, painter, Parviz Kalantari, Bahman Mohasses, painter, Na'der Na'derpour, poet, Nosrat Rahmani, poet, Sa'degh Tabrizi, painter, and Parviz Tanavoli, sculpter. Around this time he also met Biyuk Mostafavi a long- life friend, to whom Sepehri later dedicated Hajm-e Sabz (the expanse of green).

Contemporary Persian Poetry

In 1953 upon graduation from Tehran University, took a position with the Organization of Public Health and collaborated with the art magazine, Panja Khorus. This same year he participated in a number of group exhibits and published his third book of poetry, Zendegi-e Kha'bha' (The life of dreams), with one of his own paintings on the cover. In 1954 took a position in the Office of Fine Arts, and started teaching in the school of Fine Arts. (Honarest'an-e honarhay-eziba'.) During the course of the next two years Sepehri published translations of Japanese, French and English poetry along with some of his own poems. In 1956 he participated in a group show at the Mehregan Club, and in August 1957 he travelled to Paris, where he enrolled in a lithograph course at the Ecole Nationale Superieure des beaux–arts. His letters from his stay in Paris provide a candid vista into Sepehries' growing connection to nature and his painful awareness of people's disconnect from their surroundings, both themes characteristic of his later poems. On August 1958 a number of his paintings were exhibited in the first Tehran Biennale. Four were selected together with works by other Persian artists and sent to the Venice Biennale. Later that spring Sepehri participated in the Venice biennale before returning to Tehran, where he worked at the Ministry of Agriculture as a supervisor of audio-visual programs.

In January 1960 Sepehri briefly travelled to Tokio before returning to Tehran to participate in the second Tehran biennale, where he won the grand prize of the arts. Very soon Homayun Sanatizadeh, director of the Franklin Book Program purchased 150 of Sepehrie's paintings depicting desert scenes. That August Sepehri used the proceeds from his sale to return to Tokyo to study woodlock with Unichi Hiratuska, one of the most noted names of the 20th century Japanese art. On his way home in late winter 1961 he travelled to India for the first of several visits that would leave a permanent mark on his creative life. Back inTehran Sepehri had his first solo exhibit at Reza' Abbasi Gallery and a group show at the Export Bank of Iran (Bank Sa'derat Iran). In September he took a teaching job at the school of Decorative arts (Honarkadeh-e Honarhay-e Tazieni) and gave up his post six months later. This same year three of his poems appeared at an anthology of modern Persian poetry called Nemuneha'y-e sh'ear –e Aza'd. He also published his next book of poetry A'va'r-e a'fta'b (The downpour of Sunshine). In May- June of 1962 Sepehri had another solo exhibit at Farhang Gallery and published, along with a number of his poems, translation of Chinese poetry in Sokhan, a prominent academic literary journal edited by Parviz Natel Khanlari.

Chapter 10

In 1963 Sepehri had six solo and group exhibition, and one of his paintings appeared on the cover of Na'derpour's selected poems entitled Bargozide-ye asha'r- Na'der Na'derpour. That same year Abby Weed Grey purchased a number of his paintings for the Ben and Abby Grey Foundation. These pieces were subsequently included in a show called fourteen contemporary Iranian Artists, which opened in Tehran before circulating in the Unite States for four years under the auspices of the Western Association of Art Museums. A selection of these and other paintings by Sepehri were later included in other exhibits funded by Grey Foundation, namely Contemporary Art of India and Iran, which circulated throughout the United States by the Smithsonian Institutute Travelling Exhibition program from 1967 to 1969, and One World Through Art, at the Minesota State Fairgrounds Gallery in 1972.

In 1964 the journal Musiqi (est.March 1939, Tehran) a prominent literary and artistic journal edited by Ghola'm- Hossein Minba'shia'n, published Sepehrie's translation of a Japanese play, A'han (Iron) written and directed by Khojastea Kia. This same year he travelled extensively throughout India, Pakistan, and Afghanistan. In 1965 he had one group and one solo exhibition in the Borghese Gallery in Tehran, and published his poem "Seda;-ye- Pa'ye-a'b" (The Sound of Water's Footsteps)" in A'rash, a popular modern literary journal of the 1960's edited by Sirus Ta'hba'z. The poem, which made a great impact at the time also, showed that the poet had at last found his own voice and style. The year also marked the beginning of Spehri's decade-long work on his famous tree trunk painting series. For the next two years Sepehri continued his extensive travels visiting Munich and London in 1965, and France, Spain, Holland, Italy, and Austria the following year. In 1966 he published the "Mosafer" (Traveller), again in A'rash, and translations of hymns from the Rig Veda.

The death of Forough Farokhza'd in a car accident on 13 February 1967 had a profound impact on Iranian literati in general, and Sepehri in particular. As reflected in his famous elegy for her called "Doost" (Friend, Hajm-e sabz, 1968). With her death Sepehri lost not only a friend, but a fellow poet who shared much of his world, vision and sensibilities, both emotional and poetic.

In 1968 Sepehri published Hajm-e sabz. Its release coincided with the opening of his exhibit at Seyhoon Gallery in February 1968. In the next decade he published few poems yet he remained extremely active as a painter. In April and March 1969 he travelled to London and then to Cagnes-sur- Mer in

South of France where he exhibited his work at the town's International Art Festival. In late spring 1970, Sepehri went to New York and briefly stayed with his friend Manuchehr Yekta'i in Long Island before moving to Manhattan in the August for eight months, during which time he had a group show in Bridgehampton. After a brief return to Tehran he was back in Manhattan for a solo exhibit at Elain Benson Gallery. He had an extended stay in Paris in 1974 and travelled to Greece and Egypt on his way back to Iran. In 1975 he parcipitated in Tehran's International Arts Festival, and later that year he received the Forough Farokhzad Poetry Award. In winter 1977 Sepehri moved back to Kasha'n, purchased a home and published Hasht keta'b (Eight books), an almost complete collection of his published work since Marg-e rang with the addition of the new collection Ma'hich, ma'nega'h (We nothing but gaze.).

In 1978 Sepehri had another solo exhibit at Seyhoon Gallery.
This would be his last exhibit before his untimely death; in fall of 1979 Sohra'b Sepehry was diagnosed with leukemia. He travelled to London with his sister Paridokht in December 1979, where they stayed until January 1980 for treatment, before returning to Tehran. On 2 April 1980 Sohra'b was admitted to Tehran's Pa'rs Hospital where he died at 6.00 PM on 21 April 1980.

And let's not fear death.
Death is not the end of the pigean
Death is not a chain turned inside out.
Death flows in the memory of acacia,
Death lives in the thought's happy trend.
Death speaks of the arrival of morning in passage through the village night.
Death comes to the mouth with a bunch of grapes!
Death sings a song in the laryncs of the throut
Death is responsible for the beauty of the wings of the papillon.
Death sometimes picks a bunch of basil.
Death sits in the shadow sometimes, looking at us!
And we all know that the lungs of pleasure are filled with the oxygen of death.

و نترسیم از مرگ
مرگ پایان کبوتر نیست
مرگ وارونه یک زنجیره نیست
مرگ در ذهن اقاقی جاریست
مرگ در آب و هوای خوش اندیشه نشیمن دارد
مرگ در ذات شب دهکده از صبح سخن میگوید
مرگ با خوشه انگور می آید به دهان
مرگ در حنجره سرخ گلو میخواند
مرگ مسول قشنگی پر شاپرک است
مرگ گاهی ریحان می چیند
گاه در سایه نشسته است به ما مینگرد
و همه میدانیم ریه های لذت پر اکسیژن مرگ است.

روی سنگ مزارش با خطی خوش این
سه بیت از او نقش بسته است

به سراغ من اگر می آیید
نرم و آهسته بیایید-مبادا که ترک بردارد
چینی نازک تنهایی من

If you come to call on me, Tread gently, and step softly lest you crackThe fine porcelain of my loneliness

Sohra'b was a child of nature. Just like a child nestled in the bosom of his mother, Sohra'b finds rest in the bosom of nature. He regards great respect for nature and whatever is relevant to it. He looks at nature and the creatures within it in the manner of a lover who sees no fault with the beloved. He is a true worshiper who loves God and his creatures, believing that one has planted the flower of love in his heart for the entire universe. To Sora'b, love is everything. Well-versed in Buddhism, mysticism and western traditions, he mingled the western concepts with those of the east, thereby creating a kind of poetry unsurpassed in the history of modern Persian literature. To him, new forms are new means to express his thoughts and his feelings. His poetry is, indeed, like a journey. Every time you read him you understand him differently. There is a bottomless ocean of meanings in his poetry.

Sohrab takes onto a journey of an unknown world where ugly things become beautiful and despised objects become a centre of attention to the readers:
I don't know,
Why a horse is a noble animal and a
dove is lovely?

And why no one keeps a vulture.
I don't know why a clover should be
inferior to a red tulip.

We need to rinse our eyes, and view
things differently.

We should wash our words
To both wind and rain.

In Sohrab's worldview, beauty is not an abstract concept: it is created and strengthened by people. He follows Shakespeare in that there is nothing good or bad but thinking makes it so. Therefore, he invites us to wash our eyes and view the world differently. Sohra'b left us a miracle of words and meanings.

Water

Let us not muddy the brook!
Perhaps a pigeon is drinking the
water at a distance,

آب را گل نکنیم
در فرودست انگار کفتری میخورد آب
یا که در بیشه ای دور سیره ای پر میشوید

Or perhaps in a farther thicket a
goldfinch is washing her feathers.
Or a picher is being filled in a
village.
Let us not muddy the brook;
Perhaps this brook runs to a
poplar's foot,
To wash away the grief of a lonely
heart!
A dervish may be dipping dry bread
in the brook.
A beautiful lady walked to the brink
of the brook.
Let us not muddy the brook.
The lovely face has been doubled.
What refreshing water!
What a spring river!
How friendly seem the folk at the
upper village!
May their springs always gush; may
their cows always render milk!
I have not seen their village,
Surely God's footprints lie at the
foot of their huts.
There moonlight enlightens the
expanse of words.
Surely in upper village the hedges
are low;
There the folk know what sort of
flower is anemone!
Surely there the blue is blue.
A bud is blossoming, the village
inhabitants know.
O what a fine village it must be!
May its orchard–lanes be full of
music!
The folk upstream understand the
water.

یا در آبادی کوزه ای پر میگردد
آب را گل نکنیم
شاید این آب روان می رود پای سپیداری
تا فروشوید اندوه دلی.
دست درویشی شاید نان خشکیده فروبرده
در آب
زن زیبایی آمد لب رود
آب را گل نکنیم
روی زیبا دو برابر شده است
چه گوارا این آب !
چه زلال این رود !
مردم بالا دست چه صفایی دارند !
چشمه هاشان جوشان گاوهاشان شیر
افشان باد
من ندیدم دهشان
بی گمان پای چپرهاشان جا پای خداست
ماهتاب آنجا می کند روشن پهنای کلام
بی گمان در ده بالا دست چینه ها کوتاه
است
مردمش میدانند که شقایق چه گلی است
بی گمان آنجا آبی آبی است
غنچه ای میشکفد اهل ده باخبرند
چه دهی باید باشد
کوچه هایش پر موسیقی باد !
مردمان سر رود آب را میفهمند
گل نکردندش ما نیز
آب را گل نکنیم.

They did not muddy the brook. We must not either!

Address

خانه دوست کجاست؟

"Where is the friend's house?" The rider asked in the twilight.Heaven paused; the passerby bestowed the bough of light on his lips to darkness of sands and pointed to a poplar and said:
(Just before the tree)
There is a lane greener than God's dream
Where love is as blue as the feathers of truth!
Go to the end of that lane that leads behind puberty
Turn toward the flower of solitude,
Two steps before the flower,
You will stop next to the immortal fountain of earthly myths
Where a translucent feat takes hold of you!
There, in the fluid sincerity of the atmosphere,
You will hear a rusling:
You will see a child,
Who has climbed up a pine tree!
To take a nestling from light's nest.
And there you ask the child:
Where is the friend's house?
(Hasht Keta'b, p.359

خانه دوست کجاست؟ در فلق بود که پرسید سوار
آسمان مکثی کرد
رهگذر شاخه نوری که به لب داشت به تاریکی شب ها بخشید
و به انگشت نشان داد سپیداری وگفت:
"نرسیده به درخت
کوچه باغی است که از خواب خدا سبز تر است
و در آن عشق به اندازه پرهای صداقت آبی است
می روی تا ته آن کوچه که از پشت بلوغ سر به در می آرد
پس به سمت گل تنهایی می پیچی
دو قدم مانده به گل
پای فواره جاوید اساطیر زمین می مانی
و ترا ترسی شفاف فرا میگیرد
در صمیمیت سیال فضا خش خشی می شنوی
کودکی می بینی
رفته از کاج بلندی بالا جوجه بردارد از لانه نور
واز او میپرسی
خانه دوست کجاست

Beyond the Seas

پشت دریا ها

I will build a boat
And cast it into water
And I will sail far away from this
strange land
Where no one awakens the heroes
In the glade of love;
A boat with no nets
And a heart with no desire for pearls
I will keep sailing
And will lose no heart to the blue of
the sea,
Or to mermaids
Emerging out of water to cast the
charms of their locks
Upon the glowing solitude of the
fishermen.
I will keep sailing
I will keep singing: "Away should
we sail".
Men of that town had no myths
Women of that town were not as full
as a bunch of grapes
No hall mirrors reflected joys
We should sail away and away
Night has sung its song
It is now the window's turn
I will keep singing
I will keep sailing
Beyond the seas there is a town
Where windows are open to the
epiphanies
The rooftops are inhabited by
pigeons
Gazing at the fountains of Human
Intelligence
Every ten-year –old child holds a
bough of knowledge
The townfolks see in a brick row a
flame,

قایقی خواهم ساخت
دور خواهم شد از این خاک غریب
که در آن هیچ کسی نیست که در بیشه ی
عشق
قهرما نان را بیدار کند.
قایق از تور تهی
و دل از آرزوی مروارید.
همچنان خواهم راند.
نه به آبی ها دل خواهم بست
نه به دریا
حوریان دریایی که سر ار آب به در می
آرند
و در آن تابش تنهایی ماهی گیران
می فشانند فسون از سر گیسو ها شان.
همچنان خواهم راند. همچنان خواهم
خواند:
"دور باید شد دور".
گرد آن شهر اساطیر نداشت.
زن آن شهر به سرشاری یک خوشه
انگور نبود.
هیچ آیینه ی تالاری سرخوشی ها را
تکرار نکرد.
دور باید شد دور.
شب سرودش را خواند
نوبت پنجره هاست."
همچنان خواهم راند. همچنان خواهم راند.
پشت دریاها شهری است
که در آن پنجره ها رو به تجلی باز است.
بام ها جای کبوتر ها یی است که به فواره
ی هوش بشری می نگرند.
دست هر کودک ده ساله شهر خانه
معرفتی است.
مردم شهر به یک چینه چنان می نگرند
که به یک شعله به یک خواب لطیف.
خاک موسیقی احساس ترا می شنود

Or a delicate dream;
Dust can hear the music of your feelings
The fluttering wings of mythical birds are audible in the wind
Beyond the seas there is a town
Where the Sun is as wide-open as the eyes of early-risers
Poets are the inheritors of water, wisdom, and light
Beyond the seas there is a town.
So one should build a boat.

و صدای پر مرغان اساطیر می آید در باد.
پشت دریا ها شهری است
که در آن وسعت خورشید به اندازه ی چشمان
سحر خیزان است.
شاعران وارث آب و خرد و روشنی اند.
پشت دریا ها شهریست !
قایقی باید ساخت.

From "Water's Footfall"

صدای پای آب

From Kashan I came, and I do all right.
I have a piece of bread, some smarts, a little bit of wit,
I have a mother, better than the bright green leaf,
And my friends like the river streaming.
I have a God as well who lives right around here somewhere…
Among these night blooms, or there at the foot of the white pine,
Past the streams consciousness, past all the statutes and laws of the reeds'
I am a Muslim;
The rose is my qibla.
The stream my prayer-rug, the sunlight my clay tablet.
My mosque; the meadow.
I rinse my arms for prayers along with the thrum and pulse of windows.
Through my prayers streams the moon the refracted light of the sun.

اهل کاشانم   روزگارم بد نیست
تکه نانی دارم   خرده هوشی سر سوزن ذوقی
مادری دارم بهتر از برگ درخت
دوستانی بهتر از آب روان
و خدایی که در آن نزدیکی است
لای این شب بو ها پای آن کاج بلند
روی آگاهی آب روی قانون گیاه
من مسلمانم   قبله ام یک گل سرخ
جا نمازم چشمه   مهرم نور
دشت سجاده من   -- من وضو با تپش پنجره ها میگیرم
در نمازم جریان دارد ماه جریان دارد طیف
سنگ از پشت نمازم پیداست
همه ذرات نمازم متبلور شده است
من نمازم را وقتی میخوانم
که اذانش را باد گفته باشد سر گلدسته سرو
من نمازم را پی " تکبیره الا حرام " علف میخوانم

Through translucent chapters I look down at the stones in the stream—bed.

Every part of my prayer is clear straight through.

I begin my recitation when I hear the wind's call from the cypress tree minaret.

I start to whisper after the grass proclaims the allahu-akbar,

After the stream's surface sings qad-qa'mat-as-salaat-prayer time has arrived!

My Ka'aba is there on the stream-bank, in the shade of the aqacia trees.

Like a light breeze, my Ka'aba drifts from orchard to orhard, town to town.

My black stone is sunlight in the flowers.

From ka'sha'n I am, a painter by trade.

Sometimes with paint and paper I build a cage of colors and

Offer it at the Market to free your lonely heart with the song of the poppies.

پی "قد قامت" موج

کعب ام بر لب آب

کعبه ام زیر اقاقی هاست

کعبه ام مثل نسیم میرود باغ به باغ

میرود شهر به شهر

حجر الاسود " من روشنی باغچه است "

اهل کاشانم   پیشه ام نقاشی است

گاه گاهی قفسی میسازم با رنگ میفروشم

به شما

تا به آواز شقایق که در آن زندانی است

دل تنهایی تان تازه شود

Simin Behbahani 20 th century poet

Simin Behbahani is one of the most prominent figures of the modern Persian literature and one of the most outstanding among the contemporary Persian poets. She is Iran's national poet and an icon of the Iranian intelligentsia and literati, who affectionately refer to her as the lioness of Iran. She has been nominated twice for the Nobel Prize in literature, and has received many literary accolades around the world.

Simin Behbahani was born on July 20, 1927 in Tehran. Her maiden name was Simin Khalili, daughter of Abba's Khalili, poet, writer and editor of the Eghda'm (Action) newspaper and Fakhr-Ozman Arghun, poet and teacher of the French language .Abbas khalili (1883-1971) wrote poetry in both Persian and Arabic and translated some 1100 verses of Ferdowsi's Shahnameh into Arabic. Fakhr-Ozman Arghun (1898-1966) was one of the progressive women of her time and a member of Kanun-e Nesvan-e Vatankha'h (Association of Patriotic Women) between1925 and 1929. In addition to her membership in Hezb-e Demokrat (Democratic Party) and Kanun-e Zanan (Women's Association), she was for a time (1932) Editor of Ayand-ye Iran (Future of Iran) newspaper. She taught French in a number of schools in Tehran.

The marriage ended in divorce. Soon after both father and mother re-married, and Simin was raised by her mother, who married A'del Khal'atbari, the journalist and founder of A'yanda-ye Iran. It was in their house hold that Simin encountered such prominent literary figures as Mohammad Hossein Shahriar, Malek-ol-Shoara' Baha'r and Saied Nafisi, and was introduced to Persian poetry. She attended Na'mus elementary school and Hassana't high school in Tehran and enrolled in the school of Midwifery in 1345. Her membership in the youth branch of the Tudeh party resulted in allegations that she was responsible for newspaper articles critical of the school, and she was expelled. "Without any preliminaries the Colledge President Dr Jaha'nsh'ah Sa'leh directed a barrage of curses and insults at me, she remembers, I answered back... He responded by immediately slapping me in the face. Quickly I returned the slaps...I was seventeen years old and beaten by forces stronger than me...From that time the purpose of my poetry has been to fight injustice."
Several years after her expulsion, Simin resumed her education and enrolled in 1958 at Tehran University's Faculty of Law; She graduated three years later with a Bachelor's degree in Judicial Law. She was employed by the Ministry of Education as a high school teacher in1951and held the position for thirty years.

In March 1947 she married Hassan Behbahani, an English teacher.The marriage ended in divorce in 1969. Her progeny from that 22-year union were two sons and a daughter. In 1979 she married Manuchehr Kushia'r whom she lost to a heart ailment in 1984. Simin recounts the devastating effect of the loss in," A'n mard, mard-e- hamra'ham" (That man, my fellow companion).

Chapter 10

Simin passed away on August 2014 inTehran from cardiac and respiratory complications. Her body was buried in Behesht-Zahra. Thousands attended the funeral ceremony, including prominent intellectuals, artists and human rights activists. Her death received wide coverage. Several commemorative celebrations were held in different countries, including a special session of the Iranian Studies Seminar of Colombia University in New York.

Simin started writing poetry at twelve and published her first poem at the age of fourteen. She used the "char pareh" style of Nima Youshij and subsequently turned to ghazal. She contributed to a historic development by adding theatrical subjects and daily events and conversations to poetry using ghazal style. She expanded the range of the traditional Persian verse forms and has produced some of the most significant works of Persian poetic literature in 20th century.

Simin's first poetry collection, Setar'-e shekasteh (the broken sitar) consisted mostly of cha'h'rpa'reh (foursome), a quatrain, which highly mitigates, but remains within the classical requirements of meter and rhyme in Persian poetry. Although love, separation, and lonliness emerge as the dominant motifs in the majority of the poems, faint echoes of social concern are also discernible in portions of the collection. It was followed by the publication of Ja'-ye pa' (the footprints) which included 76 poems, mostly ghazal or cha'r pa'reh and its variations. Neo-traditionalist in form, the poems are either love poems or hold social messages depicting injustices that at times beset ordinary people."Her attention to intimate details of daily life protects her from making facile sweeping generalizations."

Ja'-ye pa' serves as a turning point when one considers Simin's ouvre. It is in this collection that her language comes of age, catches the attention of a number of critics, and earns her a place of prominence among contemporary Iranian poets. The collection was reprinted in 1971.

During the interval between the publications of her first collections, Simin was associated for a period with the literary pages of Tehran-e Mosavar and Omid-e Iran and also started working with Radio Iran as a lyricist in 1954. Over the course of collaboration with Radio Iran, she composed several hundred songs, a number of which were set to music by the leading arrangers and performed by prominent musicians.

Contemporary Persian Poetry

In her next collection of poetry, Chelchera'gh (Candelabrum) in which cha'ha'rpa'reh and ghazal appear in almost equal proportions, her command of poetic language was further heightened. Mostly love poems, some with erotic imagery, the collection also featured confessional poems, describing the poet's personal life and lamenting of longing and loneliness, as well as several poems on social ills and predicaments. In 1962 Simin published Marmar (Marbel). A great number of her ghazals, which comprise the outright majority of this collection, support the contention that, after hesitations expressed earlier, she had ultimately opted for the ghazal, a very popular form of lyric poem of seven to fourteen lines with deep roots in Persian literature, defined "by a set of prosodical rules, certain thematic and stylistic conventions, and an equally conventional stock of imagery," as her preferred means of expression.

One of her most popular poems, dated March 1982, was composed during one of the bloodiest phases of Iran Iraq war. The poem, titled "Dow-ba'reh misa'zamat vatan" which soon turned to a generational anthem, not only encapsulates a moment frozen in history, but a mood and a sentiment that generation after generation recognizes as authentic and true. The poem is dedicated to Simin Da'neshvar.

My homeland, I will rebuild you	دوباره میسازمت وطن
Although with the bricks of my soul	اگرچه با خشت جان خویش
pillar on your roof	ستون به سقف تو میزنم
Even though with my bones	اگرچه با استخوان خویش
We smell it again with our bones,	
	دوبلره میبویم از توگل
We become flowers again,	به میل نسل جوان تو
At the will of your young generation,	دوباره میشویم از توخون
We bleed from you again	به سیل اشگ روان خویش
To the flood of our tears again on a familiar day	
	اگرچه صد ساله مرده ام
Black comes out of the house, I paint my poem,	به گورخود خواهم ایستاد
From the blue of my sky	که برکنم قلب اهرمن
	به نعره آنچنان خویش
	اگرچه پیرم ولی هنوز

Chapter 10

Even though I have been dead for a
hundred years,
I will stand in my grave to take the
heart of the devil
From the cry of so much.

مجال تعلیم اگر بود
جوانی آغاز میکنم
کنار نو باوگان خویش

Although I am old, but still, if I have
the opportunity to teach
I will start a youth with my new
comers.

Simin's Dasht e Arzhan (Arzhan Plain) was followed by K'ghazin ja'ma
(paper dress), a collection that boasts an explicitly socio-political title by
alluding to paper dresses worn by plaintiffs and complainants who used to line
up along a road the king was expected to cross, counting on their unusual
outfits to draw attention to their plight. In addition to Yek darya a'za'di (a
window to freedom), which was published in Tehran in 1995 and 2000.
Respectively, plus re-publishing of Simin's other previous works.

From an early age and over the entire course of her life, Simin participated in
and was a member of numerous poetic associations and societies and used her
prominence to advance and promote human rights and freedom of expression.
Her closed literary friendships were with Nader Naderpour, Freidoon Moshiri,
Simin Daneshvar, Mehdi Akhavan-e Saless and Hamid mossadegh. Her
relations with her cntemporary female poet, Forough Farokhzad, were
flavored by a mutual sense of competition.

Simin delivered lectures and recited her poems at many universities, seminars
and conferences all over the world. In celebration of her life and poetry,
international symposiums were held in 2006 at the University of Toronto,
University of California at Berkley and New York's Asia Soociety.
A collection of nine DVDs on her life and poetry were released in 2006, as
well as a documentary, entitled "Simin; Nima'-ye ghazal" directed by A'rash
Sanja'bi.

Simin received numerous national and international awards and prizes, both
for her poetry and for her promotion of human rights. She was nominated for

the Nobel Prize in Literature in 1999 and 2002', was awarded the Human Rights Watch Hellman-Hammet grant, as the "voice of freedom rising against repression everywhere" in 1998; and the Carl von Ossietzky Medal by the International League for Human Rights in 1999. She was honored in 2002 by the Encyclopeadia Iranica Foundation for the unparralled beauty of her poetry and her lifelong devotion to freedom and social justice; received the Freedom of Expression Award from the writers Union of Norway, in 2007.The Latifeh Yarshater Award in 2008 for her life long dedication to the improvement of Iranian women's human rights; and the Bita Daryabandari Prize for Literature and Freedom from Stanford University in 2008.

The man with a missing leg

مردی که یک پا ندارد

A man who does not have one leg has folded his pants,
I shine my face at him, but he is sitting
He is Quite a teenager and may be not over twenty
There is rage and fire in his eyes, Meaning there is nothing to see
I thought with kindness, I shall ask patience for him,
I shall offer motherly counsel even if he is unmindfull,
I turn to him again to start a conversation,
His place is empty, he is gone, the man with a missing leg.

شلوار تا خورده دارد مردی که یک پاندارد
خشم است وآتش نگاهش یعنی تماشا ندارد
رخساره می تابم از او اما به چشمم نشسته
بس نوجوان است وشایداز بیست بالا ندارد
بادا که چون من مبادا چل سال رنجش پس از این
خود گرچه رنج است بودن بادا مبادا ندارد
با پای چالاک پیما دیدی چه دشوار رفتم
تا چون رود او که پایی چالاک پیما ندارد؟
تق تق کنان چوب دستش روی زمین مینهد مهر
با آنکه ثبت حضورش حاجت به امضا ندارد
لبخند مهرم خاری شدودشنه ای شد
این خوی گر با درشتی نرمی تمنا ندارد
بر چهره سرد وخشکش پیدا خطوط ملال است
یعنی که با کاهش تن جانی شکیبا ندارد
گویم که با مهربانی خواهم شکیبایی از او
پندش دهم مادرانه گیرم که پروا ندارد
رو میکنم به باز تا گفت و گویی کنم ساز

Chapter 10

رفته است وخالی است جایش مردی که
یک پا ندارد
وبلاگ غلامرضا ارژنگ"
"

The ghazal offered Simin an extensive reservoir of amorous and love themes—the genre's mainstay. In most of Simin's works love and amorous relationships are flavored by autobiographical overtones. Contrary to the traditional ghazal that deals with stock images and allusions and seldom elucidates on the poet's personal experiences, her amorous ghazals often address a particular issue in the emotional relationships between two people.

You said I will kiss	گفتگو "از مجموعه اشعار"
you, I said it is what I wish You said what if someone sees? I said I will deny it	گفتی که میبوسم ترا گفتم تمنا میکنم گفتی اگر بیند کسی گفتم که حاشا میکنم
You said what if from my ankles I remove the shakles of your love I said crazier than you, you know I shall find	گفتی اگر از پای خود زنجیر عشقت واکنم؟ گفتم ز تو دیوانه تر دانی که پیدا میکنم

Simin, as per her own poems indicate, writes from the point of view of a woman in love. Many of her ghazals, even the less explicit compositions, clearly express the love of a female for a male lover and herald a departure from traditional ghazals composed primarily by men and reflecting a masculine outlook and emotions. Her efforts in capturing a feminine perspective in the ghazal were not without controversy. Some critics have praised her for having been successful and even trend setting, while others who have considered her love poems from a feminist point of view find her, for the most part, to have sustained the male-oriented tradition which prevailed in ghazals throughout the centuries. A good number of the most famous and most recognized contemporary Persian love poems marked by a precise description of emotions, innovative use of similes and metaphors, and above all, the musicality of words have been composed by Simin.

The stars have closed their eyes and
gone to sleep, come
The wine of light courses in the
veins of the night, come
In waiting I have cried so many
tears at night's feet
That the flower of dawn has
blossomed and day breaks, come.

I want a Cup of Sin

He said I want that which cannot be
found.
-- {Mowlavi}
I want a cup of sin, a cup of
corruption,
And some clay mixed with
darkness,
From which I shall mold an image
shaped like
"Adam"

Wooden-armed and straw-haired!
His mouth is big.
He has lost all his teeth.His looks
reflect his ugliness within,
Lust has made him violate all
prohibitions,

And to grow on his brow, an "organ
of shame."
His eyes are like two scarlet beams,
One focused on a sack of gold,
The other on the pleasures found in
bed.
He changes mask like a chameleon,
Has a two-timing heart like an eel.
He grows tall like a giant branch,

شراب نور از مجموعه اشعار

ستاره دیده فروبست و آرمید بیا
شراب نور به رگهای های شب دوید
بیا
ز بس به دامن شب اشگ انتظارم ریخت
گلل سپیده شکفت و سحر دمید بیا

جامی گناه خواهم

گفت آنچه یافت مینشود آنم آرزوست ــ "
مولوی
جامی گناه خواهم
/ پیمانه تباهی
وانگاه توده ای خاک/ آلوده با سیاهی
زان مایه ها بسازم
انگار شکل آدم

با دست های چوبی/با زلف ها ی کاهی
کام ودهان گشاده/دندانش اوفتاده
برزشتی نهادش/
سیمای او گواهی

چشمی به کیسه زر/
چشمی به عیش بستر
همچون شعاع سرخی/تابیده از دوراهی
تن در شبیه سازی/
چون سوسمار رنگین
دل در دو گانه بازی/همتای مارماهی
سربرکشد بروید
چون شاخه ای تناور
گویی گرفته جسمش/خاصیت گیاهی
وانگاه سویم آید/
دست ستم گشاید

As if his body has acquired
vegetable properties'
Then he will come to me,
Intent on my oppression, I will
scream and protest against him.
And that ogre called man
Will tame me with his insults.
As I gaze into his eyes, innocently
and full of shame,
I will scold myself: you see!
How you spent a lifetime wishing
for "Adam"

Here you have what you asked for.

وز هیبتش بر آرم/فریاد د اد خواهی
وان غول آدمی نام
/رامم کند به دشنام
من خیره در نگاهش
/با شرم وبی گناهی
گویم به خود که دیدی
:/در آرزوی "آدم" عمرت گذشت واینک
/اینست آنچه خواهی

Mother

Gracefully she approached,
In a dress of bright blue silk;

With an olive branch in her hand,
And many tales of sorrows in her eyes.

Running to her, I greeted her,
And took her hand in my mine:

Pulses could still be felt in her veins;
Warm was still her body with life,

"But you are dead, mother",I said;
"Oh, many years ago you died"

Neither of embalmment she smelled,
Nor in a shroud was she wrapped.

I gave a glance at the olive branch;
She held it out to me,

And said with a smile,

Contemporary Persian Poetry

"It is the sign of peace; take it."

I took it from her and said,
"Yes, it is the sign of …", when

My voice and peace were broken
By the violent arrival of a horseman.

He carried a dagger under his tunic
With which he shaped the olive branch
Into a rod and looking at it

He said to himself:
"Not too bad a cane

For punishing the sinners!"
A real image of a hellish pain!
Then, to hide the rod,
He opened his saddlebag.

In there, o' God!
I saw a dead dove, with a string tied
Round its broken neck.

My mother walked away with anger and sorrow;
My eyes followed her. Like the mourners she wore
A dress of black silk.

Che khosh ast as do yekdel sar-e harf baz kardan
Sokhan-e gozashta goftan gela-ra daraz kardan
Ga'hi az neya'z- panhan nazari be-mehr didan.

چه خوشست از دو یکدل سر حرف باز کردن
سخن گذشته گفتن گله را دراز کردن
گهی از نیاز پنهان نظری به مهر دیدن

Chapter 10

Mohammad Hosseyn Behjat Tabrizi"Shahriyar"20th century Persian poet

Mohammad Hossein Behjat Tabrizi "Shahriyar" was born in Tabriz. He spent his elementary school and high school years in Tabriz graduated from Talebieh school. He also studied Arabic literature, and French with private tutor. His school years in Tabriz brought him into contact with friends, classmates, and teachers, many of whom went on to become distinguished scholars and poets later on.

In February 1920 Shahriyar relocated to Tehran. He completed his education at Dar-ol-fonoun in1924 and following his father's advice, enrolled at the school of Medicine. In Tehran, he made close acquaintance with the musician Abu'l-Hassan Saba' and the young poet Amiri Firoozkuhi. His elegiac mathnavi (rhymed couplets) in memory of the noted singer, Parva'neh, and his ghazal in praise of the pioneering singer Qammar-ol-Moluk Vaziri, earned him instant recognition:

Spitting in heaven' eye tonight is the moon here;(Qammar-Moluk) Yes, by God, tonight till dawn, the moon is here	از کوری چشم فلک امشب ّقمر اینجاست آری قمر امشب تا سحر اینجاست

His first poetry collection, entitled Diva'n-e Shahrya'r was published in Tehran in 1931, with introductions by such celebrated poets and scholars as Sa'id Nafisi, Hosayn Pezjma'n Bakhtiari, as well as Malek-ol-Shoara' Baha'r, who praised his eloquent language, and his innovative and well crafted imagery in Bah'ar's "introduction" to the collection. The collection included some Shahryar's most celebrated ghazals, strongly tinted by the reverberations of his ill-fated love for a girl whose parents disallowed their marriage and instead married her off to another man. Emotionally distraught, Shahryar left the School of Medicine in his final year in 1924 and never resumed his medical education. His father became angry at his dropping off from the School of Medicine and the incident created a rift in the their relationship that was never mended.

In 1931, Shahryar began work at the State Office for the registration of Deeds and Properties, and he was commissioned to Nisha'bour the following year, where he met the painter Kama'l-ol-Molk. During his stay in Nisha'bour, Shahrya'r was a valued presence in literary circles and was among those who participated in Ferdowsi's millennial celebration. A year after his father's death in1934 Shahryar returned to Teheran and was employed by the Ministry of Health as an inspector. He was later transferred to the Bank of Agriculture, where he worked as an accountant. His poems in glorification of Iran's national unity during the ascendancy of the Democratic Party of A'zerba'ija'n earned him an exemption from showing up in the bank by the order of Ali Mansur (Mansurol-molk), the then prime minister of Iran.

Following his mother's death in 1953, Shahryar returned to Tabriz and continued to live there for the rest of his life. In Tabriz he married Azizeh Abd-al-khal'eghi, a distant relative, a primary school teacher. They had three children; Shaherza'd, Maryam, and Ha'di.

He retired from the bank in 1965. In appreciation of his achievements as a poet, Tabriz University awarded him an honorary professorship in 1967, and the day: '16 of the month of Esfand' was announced as "Ruz-e Shahryar" in the cultural calendar of the province.
Shahryar was a competent calligrapher and wrote his own copy of the Qura'n. He had a keen interest in music, had many friends among musicians, and, for a time, used to play the instrument; ta'r and seta'r.

Following a period of hospitalization in Tabriz, Shahryar was transferred to a hospital in Tehran, where he died on 18 September 1988. He was buried in the poet's graveyard (Maghbaret-ol-Shoara') of Tabriz, where Kha'ghani Sherva'ni is also interned. His house was transformed to a museum.

Shahryar's passion for poetry came alive at an early stage of the poets'life, when he was a student at high school under the pen-name Behjat. Although his verse has taken diverse forms throughout his life, he composed some of his most appreciated poems in the traditional genre of ghazal:

My sitar weeps for my sorrows to-night That source of solace in my dark and dismal nights.	نالد به حال زار من امشب ستارمن آن مایه تسلی شب های تارمن

Chapter 10

Oh moon; you comfort my heart to
night
After all, o moon, in my` anguish
you share
That slow waning of your life, I
know, and only I know
How, in separation from the sun,
you suffer

امشب ای ماه بدرددل من تسکینی

آخر ای ماه تو همدرد من مسکینی

کاهش جان تو من دانم و من میدانم

که تو ازدوری خورشید چه ها میبینی

Shahryar's lyrical poems that earned him the applaues of A'ref Ghazvini among many others could be roughly divided into three broad categories of religious, panegiryc, and love poems, although the line between the three is often blurred. His poetical sensibility, combined with his undersanding of Persian music, is echoed in his skillful employment of internal rhyme and alteration, which by extension, has made his ghazals rewarding choices for some of the great composers and vocalists of his time. "Ha'la' chera' (why now), one of his love poems in which letter"a'" is repeated in various arrangements, was set to music by Ruh-ollah Khalleghi, and sung by Gholam-hoseyn Bana'n, the renound singer, who paid carefull attention to his choice of lyrics:

Oh, sweetheart! you are here!, I am
so delighted, but why now?
Now that I am old and feeble!, why
now"?
You are the ultimate cure!.But you
have come too late!
You, heartless! Why now? Why did
you not come earlier?

آمدی جانم به قربانت ولی حالا چرا

بی وفا حالا که من افتاده ام از پا چرا

نوشدارویی وبعد ازمرگ سهراب آمدی

سنگدل این زود ترمیخواستی حالا چرا

The first piece by Shahryar was entitled 'Soul of the Butterfly'. Defining poetry, Shahryar says: "The essence of a poem is its mild and at the same time touching influence which quite unconsciously leaves its imprint on the human mind. A poem should be the poet's mind acquired from the nature and life and presents to other minds in the form of a poem. Shahryar not only was good in lyrics; he was also a master of odes. Shahryar made use of almost all styles and proved unique in all of them. His poems are filled with the most delicate sentiments and he is sincere in everything that he says or writes. As regards his diction, Shahryar was deeply influenced by classical Persian poets, such as Era'qi and Saadi.

Shahryar was deeply concerned with human sufferings and utilized that in the core of his poems and believed that a true poem is one which is inspired by love and mysticism both. He is a very emotional and sensitive poet. His sincere emotions are well reflected through all the pieces he composed and in particular in his lyrics. Contrary to many literary figures of his time Shahriar barely involved himself with the political problems and ideologies. He was, however, known for his avid nationalism.

Shahryar's poetry is characterized by his skillful placing of non-literary words in his poems, bringing the genre of ghazal close to unadorned colloquial idiom and slang language. His intimate, idiomatic mode of expression and almost conversational tone initiates a new trend in ghazal and enriches the genre's lexical repertoire by drawing on popular culture and expression. The sincerity of his language makes his poems readily comprehensible by a broad segment of the public.

Sharyar's effortless use of slang and colloquial languge, and his fame has surpassed almost all the poets of his time. His familiarity with the music, along with his fascination with the musical harmony and the intricate aesthetics of the poetry of Hafez is well manifested in his conscious attempts to employ phonetic pattering, particularly consonance and assonance, not too often stipulated as stylistic objectivity occasionally betray his attempts in modern poetry. As noted by others, however, Shahryar's ghazals to immitate the lyrical mood and typical expressions of other classical lyricists, often fail to conjuer the elegant language of a poet like Saadi, or the resourceful ambiguity by which the lyrics of a poet like Hafez is recognized and appreciated.

Chapter 10

Shahryar's poems in rhymed couplets (mathnavi), most noted among them"
Afsa'neh-ye shab" (The tale of the night) in 1624 lines has further earned him
popular recognition and critical eminence. The poem consists of 40 sections,
which follow the same meter.

"Takht-eJamshid", a poem related to "Afsa'neh-ye shab" in 571 lines also in
the genre of mathnavi, sets forth in an emotional and archaic language a
glimps into turbulent history of Persepolis. Although his early poems were
mostly composed in classical meters, he also experimented with the modernist
trends in literature:

"There are times that Hafez leads me to Shiraz with the song of his ghazals, And times that Nima takes me to Yush with his Afsaneh"	گاه با ساز غزل حافظ به شیراز م برد گاه با افسانه اش نیما به یوش آرد مرا

Shahryar speaks of his notion of poetry as a medium to express love and
passion in various contexts, including epilogues of his poetry collections and
interviews. His conviction that poetry should epitomize the poet's affection
and moods is well manifested in his turning the rhymes and language of
everyday speech into a medium for rendering a wide range of emotions. Quite
a number of his ghazal's and most of his qet'as (topical verse) seems to have
been composed as his spontaneous reflections on incidents he has
witnessed.and marked by his insertion of references to actual circumstances.

Shahryar was a man of intense nationalistic sensitivity. Imageries in praise of
Perspolis, Zaroaster, and Ferdowsi are returning motifs in his poetry. Heydar
Ba'ba'-ye sala'm, a long poem in two parts addressed to Heydar Ba'ba', a
mountain near Tabriz, is Shahryar's most acclaimed poem in his mothere's
language, a colloquial Azeri Turkish idiom. The poem was first published in
1951 Era'deh-ye A'zerba'ija'n. In this poem that Shahryar reflects on and
speaks about his years of childhood spent near this mountain quickly became
famous, not only in Azerbaija'n but across the rest of the Turkish speaking
world. Shahryar "turned the Azeri Turkish into a masterly literary language.

Written in a lively, stanzaic form Heydar Ba'ba' contains a wealth of local
tales, songs, proverbs, sayings, aphorisms, and refrences to festive and funeral
rites, historical and religious beliefs, and food and clothing, as well as

descriptions of nature. Heydar Baba Salam is written in two parts and consists of 76 segments, each of five hemistiches with even syllables. The first three hemistiches end in the same rhyme, while the other two are rhymed differently. The prosodic meter of this poem is well known in Azerbaija'n and frequently used in the composition of love songs.

The widespread success of this poem is mainly due to its folkloric and pleasant popular language. Heydar Baba Salam has earned the immense affection of both Turkish and Persian speakers. It has been translated into many languages and has been adopted into a few plays. The text as commented by Shahryar himself, is his adaptation of the two translations of the poem into Persian by Pari Jaha'nsh'hi and Nahid Hadi. The poem is also available in Persian translation by Hoseyn Monzavi and a few others.

Greetings to Heydar Baba By Shahryar, English translation :Dr.Hassan javadi	سلام بر حیدر بابا شعر سروده شهریار ترجمه دکتر حسن جوادی

Heydar Baba, when the thunder resounds across the skies,
When floods roardown the mountain sides,
And the girls line up to watch it rushing by,
Send my greetings to the tribesmen and the village folk,
And remember me and my name once more.
Heydar Baba, when pheasants take flight,
And the rabbits secure from flowering bush,
When your garden burst into full bloom,
May those who remember us live long!
And may our saddened hearts be gladdened.

حیدر باباچوابرشخد غرد آسمان
سیلاب های تند وخروشان شود روان
صف بسته دختران به تماشایش آنززمان
بر شوکت و تبار توبادا سلام من
گاهی رود به زبان تو نام من
حیدر بابا چوکبک تو پرد زروی خاک
خرگوش زیر بته لرزد هراسناک
باغت به گل نشسته وگل کرده جامه پاک
ممکن اگر شودزمن خسته یادکن
دل های غم گرفته بدان یاد شاد کن
چون چارتاق را فکند باد نوبهار
نوروز گلی وقارچیچکی گردد آشکار
بفشارد ابر پیرهن خود به مرغزار
از ما هرانکه یاد کند بی گزند باد
گو:درد ما چو کوه بلند وباد
حیدر بابا چوداغ کند پشتت آفتاب
رخسار تو بخندد و جوشدزچشمه آب
یک دسته گل ببیند برای من خراب
بسپار بادرا که بیارد به کوی من
باشد که بخت روی نماید به سوی من

When the March wind strikes down
the bowers,
Primerose and snowdrops appear
from the frozen earth,
When the clouds wing their white
shirts,
Let us be remembered once again
Let our sorrows rise up like a
mountain.
Heydar Baba let your back bear the
mark of the sun
Let your stream weep and your face
beam with smiles,
Let your children put together a
bouquet
And send it to us when the wind
blows this way
So that, perhaps, our sleepy fortune
be awakened.
Heydar Baba may your brows be
bright.
May you be circled by streams and
gardens!
And after us, may you live long.
This world is full of misfortunes and
losses.
The world is replete with those
bereaved of sons and orphaned.
Heydar Baba, my steps never
crossed your pass.
My life was spent, becoming too
late to visit you
I know not what became of all those
beautiful girls.
I never knew about dead-ends,
about paths of "no return"
I never knew about separation, loss
and death

حیدربابا همیشه سرتوبلند باد
ازباغ وچشمه دامن تو فرهمند باد
ازبعد ما وجود تو دور از گزند باد
دنیا همه قضا وقدر مرگ ومیر شد
این زال کی زکشتن فرزند سیرشد
حیدربابا زراه تو کج گشت راه من
عمرم گذشت و ماند بسویت نگاه من
دیگرخبرنشد که چه شد زادگاه من
هیچم نظر براین ره پرپیچ وخم نبود
هیچم خبرزمرگ وز هجران وغم نبود
برحق مردم است جوانمردرانظر
جای فسوس نیست که عمراست درگذر
نامردمرد عمربه سر میبرد مگر
درمهرودروفا به خدا جاودانه ایم
مارا حلال کن که غریب آشیانه ایم
میراژدرانزمان که زندبانگ دلنشین
شورافکند به دهکده هنگامه درزمین
ازبهر رستم عاشق بیا به بین
بی اختیارسوی نواها دویدنم
چون مرغ پر گشاده بدانجا رسیدنم
درسرزمین شنگل آواسیب عاشقان
رفتن بدان بهشت وشدن میهمان آن
باسنگ سیب وبه زدن وخوردن آنچنان
درخاطرم چوخواب خوشی ماندگارشد
روحم همیشه باروراز آن دیارشد
حیدر بابا قوری گل وپرواز غازها
درسینه ات به گردنه هاسوزسازها
پاییز تو بهار تو در دشت نازها
چون پرده ای به چشم دلم نقش بسته است
وین شهریار تست که تنها نشسته است

Contemporary Persian Poetry

Shahryar's "Sahandieh" is his patriotic response to a versified letter by Bolud Qarachorli Sahand (1926-1970) another poet from A'zerbaija'n who denigrates Shahryar for rendering his poems in Persian, rather than Azeri Turkish. Sahandieh begins by Shahryar's romanticized depiction of Sahand Mountain and ends with his portrayal of himself as a poet who narrates the sufferings of his birthplace in Persian language.

Shahryar has been regarded as "amongst the very last guardians of classical Persian poetry. He has also earned the praise of a literary scholar as the most noted representative of the short-lived Persian romanticism, whose poems are romantic and lyrical in imagery and tone, and is often composed in intense moments of epiphany. Shahryar's poetry has influenced many of his traditionalist and neo-traditionalists contemporary poets, noted among them Fereydun Moshiri, Na'der Na'derpur, and above all Hushang Ebteha'j (Sa'yeh), who has praised Shahryar in several poems, including in "Be Shahryar", a poem he has dedicated to Shahryar following the death of Nima'Yushij:

Now that I am forlorn and alone, dear companion, you stay
All have forsaken this house, by God, you stay

همه با من بیکس تنهاشده یارا تو بمان
رفتند از این خانه خدا را تو بمان

Me, the leafless autmn tree, shall soon depart
You, so full of bound and promise, fresh as spring, you stay.

تو من بی برگ خزان دیده دگر رفتنیم
همه باروبری تازه بهاران تو بمان

Chapter 10

Contemporary Persian Poetry

Forough Farokhzad 20ᵗʰ century Persian poet

Forough Farokhzad was born in January 5 1935 in Tehran into a middle class family of seven children. She attended public schools through the nineth grade, thereafter graduating from junior high school at the age of fiftheen; she transferred to Kamal-ol-molk technical school, where she studied dressmaking and painting.

In 1951 she married her causin Parviz Shapour over the objection of her families mainly because of Shapour's age. A year later Foroug's first and only son "Ka'mya'r" was born. Forough separated from Parviz Shapour in 1954. She relinquished the custody of her son to her ex-husband's family in order to pursue her calling in poetry and independent life style.

In 1955 Forough's first collection, titled Asir (The captive) which contained forty five poems was published. In September of that year she suffered a nervous breakdown and spent sometime in a psychiatric clinic. In July 1956 Forough left Iran for the first time on a nine months trip to Europe. In this year the second volume of her poetry containing twenty five short lyrics, called Divar (The Wall), was published, dedicated to her former husband.

In 1958 Forough's third collection Esia'n (Rebellion), appeared and securely established her as a promising yet notorious poet. Forough's relationship with the controversial writer and cinematographer Ebrahim Golestan began and remained important in the poet's personal life until her death. In 1962 she made a documentary movie about a leper's colony, titled, "The House Is Black" The movie was acclaimed internationally and won several prizes.

In 1963 UNESCO produced a thirty minutes movie about Forough. Also Bernardo Bertoluchi came to Iran to interview her and decided to produce a fifteen minutes movie about the poet's life. In 1964 Forough's fourth poetry collection, Tavalodi Digar (Rebirth), contained thirty-five poems which the poet had composed over a period of nearly six years was published. In 1965 Forough's fifth collection of poems called "Let Us Believe In The Beginning Of The Cold Season" went to prints and was published after her death.

On Monday February 14.1967 Forough visited her mother, who later recalled their conversation over lunch as the nicest that they ever had. From her mother's home, on the way back, while driving, at the intersection of

Chapter 10

Marvedasht and Loghmanol-Doleh streets in Darrus, Tehran her Jeep station wagon swereved to avoid an oncoming vehicle, struck a wall. She was thrown out of the vehicle, at the height of her creativity and barely thirty two years old, Forough Farokhzad died of head injuies. She was buried, under falling snow, in Zahirol-Doleh cemetery inTehran, as she had predicted in her last book " Ima'n biavarim be a'gha'z-e fasl-e sard":

"Perhaps the truth was this young pair of hands/ buried beneath the falling snow/and next year, when Spring/mates with the sky beyond the window/and stems thrusts from her body/fountains of fragile green stems/will blossom, o my love, o my dearest only love".

She clearly voices her feelings in the mid-1950's about conventional marriage, and her own situation as a wife and a mother no longer able to live a conventional life in such poems as "The Captive", "The wedding Band", and "To My Sister". As a divorcee poet in Tehran, Farokhzad attracted much attention and considerable disapproval. She had several short lived relationships with men, and "The Sin" describes one of them.

The Captive (Asir)	"اسیر"

I want you, yet I know that never
Can I embrace you to my heart's content!

ترا میخواهم و دانم که هرگز
به کام دل در آغوشت نگیرم

You are that clear and bright sky.
I, in this corner of the cage, am a captive bird.

تویی آن آسمان صاف وروشن
من این کنج قفس مرغی اسیرم

From behind the cold and dark bars
Directing towards you

زپشت میله های سرد و تیره
نگاه حسرتم حیران به رویت

my rueful look of astonishment!

I am hoping that a hand might come
And I might suddenly spread my wings in your dirction.

در این فکرم که دستی پیش آید
و من ناگه گشایم پر به سویت

I am thinking that in moment neglect

در این فکرم که در یک لحظه غفلت
از این زندان خامش پر بگیرم

I might escape from this silent prison,

Laugh in the eyes of my jail-keeper,
And by your side start a new life.

I am pondering over these thoughts, yet I know,
That I cannot dare leave this prison!

Even if the jail-keeper would let me!
I am left with no breath or breeze to fly.

From behind the bars, every bright morning
The look of a child smile in my face;

When I begin a song of joy,
His lips come towards me with a kiss.

O Heaven! If I wish one day
To fly out of this silent prison,

What shall I say to the child with tears in his eyes?
Forget about me, for I am a captive bird?

I am the candle that illuminates a ruin!
With the fire that is burning in her heart!

If I choose silent darkness
I will bring the nest to ruin!

به چشم مرد زندان بان بخندم
کنارت زندگی از سر بگیرم

در این فکرم من ودانم که هرگز
مرا یارای رفتن زین قفس نیست

اگر هم مرد زندان بان بخواهد
دگر از بهر پروازم نفس نیست

ز پشت میله ها هر صبح روشن
نگاه کودکی خندد به رویم
چو من سر میکنم آواز شادی
لبش با بوسه می آید به سویم

اگر ای آسمان خواهم که یک روز
از این زندان خامش پر بگیرم

به چشم کودک گریان چه گویم
ز من بگذر که من مرغی اسیرم

من آن شمعم که باسوز دل خویش
فروزان میکنم ویرانه ای را

اگر خواهم که خاموشی گزینم
پریشان میکنم کاشانه ای را

Chapter 10

Forough's personal life has attracted a kind of fantasy literature. She has been idolized and demonized, respected and rejected. The Persian reading public, critics, and commentators are both attracted and repelled by her iconoclasm. Her detractors like her admirers have made her personal life the focus of much debate and attention.Yet, throughout her short literary career, Forough, who wrote in an authbiographical voice showed a pronounced aversion to give away even the scantiest biographical data on herself. Most likely she was reacting to the obsessively sensation-seeking interest of the critics in her personal life, an interest that all too often replaced (and still replaces) the more serious attention that her work deserves.

The whole body of her work as indicated before resists the dominant cultural assumptions that framed her writing and its reception. It is a struggle against the institutions of both literature and society, an oasis of the conventionally forbidden –sexual, textual, and cultural. It disrupts social systems and heierarchies at their most intimate level. It reveals the joy and pain of transition from one cultural pattern to another. It personifies the pleasures of hybridization of mingling the old and the new.

A confrontational stance towards gender categories and attributes, a merciless reflexivity and meditation on the nature of the self, an exploration of the exhilaration and the violent love, and a candid portrayal of the high price paid by a literary woman to nurture her creativity—these are some of the issues that Forough explores in her writing. Not many of her contemporaries risked the creation of so complex, layered paradoxical, and so vulnerable a world.That daring, radical, reformulation of ideals, relationships, and norms; that candor, have earned her a pariah status, but also made her central to modern Persian literature. It is hard to freeze Forough's fluid poet- persona in a moment or in a familiar frame. She crosses boundries, and refuses to be classified. Throughout her five poetry collections we witness the development of a female persona whose complexity defies the stereotype; a woman priviledged with emotional, psychological, and intellectual awareness; a woman contradicting prevailing notions of "feminine" and asserting, with however much awe and confusion, her sense of herself as different from that conventionally defined as belonging to women. With the intimate and the personal as an ever-present background, Forough's fourth collection (Tawalod-I digar) and (Ima'n biavarim be aghaz-Fasl-e sard) celebrate the birth of a female character who rejoices in her independence. Her own model, and in the process gives birth to a self in the image of her own liking and aspirations.

The Sin

I sinned a sin full of pleasure,
In an embrace which was warm and fiery,

I sinned surrounded by arms
That was hot and avenging and iron.

In that dark and silent seclusion
I looked into secret-full eyes.

My heart impatiently shook in my breast
In response to request of his needful eyes.

In that dark and silent seclusion,
I sat disheveled at his side

His lips poured passion on my lips,
I escaped from the sorrow of my crazed heart.

I whispered in his ear the tale of love;
I want you o life o life of mine,

I want you, o life-giving embrace,
O crazed lover of mine, you.

Desire sparked a flame in his eyes;
The red wine danced in the cup.

In the soft bed, my body
Drunkedly quivered on his chest.

I sinned a sin full of pleasure,
Next to a shaking stupefied form.

O God, who knows what I did

Chapter 10

In that dark and quiet seclusion!

But it is not only the woman portrayed in Forough's poetry who is unconventional. Men, too, are on a journey of their own. They break conventional codes. They free themselves from stringent codes of masculinity (marda'negi). "The one I love/ is a simple man/ I have hidden/ between the bushes of my breasts/ like the last relic of a wonderous religion, in his ominous land of wonders" (Mashugh-eman), "Tawallod-I digar".

Before Forough, individualized reflections of men barely existed in women's writings in Persia. The few men portrayed usually lack any personal idiosyncracies of nuances of character. They are captives of cultural cannon of masculine images and steriotypes. They are types rather than characters. They are in effect, veiled. Forough strips away in veil of mystery and presents them in their all- too-human frailities, contradictions, and strengths. These are men who can choose and be chosen, desire and be desird, gratify and be gratified. No longer Phantom personalities dreams, figments of imagination; no longer prisoners in the prisons of their own making; No longer compromised in their capacity for intimacy. Forough gives men a new life by giving them clearer focus. Liberated them from sex-stereotyped modes of thought and emotions, commited to the expansion of their possibilities and potentials, they celebrate reciprocity and intimacy in relationships.

But the bliss enjoyed by men and women in Forough's poetry is Short-lived. A recurrent theme, a topos, which links Asir to Ima'n bia'varim, be aghaz-e fasl-e sard is, in fact, the relentless flow of time. Everything, even the moment of acstasy, is ephemeral. Nothing can suspend temporarily. The poet repeatedly mourns the quick, irreversible passage of time. Anxiety regarding the evanescent nature of everything breaks through her poems. Passionate love proves to be a transient illusion. Her constant quest for an ideal love, timeless and ethereal, ends in bitter disillusionment. Images emerge—of death, especially of the "sucking mouth of the grave" ("wahm-e sabz", Tawalod-i digar). Living on the fringes of her society, alone and lonely, bothered by and conscious of her ephemerality, Forough foresees the coming of black clouds, of cold seasons. A rebel conscious and perhaps tired of her rebellion, an exile in her native land, she sees herself, time and again, as a lonely woman."And here I am / a lonely woman/ at the threshold of a cold season/ coming to understand the earth's contamination / and the elemental, sad despair of the sky":

Let us believe in the beginning of
the cold season
And this is I
A woman alone
At the threshold of a cold season
At the beginning of understanding
The polluted existence of the earth
And the simple and sad pessimism
of the sky
And the incapacity of these cement
hands.

Time passed,
Time passed and the clock struck
four,
Struck four
Struck four.
Today is the winter solstice
I know the seasons's mystry and
Understand each moments words.
The savior lies in his tomb and
The soil, the accepting soil,
Represents peace.

Time passed and the clock struck
four.

In the street the wind is blowing and
I am thinking about the flowers
mating,
about buds on thin anemic legs and
this exhausted, tubercular time
and a man
is passing by the soaked trees, the
man
whose threads of blue veins like
dead snakes
have crawled up the two sides of his

ایمان بیاوریم به آغاز فصل سرد
واین منم زنی تنها در آستانه فصلی سرد
در ابتدای درک هستی آلوده زمین
ویاس ساده و غمناک آسمان
وناتوانی این دستهای سیمانی
زمان گذشت

زمان گذشت و ساعت چهار بار نواخت
چهار بار نواخت
امروز روز اول دیماه است ـ من راز فصل
ها را میدانم
و حرف لحظه ها را می فهمم
نجات دهنده در گور خفته است و خاک
خاک پذیرنده اشارتیست به آرامش
زمان گذشت و ساعت چهار بار نواخت.
در کوچه باد می آید در کوچه باد می آید
ومن به جفت گیری گلها می اندیشم ـ به
غنچه هایی با ساق های لاغر کم خون
و این زمان خسته مسلول
و مردی از کنار درختان خیس میگذرد
مردی که رشته های آبی رگهایش ـ مانند
مارهای مرده از دوسوی گلوگاهش
بالا خزیده اند و در شقیقه های منقلبش آن
هجای خونین را تکرار میکنند
سلام ـ سلام
و من به جفت گیری گلها می اندیشم

در آستانه فصلی سرد
در محفل عزای آینه ها
و اجتماع سوگوار تجربه های پریده رنگ
و این غروب بارور شده ازدانش سکوت
چگونه می شود به آن کسی که می رود
اینسان
صبور سنگین سرگردان فرمان ایست داد

throat and repeat
into his panicked temple the blood-
stained
syllable.
"Hello!"
"Hello!"
And I am thinking about the flowers
mating.

At the threshold of a cold season
Among the mirrors gathered in
mourning
And the huddled experiences,
grieving and pale,
And in this sunset pregnant by the
knowledge of silence
How can one tell that person passing
by-
Patient,
Heavy,
Bewildered-
To stop?
How can one tell that man he is not
alive, that he has never lived?

In the street the wind is still blowing
and the isolated crows of solitude
circle in the old gardens of apathy
and the lather, how stubby it is.
Translated by Elizabeth T. Grey, Jr.

چگونه میشود به مرد گفت که او زنده
نیست او هیچوقت زنده نبوده است

در کوچه باد می آید- کلاغ های منفرد
انزوا
باغ های پیر کسالت میچرخند ونردبام
چه ارتفاع حقیری دارد
آنها ساده لوحی یک قلب را با خود به
قصر قصه ها بردند واکنون
دیگر چه گونه یک نفر به رقص بر
خواهد خواست
و گیسوان کودکیش را در آبهای جاری
خواهد ریخت
و سیب را که سرانجام چیده است وبوییده
است- در زیر پا لگد خواهد کرد؟
ای یار ای یگانه ترین یار چه ابرهای
سیاهی در انتظار روز میهمانی خورشیدند
انگار در مسیری از تجسم پرواز بود که
یک روز آن پرنده ها نمایان شدند
انگار از خطوط سبز تخیل بودند- آن
برگهای تازه که در شهوت نسیم نفس
میزدند
انگار آن شعله های بنفش که در ذهن پاک
پنجره ها میسوخت
چیزی بجز تصور معصومی از چراغ
نبود..
.

In these opening lines, "Let us believe in the beginning of the cold season" echoes the closing lines of "Those Days," which Forough had composed some five years eaelier. In a sense, the conclusion she had reached in 1960 in her realization that "those days" of childhood and adolescent wonder and innocence and authomatic harmony with the world about one were gone, leaving her a "lonely woman," has become a premise for her in the later poem.

Of course, the concluding lines of "Those Days" are not unproblematic in literary critical terms insofar as lonliness is not an inevitable sense consequent upon the realization that youthful innocence and vitality have for ever departed. In other words, the poem does not make the casual connection between the nostalgic review and the haunting refrain about "that girl" who "now is a lonely woman". Nevertheless, in "Those Days" the poet remains honest to her feelings, reflecting as ever in her poetry, her true mood and perceptions of the moment. On the other hand, in such poems as "Those Days" and "Let us believe in the beginning of the cold season" as at least Baraheni noted, Forough's unswerving commitment to veracity makes it possible to avoid the pitfalls of the main stream modernist commitment to social and political engagement in verse. Her poetry of life may occasionally suffer because of its subjectivity but at least life's vitality shows through, where as in poetry of social commitment sometimes only ideology is communicated, often lacking both verisimilitude and the subjective truth of personal experience.

In "Let us believe in the beginning of the sold season" Forough looks into both the past and the future:
Time passed,
Time passed and the clock struck four,
Struck four times.
Today is the winter solstice.
I know the season's secrets
The wind is blowing through the street, the beginning of ruination
I am cold,
 I am cold, and it would appear that it will never be warm again?
I am cold and I know that nothing will be left
Of all the red dreams of one wild poppy,
But a few drops of blood.
I shall give up lines and give up counting syllables too,
And I will seek refuge from the mob
Of finite measured forms in the sensitive planes of expanse.
I am naked, naked, naked,
I am naked as silence between words of love,
And all my wounds come from love, from loving
Will I once again comb my hair with wind?
Will I ever again plant pansies in the garden?
And set gerenumes in the sky outside the window?

Chapter 10

Will I ever again dance on wine glasses?
Will the doorbell call me again toward a voice's expectation?
I said to my mother it's all over now.
I said, Things always happen before one thinks;
We have to send condolences to the obituary page...
Time passed,
Time passed and nit fell over the acacia's naked limbs,
Night slithered on the side of the window panes,
And with its cold tongue
Sucked in the remains of the departed day.
Where am I coming from?
How loving you were when you...
Carried me to love's meadows
Through an oppressive darkness
Until that whirling smoke, the last gasp
Of fiery thirst settled down upon the field of sleep.
And those cardboard stars circled about infinity.
Why did they call sounds speech?
Why did they welcome the glance into the house of vision?
Why did they carry caresses to virginity's timid hair?
Look how here the soul of a person, who uttered words,
And whom a glance caressed
And whose shying away caresses calmed
Has been nailed to the scaffold of beams of misgivings,
And how the tracks of your five-finger branches
That was like five words of truth
Have remained upon her cheeks.
What is silence, what is it, o dearest one?
What is silence but unspoken words?
I am bereft of speech, but the sparrow's language
Is the language of life, of flowing sentences?
Of nature's celebrations
 The sparrows speak of spring leaves, spring.
The sparrows speak of breeze, fragrances, and breeze.
The sparrows' language dies in a factory.
Who is this, this person headed for the moment of oneness?
Over the highway of eternity
And who winds her everpresent watch
With the mathematical logic of division and reduction?

Who is this, this person?
For whom the rooster crowing is not the day's first heartbeat
But the smell of breakfast time?
Who is this, this person? Who wears love's crown
And is withering in her wedding clothes?
Greetings, o alienation of loneliness,
I am relinquishing the room to you,
Because the black clouds always
Are prophets of new messages of purity?
And in a martyrdom of a candle is an incandescent secret which
The last and longest flame well knows.
Let us believe in the beginning of the cold season.
Let us believe in the ruins of the garden of imagination.
Look, what a heavy snow is falling!
Perhaps the truth was in those two young hands,
Those two young hands
Buried beneath the never ending snow.
And next year, when spring
Sleeps with the sky beyond the window
And her body exudes
Let us believe in the beginning of the cold season

Both the mood and premise of "Let us believe in the beginning of the cold season," i.e, "a woman alone" at the beginning of the season, provide the fairest and saddest perspective from which to appreciate Forough's life and art, especially insofar as it was one of her last major poetic statements. In fact according to one critic the poem is "a review of her whole life, a look at exciting past moments and empty present ones….an expiration in the depth of innocence… the last look of a drownining person who will be silenced by a coming wave.

Mohammad Hassan Moayeri (Rahi) 20th century Persian poet

One of the most distinguished and popular Persian poets of Iran in recent times, Mohammad Hassan Moayeri who elected "Rahi", (meaning dust under the feet) as his pen-name at the age of 25, was born in Tehran on April 1 1909. He was named Moayeri after his father's name Mohammad Hassan Moayed

Khalvat who had passed away six months before his birth. His grandfather Moayer-ol-Mama'lek Neza'm-ol-Dowleh, was the treasurer to Na'ser-el-Din Sha'h Gha'ja'r. Rahi completed his high school education at the famous Dar-ol-fonoon in Tehran. The school was established by "Amir Kabir" who was prime minister to Na'ser-el-Din Sha'h. Rahi's first government job after graduation was at Tehran Municipality followed by successive jobs at other Government jobs until his retirement.

Like most other contemporary Persian poets Rahi's love of poetry commenced in his youth and continued to grow through his contact with literary figures and poets and his participation in literary societies, a feature of Persian urban literary life that began in the 18th century and became widespread after the Constitutional Revolution. His membership in the Hakim Nez'ami Literary Society, founded by Hassan Vahid Dastgerdi in 1932 and his participation in editing and annotating Neza'mi Ganjavi's Panj Ganj or Khamseh further contributed to his fascination with Persian classical literature.

Unlike most of his contemporaries, Rahi barely departed from the conventions of Persian classical prosody (Arooz). His poems are marked by the innovative employment of similies and metaphors, and a harmony of rhythms and rhymes with the poem's content. Nature, human desire, solitude, sorrow, flowers and wine are recurrent motifs in his poetry:

"Like a climbing lily around an eglantine branch Tender and delicate she rests in my embrace tonight, Rahi"	همچو نیلوفر به ساق نسترن پیچیده ام نازک اندامی بود امشب در آغوشم رهی

(From the poem Ba'ra'n-e sobhga'hi)

His familiarity with music is well reflected in his skilful employment of internal rhyme and alliteration in his poetry:

"The one who by your sweet lips, O fountain of life Has serenaded your praise and received reproach, is me!"	آنکه پیش لب شیرین تو ای چشمه نور آفرین گفته و دشنام شنیدست منم

Contemporary Persian Poetry

(From the book, Sa'ya-ye 'omr)

The repetition of 'sh' and 'n' in various arrangements works to creat a melody in the poem that has further bolstered by the use of words commonly paired with, and therefore serving to evoke, other words employed elsewhere in the poem. Many of his ghazals, not too far from the masterpieces of Persian classic poetry, are among the most popular and the most appreciated verses of his period.

در پیش بی دردان چرا
فریاد بی حاصل کنم

"Why should I lament in vain
amidst the sober and pain free?

ساقی بده پیمانه ای ز ان
می که بیخویشم کند

O Cup bearer, bring me cup strong
enough to free me from self!

(From the book, Ba'ra'n-e sobhga'hi)

He also joined the ranks of many of his contemporaries—Fereydoon Tavalali,(1919-1985), Abu'l-Qa'sem Ha'lat (1919- 1992), and Mohammad Ali Afra'shta (1908-1959)—who, albeit from different political backgrounds, delighted in composing humorous, burlesque and satirical poetry during the short-lived period of freedom of expression which followed the invasion of Iran by the Allied Forces and the subsequent abdication of Reza Shah in 1941.

His satirical poems, under such names as Za'ghcheh, Gushe-gir, Hagh-gu, and Sha'he-pariyun, appeared in the weekly Tehra'n-e mosavar and more significantly, in B'aba' Shamal a weekly satirical periodical founded by Rez'a Ganjian in April 1943. In one such poem Rahi exercises his wit in describing the election of women representatives to the Parliament, alluding throughout to the names of prominent male representatives, who, as the poem goes to satirize, were mesmerized by the beauty of their newly-arrived counterparts. His talent for nuance, the art of ambiguity and the double entendre was also exercised, as held by Amiri Firuzkuhi, to a degree of perfection in both his humorous and serious verse, and indeed, on friend and foe alike.

His biting and critical verses, directed at Iranian collaborators who were nothing but a group of traitors attempting to separate A'zerba'ija'n and surrendering it to the forces of USSR during the occupation of this important province by invaders thus giving away for ever an important part of our home-land , reflect his penchant for patriotism, and remain remarkably poetical. Some of these verses were set to music and aired by Radio Iran for several years to come:

Oh you!, The jewel laiden land of Iran You are more gracious thant the paradise Art and culture is alive by the light of your name The world is intoxicated with the wine drunk from your cup May this country and its people be alive forever	تو ای پر گهر خاک ایران زمین که وا لاتری از بهشت برین هنر زنده از پرتو نام تست جهان سر خوش از جرعه جام تست بر و بوم این ملک پاینده باد

Rahi's appointment as the literary director of radio Iran's music program in the later years of his life gave him the greatest professional satisfaction and was most in keeping with his artistic inclination. Rahi exhibited both artistic fervor and skill in composing lyrics to be set to music for the Golh'a program that brought quality performances by the best performing artists to a vast audience. Some commentators have pointed out his debt to his predecessor A'ref Qazvini. As noted by a critic; however, the incongruous repetitions and breaks in flow at times encountered in A'ref's verses are abscent from Rahi's work. His verses are recognized from his elegant and delicate language and for the highly informed coordination of lyrics and melody. Rahi's compositions, often exemplary, were emulated by many and played an instrumental role in extracting lyrical poetry from the worn out rut into which it had fallen.

Throughout his years with the Radio, Rahi enjoyed the friendship and collaboration of such eminent composers and vocalists as Morteza Mahjubi (1900-1965), Ruh-Olla'h Kha'leghi (1906-1965), Ali Tajvidi (1919-2006) Abd-ol-Ali Vaziri (1887-1979), and Ghola'm Hosein Ban'n (1911-1986). Rahi's political sensibilities, and his ability to fit words to music, combined with his deep understanding of Persian music made him the poet of choice for

Contemporary Persian Poetry

many composers of his time (A set of his verses that were set to music is recorded and published as Ya'd bood-Rahi: Barna'me-ye 485 golh'ay-ye Ta'za. He had an extensive following, not only in Iran, but also in Afghanistan and Pakistan, where his cassettes were circulated hand to hand, including the following famous composition that began:

"All night I cry, like the reed
I bear sadness, I bear sadness".

همه شب نالم چون نی
غمی دارم غمی

Rahi has been described as tall, well-groomed, and attractive man. Characteristics that were not lost on the opposite sex. Much has been written of his romantic affairs. Mohammad Hejazi (Moti-ol-Doleh (1901-1974) who was distantly related and shared an office with him at the Ministry of Culture and Art, found inspiration for a number of his stories, in particular A'yeneh '(Mirror) in Rahi's romances and romantic escapades. The noted historian Ba'sta'Ni Parizi has also alluded to the love between Rahi and Maryam Firuz for whom Rahi composed some of his most celebrated ghazals. This romance was short lived, however, as soon thereafter, Maryam Firuz met Nur-el-Din Kiyanoori, the prominent member, and sometime leader, of the Hezb-Tudeh (Tudeh) party, the man she would eventually marry.

Rahi died of cancer on November 14, 1968, and was buried in the Zahir-al-Dawleh Cemetery in Tehran. At the time of his death, Rahi was at the hight of his fame, both in Iran and abroad, just before his death, he was praised by Khalil-Alla'h Khalili, a notable Afghan poet, in a long and eloquent Qasida:

"Dar sepehr-sokhan cho badr-e monir
Ghazal ta'bnak-tost, Rahi"

در سپهر سخن چو بدر منیر
غزل تابناک توست رهی
در آسمان سخن غزلت
چو ماه تابان است رهی

(In the heaven of words, your ghazals,
Are like the shining moon, Rahi

(From the book; Sayeh-e omr)

His loss received wide coverage in Iran and the Persian- speaking countries. A memorial service was held at Sepahsa'la'r Mosque, attended by Mohhamad Reza Shah Pahlavi, Prime Minister Amir Abbas Hoveyda and the political and social elite. He was remembered as "one of the most eminent poets of the period, whose life and death immitated his poetry. Several poets wrote eulogies in his memory, including his old friend Amir Firuzkuhi, Ra'di A'zarakhshi, A'sef Fekrat, the noted contemporary Afghan poet.

Rahi's poems, songs, compositions, satire and humor have been brought together in a number of collections, of which Sa'yeh-e omr is the only collection edited under the supervision of Rahi himself. The list of publications includes:

A'za'deh (poetry collection) Tehran, 1969.
Ba'ra'n-e Sobhga'hi, Tehran 1999
Diva'n-e Ka'mel-e Rahi Ed; Bahman Kalifa Bana'rva'Ni.
Kolliya't-e Rahi, ed; Reza' Saja'di
Majmua-ye Asha'r, Said Q'ne'i,
Raha'vard-e Rahi, Ed; Da'rush Sabur,
Tanzha'-ye Rahi Moa'yri, Ed; Rahim Cha'voshi Akbari.

Rahi also contributed to Ettela'a't-e haftegi and other periodicals, at times selecting from other poet's works, and describing their lives. He has also contributed articles on the poets who composed in Persian in the Indian subcontinent. His writings are published in two collections under the same title Golha'-ye ja'vida'n.

Ahmad Shamlou 20th century Persian poet

Ahmad Shamlou was born on December 12, 1925, in Rasht in the province of Gilan, His father was an army officer and as such the family moved from city to city depending on his father's job assignment. They lived in the province of Sistan for a while and then in Mashhad, in the province of Khorasan. Shamlou had a rather hard childhood life in particular because of having to move from city to city.

In 1941 he left Birjand a city in Khorasan and moved to Tehran with his high school education still incomplete. In Tehran he got admitted to German technical school, but soon that also had to be interrupted because the family had to move to Gorgan and then to Uromieh finally failing to obtain his high school diploma. At the age of 29 following the fall of Prime Minister

Contemporary Persian Poetry

Mohammad Mossadegh, Shamlou was arrested for being a member of communist Tudeh Party and spent a year in prison.

Remembering his introduction to Persian poetry Shamlou explains how he first learned writing poetry from foreign poets like the Spanish writer Lorca, the Frenchman, Eluard, the German Rilke, the Russian, Mayakovsky and the American Langston Hughes; and only later, with this education he turned to the poems of his mother language to see and to know, say, the grandeur of Hafez from a fresh perspective.

Shamlou's debut work, Forgotten Songs was a collection of classical and modern poetry which was published in 1947 with an introduction of Ebrahim Dilmaghanian. In 1948, he started to write in a literary monthly called Sokhan-no. Two years later his first short story, "The Woman behind the Brass Door" was published. His second collection of poems, Manifesto was published in 1951. He showed inclinations toward social ideology. He got a job in the Hungarian embassy as their cultural advisor.

His third collection of poems, Metals and Sense (1952), was banned and destroyed by the police. His translations of Gold in Dirt, by Sigmund Motritz, and the voluminous novel The heartless Man's Sons by Mo'r Jokai, together with all data gathered for his work on the colloquial culture of urban Iranian life (to be known as The Book of Alley) were also confiscated and destroyed. In 1954 he was jailed for 14 months. In 1955 he translated and published three novels by European writers. He became the editor-in-chief of Bamshad literary magazine in 1956.

He rose to fame from his next volume of poetry, Fresh Air, published in 1957. Zia Movahed, poet and philosopher commented that "Anyone who reads Fresh Air today can see that this language, this texture, is different from anything else. In contemporary poetry, few have accomplished this kind of rhyme as Shamlou has. Fresh Air was the greatest event in our poetry—after Hafez". He also published a few studies on classical Iranian poetry. His translation of Barefoot, a novel by Zaharia Stancu, was released in 1958, establishing Shamlou's authority as a translator. In 1959 he began publishing short stories for children, as well as directing documentary films and working for film studios.

Chapter 10

In 1967, he became editor-in-chief of Khusheh. His new translation of Erskine Caldwell was published, and he participated in the formation of the Union of Iranian writers and gave several poetry readings at Iranian universities. In 1968, he began his study of Hafez, the classical grand poet of the Persian language; translated Garcia Lorca's poems and Song of Solomon from the Old Testament, organized a week of poetry reading for established and new Iranian poets, which was very well received. In 1969, his weekly magazine was closed down by the police. Of The Air and Mirrors, a selection of older poetry, was published, together with his collection of new poems, Odes for the Earth.

In 1970, Blossoming in Mist was published. He also directed a few documentary films for television and published several short stories for children. In 1971, he redid some of his earlier translations. In 1972, he taught Persian literature at Tehran University. Several audio cassettes were released of Shamlou reciting other classical and modern poet's work. He obtained membership in the Language Academy of Shamlou, published several new translations and wrote a few film scripts. He travelled to Paris for medical treatment. In 1973 two new collections, Abraham in Fire and Doors and the Great China Wall, were released, along with several new translations. "The Song of Abraham in Fire"is one of the most well-crafted and famous contemporary Persian poems written by Ahmad Shamlou. Shamlou connects his poem to the collective consciousness of the whole world, presenting characters of heros and even the social scapegoat rather in a curious way as we read about the case of a man who sacrifices himself for land and love and, yet, who is betrayed by others due to their ignorance and biases. In 1975, he published his work and study of Hafez. In 1976, he travelled to the United States and gave poetry readings in many cities. He participated in the San Francisco Poetry Festival before returning to Iran. In 1977, he published his new poem, Dagger on the Plate. He left Iran in protest of the Shah's regime and stayed in the United States for a year giving lectures in American universities.

In 1978 he left the United States for Britain to act as the editor-in-chief for a new publication called Iranshahr. He resigned after12 issues and returned to Iran just after the advent of revolution. He rejoined Union of Iranian writers and began publishing a new periodical, Ketab-e Jom'e to great success. 1978 was a very active year in his life, and he published many poems and translations, as well as giving numerous lectures and readings. He was also elected to the membership of the Writer's Union's leadership. 1979 was also a year of intense activity. The first and second volumes of The Book of Alley went in print. He was also re-elected as member of the Writer's Union's leadership.

Starting in 1980, owing to the harsh political situation in Iran, he led a rather secluded life that would last for the next eight years; working with Ayda on The book of Ally, as well as many other literary endeavors, including a translation of The Don by Mikhail Sholokhov. In 1984 he was nominated for the Noble Prize in literature. In 1988 he was invited by Ingterlit, the World Literary Congress. He toured Europe givng many lectures and readings. His complete collection of poems was printed in Germany, and he returned to Iran. In 1990 he toured the United States. Human Rights and the Fund for Free Expression presented him with their annual award. Several works were published on his poetry and his overall literary contribution. In 1991 he toured Europe again and returned to Iran for another four years of intensive work. That same year, he won the Freedom of Expression Award given by the New York based Human Rights Watch. In 1992, his work sacred words appeared in Armenian and English. In 1994 he toured Sweden, invited by his Swedish editor Masoud Dehghani Firouzabadi, giving numerous lectures and readings.

In 1995, he finished the translation of And Quiet flows the Don. There was a special gathering in Toronto of Iranian writers and critics to discuss Shamlou's contribution to Persian poetry. His Aurora was also published in Spanish. In 1999, he was presented with the Stig Dagerman prize by the Swedish Foundation.

Shamlou was married three times. In 1947, he married Ashraf Islamniya and together they had three sons and a daughter. They divorced in 1957 after several years of conflict and long separation. His second marriage to Tusi Hayeri who was fourteen years older than Shamlou, ended in divorce in 1963 after four years of marriage. He met Aida Sarkisian in the spring of 1962 and they were married two years later in 1964. Aida came from an Armenian-Iranian family who lived in the same neighborhood as Shamlou. Her Christian family objected to the marriage on the basis of the Islamic background of Shamlou's family. Moreover, Shamlou was older; and had been divorced twice. She became an instrumental figure in Shamloo's life and they remained together until his death in 2000. Her name appears in many of his late poems.

Chapter 10

Suffering from several illnesses at the same time, Shamlou's physical condition deteriorated in 1996. He underwent several operations and in 1997, his right foot was amputated due to severe diabetic problems. He died on Sunday, July 23, 2000 at his home in Karaj due to complications from his diabetes. On July, 27, thousands took part in his funeral. He was buried in Emamzadeh Taher, Karaj.

Works and style
Ahmad Shamlou has published more than seventy books; 16 volumes of poetry; 5 Anthologies of poetry; 5 volumes including novels about kids, short stories & screenplays, 9 volumes of children's literature about Clifford; 9 translations of poetry into Persian; 21 novels translated into Persian; 5 collections of essays, lectures and interviews; 10 volumes of The Book of Alleys.

Ahmad Shamlou's poetic vision accords both western Modernist concepts and modern transformation of classical Persian poetry. The Spanish poet, Federico Garcia Lorca, the African American poet Langston Hughes, The French thinker, and writer Louis Aragon, and Nima Youshij are among the figures that influenced him. One of the disciples of Nima Youshij, Shamlou, standing among the generation who adopted his techniques, constantly sought untried ways, new poetic realms. He quickly became the flag bearer of young Iranian poets and writers that included Forough Farokhzad, Sohrab Sepehri, Mehdi Akhavan Sales, Nosrat Rahmani, and Nader Naderpour.

Shamlou's poems are filled with mythological concepts and symbols to glorify seemingly simple and ordinary figures who are politically condemned for their revolutionary beliefs that, regardless of governmental suppression, actually reflect the activist's deep love of their nation and people. Even though his focus is the purity of such individuals, many of whom were his close friends, Shamlou writes his elegic poems boldly and does not hold back from criticizing and denouncing hypocrisy and cruelty of his society.

Public Love by Ahmad Shamlou	عشق عمومی شعر احمد شاملو
Secret of tears, The smile of secrets,	اشگ رازی ست لبخند رازی ست اشگ آنشب لبخند عشقم بود

Tears, that night was the smile of
my love
I am not a story to tell
I am not a song to sing I am not a
Voice to hear
Or something to see
…or something to know
 I cry out in pain
The tree speaks to the forest
Grass to the desert
Star to the galaxy
And I to you I say
Tell me
Your name, give me your hand, tell
me the trick
Give me tour heart, I have found
your roots, I have spoken
With your lips to all lips, and, your
hands are
Familiar with my hands
In the light of solitude I have wept
with you
For the sake of the living
And in the dark graveyard I have
sung with you the
Most beautiful hymns because the
dead
Have been the most beloved of the
living this year'
Put your hand Give me
Your hands to me aware
Of Dyryafth you speak
Like a cloud that storms
Like the grass of the field
As the rain that in the sea
Is like a bird with spring
As the trees that the forest talks Says
Because I have understood your
roots

قصه نیستم که بگویی
نغمه نیستم که بخوانی
صدا نیستم که بشنوی
یا چیزی که ببینی
یا چیزی چنان که بدانی...
من درد مشترکم
مرا فریاد کن
درخت با جنگل سخن میگوید
علف با صحرا
ستاره با کهکشان
ومن با تو سخن میگویم
نامت را به من بگو
دستت را بمن بده
حرفت را به من بگو
قلبت را به من بده
من ریشه های تو را دریافته ام
با لبانت برای همه لب ها سخن گفته ام
و دست هایت با دستان من آشناست
درخلوت روشن با تو گریسته ام
برای خاطر زندگان
و در گورستان تاریک با تو خوانده ام
زیباترین سرود ها را
زیرا که مردگان ای سال
عاشق ترین زندگان بوده اند
دستت را به من بده
دستهای تو با من آشناست
ای دیر یافته با تو سخن میگویم
به سان ابر که با توفان
به سان علف که با صحرا
به سان باران که با دریا
به سان پرنده که با بهار
به سان درخت که با جنگل سخن می گوید
زیرا که من
ریشه های تورا دریافته ام
زیرا که صدای من
با صدای تو آشناست

Because my voice is familiar with
your voice"

The Fish
Poem by Ahmad Shamlou

شعر ماهی
سروده احمد شاملو

I don't suppose, my heart was ever
Warm and red like this before
I sense that in the worst moments of
this black
Death-feeding repast
 A thousand thousand well-springs
of sunlight
Stemming from certitude,
Well up my heart, I sense, further,
that
In every nook and cranny of this salt
Barrenness of despair
A thousand thousand joy forests
stemming from the soil,
Are suddenly springing,
Oh, lost certitude, oh, sea-creature
Fleeing in the concentric, shivering,
mirroring pools
I am the clear pool, mesmerized by
love,
Search out a path for me among the
Mirror pools
I don't think my hand was ever
strong and alive
Like this, before.
I sense that in my every vein,
In time with my every heart beat,
The warning bell of a departing
caravan toils.
She, bare, came one evening
through the door
Like the soul of water.

من فکر میکنم
هرگز نبوده قلب من
اینگونه
گرم و سرخ
احساس میکنم
در بدترین دقایق این شام مرگ زای
چندین هزار چشمه خورشید
در دلم
میجوشد از یقین
احساس میکنم
در هر کناروگوشه ای این شوره زار یاس
چندین هزار جنگل شاداب
ناگهان
می روید از زمین

آه ای یقید گم شده ای ماهی گریز
در برکه های آینه لغزیده تو به تو!
من آبگیر صافی ام اینک ! به سحر عشق
از برکه های آینه راهی به من بجو!

من فکر می کنم
هرگز نبوده
دست من
این سان بزرگ و شاد:
احساس میکنم
در چشم من
به آبشار اشگ سرخ گون
خورشید بی غروب سرودی کشد نفس
احساس می کنم

At her breast two fish
In her hand a mirror, her wet hair,
Moss fragrance, intertwined moss.
On the threshold of despair,
I bellowed: Ah, oh retrieved certitude.
I won't put you again aside.

در هر رگم
به هر تپش قلب من
کنون
بیدار باش قافله ای می زند جرس.

آمد شبی برهنه ام از در
چو روح آب
در سینه اش دو ماهی و در دستش آینه
گیسوی خیس او خزه بو چون خزه به هم
من بانگ برکشیدم از آستان یاس:
"آه ای یقین یافته بازت نمی نهم!"

Mehdi Akhavan Sales 20th century Persian poet

Mehdi Akhavan-e Sales was born in Mashhad in February 1928. He died in Tehran in August 1990. He completed his elementary school in Mashhad and entered a technical school to train as a welder. He became interested in music and because he knew that his father does not approve he tried to learn playing the ta'r {instrument} secretly. Akhavan was first a student of the traditional Persian poetry and started his poetic career as a classist. Apparently Parviz Ka'vian Jahromi an instructor in the technical school in Mashhad familiarized him with the elementary principles of classical Persian prosody. Akhavan soon found his way to the literary circles of Mashhad, the most notable of which, the Khorasan Literary Society, was directed by "Abdol-Hoseyn Nosrat Monshi-Bashi and regularly attended by such literary figures as Ali-Akbar Golshan Azadi and Mahmud Farokh. Akhavan opted for M.Omid as his pen name. As he grew older, however, "He began to play with the meaning of that poetic name with a dubious, gradually deepening sense of irony."

Soon after, however, Akhavan along with Reza Marzban, Ali Milani, and a few others, formed Baha'r, a literary circle more in tune with modernist trends in poetry. It was during this period that Akhavan became involved with leftist politics, which was popular among the intelligentcia and artists during the

1940's. He soon became a member of the provincial committee of the recently established Youth Organization of the Tudeh Party.

In 1947 Akhavan moved to Tehran, having seen already his poems appear in print in Mashhad's local papers. In Tehran, Akhavan began work in editing, and in 1948 was employed by the Ministry of Culture and sent to the outskirts of Vara'min as a teacher, a position that gave him ample time to further familiarize himself with classical Persian poetry. He continued to be engaged in the political activism he had initiated in Mashhad. In 1950 Akhavan married his cousin, they had six children.

In 1951 Akhavan's first collection of poetry Arghanun dedicated "to all freedom fighters," was published with an introduction by Reza Marzban. The first edition of the collection consisted of his classical poems, as well as some poems which exhibited his gradual departure from the prosodic rules of Persian classical poetry. In later editions, Arghanun was altered substantially as Akhavan added more classical poems and removed several others. In 1951 he was appointed literary editor for the newspaper Javanan-e democrat, (Young democrats), a position that expanded his contact with the poets of his generation.

The oil crisis of the early 1950's and the ensuing political scenery in 1953 created much frustration among the young, active generation of Akhavan's time. He was apprehended twice for political activism and involvement with the Tudeh Party, first for a short period of time in winter of 1953 and then a month later, at which point he was imprisoned for roughly a year. Disappointed by the failure of democratic overtures in Iran, Akhavan refrained from political activity and settled into a slf-devised and idealized figure that he called "Mazdosht," a composite of aspects of Zarathus, the Persian prophet, and Mazdak, the archetype of the rebel prophet in ancient Iranian culture, with a small sprinkling of ideas from Ma'ni and Buddha ("Tak o tanha' rah-e Mazdosht puyam,") and in "To ra'ey kohan bum o bar dust da'rum,".

After his release he was sent into the environs of Kashan to teach. He soon quit the job and returned to Tehran. In order to pay his keep he found employment in journalism, publishing at times under aliases and pen names. In the years following his imprisonment Akhavan, along with Hoseyn Ra'zi was in charge of the literary section of Ira'n-ema', a political journal published by Jaha'n Tafazoli.

Zemestan (winter, 1956), Akhavan's second collection of poetry consisting of 39 poems, demonstrates in no uncertain terms his familiarity with, and positive disposition toward, Nimaie poetry. The collection earned Akhavan celebrity status in the Persian society of the time. The title poem of the collection, as held by a critic, not only Akhavan's rich poetical disposition and his studied familiarity with classical poetry, but also paints a penetrating image of wintery outlook of Persian society in the gloom-ridden years of 1950's.

Following the publication of Zemestan, Akhavan began work with Ebrahim Golestan, the author and filmmaker, in his film production company. There, his responsibilities included editing film scripts and supervising soundtrack recordings. His colleagues included Forough Farokhzad, Fereidun Rahnema, Karim Emami, and Najaf Daryabandari, among others.

Having turned to Nima Yushij, Akhavan spent years introducing Nimaie poetry to Iranian audiances to good effect. Throughout his books and essays, Akhavan draws a basic distinction between Nima's approach to poetic signification and the manner in which he invites his readers to participate in the act of creating meaning, on the one hand, and that of certain classical poets, on the other, who worked with a complex set of inherited concepts linked together throughout the centuries, and whose readers have been conditioned to anticipate adherence to conventions now defunct.

In 1959, Akhavan's third collection of poetry, A'kher-e Shah-name (The ending of Shahname), was published, containing what could prove to be some of his most acclaimed poems. The title poem of the collection not only reveals Akhavan's meditation on Iran's glorified pre-Islamic past, but also conveys his elegiac conviction on the impossibility of its survival.

...We	...Ma'
Are the conquerors of cities gone with the wind?	Fa'teha'n-e Shahrha-ye rafteh bar ba'dim.
With a voice too weak to come out of the chest	Ba seda'-I natava'n-tar za'n-ke birun a'yad AZ sineh,
We relate the forgotten tales.	Ra'vian-e ghasrha-ye rafta AZ ya'dim.
	(A'kher-e Shah-na'ma)

Akher-Shahnama was extremely well received by readers and critics alike. Forough Farokhzad regarded the collection's title poem to be "one of the most powerful poems to be composed since the inception of She'r-now. Jala'l A'l-Ahmad, while at times critical, was complimentary, especially of the poet's sensivity to social and political issues. In 1961 Akhavan left Golesta'n Film Studio and began a period of cooperation with Radio Iran, where he was engaged in writing cultural and literary programs. In 1965 he published his fourth poetry collection, Az in Avesta'. The collection, in which approximately three quarters of the poems are composed in what is generally recognized as Nimaie style of poetry, "The style that Akhavan first explored in a number of his last poems in Zemesta'n and which has good renditions in Akher-e Shahnama, comes to fullness and perfection in this collection"

Akhavan's world view, suggestive of his obsessive engagement with the eternal struggle between light and darkness, earned him a critical attack by Reza'Bara'heni. It should be noted, however, that an increasing deterioration in the human condition is discernible in Akhavan's conception of history and his "flight into past," as held by a critic, "is the strong yearning of a refugee, who at the end arrives at bolted doors."

In 1969, he moved to Abadan to find employment with the local television station. There he researched and wrote literary and cultural programs as well as pamphelets on the historical geography of several regions. In that same year his fifth collection of poetry, Pa'iz dar Zendan (autumn in prison), was published. The collection includes a number of poems composed during his incarceration, mostly in Nimaic meter. With a few notable exceptions, most are devoid of the literary quality and significance encountered in his earlier collections.

In 1974, following his daughter's death, he returned to Tehran and began work at Iranian National Television, appearing frequently in literary programs in the period preceding the Revolution. In 1977 he accepted positions teaching the literature of The Samanid period as well as contemporary literature at Tehran University, the National University, and the Teacher Training College. Zendegi miguyad: amma' ba'z ba'yad zist... (Life says; still we must live)...

Akhavan's sixth poetry collection was published in 1978. The book, as noted by Akhavan in his introduction, is more a "recollection in verse," and "not poetry in the customary or usual sense". Akhavan's seventh collection is a composite of classical and Nimaic verse as well as a poem entitled "A'ha'y, b'a to-am" (Hey, I'm talking to you!), that is significant in that it is devoid of meter; a form with which Akhavan rarely experimented.

Akhavan's Nimaic verse in this collection fails to attain the heights encountered in his earlier works. The collection also includes a number of poems in new "Khosravani", a term he coined after the pre-Islamic poetry known as Khohsravani.

In 1979, Akhavan commenced work as Editor in Chief of the Sa'zema'n-e Entesha'ra't VA a'muzesh-e Enqela'b-e Esla'mi, or what had been Moassessa-ye entesha'rat-e Feranklin before; (Franklin Book Program), but he did not last there for more than a few months. In 1981, despite his long years of employment in governmental organizations, he was retired without pay. In 1989 Akhavan's eight collection of poetry, "To ra' ey kohan bum o bar dust da'ram" was published. It contains some of Akhavans best poems in classical prosody. His complete abandonment of Nimaic meters in the collection, however, raised eyebrows in modernist literary circles to the extent that it was regarded by some as a "hollow shell"

Poem "Ancient Land (Kohan Bum)" by Mehdi Akhavan Sales:	ترا ای کهن بوم وبر دوست دارم ز پوچ جهان هیچ اگر دوست دارم
O You Ancient Land, (I love Thee) From all the meaningless earthly possessions, if I acclaim	ترا ای کهن بوم وبردوست دارم ترا ای کهن پیر جاوید دوست دارم
Thee oh ancient land, I adore Thee oh ancient eternal great, If I adore any thee I adore	ترا دوست دارم اگر دوست دارم ترا ای گرانمایه دیرینه ایران
Thee oh priceless ancient Iran, Thee oh valuable jewel, I, adore	ترا ای گرا می گهردوست دارم ترا ای کهن زا د بوم بزرگان
Thee ancient birthplace of the great nobles	بزرگ آ فرین دوست دارم هنروار اندیشه ات رخشد و من
	هم اندیشه ا ت هم هنر دوست دارم

Thee famous creator of the greats, I adore	اگر قول افسانه یا متن تاریخ
	وگر نقد ونقل سیر دوست دارم
Thine art and thoughts shines through the world Both thine art and thine thoughts I adore	اگر خامه تیشه ست وخط نقش در سنگ بر اوراق کوه و کمر دوست دارم
	وگر ضبط دفتر ز مشگین مرکب
May it be legend or history? Critics and ancient stories, all I adore	نبین خامه یا کلک پر دوست دارم گمان های تو چون یقین دوست دارم
Thine fantasy, I worship as truth Thine reality, as news I adore	هم اورمزد وهم ایزدانت پرستم همان فره وفروهر دوست دارم
Thine Ahuramazda and Yazatas, I revere Thine glory and Farahvafar, I adore	به جان پاک پیغمبر با ستانت که پیری ست روشن نگر دوست دارم
To thine ancient prophet, I take an oath Who is a bright and wise sage, I adore	گران مایه زردشت را من فزونتر ز هر پیر و پیغام بر دوست دارم
The noble Zarathustra, more so than All other sages and prophets, I adore	بشر بهتر از او ندید و نبیند من آن بهترین از بشردوست دارم
Humanity better than him has not seen and will not see This noblest of humanity I adore	سه نیکش بهین رهنمای جهان است مفیدی چنین مختصردوست دارم
This great Iranian was a leader This Iranian leader I adore	نه کشت ونه دستور کشتن به کس داد از این روش هم معتبردوست دارم
His trios are the greatest guide for the world This impactful yet brief guide, I adore	هم آن پیر بیدار دل با مدادت نشا بوری هور فر دوست دارم
	فری مزدک آن هوش جاوید اعصار که اش از هر نگاه ونظر دوست دارم
	دلیرانه جان باخت در جنگ بیداد

من آن شیردل دادگر دوست دارم

He never killed, nor asked others to kill
This noble path I adore

جهانگیر وداد آفرین فکرتی داشت

فزونترش زین رهگذردوست دارم

This truthful ancient sage
Who went beyond the legend, I adore

ستایش کنان مانی ارجمندت

چو نقاش وپیغا موردوست دارم

The eternal intellect of the glorious Mazdak
From all angles and aspects, I adore

همان نقش پرداز ارواح برتر

هم ارژنگ آن نقشگردوست دارم

He died bravely in the war with injustice
That just lion-heart I adore

همه کشتزارانت ازدیم وفاراب

همه دشت ودر جوی وجر دوست دارم

Global and just thought he had
More of his thoughts in our path I adore

شهیدان جانبازوفرزانه ات را

که بودند فخربشردوست دارم

Praising thine great Mani
The artist and messenger I adore

به لطف نسیم سحرروحشان را

چنان چون زآهن جگردوست دارم

That painter of the higher spirits
The truth of his paintings I adore

هم افکار پرشورشان را که اعصار

از آن گشته زیروزبردوست دارم

All types of your fertile land
All your fields, deserts, springs and rivers I adore

هم آثارشان را چه پند وپیام

وگرچند سطری خبردوست دارم

Thine brave and noble martyrs
Who were prides of the humanity, I adore

من آن جاودان یاد مردان که بودند

به هر قرن چندین نفردوست دارم

With the help of the morning breeze, their spirits
Made of iron, I sense and I adore

همه شاعران تو و آثارشان را

به پاکی نسیم سحردوست دارم

ز فردوسی آن کاخ افسانه کافراخت

در آفاق فخر وظفردوست دارم

زخیام خشم وخروشی که جاوید

Their works of experience and messages
Or may be a few lines of news I adore

کند در دل وجان ا ثردوست دارم

ز عطار آن سوزوسودای پردرد
که انگیزد از جان شرردوست دارم

These legendry noblemen of
Just a few in each century, I adore

زسعدی واز حافظ واز نظامی
همه شوروشعروسمردوست دارم

All thine poets and poems
Same as the morning breeze I adore

خوشا رشت وگرگان ومازندرانت
که شان همچو بحرخزردوست دارم

Thine Ferdowsi, the legendry literary tower he erected
Placed in the hall of fame and glory, I adore

فری آذرآبادگان بزرگت
من آن پیشگام خطردوست دارم

Thine Khayyam, the eternal anger and passion he created
In our hearts and souls I adore

صفاهان نصف جهان تورا من
فزون ترزنصف دگردوست دارم

From that admirer of Shams, the passionThat inflames the heart, I adore

خوشا خطه نخبه زای خراسان
زجان ودل آن پهنه ور دوست دارم

From Saadi, Hafez and Nezami
All the cheers, poetry and fruits I adore

زهی شهر شیراز جنت طرازت
من آن مهد ذوق وهنردوست دارم

Great art thine Rasht, Gorgan and Mazanderan
The same as Caspian Sea I adore

بروبوم کرد وبلوچ تو را چون
درخت نجابت ثمردوست دارم

Great art thine Karoun river and Ahvaz
Sweeter than sugar I adore

خوشا طرف کرمان ومرزجنوبت
که شان خشگ وتر بحروبردوست دارم

من "افغان" هم ریشه مان را که باغی
ست
به چنگ بتر از تتر دوست دارم

Glory to thine Azerbaijan
That first step to danger I adore

کهن سغد وخوارزم را با کویرش
که شان باخت دوده ی قجردوست دارم

Esfahan, thine half of the world
More than the other half I adore

Great art Khorasan the birthplace of
the wise
With all my heart and soul, that vast
land I adore

Great art thine beautiful Shiraz
The center of talent and art I adore

Thine lands of Kurdistan and
Baluchistan, same as
The noble fruit tree I adore

Great art thine Kerman and southern
borders
Thus dry and wet, sea and desert I
adore

Soqd and Kharazm and their desetrs
Alas Qajars had lost, but I adore

Thine Iraq and the long strips of
Persian Gulf
Similar to wall of China I adore

Our ancient Caucasia to Iran
A son in father's house I adore

Thine yesterday's legends and
tomorrow's dreams
In each its own, both I adore

Thus better than these two, art thee
alive
Thine today's entity I adore

عراق وخلیج تورا چون ورآ زرود
که دیوار چین راست دردوست دارم

هم ا ران وقفقا ز دیرینه مان را
چو پوری سرای پدردوست دارم

چو دیروزا فسا نه فردای رو یات
به جان این یک و آن د گر دوست دارم

چو رویا و افسا نه دیروزوفردا ت
به جای خود این هردو سردوست دارم

و لیکن از این هردو ای زنده ای نقد
من امروزتوبیشتردوست دارم
تو در اوج بودی به معنا و صورت
من آن اوج قدرو خطر دوست دارم
دگر بار بر شو به اوج معانی
که تاین تازه رنگ وصور دوست دارم
جهان تا جهان است پیروز باشی
برومند و بیدارو بهروز باشی

Thine beauty and depth were on top
of the world
That ultimate value and danger I
adore

Once more arise to the maximum
depth
This new color and beauty I adore

Not   Easternization,   Not
Westoxication, Not Tazi-fiction
For thee O Ancient Land I adore

Until the world remains, victorious
thou shalt be
Strong, awake and fortunate thou
shalt be

Akhavan-e Sales holds a place of special distinction among the Iranian poets
of the modern times. His style is, however similar to the works composed by
most of his contemporary authors and poets of our time who pursued
enthusiastically the achievements of the National Movement and were not
immune from the consequences of the political and social crisis of the time.
Specifically the most vivid feedbacks of these may be found in Akhavan's
poetry. He is a poet whose attitude about historical and political events is more
emotional, because he is by nature neither a politician nor historian. This
emotional trend provides the ground for reflection of romanticism in his
poetry. His poetry may not fully and in all of its aspects be categorized in
romanticism school because some of the components and features are
expressed outside the romantic scope.

The trend of Akhavan to romanticism or the romantic aspect of his poetry may
be sought in his frustrating political-social poems within the scope of
emotional reflection of defeat. "winter" is one of the most famous poems
composed by Akhavan that reflects the frustrated and sad voice of a generation
in a symbolic expression. What is found in "winter" as the expressions of

romanticism, indeed are the conceptual axes and general atmosphere governing the poem. From this view point, naturalism, symbolic and methaphoric expression, seclusiveness, and frustration are also considerd as the most important and significant aspects of the poem. Although socio-political issues find"the most sincere expression in his poetry" Akhavan often lends his verses to the implicative power of imagery rather than the explicative nature of literal language. In contrast to the blunt advocacy of political ideologies with which much of the literature of the period is stamped, and to which time has already proved to be an enemy, Akhavan, in the best of his poems creats two fully independent semantic fields, each complete in itself; one of which, however, is intricately embedded in the poem, requiring more subtle intellectual involvement for revelation"Ba'ghe-man in Zemesta'n" offers a rewarding example:

From zemestan, poem by Akhava'n Sa'les
The leafless Garden:

باغ بی برگی-شعر زمستان سروده
اخوان ثالث

The leafless garden
Is alone day and night
With its pure and sad silence.

باغ بی برگی
روزوشب تنهاست
با سکوت پاک نمناکش

Its lyric is the rain and his song the wind,
Its garment is of nudity cloak,
And if another garment it must wear ,
Let its warf and woof be woven by golden ray.

آسمانش را گرفته تنگ در آغوش
ابر با ان پوستینش سرد نمناکش

ساز او باران سرودش باد
جامه اش شولای عریانی ست
ور جزینش جامه ای باید
بافته بس شعله ی زرتار پودش باد

They can grow or not grow, wherever they want or don't;
There is neither a gardner nor a passerby.
The depressed garden
Expects no spring.

گو بروید یا نروید هرچه در هرجا که
خواهد یا نمی خواهد
باغبان ورهگذاری نیست
باغ نومیدان
چشم در راه بهاری نیست

If its eye sheds no warm luster
And on its face no leaf of smile grows,
Who says the leafless garden is not beautiful?
It relates the tale of fruits, once reaching to heavens, now lying in the cold Coffin of earth.

گرزچشمش پرتو گرمی نمی تابد

The leafless Garden ,
Laughs in tearfull blood,
Eternal, mounted on his wild yellow
stallion,
Roams autumn, the king of seasons.

وربه رویش برگ لبخندی نمی روید
باغ بی برگی که میگوید زیبا نیست؟
داستان از میوه های سر به گردون
سای اینک خفته در تابوت پست خاک
میگوید

باغ بی برگی
خندهاش خونی ست اشگ آمیز
جاودان بر اسب بال افشان زردش
۱ می چمد در آن پادشاه فصل پاییز

An alluring image of ancient Iran flavors Akhavan's poems creating a sharp, and often unfortunate, binary between Persians and Arabs. His fifty–seven-line long qasida, "To ra' ey Kohan bum bar dust da'ram" wherein he takes readers on an imaginary journey around Iran, roaming up and down its history and territory, noting all that he loves and adores, is replete throughout with his expression of a burning love for Iran
(See on page 302 above, the poem in its entirety in Farsi and English)

Akhavan's ease with qasidah, a genre rarely attempted by his contemporaries, brings to mind the erudition of the old masters. His melancholy mood of dashed hopes is occasionally expressed by a certain characteristic wit and irony "Another feature not frequently seen in the poetry of his contemporaries" His often ribald introductions to his collections of poems, particularly the one he wrote for The End of Shahnama, are fascinating examples of his satiric gifts. Akhavan's poems are translated into many languages, including English.

Karim Amiri Firuzkuhi 20th century Persian poet

One of the most distinguished contemporary Iranian poets and writers Karim Amiri Firuzkuhi was born in 1910 in Farahabad a suberb of Firuz Kuh in the province of Ma'zanderan. His ancestors had been governors and military commanders from the reign of Karim Khan-Zand to the end of the Qajar rule in Iran, so that their names all included the title of Amir, meaning emir or king. His father was a modernist under the Qajar Muzaffar Ed-Din Shah accompanying the shah to Europe as a commander and dignitary, thus having the opportunity to directly observe the latest developments of Western civilization.

At the age of seven, Karim was taken by his father to Tehran, though this great change in his life tragically coincided with his father's death. His grandfather, Amir Muhammad Huseyn Khan Sardar (Chief Commander) became an influencial guardian for Karim. Amir Muhammad Huseyn Khan Sardar is historically noted for receiving the Legion of Honor from the French government for his translation and implementation of the Belgian military doctrine in Iran as well as the successful siege of Hera't in the course of a campaign. He is also the founder of the first school orphanage in Tehran, now well known as the Firuzkuhi Elementry School which utilized resources from the Firuzkuh land holdings to privately fund a vocational school for young boys and orhpans.

Karim received his primaery education in Tehran at the Siruz, Servat, Alliance, and Sultani schools, and going on to study elementary science course, logic, theology, and philosophy at the American College inTehran. He later pursued private study in the circles of learned scholars such as Vahid Dastgerdi, the director of the Armaghan journal and president of the Hakim Nezami literary Society, with whom he studied subjects such as the principles of Philosophy, rhetoric, and belles-lettres.

At the age of 28, Karim turned to the traditional sciences, studying six years with a number of prominent scholars studying Arabic literature, logic, theology, Islamic jurisprudence and religion. He mastered Persian literature and poetry as well as writing and prose and the composition of poetry in both Persian and Arabic.

Amir came to head the Documents Registration and Real Estate Administration from 1947 to 1957 but resigned from government service altogether to pursue freelance writing. During his writing and literary career his contributions were not limited to the Literary Society of Iran, the Hakim Nezami Literary Society, and the Farhangestan Literary Society. Amir was also associated with scholars, writers, and poets in the likes of Rahi Mo'ayeri, Professor Bahmanyar, Mohammad 'Ali Bamdad, Vahid Dastgerdi, and

Chapter 10

Sadegh Hedayat as well as with musicians like Habib Sam'aie, Abol-Hassan Saba, and "Abdol-Husain Shahnazi. Amiri Firoozkuhi died inTehran in October10 1984 at the age of 73.

Amiri Firuzkuhi began composing ghazals at the age of twelve. When he discovered Sa'eb Tabrizi, he was captivated by his style and, as a result, became a distinguished adherent of the Indian genre of Persian poetry through his ghazals. His expression in ghazals are straight forward, clear, smooth, and thematic. In his qasidas his rhetoric is reminiscent of Khagani's lucidity and eloquence, and his poetic nostalgia that of Mas'sud SA'd. In his qasida composition he interwins a legacy of the khorasani genre with developments of the restoration in such a way, bringing grace to qasidas that are predominantly melancholic.

His qita's stylistically follow on the model of his qasida's. He chooses mathnavi {ryming couplet genre} to set the mood with an expression reminiscent of Nezami. His poetry runs to 3000 couplets, in the composition of which he exercises the utmost precision and through a diversity of rhymes crafted in a multiciplity of couplets, he provides inventive imagery stemming from the interaction of his thoughts and feelings. He was acquainted with the subtleties of Persian poetry, which he applied to his compositions in the Indaian genre in such forms as ghazal and qasida. He also had a thorough knowledge of Arabic, in which he composed poetry as well.

The majority of Firuzkuhi's poetic work was composed after he turned fifty. He was celebrated in literary societies throughout Iran, whom he had worked with actively. His admiration for Sa'eb Tabrizi is not only reflected in his poetry but also in his critical edition of that poet's work which he penned in a detailed introduction. Amiri Firuzkuhi was at odds with the conventional terming of the Sa'eb style as Indian insisting that it was in a separate 'Isfahani genre. Apart from his work in qasida and ghazal, he is noted for composing poetry in the form of tarkib-band in contrast to his ghazals. Amiri tended to compose his qasidas in the Khorasani genre, following the precedents of Khaghani, Naser Khusrow, Mas'ud SA'd and Anvari.

His poetry is fraught with the bemoaning of life with its evanescence and vissitudes, along with his own personal lack of fulfillment, his lyrically expressed pain and frustration. His home in Tehran was known as a haven for the deeply feeling, where cultured people like'Abdel-Rahman

Contemporary Persian Poetry

ParsaTuysirkani, Ahmad Mahdavi Damghani, Habib Yaghma'I, Gholam Husayn Ra'di Azarakhshi, and prominent classical musicians gathered in a convivial atmosphere for fruitful discussion of poetry, belles-letters, and art.

Being independently able to live off the proceeds of his inherited lands in Firuzkuh, he could spare his sensitive nature from the burden of the duties of professional involvement with the government. After his death, his daughter Amir Banoo Karimi published his divan in two volumes and made his passionate ghazals available to eager readers. Amiri's works include translations of texts of the Nahj al-Balagha, two volumes of his own divan, a critical edition of Saeb Tabrizi's divan along with an introduction, a 'Ihqaq al-Haqq' in support of the poets of the Safavid era.

Pezhman Bakhtiari 20th century Persian poet

Amir Hossein Bakhtiari (Pezhman Bakhtiari) was born in Tehran on November 1900. He was the only child born to Ali- MoradKhan Mirpanj-Bakhtiari, constitutionalist and noted Kha'n of the Bakhtiari tribe and A'lamtaj Qa' em-maghami better known as Zha'leh, a renowned poet and advocate of women suffrage and a descendent of Mirza' Abul- Qa'sem Qa'em- maqam-e Fara'h'ni (1779-1835), the poet and prose stylist, and the prime minister of Mohammad Shah Qa'ja'r.

Pezhman's parents separated when he was just one year old. His mother left the house and, depite her efforts, was not allowed to see her son. The indelible pains of loneliness marked Pezhman's childhood and persisted in his poems. He sought out his mother when he was 27 years old and lived with her the remaining years of her life:

I was just an infant when my mother left me alone	طفلکی بودم که مادر خواست بی یاور مرا
And I was only nine when I lost my father	رفت در نه سالگی سایه ی پدر از سر مرا

Pezhman spent his early childhood years in the tribes' territory, and at the age of six, he attended a maktab (private tutoring) in the village of Dastak of Cha'har Maha'l, one of the two administrative provinces of the tribe's territory. After the death of his father in 1909, he came under the guardianship of Aliqoli Khan Sardar Asa'd Bakhtiari II, the head of Bakhtiari tribe, and his son, Ja'far Qoli Khan Sarda'r As'd Bakhtiari III. However, he never received any of his inheritance and was not sent to Europe to study, which was against his father's will. Pezhman returned to Tehran several years later and enrolled in Ashraf primary school before entering the St.Louis School, Iran's first Catholic Mission school. In St Louis, he was a classmate of Nima Yushij, who attended the school from 1909 to 1917, and the pupil of Nezam Vafa, a noted poet of the time. After graduating from St.Louis, he went to Mashhad, where he studied classical Persian literature with Adib Nisha'boury and Arabic with Badi-ol-Zama'n Forouzanfar.

He returned to Tehran in 1925, where he bagan his two-year compulsory military service. As he was familiar with the French language, he was transferred after military training to the newly established Department of Wireless communications, affiliated with the then Ministy of War. He was later employed by the department, which was subsequently integrated into the Ministry of Post, Telegraph, and Telephone. He worked there until his retirement in 1958. During the years 1924-1925, he also was the chief editor of the newspaper Fekr-e A'zad, published by Ahmad Bahmanyar in Tehran. In 1948, he published a book on the history and development of mail, telegraph, and telephone service in Iran. He also published the first issues of Majalleh-ye post-e Iran in cooperation with Nasr-ollah Falsafi.

Following Rahi Mo ayeri's death in 1968, Pezhman succeeded him as the literary director of Radio Iran's Barna'ma-ye Golha program. His skill in composing lyrics to be set to music for the Golha'program soon earned him high recognition. He was also a member of Radio Iran's Shora'yeh Sher o Taraneh and played an instrumental role in documenting and reviving Bakhtia'ri folk songs and music in Radio Iran. The bucolic backdrops of childhood never departed from Pezhman's imagination and were, in turn, reflected in his poetry. One of his more notable poems is about the traditional homeland of the Baktia'ris, in the last line of which he portrays the land as his God:

You are guiding me towards the deities	سوی ایزدان رهنمای منی
You, O Bakhtiari, are my God!	تو ای بختیاری خدای منی

Contemporary Persian Poetry

His cooperation with Radio Iran, which continued until 1973, brought him into contact with many vocalists and composers such as Ali Tajvidi, Parviz Ya'haghi, Mahmud Khonsari, and Java'd Ma rufi, and Abdol- Vaha'b Shahidi. He was also instrumental in the establishment of the Gowhar Literary Society. His poems and articles were published in such literary journals as Yaghma, Gowhar, Armagha'n, Sokhan, Vahid, A'muzesh o Parvaresh and Nou-baha'r.

Pezhman died of cancer and was buried in Behesht-Zahra Cemetery of Tehran in December 1974. The date of his death is recorded in Chronograms composed by such poets as Bagha'i-e Na'ini and Ria'zi-e Yazdi.The inscription on his tombstone, taken from one of his famous poems, reads:

Since my broken body became the
wayfarer on nonbeing,
My tired organs felt amazingly
rested

تا رهروی آدم شد جسم شکسته ما
آسایشی عجب یافت اندام خسته ما

Pezhman has been described as a humble, intimate, hardworking, passionate and knowledgeable poet with so much feeling for his homeland and a profound sense of philanthropy. He began composing poetry in his youth. At first, he chose "Sarmast" (enchanted), and then "Pezhman", as his pen names. He was fascinated with classical Persian literature and spent most of his time reading poetry. In 1932, he joined the Anjoman-e Hakim Nezami, a literary circle founded by Hassan Vahid Dastgerdi in 1932 and he parcipitated in editing and annotating Nezami Ganjavi's Panj ganj or Khamseh, further contributed to his fascination with Persian classical literature.

Approximating such contemporary poets as Rahi Moa'yeri and Amiri Firuzkuhi, Pezhman rarely departed from the conventions of Persian classical prosody. Although he tried his hand at almost all classical styles, he appeared at his best in the genre of ghazal. Pezhman's poetical and musical sensibilities, well exhibited in his skillful employment of internal rhyme and alliteration, earned him the praise of many and offered rewarding choices to such eminent vocalists of his time as Manuchehr Homa'yunpur and Mohammad Reza Shajarian among others:

No one's love resides at the depth of my heart
Nobody stays in this ruined hut

در کنج دلم عشق کسی خانه ندارد
کس جای در این خانه ویرانه ندارد

Whoever I gave my heart to, brought it back
Nobody tolerates a so madly in love heart

دل را به کف هرکه نهادم بازپس آرد
کس تاب نگهداری دیوانه ندارد

At the feast of the world, there is no one but our lomging heart
Ah ! that candle that burns and has no butterfly

در بزم جهان جز دل حسرتکش ما نیست
آه ! آن شمع که میسوزد پروانه ندارم

I said, "My Love why is it that you do not fall in the trap that I have set?
She said, " what can I do! your trap has no bait!

گفتم مه من از چه تودر دام نیفتی
گفتا چه کنم دام شما دانه ندارد

O', Ah! do not trouble yourself in vain!, there is no way to access the privacy of a crazy heart!

ای آه! مکش زحمت بیهوده که تا ثیر
راهی به حریم دل دیوانه ند

In the society of sane men, I do not set foot,
The insane has no patience to listen to the words of sane.

در انجمن عقل فروشان ننهم پای
دیوانه سرصحبت فرزانه ندارد

For how long you want to narrateThe story of Alexander and Dara?
Life is far too short to listen to so many tales!

تا چند کنی قصه اسکندرودارا ؟
ده روزه عمر این همه افسانه ندارد

I have an eternal fire in my chest
My existence is death, named life

آتشی در سینه دارم جاودانی
عمرمن مرگیست نامش زندگانی

Contemporary Persian Poetry

Laden with a deep sense of loss, remorse, and solitude, Pejman's poems are, on the one hand, romantic depictions of human desires and needs, occasionally bordering on eroticism, On the other, they are an exaltation of the patriotic discourse of the period in praise of freedom and are colored by an unconditional love for the homeland. His poem "Iranzamin" offers an example:

Even if Iran is naught but a wasteland, I am in love with this waistland	اگر ایران بجز ویران سرانیست من این ویرانسرا را دوست دارم
If our history is tainted with legends I love these legends!	اگر تاریخ ما افسانه رنگ است من این افسانه ها را دوست دارم
The sounds of our flute although is heart-rending, I love this heart rending sound of the flute.	نوای نای ما گرجان گداز است من این نای و نوا را دوست دارم
If its climate is not pleasant, I love this climate	اگر آب و هوایش دلنشین نیست من این آب و هوا را دوست دارم
The delight with the thorns of its dry deserts is so much that, makes me love this worn-out foot.	به شوق خار صحرهای خشگش من این فرسوده پا را دوست دارم
I love this beautiful land with all my heart, I love this enchanting bright sky.	من این دلکش زمین را خواهم از جان من این روشن سما را دوست دارم
If harmed by hand of a fellow Iranian, I love the man who caused me the harm	اگر بر من ز ایرانی رود زور من این زور آزما را دوست دارم
If you are pure or you are sinful,	اگر آلوده دامانید اگر پاک امن ای مردم شما را دوست دارم

Chapter 10

O' people of Iran, I LOVE you!

Pezhman versified the history of the Ashka'nia'n (Arsacid) dynasty in the genre of mathnavi (rhymed couplets) and was particularly noted for the patriotic qasidas that he composed when Iran was under the occupation of British and Russian forces during World War II (e.g.,"Nameh be Stalin" (letter to Stalin), "Nameh be Winston Churchil", and "Azerbaieja'n," .Pezhman also tried his hand, occasionally, in the semi-traditional genre of Chaha'rpa'reh (foursome).

His choice of theme in one of his foursomes, entitled, "Dud-keshha'" (The chimneys), which is characterized by innovative imagery, has inspired critics to trace similarities between the poem and the English poet William Blakes. (1757-18227) "The Chimney Sweeper" poems in his Songs of Innocence and Songs of Experience.

The chimneys on rooftops,	دود-کشها برفراز بامها
Sigh with sorrow in every breath	هر نفس آهی ز دل برمیکشند

Pezhman's poetry benefits from simple language and innovative, yet easily accessible imagery. As recalled by a critic and friend, Pezhman regretted publishing two of his collections, entitled Siyah-ruz and Zan-e bicha'reh, and burnt an unpublished collection of his poems titled "Bicha'regi-e zana'n" in 1931. Pezhman's edition of the poetry of Hafez was published in 1936. It was followed by the publication of Kolliyat-e Ja'mi and Nezami Ganjavi's Khosrow o Shirin, Makhzan-al-asra'r, Haft Peykar, Leyli o Majnun, and Sharafna'meh" generally known as the first part,"of Nezami's Eskandar-Na'meh. The second part of the book is known as Eqbal-na'meh or Kherad-na'meh, "Although there is no strong evidence that the author used these names to distinguish the two parts, and in quite a few manuscripts the name Sharaf-Nameh is in fact applied to the second of the two poems.

Pezhman also published the collection of his mother's poems, with a comprehensive introduction on her life, as Diva'n-asha'r- Zhaleh Qa'em-maqa'mi in 1964. The book has been republished several times since then. Pezhman was a keen student of French language and literature. He dedicated poems to such renowned French poets as Paul Valery and Charles Baudelaire and translated some notable French literary works into Persian.

Nader Naderpour 20ᵗʰ century Persian poet

Nader Naderpour was born on June 6, 1929 in Tehran. His parents were both fluent in French and had a deep love for art, music and history. His father was a descendent of Reza Gholi Mirza, the eldest son of Nader Sha'h. The eldest of two brothers and three sisters, Naderpour grew up under the supervision and care of his culturally rich parents. His father, who died when Naderpour was only fourteen, was a skilful painter and also a man familiar with poetry and literature. It was he who taught young Naderpour Persian literature and classic poetry. When he was a preschooler, Naderpour would sit in his father's lap and be encouraged to read the newspaper every night. His father also had Naderpour memorize classical and modern poetry. His mother was a talented player of the string instrument the tar, and she helped Naderpour to develop an appreciation of music.

In 1942 during World War II, Naderpour entered Iran-Shahr High School in Tehran. A year later when Iran was occupied by the Allied military forces, Naderpour like many other students of the time, got involved in Politics, and he participated in a small nationalist party group. Later he joined the Tudeh Party of Iran, which became the major Communist Party of the country. Like Nima Yushij, Naderpour also published a number of poems in journals such as People and Leader, and Our Iran (Mardom, Rahbar and Iran-e-Maa') , all leftist publications; Press Arms of Tudeh Party and supported byTPI at the time.

By the time Naderpour graduated from high school in 1948, he had already left the Tudeh Party. In fact, since 1946 Naderpour had been unhappy about the Iran-Azerbaijan crisis, and like many other nationalist students, he was convinced that Soviet Commumism could not make any provision for the independent nationalist communist movements in other countries. Subsequently, Naderpour worked wholeheartedly to ensure that Iran's parliamentary elections would be open, honest, and fair. He therefore became sympathetic to the National Front;(Jebhe-ye Meli) and its leader, Mohammad Mosadegh, and other nationalists in those elections.

In 1950 Naderpour was sent to Paris, France, to continue his education in French language and literature at the Sorbonne University. During his stay in Paris he not only became a freelance writer for various publications but he also wrote for the Third Force Party (Niroy-e Sevvom), which Iranian ideologue and writer Khalil Maleki had established under the aegis of the National Front Party in Iran. After having received his BA degree, Naderpour returned to Tehran and started working in the private sector. In 1960 Naderpour arranged the first modernist Persian poetry reading in Tehran, held at the Cultural Society of Iran & America (Anjoman-e Farhangi-e Iran-o Amrica). Later, he worked as a consultant at the Office of Dramatic Arts of the Ministry of Arts and Culture (Veza'rat-e Farhang-o Honar). He was also appointed as the Editor of Theater Magazine (Majaleh-ye Nemayesh), and as the Editor- in -Chief of the Monthly Journal of Art and People (Honar-o Mardom).

In 1964, Naderpour travelled to Europe. In Rome, he continued his studies in the Italian language and literature. He also spent some time in Paris, studying French cinema, and devoting time to his own poetry. In 1968, Nadaerpour became one of the thirty or so founding members of the first Association of Writers of Iran (Ka'noon-e Nevisandegaan-e Iran). He was also one of the signatories of its manifesto, along with several other famous Iranian writers and poets. When Jalal Al-e Ahmad, the driving force behind the Association, died in 1969, theAssociation chose Naderpour to speak on its behalf at the internment ceremony. For two consecutive years Naderpour was elected as a member of the steering committee for the Association of writers of Iran. Later on, in 1977, he decided not to participate in the rejunivation of the Association due to differences of opinion.

In 1971, Naderpor took over as the director of Contemporary Literature Department (Gorooh-e Adab-e Emrooz) in the National Iranian Radio and Television, where he directed many programs on the life and works of contemporary literary figures. Naderpour fled the Iranian Revolution in 1980 for France and resided there until 1987. He was elected to France's Authors' Association, and participated in several conferences and gatherings. In 1987, he moved to California. During his residence in the United States, Naderpour gave several speeches and lectures at Harvard University, Georgetown University, UCLA, and UC Berkley. Naderpour was considered as the first Iranian poet who opened up exciting vistas of the new Persian poetry, and he was considered one of the leaders of the movement for the New Poetry or She'r-e Nou in Iran and among other Persian speaking nations like Afghanistan, Tajikistan and Pakistan.

Naderpour was nominated for the Nobel Prize in literature in 1993. He was also the receeipient in 1993 of the Lilian Hellman and Dashiell Hammett Prize, awarded to writers whose works are banned in their homeland, and the Ehsan Yarshater Award, conferred by the Rudaki Cultural Foundation, in 1998, which was presented to him in a ceremony held in the Foundation's headquarters in Vancouver, Canada. Naderpour's career as a poet and literary critic was celebrated at a conference held on the occasion of his sixtieth birthday at the University of California in Los Angeles in 1989. In appreciation of his lifetime achievements as a poet, a ceremony was also held in Washington D.C., in which scholars and literary critics participated.

In the morning of Friday, 18 February 2000, Naderpour died of a heart attack in his home in Los Angeles; he was buried at Westwood Village Memorial Park and Mortuary, while his melodic voice rang out over loudspeakers. His death received wide coverage outside Iran, and several commemorative celebrations were held in different countries. Shortly after his death, his wife established the Naderpour Foundation, dedicated to the preservation and propagation of his work and legacy.

Naderpour's refined language and the rich poetical imagery of his well-crafted poems, imbued with a new and modern system of signification, has transformed him into a central figure in popularizing modern poetry and familiarizing the growing Persian audiences with central tenets of Nima's poetic discourse. Many of his contemporary poets have commended his style for clarity and musicality, thematic and organizational coherence, and innovative use of imagery. They have praised him as a poet whose poems are his signature and as a clairvoyant poet with a penetrating lucidity that permits him to see the reality of things beyond formalism, and foresee the course of future events. He is regarded as "the most emulated poet, particularly among Persian speakers of Afghanistan and Central Asia and as a poet whose poetry has already been recognized as a modern classic of Persian literature

The Winter Homily, a poem by Nader Naderpour: Translated by Farhad Mafie	شعر نو "خطبه ی زمستان" از نادر نادرپور:
"O, the fire that flames from inside the night rose to dance, But turns to stone by morning! O. the memory of the earth's seething anger	ای آتشی که شعله کشان از درون شب برخاستی به رقص اما بدل به سنگ شدی در سحرگهان ای یادگار خشم فروخرده ی زمین

In the days when the sky's rage was spreading!
O, the sense of pride
O, the point where epics begin and end
O, the magnificient summit of old epics
O, the house of Ghobad!
O, the Land of Zal the Champion's childhood."

O, the astonishing summit!
O, the anonymous grave of the unfortunate Jamshid!
O, the cliff of anguish of Zahak the black-hearted!
O, summit! O, valiant champion! O, combatant of old!
O, he who was thrown into his brother's well!
But the king's crown
At the moment of the fall
Was saved for the world from the well's narrow pass!

O, the white summit on the horizon of childhood!
So like a whitened sugar cone on blue paper.
O, the summit new in appearance to the poet's imagination!
Like a gigantic stone that lasts forever!
I am on a night when even the crickets are sleeping,
The lonliest voice in the world,
Never reaching anyone else, from any direction.
I am in the frozen silence of this dark night,

در روزگار گسترش ظلم آسمان
ای معنی غرور
نقطه ی طلوع و غروب حماسه ها
ای کوه پرشکوه اساطیرباستان
ای خانه قباد
ای آشیان سنگی سیمرغ سرنوشت
ای سرزمین کودکی زال پهلوان

ای قله شگرف
گور بی نشانه جمشید تیره روز
ای صخره ی عقوبت ضحاک تیره جان
ای کوه ای تهمتن ای جنگجوی پیر
ای آنکه خود به چاه برادر فروشدی
اما کلاه سروری خسروانه را
در لحظه ی سقوط
از تنگنای چاه رساندی به کهکشان
ای قله سپید در آفاق کودکی
چون کله قند سیمین در کاغذ کبود
ای کوه نوظهور در اوهام شاعری
چون میخ غول پیکر بر خیمه زمان
من در شبی که زنجره ها نیز خفته اند
تنها ترین صدای جهانم که هیچ گاه
از هیچ سوی به هیچ صدایی نمی رسم
من در سکوت یخ زده ی این شب سیاه
تنها ترین صدایم وتنهاترین کسم
تنها تر از خدا
در کار آفرینش مستانه جهان
تنها تر از صدای دعای ستاره ها
در امتداد دست
درختان بی زبان
تنها تر از سرود سحرگاهی نسیم
در شهر خفتگان
هان ای ستیغ دور
آیا بر آستان بهاری که میرسد
تنها ترین صدای جهان را سکوت تو

The loneliest voice in the world,
Never reaching anyone else from any
direction.
I am, in the frozen silence of this dark
night,
The lonelist voice and the loneliest
person,
Lonelier than God
Working on the numinous creation of
the world,
Lonelier than the star's praying sound
Along the hands of speechless trees,
Lonelier than the breeze's morning
anthem
In the city of sleepers.
You, O, far summit!
In the beginning of the upcoming
spring,
Will the loneliest voice in the world
Be allowed to echo in your quietness?
Will my lost voice, panting,
Be able to find a path to your hight?
Will your cold mouth, by my warm
tune,
Be able to erupt again?
Ah, O the tranquil and the virtuous!
O, the dour wintery face!
O, the angry lion!
Will I, from the small door of this
strange exile,
Again see the rising of the sun
From your summit peak?
Will I be able to see you again?

كان انعكاس تواند داد؟

آيا صداى گمشده ى من نفس زنان
راهى به ارتفاع تو خواهدبرد؟
آيا دهان سرد تو را
لحن گرم من
آتشفشان تازه تواند كرد؟
آه اى خموش پاك
اى چهره ى عبوس زمستانى
اى شير خشمگين
آيا من از دريچه ى اين غربت شگفت
بار دگر برآمدن آفتاب را؟
از گرده ى فراخ تو خواهم ديد؟

There have, a number of remarks over time, been made about Naderpour and
his poetry as cited by some Iranian scholars and researchers. Here is one made
by Professor Ehsan Yarshater:

Chapter 10

"In my opinion, Naderpour's poems are lasting poems. Undoubtedly, his works will be counted among the classics in the Persian language. In the last twenty years we owe thanks to Naderpour for many expressions that have now become popular and universal, such as the sadness of exile, being cut from our own roots, disheartened by the homeland that is being traumatized. In addition, he has given life to his poems through his beautiful descriptions, and through new, effective explanations he has made apparent to us the ambiguous, complex conditions of our own hidden conscience. His poem is the poem of our sadness, our worries, our hopes, and our disappointments."

Here is another comment made by Iraj Bashiri together with his translation into English of Naderpour's poem "A Man with Two Shadows:

"Naderpour supported the three principles established by Nima. First, he believed that like natural or conversational speech, poetry must convey the meaning; the number of words as well as the simplicity or complexity of the phraseology must be dictated by the requirement of the expression of the thought being expressed. In other words, he believed that the phrases expressing single thoughts do not have to be of the same length. Secondly rhythm, Naderpour believed, need not follow an established, monotonous form. Rather, like natural speech, it should be allowed to vary depending on the requirements of the thought structure being expressed. Thirdly, rhyme must appear at the end of each completed thought pattern. Rather than forced on thought segments. Naderpour believed, rhyme must serve as a unifier; it must join complete thought segments and present them as a cohesive expression of the poet's sentiments". His poem "Man with Two Shadows" is a good example of this, especially regarding his use of shadows, its interansigence vis-à-vis the night.

"A Man with Two Shadows" by Nader Naderpour translated by Iraj Bashiri:

مردی با دو سایه شعر نادر نادرپور

من در غروب سرد جهان ایستاده ام
خورشید سرخ شامگهان سایه ی مرا
از زیر پای ظهر به تدریج و احتیاط
بیرون کشیده است و به من باز داده است

وین
سایه ی دراز همان آفریننده نیست
کز بامداد همسفرم بوده تا غروب
و زکودکی به پیری من ره گشاده است

Standing amid a cold global sunset,
My shadow is cast
By the burning evening sun
This has in turn,
Gradually but carefully,
Pulled it away

From beneath the feet of the mid-
day sun.
But, this elongated shadow
Is not the creature that has,
Accompanied me from dawn to
dusk
The creature that has led me from
childhood to senility,
That shadow was born to the
morning light
This shadow is sired by the evening
glow.
One day, when suddenly,
Through the frame of my bright
adolescence window
I discovered "future",
Golden and glowing,
That shadow, too, was born with the
light.
Alongside that future
Prepared to climb to the peak,
I rode, I felt, while
The rest of the world walked beside
me.
But the appearance of noon
Like light to which a film is exposed
Destroyed my morning dreams of
"future"
It destroyed all the shadows that
graced the earth
Lonely and suddenly
The shadow that had accompanied
me
The shadow that had perished by the
warmth of the sun
That shadow alone was revived
And now, in the fleeting sunlight of
my life

آنسایه را درخشش صبح آفریده بود
وین سایه را فروغ شبانگاه زاده است
روزی که ناگهان
از چهارچوب پنجره ی روشن بلوغ
آینده را طلایی وتابنده یافتم
آن سایه نیز همره
نور آ فریده شد
من پا به پای او
آماده ی صعود بدان قله ی بلند
از منزلی به منزل دیگر شتافتم
گویی که من: سوارم وعا لم :پیاده است
اما ظهور ظهر
رویای صبحگاهی آینده ی مرا
چون عکس نور دیده سرا پا سیاه کرد
تنها وناگهان
آن سایه ای که در پی من ره سپرده بود
وز هرم نیمروزی خورشید مرده بود
جننی دوباره یافت
وینک در آفتاب گریزان عمر من
رو بر گذشته پشت برآینده پا به گل
در انتظار مقدم شب ایستاده است

Chapter 10

> Standing amid the mud, it waits for
> the night
> Its face to the "past", its back is to
> the future

Chashmha o dastha (Eyes and Hands), Naderpour's first collection of poetry with 37 poems, was published in 1954. It was followed by the publication of Dokhtar-e JA'm (Daughter of the cup) in 1955, a collection of 17 poems, which won him more prominence. Although death and loneliness lurk in the background of most of the poems in these collections, many poems nevertheless, glitter in the light of wine, love, and pleasure. Naderpour married Shahla Malekza'deh Hirbod in 1957, and his only daughter, Pupak, was born in August 1959. The couple separated in 1961.

Naderpour's third collection of poetry, entitled She'r-e angur (The grape poem): (1984), was published in March 1958. Khanlari, then a towring presence in the literary scene praised Naderpour as a leading poet of the modernist school. Before joining the newly established periodical Honor o Mardom by the end of 1959, Naderpour worked for a brief period of time with Namayesh magazine, which was published by the Office of Dramatic Arts at the Ministry of Arts and Culture as well as Majalla-ye Musiqi, a literary and cultural journal edited by Gholam –Hosayn Minba'shia'n. His cooperation with Honar o Mardom lasted until 1964.

Throughout these years Naderpour's standing in Iranian literary circles soared. He used his prominence to advance and promote modernist poetry. He was influential in the publication of Hava'-ye ta'ze (Fresh air) by Ahmad Shamlou.

Sorma-ye khorshid (The healing kohl of the sun), his fourth collection of 41 poems, was published in 1960. The collection was recognized as the best book of the year by Anjoman-e ketab founded in1957 by Ehsan Yarshater in collaboration with Iraj Afshar, Abdol-Hoseyn Zarrinkub, and several other scholars. A selection of Naderpour's poems, entitled Bargozida-ye asha'r-e Nader Naderpour was published in 1963, with a painting by Sohrab Sepehri on its cover; it was reprinted several times.

Contemporary Persian Poetry

Naderpour, as his introductions to his poetry collections indicate, grants essential characteristics of modern poetry in Nima's discourse, and agrees with him that phrases expressing single thoughts in a poem do not have to be of the same length; rhythm need not follow an established, monotonous pattern; and rhyme, rather than being forced on thought segments, could appear at the end of each completed thought pattern. Of special note is Naderpour's common introduction to the three collections that he published in 1978 (Giya'h o sang na a'tash, Az a'sman'n ta'risma'n, Sha'm-e ba'z pasin), in which he contends that a good poem, as an organic set of elements, must also benefit from the harmony of rhythms and rhymes with the poem's content, and not least, should stay in tune with the poet's imagination and affections, rather than his political predictions.

Naderpour's early poems are mostly composed in chaha'rpa'ra (foursome), a distinct type of quatrain sequence format in abcb rhyme, which remains within, but slightly loosens, the classical requirements of rhyme in Persian poetry. Although romantic and lyrical in imagery and tone, they often manifest leftist proclivities.

"Old smiths, all, hammer in hand, With burnt complexions under the sun	آهنگران پیر همه پتک ها به دست با چهره های سوخته در نور آفتاب
Like crimson stars in the gloom of dusk Eyes filled with the glad tidings of revolution ("Sorud-e khashm," 1952)	چون اختران سرخ به تاریکی غروب چشمان پر از نوید فرحبخش انقلاب

After this early period, Naderpour's conception of commitment in literature was transformed, conveying a vision of existence above and beyond the dynamics of the period, his poetry veered toward the philosophically sad and pessimistic end of the late nineteenth /early twentieth-century spectrum of Western literature, loneliness, despair, and death lingered in growing intensity in the background of most of his poems throughout his life, and loaded his voice with a quality and tone reminiscent of late nineteenth-cntuny French symbolists, whose works he had introduced to Persian readers in Sokhan.

From this prison called life
I will never have the power to free
myself
Why should I set my heart to the
hope of death!
I am no longer separated from death

زین محبسی که زندگانیش خوانند
هرگز مرا توان رهایی نیست

دل بر امید مرگ چه می بندم
دیگر مرا ز مرگ جدایی نیست

A distinct feature of Naderpor's poetry is his unique personification of nature, which neither resembles the idyllic pastorals depicted by writers and poets of the Constitutional period nor emulates the blend of regional imagery with social elements in Nima's poetry, or the translucent connection with nature by which Sepehri's poetry is best recognized. Sky, sun, moon, and stars, along with birds, trees, mountains, and other natural elements are often personified and called upon as the psychological landscape of Naderpour's poems and the organic repository of his sorrows and despair. His sensibility to hear' the natural world's often muted voice and his ability to impart soul to natural objects has led critics to discern reverberations of Manuchehri's nature poems in Naderpour's poetry.

"Night, like a woman who,
Closes the windows one by one,
And turns off the lights of her room
Turned off all the stars and went to
bed"

شب چون زنی که پنجره ها را یکان یکان
می بندد و چراغ اطاقش را خاموش میکند
یک یک ستاره ها را خاموش کرد و خفت

"With red fish of her lips
In the pallid water of her face
Serenely and silently I swam"

با ماهی سرخ رنگ لبهایش
در آب پریده رنگ سیمایش
آهسته و بی صدا شنا کردم

Among his most celebrated poems is the title poem in his fourth poetry collection Sorma-ye Khorshid, in which he portrays himself as a 'blind bird' who simmers 'like a wet log', in the 'forest of night,' until he is touched by the warm hand of the sun of love, whose 'healing kohl restores his sight,' By repeating the first line of the poem, "I was a blind bird in the forest of night"

(Man morgh-e kur-e jangal-e shab budam), at the beginning of several stanzas that follow, Naderpour not only creates a harmony in the poem, but also unites the thoughts and sentiments that have inspired it. However, Naderpour's poetry exhibits an urban sensibility, often colored by a cynical and ironic overtone.

Mirror imagery appears in high frequency and plays a crucial role in the poetry of Naderpour. More than refracting which is before them, the mirrors shed light on the unseen, affording the onlooker insight into both, his own psychic set-up as well as the community in which he partakes.

The image of woman, real or imagined, has undergone radical transformations in Naderpour's poetic repertoire. From an object of desire and a source of transitory respite in the explicit language of his early poems, which on occasions border on the erotic, it has moved toward a magnitude of representations in the implicative power of imageries in his later poems.
Not all commentators, however, concurred with what they defined as Naderpour's exaggerated engagement with imagery at the expense of the poem's content, a quality that they held central to the effectiveness of any poem. "The kind of popular modern poetry that Naderpour's work represents" as held by a critic, "…lulls the heart, pleases the senses, or elicits some stock emotional responses. Otherwise, its pains and passions are skin-deep, as are its joys and pleasures.

Naderpour also experimented, more in the depiction of love and the rememberance of bygone days, both in Iran and abroad, with the traditional mono-rhyme poetry and the genre of ghazal. Unlike classical ghazal, however, whose lines and statements are often independent of each other, Naderpour's ghazals have unified themes. His rendition of his ghazals as narratives has inspired critics to trace an epic disposition in his poetry.

Verses from classical poets often appear in Naderpour's ghazals either as an epigram, or within the poem, and broadens the poems strata of signification. He skillfully employs internal rhyme and alliteration in his poetry. The repetition of 'a' in various arrangements in "Kohan diara", a vastly popular mono-rhymed poem, composed on the eve of the revolution of 1979 and addressed to Iran, works to highten the nostalgic mood of the poem:

کهن دیارا دیاریارا دل از تو کندم ولی ندانم

که گر گریزم وگر بمانم کجا بمانم

"O, my ancient land! Land of the beloved! My severance from you is done, but I know not
If I flee, to where shall I flee, and if stay, where shall I stay"

While in Iran, Naderpour was criticized by his engage' contemporaries for showing no interest in political issues after his intial, perhaps lukewarm, forays into the political arena. Away from Iran, however, many of his critics preferred to remain silent.

A complete edition of Naderpour's poetry collections was posthumously published as Majmu'a-ye asha'r- Nader Naderpour in two volumes. The edition also includes Naderpour's previously mentioned introductions. His poetry has been translated into many languages. In addition to English, selections of Naderpour's poetry were translated into Dutch and several times into French and Italian.

Mohammad Reza Shafie Kadkani 20th century poet & literary critic

Mohhamad Reza Shafiei Kadkani is an outstanding writer, poet, researcher and literary critic of Persian literature of our time. He was born on October 10 1939 in the village of Kadkan, a suberb of Torbat Heydariye in the province of Khorasan. He never attended primary, nor secondary public school; instead, he was taught and tutored at home by his father who was a learned and highly educated man. He was taught Arabic language and literature by the famous literary scholar Adib-e Neishabouri and later was taught Islamic Jurisprudence, Theology, and classical Persian literature by Shaykh Hashem Ghazviny another prominent scholar in Khorasan. He was admitted to Ferdowsi University to pursue his higher education in Persian language and literature, graduating with a Master's degree and then was admitted to the Tehran University where he got his Ph.d in literature. He was a student of prominent figures such as Badiozzaman Forouzanfar, Mohammad Moin, and Parviz Natel-Khanlary. While studying in Mashhad and Tehran he took part in various poetic circles and became well-known among literary elite.

Contemporary Persian Poetry

Although known for his modern poetry, Kadkani started with the classical form of ghazal which consists of rhyming couplets and a refrain, with each line sharing the same meter. He published his first poetry collection, Zemzeme-ha (whispers) in 1965. In his following poetry books Nocturnes (Awazhaye shabaneh) and Through a Leaf's Eyes (Az Zaba'n-e Barg) Kadkani departs from lyrical poetry and adopts the new form known as Nimaic poetry (Sher-e-nou/modern poetry). In Kadkani's writing with this new form come new social concerns as well, and with an elevated epic tone. His fourth collection, In the Garden Alleys of Nishabour (AZ kouche-bagh-haye Nishabour) was published in 1971 and is considerd by many to be the epitome of Kadkani's mastery in style and poetic language. This collection became so popular that lines from it now are used regularly in everyday conversations. Echoing the voice he had reached in The Garden Alleys of Nishabour, Kadkani released three new poetry collections six years later: Like a Tree in a Rainy Night (Mesl-e Derakht dar Shab-e Barani), The Scent of Moulian Brook (Booy-e Jooy-e Moulian), The Second Millenium of the Mountain Deer (Hezareh-e Douvom-e Ahouy-e Kouhi) emerged. In this collection Kadkani took the voice and style he had perfected to a new level. The philosophical complexities of his poetry in The Second Millenium correspond to the poem's formal strengths and linguistic intricacies.

After finishing his Ph.d Kadkani was invited to remain in the University of Tehran as a professor, a position he still holds to-day. As a literary critic and scholar, Shafie Kadkany has written on imagery and rhythm in Persian poetry, edited the poetry of classical Persian poets and translated work on Islamic mysticism.

Shafiei Kadkani is known for his works on literary criticism and modern Persian poetry. He has written several books on the art of poetry, the first of which was completed in 1943, and published about ten years later.Two of his most famous books are the following:
Poetry and Music
Poetry and Imagination
Kadkani has also researched, edited and compiled several classical books of Persian poetry, including all major works of Atta'r; Asrar al-Tohid, Mosibat-nameh, El'ahi-n'ameh, Mantegh al-Touour, Asra'r-na'meh. He has dedicated some of his books on Atta'r to his father. He has been also the only critic who has edited and compiled the History of Keramiyeh, and a number of other highly important works.

Chapter 10

In 2018 Kadkani published a 3-volume treatise on the Persian poet Hafez. Two of these are based on his lectures at the University of Tehran. The third consists of a collection of his notes on Hafez'poetic lexicon. He credits his mother for having introduced him to Hafez and dedicated this 3-volume work to her.

Kadkani started publishing his poems in local publications in the Khorasan province of Iran. Originally, he used the pen-name of "Sereshk", which in Persian means "tear". This pen-name was also based on the Persian abbreviation of his full name. His most famous poem; Happy Journeys!—has brought him international attention. It has decorated a wall in Leiden in Netherlands. It has also been inscribed on tombstones of many Persians, abroad and at home. (Use of poetry on tombstones is a long-standing tradition in the Persian-speaking world.)
Here is that famous poem;"Travel Safely!"

Where are you going, in such a hurry?" The desert-thorn asked the wind.	سفر به خیر "به کجا چنین شتابان؟" گون از نسیم پرسید
My heart is in torment here – Don't you want to get away "From this dusty desert?" "	"دل من گرفته زینجا هوس سفر نداری ز غبار این بیابان؟"
"It's all I long for, but What can I do, with my feet tied like this…"	"همه آرزویم اما چه کنم که بسته پایم..."
"Where are you going in such a hurry?"	"به کجا چنین شتابان؟"
Wherever it may be, except here, where I am	به هر آن کجا که باشد به جز این سرا سرایم
Travel safely then! But my friend, I beg you,	

When you have passed safely from this brutal wasteland	سفرت به خیر! اما تو و دوستی خدا را
And reached blossoms, and the rain, Greet them for me."	چو از این کویر وحشت به سلامتی گذشتی

به شکوفه ها به باران
برسان سلام ما را"

Shafiei Kadkani is one of the most capable contemporary poets who can clearly see the effects of the romanticism school and its principles in his poems. Cases such as empathy with nature, nostalgia, discovery and intuition, imagination, village praising, mental journeys, despair, contemplation in the course of life, the expression of suffering and sorrow, love, etc. are prominent contents of poet's poem that has provided field for the study of romanticism in his poetry and made him a romantic poet. Studies show that most of the principles and components of romanticism school are manifest in the poet's poems. Like romantics, when he speaks of nature, he sees his spirits and emotions in the parts of nature and he is sympathetic with it. He welcomes the village in front of the city and refuges to it. Or sometimes he immerses in the imagination and discoveries of a universe that romantic poets know such world. He occasionally talks about his grieves. Sometimes he realizes the passage of time and life and he thinks about it. In some cases, as romantics, he hugs frustration. There are such categories in his poetry which gives him a romantic quality.

Three odes to spring by Shafiei Kadkani:

Inevitability

It is coming; it is coming; like spring from all directions.
It is coming.
Neither wall, nor barbed wire does it recognize. It is coming
It does not linger at a walk or gallop.
Oh,
 Let me be like a drop of rain,
In this desert,
That brings good news of this arrival to the earth,
\or the throat of a small lark

Chapter 10

That in mid-winter
Is singing of the spring pennyroyal mit
When by the lead bullet.

Drop of its blood
On the non-stop monotonous music of snow
It bestows the purple refrain.
Of Fluid Moments
At the height of spring when the dawn is awake
Render me like the rain
Like the flower
To that wavelike river of luminosity
In that azure spring
-those two fields of resurrection
In that receptive and elusive silence
Like a song,
Once again,
Repeat me.
With the Green Sprouted wheat of Changiz
Here they have sprinkled
A pink and green dust on the trees in the distance,
That is still floating,
Suspended,
In the air

From far away
I can still sense the scent of young spring,
Mingled with the blood of autumn
Oh meadow, the fragrance of departure
Wafts from every single leaf of your garden,
And your spring
I see,
Ah,
There, the sparrows
On the edge of the pool,
Speaking with the red fish
About leaving
With the green sprouted wheat of Changiz
The farmer of Tus and Tabriz!

May the ancient New Year be auspicious!

Fereydoon Tavalali 20ᵗʰ century Persian poet

Fereydoon Tavallali one of Iranian prominent contemporary poets was born in Shiraz in the year 1919. His father Jalal Khan was a descendant of the Tavallali clan from the 'Amala branch of Qashqa'iei tribe whose family had migrated to Shiraz. He lost his mother when he was six years old. He attended Nama'zi primary School and Soltani Secondary School in Shiraz. He graduated from Tehran University with a degree in archeology in 1941, and was subsequently employed in the Notary Public of Shiraz. In 1943, he married a novice writer, Mahindokht Farbod, the author of a collection of short stories, entitled Sanjagh-e Morva'rid (The Pearl Pin). They had three children.

Tavallali started writing poetry and prose at a young age, and was involved with the period's politics of descent from early on. Much of his early work displays the hallmarks of left-learning, which had gained ground among the youth and intellectual communities of the period. During the intial decade that followed the occupation of Iran by the Allied forces in 1941, and the subsequent abdication of Reza Shah, the Iranians enjoyed a rare and short-lived period of freedom of expression, which proved to be a strong stimulus to the arts and letters, and had a powerful and lasting effect on Iran's intelligentsia. In 1943 Tavallali and a group of his friends, including Hamidi Shirazi established Anjoman-e azadega'n-e Fars. It was dissolved, however, when the Tudeh party opened its first branch in Shiraz in April 1944, and all its founding members (aside from Hamidi Shirazi) joined the party.

It was during this period that Tavallali began experimenting with satirical pieces that were known and later published under the title of al-tafa'sil. In these pieces, he criticized the traditional social values and ridiculed such well-established political figures as Ahmad Ghava'm and Sayyed Zia' ed-Din Tabataba'ie. Al-Tafa'sil, reminiscent of the maqa'ma genre in classical Persian literature, was composed in a mixture of poetry and prose. The eloquent language of these satirical pieces which were inspired by social discontent, found an eager audience and earned the praise of many, including Ghava'm and Tabatabai, who were subjected to Tavallali's poignant critiques, to the extent that they even, helped to shield him against State censorship. Mohammad Taghi Baha'r the prominent poet and scholar, praised the skill exhibited in these pieces and commended Tavallali as a rising star in Iran's literary scene. In 1945 Baha'r was appointed as the Minister of Culture and helped Tavallali secure a job in the archaeology department of the Ministry of Finance in Fars. A year later, Tavallali was assigned to oversee the excavations carried out in the Susa region by Roman Girshman, the French archeologist and one of the pioneers of archeological research in Iran.

Tavallali was amongst the poets, who participated in the First Iranian Writers Congress, a gathering with predominantly leftist sympathies, sponsored by the Perso-Soviet Society of Cultural Relations (Anjoman-e rava'bet-e farhangi-e Iran va Eteha'd-e Jamahir-e Shoravi) in 1946. The congress provided a forum for airing various opposing views and contributed significantly to the development of "engag'e literature" in Iran, which attracted a large group of writers in later years. The poem that Tavallali recited in the Congress was entitled "Farda'ye enghela'b" ("The Day after the Revolution"). It earned him immediate fame as a leftist poet. In 1947, as the conflicting interests within the Tudeh party's leadership unfolded, Khalil Maleki and a number of other staunch desenters resigned from the party. The separatists (ensh-e a'biyun), as they were labled included nine prominent members—Jala'l A'l-e Ahmad, Rasul Parvizi, Na'der Na'derpour, and Fereydoon Tavallali—were poets or writers of eminence.

After leaving the Tudeh Party, Tavallali, became increasingly involved in the political movements that culminated in the nationalization of Iran's oil industry, led by Mohammad Mosadegh, who later became prime minister. After the fall of Mosaddegh in 1953, Tavallali, whose residence was looted by his political opponents, was forced into a period of hiding, and subsequently fled to Tehran. Several years later in 1959, however, with gradual ebing of political turbulances he assumed the directorship of the Department of Archeology of Fars.

Despite his education and career, it was literature that most fascinated him. Beginning his literary career in a time in which the nature and pace of change in Persian poetry were the subject of a heated debate. Tavallali joined a number of his contemporaries who tried to articulate a middle position between the traditionalists, who adhered to age-old rules of meter and rhyme of Persian poetry and the modernists who, "not only dispensed with the necessity of rhyme and consistent meter, but also rejected the imagery of traditional poetry and departed noticeably from its mode of expression".

Contemporary Persian Poetry

Although varied from one another in the degree from which they departed from the Persian classics, most of these modern-traditionalists—notable among them Majd-ed Din Mirfakhra'ie (also known as Golchin Gila'ni), Parviz Natelkhanlari and later, Hushang Ebtehaj (known as Sa'ya), Fereydoun Tavallali, Nader Naderpour and Fereydoon Moshiri—acknowledged the significance of Nima' Youshij as the founder of modern poetic discourse in Iran. Well versed, albeit to different degrees, in classical Persian literature, and familiar with Western literature and literary modernism, they strove to demonstrate the capacity of modern Persian poetry to maintain imperative and perceptible connections with the classical tradition, and at the same time, to enlarge the capacity to incorporate images perceived as belonging to the modern world. Since all of these poets were affiliated with the journal Sokhan, founded and edited by Parviz Natel Khanlari, they were later known as the poets of the Sokhan School, with Nader Naderpour as its most noted representative, were also known as the "New Romantics," or "New Classcists,". The Sokhan School of Poetry was enthusiastically received by many, and at the same time, stirred harsh criticism. It was criticized as a reactionary movement that had impeded the fruition of modern Persian poetry and was commended as a significant current in the history of Persian poetry.

At the first stage of his literary career, Tavallali was fascinated by some of Nima's early poems, in particular "Afsaneh" and "Ey Shab". His acquaintance with Nima, through Rasul Parvizi, developed into a short-lived period of friendship between the two poets. Tavallali named his first daughter after Nima' which had dedicated his poem, "Ta'r-e Shab-pa'" to Tavallali. It should be noted however, that Nima's dedicatory note "Be Tavallali-e 'azizam" ("To my dear Tavallali") was omitted in his Collection of Poems, published in 1992.

Despite his early intimate association with Nima,Tavallali soon distanced himself from the new literary movement brought on by such poems of Nima as "Gorab"(Raven), published for the first time in Majalla-ye musighi (journal of Music, 1939). In his introduction to his first collection of poetry, Raha, Tavallali, though not explicitly mentioning Nima's name, comments negatively on his school of poetry, "{This group of modernists} have forgotten all about Persian grammar and, by using such erroneous phrases as 'ruza-ash zemestani' (his days wintery) instead of 'ruzha-ye zemestani-ash (his wintery days), complicate their novel ideas so much that they could not be understood unless explained and clarified by the poet himself".

In his elaboration on the essential characteristics of a good poem, Tavallali, although in favor of a studied breakaway from the traditional prosodic rules, emphasizes the harmony of rhythms and rhymes with the poem's content and spirit; its innovative similes and methaphores; its being devoid of obsolete rhythms, rhymes and rhetorical devices; its being open to new melodious phrases and the extant but forgotten words; and its precise description of emotions, scenes and events.

Tavallalie's early poems, mostly romantic depictions of human desires and needs, benefit from his studied choice of descriptive compound imageries and his awareness of the music of words. Although at times he speaks of the "the cry of the people," "the uproar of the workers," "and "the cheers of the oppressed," (Tavallalie's Sho'la-ye kabud) in his more successful poems such concepts as love, nostalgia and death prevail. The smooth blend of Persian lyricism and European romanticism in most of these poems, that often follow a storyline, and by which his poetry is distinguished, influenced many modern-traditionalist poets throughout the 1940's and 1950's, most notable among them Fereydoon Moshiri, Nader Naderpour, Sohrab Sepehri, Siavash Kasraie, Nosrat Rahmani, and Forough Farokhzad. The opening lines of four of his poems in Sho la-ye Kabud—"Maryam," "Ba'stan-shena's,"Na'-A'shena-parast, and "Karun"—read as follows;

"In the midst of dusk, when the moon yellow and broken,
Rises from the East half way through nightfall,
Standing Salvia quite and pensive,"

در نیمه های شامگهان آنزمان که ماه
زرد و شکسته میدمد از طرف خاوران
استاده در سیاهی شب مریم سپید
آرام وسرگران

"Delving deep in the black soil, the archeologist,
In search of the dark torch of the dead,
Pinning for a warm torch in the cold grave,
Gives away the ashes of ancient centuries to the wind,"

در ژرفنای خاک سیه باستان شناس
در جستجوی مشعل تاریک مردگان
در آرزوی اخگر گرمی به گور سرد
خاکستر قرون کهن را دهد به باد!

"The boat gently, like a graceful swan moved on the Karoon,

بلم آرام چون قویی سبکبار به نرمی بر سر کارون همی رفت

Into the palm grove on the shore, the sun the edge of the horizon sunk in,"

به نخلستان ساحل قرص خورشید زدامان افق بیرون همی رفت

Although Tavallali, in this period of his literary career, often experiments with the classics forms of mostaza'd, a variant of ghazal or qasida, with an additional phrase repeating the same pattern as the main meter, and mossamat, in which the couplet basis is abandoned and the stanza consists of a number of hemistiches with a rhyme that usually changes at a fixed point, most of his poems are in cha'har pa'ra, a four line stanza. His polished and lyrical language in these poems earned the praise of many critics who commended him for achieving a distinct style in love poetry, and a poet whose relax experimentation with rhymes and rhythmes spares his poems from the rigidity of Nimaic modern style.

Mohammad Ba'heri and Rasul Parvizi, Tavallali's old friends in the Tudeh Party were also the close friends of Asad-Allah 'Alam, a confident of Mohammad Reza Shah Pahlavi, who occupied such key positions as minister of interior, prime minister, and later, Minister of Court for many years. The friendship earned them high positions in the government. Mohammad Baheri was appointed as the Minister of Justice, while Rasoul Parvizi was first elected as a deputy in the parliament (majles), and then was appointed as the Deputy Prime Minister. In 1965, when Amir Asad-allah 'Alam was appointed as the Dean of Pahlavi University in Shiraz, he assigned Tavallali to the advisory board of the university; a position he held till his retirement.

Tavallali's poems in this period, while at times implicitly critical of the Sha'h's policies and sprinkled with praise for those who fought against dictatorship (Tavallali's Shola-ye kabud) are, for the most part, marked by the sorrows and disappointments of a self who is entangled in harsh criticism. The indelible print of betrayed hopes, although visible in some poems of the collection Na'fa, appears as the central motif in the poems he composes throughout these years.

"Like an owl with broken wings, in this hopeless feast

چون بوم پرشکسته در این عید بی امید

I sit in my sorrowful cave ;" "Sho'la-ye kabud"	بنشسته ام به دخمه ی اندوه بار خویش

The macabre overtone and the frequency of words and images that in Tavallali's poetry revolve around death, soil, grave, and grave-digging, to mention a few among many, has led a critic to notice a profound relationship between his field of study and professional career as archeologist, on the one hand, and his poetry on the other.

In this period of his life Tavallali shuns political engagements and turns to farming in a village he had inherited from his father. Getting closer and closer to Alam he praises him in such poetic appellations as the "Sire of Idols," and addresses him as the "Great Man" and the "Emir," in his third collection of poetry, entitled Puya. Tavallali's shift from communism in his early adolescence to supporting the political movements that led to the nationalization of oil industries in 1950's, and on to enjoying close ties with the Pahlavi court digintaries in the last decades of his life, subjected him to harsh verbal and, to a lesser extent, written criticism.

However, Tavallali composed some of his most celebrated poems in this period. Drawing on his earlier experimentations with literary techniques, in particular compound imageries, he returns to the genre of ghazal, a traditionally apt mode for depiction of love, description of nature, and rememberance of the bygone joyful days of life:

"In the sorrow-stricken garden, the maple leaf is on fire, The tired crow heralds the coming of the rain,	به باغ غمزده آتش گرفت برگ چناران کلاغ خسته خبر می دهد زریزش باران
The cries of the down hearted ravens have mounted, Instead of the sweet song of doves and nightingales	غریو شیون زاغان دلفسرده برآمد به جای نغمه شیرین قمریان و هزاران
Release me to the lap of the mourning fall	مرا به دامن پاییز داغدیده رها کن
	که مست باده مرگم کند چو باده گساران

So that it makes me drunk on the
wine of death."

Tavallali develops an increasingly critical approach toward modernist poetry
in these years and even describes the poetry of Nima Yoshij as a half-formed
fetus (jenin-e nimband). In contrast to his earlier poems, this period of
Tavallali's poetry is characterized by his sensual expressionism and his
description of physical love bordering on erotica. The sexual overtone of the
Poya collection, described by a commentator with psychoanalytic bent on
grotesque sexual anarchism, earned Tavallali harsh criticism. In his later
poems, however, sensuality and sexual aspirations gradually faded away, and
were substituted by a fascination for opium.

Tavallali's life and literary career have journeyed and changed shape in parallel
with the dominant social, political, and literary trends of the mid decades of
the 20th century Iran. His poetry, in which personal experiences are
inseparably interwoven with political and historical events, exhibits the major
characteristics of a period of transition in Iran's modern literature. The most
enthusiastic admirers of his poetry, however, were the traditionalists and
modern traditionalists. Little is known regarding his poems from 1980 until
his death in 1985.

Tavallali was in poor health throughout the last decade of his life and died of
a heart failure. He was buried next to his father in Hafeziye. One year after his
death his wife established a literary center in their residence, calling it
Anjoman-e Fereydun. Tavallali was an amature player of tar, setar and piano.
His loss was widely reflected upon in the literary circles of the period. As
commented by Khanlari, with the "silence of this great man of letters, modern
Persian poetry has lost one of its pillars

Dr. Mehdi Hamidi Shirazi 20th century Persian poet

Dr Mehdi Hamidi Shirazi was one of the most prolific and innovative poets,
and writers in the contemporary domain of Persian litrature in Iran. He was a
brilliant scholar, a great teacher as well as a most sincere and knowledgable
believer and fighter to protect and ensure the continuity of classical style of
our Persian literary legacy which had come under criticism and attack by the

promoters and supporters of the new school of literary modernity (the new style; shera nou).

Hamidi was born in Shiraz in May 1914 .He lost his father when he was only three years old and was raised by his mother who was an intellectual and supporter and promoter of public education for all Iranians and in particular the women who had been deprived of the opportunity up to that time. Hamidi got his elementary and secondary school education in Shiraz. He was lucky to have Dr. Lotf-Ali Soratgar as one of his teachers who discovered his literary talent at an early age and helped to promote it. Hamidi left Shiraz after graduating from high school and continued his education at Tehran Teachers College an affiliate of Tehran University where he received his B.A degree in Persian literature in 1937. He then returned to Shiraz to teach at a public high school. One year later he published his first collection of poems entitled "Blossoms" (Shokoof-e ha), followed by a poem called "A'ra'mga'h-e eshgh" (The graveyard of love) in memory of the death of his fianc'e.

In 1939 he passionately fell in love with and was engaged to Manije-h Sha'drava'n, a girl distinguished in her native city Shiraz, for her beauty. This was a rousing love that broke Hamidi's silence with the publication of Ba'd az yek sa'l "After one year" in which he illustrated his brooding silence in a poem titled "Chaka'ma-ye Safid"(blank poem). Meanwhile, he was drafted for military service and had to leave Shiraz for six months. Manija's father who opposed their marriage, eventually succeeded in annulling their engagement after six months. This left a lasting effect on Hamidi and set the tone for a good number of his later poems. Hamidy immediately expressed his deep frustration in a number of poems that he published in 1940 in Shiraz newspapers and later in a three-volume prose work called Eshgh-e dar ba dar (two volumes, were censord for sometime), making his own love affair the talk of the town.

After doing the military service and a year of teaching at Shiraz high schools, Hamidi went to Tehran and married Nahid, a girl of Shirazi descent. She bore him a son and a daughter. In the same year he published Ashg-e- mashugh (The tears of the beloved), a collection of his poems in two sections : Eshgh va Entegham (Love and Revenge), in which he most passionately exposed his love story with outright, and not always complimentary, references to his beloved who, in the meantime, had been married. Ashg-e-mashugh soon became popular, particularly with the younger generation, and went into its

10th impression during the author's lifetime, disseminating Hamidi's name the story of his frustrated love affair as common knowledge.

"Whether you die or stay alive, you are my beautiful sweet heart
You are my only beautiful beloved, though you annoy me

Though you are not near me but always in my heart
Oh! I wonder! Like a dream, you are in my awaken eyes

You are escaping from me and you come following me too
You are the shadow, for thou are not my sweetheart, but mine!

Hamidi wrote a thirty four fraction poem (Charpareh) which is unique or to say the best nostalgic homeland poetry in our literary history. The piece is an incredibly beautiful poetic, and emotional epic and was to take part in 1954 C.E contest in Tehran and won the first place. The original story in prose was written by the historians. However, Hamidi by adopting and versifying this true story has created a nostalgic drama that has been considered by the literary critics a true poetical masterpiece. Hamidi has arranged this great epic into a number of separate frames. Scene one depicts the start of the battle titled "In the waves of Sind (Indus) River" between the armies of Prince Jallal-ed Din Kharazm Shah & Genghiz, the Mongol.

"To the west, the crawling Sun it was hidden behind mountains

به مغرب سینه مالان قرص خورشید
نهان میگشت پشت کوهساران

Pouring down saffron color powder on spears and the Spearmen

فرو میریخت گردی زعفران رنگ
به روی نیزه ها و نیزه داران

By the horse's hooves turned on the ground the heads like bloody balls,

ز سم اسب میچرخید برخاک
بسان گوی خون آلود سرها

By the sword sparkled fell on the plain successively, hands away from shields

زبرق تیغ می افتاد در دشت
پیاپی دستها دور از سپرها

Chapter 10

And the heart and chest that were torn apart by the long and short spears, especially in the war unequal in terms of human resources, so agonizing and painful beyond description.

Among the dark dust as cloud sparkling spearheads peaks Life burning sword blades kissing the crowns of heads	میان گرد های تیره چون میغ زبان های سنان ها برق می زد لب شمشیرهای زندگی سوز سران را بوسه ها بر فرق می زد

At this point of Jala'l-ed Din's battle against the Mongols, his prime-secretary Nuredin Mohammad Zeidari Nasavy, has reported briefly and precisely:

[This war was great combat and a great calamity. Long time ago, when Jala'l ed- Din gathered the great army, Genghiz was attacked and defeated by him) but now Genghiz reached the shores of Indus river at the head of a new greater army. The two armies clashed and put knife in each other… Jala'l ed-Din, with a small army of men stood manly against Genghiz, and personally attacked the heart of his army, and scattered them apart and pursued. When Genghiz saw the failure, turned his back retreated and fled hastily. Genghiz soon returned again with ten thousand of the elite guards , who had the title of valiants (Bahadurs) and the war was resumed. but when, the ambush, on the right side of the army of Jala'l ed-Din that "Amin-al molk" was on it broke, the order turned into chaos, and they could no longer resist].

In the turbulent battle, although Jala'l ed-Din along with his brave soldiers, made fatal blows on the Mongols, but the numerous of the Mongol armies offset these impacts. According to the History book of the Mongul conquests, "Jala'l ed- Din and his assistants were so valiant but the discipline and organization of the Mongols were dominant on their courage". On the other hand every moment the number of Iranian army was reduced and the Mongol war invaders went on their victory. The brave commander of Iran, along with the sunset, also saw the sun of his life declining.

"The bright face of the day was becoming hidden under the night's dark skirt	نهان میگشت روی روشن روز به زیر دامن شب در سیاهی
	در آن تاریک شب میگشت پنهان

It was being hidden in the dark night the brightness of Kharazmshahi camp	فروغ خرگه خوارزمشاهی به خوناب شفق در دامن شب به خون آلوده ایران کهن دید
In the red sunset, by the night's fall He saw the ancient Iran sunk in blood. In a sea of blood, in the full sun He saw his own vision in the sunset"	در آن دریای خون در قرص خورشید غروب آفتاب خویشتن دید

At this time, perhaps what he feared the most fare and the most important concern of the brave and young prince was the respect and honor of the privacy of his wife and women in the kingdom court. However, he knew that in case he was killed at the Mongol dominion, they will have no mercy, and with the full brutality they would not refuse any defamation.

With such notions in his mind, he saw himself and his family on the verge of destruction. He shed tears of regret and grief. In the meantime, staggering in his mind was a surprising idea: the possibility of the enemy victory was very strong. If I get killed (he said to himself), I am sure they will attack the privacy of my family. So the best decision that I have to make to ensure the honor and dignity of the family and my wife would be that this very night before the Mongol oppression and invasion, throw women and children in the Indus river so that the Mongols do not get access to them and I would then be able to cross the river safely to gather troops and embark on attacking the enemy.

"If tonight women and children fearing a bad name throw in the water	اگر امشب زنان و کودکان را زبیم نام بد در آب ریزم
If tomorrow I do not gain victory I would escape through the sea"	چو فردا جنگ بر کامم نگردید توانم کز ره دریا گریزم

Hence, he spoke with his wife and other women and informed them of his plan. They agreed to stand by his decision.

Zeidary Naseri has written:
{...When defeated Jalla'l ed- Din, came back to the Indus River Shore, he saw his mother and his wife and some of the family in his shrine, tangled in crying and started moaning. They made him swear to God to kill them, and free them from the scourge of captivity, he orderd that they be thrown in the water on their demand. And this catastrophe happened as a strange and rare tragedy.}
(Zeidari Nasery)

Then asked for the children one by one Looked angrily up at the sky	پس آنگه کودکان را یک به یک خواست
First, washed them by tears then threw them in the river!	به آب دیده اول دادشان غسل سپس در دامن دریا رها کرد
When women saw children in the water, they became distracted alike hairs	زنان چون کودکان را در آب دیدند چو موی خویشتن در تاب رفتند
Of the costly pain, without the king's word, they Rushed into the waters like a fish	وزآن درد گران بی گفته شاه چو ماهی در دهان آب رفتند
The King saw at a glance on water the contortion of twisted locks	شهنشه لمحه ای بر آبها دید شکنج گیسوان تاب داده
What did he do then, knows history; Seeking flower on the water	چه کرد از آن سپس تاریخ داند به دنبال گل بر آب داده
From one night to another with the small army, He cast the Heads from bodies and the helmets from head	شبی را تا شبی با لشگری خرد زتن ها سرسرها خود افکند
When the army surrounded him he cast the horse as ship in the river	چو لشگر گرد بر گردش گرفتند چوکشتی باد پا در رود افکند
	چوبگذشت از پس آن جنگ دشوار
	از آن دریای بی پایاب آسان
	به فرزندان ویاران گفت چنگیز
	که گر فرزند باید باید اینسان

As he passed through the difficult
war from that very deep sea, easily

Genghiz said to his children and
friends

 if must son, must be like this

Yes, those who were here before us,

This was how they fought off the
Turks and Arabs.

I narrated this story here,
So that you know the value and
appreciate;

 How hundreds of brave ones
sacrificed,

 Their lives to safe keep every
square inch of this Land

بلی آنان که از این پیش بودند
چنین بستند راه ترک وتازی
از آن این داستان گفتم امروز
که دانی قدر و بر هیچش
نخوانی
به پاس هر وجب خاکی از این ملک چه
بسیار
است آن سرها که رفته
زمستی برسر هرقطعه زین خاک خدا
داند چه افسرها که
رفته

Hamidy in 1942 published two prose works Fereshteg'n-e zamin (Angels of
the earth) and Sabok sarihay-ghalam (The frivolities of the pen), and a year
later he joined his old friend Torab Basiri to publish the weekly paper
Oghianous (Ocean) in Shiraz. Fereydoon Tavallali, a former student of
Hamidi, was a regular contributor to this paper with his critical essays written
in the same humorous style that he later used in his Al-tafa'sil. Hamidi has
written several national nostalgic poems such as odes "What Iran says?",
"Ferdowsi and Iran", "Black skys", "The 2nd of March", and poem
(Charpareh) of "In the Waves of Sind (Indus) River". In some verses of the
mathnavi sonnet "The Straw Story", with great sadness and yearning, he
criticizes the chaotic homeland condition after the Allied invasion of Iran in
World War II:

My land, the territory of Iran! Is this you?

Chapter 10

The destroyed and cultivated habitat, is this you?

Is this you, Oh, the chamber of Darius?
Is this you, Oh, the cradle of lions, is this you?

Oh, the respectable mother of Jacob Layth,
The fostering place of princes! Is this you?

Oh, the respectable cradle of Bouzarjomehr!
The art nurturing of Ministers! Is this you?

Do you remember you had a Bijan?
Do you also remember a Bahman?
Do you remember among the wars
You had a Rostam and one immortal too? The pitch sky!,

Do you remember!,that you had also a Bright sun?
We are not those male lions;

These boys are not similar to their fathers!

Siavash Kasraie 20th century poet

He was born in Isfahan in 1926 and shortly after, his parents moved to Tehran where he attended Adab school for his primary education and continued his secondary education at the military high schhool (Madress-eye Neza'm) and finally at Darol-Fonoon where he graduated and continued to University of Tehran Faculty of Law. He worked after graduating from the Law school at a number of government offices in Tehran and at the same time taught Persian literature at the University of Sista'n and at the Faculty of Fine Arts of Tehran University. He married Mehri Nawdari in 1962 and had two children.

While still in high school Kasra'ie made friends with the leftist political figures such as Mohsen Pezeshkpur and Dariush Forohar and was influenced by their nationalistic sentiments. As a college student, however, he became excited by the ideas of Marxism Leninsm doctrines along with other modernist young poets and became a loyal member of Tudeh Party. In the 1940s, along with some other avant-garde writers with a sense of political mission, including Ahmad Sha'mlou, Hushang Ebteha'j, and Mehdi Akhava'n-e

Contemporary Persian Poetry

Sa'les, Kasra'ie joined the circle of Nima'Yushij who is generally acknowledged as the founder of modern Persian poetical discourse, (She're-Nou) .

Following the line set by Nima' and attempting a freer and more independent mode of expression, Kasraie was a central figure in familiarizing the growing Persian audiences with Nima's poetry. His early poetry, although implicitly burdened by his ideological views, is nevertheless romantic and lyrical in imagery and tone.

In 1953 at the age of 27 with the suppression of the Tudeh Party he was arrested and imprisoned for a short time.Throughout the second half of the same period he was increasingly involved in political activities and, in turn appropriated the ambiguous and methaphoric language of the period's politicized poetry, developed from the commited poet's need to escape censorship. Under different pseudonyms, he wrote poems in praise of such Marxist figures as Taghi Ara'ni and khosrow Golesorkhi. He dedicated his most famous collection of poetry A'rash-e Kama'ngir (Arash the Archer) to the memory of Khosrow Ruzbeh, an inflencial member of the military branch of the Tudeh Party who was executed in 1958.

The epic of Arash the Archer Written by Seyavash Kasraii	حماسه ی آرش کمانگیر سروده سیاوش کسرایی
Morning was arriving, the old man quietly begun:	صبح می آمد پیرمرد آرام کرد آغاز
"Iran's army was in a fiercely painful worry,	لشگر ایرانیان در اظطرابی سخت دردآلود
Whispering they teamed up in twos, in threes… Children on roofs; girls sitting at windows, mothers sad by doors	دو دو وسه سه به پچ پچ گرد یکدیگر پیش روی لشگر دشمن سپاه دوست
The plain was completely. As far as eyes could see, coverd black with the enemy's army	دشت نه! که دریایی از سرباز آسمان الماس اخترهای خود را داده بود از دست

The muted murmur it rose to a
crescendo.

The people, like a disturbed sea,
Came to rage
Turned to roar;
Fell to waves
Cleaved its chest like a shell
And did a manit bear forth."
"

Arash am I, -
So begun the man facing the foe; -
Arash am I, a free warrior,
Armed with the arrow in my quiver
All ready to take your bitter trial.
Seek not my roots, -
Son of toil and torment am I;
As a meteor that flees the night,
As rising sun that shines alight.
Hallowed be the armor worn in war;
Blessed be the wine they drink in
triumph,
Hallowed and blessed your armor
and wine!
My heart I hold in hand
And cluch it tight, -
The heart, the vengeful cup of blood
The heart, the restless, the wrath-
toned…
May I in a feast drink to your
triumph?
May I in a fight clinck to the cup of
your heart!
For the cup of hatred is of stone.
In our feast, in our fight, stone and
jar are at war;
In this battle,
In this trial,

منم آرش
چنین آغاز کرد آن مرد با دشمن

منم آرش سپاهی مردی آزاده
به تنها تیر ترکش آزمون تلختان را
اینک آماده

مجوییدم نسب
فرزند رنج و کار

گریزان چون شهاب از شب
چو صبح آ ماده دیدار

مبارک باد آن جامه که اندر رزم پوشندش
گوارا باد آن باده که اندر فتح نوشندش

شما را باده وجامه
گوا را ومبارک باد

دلم را در میان دست میگیرم
و می افشارمش در چنگ

دل این جام پر از کین پراز خون را
دل این بی تاب خشم آهنگ

که تا نوشم به نام فتحتان در بزم
که تا کوبم به جام قلبتان دررزم

جام کینه از سنگ است
به بزم ورزم ما سبو وسنگ را جنگ
است

در این پیکار
در این کار

It is the heart of the people in my hand;
And the hopes of a silent people my helper.
The arc of the heavens in my hand
The bowman is I, the archer;
The swift-winged meteor;
The lofty crest of mountain, my haven;
The early-rising sun's eye is my den.
Fire the feather of my arrow;
And the wind is my servant.
Yet,
Today the cure shall not be might and valor.
Freedom may not be by iron body and youth power.
In this field,

On this very life-taking

and home-making arrow,
A feather of life shall be to fly with no rest"
Then he turned his head heavenward,
And in an altered tone yelled out words of else;
"Salute, O, Last morn! Farewell, O Dawn!
For it's last sight of Arash.
I swear to true morn!
I swear to the veiled sun, the pure-eyed, and the love-raining!
Arash his life in the arrow shall fly,
And fast he shall fall.
The earth knows this, so do the heavens,

دل خلقی است در مشتم
امید مردمی خاموش هم پشتم

کمان کهکشان در دست
کمانداری کمانگیرم
شهاب تیزرو تیرم
ستیغ سر بلند کوه ماوایم

به چشم آفتاب تازه رس جایم
مرا تیر است آتش بر
مرا باد است فرمانبر

و لیکن چاره را امروز زور و پهلوانی نیست
رهایی با تن پولاد و نیروی جوانی نیست

در این میدان
بر این پیکار هستی سوز سامان ساز
پری از جان بباید تا فرو ننشیند از پرواز

بس آنگه سر بسوی آسمان بر کرد
به آهنگی دگر گفتار دیگر کرد

درود ای واپسین صبح ای سحر بدرود
که با آرش ترا این آخرین دیدار خواهد بود

به صبح راستین سوگند
به پنهان آفتاب مهربار پاک بین سوگند

که آرش جان خود در تیر خواهد کرد
پس انگه بی درنگی خواهدش افکند

زمین می داند این را آسمان نیز

That my flesh is flawless and pure my soul.
Neither a trick, nor a charm in my work dwells;
No fear in my mind, or dread in my heart's lair"
He stopped then and said no word awhile.
Breaths in chests were restless.
"Before me Death,
Wearing a fearsome mask lumbers forth.
At each dreadfull step,
Bloodily he eyes me up.
On the vultures' wings he hangs over me,
He lingers and looms ahead;
And deadly cold laughs at me;
There resounds in the mounts and vales,
A baneful sneer he yells at me,
He then claims it back anew.
My heart loaths death;
For the evil Death is flesh-consuming,
Yet, once the lifs'soul is dimmed by pains;
When good and evil are at war;
It is sweet to go into the mouth of death.
It is all that freedom shall want.
Thousands of telling eyes 'n' silent lips
Know me their herald of hope.
Thousands of trembling hands and thrilling hearts
Bar me now and push me forth then.
With human charms I adorn my heart and soul.

که تن بی عیب وجان پاک است

نه نیرنگی به کارمن نه افسونی
نه ترسی در سرم نه در دلم باکی است

درنگ آوردو یک دم شد به لب خاموش
نفس در سینه های بی تاب می زد جوش

زپیشم مرگ
نقابی سهمگین بر چهره می آید

به هر گام هراس افکن
مرا با دیده خونبار می پاید

با بال کرکسان گرد سرم پرواز می
گیردبه راهی می نشیند راه می بندد
به رویم سرد می خند د

به کوه ودره می ریزد طنین زهرخندش را
و بازش باز می گیرد
دلم از مرگ بی زار است

که مرگ اهرمن خو آدمی خوار است
ولی آندم که ز اندوهان روان زندگی تار است

ولی آندم که نیکی وبدی را گاه پیکار است
فرورفتن به کام مرگ شیرین است
همان بایسته آز آدگی این است

هزاران چشم گویا ولب خاموش
مرا پیک امید خویش می داند

هزاران دست لرزان ودل پرجوش
گهی میگیردم گه پیش می راند

And I tread forth.
And by all power life has in eyes
and smiles,
I the fearful face of death shall
unveil."
He knelt in prayer,
Holding his hands towards the
peaks;
"Rise, O Sun, O provision of Hope!
Rise, O veines of Sunlight!
The flowing spring you are, thirsty
and restless am I.
Rise and fill the soul to the rim 'till
it quenched shall be.
As I've got my foot in the mouth of
ireful Death,
As in my heart I've got a fight with
the war-lusted evil,
I wish to bathe in your sea of light;
I seek the scent and hue in your
petals, O golden Flower!
Yea, O the rebel peaks of silence,
That scrapes your forehead against
the dreadful thunders,
And overlook the dreamy view of
the porch of night,
That rams the silvery pillars of
gilded day on your shoulder,
And shelter the fiery clouds;
Be lofty and proud!
My hope let it rise,
As flags of dawn breeze over your
ridge.
Save my pride
As the leopards you hold in your
rocky slide."
The earth still and the sky silent
were.

پیش می آیم
دل و جان را به زیورهای انسانی می آرایم

به نیکیی که دارد زندگی در چشم و در لبخند
نقاب از چهره ترس آفرین مرگ خواهم کند

نیایش را دوزانو برزمین بنهاد
به سوی قله ها دستان زهم بگشاد

برا ای آفتاب ای توشه امید
برا ای خوشه خورشید

تو جوشان چشمه ای من تشنه بی تاب
بیا سرریز کن تا جان شود سیراب

چو پا در کام مرگی تند خو دارم
چو در دل جنگ با اهریمنی پرخاش جو دارم

به موج روشنایی شستشو خواهم
زگلبرگ تو ای زرینه گل من رنگ و بو خواهم

شما ای قله های سرکش خاموش
که پیشانی به تندرهای سهم انگیز می سایید

که بر ایوان شب دارید چشم انداز رویایی
که سیمین پایه های روز زرین را به روی شانه می کوبید
که ابر آتشین را در پناه خویش می گیرید

غرور و سربلندی هم شما را باد

As if the world were all ears to hear Arash's words.
The sun's paw slowly slid down the mountains' mane.
And flew a thousand spears of gold at the sky's eye.
Arash calmly threw a look at the land beyond.
Children on roofs;
Girls at windows;
Mothers sad by doors;
Men on road.
That song of no word with a heart-rending sorrow,
From eyes soared up on the morning breeze.
What song can sing?
What melody can play?
The resounding rhythm

of the firm steps
Manly taken towards doom?
The refrain of steps taken surely forward.
His foes in a mocking silence gave way.
The children on roofs called his name.
Mothers for him prayed.
The old men turned their eyes.
Girls, clutching their necklaces,
Sent him power of love and loyalty.
Arash, yet silent,
Mounted up the Alborz side,
And did veils of tears ceaselessly after him drop."
Closed his eyes a wink Amoo Nowruz,

امیدم را برافرازید

چو پرچم ها که از باد سحرگاهان به سر دارید
غرورم را نگهدارید
به سان آن پلنگانی که در کوه وکمر دارید

زمین خاموش بود و آسمان خاموش
تو گویی این جهان

را بود با گفتار آرش گوش

به بال کوه ها لغزید کم کم پنجه خورشید
هزاران نیزه زرین به چشم آسمان پاشید

نظر افکند آرش سوی شهر آرام
کودکان بر بام
دختران نشسته بر پنجره ها
مادران غمگین کنار در
مرد ها در راه

سرود بی کلامی با غمی جانکاه
زچشمان بر همی شد با نسیم صبح دم همراه

کدام آهنگ آیا می توان ساخت
طنین گامهای استواری را که سوی نیستی
مردانه می رفتند

دشمنانش در سکوتی ریشخند آمیز
راه وا کردند
کودکان از بامها او را صدا کردند
مادران او را دعا کردند
پیرمردان چشم گرداندند
دختران بفشرده گردن بندها در مشت
همره او قدرت عشق ووفا کردند

His lips smiling, he was drowned in
dreams.
Children with weary querying eyes,
Were in wonder at the bravery!
Flames in the furnace were flying,
Wind was roaring.
"At night,
The trackers who traced Arash up
on the peaks,
Climbed down
Bearing no sign of him,
Save a bow, and an empty quiver.
Yea, yea,
Arash did his life with the souring
arrow fly;
He did the work of hundreds of
thousand thousands swords.
The arrow of Arash
The horsemen who rode along
Jeyhun,
The noon after that day,
Saw landed on a great walnut
bough.
And there ever after,
Border of Iran and Turan they
called.
Sunlight,
In her slow fleeing,
For years strolling passed over the
roof of the world.
Moonlight,
Her nightly journeys all in vain,
In the heart of every land and lane,
Silently peeked into each porch and
doorway,
Sun and moon in flight
Many years passed,
For years and again,
On all the vastness of Alborz,

آرش اما همچنان خاموش
از شکاف دامن البرز بالا می رفت
وز پی او
پرده های اشک پی در پی فرود آمد

بست یکدم چشم هایش را عمونوروز
خنده برلب غرقه در رویا

کودکان باد دیده گان خسته وپی جو
در شگفت از پهلوانی ها

شعله های کوره در پرواز
باد در غوغا

شامگاهان

راه جویانی که می جستند آرش را به
روی قله ها پیگیر
باز گردیدند

بی نشان از پیکر آرش
با کمان وترکشی بی تیر

آری آری جان خود در تیر کرد آرش
تیر آرش را سوارانی که می راندند بر
جیحون

به دیگر نیمروزی از پی آنروز
نشسته بر تناور ساق گردویی فرو دیدند
وآنجا را از آن پس

مرز ایرانشهر وتوران بازنامیدند

آفتاب در گریز بی شتاب خویش
سالها بر بام دنیا پا کشان بود

The entire doleful dumb

peak there you see,
And in those snow-swept vales you
know,
The helpless wayfarers lost at night
In heart of the mountains call Arash
over and over,
And seek their needs.
By the mouths of the stones on the
mountain
Arash answers.
Help them know the rise and fall of
paths;
Gives them hope,
Shows them the way."

Translated by: Abbas Mehrpooya,
Azad University of Hamadan

ما هتاب

بی نصیب از شبروی هایش هم خاموش

در دل هرکوی و هر برزن

سر به هر ایوان و هر در زد

آفتاب و ماه را در گشت

سالها بگذشت

سالها وباز

در تمام پهنه البرز

وین سر اسرقله مغموم وخاموشی که می
بینید

وندرون دره های برف آلودی که می دانید

رهگذرهایی که شب در راه می مانند

نام آرش را پیا پی در دل کهسار می
خوانند

و نیاز خویش می خواهند

با دهان سنگ های کوه آرش می دهد
پاسخ

می کندشان از فرازواز نشیب جاده ها

آگاه ـ می دهد امید می نماید راه

The indelible prints of betrayed hopes and a deep sense of loss marks Kasra'is
exilic poetry Most of his exilic poems witness to the fact that he had difficulty
in adjusting to life away from his native land. In one poem addressed to Iran,
he writes
:

"Here is one alienated and
distraught devoted to you,
and awaiting no one."

کاینجا غریب مانده پر|آکنده خاطریست
دلبسته شما و به امید هیچکس

Kasraie has also experimented, although without much success, with the genres of ghazal (lyrics) and mathnavi (rhymed couplets). His poems in roba'ie, do' beiti (quatrains), and the modern genre of cha'ha'r pa'reh have enjoyed critical acclaim. An example is the following:

"We were asleep by the side of a brook, You stole the moon from the water with a cup	کنار چشمه ای بودیم در خواب تو با جامی ربودی ماه از آب
When we drunk from that refreshing cup You turned into a water lily, and I into tears shed by moonlight."	چونوشیدیم از آن جام گوارا تو نیلوفر شدی من اشگ مهتاب

In fact, with the exception of few poems like (From Curfew to Cock Crow), Kasraie never abandoned the variations on the metrical traditions of classical Persian poetry. As a stylistically follower of Nima with a more refined language and a poet whose poetry is better known than himself, Kasraie is among the Persian poets with modernist tendencies who "have introduced sufficient novelty into their poetry to set it aside from the poetry of the past, and yet have preserved enough affinity with tradition to save their works from sounding alien or incomprehensible"

Kasra'ie is also the author of several stories for children, of which' Ba'd az zemestan dar a'ba'di-e ma' (After winter in our village) was voted by Shora'-ye keta'b-kudak (The Council for Children's book) as the best book of the year for children. Kasraie's essays, short stories and interviews are published in a collection entitled Dar hava'-ye morgh-e a'min (In the sphere of the Amen Bird).

Early in February of 1996 Kasraie had a heart operation in Vienna and died a few days later. He was buried in the artist's section of Vienna's central Cemetery.

Hushang Ebtehaj (Sayeh) 20th century Persian poet

Chapter 10

Hushang Ebtehaj (pen name Sa'yeh) was born in the city of Rasht, province of Gilan on February 26 1928. He completed his primary education there before moving to Tehran. S'aye published his first book of poetry at the age of 19. In Tehran he got involved in various literary circles and got to know Dr Mehdi Hamidi Shirazi who wrote a preface to his first poetry collection praising his literary talent. During this period after the end of the Second World War, Tehran was flourishing with a great number of modernist poets and writers in particular the followers of the new poetry style introduced by Nima Yushij called "she'r-e nou". Sayeh became a contributor to a number of magazines and periodicals such as Sokhan, Kavian, Sadaf, Maslehat and others. Like many other literary writers of contemporary Persian literature who were strongly indoctrinated with leftist democratic tendencies Sayeh in his verse and life, has been politically engaged.

Active in the communist Todeh Party, he was imprisoned following the Iranian Revolution of 1979. However, viewing his literary life exclusively through the lens of political historicity is a reductionist endeavor. Through his short introduction, Sweeney (co-translator of a number of Sa'yeh's poems into English) alludes to Sayeh's multilayered identity, namely the literary humanism that emerges from his love poems. He also references "Hafez be sa 'y-e Sayeh", a colossal undertaking of a comparative verse- by- verse study of existing versions of Hafez that took Sayeh around the Persian speaking world. And he highlights some of the challenging aspects of translating Sayeh and provides useful background information on the aesthetic force and social power of his verse. Marashi and Sweenedy must be commended for vigorously and critically engaging with Sayeh's variegated poetics in translation.

Sayeh is an outstanding literary figure of Persian contemporary poetry. He is extremely popular amongst a majority of Iranians in particular the younger generation of post Iranian Revolution of 1979. Sayeh's poetry expresses the aspirations, sentiments and heart desires of many Iranians; young and old. Sayeh is a highly regarded figure on the Iranian literary landscape. A dozen volumes of his poetry were published between 1946 and 1999 giving Sayeh a great start to establish for himself a special place amongst the new upcoming young poets of mid-twenty century. A selection edited by Mohammad Reza Shafei Kadkani, 'A'yeneh dar A'yeneh was first published in 1990 and is now in its 12th edition'.

Contemporary Persian Poetry

Sayeh's verse profoundly engages aspects of Iranian political history without compromising poet's independence. His love poems, recited with Hafezian lyricism, are amongst the most treasured works of Persian contemporary poetry. Fortunately, and thanks to the special work and collaboration of Chad Sweeny, an author of four books of poetry who lives in California and Mojdeh Marashi, an artist, writer, and translator based in northern California,". The two have collaborated on this project for several years, during which their translations appeared in various peer-reviewed literary journals such as Poetry International, Washington Square Journal, and Indiana Review. With more than 50 poems from 12 books, the selection spans half a century of Sayeh's verse and offers a thorough picture of his literary development through various poetic forms (rubai, ghazal, and Sher-e-sepid) and modalities (love poems, elegies, and politically charged verses).

"Love is the heat that multiplies itself
The birth of a birthing cosmos"
"Youth is a shimmering image
The heart eventually lets it go
Startled from sweet morning sleep
Come, my heart, it's late."

The translators; Chad Sweeney and Mojdeh Marashi have not shied away from footnoting mythological and intertextual allusions, providing guidance to curious readers who wish to explore the literary tradition to which Sayeh belongs. For instance, in the poem "Shabikhoon," translated as "Night Raid," the literal meaning of the term (night blood) has been footnoted, which brings the alterative of the source language into English, revealing some of Persian's semantic peculiarities. Though in the same poem, the translators have opted for a more domesticating translation of saghi, rendering it as "wine maid" – close to the conventional translation for Arabic saqi, "wine server" –which flattens the deeper connotations of the term in Persian literary tradition. (The saghi pours the wholesome wine of life into the empty bowl of the poet. At times, he inspires the poet and at other times he serves as a spiritual teacher, the symbol of the existence of the beloved on earth.) Though this collection is not bilingual, each translation is accompanied by the Persian title, which makes locating the original poems easier.

My bed
Is the empty shell of loneliness!

Chapter 10

You are the pearl
Strung from other men's necks

'The Art of SteppingThroughTime' captures the variety of his verse in bright and engaging English. While the original rhyme and meter schemes of Sayeh's ghazals are lost, the simplicity of these translations, in form and verbiage, create their own music in English. "Musical congruence rather than musical equality"—this is what Marashi and Sweeney have opted for. A poem by Sayeh, from that collection translated into English by Chad Sweeney and Mojdeh Marashi:

"The world does not begin or end today
Sad and happy hide behind one curtain

بازیچه ایام دل آ دمیان است". شعر از سایه
امروز نه آغاز و نه انجام جهانست
ای بس غم وشادی که پس پرده نهانست

If you are on the path don't despair of the distance
Arrival is the art of stepping through time

گر مرد رهی غم مخور از دوری و دیری
دانی که رسیدن هنر گام زمان است

A seasoned traveler on the road to love's door
Your blood leaves its mark on every step

تورهرو دیرینه سر منزل عشقی
بنگر که ز خون توبه هر گام نشان است

Still water soon sinks into the earth
But the river rolling grows into a sea

آ بی که بر آسود زمینش بخورد زود
دریا شود آن رود که پیوسته روان است

Let's hope that one reaches the target
So many arrows have flown from this old bow

باشد که یکی هم به نشانی بنشیند
بس تیر که درچله این کهنه کمان است

Time taught me to fall out of love with your face
That's why these tears are tinted with blood
Shame the long game of decades

از روی تو دل کندنم آموخت زمانه
این دیده از آن روست که خونابه نشان است

Plays the human heart as a toy

درد و دریغا که در این بازی خونین
بازیچه ایام دل آدمیان است

A caravan of tulips crossing this meadow
Was crushed under hoof by the riders of autumn

دل بر گذر قافله لاله وگل داشت
این دشت که پامال سواران خزان است

The day that sets springs breathe in motion
Will birth flowers and grasses from shore to shore

روزی که بجنبد نفس باد بهاری
بینی که گل وسبزه کران تا به کران است

Mountain, you heard my cry today
The ache in this chest was born with the world

ای کوه تو فریاد من امروز شنیدی
دردی است در این سینه که همزاد جهان است

All praised brotherhood but did not live it
God, how many miles from tongue to hand?

از داد وووداد آن همه گفتند ونکردند
یا رب چه قدر فاصله دست وزبان است

Blood trickles my eyes in this corner of enduring
The patience I practice is squeezing my life

خون می چکد از دیده در این کنج صبوری
این صبر که من میکنم افشردن جان است

Come on, Sayeh, don't swerve from the path
A jewel is buried beneath each step

از راه مرو "سایه" که آن گوهر مقصود
گنجی است که اندر قدم راهروان است

O joy! Poem by Hushang Ebtehaj

شعر آزادی سروده هوشنگ ابتهاج

O joy!
O liberty
O joy of liberty!
When you return,
What shall I do?
With this melancholy heart!

ای شادی
ای آزادی
ای شادی آزادی
روزی که تو بازآیی

Chapter 10

Our sorrow is heavy,
Our hearts are bleeding,
Blood spurts from our heads to our
feet,
From head to foot we are all pain,
We have exposed our loving heart to
hazards
For your sake!
When the tongue feared the lip,
When the pen doubted the paper,
Even, even our recollection dreaded
to speak during dreams,
We used to engrave your name in
our heart
Like an image on turquoise,
When in that dark street,
Night followed night,
Created on the closed window,
We spread your voice like spurting
blood
Like a stone thrown in the swamp
On the roof and at the door.
When the deceit of the beast,
Disguised in Solomon's garment,
Wore the ring on his finger,
We mused to rhyme your secret,
like God's mightiest name
In poetry and ode.

We spoke of
Wine, of flower, of morning,
Of mirror, of flight,
Of Phoenix and of the sun.
We spoke of light, of goodness,
Of wisdom, of love,
Of faith and of hope.
That bird that journeyed in the cloud

با این دل غم پرورد
من با تو چه خواهم کرد؟
غم هامان سنگین است
دل هامان خونین است
از سر تا پامان خون می بارد
ما سر تا پا زخمی
از سر تا پامان خون می بارد
ما سر تا پا دردیم
ما این دل عاشق را
در راه تو آماج بلا کردیم
وقتی که زبان از لب می ترسید
وقتی که قلم از کاغذ شک داشت
حتی حتی حافظه از
وحشت در خواب سخن گفتن می آشفت
ما نام ترا در دل
چون نقشی بر یاقوت میکندیم
وقتی که در آن کوچه تاریکی
شب از پی شب میرفت
و هول سکوتش را
بر پنجره فروبسته فرومیریخ
ما بانگ ترا با فوران خون
چون سنگی در مرداب
بر بام و در افکندیم
وقتی که فریب دیو
در رخت سلیمانی
انگشتر را یک جا با انگشتان می برد
ما زمزمه ترا چون اسم اعظم
در قول و غزل قافیه می بستیم

از می از گل از صبح
از آینه از پرواز
از سیمرغ از خورشید
می گفتیم
آن مرغ که در ابر سفر میکرد
آن بذر که در خاک چمن می شد
آن نور که در آینه می رقصید

That seed in the ground that grow
into a lawn,
That light that danced in the mirror,
And murmured to our heart's
solitude,
Spoke of meeting you at every
breath,
In the school, in the market,
In the mosque, in the town square,
In jail, in chains,
We murmured your name;
Liberty!
Liberty!
Liberty!
Those nights of nightmare,
Those nights of tyranny,
Those nights of faith,
Those nights of shouting,
Those nights of patience and
awakenings,
We sought you in the street,
We called your name on the roofs;
Liberty!,
Liberty!,
Liberty!
I said;
"When you return
I will lift my young heart
Like the banner of victory,
And will hoist
The bloody banner
On your lofty roof
I said
"On the day that you return,
I will strew this blossoming blood,
Like a bouquet of rose,
At your foot,
And will hang
My rolling arms

در خلوت دل با ما نجوا داشت
با هر نفسی مژده دیدار تو می آورد
در مدرسه در بازار
در مسجد در زنجیر
ما نام ترا زمزمه میکردیم
آزادی!
آزادی!
آزادی

آن شب های ظلمت وحشت زا
آن شب های کابوس
آن شب های ایمان
آن شب های فریاد
آن شبهای طاقت وبیداری

در کوچه ترا جستیم
بر بام ترا خواندیم
آزادی!
آزادی!
آزادی!

می گفتم
روزی که تو باز آیی
من قلب جوانم را
چون پرچم پیروزی
بر خواهم داشت
وین بیرق خونین را
بر بام بلند تو
خواهم افراشت
می گفتم
روزی که تو باز آیی
این خون شکوفا را
چون دسته گل سرخی
در پای تو خواهم ریخت
وین حلقه بازو را
در گردن مغرورت

Around your neck
O liberty!
See!
Liberty!
This carpet lying under your foot,
Is dyed with blood
This flower garlands is made of blood,
It is the flower of blood...
O liberty!
You come through the alley of blood,
But
You will come and I tremble in my heart;
What is this which is concealed in your hand?
What is this which is twisted around your leg?
O liberty!
Are you coming with cbains?

خواهم آویخت
آی آزادی!
بنگر!
آزادی!

این فرش که در پای تو گستردست
از خون است
این حلقه گل خون است
گل خونست
ای آزادی
از ره خون می آیی
اما
می آیی و من در دل می لرزم
این چیست که در دست تو پنهان است
این چیست که در پای تو پیچیده ست
ای آزادی!
آیا با زنجیر می آیی؟

The Wall, poem by Sayeh:

شعر دیوار سروده هوشنگ ابتهاج

Behind this lofty mountain,
Beside the pale sea,
There was a girl
With whom
I was madly in love
As if Gali
Had been created
That I should love her fervently,
And she should love me sweetly...
And you know

پشت این کوه بلند
لب دریای کبود
دختری بود که من
سخت میخواستمش
و توگویی که گالی
آفریده شده بود
که منش
دوست بدارم پرشور
ومرا دوست بدارد شیرین
وشما می دانید

O silent stars!
How happy we were,
I and she were drunk in the sweet
sleep of hope,
And what pure happiness
Laughed in my eyes and hers…..
And now, O coy maidens,
If you aren't dumb.
Open your mouths
And say what happened from that
calumny?
What happened to this clouded
spring!
And between me and she,
Now lies this vast plain,
And this lofty mountain…

آه ای اختران خاموش
که چه خوشدل بودیم
من و او مست شکر خواب امید
وه چه خوشبختی پاک
در نگاه من و او میخندید
وینک ای دخترکان غماز
گر نه لالید و نه گنگ
بگشایید زبان
وبگویید که از
یک بهتان
چون شد این چشمه غبار آلوده
و میان من و او
اینک این دشت بزرگ
اینک این راه دراز
اینک این کوه بلند

Translated into English by M.Alexandraian

Ali Akbar Dehkhoda' 20th century Persian scholar, author & critic

Mirza Ali Akbar Ghazvini, known as Dehkhoda, the Persian literary scholar, poet, author, and a political and social critic, was born in Tehran in 1870 . He came from a traditional land-owner's family in Qazvin, but his father, Khan Baba Khan Qazvini, had moved the family to Tehran from not long before Dehkhoda was born and died when the boy was only nine years old.

Dehkhoda studied Theology and Islamic law and literature under the tutelage of Shaykh Gholam-Hosseinn Borujerdi, but was also influenced by the liberal attitude and teachings of his neighbor, Shaykh Hadi Najmabadi. On December, 1899, Dehkhoda enrolled in the school of Political Science (Madresseh Oloom Siasi) which had just been established primarily to educate the sons of aristocracy for later careers in the government. According to Dehkhoda's classmate, Abdollah Mostofi, the initial enrollment was 16 students though apparently more enrolled later, and the Minister of Foreign Affairs, Moshir-al-doleh and his secretary Moshir-al-Molk lectured at their school. After completing his studies, Dehkhoda' was retained as a secretary by the Gha'ja'r dignitary and ambassador to Balk'an countries, Mo'aven-al-Doleh Ghafari (later Ahmad Shah's Foreighn Minister in 1915), a man of substantial means. Around 1903, Dehkhoda accompanied Ghafari on a mission to Europe where he travelled and studied for the next two years, primarily in Vienna, Austria.

In 1905 Dehkhoda returned to Iran and was engaged by Ha'ji Mohammad-Hoseyn Amin al- Zarb as interpreter for the French engineers who were building the highway between Khorasan and Tehran. After the promulgation of the constitutional decree in 1906 the first Persian newspaper Sur-e Esra'fil was conceived and published and Dehkhoda was hired as editorial secretary and contributor.

The constitutional period was an era of journalistic efflorescence. Most journalists, however, had no real writing skill, were ill acquainted with the world outside Persia, and lacked understanding of such concepts as freedom, equality, and constitutional government. The journals for which they often worked disappeared after the first few issues. Sur-e Esrafil, however, reflected its founder's passionate devotion to liberal ideas. Dehkhoda a gifted writer, was trained in political theory, and thanks to his knowledge of French and his European travel, he also had a sophisticated understanding of world affairs. He was thus able, through his well-reasoned and clearly written political articles in Sur-e-Esrafil, to attract a wide audience, particularly for his satirical series Charand parand, which was the main reason for the rise in the number of printed copies of the newspaper to a high of 24,000 far higher than those of even the best contemporary publications.

After the coup d'etat of Mohammad-Ali Shah (1907-1909) in 1908 Dehkhoda, fearing retaliation from the court and the reactionary clergy, joined several other notable constitutionalists in taking refuge at the British legation in Tehran. Owing to the intervention of British officials, he received a safe-conduct and left for Baku and eventually Paris, where he remained for about a year and a half, until January of 1910. This exile was one of the most stressful periods of his life. Not only did the agents of the Persian government persecute his relatives and associates, but he himself was also suffering from depression and poverty, yet he never slackened in his literary and journalistic activity. From Paris he went to Switzerland, where in Yverdon he published a new series of Sur-e-Esrafil, which appeared January 23 to March 6 1909 printed in Paris. The cost of publication and smuggling copies to Persia, where distribution was not permitted, were high, but eager readers passed each copy from hand to hand. Nevertheless Dehkhoda's desperation reached such a point that he began to think of suicide. Instead he went to Germany and resumed publication there, but again there were difficulties, and he moved to Istanbul, hoping for assistance or employment from the Persian community there. With the help of Mirza'Abul-Hassan Khan Mo a'zed-al-Saltana, the head of Anjoman-e Sa a'dat, he, Ha'ji Mirza' Yahya' Dowlata'ba'di, and Hoseyn Danesh undertook publication of a newspaper called Sorush. It seems that Persian merchants living in Istanbul assumed the cost of the early numbers of this journal! Again, however, the difficulties of ensuring that copies reached Persian subscribers caused the cessation of publication after fourteen or fifteen issues.

After the overthrow of Mohammad-Ali Shah, Dehkhoda returned to Persia, on 23 January 1910. In the same year he was elected by the people of both Kerman and Tehran to represent them in the second Majles. His popularity in Kerman was owing to his criticisms in Charand parand of the heavy-handed government of Firuz Mirza Nosrat-al-Dowla. In 1914, with Persia in the grip of British and Russian occupation, Dehkhoda took refuge with the Bakhtiari tribes in Chaha'r Maha'l. After his return he served for a short period in the Ministry of education (Vezarat-e ma a'ref) with the title "head of secretariat" (rais-e kabineh) and in the Ministry of Justice (Wezarat-e adlia-h) with the title "head of the office of investigation" In 1924 he was appointed director of the Madressa-ye olum-e siasi, where he served until 1941.

Dehkhoda's satirical column and his humorous but vitriolic commentaries was one of the reasons for the paper's popularity. In general Dehkhoda's commentaries dealt with socio-economic and political issues often deriding the courts, the Royal court and the reactionary clergy while exposing their tyranny, dependency, and corruption. For this reason, both Sur-e Esrafil and Dehkhoda provoked the wrath of the Royal court for which Sur-e Esrafil eventually paid with his life.

Dehkhoda's reform minded ideas soon made him a target of the clergy. Among these were his support for educational reforms and land distribution, both of which threatened the clergy as major landowners and the main influence and players in an anachronistic system of education. At this time, the reformists were just beginning to demand and institute changes in the system of education which was essentially based on private schooling, often taught by a clergy, with the skills of writing and reading learned through Quranic readings, advancing to studying Islam, and Islamic jurisprudence accompanied with limited instruction in mathematics, history, and literature.

These reforms were led by Mirza Hassan Roshdieh with the first modern schools; Dabestan, using blackboards, instruction books and maps, opening in Tabriz in 1887, Tehran in 1888, and later serving as model schools for the establishment of modern education in Iran. The clergy considered these schools as undermining Islam and they were routinely attacked by thugs dispatched by the clergy burning and destroying the books and supplies and shutting down the school.

Both the clergy and the monarchy had vested interest in preserving the status quo. They both controlled vast amounts of fertile land under a feudal system of production and management; exercised a considerable power and control over the Iranian society mired in corruption and frequent manipulation by foreign interests, particularly Britain and Russia; and they both demanded blind obedience. For this reason, a good portion of the clergy sided with the Monarchy, resisting change and considered reforms as heretical measures instigated by Babis and western stooges. Among these was the powerful Shaykh Fazlolah Noori, who preached publicly that modern education and educating women was Ba'bi conspiracy realizing well that it would undermine the clergy's power and income. Although there were some pro Constitution clergy, the majority of the clergy considered the constitution as a western idea in conflict with Shari'at. Dehkhoda's satirical pieces ridiculing these views and attacks on Noori and his ideas led to the temporary banning of the newspaper Sur-e Esrafil. Sur-e Esrafill himself was executed by the order of the Shah. Other major leaders of the movement that were killed or executed by the Shah's order were Malek-al-Motekalemin, Judge Ardaghi Ghazvini and Seyed Jamal-aldin, the father of the famous contemporary writer and critic Jamalzadeh.

The idea of compiling an encyclopedic dictionary of the Persian language was conceived during his stay with the Bakhtiari tribe in Chaha'r Ma'ha'l, and on his return to Tehran he applied himself to assembling the preliminary materials. He also continued his literary and scholarly activities, publishing articles in such journals as Iran-e konouni, Aftab, and Da'nesh.

In the atmosphere of strict censorship under Rez' Shah, Dehkhoda put aside his political activities and devoted himself entirely to scholarly and literary work. The fruit of this period of his life includes the four-volume collection of aphorism (Amsal o hekam, 1925-1932) and the first volume of his Loghat-na'ma, which appeared in 1939, as well as a number of scholarly articles on Persian literature and language. He continued to concentrate on the Loghat-nama through the first decade of the reign of Mohammad Reza Shah. In 1951 Mohammad Mosaddegh came to power, and the movement to nationalize the oil industry was gaining momentum; in the prevailing atmosphere of political excitement Dehkhoda once more turned to politics, joining the Anjoman-e havadaran-e solh (Society of the supporters of peace), and a group with socialistic tendencies. Although the leaders of the Tudeh party sought to attract the support of well-known Persian cultural figures, Dehkhoda instead declared his support for Mossadegh. Soon after Dehkhoda withdrew entirely from political activity and devoted the rest of his life to Loghat-nama.

"Loghat-Nameh Dehkhoda" was established at his home located on Tehran's Iranshahr Avenue attracted a significant number of progressive scholars and linguists to collaborate in the writing of his Loghat-nama. In those days, Iranshahr was located on the outskirts of the city away from hustle and bustle of the city and mixed noise of automobile and doroshkeh (horse drawn carriages)) traffic, but Dehkhoda's home was busy with scholarly and intellectual activities. A significant library was built and each person was assigned a special letter of the Persian alphabet or other tasks. By the time of his death in March 1st 1956, the work had surpassed 80 volumes.

In 1945 Dehkhoda's home was designated as the Dehkhoda Institue. After his death the Institute was transferred to the Parliament which assumed its responsibility and the administrative duties of Loght-nameh was assigned to Dr. Mohammad Moin, one of his assistants and collaborators since 1945, by the Majlis, in accordance to Dehkhoda's wishes enunciated in his will. In 1958, the responsibility of Loghat nameh was transferred to the Tehran University's Literature Department and Dr Moin was appointed as the head of the Dehkhoda Institute. Later Dr Moin, an outstanding scholar in his own right, was replaced due to his illness, by Dr Seyed Jaffar Shahidi as the head of the Dehkhoda Institute. Dr Shahidi had once collaborated with the group task of translating Arabic terms into Persian and was also responsible for supervising the publication of Moin's own work, Farhang-e Farsi, in 1972. It still continues as a branch of the Tehran University located on Vali Asr Avenue in Shemiran.

Although Dehkhoda never enjoyed wealth or affluence, he was always open-handed. He devoted the royalties from Amsa'l o hekam to subsidise for printing new books and for the care of the sick.

Dehkhoda's youth coincided with the last decade of Na'ser-al-Din Sha'h's rule, when, owing to the major role of the clerics in the successful campaign against the tobacco concession, new populist forces were unleashed in Persian politics. Religious leaders wielded considerable influence in everyday life, and many of them became prominent landowners. Dehkhoda was a believer in equality before the law regardless of religious belief and he fervently supported emancipation of women, particularly abolition of the veil. Owing to his early exposure to the ideas of Najmabadi, he was convinced that, over the course of centuries, Islam itself had been unduly manipulated by religious jurists. He himself, as one who had to earn his living, was aware of the difficulties faced by ordinary folks and the widespread injustices of the landlord-peasant system. Aside from his campaign against what he considered religious superstition, the greater part of his articles was written in support of the peasants and laborers. One of his most important proposals was for the establishment of an agricultural bank, to which large landowners would turn over one-tenth of their holdings at a reasonable price, to be converted into small shares and transferred to the peasants, who would pay for them in installments.

Dehkhoda also wrote and translated a series of articles on the Russian Revolution, to familiarize his readers with social and political topics through explanation and criticism of the various political and factions involved. He was personally convinced that, in the conditions prevailing in Persia, the program of the social democrats was most appropriate. After he was elected to the Majles he joined the E'teha'dion (Moderates) faction.

Dehkhoda's prose enjoys a special distinction in the Persian literature of this century. His profound familiarity with Persian classical literature, both prose and verse; his prodigious store of current proverbs partly derived from his work on Amsa'l o hekam; and his early involvement in journalism, with the concomitant need to attract large number of readers, all helped to develop a clearly understandable style far removed from the ornate artificiality that characterizes the prose of the Qajar period. His knowledge of French, though it brought him familiarization with Western literature, never led him to adopt a "Western coloration or to incorporate French borrowings into his own work". Even Charand parand which was filled with puns, ambiguities, allusions, and intimations (iha'ama't, kena'ya't, talmiha't), owed its success to the fact that it was intelligible to ordinary folk and at the same time entertaining to the intellectual elite and sophisticated men of letters. In Dehkhoda's serious political articles convoluted and artificial expression is also lacking though his editorials in Soroush and his satirical pieces for Iran-e kononi do not do the same bite as the original Charand parand series in Su'r-e Esrafil. The difference is so great in fact that some have suspected that the latter was actually written by Mirza Jahangir Khan. The pieces in the numbers of Su'r-eEsrafil printed in Switzerland were, however, written months after the execution of Mirza Jahangir Khan, and it therefore seems certain that Dehkhoda himself wrote them after what he called five months of silence. The disparity in tone may instead be attributed to the change in Dehkhoda's own circumstances. He wrote for Su'r-eSrafil as a member of the disenfranchised elements in Persian society, but six years later he had become a deputy in the Majles and himself a member of the ruling elite.

Although Dehkhoda was not primarily a poet and his poems are mainly exercises in versification, he has nevertheless earned a place in the history of contemporary poetry. His modest output includes ghazals and other pieces in the classical style, each written exclusively in the language of the time of the poet being emulated. For example, in "Lisak which was composed in imitation of Rudaki", there is not a single word or expression that was not in the Persian lexicon of the 10th century. Similarly, at the request of Habib Yaghma'ie he composed a poem in the style of Bahra'mi Sarakhsi. Some of these "imitations "are actually superior in lucidity, expository power, and elegance of expression to the originals, including even some from Saadi's Bustan.

Dehkhoda also wrote a mussamat and two masnavi's (in both Turkish and Persian ;) also in the popular (awa'ma'na) manner. Because of his ingenious use of slang expressions his poetry includes the best examples of popular Persian verse ever written. A third group of poems consists of mathnavis in which he used allegory and narrative to expound his social ideas; as these pieces were aimed at the educated class, he did not hesitate to use all manner of allusions to the Kura'n and words of fegh and belles letters, as well as archaic expressions. In " Ensha' Allah gorba ast" (God willing it' s cat) his powerful portrayal of the mien and behavior of a hypocritical a'khund is almost without equal in Persian literature. Among other literary works were annotations to the Divan of Na'ser Khosrow and the Diva'n of Hafez, which appeared in the journals of Yaghma' and Da'nesh; he also wrote a biography of Abu Rayha'n Biruni, called Seh'ah al-fors by Hendushah Nakhjavani and the diva'ns of Manuchehri Damghani, Farrokhi Sistani and parts of Masud-e Sa'd-e Salma'n's.

In all his writings Dehkhoda was a perfectionist and meticulous craftsman. He was a nationalist, outspoken in his convictions, indifferent to the wrath of powerful men, and a firm believer in Persian culture.
Two of Dehkhoda's masterpieces; "Charand –o Parand" and "God willing it is a cat" have been, in recent years, translated into English and published. For information how to obtain them please go to Www.google.com.

Hassan Nikbakht 20th century Persian poet

Hassan Nikbakht was born in 1937 in Tehran. He completed his higher education in Tehran and entered professional career in editorial and publishing. His love of poetry and writing in the early years of his life brought him to the literary circles in Tehran. He soon got acquainted with famous writer, literary critic and poet Dr Mohammad Ebrahim Bastani Parizi who supported and guided his poetic talents as well as other literary masters of modern Persian poetry in Tehran. Dr.Bastani Parizi wrote a preface to his first collection of poetry, "Harir-e Arezo" which was published 1989 in Tehran. Nikbakht is an extremely sensitive poet whose poetry is inspired by the people's pains, sufferings, and daily problems which have their roots in the social and political chaos that has entangled the daily lives of his fellow country men for many years. Nikbakht has for long considered poetry's main role to be a media through which people's hopes and aspirations, pains and problems can be conveyed and has found it to be the most effective vehicle.

Nickbakht has witnessed these social pains and hardships from the early years in his life and is well aware of them and their nature as well as their source. He calls himself "the poet of patience and aspirations" He has wrapped these aspirations and hopes as well as the life's beautiful gifts into a poetic mould and has gathered them in his first poetry album titled the "Harir-e Arezoo" (Aspirations wrapped in Silk) Here is a sample of the poems from that collection:

We remained behind in the lover's
abode
We remain ,with no excuse,

The wayfarers already left, and we,
Are left all alone in this night of
envy,

We got lost in the silk –wrapping of
our aspirations
We are lagging-behind in search of
our destination.

Fog has covered-up our vision
We have become love-sick in search
of a light

A fire is spread to our nest
We are left behind in the middle of
the flames

An effort is needed to, perhaps,
break open the cage
Why are we being so patient in this
darkness!.

We do not have much wealth,but as
ever,
Continue to stay; although with a
worn-out pride.

The yellow leaves are trembling and
about to fall,
We are a green forest and standing
up strong!

O'   you   our   sympathetic
clouds,where is the   rain?

در دیار عاشقان ما مانده ایم
بی بهانه فکر فردا مانده ایم

راه پویان زود کوچیدند وما
در شب حسرت چه تنها مانده ایم

در حریر آرزوها گم گشته ایم
در پی مقصود خود وامانده ایم

مه فضای دیده را پوشانده است
در پی نوری چه شیدا مانده ایم

آتشی میسوزد این کاشانه را
در میان شعله ها جا مانده ایم
همتی شاید قفس را بشکنیم
از چه در ظلمت شکیبا مانده ایم

دستمان پر نیست اما همچنان
با غروری خسته اینجا مانده ایم

برگهای زرد لرزانند وسست
جنگل سبزیم وبرپا مانده ایم

ابرهای همدلی! باران کجاست

تشنه لب در پای دریا مانده ایم

تا چه پیش آید نمی دانم ولی
منتظر بر لطف فردا مانده ایم

We are standing by the sea, but
thirsty we are !

I have no idea what is in-store for
us,!
But we are still looking to tomorow
for a favor.

This ghazal (ode) is a good example of the amourous and gnostic ghazals that
form most lyrical poems in Nikbakht's poetry collection. Lyircs have been
mostly one of the most desirable poetical vehicle for the Persian poets
throughout the years to express their inner and common feelings of pain,
aspirations and hopes. It is Nikbakht's preferred style of writing poetries too.
He has written a number of amouros, Gnostic and social lyrics.

Pain afflicted ones! Where is cure?
In the lover's abode where is peace?
We have lost our way in search of
destination.
How can we make up for the love's
fault?

در دیار عاشقی سامان کجاست؟
در پی مقصود ره گم کرده ایم
این خطای عشق را تا وان کجاست؟

The mirror's face is made up of hard
rock!
Where is the light to illuminate our
comrade's heart?

سینه آیینه ها از سنگ سخت
نور باران دل یاران کجاست؟

They afflicted our lives with
anguish, where is the relief?
My life is burning with the fire of
envy!

درد را با جان ما آمیختند
دل به جان آمد مگر درمان کجاست؟
آتش حسرت به جانم بوسه زد
آب لطف بوسه جانان کجاست؟

Where is beloved's Soothing kiss ?

Contemporary Persian Poetry

Nikbakh's heart is completely filled with pain and he deeply agonizes over the social injustices of his time and the extremely rough road ahead to freedom. In the following poem he is clearly grieving and sheds tears of pain over the predominant oppresions of time.

Come let us mourn the arrival of spring, Come a thousand times to shed tears a thousand times'	بیا به ماتم فصل بهار گریه کنیم هزاروار بیا تا هزاروار گریه کنیم
Coming of calamity is being heard from in the distance Come let us cry for feeling exiled in these times.	صدای فاجعه از دوردست می آید برای غربت این روزگار گریه کنیم
The arrow of oppression is always in the hunters' bow. Come let us shed tears in the spring	همیشه تیر ستم در کمان صیاد است بیا من و تو به فصل بهار گریه کنیم
In the rough road to freedom; Come let us shed tears for the injured feet of that lonely rider	درون جاده پر سنگلاخ آزادی به پای زخمی آن تکسوار گریه کنیم
My heart is filled with agony for the oppression in our time, Come let us shed tears to the tunes as being played on citar.	دلم گرفته ز بیداد این زمانه بیا به همنوایی بانگ ستار گریه کنیم

Nikbakht's lyrical poems are charming. His sensitive poetic gift and his outstanding literary talent have helped to write lyrics that are rich in poetic wit as well as fine figures of speech. He constantly lives and hopes for change and therefore has no alternative but to be patient!:

Other than being patient waiting for you, what else could I do! Other than believing in the illusions of you, what else coud I do!	اگر با انتظارت سر نمی کردم چه میکردم خیالت را چنین باور نمیکردم چه میکردم

دو چشمت آیه های آبی شبهای مهتابی

اگر این آیه ها از بر نمیکردم چه میکردم

Your eyes: "the blue verses of moonlit nights"!
Other than memorizing those verses, what else could I do!

به گرد غنچه غم پرزند پروانه جانم

اگر این غنچه را پرپرنمیکردم چه میکردم

The butterfly of my soul, flutters around the blossom of my grief
Other than plucking its petals , what else could I do!
In the season of the draught of "Humanity";
Other than being patient by shedding tears, what else could I do!

اگر در خشکسال مردمی دامان صبرم را

به آب دیدگانم تر نمیکردم چه میکردم

Literature and in particular poetry has for ever been the reflection of the people's lives in human societies and their social behavioures. Poetry that has direction and embodies messages demonstrates the ups and downs of their lives. Poet considers himself committed to demonstrate in the language of verse whatever that is going on around him. Sometime, use of metaphors and equivocations afford these kinds of poems hundreds of excegies and assimilations:

Why the green fields of wheat are burning in fire!
The gloomy flames of fire have engulfed the Reed-bed!

چرا آتش به جان سبز گندم زار افتاده

لهیب شوم آتش بر تن نیزار افتاده

All friends were friendly and kind with one another,
Why there is now a wall between those sympathetic friends!

تمام دوستان با هم انیس ومهربان بودند

چرا بین رفیقان همدلان دیوار افتاده

Why broad-mindedness has now left our spirits!
Why are thorn-fields between friends in place of green-fields!

چرا آزادگی از روح ما رخت سفربسته

به جای سبزه زاران بین یاران خار افتاده

چرا همسایگان از حال همدیگر نمی پرسند

چرا گل های یاری خار گشته خوار افتاده

تمام چشم ها مان در افق سوی آینده ست
در آنجا اتفاقی دلنشین انگار افتاده

Why the neighours do not enqire of
one another's well-being!
Why the flowers joining friends
have turned thorns!

All our eyes turned to the horison
staring into the future!
As if something heart-warming and
cheerful is happening there!

And finally Nikbakht has determined that the cure lies in "patience" and
laughter's place is in "jail" He becomes content with shedding hidden tears

In the dark, moonless night:
  Night is long, we must be patient?
  Laughter is in jail, we must be
  patient?

  Tears have frozen on the cheeks,
  Tears must be hidden, we must be
  paient?

  It is the roar of thunder and the
  home-burning lightning
  City is under the threat of storm we
  must be patient?

  Sky, like the eyes of the lovers,
  Is pouring down with rain we must
  be patient?

  The alley is filled with hesitation,
  the homes
   On verge of destruction, we must
  be patient?

شب چه طولانی ست باید صبر کرد
خنده زندانی ست باید صبر کرد؟

اشگ ها بر گونه ها ماسیده است؟
گریه پنهانی ست باید صبرکرد؟

غرش رعد است وبرقی خانه سوز؟
شهر طوفانی ست باید صبر کرد؟

آسمان مانند چشم عاشقان
سخت بارانی ست باید صبرکرد

کوچه پر تردید مانده خانه ها
رو به ویرانی ست باید صبر کرد

Nikbakht has demonstrated a keen interest in writting melodies. His melodies, form a charming part of his poetry collection and have been put to music and song by a number of singers and musicians in Iran in recen years.

Maryam Nezami 20th century Persian poet

Maryam Nezami was born in Isfahan, in 1948. Her father Abdolhossei Nezami, was a well-read scholar of Persian classical literature. He was trained in classical Persian music by musical masters of his time in Isfahan, such as Maestro Ta'j Isfahani, Hassan Kassa'I, Jalil Shahna'z and others. He had inherited a great voice from his father and got the initial musical training to become a tenor. He was a very humble man and did never put his musical talent at the service of commercial musical entertainment in Radio or television nor sung in public gatherings to earn financial gains or national fame. He, however, in Maryam's early years of life recognized her musical, artistic, and literary talents and applied his own musical and literary expertise to teach, train and guide her into the world of art, music and poetry.

Maryam started to learn to play piano and singing around the age of twelve under the tutoreship of the masters of classical music in Tehran. She also started attending regular schooling and continued her higher education by entering the faculty of political science of the Teheran University. After graduation, she worked at the legal office of Iran's Bank Sepah for couple of years, but soon left the bank to pursue her career in music, painting and literature.

In the arena of the contemporary Persian poetry Maryam Nezami is one of the most outstanding poets of our time empowerd with an exceptional literary talent, verve and poetic gift. However, she has remained unknown within the poetic circles and in the community of poetry lovers. This has been mainly due to the fact that this lady poet has declined to publish her poetry because of her extraordinary humility and her deep knowledge and awareness of the superior quality of the vast and exceptionally great treasures of Persian poetry. She is truly of the opinion that the domain of Persian poetry exclusively belongs to the great classical poets such as Hafez, Sa'di, Ferdowsi, Mowlavi, Eraghi, Ja'mi and others and therefore would be discourteous to encroach upon it. There are many poets and poetry lovers who of course disagree with her saying that every flower has a different scent and beauty of its own and evolutionary progress should not be stopped and must be allowed to continue.

Although Maryam has refused to publish her vast and beautiful collection of poetry, notwithstanding throughout the years has continued to write a great number of poems in all different varieties of Persian poetic genre including ghazals, roba'ie, qasida, qeta, mathnavi, dobeiti, and more; in Khorasani, Araghi, Hendi, and Modern (Nimaie) styles.

Maryam is gifted with a poetical verve, pensive, thoughtful, and deeply imaginative. She is highly educated in the field of literature, languages, history and gnosticism. She is a poet with a soul that is extremely sensitive, full of love for all human beings, and cares deeply about our environment. She adores the natural beauties that have surrounded us in this world and is greatly concerned about the health and preservation of all natural elements that have made life on this plant possible; water, soil, air, plants, and in particular trees that she considers them to be of vital importance for the healthy continuation of life on our planet.

A review of Maryam's poetic treasure clearly demonstrates how skillfully she has journeyd through the entire twelve centuries literary panorama of Persian poetry and has applied her outstanding poetic talent to this arena, creating poetry in all the major poetic styles from Khorasani, to Eraghi, to Indian,and finally to modern and contemporary "Shereh Now" (new poetry).
Maryam, has throughout her life, been successfully creative on other branches of art, in particular, painting. Her work covers a variety of styles,from classical to modern, and does water-colors as well as oil-painting.

As it was briefly mentioned, she started to learn to play piano and singing in Persian and classical western music. She got her training in Persian music from her late father and opera under the tutorship of one of the outstanding opera masters and singers in Tehran. She was offered a job for a few years in a music college in Tehran tutoring students to sing in opera choirs. She has also continued to tutor privately at her home. She taught her son Ramin to play piano and singing from an early age and he is at present working as an opera singer in Germany at one of the many government sponsored theaters there.

Maryam has been inspired by the poetry and or thoughts and philosophy of the great classical poets and writers such as Jalale-Din Muhammu Mowlavi, Eragh Ferdowsi, Nezami, Omar Khayam, Sa'di, Hafez, and to a lesser degree modernists like Parvin Etessami, Malek-al Shoara Bahar, Fereydoon Moshiry, Sohrab Sepehri and others.

The poem "Elegy of the tree" is a beautiful poem that shows her extreme concern about the quality and health of our environment and brings to our attention how fast greedy and irresponsible individuals are undermining and jeopordizing the life and health of this one of the greatest gifts of nature and as a result putting the quality of life, prosperity, health, happiness, and continuity of all living species on earth. Following is that poem:

The tree's elegy	مرثیه درخت

He who discovers the hidden treasure contained within the tree.
May God help him if he is a protector of the tree

هرکه ره یافت به گنجینه سرشار درخت
حق نگهدارش اگر هست نگهبان درخت

Splendour of the garden, brightness of the meadows, glory of the flower, are all indebted to the brisk market of the tree.

رونق باغ وفروغ چمن وفخر گل است
جملگی در گرو گرمی بازار درخت

Tree's eyes forever are staring at the source of light,
Our eyes light up when looking at the splendor of the tree

دیدگان دوخته همواره به سرچشمه نور
دیده روشن شود از دولت دیدار درخت

Life's blood flows through the green veins of the tree,
Life's burden is carried on the tree's fruit laden by the tree

دارد اندر رگ سبزش جریان خون جهان
بار هستی همه بر شانه پربار درخت

Tree's green soul is burdend to purify our contamination
With every breath that its body breathes out,

روح سبزش پی پالایش آلایش ماست
هرنفس چون بد مد پیکر هشیار درخت

می وزد باد طرب خیز به پهنای سپهر
چه دل انگیز بود رقص سبکبار درخت

فیض فردوس نهان در دل سبزینه اوست
نازم آن سینه که شد عارف اسرار درخت

خود ثمرگیرد وبخشد ثمر از خاک به خاک

How delightful is to witness, the
tree's care-free dance,
In the wind when it blows across the
world!

The grace of paradise is hidden in
the tree's deep of the green
Glory be to the mind that is aware of
the tree's hidden secrets.

Proud is tree to be free from want
from the the entire world;
As it gets its fruit from the earth and
gives it to the world!

Tree's green leaves that give it its
beauty
Are truly considered to be a
manifestation of God's wisdom.

Tree hurts from the claws of the
vagrants, but is helpless;
As its feet are permanently chained
to the ground!

Passerbyes have cut their names on
its trunk.
A permanent shameful impression
on the tree's memory.

Fruits of the tree are more superior
to the jewels from the mines,
People do not appreciate the true
value of what the tree produces!

Homes and gardens are being wiped
out due to the builders' greed;

بی نیاز از همه عالم سر سالار درخت

مظهر معرفت حق شمرند ش چه به حق
برگ سبزی که دهد جلوه به رخسار
درخت

رنجد از پنجه ولگرد و گریزش نبود
بسته زنجیر زمین پای گرفتار درخت

باشد از رهگذران بر تنه اش نام و نشان
نقش ننگی ابدی مانده به تذکار درخت

بر تر از گوهر کانی گهر آورده به بار
نشنا سند کسان قدر گهر بار درخت

خانمان میرود از حرص عمارت بر باد
فتنه ها میکند این فاجعه در کار درخت

شب مهیای شبیخون و کمر بسته کنون
خیل غارتگر شبگرد به کشتار درخت

غرش اره و تنبور تبر زوزه کشان
می درد مخمل رویای پری وار درخت

فتنه گر لشگر سلطان زمین چون طاعون
می شکافد به قساوت تن تبدار درخت

برج عمال تجارت برود تا افلاک
نقش خاک است مهین قامت مهیار درخت

دیگر این شهر عمارت زده گورستان است
از کران تا به کران ریخته آوار درخت

برهوت است به جا زان همه باغ ملکوت
سوخت هستی گه ما آه شرر بار درخت

منظر سبز طراوت سیه از سایه دود
تیره چون چادر شب پرده زنگار درخت

اندر این وادی ویرانه قدم تا به عدم
می رود توده آ لوده به آثار درخت

دامن دشت و دمن سوخته از داغ و هنوز
دست ما دوخته بر دامن ایثار درخت

بایدش در فکند تیغه تنبیه زبن
دست جوری که بر آید پی آزار درخت

خون دل میخورد از غفلت تاریک دلان
دیده کو تا نگرد دیده خونبار درخت

خنک آن دوست که سبزینه نهالی بنشاند
سبز بخت آنکه بود یار وفادار درخت

The tragedy brings calamity to the
life of the tree.

It is night and time for the surprise
attack by,
The army of plunderes waiting to
wipe out the tree.

The roar of the saws, and the
hawling of the large axes,
Tearing apart the fairy dream of the
tree.

The seditious army of the king of the
earth,
Like plague splits up into pieces the
feverish body of the tree.

The tower of the agents of
mercantiles rises up to the sky,
Turning to dust is the tall and
graciously beautiful body of the
tree.

This once green covered city is now
turned into a cemetery
Buried, end to end with the debries
of the dead tree.

That kingdom of heaven is now
nothing more but a desert,
Alas for the vicious scintilla that
was set to wipe out our tree.

That green fresh landscape is now
smokey black,
Dark like, the wrapper for bed
clothes, are the leggings on the tree.

From here to eternity, in this desert,
Nothing is seen other than the dark
burnt remains of the tree.

Plateaus and plains are bereaving
the loss of the tree
And yet we are looking to the
generosity and blessing of the tree

Blade of punishment ought to
cutoff,
The hands of the oppressor who
attempts to harm the tree.

The negligence of the dark-hearted
causes great hearhache,
Where are the eyes to see tears of
blood shedding by tree!

Blessesd be the friend that plants a
new tree!
Blessed be the one that is forever a
loyal friend of the tree.

Maryam's poetry`is rhythmical and eloquent, lucid, free and easy, and void of
any artificiality. Truethful and pleasant overflowing with freshness and
beauty. It is highly imaginative with original subject matter, novel simile, new
and rhyming diction.This ghazal, (ode) is a realistic and beautiful narrative of
the legend of life:

Life passesd away and time went by, Immersed incessantly in a fancy or a thought.	آسان گذشت عمری و طی شد زمانه ای هردم به سر خیالی و در دل بهانه ای

Memories of long bygones return like in a dream,
Mirage-like dreams; water and deceiving stories'

بگذشته های دور چو خواب آیدم به یا د
خواب سراب و آب و فریب فسانه ای

Rose-garden a ruin and the nightingales recite sad songs,
In mourning for the death of the flowers.

ویرانه گشت گلشن و بلبل به سوگ گل
با ناله ای حزین بسراید ترانه ای

Angle of Death; the worlds' covetous hunter, sitting in wait,
With its net set ready to lure in its next prey.

صیاد دهر طعمه نگسترده بی طمع
دامی نهاده تا که دهد آب و دانه ای

In gain of fame and fortune much toil you suffer,
In the wink of an eye,you and all your gains will be naught!

بس بار بی ثمر بری از نام وازنشان
در هم زنی چو دیده نماند نشانه ای

Crown of glory on head like the one worn by Solomon!
Burden of greed on shoulder like the ant carrying to its nest!

تاج شرف به سرچو سلیمان به بارگاه
بار طمع به دوش چو موری به لانه ای

Fortunate the one who can, burn in love, like a candle,
To light up, with flame, a lover's night!.

خوش آنکه همچو شمع بسوزد زسوز عشق
روشن کنند به شعله شب عاشقانه ای

We drowned and the high waves pushed me down into the deep,
That was the sea of love with no shores in sight.

گشتم غریق و موج گران ز سر برفت
دریای عشق بود ونبودش کرانه ای

Tomorrow my Gnostic will proclaim in my ear,

فردا به گوش خفته دهد عارفم ندا
فانی به بست رخت وبشد جاودانه ای

The mortal left the world and turned
immortal!.

Maryam, not only is an outstanding poet with deep knowledge and great skill
in Persian poetry from classics to modern; she is also a painter, a musician, a
teacher of classical music, in particular, Opera. She has trained many students.
She also sings and plays piano beautifully.

Maryam started painting at the age of eighteen. She is extremely talented in
different styles using oil-paint and in particular water-colour. Another field of
Maryam's expertie's is translation of German poetry into Persian and vice-
versa. She knows Esperanto and has translated and published Parvin
Ettesamie's poetry collection from Persian into Esperanto.

Come back for there is no rose garden without you, Flower turns vexatuios thorn without your presenc here!	باز آی که بی روی تو گلزار نباشد گل بی تو به جز خار دل آزار نباشد
Nightly my eyes are fixed at the door and awake, Hoping and praying that you might suddenly appear.	شب نیست که این دیده بردوخته بر در از حسرت دیدار تو بیدار نباشد
'Intoxicated' is 'not' who just boasts of having taken the Cup; No matter how drunk he be. If 'Enlightened"; he is not!	از باده پرستی چه زند لاف هر آن مست کز جام تو می نوشد و هوشیار نباشد
If I set eyes on that beautiful thornless flower, All other flowers, will become worthless in my eyes!	بر دیده نشیند چو به ناز آن گل بی خار گل نیست که در دیده ما خوار نباشد
The nobles will not have much regard,	آزاده دلانش سر مویی نشمارند آن دل که به موی تو گرفتار نباشد

For the heart that does not deeply revere your love

Your image which illuminates the veil of the soul,
Wuold be visible if it was not for the veil of the thought.

نقش تو که بر پرده جان است منور
پیدا ست ا گر پرده پندار نباشد

In the eyes of the hypocrites, it is worthless, 'the faith',
That its followers fail to wear rosary and girdle!

در دیده ارباب ریا هیچ نیارزد
ایمان که به تسبیح و به زنار نباشد

From the eloquent preacher that is a master of slogans, Much talk it is heard but no action it is seen.

از واعظ خوش لهجه که استاد شعارست
گفتار بسی باشد و کردار نباشد

This caravan is being led into non-existence,
For its Leader is none but a highwayman.

ره سوی عدم میبرد این قافله کامروز
جز راهزنش اش قافله سا لار نباشد

Maryam, the multi-talentd poet of our time has also tried her hand in writing new-style poetry. In this arena, she has been deeply inspired by the contemporary and outstanding poet; Sohrab Sepehery. She has remembered

Sohrab's style in the following poem addressed to her son "Ramin" :

"How green you are, to-day, my flower....!"
"And how sober is your body....!
Do you want a poem; in new or old style?
Certainly this would not be your concern.
Your Pure poetry is your companion
You recite your poems well and load

تو چه سبزی امروز گل من...!
و چه اندازه تنت هوشیار است...!
شعرنو خواهی یا شعر کهن؟
غمت این نیست یقین
شعرناب ات یاراست
شعر می خوانی گویا ورسا
وتپش های دلت
از مضامین وزین سرشاراست
می دهی گوش به موسیقی شعر

And your heart's palpitations,
 Overflowing with firm and witty remarks.
You listen to the music's poetry
Poetry is your companion, And your lips thirsty for a rhythmic drink,
That from the inspiring source of speech,
Flows out the edge of thought.
Cheerio that drink of luent poetry;
The   Cup,   overflowing   with messages.

Remembering Sohrab and his night of poetry.
 An intoxicating and aged wine in a new Cup.
His memory: a charming bed of flowers,
A colorful painting,
The green leaf that he painted,
The red line that he drew
Eight kooks
Eight   flower-gardens,   garden, paradise….
The green heavenly plains.
His pen believed the wisdom of the grassy plains,
And a thousand eyes watching in the flower-garden.

How patient are you, my flower, how patient….!
The big-hearted man from the expanse of The salt-desert.
A soul-searcher!
Sand –dunes under your feet,
Slipping away,

که رفیقی با شعر
و لبت تشنه نوشی موزون
که ز سرچشمه الهام کلام
جوشد از مطلع فکر

نوشت باد جرعه ای شعر روان
جام جوشانی لبریز پیام
یاد سهراب وشراب شعرش
کهنه شرابی گیرا در جام نوین
خاطرش فرش فریبنده گل
نقش ونگاری رنگین
برگ سبزی که نگاشت
خط سرخی که نوشت
هشت کتاب
هشت گلشن باغ بهشت....
دشت سبز ملکوت
قلمش هوش علفزار را باور داشت
و هزار دیده در دامن گلزار تماشاگر داشت

چه صبوری گل من چه صبور.....!

مرد دریا دل پهنای کویر
عاشق سیر وسلوک
زیر پایت شنزار
می لغزد دیر چه دیر.....!
می رود تا افق کشف وشهود
راهی دور چه دور.....!
رهرو خسته و خاموش بیابان فراق
پای تبدار بر راه طلب
می تازی بر لشگر شب
در عبوری روشن تا اشراق
تا مشرق نور

کودکی یادت هست...؟

Travelling the horizon of Discovery
and Intuition.
A road far, how very far!
The tired and silent wayfarer of the
desert of separation
In search with feverish feet
Rushing the army of night
In a clear move towards
Enlightenment
To the East of Light

Do you remember the
childhood....?
At the night of poetry.
Lovimg friends, afflicted by the
fever of poetry.
Cups of poetry going round
Intoxicated partners
Grabbing kisses from the lips of
poems.
My ingenious child,
Sleeping on the shore of dreams
Listening to the poetry's lullaby
His eager, awakend ready to learn
mind,
Submerged in the dream world of
poetry.
The tinly little fish of the sea of the
dreams,
Gets carried by the wave of his
eloquence,
To the expanse of the sea of poetry
To-day, you're the tall cypress
How young, my flower....!
You were seeds, now grown to a
garden
You turned into a river, flowing like
water

کنار شب شعر
دوستانی دلبند مبتلای تب شعر
جام شعری سرگردان دست به دست
می گرفتند حریفان سر مست
بوسه ها از لب شعر
کودک زیرک من
آرمیدست بر ساحل خواب
می دهد گوش به لالایی شعر
ذهن بیدار ادب آموزش
غرق در عالم رویایی شعر
ماهی کوچک دریای خیال
میبرد موج سخن پردازش
تا وسعت دریایی شعر
سرو سالاری امروز
چه برنا گل من....!

بذری بودی باغ شدی
رود گشتی رود جاری چون آب
دیگر ابعاد خیال انگیزت
نیست اندازه قاب
ابر گشتی ابر بر شانه کوه
می بری گوهر باران انبوه
بر دوش ستبر
شعر شیوایی امروز
چه موزون گل من....!
غزلی روشن در مدح سحر
تو چکامه ای دل انگیز در وصف بهار
در کتاب دل من مثنوی جان وتنی
تو روایتی روان در رگ ذهن
قصه ای جاری در فکر منی
برتن نازک اندیشه من
پیرهنی
بهترین شعر منی

No longer the dimensions of your
imagination,
Fits the size of the frame.
You became cloud on the shoulder
of the mountain.
You carry the jewels of the rain,
Upon your sturdy shoulders;
Today's poetry of eloquence.
How rhythmic and elegant; my
flower....!
A lucid ode in praise of the dawn.
You are a delightful elegy in praise
of spring.
In the book of my heart you are the
mathnavi of body and soul.
You are a luent narrative in the vein
of the mind
An ever present story in my
thoughts
Over the tender body of my
reflections;
You are a delicate trim over the
body of my thoughts!
You are my best poem.

As it was mentioned before, Maryam is a bilingual poet . She has written
poetry in English, German and Spranto. We are including here three single
pieces of her poetry written in these languages:

A poem written in English and Persian by Maryam Nezami, in honor of
Meister Gerhard Geretschlager celebrating Piano-Recital Event at Austrian
Cultural Institute in Teheran

When he went on beautifully playing	آن زمان که او
Fascinating sounds of paradise,	با نواهای خیال انگیزبهشت
As it were the angles choral playing	نواختن آغاز کرد
Till pure delight the humans realize;	گویی انسان با نغمات ملکوتی

Chapter 10

Then our souls desireing graceful and bless
Came by the music calmly to confess.
Charmmly fluttering virtuous fingers,
For birds wings swinging high above with fair;
Made magic tunes of the nature's whispers;
Ecstacy nailed everyone on the chair;
Melodies absorbed us hearing so clear
That the whole bodies became all ear
How far could fly upon the apogee
Our vision by that glorious sentiment;
Like the light clouds soaring gaily and free
Wether the time and earth seemed to be absent.
The hearts ravished as if forgot to beat
And the whole matter became all spirit
Fancyfully flowed into a cheerful dream
The feeling by intensive affection,
As eagerly gliding torrential stream
Runs to reach the widethe wide see of perfection;
Warble vibrations left us deeply to drown
So that in silence voice of our own

Januarry1995
Teheran

فرشتگان به سمت ادراک سرمستی
مطلق پرواز کرد
وروح وروان ما
با اشتیاق وآرامشی آسمانی
همراه موسیقی لب به سخن باز کرد
انگشتان ماهرنغمه گر
همچون پرندگان بلند پرواز
پروبال زنان گرم پرواز
نغمه های جادویی طبیعت...
وشنوندگان مجذوب نواهای دل انگیز
میخکوب بر جایگاه خویش
پیکر ها همه یکپارچه گوش
پرنده خیال همچون ابرها
شادمان وآزاد در عروج
به اوج واحساسی شکو همند
عرصه ای بی حضورزمین وزمان
وعناصر مستحیل در تبدیل ماده به معنا
رویاهایی شکو همند احساسی تاثیرگذار
گویی رودباری سیل اسا روان بود
در اشتیاق رسیدن به دریای کمال
طنین سرایشی دلنشین همگان را
همچون غریق به اعماق پیوسته بود
آنگونه که صداهای ما
همه در سکوت شکسته بود

A poem written by Iraj Mirza,
Translated into Esperanto by Maryam Nezami

Naske min patrino cemame
Sucadon sufere lernigis,
Dumnokte ce lulio maldorme
Dormadon kvere lernigis
Rideton metis sur mian lipon
Floreton floradi tenere lernigis,

گویند مرا چوزاد مادر
پستان به دهان گرفتن آموخت
شب ها بر گاهواره ی من
بیدار نشست وخفتن آموخت
لبخند نهاد بر لبانم
برغنچه گل شکفتن اموخت

Je la buso min parolige
Vortadon litere lernigis,
Manprene pason post laso
Iradon tiamaniere lernigis,
Mian vivon si kreadis kerne
  Patrinon mi amas eterne

یک حرف ودوحرف بر زبانم
الفاظ نهاد وگفتن آموخت
دستم بگرفت وپا به پا برد
تا شیوه راه رفتن اموخت
پس هستی من ز هستی اوست
تا هستم وهست دارمش دوست

Pflugst du schoner Baum....
Pflugst du schooner Baum dein Blatter
herum
Und die Nachtigallen bleiben all'
stumm warum?
Ach ja da Herbst trau lisch hin und her
doch siegt,
Verliesst der Vogel Nest und nach
Ferme fliegt.

درخت زیبا پراکنده اطراف ت برگریزان
و بلبلان همه لال در سکوت ...چرا؟

آه .. آری پاییز غم انگیز همه جا چادرزده
است
پرنده از آشیان پریده در پرواز به
دوردست ها.
عنقریب هوا روبه سردی .. آبی
خاکستری

Wird bald wohl blau und kalt und grau
das Wetter,
Gelb und ros und rot dein blatter
Dir   Teppisch farbenfroh herum so
legen,

و برگهای تو زرد و سرخ وصورتی

گسترده فرشی رنگین از رنگهای
رخشان

Sei doch Frisch du schooner Baum
beim Regen.

بر خویش ببار درخت زیبا طراوت باران
را.

Keine Sorge aber hast du meiner Baum
Da in kuzem ja vergeht das trube
Traum,
Fleigt die Zeitim Augenblick so wart ab
nur!
Neu wird wieder gleich beim
Wiedergeburt die Natur.

غم واندیشه به خود راه مده درخت من...
زیرا این رویای تیره وتار دیری نخواهد
پایید

Belegt sie mit schonen helgrunen
Schleier

زمان در چشم بر هم زنی سپری می شود

Dain Stamm, deine Zweigen vor Fruhlingsfeier ,
Dann sag' ich dir ein Geheimnis meiner Baum;
Schau mal macht aber mich die Zeit wieder Jung kaum!

و طبیعت بار دیگر از نو متولد خواهد شد.

بزودی در جشن بهار طبیعت چادر سبز بر پا می دارد
و رخت سبز تو بر شاخ و برگ ات می پوشاند..

و آنگاه درخت من .. رازی پنهان در گوش ات می گویم
در گذر زمان تو دوباره جوان می شوی
ومن پیر...

Bibliography

E.G.Brown, Aliterary History of Persia
Sa'id Nafissi, Tarikh Nasr va nazm dar Iran
John Rypka History of Iranian Literature
Shebli Noma'ni, Sher al-a'jamZabiholla'h Safa' Tarikh-e Adabiat dar Iran
Abd-al-Hosayn Zarrinkub, Seyri dar Sher-e Farsi
Zahhireddin Mohammad Awfi, Labab al-alba'b
Lotf-Ali Beyg A'zar, (Ateshkadeh, Tazkeras and critical anthologies)
Nezami Aruzi, (Chaha'r Magha'leh)
Gha'boos ibn Woshmgir (Gha'bous-Na'meh)
Neza'mol Molk, (Siasatna'meh)
Abolfazl Beyhaghi (Tarikh-e Beyhaghi)
Ata'-Malek Juvayni (Ta'rikh Jaha'ngusha')
Atta'r Neisha'bouri (Tazkerat-ol-Owlia')
Badi-al-Zama'n Foruza'nfar (Sokhan va sokhanvaran)
Dawlatsha'h Samarghandi, (Tazkerat al-Shoara')
Mir Ali Shah Navai (Maja'lesat-Nafa'es)
Sa'm Mirza' Safavi (Khamsetal-Mottohayerin)
Reza'Ghopli Khan Hedayat (Haft Ighlim)
Mohammad Ali Hazin-e La'hiji (Tazkerat al-moa'serin)
Jama'l Khalil-e Sherva'ni (Nozhat al maja'les)
Reza' Gholi kha'n Hedayat (Maja'ma al-fosaha)
Shams al-Din Ahmad Afla'ki, (Mana'gheb al-A'refefin)
Hossein Mirza Ba'yaghra' (Maja'lesul Usha'gh)
Mohammad Ta'her Nasra'ba'di (Tazkerat al-Shoara')
Abd-al-Nabi Ghazvini (Tazkera-ye meykha'na)
Ba'ba' Ta'her Orya'n, Quartine (do-beyti)
Farid-al-Din Atta'r (Ela'hi-na'ma)
Mohammd Ali Ra'vandi (Ra'hat al-sodur va A'yat al-sorur)
Abu'l-Fazl Bayhaghi (Ta'rikh-e Mas'udi)
Tarikh –na'meh Tabari
Abu' Ali Mohammad Bal'ami (Ta'rikheh Bal 'ami)
Jerome Clinton (The Diva'n of Manuchehri Damgha'ni)
Abu'l-Gha'sem Ferdowsi, Sha'h-na'ma, ed. Jala'l Khaleghi-Motlagh.
Richard Frye, (The Golden Age of Persia)
Ruba'iya't Hakim Omar Khayyam

Bibliography

Abd-al Rahma'n Ja'mi, (Diva'n-e ash a'r)
Said Nafisi, (Ahva'l va Asha'r- Rudaki)
Vahid Dastgerdi, (Neza'mi Ganjavi, Khamsa' Neza'mi).
Fereydoon Moshiri, (Collection of Poems)
Mohammad Jafar Mahjub, Complete works of Iraj Mirza
Dr. Mehdi Hamidi Shirazi, Collection of poetry (after one year)
Reynold A. Nickolson (Lover's secret told in the talk of others)
Reynold Nicklson (Translation of Mathnavi of Jalal al-Din Rumi)
Cyrus Tahba'z (complete works of Nima Yushij)
Dr.Gholam-Hossein Yousefi, (Cheshmeh Roushan)
Shebli Noma'ni- Dr.parviz Khanlari, (Complete works of Sa'eb)
Ivgeni Edward Berteles (Ta'rikh Adabia'te Farsi)
Badi al- Zaman Forouzanfar, (Koliya'te Shams Tabrizi)
Wikipeadia, the free encyclopeadia.
Dr.Salim Neisa'ri (Diva'n Ha'fez Shirazi)
Jala'l al-Din Homa'ie (Mowlavi –na'meh)
Dr. Abdol Hossein Zarkoob) Peleh-Peleh ta' Mola'gha'te Khoda')
Dr.Saied Hamidia'n (Sha'h-na'mehe-ye Ferdowsi)
Mohammad Ali Foroughi (Kolia'te Sa'di Shira'zi)
Ka'mia'r A'bedi, (Sure-Esraphil, va Ali Akbar Dehkhoda')
Encyclopeadia Britanica
Majma al-Tava'rikh Val Ghessaes
Ebn-al Nadim (Al fehrest)
Zabihola'h Safa' (Hema'se-sara'ie dar Iran)
Al asra'r al-Ba'ghie
Mohammad Hossein Khalaf Tabrizi (Borha'ne-Gha'teae)
Ebne-Esfandia'r (Ta'rikhe-Tabarestan)
Ta'rikhe-Tabari
Ghazvini, (Moghadameh Sha'h na'me Abu-Mansuri)
Asra'r al- Ajam

Asadi (Loghateh-Ferse)
Ta'rikheh-Bokhara'
Zabiholah Safa (Asra'r al-Tohid)
Kh'ghani Sherva'ni, (Za'd al-Mosa'ferin)
Zabiholah Safa, (Ta'rikhe –Oloome-Aghli)
Badi-al zama' Forouzanfar, (Tarikhe adabiyat)
Mohammad – ben Zakaria Ra'zi (Resa'late Al Biruni)
Tarjoma'n' al-Bala'gheh

Bibliography

Ta'rikhe Gerdizi
Ta'rikhe Yamini
Henry Corbon va Dr.Mohammad Moin (Ja'ma't al –Hekmatein)
Aba's Eghbal Ashtiani (hadadgh Al-Sahar)
Dabir Sia'ghi, (Hava'shi diva'ne-Manouchehri)
Mojmal al-Tava'rikh
Reya'z al-A'refin
Ha'j khalifeh, (Kashf al-Zonoon)
Ghatra'n Tabrizi, (Diva'n Asha'r)
Rashid Yasami (Masoud, Sa'd Diva'n Asha'r)
Dr Reza' za'deh Shafagh, (Tarikh adabiate Iran)
Shahrzoori, (Ta'rikh al-Hokama')
Modares Razavi, (Diva'ne Sana'ie)
Diva'n a'sha're J ama'l al-Din Esfaha'ni
Mousa Ansa'ri, (Diva'n Asha'r Zahir Farya'bi)
Kha'gha'ni Shervani, (Tofat al-Ara'ghein)
Abdol Rasouli, (Diva'n Asha'r Khaghani Sherva'ni)
Saiid Nafisi, (Diva'n ghasa'yed va ghazalia't Atta'r Neisha'bori)
Edward Brown, (Az Sa'di ta Ja'mi)
Jala'l al-Din Homa'ie, (Moghadameh Valad –na'meh)
Badi al-Zaman Forouza'nfar, (Biography of Mola'na Jala'l al-Din)
Moayed Sa'beti, (Moghadameh Diva'n Homa'm Tabrizi)
Obeyd Za'ka'ni, (Osha'gh-na'meh)
Mohammad Ali Tarbiat, (Da'neshmanda'ne A'zerba'ija'n)
Mohammad Moba'rak Alavi & Neza'm al-Din O'liya'. (Seir al-Oliya')
Tarikhe Fereshteh.
Modares Razavi, (Diva'n Asha're Seied Hassan Ghaznavi)
Amir Khosrow Delhi, (Diva'n Ka'mel Asha'r & his Khamseh)
Soheili Khonsa'ri, (Divane Asha'r, Kha'jooye Kermani)
Kuhi Kerma'ni, (Rozat al-Anva'r)
Said Nafisi, (Moghadameh Diva'neh Ghataa't va Roba'iya't Ebn Yamin)
Aba's Eghba'l A'shtiya'ni, (Kolia'te Obeyd Za'ka'ni)
Herma'n Ete', (Ta'rikh adabiyat Fa'rsi)
Osta'd Avesta', (Koliya't Asha're Salma'n Sa vaji)
Masoom Ali Shah, (Tara'yegh al- Hagha'yegh)
Saiediyan, (Asha'r Amir Sha'hi)
Maja'les al-Nafa'yes, (translated by Sha'h Mohammad)
Resa'ley Ja'mi, (Rashaha't ein al- Haya't)
Ahmad Soheili Khonsa'ri, (Diva'n Asha're Ba'ba' Fagha'ni)

Bibliography

Sahafeh-Ebra'him.
Ahmad Golchin Maa'ni, (Tazkerhe Meykha'neh)
Saied Nafisi, (Moghadameh Diva'n Hela'li Joghataie)
Romlo, (Ahsan al-Tavarikh)
Ha'med Raba'ni, (Diva'n Asha're Ahli Shira'zi)

–